PLAY AND CHILD DEVELOPMENT

SECOND EDITION

JOE L. FROST
University of Texas

SUE C. WORTHAM
University of Texas at San Antonio

STUART REIFEL
University of Texas

PEARSON
Merrill
Prentice Hall

Upper Saddle River, New Jersey
Columbus, Ohio

Library of Congress Cataloging in Publication Data
Frost, Joe L.
Play and child development / Joe L. Frost, Sue C. Wortham, Stuart Reifel.— 2nd ed.
p. cm.
Includes bibliographical references and index.
ISBN 0-13-113123-0 (pbk. : alk. paper)
1. Play—Social aspects. 2. Child development. I. Wortham, Sue Clark. II. Reifel, Robert Stuart. III. Title. HQ782 .F75 2005
305.231--dc22 2003025140

Vice President and Executive Publisher: Jeffery W. Johnston
Publisher: Kevin M. Davis
Editor: Julie Peters
Editorial Assistant: Amanda King
Production Editor: Sheryl Glicker Langner
Production Coordinator: Erin Connaughton, nSight, Inc.
Design Coordinator: Diane C. Lorenzo
Photo Coordinator: Lori Whitley
Cover Designer: Terry Rohrbach
Cover Image: Index Stock
Production Manager: Laura Messerly
Director of Marketing: Ann Castel Davis
Marketing Manager: Autumn Purdy
Marketing Coordinator: Tyra Poole

This book was set in Zapf Humanist by Laserwords. It was printed and bound by R. R. Donnelley & Sons Company. The cover was printed by Coral Graphic Services, Inc.

Photo Credits: p. 2 Kinderspiele [Child's Play], by Pieter Breugel, from the Kunsthistorisches Museum, Vienna; p. 6 Athenian Red Figure Vase, reproduced by permission of Hirmer Fotoarchiv München; p. 10 Children with blocks, ca. 1900, Photography Collection, Miriam and Ira D. Wallach Division of Art, Prints, and Photographs, The New York Public Library, Astor, Lenox and Tilden Foundations; pp. 16, 56, 91, 106, 109, 146, 150, 212, 227, 269 by Anne Vega/Merrill; pp. 26, 32, 37, 114 by Todd Yarrington/Merrill; pp. 77, 144, 234, 290 by Scott Cunningham/Merrill; pp. 86, 156 by Laima Druskis/PH College; pp. 120, 205, 276 by Teri Leigh Stratford/PH College; pp. 161, 178 by Larry Fleming/PH College; pp. 173, 327, 379 by Shirley Zeiberg/PH College; p. 188 from the National Museum of Taipei, reproduced by permission; pp. 197, 246 by Barbara Schwartz/Merrill; p. 241 by Andy Brunk/Merrill; pp. 292, 293 courtesy of the Austin Children's Hospital; pp. 300, 330, 341, 345, 362, 375 provided by Joe L. Frost; p. 304 from *American Playgrounds*, by E. B. Mero (Boston: American Gymnasia Co., 1908); pp. 314–315 courtesy of Rusty Keeler, Planet Earth Playscapes; pp. 319, 324 by Ken Karp/PH College; p. 353 by KS Studios/Merrill.

Pearson Education Ltd.
Pearson Education Singapore Pte. Ltd.
Pearson Education Canada, Ltd.
Pearson Education—Japan
Pearson Education Australia Pty. Limited
Pearson Education North Asia Ltd.
Pearson Educación de Mexico, S.A. de C.V.
Pearson Education Malaysia Pte. Ltd.

PEARSON
Merrill
Prentice Hall

10 9 8 7 6 5 4 3 2
ISBN: 0-13-113123-0

We dedicate this book to our families, who support our work and endure our mood swings—lovingly and patiently.

Educator Learning Center: An Invaluable Online Resource

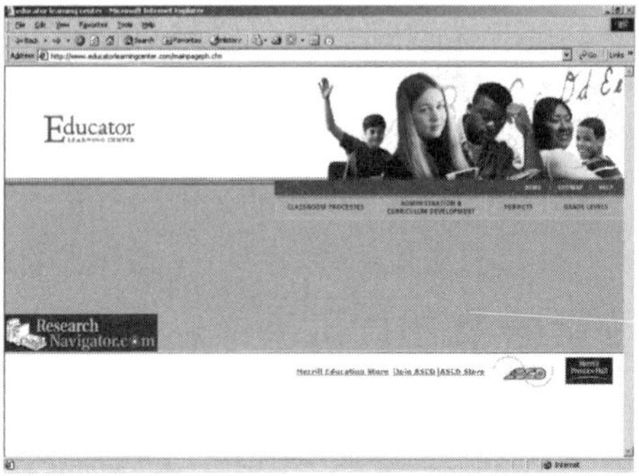

Merrill Education and the Association for Supervision and Curriculum Development (ASCD) invite you to take advantage of a new online resource, one that provides access to the top research and proven strategies associated with ASCD and Merrill—the Educator Learning Center. At **www.EducatorLearningCenter.com** you will find resources that will enhance your students, understanding of course topics and of current educational issues, in addition to being invaluable for further research.

How the Educator Learning Center will help your students become better teachers

With the combined resources of Merrill Education and ASCD, you and your students will find a wealth of tools and materials to better prepare them for the classroom.

Research

- More than 600 articles from the ASCD journal *Educational Leadership* discuss everyday issues faced by practicing teachers.
- A direct link on the site to Research Navigator™ gives students access to many of the leading education journals, as well as extensive content detailing the research process.
- Excerpts from Merrill Education texts give your students insights on important topics of instructional methods, diverse populations, assessment, classroom management, technology, and refining classroom practice.

Classroom Practice

- Hundreds of lesson plans and teaching strategies are categorized by content area and age range.
- Case studies and classroom video footage provide virtual field experience for student reflection.
- Computer simulations and other electronic tools keep your students abreast of today's classrooms and current technologies.

Look into the value of Educator Learning Center yourself

A four-month subscription to Educator Learning Center is $25 but is **FREE** when used in conjunction with this text. To obtain free passcodes for your students, simply contact your Merrill/Prentice Hall sales representative, and your representative will give you a special ISBN to give your bookstore when ordering your textbooks. To preview the value of this website to you and your students, please go to **www.EducatorLearningCenter.com** and click on "Demo."

Preface

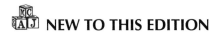

NEW TO THIS EDITION

This book is about children's play and development. Changes to this new edition include new information and research on the following:

- History, theories, and culture of play
- Montessori and child development views of play
- Examples of play in Chapters 1 and 2
- Nature and consequences of play deprivation
- Benefits of playground play, more on safety in both indoor and outdoor play, and additional emphasis on nature, gardens, and wild places in children's play
- Effects of electronic play (video games, computers, immersive reality) on children's development
- Roles of play leaders
- Strategies for adults for facilitating play with children with disabilities
- Bullying and aggressive behavior in school-age children and characteristics of these children

CONTENTS AND ORGANIZATION OF THIS TEXT

To understand any human activity, such as play, it is necessary to explore that activity as it has evolved over time. We begin in Chapter 1 with a look at "Play's History: Ideas, Beliefs, and Activities." Indeed, play does have an epic history, dating back thousands of years. As we state in Chapter 1, play activities existed long before recorded history. As a result, we have both prerational knowledge of play, which has remained with us since before the onset of recorded history, and rational knowledge of play, those aspects of play that we have come to be aware of by means of scholarship.

Our earliest rational knowledge of Western play can be described in terms of three themes: *agon*, *mimesis*, and *chaos*. These themes continue to describe play across the centuries, although the relative weight of each is seen to vary over time. *Agon*, or conflict, appears in competitive games and has its present manifestation in sport. *Mimesis*, or imitative action, is associated with theater, role play, and creative forms of play. *Chaos*, or leaving things to the Fates, is reflected in games of chance. During the Enlightenment and Romance periods of history, versions of *mimesis* were exalted, to call attention to humankind's creative spirit. It was during these times that particular attention from scholars began to focus on children's play. Freedom and the human spirit were associated with play by educators such as Johan Pestalozzi and Friedrich Froebel. This belief has remained with us and forms a cornerstone for understanding children's play.

The history of children's play developed a life of its own during the 19th century, with the scholarly research efforts of individuals such as G. Stanley Hall, John Dewey, and child development researchers who soon followed them. Although these scholars reflected differing assumptions about play, their combined efforts, building on the work of earlier philosophers, kept play at the center of children's development.

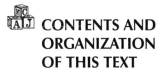

Our history of prerational and rational experience with children's play serves as a basis for our current efforts to study play. Through the past century, research on children's play contributed to theories about play and its role in development. As we look at our efforts to make sense of play, we see a variety of rhetorics for play and a wider variety of theories to make sense of it. Chapter 2 introduces a number of theories that dominated play scholarship throughout the 20th century, as well as a number of emerging theories that are leading us into the 21st century. These theories are illustrated with an example of children at play, showing how play must be understood from multiple perspectives. Being able to put on different theoretical lenses allows the observer of play to understand its many meanings.

Chapter 2 also provides a model for deciding which theory may be most useful for professionals who are supporting play. Theory is placed in the model as a tool for assisting teachers to plan, observe, and assess children as they play. Values and beliefs about play must be articulated and aligned with relevant play theories. The model is supplemented by research on teacher beliefs as they relate to theory and practice.

History and theory are invaluable tools for understanding play and for seeking keys to practice. During the 20th century, additional tools emerged from research in several disciplines. Chapter 3 details the work of behavioral scientists who, during the 1960s, introduced the notion of plasticity of the human brain with particular reference to very young children. This set the stage for national attention to early development in playful contexts. More recently neuroscientists, employing high-tech brain imaging, have opened a new front in understanding children's behavior, including play, and implications for practitioners are tenuously being drawn.

Chapter 3 also discusses the growing tendency among educators and politicians to substitute academic rigor and high-stakes testing for free, spontaneous play, resulting in loss of time for recess, physical education, and the arts. A parallel trend, substituting technology play and pay-for-play, also impose impediments to spontaneous play, presenting an ever-growing threat to children's health and development.

Three chapters address play and development. The first, Chapter 4, discusses the first 2 years of development. The preschool years are discussed in Chapter 5, and school-age children in Chapter 6.

Issues of culture and gender are addressed in Chapter 7. Because so many societies are multicultural at this time, there are always questions about the traditions, meanings, relationships, and communications that may vary with different groups of people. Building on earlier reviews by Schwartzman and Slaughter and Dombrowsky, we present research on the topics of continuities and discontinuities in children's play. Gender differences in play are universal and apparent from many studies. A discussion of theories of gender development introduces a description of the continuing debate on the nature and nurture of play. Studies, while not resolving the debate, illustrate girl/boy differences in social patterns, toys used, and texts dramatized in play.

Implications for practice in child care center and school contexts naturally arise from discussions of play theory and research. Over recent decades, a number of approaches have evolved which address the integration of play into curriculum and the roles of teachers. In Chapter 8, we examine the dominant approaches, ranging from hands-off play to broadly and narrowly focused play intervention. Since all these approaches are drawn from serious examination of theory and research, practitioners may borrow relevant dimensions from more than one model. In a multi-ethnic, pluralistic society, the developmental needs of individuals and groups may not be appropriately met by a single approach. Play is not all that children need, but knowledge is constructed through play, and, through sensitive adult intervention, play and work become complementary activities.

The questions of how children with disabilities engage in play and what adaptations need to be made to adult roles and the environment to expand play are the focus of Chapter 9. Researchers interested in the nature of play in children with disabilities have conducted studies comparing the play of children with specific disabilities with the play of peers who have typical development. The play of children with specific disabilities has also been studied to determine how changes in the environment and adaptations of toys can enhance play opportunities for children. The use of technology, particularly computers, for modification of play possibilities for all children in the classroom is becoming more prevalent. Most significantly, modification of the outdoor environment has become a significant design challenge within the last two decades as play specialists have sought to make outdoor play more accessible to children with all types of disabilities.

The natural therapeutic qualities of play lend even greater emphasis to the importance of play for child development. As seen in Chapter 10, play therapy has its roots in the psychoanalytic tradition, but, over the years, theorists and practitioners modified the practical applications of this tradition to develop several approaches. The fundamental tenets of child-centered play therapy are rooted in the beliefs that children play out their phobias, feelings, and emotions and that play has natural healing powers. Play therapy is now successfully conducted with children of all age groups and in individual, family, clinical, school, hospital, and group contexts.

Since play is an important ingredient of both indoor and outdoor activities, Chapter 11 focuses on the creation of special, magical, creative outdoor play environments. (Indoor play environments and indoor safety are discussed in Chapter 8). This section is intended to counter the growing pattern of cookie-cutter (standardized) playgrounds in U.S. child care centers, schools, and public parks by focusing on comprehensive environments featuring natural elements such as sand, water, tools, materials for construction, nature areas, and "special places." Fundamental to countering this trend is convincing adults that recess and outdoor play are essential to children's healthy development. Even the best outdoor play environments have little effect unless children have ample time to experience and create over extended periods of time.

The extensive analysis of child safety in public places, discussed in Chapter 12, is unique in child development texts, perhaps because of the prevailing view that accidents and injuries are inherent in growing up. Safety experts and a growing body of safety research conclude that accidents can be prevented, especially those that expose children to risks of permanent injury or death. We wish to make one point crystal clear: We do not advocate "dumbing down" playgrounds or play venues in an effort to make them safe. Quite the contrary—play environments can be made safer than traditional settings while simultaneously expanding challenges and opportunities for physical development and other areas of development. Risk is an essential element in developing safety skills.

The discussion of play leadership in Chapter 13 promotes the concept that all adults who supervise children at play—parents, aides, teachers, youth workers—need certain skills. The term *play leader* is intended to apply to all such workers/players. The skills needed appear to be inherent or natural for many adults. For example, most parents play peek-a-boo with infants and toddlers, cuddle them, talk to them, and provide toys. But as the child matures and is passed from one caretaker to another, play leadership skills frequently take a back seat to didactic instruction, scheduling, and academic pursuits. Good play leaders respect children and play; they sense the flow of children's play, recognize this as the release of ultimate creative impulses, and know this is the stuff from which learning and development emerge.

ACKNOWLEDGMENTS

The authors wish to acknowledge and express appreciation to those who helped prepare this book. To John Sutterby, Seunghwa Kim, Dottie Hirshman, Jim Therrell, Shu-Fen Cheng, Shelley Nicholson, and Debora Wisneski for comments on chapter drafts; to Rusty Keeler who assisted with photographs; to Laura Havlik who helped with computer foul-ups and various tasks; to our colleagues at other universities who provided valuable, extensive analyses and suggestions for improving the manuscript: Genan Anderson, Utah Valley State College; Amanda Wilcox-Herzog, California State University, San Bernardino; Dana Bryant Biddy, University of Houston, Clear Lake; Susan Macy, California State University, Fresno; and Susan Churchill, University of Nebraska, Lincoln, and to the many students who contributed in countless ways.

Discover the Companion Website Accompanying This Book

THE PRENTICE HALL COMPANION WEBSITE: A VIRTUAL LEARNING ENVIRONMENT

Technology is a constantly growing and changing aspect of our field that is creating a need for content and resources. To address this emerging need, Prentice Hall has developed an online learning environment for students and professors alike—Companion Websites—to support our textbooks.

In creating a Companion Website, our goal is to build on and enhance what the textbook already offers. For this reason, the content for each user-friendly website is organized by topic and provides the professor and student with a variety of meaningful resources. Common features of a Companion Website include:

FOR THE PROFESSOR

Every Companion Website integrates **Syllabus Manager™**, an online syllabus creation and management utility.

- **Syllabus Manager™** provides you, the instructor, with an easy, step-by-step process to create and revise syllabi, with direct links into Companion Website and other online content without having to learn HTML.
- Students may logon to your syllabus during any study session. All they need to know is the Web address for the Companion Website and the password you've assigned to your syllabus.
- After you have created a syllabus using **Syllabus Manager™**, students may enter the syllabus for their course section from any point in the Companion Website.
- Clicking on a date, the student is shown the list of activities for the assignment. The activities for each assignment are linked directly to actual content, saving time for students.
- Adding assignments consists of clicking on the desired due date, then filling in the details of the assignment—name of the assignment, instructions, and whether or not it is a one-time or repeating assignment.
- In addition, links to other activities can be created easily. If the activity is online, a URL can be entered in the space provided, and it will be linked automatically in the final syllabus.
- Your completed syllabus is hosted on our servers, allowing convenient updates from any computer on the Internet. Changes you make to your syllabus are immediately available to your students at their next logon.

FOR THE STUDENT

- **Introduction**—General information about the topic and how it will be covered in the website.
- **Web Links**—A variety of websites related to topic areas.
- **Timely Articles**—Links to online articles that enable you to become more aware of important issues in early childhood.
- **Learn by Doing**—Put concepts into action, participate in activities, examine strategies, and more.
- **Visit a School**—Visit a school's website to see concepts, theories, and strategies in action.
- **For Teachers/Practitioners**—Access information you will need to know as an educator, including information on materials, activities, and lessons.

- **Observation Tools**—A collection of checklists and forms to print and use when observing and assessing children's development.
- **Current Policies and Standards**—Find out the latest early childhood policies from the government and various organizations, and view state, federal, and curriculum standards.
- **Resources and Organizations**—Discover tools to help you plan your classroom or center and organizations to provide current information and standards for each topic.
- **Electronic Bluebook**—Paperless method of completing homework or essays assigned by a professor. Finished work can be sent to the professor via email.
- **Message Board**—Virtual bulletin board to post and respond to questions and comments from a national audience.

To take advantage of these and other resources, please visit the *Play and Child Development* Companion Website at

www.prenhall.com/frost

Brief Contents

Contents

CHAPTER 11

Creating Play Environments 300

CHAPTER 12

Child Safety in Public Places 330

CHAPTER 13

Play Leadership in American and European Playgrounds 362

APPENDIX

Playground Checklist 383

References 388

Name Index 433

Subject Index 443

NOTE: Every effort has been made to provide accurate and current Internet information in this book. However, the Internet and information posted on it are constantly changing, and it is inevitable that some of the Internet addresses listed in this textbook will change.

Chapter 1

Play's History

Ideas, Beliefs, and Activities

RECREATION is as necessary, as Labour, or Food. But because there can be no Recreation *without Delight, which depends not always on Reason, but oftener on Fancy, it must be permitted* Children *not only to divert themselves, but to do it after their own fashion.*

(Locke, 1693/1968, p. 211)

THE BAKER cannot bake if the miller grinds him no meal; the miller can grind no meal if the farmer brings him no corn; the farmer can bring no corn if the field yields him no grain; the field can yield no crop if nature does not work towards it in inner harmony; she could not work in this inner harmony if God did not place in here power and material, and if His love did not guide everything to its fulfillment.

It is doubtless with these ideas that the children are brought up, who are playing at baking and feasting on bread. . . .

(Froebel, 1844/1897, p. 148)

Play is so much a part of our lives as human beings that we may fail to reflect on the range of play activities in which we engage and on what those activities mean for us. In this text, we hope to provide a basis for understanding what play is for humans—in particular young, developing humans—as a means of enabling the reader to reflect in more depth about what role play has in our lives. As the opening quotes suggest, there are multiple meanings for play and multiple forms of activities that we call play. Locke suggests that play is necessary for children and is based on "fancy," or imagination. As Froebel suggests, children may pretend in a manner that reflects the **experiences** they have had, in this quoted example making and eating bread; play becomes an **imitation** of life that serves to educate children. Spariosu (1989) comments on how we think about play, as a reflection of Western thought whereby play interacts consciously or not with how we think. Play tells us a great deal about who we are as human beings, and scholars have many ways of treating the concept of play.

In this text we will be treating children's play as a complex variety of activities. So many layers of meaning are associated with play (e.g., its conscious or unconscious attributes; whether we are focusing on social, cognitive, motor, or cultural aspects of **development**; whether play is an innate, biological phenomenon as opposed to an indicator of **culture**) that we must constantly revisit any play activity to analyze and understand what it means to us. Play activities are complex, and how we make sense of them is complexly challenging.

How we make sense of any human activity like play is further complicated by the fact that our "thought has operated over the centuries," as Spariosu (1989, p. 12) put it. Our current thinking about play has been shaded by the centuries of thought about play that precede our own. One function of the study of history is to help us understand the evolution of our ideas over the centuries, to better situate our current thinking and beliefs. This chapter is designed to help show some of the historical origins of our ideas about play.

As Spariosu also notes, the activity of play may have both rational and irrational meanings for us. Play, as an activity that may have prehistoric roots for human beings (Bateson, 1955/2000), has been part of human experience prior to the onset of rational thought. (Studies of nonhuman, especially primate, play suggest the likelihood of play being a precursor to rationality. See Bekoff & Byers, 1998.) Human beings probably played before we evolved the civilizing institutions of philosophy, science, or teaching.

By looking at our contemporary world, we can clearly document play that is part of our "civilized" experiences. We have organized sports in our schools and out of them, including soccer for preschoolers and more traditional Little League, gymnastic, and skating programs. There are playgrounds in city parks, facilities for play in shopping malls, and a burgeoning world of play made available through personal computers. Children's play is thoroughly woven into the fabric of our daily lives, in very visible and organized ways.

Beyond the play recreation that we provide for children in our contemporary Western **society**, we also base many of our services for children and families on beliefs about the centrality of play for healthy development and **education**. Play is described as the foundation for learning and mental health in families (Hellerdorn, Van Der Kooij, & Sutton-Smith, 1994), including family intervention programs designed to counter the influences of poverty (Levenstein, 1988). Play is also a cornerstone for **developmentally appropriate practice (DAP)**, guidelines for the education of young children in group settings (Bredekamp & Copple, 1997). We, as a society, have acknowledged play as more than recreation; we have built it into some of our social institutions. We now engage in (some forms of) play consciously and for a purpose, when we join a soccer team or go to the theater with friends. We have built play into our lives, creating social institutions for its expression. Play, for human beings, is a set of cultural practices of which we are fully conscious. Play is a part of our rational thinking, especially with regard to the lives of children.

With all the visible forms of play that we encounter, whether in schools, parks, malls, or cyberspace, we still overlook or ignore many play activities. Adults tend to ignore teasing games or **pretend** that offends propriety (Opie, 1993; Opie & Opie, 1997; Reifel, 1986). While adults once overlooked play about violence, it is now receiving more attention (Beresin, 1989; Carlsson-Paige & Levin, 1987; Goldstein, 1995). And play on sexual themes may be dismissed by many as "just play," thereby relegating it to the world of the invisible. For all the ways we are rational about play, there are also many ways that we are prerational. Some forms of play are part of our lives without our acknowledging them.

Based on Spariosu's (1989) work, we can see the complexity of play evolving. We must add historical complexity to how we think about play. We must remember that some parts of play may have meaning for us on a prerational level, based on ancient patterns of play that remain nonconscious to us. Such is the power of pretense for normal humans, who can without thought shift from the here and now to an imaginary world when playing with a preschooler; it comes to us naturally, and we don't need to think about it. Other aspects of play have fully articulated, rational meanings for us. The centrality of organized sports in schools, for example, highlights play as part of institutionalized, rational experience, from the scheduling of physical education courses into the curriculum to the planning of sport seasons for soccer, basketball, and swimming. History tells us the story of what occurred. Play has not always been viewed as something worth documenting. Therefore, our understanding of the history of play is complicated by the fact that we do not have rich details describing what people actually did while they played. Mergen (1995) points out that play could be understood in terms of memories, in terms of relics, and also from our understandings generated by historians. Historians then look not at actions but at documents of actions (e.g., the images on vases or paintings) or documents about actions (e.g., records of sports competitions or reflections by participants on playing). They look at relics or objects that were acted upon (clay dolls; miniature bows and arrows), and they look at a full range of documents that may help them understand the phenomenon of play.

Given the difficulty of understanding the history of play, because of our lack of documentation of what people actually did when they played in ancient times, it may be appropriate to understand the history of play by following a number of strands in the historical literature on play. One strand in this literature highlights our historical understanding of play in general. This understanding gives us definitions of play in terms of activities in which all human beings may participate. The emergence of children's play as a subset of this broader view of play gains historical significance as writers begin to focus specifically on what children do and ought to do as they play. A second strand that we should think about has to do with the distinction between what we know about play activities as opposed to what we know about how play was described in the literature. Play is treated as an idea and described as it relates to other ideas and to the emergence of human understanding. As we will see later in this chapter, it is only with the post-Enlightenment Romantic era that we begin to see evidence of what play can be for children and an elaboration of what its significance may be for children's education and development. And it is only after the Romantic era that we begin to see efforts to document activities that we should understand in terms of their playful elements. The post-Darwinian enterprise of conducting observations as part of a controlled scientific effort altered the shape of how we understand play.

This chapter will explore the history of children's play. To acknowledge the complexity of play, we will see how the history of thought about play (philosophy, concepts, beliefs) has changed over time, offering us an increasing number of ways we can think about play. We will also see that play emerged in the 19th century as a rational phenomenon for considering the education and development of children. With play established as a rational tenet of early education, our thinking about play transformed due to evolutionary theory and the introduction of science to the study of children and education. These strands of history of play contribute to how we make sense of play, how we plan for it, how we participate in it, and whether we advocate it as an important part of children's lives.

PHILOSOPHY AND IDEAS OVER THE YEARS

The Ancients and Play

> In the cult of Artemis girls were sometimes placed in the service of the goddess for longer periods, during which they underwent puberty initiation rites. Once again the rites characteristically involved the formation of dancing groups, as well as foot-races, processions to altars and other sacred objects, and the sacrifice of an animal as a substitute for the human victim demanded by Artemis in myth. (Lonsdale, 1993, p. 170)

Play has been part of philosophical discourse since the time of the ancient Greeks. Plato (427?–347 B.C.), Socrates (470?–399 B.C.), Aristotle (384–322 B.C.), and Xenophanes (6th century B.C.) all explored the meaning of play as part of their frameworks for understanding human expression and thought (Spariosu, 1989). For example, in The Republic (1993) and The Laws (1975), Plato wrote of the importance of freedom for learning, and specifically mentioned playing at building in childhood in order to perfect knowledge that will be used later in life (Wolfe, 2002). Emerging from religious contemplation, these philosophers identified a number of forms of play that helped make sense of the world and humans' role in it (Lonsdale, 1993). How can we understand the human condition? *Agon, mimesis,* and *chaos* provided three routes

Ancient Greek players used masks in mimesis to take on new roles.

for understanding, and they all provide a basis for how we continue to think about play.

Agon, or conflict, represented one way to consider play. The ancient Greek gods were understood to play with humans in the world, to provide challenges that might take the form of war, politics, or other forms of strife that would put humans into physical or social **competition** with one another. Those who won the competition, who mastered a conflict such as winning a foot-race, were those who were blessed by the gods. Real strife was one realm where these conflicts might be played out, but as the ancients came to understand agon they created surrogate forms of real conflict in which they could determine who was to be blessed. For example, instead of fighting a real war, there would be games in which competitors threw lances (javelins), heaved stones (shot puts), shot arrows (archery), and engaged in other forms of physical competition, all to see which individual or community had the gods' support. The competitive striving of sport was one avenue for ascertaining who was gifted by divine power. Competitive play, in the form of sport or games, continues to be a major part of how we think about play to this day.

Mimesis included any number of representational forms that stemmed from actions designed to mimic the gods, as a form of adoration. Acting in ways that were thought to be pleasing to the gods, possibly by doing what the gods were imagined to do, such as dancing, were seen as ways of bringing humans closer to the gods and possibly creating divine favor for the actors. Scenarios where the gods were depicted as orchestrating human actions evolved into theater (plays), rituals (religious rites), and other forms of dramatic or symbolic depiction. Mimesis or mimicry might be imitative, interpretive, or expressive, but in all cases involved acting out of the ordinary. Imaginative or dramatic enactment by adults or children is still seen to be at the core of contemporary **symbolic play** and recreation.

Chaos, or the order and disorder of nature, provided a third route for relating to the gods and making sense of humans' role in the world. How can we learn to relate to the randomness of the gods' actions? One way is to try to predict what they want. Perhaps by throwing bones on the ground or reading patterns of entrails, we can see a pattern that is intended for us. Belief that divine order can emerge from randomness involves a trust in **chance**, a belief that from all the possible things that could occur, there will be a godly intervention to mark the player's path. The belief is that tossing bones (rolling dice), exposing images (drawing playing cards), and drawing lots all reveal to the player that he or she is selected by the gods. Games of chance (with or without divine associations) are a third form of play that continues to this day, whether in the form of gambling, drawing straws, or flipping coins to decide who will have the first turn.

> Thus we see a small boy wearing a helmet and holding a spear performing a weapon dance, a training qualification rite for ephebes [citizens]. (Lonsdale, 1993, p. 131)

The ancients argued about the meanings of these activities and refined their philosophies in relationship to them. The religious connections made between play and human actions are clear, and we can see that some of the ways we think about play (the power and skill of agon; the pretense of mimesis; the luck of chaos) are still with us, at least intuitively. The forms of play the ancients discussed applied to all people and could be seen in adult actions as well as child's play. What we do not see is a clear rationale for considering the play of children, whether the weapon dance is just a religious ritual or whether it is socialization or practice for actual adult roles. The play actions of children outside of ritual activities were not recorded, so we have virtually no idea what comprised the range of children's play in these ancient times.

Enlightenment and Romantic Thought on Play

Ideas about play, and children's play in particular, received more attention during the historic periods when thinkers such as John Locke, Immanuel Kant, and Friedrich von Schiller began to reconsider the human mind. Rational thought, rather than a nearly exclusive focus on religion and belief, became the major concern of philosophers. What we know and how we know it, whether in the realms of science, morals, or the arts, became issues for analysis. Play was considered as part of this analysis in varying ways, as a foundation for rationality, as the roots of the irrational or spiritual, or in some cases it was just mentioned in passing. Again, we shall see that play was discussed in the most general terms, and we have little evidence for understanding what people actually did (or were supposed to do) when they played. We will begin to see that the play of children is separated from human play in general, allowing us to make a special case for children's play (although it is not clear what comprised such play). And we shall see that the increasing emphasis on play and rationality does not preclude a continued connection between ideas of play and the divine or spiritual. Finally, we shall see that links between play and rational thought led to the creation of detailed articulations of what play ought to be for children; play is elevated by educator/philosophers such as Friedrich Froebel to a type of activity, with specific objects that were thought to shape the mind and spirit.

The Rational Man: Locke and the Tabula Rasa

The 17th-century British philosopher John Locke (1632–1704) is frequently credited with providing a basis for psychological behaviorism. Locke's interest in the origins of reason lead him to speculate that each human being is born as an intellectual blank slate, or tabula rasa, on which our sense impressions are inscribed. Human thought results from experiences we have, not from any mystical or spiritual internal processes. We know what we learn. Locke's thoughts about the mind and how it is formed contributed to education and child rearing in his own day and long after.

Play is not often associated with Locke, but as his 1693 writing on *Some Thoughts Concerning Education* indicates, he was aware of play as an important part of childhood experience. This chapter's lead quote indicates that Locke saw play as being a necessary part of childhood. Children are players by nature, pursuing their imaginative "fancy" for the pleasure that it brings. While such experiences were not understood to contribute to rationality and the mind, Locke saw them as contributing to children's health and spirit. While not good for the mind, per se, play did have a role in improving attitude, aptitude, and physical well-being. Locke was among the first to specify that play with toys, carefully supervised by adults, was desirable for children.

Kant: Categorical Imperative, Play, and Aesthetics

Immanuel Kant (1724–1804) was an Enlightenment thinker with important ideas that influence us still. While he drew on many ancient Greek concepts for his philosophical framework, including many of those ancient ideas about play (agon, mimesis, chaos), his primary concern was with how we know things (Spariosu, 1989). Kant's writings on reason, the use of science to create knowledge, and the ways the mind categorically treats knowledge continue with us to this day through the research of Jean Piaget and others (Piaget, 1932/1965, 1970).

What does play have to do with knowledge, within this philosophical perspective? For adult human beings (Kant did not deal with children), the imagination, or free play of the mind, is the **context** in which knowledge and reason operate. Imaginings are those things that we strive to make sense of, thereby creating the need for knowledge. Play, in this sense, drives us to pursue knowledge. Kant did not stop here. He also attributed to play the basis for the arts and morality. As spiritual and moral matters are not concrete and cannot be objectively determined, it is left to the play of the imagination to guide us to understand the more ephemeral aspects of humanity.

By rooting (adult) imagination in play, Kant argued for a more cognitive or mental view of play. Play goes on in the head. He never linked his idea of play to activities (other than, perhaps, artistic creation), so we have no clues as to what play would look like. While not being, in Kant's terms, rational, play is clearly placed in the mental world as opposed to the world of activity. And Kant's world is an adult world, where he never deals with children and their play. It would be left to those who worked decades and centuries later to address those questions.

Schiller: The Roots of Creativity in Play

Philosophical thought about the role of play and human experience took a large step forward in the Enlightenment with Friedrich von Schiller (1759–1805). In the late 18th century, his philosophical work identified play as a key part of who we are as human beings, and he wrote specifically about play as expenditure of exuberant energy. Schiller's philosophical concerns were related to the role of play with all human beings, not just with children. As we shall see, it was later philosophers and educators who refined his ideas with regard to children. Within Schiller's philosophy, the notion of play contrasting with work is explored. From Schiller's point of view, work consumes our human energy to meet our physical needs; we work to survive, and that work consumes energy. Any energy that we may have left over is dedicated to play. So play is any exuberant or extra energy that we might have after we have completed our labors. This play is used by human beings for exploring **creativity**, for transcending the reality of our life in work. This makes play a symbolic activity; it is an activity that goes beyond the here and now (Schiller, 1795).

Within Schiller's framework, there are notions of physical play as well as symbolic play. Physical play can take the form of any physical activity, such as sport or festival, that involves the use of excess material energy; therefore, one strand of play within his thinking dealt with physical actions. Far more important to Schiller, however, were the symbolic aspects of play that took the form of symbolic or dramatic activity and were most frequently expressed through the arts. Any excess mental energy that we may have on completion of our labors can be used for creation of aesthetic or pleasing activities. These activities will allow us to move beyond the rote activities of labor, to think on a higher level. Thus, play is our route to higher-level, spiritual thought. In this philosophical view, it is such thought that allows humans to transcend their condition. Play becomes emancipatory and a source of hope. Schiller's message resonated with his revolutionary times. It is also the root of contemporary thought linking play with creativity, including current beliefs in the connection between play and imagination.

From the Enlightenment, we got a progression in the ideas philosophers articulated about play. John Locke saw play as natural for children, contributing to their spirits and well-being. Immanuel Kant attributed to play an important role in higher thought; play was the mental activity from which rationality emerged, especially as a basis for aesthetic expression. Friedrich von Schiller took this view one step further, theorizing that play was excess energy from which all creative, artistic, and spiritual activity grows. Philosophical beliefs evolved during this era, but they fell short of articulating or describing the actual play of children.

Shaping Rational Man: Froebel on Play in the Kindergarten

As discussed earlier, Schiller had great influence on intellectuals and artists during the era we call Romantic. His poetry inspired the composer Ludwig Van Beethoven to include Schiller's "Ode to Joy" in his *Ninth Symphony*. He also influenced the thought of the German educator Friedrich Froebel (1782–1852). Froebel was a student of the innovative Swiss educator Johan Pestalozzi (1746–1827). Among Pestalozzi's innovations were a democratic commitment to universal education and an understanding of the educational needs of younger learners, drawing on some aspects of Jean-Jacques Rousseau's (1712–1778) *Emile* (1762/1972) and Comenius's *The Great Didactic* (1896). Instead of learning by means of rote memorization, in Pestalozzi's view, children were supposed to learn naturally from their encounters with real things, so-called "object lessons." Learning by doing was a radical concept that was put into practice in Pestalozzi's Swiss school (Wolfe, 2002).

Froebel interpreted Pestalozzi's ideas and practices based on a number of his own learning experiences. He spent time as a youth working as a woodsman, and he studied physical science before serving as curator of a natural museum's crystal collection. These experiences combined with his study of Romantic philosophy, including Schiller and Rousseau, and ideas about humankind's relationship to **nature**, the innate goodness of learning from nature, and self-initiated learning. Schiller proposed the natural role of play, as excess or **surplus energy**, as humankind's route to higher, more spiritual thought. Froebel combined these experiential and philosophical bases with the pedagogical principles he acquired in Switzerland to formulate not just an activity-based curriculum, with objects inspired by physical science, but a play-based curriculum (Brosterman, 1997).

Given the pivotal role that Froebel's educational thought has in the history of children's play, it seems worthwhile to explore his curriculum on a number of levels. What did he believe play was? How can we reconcile the co-occurrence of "natural" (i.e., not tainted by society) activity and educational (a necessarily social) activity? How can we enable activity that captures the "spiritual" qualities that are characteristic of higher forms of thought? How should we think about such play activities as a curriculum, whereby children play their way to understanding? While Froebel did not provide explicit answers to all these questions, he did draw connections between philosophical beliefs and practical actions, in particular with the play materials and activities he included in his curriculum (Shapiro, 1983).

We are familiar with many of the play materials of this Froebelian kindergarten, but classroom play practices have changed over the decades.

Gifts and Occupations. In terms of play, one of the most interesting of Froebel's contributions was his interpretation of philosophical beliefs about play. The surplus aesthetic energy that Schiller described was seen by Froebel as an avenue for the "natural" education of children. He translated beliefs about play into educational practices by means of play objects that would be manipulated in ways that supposedly lead to educational insights. These objects, or "gifts," and their related activities were situated in a "natural" setting, where children were to be nourished like flowers in a garden—the children's garden, or kindergarten. A closer look at Froebel's revolutionary form of educational play will illustrate an important step in the history of children's play and at the same time raise questions about how "natural" this view of play really is.

Froebel designed gifts and occupations to allow children to experience a universal **spirituality**, an understanding of a humanist God's universe and one's place in that universe (Froebel, 1826/1902). That universe could be understood in terms of the physical world (nature), mathematics (how we know nature), and art (aesthetics or beauty) (Brosterman, 1997). By means of play activities, children would encounter the forms of nature, knowledge, and beauty that would reveal the "Divine Unity" of the world and our place in that unity (Froebel, 1826/1902). Froebel's ambitions for play were lofty.

What were the gifts and occupations that were designed to meet these high aspirations? Froebel developed his system of education over a period of decades, but he did not make clear distinctions between gifts and occupations. Versions of his publications describe a range of play materials that were included in the kindergarten (Brosterman, 1997). Figure 1–1 includes play objects listed in his *Education of Man* (1826/1902).

What did it mean to play in Froebel's kindergarten? From the gifts and occupations listed in Figure 1–1, it may seem that children might play just as they do in contemporary early childhood classrooms. The blocks, clay modeling, painting, and colored balls sound familiar; they are common playthings that might be on the open shelves of play centers in child care or kindergartens. As it

FIGURE 1–1 Froebel's Gifts and Occupations

Gifts

First gift:	Six small yarn balls, one each in a primary or secondary color
Second gift:	A small wood ball, wood cylinder, and wood cube
Third gift:	A small wooden cube, composed of eight component cubes
Fourth gift:	A small wooden cube, composed of eight rectangular blocks
Fifth gift:	A larger wooden cube, composed of 27 cubes
Sixth gift:	A comparably sized wooden cube, composed of 27 rectangular blocks
Seventh gift:	Wooden tablets (squares, half-squares, triangles, half-triangles, third-triangles) [parquetry shaped blocks]
Eighth gift:	Wooden sticks (lines) and metal curves (circles, half circles, quadrants)
Ninth gift:	Points (beans, seeds, pebbles, holes in paper)
Tenth gift:	Peas (or pellets) construction, with sticks

Occupations

Plastic clay (solids)
Paper folding (surfaces)
Weaving (lines)
Drawing (lines)
Stringing beads (points)
Painting (surfaces)

happens, there may be great differences between traditional kindergarten practices and contemporary ones, because of very different beliefs about what play is (Kuschner, 2002). A look at some of Froebel's writings may illustrate those differences.

"Natural" Education, at Mother's Knee. Some of Froebel's earliest educational writing is *Mother's Songs, Games, and Stories* (1844/1897). Froebel thought that child's play was symbolic and developmental, and codified play was the foundation of education. As can be seen from a review of the play activities he described, it is clear that what he saw as good, "natural" play for children were the games that mothers played with their young children, symbolically reflecting very specific cultural practices and values. Games like "Beckoning the Chickens" or "Beckoning the Pigeons" (pp. 26–29) in which the toddler is encouraged to simulate the mother's actions aimed at summoning and feeding birds, are good examples. These pretend activities for the child are clearly based on assumptions about participation in a very specific form of agrarian community, where cultural practices such as animal care were seen as central to life and custom. Likewise, Froebel's "natural" game of patty-cake (1844/1897, p. 147) reflects a simulation of the (then) culturally meaningful act of baking bread; the child was asked to participate in the actions performed by the baker or mother as she mixed, rolled, and baked a loaf of bread. Froebel goes to great lengths to affirm that such games were natural for the child and mother, while at the same time claiming that "it is a link in the great chain of life's inner dependence" with society (and thereby culture) at large (p. 148).

We could continue with an analysis of the entire volume of *Mother's Songs, Games, and Stories* to see a limitless set of culturally specific play activities, such as finger games (e.g., "The Shopman and the Girl," p. 102; "The Carpenter," p. 76) and action-accompanied songs (e.g., "The Fish in the Brook," p. 30; "Mowing Grass," p. 24). These play activities all involve some sort of pretense that is seen as natural; specific cultural experiences are the "what" of the pretense. Many of us grew up playing some of these games because Froebel's beliefs and practices of mother-child play were passed on to us.

The common assumption, given Froebel's position as a post-Enlightenment, Romantic educator, is that his view of education reflects an organic, naturally-based philosophy; the frequent occurrence of the word *Natural* (many times capitalized, as if to add prominence) in his writings tends to support that view. The metaphor of the flower growing in the garden for early education strengthens that assumption.

And how are we to be educationally natural, from Froebel's point of view? The answer is play. "The plays of childhood are the germinal leaves of all later life" (1826/1902, p. 55). The naturally creative actions of children are the basis for education. But what are the natural play activities that Froebel points to as naturally educative? He identifies a number of play activities that form the core of the kindergarten curriculum: the ball (for simulating the relationship of objects in the world to one another and for representing our connection to one another through games), building blocks (construction materials to simulate, worldly structures), sticks (for pattern creation to simulate letters), "pricking sheets" (pp. 285–287) for creating patterns and sewing (sewing or lacing cards), paper folding and cutting, and a number of other simulative manipulatives. Add to these the songs and games that mothers play with children, and we have a picture of Froebel's beliefs about what is "natural" in childhood.

Kindergarten play materials are a good deal less obviously tied to cultural customs than are his "Shopman" finger plays and the "Fish-in-the-Brook" song. There is something more abstract and educational about building with blocks as compared with imitating a weather vane. Yet the educational use of **manufactured** balls, made available thanks to new, industrial means of production, or paper for folding and sewing, based on the same industrial advancements, illustrates how culturally based all of Froebel's educational play really was. The materials Froebel selected were very much reflective of the industrializing society and culture of which he was a part.

By writing his books on the kindergarten, Froebel codified and institutionalized certain ideas and practices that have been passed on to us (although not necessarily intact). It is doubtful that any contemporary practitioner of early childhood education would call her or himself a Froebelian, but go into any classroom and you will witness residue of his influence: block play, ball games, finger plays, circle time, and any number of other play activities that we can trace directly to him. Also present in teacher thinking are any number of Froebel-linked ideas, such as the naturally unfolding/developing child and the spiritual, innate goodness of the child.

As a student of Pestalozzi, Froebel saw the importance of education in shaping the rational and spiritual being. Good, thoughtful people were created by education, so a purposeful program was needed to create conditions where those ends could be reached. With Froebel, we see a shift from mere thought about practice and play to specific prescriptions about what practice should be. He began with the world of play ideas (both rational and spiritual). He translated the ideas into activities, and he prescribed what play should be in order for it to serve the ends of education. He was one of the first thinkers about play to create rational play institutions, in the form of his carefully articulated play curriculum and the schools where it would be implemented. Play would no longer be abstract (only for philosophers) and intuitive (practiced without thinking). German immigrants were impressed with Froebel's ideas and brought them to the United States in 1856, where they became extremely popular.

Froebel made many intuitive assumptions about the naturalness of play, apparently assuming the universality of play as he saw it. In a fundamental sense, he created a special form and world of children's play. How did he do this? First and foremost, he articulated a rational plan for play and linked that plan to the civilizing institution of education; he made play less a part of **nature** and more a part of **nurture**. Assumptions about either the "naturalness" of play (especially children's play) or the cultural-groundedness of play (especially for ritual, recreation, and sport) underlie much research, in spite of admonitions by Sutton-Smith (1993) and others that social and physical context have a great deal to do with what we study. Froebel is something of an anomaly in this regard, as he argued for the naturalness of play but then prescribed a remarkably detailed set of cultural play activities that were seen as basic to education.

By linking play and education, Froebel saw the benefit of particular play settings (his "garden") for the education of children. Play may take place anywhere, but educational play occurs in particular, planned settings. This effort to make play more rational, or conscious to us, suggests the idea that specific forms of children's play are *not* natural, like those found in many North American, middle-class homes, where education and schooling are significant parental concerns and the context is richly arranged with concrete play materials to engage and guide children. The material and symbolic nature of this particular play becomes a meaningful entry point for understanding particular family socialization patterns. Froebel made part of such play rational to us, while ignoring its cultural roots. His beliefs also reflected assumptions about what is "natural" for children—assumptions that would be explored later in his century.

On the Nature of Play: Scientific Approaches

The rich history of philosophical musing about play, from the ancient Greeks to the Romantic thinkers, gave way to a new perspective inspired by the revolutionary work of Charles Darwin (Schwartzman, 1978; Spariosu, 1989; Sutton-Smith, 1997). While Darwin himself was not much interested in play, his work on evolutionary science had a tremendous impact on how people subsequently thought about play. His thinking about natural selection and species' survival contributed to a scientific look at play, as opposed to the earlier philosophical speculations.

Those earlier speculations were not entirely lost, but in the post-Darwin era, they were reinterpreted and given new meanings. For example, the late 18th-century philosopher Herbert Spencer (1820–1903) revisited Schiller's notion of play as surplus energy and converted it into a psychological version of Darwin's ideas about adaptation. In this modified theory, surplus energy was seen to fuel instincts that would assist natural selection; play fighting was associated with the need for dominance, coordinated games were associated with the need for social interaction, and artistic/aesthetic play would enhance symbolic skills. Schiller's philosophical beliefs were refocused on specific human activities that were consistent with emergent thought about human adaptation.

Darwin's evolutionary theory began to influence a number of 19th-century scholars of play, including Spencer, G. Stanley Hall, Karl Groos, and, bridging into the 20th century, John Dewey. The scientific view of play, as opposed to the more purely philosophical emphasis of earlier scholars, contributed to our theoretical and research-based views of play that will be more fully described in Chapter 2. The following sections will address the historical progress of the play concept prior to the advent of systematic, empirical study of play.

Hall on Recapitulation

Just as Herbert Spencer had adapted earlier thinking about play in light of Darwin's theory of evolution, G. Stanley Hall (1846–1924) found his own way of interpreting evolution in his theoretical understanding of children and their development. Hall, a psychology professor at Clarke University and founder of the Child Study Movement in the United States, was dedicated to creating a scientific approach to understanding child development. Like other behavioral scientists of his time, he was influenced by Darwin and by the experimental scientific methods that were being created in the latter half of the 19th century. The purpose of these scientific methods was to move beyond philosophical belief and speculation toward a body of knowledge based on observation and experimentation. Philosophical ideas were to be given their due, but the proof of any idea was in its testing. Efforts to create a scientific, predictable understanding of children were increasing at this time, because of the dramatic growth of public education, with the accompanying need for teachers to understand the children they were teaching.

Play was certainly not Hall's primary concern, but he wrote on many aspects of child growth, including childhood play. Basing some of his scholarship on the new biological, theory of evolution, he articulated what he referred to as a "recapitulation theory" of play and development. The metaphor he used is fairly transparent and is now discounted, but it is of interest given the influence he had during his life and with the students who followed him. The essence of **recapitulation** theory is that each organism re-creates the evolution of the species in its organic development. In utero and after birth, the biological and cultural progress of the entire species is played out in how the individual organism grows. In utero, we supposedly see the human fetus change from a single-cell organism to a fish, amphibian, reptile, and finally mammal. Such theorizing had its appeal when it could explain the simple observations of biological development that were available at that time; of course, contemporary science shows us that the complete complement of any human phenotype is fully present in the DNA of any fetus.

Hall, with the scientific tools available to him, carried his recapitulation metaphor to the development of human behavior. As the biology of each organism had been understood to repeat the evolution of species, so did the behavioral development of each individual repeat the cultural evolution of humankind (as understood at that time). This theory predicted that observing any child would reveal a developmental sequence, and that the sequence would represent significant steps in the evolution of *Homo sapiens* (see Table 1–1).

By going through all of the play **stages** included in the recapitulation theory, children would, in essence, get the primitive past of the human

TABLE 1–1 Hall's Recapitulation Theory of Play

Evolutionary Stage	Play Forms
Animal	Climbing, swinging
Savage	Tag, hide-and-seek, hunting games
Nomad	Pet care
Agricultural/settlement	Digging in sand, playing with dolls
Tribal	Team games

species out of their system. They would then be able to focus on the higher-level mental and social skills that were expected of civilized human beings. Adult play, in the form of games such as baseball or football, was seen as an instinctual offshoot of residual, precivilized times. Play had its purposes in contemporary child development, but the purposes had to do with overcoming our uncivilized biological roots; play did not build toward a future but was seen to allow us to get rid of the past.

It is easy to dismiss the recapitulation theory on any number of grounds. It does not reflect the facts or gist of Darwin's theory of evolution, with its emphasis on the biological development of the individual, as opposed to his more nuanced consideration of populations and adaptation. Nor does it reflect an accurate picture of cultural history, with its sequence of stages that grossly simplify the progress of civilization. And, most telling, the stages of play that are predicted by the theory have not been validated by observation; child play does not progress as Hall's theory tells us it should. Despite these significant flaws, recapitulation theory continues to impact us because it does something novel: It tells us we can look for detailed, progressing stages in child play and development. Hall had the facts wrong, and he misinterpreted any number of theories; but he provided a principle for tracking the behavioral progress of children. This principle has shaped much of the research that has been done since his time, including the work of oft-cited 20th-century play researchers such as Mildred Parten, Jean Piaget, and Kenneth Rubin.

Hall's play theory is significant for us, not because of what it tells us substantively or theoretically about play; he was clearly in error in his beliefs about what play is. His theory is significant because it has provided us with a way of thinking about children's play, in terms of progressive stages that children pass through on their roads to maturity, albeit not the stages he identified. Hall gave us a way of thinking that remains with most of us to this day.

Groos and Practice Play

A more faithful and plausible interpretation of Darwin's theory of evolution was explored by the naturalist Karl Groos (1861–1946). Groos was a scholar with broad interests, including aesthetics, ethology, and psychology. Among his writings were two classic books on play, *The Play of Animals* (1898) and *The Play of Man* (1901). While philosophical speculation is still present in his theory, Groos had the insight to see play as a contributor to evolutionary adaptation.

His argument reduces to a number of basic points. The so-called lower animals, those that have not evolved as much over the course of history, do not play; we have no evidence to support the belief that insects, fish, snakes, or toads play. There is plenty of evidence that species that have evolved to higher levels, including mammals and especially great apes, do play a great deal. It is also apparent that species that have evolved to these so-called higher levels demonstrate much more play with their juvenile members; puppies play more than mature dogs, and human children play more than adults. These observations suggested to Groos that play serves an adaptive purpose, that play as defined by him functions to contribute to the survival of the species. He identified this function as **pre-exercise** or **practice.**

Groos's idea about play makes more sense when we remember that the species that he thought of as having evolved to higher levels, particularly humans, have a relatively longer period of immaturity in the spans of their lives. Immature insects, in their pupal forms, are immobile, and when most snakes or fish are hatched, they may be smaller than adults but are fully responsible for their own survival. Mammals, on the other hand, are born immature and need periods of care and weaning prior to moving into their adult roles. We humans consider nearly the first 20 years of our lives as a period of immaturity, when babies are nurtured, children are schooled, and adolescents are socialized into the culture. This period of immaturity is marked by the predominance of play, and the longer the period of immaturity, the more play. Play, during immaturity, was seen by Groos as the opportunity to practice those things that would prove to be adaptive for the species during adulthood.

The sorts of things that might be practiced would vary from species to species. We can easily imagine that a kitten chasing and pouncing on a ball or leaf is developing those very skills that an adult cat will use to prey on mice; the kitten is pre-exercising catlike hunting skills that allow cats to feed and survive. The juvenile chase games of baboons practice the social hierarchies that precede adult social structures that are necessary for social cohesion, protection, and propagation of the species. Juvenile baboon play provides a service for what comes after.

It is more complicated to imagine how human childhood play might serve this Darwinian adaptive function. Groos identified two types of human play that he saw as functional: experimental play and socionomic play. Experimental play provides sensory and motoric practice, including object manipulation, construction, and games with rules. Such play should pre-exercise adult self-control. Socionomic play provides practice for interpersonal skills, including chase and rough-and-tumble games, social and family (dramatic) play, and imitation. While Groos was aware of beliefs about play serving as a basis for symbolic and creative endeavors, he limited his view of practice play to self-control and social skills.

Groos, with his theory on practice play, provided an important rationale for valuing play. At the same time, he limited his argument to a small number of play domains that he saw as adaptive. Perhaps the biggest strength in his ideas comes from the way he argues that play is necessary and useful for adult human life, as opposed to views like Hall's, in which play was reduced to a set of activities that needed to be worked through by the growing child to allow later development. There are also many weaknesses in Groos' view, not least of which is the difficulty of testing it scientifically.

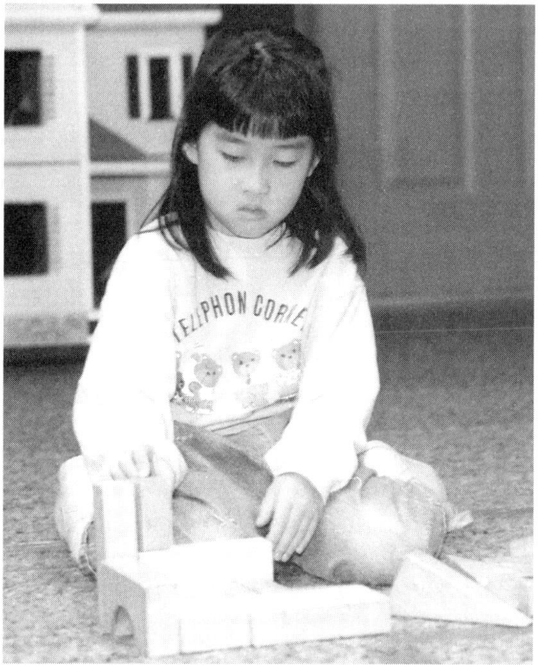

Traditional materials may be used in many ways, as children freely realize their ideas through play.

The Modern Era of Children's Play

The 19th century began with a set of inspirational beliefs about play firmly in place. Schiller's philosophical writing, in particular, highlighted the importance of play as a source of human creativity and higher thought. The growth of popular education, especially the revolutionary curriculum designed by Froebel, translated these beliefs into play activities intended to develop and educate young children. Prerational beliefs about play as mimesis (Spariosu, 1989) were translated into rationalized institutions for human development, where symbolic representation in play served educational ends. By midcentury, new scientific theory from the biologist Charles Darwin shifted discourse on play away from the spiritual and symbolic toward the biological. Agon and chaos (Spariosu, 1989) were acknowledged as possible contributors to human adaptation, although the role of culture was not yet understood. Beliefs and ideas about play were becoming more rational, but the lack of evidence about what play is and how it functions for children kept our understanding of play activities on a prerational level.

At the start of the 20th century, values and beliefs about play varied widely, and there were disagreements about play's particular role in development and education. Equally widespread was the commitment to study children, making use of the new tools of science that Hall, his students, and others were creating. The study of children inevitably lead to research on play. Many of these threads of research, beliefs, and values came together in the writings of John Dewey, one of the foremost educational philosophers of the 20th century.

Montessori and the Absorbent Mind

Maria Montessori (1870–1952) was an inspired educator who has contributed to professional and parental ideas about young children's growth and needs. The first woman to receive a medical degree in Italy as well as a Ph.D. in anthropology (Wolfe, 2002), Montessori had a rich and varied career in pediatrics, psychiatry, and what we today would call special education. Her view of child development and education was well articulated in a number of books, many of which continue to be in print (e.g., Montessori, 1913, 1917, 1964, 1995). Perhaps more importantly, she established schools for children, called Houses for Children (Casas dei Bambini), first in Rome, then around the world. In these Houses for Children, activities were conducted that were designed to meet the needs of urban, impoverished children who needed education to assist their development by allowing them to organize their environments. Activities were based on beliefs in the child's spiritual goodness, internal motivation, and propensity to act constructively in a free, properly planned environment.

Montessori's approach to education was impressive in its philosophical and pedagogical richness. Play was not central to her view of education and development, although there were two aspects of Montessori's program that seemed to relate to play. First, the teacher (or directress, as she was called) of a children's house prepared a planned environment, where children freely chose their involvement with Montessori materials. As children developed, they chose more purposefully, no longer playing with materials, but preparing for lessons that refined the senses and created order. As Hall had theorized (see Hall on Recapitulation), children in Montessori programs got play with materials out of their systems before they were ready to learn. Acting freely was important and necessary, but the purposes of education and development were reached only when children put their play impulses on hold to receive demonstrations from the directress. The directress observed the children closely, to see when they were ready for lessons.

Second, the planned environment in a Montessori school was richly provided with miniature or child-sized materials. Furniture and materials were designed with great care for developmental needs and competence. Small pitchers and glasses, miniature mops, brooms, and buckets, all suggested to the outsider that the children were engaging with toys, and so were playing. Such was not the case. Children did not play, in the sense of pretending, with these materials. Miniature objects in a Montessori school were designed to help the child master real-world skills, with objects that were crafted to their size; the child did not pretend to pour or clean, but refined motor skills in order to really pour and clean. A child pretending with any of these materials was seen as not yet ready to benefit from using them.

Her writing and schools made Montessori famous early in the last century. G. Stanley Hall, Arnold Gesell, John Dewey, and Jean Piaget were among those who knew of her work, although not all agreed with her approach (Wolfe, 2002). Montessori schools existed worldwide, and in the United States were private preschools and Head Start centers (consistent with their original design, for low-income children), and the Montessori philosophy increasingly informs the curriculum in public schools. While some saw play in her approach, others sensed that play was incidental to Montessori's beliefs and curriculum.

Dewey on Science in Planned Contexts

John Dewey (1859–1952) was a leading American philosopher who continues to have influence on academic and professional thought. He was interested in creating a pragmatic point of view in the service of society. Society in his time was changing rapidly due to immigration and industrialization. It could be argued that the quick changes Dewey saw were no less pronounced than our current waves of immigration and increasing technology. Dewey applied his philosophy to a range of political, aesthetic, and professional problems, including children's education.

As a critic of public education, Dewey articulated a number of arguments for dealing with education. He also established a laboratory school at the University of Chicago, where he taught. Among the beliefs that he elaborated were inquiry as valuable for studying practice, to understand how and why practice worked; that education is based on the experiences of students; and that the values of democracy and **freedom** need to be infused into education. In his writings and laboratory, Dewey attempted to refine those beliefs.

To what educational end or aim might play contribute, especially the aim of education for participation in a democratic society? Dewey wrote about play in two ways: (a) play as providing a more generalized internalizing of knowledge by younger children and (b) play as being the free, intrinsically interesting exploration of society and nature. To explicate more fully those trains of thought, Dewey's writing is contrasted with that of Lev Vygotsky (1978), who describes some similar features of play as a means for unifying meaning through free action. It will be argued that both scholars' views complement and explicate one another in necessary ways, although questions remain about the nature and role of social context for educational play.

Dewey's writings served as a framework of sorts, for guiding how, and what, we thought about play as an educative activity. In some of his earliest educational and psychological writing on play, Dewey (1896/1972) addressed the nursery school child's experience and the centrality of play for helping the child make ideas his or her own: "The child does not get hold of any impression or any idea until he has *done* it" (p. 195). "He acts the idea *out* before he takes it *in*" (p. 196). Intrinsically motivated, freely chosen, communicative pretense was described as *the* primary educative experience for the preschool child. Play actions, as communicative efforts, were described as the way children formed ideas. The experience of pretend play allowed children to actively make meaningful what is most important to them (i.e., their interests), but symbolic enactment also necessarily builds the shared symbol systems and community that go with them. It is a good deal less clear how this view of play, as pretend, relates to the education of school-age children.

Play, as a term relevant to older children, was more fully discussed 20 years later by Dewey (1916) in *Democracy and Education*. It is then that additional notions of play, especially his distinction of work and play, were presented. Again, freedom and intrinsic motivation were seen as defining elements of play, as a means of exploring personal and shared interests. At this point, Dewey noted that work is undifferentiated from play for younger children (p. 239), while older children presumably have more distinct notions about different purposes of work and play (King, 1982).

If school-age children's play is somewhat different than the pretend play of preschoolers, then what is play during that developmental stage (or should it be)? What *are* free and intrinsically motivating activities for elementary school-age children? Dewey gave us only the most general ideas, about exploring outdoors (Rivkin, 1997) and playgrounds (Frost, 1992). Dewey did not give us enough of his thinking about play, especially at the elementary-school level, on which to build. Also, he seemed to acknowledge that despite common component dispositions to play (such as freedom, intrinsic motivation, social engagement), we are dealing with a different play phenomenon for preschoolers (pretend) and elementary children (exploration). In terms of the educative aims of play, both of these senses of play are a model or foundation for free participation in a community of people with shared interests.

Dewey wrote eloquently of the inseparability of means and ends. To practice freedom, one must experience freedom. The same must be true for formation of any social community. Play seems to embody those experiences of freedom, but it seems that there are any number of forms of play that Dewey did not describe or anticipate: illicit play, scapegoating, peer culture, and exclusionary pretend and games. Children can be mean and antidemocratic when they play, as Sutton-Smith (1997) has argued. Dewey was working from a set of beliefs about what play was, influenced by Romantic and Enlightenment thinkers. He did not have an extensive database on play in its many forms. What he was able to do was articulate his belief in the freedom inherent in play and weave that belief into his view of education.

Today, Dewey is more typically cited in support of philosophical perspectives or ideological points of view regarding the child-centered curriculum. His specific notions about play are ignored as scholars explore more contemporary theorists, such as Vygotsky (1978), with whom Dewey has a certain degree of agreement regarding play. Dewey's view, as outlined earlier, appeared to be reducible to two strands: play is a form of activity that for young children *is* their form of thought, and play is freely chosen activity. Vygotsky's view of play resonates with Dewey in a number of ways. Vygotsky writes of play being the way "thought is separated from objects and action arises from ideas rather than things" (1978, p. 97), as well as "the development of will, the ability to make conscious choices" (p. 101). Both authors appear to see play as action that allows meaning creation for young children and as an expression of will. While Vygotsky's contributions to play theory will be presented in more detail in Chapter 2, it is worth noting a few commonalties between his ideas and Dewey's here.

Vygotsky (1978) places play in a central location in his contextualist view of development. Play is identified as a key developmental phase, from the preschool to the early school years. It is a zone of proximal development (ZPD), within which "the child can stand a head taller than he really is" (p. 102). Play is a developmental mechanism that allows young children to turn actions into meanings and to internalize (or to make abstract) those meanings. Play is supposedly developmentally meaningless for infants and older children, but for preschoolers it is the epitome of mental life, whereby they acquire the symbol system and ideas of our culture(s). Vygotsky's ZPD appears to match Dewey's "realization of an idea" (1896/1972, p. 195) from the "totality of life" (p. 197).

Vygotsky and Dewey also seem to be agreeing when they describe experience (using Dewey's term) and consciousness (Vygotsky's term), linkages of perception and action, play as the internalization of (self-) control, and play being characterized by free choice. These similarities in belief are in contrast to several differences, including when play is a significant activity for children (for Vygotsky it is salient only during early childhood) and the nature of freedom (for Dewey it is the action-based foundation for participating in society, while for Vygotsky it is illusory and tied only to any meaning being enacted). Dewey's freedom has more implications for social and societal relationships; Vygotsky's freedom primarily shapes thinking.

Social context is important for both, but Dewey specified his relevant context in terms of democratic society; the values of democracy have their roots in the choices of play. He also gave schools, as institutions that shape the minds and beliefs of citizens, a challenge to include play and study by means of play as part of the curriculum for a democratic society. How must we think about play differently, to support it and make it a better educational tool for promoting democratic relationships? This is a question that was not asked by Froebel, Hall, or earlier thinkers who shaped our beliefs about play. Dewey also shifted thinking about play from the evolutionary, biological thinking of Darwin and Groos toward beliefs about play as a social institution.

As a pragmatic philosopher, Dewey bridged the era when scholars elaborated their beliefs and the contemporary era when scientists tested their beliefs. Dewey built systematic inquiry into his philosophy, challenging his followers to test their ideas in the laboratory of life. If we "create" play customs in classrooms, then we should study those customs to understand how they work. Children's play was gaining more legitimacy as a scholarly interest, and what follows in this book is a record of that scholarship. And as we came to know more about play, it was studied by scholars in a variety of disciplines, including history.

Academic Child Development in the Early 20th Century

The growing field of scientific child study in universities and colleges combined with the growth of kindergarten education and the emergence of the nursery school movement to stimulate research and academic writing on children's play in the first half of the 20th century. Ideas about play in the kindergarten were being tested and refined in light of newer theories of development (Kuschner, 2001). Nursery school laboratories were beginning to provide play-based settings for describing children's growth in rigorous ways. Ideas about play and development became increasingly differentiated during this period, and the issue of play as an indicator of child interests emerged.

While Froebel's vision of the child as a natural player, using gifts and occupations to learn about forms of beauty, life, and knowledge, was still popular in some circles, others were adapting his activities to a Child Study Movement notion of "the whole child." Prominent educators such as Patty Smith Hill were among those who wanted to adapt a playful kindergarten to more of the needs of children and the school curriculum (Wolfe, 2002). She, and many others, attempted to incorporate John Dewey's thinking about studying children in school as a way to understand their education. Using kindergartens, and then nursery schools, as laboratories for studying children's education became important (e.g., Burk & Burk, 1920; Hall, 1911; Jersild & Fite, 1939).

Laboratory schools, still influenced by a version of the Froebelian idea of play as the primary avenue for learning for young children, were settings where play was described and researched. Prominent texts on child psychology and development asserted "We have already pointed out that much of the child's learning takes place during play" (Jersild, 1933, p. 431), while describing the child in terms of motor, language, social, emotional, cognitive (i.e., "understanding"), and imaginative development (e.g., Jersild, 1933, 1942, 1946; Morgan, 1935). Classroom play was seen as the norm for young children, where optimal learning occurred in all aspects of development. Some effort was made to describe laboratory play settings (Hill & Langdon, 1930; Jersild & Fite, 1939) that were considered optimal.

Much of the research and writing produced during this period tended to describe play development in terms of children's chronological age (e.g., Gesell, 1934, 1939; Jersild, 1933; Rasmussen, 1920). The sorts of writing that had existed 50 years before, such as Froebel's mystical writing about children's nature, and Montessori's writing about the spiritual child, were being replaced by normative descriptions of children at different ages (e.g., Parten, 1932). (Most of the children being described were Caucasian and from university communities.) The dominant impression was that children could be understood in terms of how they play at different ages, and their play could be understood in terms of aspects of development (motor, language, social, emotional, cognitive, etc.) (Thomas, 1996). The convergence of play, learning, and development of the whole child was standard in textbooks and research. An age and stage understanding of play provided a guide for teachers and parents, as they looked to age norms as a way of understanding the progress that children were making. Such an age and stage approach to understanding children perhaps had the unanticipated consequence of suggesting that aging by itself (i.e., maturation) was enough to ensure developmental progress. The role of social context and support for play (i.e., the nurture of play), took a back seat to the assumed nature of play (that which the child brings with her while playing).

Issues of culture and context were not totally ignored, although they are almost afterthoughts in the description of the Child Study Movement whole child as player. One way that the educational context appeared was in the recurring emphasis on play as an avenue for understanding children's interests. Dewey had proposed education as a developmental process where we pursue our individual and socially shared interests. Child development researchers, building on Hall's survey approach, saw the study of children's play as an important way of understanding children's interests and the context of their development. By looking at children's play, teacher/researchers could learn about children's interests and prepare the curriculum to build on children's intrinsic interests. Play was not just a natural process; it was a window to the things that motivated children. Children's play interests were an important feature of child psychology in the 1930s and 1940s (e.g., Jersild, 1933, 1942, 1946), but had virtually disappeared as a topic 30 years later (e.g., Jersild, Telford, & Sawrey, 1975).

The abstractions of 19th century thought about play were being refined and replaced in the early 20th century. Development of the whole child, as a physical, social, thinking being (who, to a lesser degree, operates in a culture) had become our way of thinking about play; play was seen as how children learn and develop. Scientifically established age norms replaced Romantic ideas, and debates about the freedom and meaning of play began (e.g., Burk & Burk, 1920; Kuschner, 2001). While age and stage descriptions of the development of play became firmly entrenched, there was still some acknowledgement that observations of play should not discount the social setting within which they take place.

Huizinga on Cultural Change

During the early 20th century, children's play emerged as a topic of study. Continuing today, researchers focused on aspects of play and development or on play itself. Play scholars may view children's play as part of the larger picture of human play (e.g., Caillois, 1961; Figler & Whitaker, 1991; Reifel, 1999; Spariosu, 1989; Sutton-Smith, 1997). The Dutch historian Johan Huizinga (1872–1945) attempted an ambitious cultural history of play, parts of which have been very influential for children's play scholars.

In his 1938 book *Homo Ludens: A Study of the Play-Element in Culture*, Huizinga brought together descriptions of a broad range of anthropological, sociological, and artistic activities from around the world. His purpose was to demonstrate "that civilization arises and unfolds in and as play" (Huizinga, 1938, foreword). Play, both children's and adults', serves social and cultural functions: forming social groups; creating distinct communities within society; creating social status among groups and individuals; enabling social cohesion; transforming culture; displaying social oppositions; reaffirming social concerns. (See Henricks, 1999, for a critique of these functions.) Musical performance, adult festival, sport, and children's play are all part of this analysis, and are all part of what makes civilization exist and change.

FIGURE 1–2 Huizinga's Characteristics of Play

1. Play is voluntary.
2. Play is not ordinary or real.
3. Play is secluded or limited.
4. Play creates order, is order.
5. Play tends to surround itself with secrecy.

Play, as seen by Huizinga, has great power over who we are as members of society. It defines our social position, supports our values, and contributes to our identities as members of the group. Even more powerfully, play does not merely replicate existing social and cultural standards. Because of the social dynamic created by play, it is a force for challenging and advancing society. The "play" of social strife and resolution is not metaphoric; it has real consequences.

Most researchers of children's play do not consider simultaneously the cultural, social, and historical dimensions that Huizinga did. They do acknowledge the characteristics of play that he devised (see Figure 1–2). The qualities of play that he saw as descriptive and transformative for society have become useful definitions for what play is, including its voluntary nature (we must chose to play), its nonordinariness (pretend is not real), the seclusion or delimitation of play (it takes place in particular places such as a playing field or is private like computer games), its orderliness (there are rules inherent in most play), and its secrecy (we keep key information from nonplayers). Duncan (1988) argues that too much of Huizinga's understanding of play is based on competitive or conflict forms of play. In spite of possible biases in Huizinga's work, these characteristics have been adapted for child play scholarship, whether in the form of descriptive dispositions to play (Rubin, Fein, & Vandenberg 1983; Spodek & Saracho, 1988) or refinement of other theoretical constructs.

Materials for Play

The study of the history of play has been made difficult by the lack of extensive documentation of play activities and, to some degree, by the lack of play objects that tell us about how people played in the past. Growth of the toy industry, caused by the technology and wealth of the industrial revolution in the 19th century, contributed to new forms of play research: the study of toys (Cross, 1997). Interest in and nostalgia for the toys of our childhood have created new understandings about what play is and how play objects may shape our play.

The most comprehensive study to date of the history of toys is Cross's (1997) survey of manufactured toys and beliefs about them. Cross describes the transition from locally crafted playthings to the mass market of toys in the United States. The tradition of craftspeople (often from Germany; see also Brosterman, 1997) preparing limited numbers of dolls and building sets for the few families who could afford them was replaced by the trend of less expensive, machine-made toys for the general public. Such toys became more available, thanks to new institutions such as 5- and 10-cent stores and catalog shopping. Growth in this new market sparked debates during the 20th century about what toys were good or bad, the appropriateness of certain toys for boys and girls, parental roles in play, and social class and race. Cross documents these debates in both academic publications and popular magazines.

Themes that Cross explores include a number of beliefs that have spanned the history of play. Do manufactured toys shape a child's future, as a type of pre-exercise? Do toys affect personality and character? To what extent do manufactured toys expand or suppress children's imaginations? These debates have been going on for a century, prior to concerns about whether Barbie dolls damage girls' body images or GI Joe dolls make boys more violent.

The role of manufactured toys in play continues to be of interest for play researchers. As new technology creates new play objects, new questions arise about how children are playing and what that play means for them.

EMERGING ISSUES

> A gaggle of hilarious boys gathered around, almost drunk with jollity, wanting to know what I had written down. "It's War this morning," they said, waving their plastic pistols. One of them was wearing the top part of a camouflaged battledress. (Opie, 1993, p. 60)

Industrial and technological society creates a new context within which play has new meanings. War play is no longer seen as a ritual for citizenship, as it had been in ancient Greece (see The Ancients and Play); contemporary scholars see it as a kind of fun mass marketed by the toy industry. Communities where play takes place have changed, and parental supervision is not what it once was; suburban neighborhoods and mobile professionals provide more change in children's lives than stability. Television and other media contribute to play, providing ideas to mimic and objects for play; every new summer movie has a shelf of toys that represent it. Toys are available in a wider variety of places, including every fast-food restaurant that caters to children; having popular playthings, rather than making things, is the norm.

> The hand-clappers were still clapping when the bell rang. With half an ear I had overheard them singing the favourite Brownie song "I went to the animal fair, the birds and the beasts were there," and chanting the newest version of "When Susie was a baby." (Opie, 1993, p. 200)

History provides some perspective on these emerging conditions in which play continues to be important. Girls in ancient times danced to prepare for womanhood, sometimes imitating animals in their ritual play (see The Ancients and Play). Contemporary girls sing about animals and join play groups to celebrate their friendships. Themes that have withstood millennia will be useful, but they must be interpreted in light of new circumstances.

SUMMARY

Spariosu (1989) tells us that our core concepts about play—mimesis, agon, and chaos—have a venerable history in Western thought. The imitative, competitive or aggressive, and random qualities of play remain commonalities as we participate in play, whether as adults or children. Over the past 2,000 years, we have become more aware of these qualities and moved them from the prerational to the fully rational parts of our minds, where we can fully think about them. The ancient Greeks emphasized more of the competitive in play; their games were imitations of conflict. They also valued the imitative in their religious rites and theater. The innate, natural quality of play was assumed. But it was not until the 18th century that we began to value the rational, creative, and imagination-provoking qualities of mimesis.

The Enlightenment began to link play with the mind and thinking, as a source of creativity. Kant and Schiller made play a key element of their philosophies, allowing subsequent thinkers to apply those ideas to children and child development. Other thinkers, such as Locke, at least acknowledged the value of play for recreation and identifying aptitudes. Froebel, building on ideas from Schiller, Rousseau, and Pestalozzi, made his form of play rational. He took the prerational cultural customs of German life and made them into a tool for shaping the spiritual, creative, and intellectual lives of children. Froebel was one of the first thinkers in history to translate ideas about children's play into practice. His popular ideas helped shape thinking about play in the United States and elsewhere.

Developments in natural science, especially Darwin's theory of evolution, began to provide new ways to think about play as a natural phenomenon. From the mid–19th century to the beginning of the 20th, it was assumed that play was a biological mechanism, a part of what we are as human beings. Psychologists such as Hall saw play as a necessary stage that children must go through, repeating the biological development of the species, before they can transcend our "primitive" history. Images of play as imitation predominated. Groos interpreted child play as practice for what was to come, a form of preparation for helping the species adapt. While the biological bases of play continue to interest scholars, the lasting contribution of these thinkers was the idea of stage theory for play. This influence continues in educational programs for young children and in the child development research that guides our understanding of play.

More recent history has seen not only the mimesis of play, in the form of pretend, but also the agon of play return as topics of interest. Conflict, and its resolution in the service of democratic principles, were part of Dewey's play legacy, in addition to his interest in enactive pretend play. From a different perspective, Huizinga pointed to the socially generative functions of play, based not only on symbolic action (as during festivals) but also on the social stratification of play (as with team formation). He made us aware of how we might be using play to transform our culture; he made the unconscious conscious. These scholars also point to the emergence of evidence, or research findings, in our efforts to know more about play, whether in the world of children or in society as a whole.

The imaginary, the challenging, and the purely fanciful come together in contemporary studies of the history of play. Play has become a predominant element in our materialistic society. The study of toys and the play that goes with them seems to return to questions about our historically rooted, philosophical beliefs. What do toys and our culture do to our imaginations, and how does that shape who we are? Does play require conflict and violence, or challenge us to improve our human skills? Is fun just fun, or does it do something more important for us? And how do our current cultural conditions alter any of those questions? The answers to these questions, while based in historical beliefs, may depend on which theoretical lenses we use to inspect play (Sutton-Smith, 1995).

KEY TERMS

Chance
- *Chaos*

Competition
- *Agon*
- *Games*

Context
Creativity
Culture
Development
Developmentally appropriate practice (DAP)
Education
Experience
Freedom
Imitation
- *Mimesis*
- *Pretend*
- *Symbolic play*

Manufactured
Nature
Nurture
Pre-exercise/practice
Recapitulation
Society
Spirituality
Stages
Surplus energy

STUDY QUESTIONS

1. How did the ancient Greeks think about play?
2. What was the role of religious belief in ancient Greek play?
3. What are the characteristics of *agon, mimesis*, and *chaos*?
4. How did the Enlightenment alter how people thought about play?
5. How did various Enlightenment philosophers (Locke, Kant) see play as contributing to rational thought?
6. How did various Romantic philosophers (Schiller, Froebel) see play as contributing to a rational spirit?
7. In what ways are play and creativity linked?
8. How did the following researchers/theorists contribute to how we think about play: Locke, Kant, Schiller, Froebel, Groos, Hall, Huizinga, Dewey, Vygotsky? What were their specific contributions?
9. How did Darwin's theory of evolution alter thoughts and beliefs about play?
10. Contrast two biologically based theories of the development of play. How does play serve different developmental ends from these points of view?
11. What basic beliefs did Dewey have about play and its role in education? How did he propose to verify that his beliefs were correct?
12. How does this historical era influence how we think about play and how we look at play? Why does 20th-century play look different than 19th-century play?
13. With a friend, observe children playing. Compare your beliefs about what the children are doing as they play. What are the historical origins of the beliefs you have?
14. Why is it useful to understand the history of play (a) for understanding a particular play activity such as block play and (b) for gaining insight into how we think about play in general?
15. How might play contribute to who we are as individuals and to the society within which we live?

Chapter 2 Theory as Lenses on Children's Play

SOME STUDY the body, some study behavior, some study thinking, some study groups or individuals, some study experience, some study language—and they all use the word play *for these quite different things. Furthermore their play theories, which are the focus of this present work, rather than play itself, come to reflect these various diversities and make them even more variable.*

(Sutton-Smith, 1997, p. 6)

What is "play theory," and why should it matter to us? Play is a fun, natural activity for children and adults. Why bother to confuse ourselves, and possibly ruin our actions, by adding theory? The fact is that we cannot escape theory, in the sense that we are always using it. As parents, teachers, or others who may have an interest and participate in play, we will bring to play experiences our own understandings of what play is and what it means to play. The previous chapter reviewed historical ideas about play, including theories. Those ideas allow us to see play as part of our thinking about biology, nurture, aesthetics and social relationships. In this chapter, we will explore the reasons scholars devise to explain play, including current theories, views of **theory** and **beliefs** about play, a number of theories that have proved to be useful for understanding children's **play,** and current issues that are shaping our theoretical understanding of children's play.

As Sutton-Smith's (1997) opening quote suggests, there are many ways of thinking about play, as well as many play activities to think about. We think of a baby shaking his rattle, a girl playing hopscotch, an adult playing tennis, and we can call all these activities play. Yet, we must think about these activities differently. We do not associate the same sort of skill, strategy, and purposefulness with shaking a rattle as we do when we think of tennis, and hopscotch brings to mind an entirely different set of ideas. Reflecting about play, however, is not so simple. Deciding how to think about play, what to observe or listen to, and how to understand its meaning is very complicated. Theory is one tool we have to help us. But how does theory help us?

What ideas do we have when we think about play activities, and how do we make sense of them? When we think of play, do we think of hopscotch and tennis? Do we think about play more often when we think of children, adults, or other species of animals? Do we think about play when we turn on the computer, or do those thoughts occur to us only some of the time? What does research tell us about these activities? Theory is part of our thinking, and it guides research on play. It tells us how hopscotch and tennis share common play attributes (e.g., they are both games) and how they differ (children play hopscotch, either alone or with playmates; adults play tennis with others). It tells us who plays what (e.g., children play house, while adults play card games like bridge; we play fetch with dogs, but not with cats or other people). It informs us that computers are popular game venues for children, but that adults use computers for both work and play.

The sections that follow are intended to help us understand theories that have been promoted by 20th-century play scholars (Rubin, Bukowski, & Parker, 1998). We will see how theories contribute to commonly shared conceptions about play (e.g., that it promotes children's cognitive, social, creative, motor, and moral development), but we will also see how each of us, as we engage in play, have our own theories about play. We will explore how our beliefs about play combine with scholarly theory to provide us with ways of thinking about play in our particular contexts. Our experiences, informed by research and theory, allow us to generate our own ways of thinking about play.

WHY STUDY THEORIES?

In *Webster's Third New International Dictionary of the English Language Unabridged*, theory is defined, among other things, as "imaginative contemplation of reality: direct intellectual apprehension: insight"; as "a belief, policy, or procedure proposed or followed as the basis of action"; as "a field of intellectual inquiry"; as "a judgment, conception, proposition, or formula"; or as "something taken for granted, especially on trivial or inadequate grounds: CONJECTURE, SPECULATION, SUPPOSITION" (Gove and the Merriam-Webster Editorial Staff, 1986, p. 2371). Whenever we think about something, judge it, or form a belief about it, we are by definition in a world of theory. We may not be aware that we are theorizing, but we are. Theory may be a more formally derived set of empirically verified principles (Williams, 1996) or a conception that may emerge from experience. Others, like Beyer and Bloch (1996), see theory as a conceptual lens for developing and communicating meanings and understandings. There are many ways to think about what a theory is. We might use theory to help us understand ordinary and extraordinary aspects of our lives.

In their analysis of theory and practice related to teaching young children, Chafel and Reifel (1996) conclude that (a) every experience is theory-laden, (b) theory is contextually bound, (c) theory and practice are distinguishable but inseparable concepts, and (d) alternate theoretical paradigms are needed to understand early childhood experiences. To the degree that play is part of child-rearing and classroom practice, it is something that we think about and for which we have theories. We need to think about what play means for children as they are playing; every time children play, it means something for them. We need to think about how to plan the settings in which they play; the context in which children play shapes that play and gives it unique meaning. We need to think about how we will participate with them as they play; adults are part of the play context for children. To do all these things, we must know how others have thought about play, as well as what the children we observe are telling us as they play; we can make sense of our own play experiences by understanding how others have made sense of theirs.

We will see in this chapter how each theory provides a lens with which we can look at play. Depending on our reasons for observing play, we may best be served by having a variety of theoretical lenses at our disposal.

CURRENT THEORIES OF PLAY

We think about play in many different ways. We think about it in terms of how we have fun. We think about games we play. We think about children as they pretend. We think about things we do when we are not working or doing the things we must do. What do scholars tell us about play? And how might their ideas about play help us understand more about what we see when children are playing?

In *The Ambiguity of Play*, Sutton-Smith (1997; see also 1999) reviews numerous studies on play from far-ranging disciplines. He looks at research from biology, anthropology, literary studies and performance, risky and vicarious play, along with the pretend and games that we see in our daily observations of children. From this view, he argues that play scholarship appears to coalesce into seven broad **rhetorics**, in the sense that fields of scholarship adopt belief systems, underlying ideologies, and the values of those who participate in such scholarship. He traces four rhetorics to the ancient Greeks (Fate, Power, Identity, Frivolous) and identifies three modern rhetorics that stem from post-Enlightenment thought (**Progress, Imaginary, Self**). While rhetorics may be associated more with a discipline or disciplines and related epistemologies, they inevitably have broader cultural meanings. These rhetorics are summarized in Table 2–1.

A particular problem for researchers and childhood specialists is how we think about the play. What activities do we define as play for children, and what activities are not play? Many people think that children's play is good for them, that it promotes learning, that it creates social competence. Some argue that play is the way we learn to solve problems, whether cognitive (Bruner, Jolly, & Sylva, 1976) or social (Sutton-Smith, Gerstmyer, & Meckley, 1988). We make sweeping assertions about play, but as Table 2–1 illustrates, there are many forms of play and many ways of thinking about it. When children play house, is it pretend, leisure, fantasy, or nonsense? Are children learning about "house," each other, or just fooling around? When children watch television, are they experiencing leisure, imagining, or just wasting time? When children play soccer, is it an athletic, leisure, or game experience? Or are all of these perspectives in some sense true? We need theory as a tool to help us think about what we mean when we talk about play, especially when we

TABLE 2–1 Rhetorics of Play and Their Respective Disciplines and Theorists

Rhetoric	Discipline	Play Form(s)	Scholars	Child Play Research
Progress	Biology, psychology, education	Pretend, games	Erikson, Piaget, Vygotsky	Smilansky (1968)
Fate	Mathematics	Gambling	Abt, Fuller	
Power	Sociology	Athletics	Spariosu, Huizinga	Yeatman & Reifel (1997)
Identity	Anthropology	Festivals, parties	Turner	Fine (1983)
Imaginary	Art, literature	Fantasy	Bateson, Bakhtin	Dyson (1997)
Self	Psychiatry	Leisure	Csikszentmihalyi	Kelly-Byrne (1989)
Frivolity	Pop culture	Nonsense	Stewart, Welsford	Opie & Opie (1959)

Source: Adapted from Sutton-Smith (1997, p. 215).

make assertions about how important play is or claim that play is allowing us to meet educational or developmental purposes.

Educational and developmental literature refers to play in all sorts of ways that conceal what is meant by the term play. Most scholarship on children's play has kept theory, ideology, or philosophy implicit, making some meanings presented in the research literature seem obscure. While early childhood education and play have an affinity that dates back hundreds of years (the educational uses of play can be traced to Comenius (1896) in the 17th century; see Chapter 1 of this text), it is not always clear what activities are implied or what ends are being met. This problem continues today, in the way play is included as a significant factor in the National Association for the Education of Young Children's developmentally appropriate practice (DAP) guidelines (Bredekamp & Copple, 1997). The assumption seems to be that play is good for children, and that children benefit from play in a number of ways. (That assumption is, in fact, one of the foundations for this book.) This perspective appears to reflect Sutton-Smith's rhetoric of Progress, within which he discusses play as an avenue for learning or development. He cites many of the play studies that serve as part of the knowledge base for teaching young children. Many who have responded to *The Ambiguity of Play* (e.g., Fein, 1999; Rivkin, 1999; Samaras, 1999) appear to assume that Progress, in the form of learning or development, is what we are talking about when we speak of play and children (Reifel, 1999).

Rhetorics of Progress and the Imaginary may serve more like philosophical bases for the field; commonplaces that support our beliefs. Fein (1999), in her logical analyses of Sutton-Smith's rhetorics, goes further by arguing that empirical and theoretical descriptions of play (the sorts of things that Sutton-Smith includes in his argument) may have nothing to do with what classroom play is really about. Fein tells us that what is implied by the rhetoric of Progress is many forms of development, whereas classroom play should be about consolidation of experience, vividness, and even happiness.

Given all these views on what play may be, we need theory to help us sort out the complexity of play as we plan, observe, and participate in activities we call play. We want to make sure that we are not talking about different things, conceptually, by resorting to a vague term that glosses over what we really mean by play. We want to ensure that our contemplations and judgments about reality (in this case, play) are clear and articulate. Becoming aware of our beliefs and purposes is necessary as a step in our selection and use of play theory. This step must be used by researchers as they study activities that we recognize as play and by practitioners as they engage children in play activities. A number of theories have proved useful as lenses through which we can look at play in order to understand more about children's play.

DOMINANT CONTEMPORARY THEORIES

Let's look at an early childhood play interaction as one avenue for understanding how dominant contemporary theories guide what we look for and what we see when we are viewing play.

> The interaction began during a regularly scheduled free play time as Anna joined Zoe at a[n] easel supplied with newsprint, green, orange, and purple paints, and brushes.
>
> *Anna:* I'm makin' pumpkin.
> *Zoe:* Me, too. [singing, humming]
> *Zoe:* Wanna call this a pumpkin?
> *Anna:* Yeah.
> . . . .
> *Zoe:* Yeah, make a Halloween picture.
> a verbal exchange of opinions with peers who passed by
> *Julie:* Well, a pumpkin doesn't look like that.
> *Zoe:* I know but I'm just making it the way I want.
> *Julie:* Did you know Zoe's makin' a pumpkin the wrong way?
> . . . .
> *Zoe:* Let's make a big blump and then finger paint.
> *Anna:* OK. I'm just gonna keep on finish painting.
> . . . .
> *Anna:* I'm a witch so I make purple stew.
> *Zoe:* Oh, I make green stew.
> *Anna:* I'm a witch cuz I make purple stew.
> *Anna:* Hehehehe. We are witches, we are making [chanting]
> *Zoe:* We are witches, we are witches.
>
> Moving further into their imaginary Halloween frame, the girls exchange loud and excited "Boo's!" as they squat down and jump up, peeking around the sides of the easel.
>
> *Anna:* I have another idea that we can do [chanting]
> I have a black cat, her name is Black Cat.
> *Zoe:* [chanting, inaudible]
> *Anna:* I have a black cat, her name is Black Cat.
> *Zoe:* [Laughter] I have a black cat! And my name is Black Cat. (Reifel & Yeatman, 1993, pp. 356–360)

As suggested in Chapter 1, many of our contemporary theories of play have their roots in 19th-century thinking. Our ideas about play, if not many of our play activities, have their origins in Romantic and Enlightenment philosophies. Coming from that perspective, we might see this play at an easel as an example of creativity in young children. Perhaps the most significant theoretical assertions that shape how we think about play today can be traced to Charles Darwin's (1859) revolutionary theory on the evolution of species (Schwartzman, 1978; Spariosu, 1989; Sutton-Smith, 1997). In his argument stating that species adapt to their environments, he includes important notions about the adaptive interplay of biological and environmental influences, or the relative contribution of nature and nurture to who we are and how we behave. Some play theorists make explicit the biological or environmental influences they see as relevant to play; other theorists keep those assumptions implicit. In the following sections, we will see how nature and nurture appear in a number of theoretical perspectives, including the work of Freud and the psychoanalysts who followed him (e.g., Erikson, 1963; Peller, 1954), communications scholars (e.g., Bateson, 1955/2000; Garvey, 1993), cognitive specialists (e.g., Piaget, 1962; post-Piagetians: Bruner, 1972; Vygotsky, 1978), social theorists (e.g., Corsaro, 1985; Parten, 1933; Sutton-Smith, 1972; the social status researchers), and, finally, work that attempts to synthesize some of these points of view. At each step along the way, we will revisit Anna and Zoe to see what theory can tell us about what they are doing as they play.

Psychoanalysis: Emotional Motives for Play

Within a matter of decades after Darwin's (1859) *Origin of Species* appeared, the medical doctor Sigmund Freud (1856–1939) began to interpret human behavior in terms of its biological and cultural influences. Freud worked with patients who had mental problems, ranging from neuroses to psychoses. To understand what had happened to these patients and how to try to cure them, he developed his version of psychoanalytic theory. This theory included a strand on normal human development, as well as a strand on what might go wrong in normal development, thereby leading to mental problems.

Basic to Freud's theory is how nature and nurture contribute to the structure of personality, including ego, id, and superego. We are born with biological drives (the id, including such things as hunger, social contact, sexuality), but society limits or guides the degree to which we can pursue those drives. For example, we may want to eat cookies all the time, because we desire them; but parents and teachers limit the number of cookies we may eat and the times when we may eat them. As we internalize those social limitations, we develop our superego, or conscience, to provide an internal representation of society's rules; we reach a point when we can tell ourselves when and how we can indulge our desires. The interplay of forces (internal id; external social restrictions) shapes who we are as a person, or our ego. Freud argues that much of this dynamic happens subconsciously or unconsciously; what we know consciously is only a small part of what we are processing in our minds (Freud, 1918). This is a key foundation for thinking of play as a rhetoric of Self (Sutton-Smith, 1997, 1999).

This theory of personality attempts to describe what motivates us (our drives), how our morality is formed (our superego), and how we emerge as human beings. Parents serve as our first contact with society, letting us know when we may eat, sleep, and pursue our interests, as well as letting us know how we should act. Teachers, playmates, and other agents of society provide additional limits on what we may or may not do. Imbalance in the forces that shape us (too much biological drive; inappropriate social restrictions) can lead to mental illness. Our personal histories, in whatever forms they may take, contribute to who we are. The balance of nature and nurture reveals itself in personality formation.

Emotions can motivate social play.

What is the role of play in this developmental process? Play has an important role in normal development, as a mechanism in childhood for resolving past pressures a child feels when drives are being curbed by societal expectations (Erikson, 1963; Peller, 1954). Play also has a therapeutic role, as an avenue for dealing with experiences that have proved to be maladaptive (Freud, 1909; Erikson, 1941; Winnecott, 1971). For most children, play provides a psychologically safe context where what is desired can be obtained, in the world of fantasy. If mother will not allow cookies between meals, then we can play tea party and pretend to have cookies. Play, in the form of fantasy or pretense, is a reflection of children's efforts to deal with those things that are out of their control (i.e., the adult world) that are placing limits on their desires. Childhood play for most children is a pressure valve that allows desires to be acted on symbolically through pretend actions that adults and others tend to ignore and not take seriously. In play, children can get away with all sorts of things that they cannot get away with in reality: children can boss around others (they would be punished by adults if they tried it in real life); they can consume all they want (adults ration consumables in real life); and they can control everything that adults control in reality (when they sleep and get up, when they come and go, how they relate to others) (Freud, 1922, 1959). Fantasy play allows children to begin to deal with reality on their own terms, and they deal with those aspects of reality that are most important to them (Singer & Singer, 1977, 1992). Play, from a psychoanalytic perspective, is an important part of early personality formation. The rhetorics of Self and the Imaginary come together here (Sutton-Smith, 1997, 1999).

Therapeutically, play is a window into the concerns of the child. Psychoanalysts (Erikson, 1963; Freud, 1964; Klein, 1955) were among the first to use play as part of child therapy. For those children who are perceived as suffering from psychological problems, therapeutic play sessions provide the analyst with an avenue for understanding the child's problems. More importantly, play is the means by which children can take charge of their problems and find routes for mastery and wellness (Axline, 1969; Erikson, 1972). Chapter 10, on play therapy, brings these psychoanalytic ideas up-to-date.

Freud's followers refined his theory of personality development and play. Erik Erikson is perhaps one of his best-known students. His *Childhood and Society* (1963) provides a more detailed analysis of early personality formation from a psychoanalytic perspective and highlights play as a key feature of early socialization. In other writings, Erikson points to play as being a number of things: a reflection of the child's past, musings about the present, or explorations about what is to come. In all cases, Erikson continues the Freudian idea of nature (biology) dealing with nurture (social relationships, culture) through play.

A different perspective is provided by Lili Peller (1954). Peller argues that in some cases, what we see in play is not just a reflection of the child dealing with reality; the child may be dealing with the ways he or she wishes reality would be. When a child hugs a doll, it may not be a reflection of the child having been hugged by an adult; it may be that the child wants to be hugged by an adult. Peller points to the difficulty of interpreting the meaning of play actions from a psychoanalytic perspective. Reality and fantasy must be seen from the point of view of each child's developmental history and from the child's personal meanings.

Play is an important theoretical concept that comes with Freudian connotations. It is one of the important developmental activities that allows us to become who we are as human beings. It allows us to deal with society's rules and to find out who we are. And, in those cases when we are having difficulties, it allows us to heal. We may have difficulty believing in some of the pieces of Freud's theory (e.g., childhood sexuality; drives as a source of **motivation**), but a number of features of his theory appear to stay with us:

- Play tells us about who the child uniquely is, as a constructor of her life history;
- Children resolve problems as they play;

- Feelings or affect is an important part of play;
- Who we are as individuals (i.e., our self-concept) is shaped in play;
- Our developmental or life histories are important for understanding who we are.

Clearly, when Zoe is challenged by Julie about the appearance of her painted pumpkin, Zoe has feelings about the challenge. Zoe opts to turn her painted pumpkin into a "big blump" that she can finger paint over; when her initial painting is found to be wanting, she reverts to a less mature stage of painting, where representation does not matter. Her play provides a safe place where she can continue playing with Anna on a level that cannot be challenged by others. In play, Zoe makes things the way she wants them to be, and in play resolves her hurt feelings.

More than most of the other theories that will be described here, psychoanalytic theory reminds us of the totality of the child, including **feelings** and motives (Biber, 1984). It gives us lenses to see each child as a biography that is being written. Zoe copes with challenges. It is not until we hear from Bruner (1990) that meaningful activity in narrative form re-emerges as a topic of developmental interest.

Communications and Play

Bateson on Play Frames

When children play, they communicate in many ways. When play is social, children must communicate with each other so that everyone knows what is happening. When children play alone, they are also communicating, although the **signals** may not be clear or obvious. The communicative aspects of play have become increasingly interesting to play researchers (Christie, Enz, & Vukelich, 1997; Garvey, 1993; Goncu, 1993; Schwartzman, 1978; see Chapter 7, "Cultural and Gender Influences on Play," for a more extensive discussion on communication studies), but the nature and nurture of play communications are not always acknowledged.

One of the earliest and most profound theories that connects play and **communication** is Gregory Bateson's "theory of play and fantasy" (2000, first published in 1955). An anthropologist, Bateson was interested in questions of **adaptation** and misadaptation (particularly mental illness) and developed his theory after observing otters playing in the surf. His insight was that many actions that would be taken seriously in reality are not taken seriously when individuals are engaged in play; when animals play fight, their nips are not mistaken for the bites that would occur in real fights. "I saw two young monkeys *playing, i.e.*, engaged in an interactive sequence of which the unit actions or signals were similar to but not the same as those of combat" (Bateson, 1955/2000, p. 179). When a 5-year-old girl asks whether we want to go to a tea party, as an adult we do not expect to be less hungry when we are done; and if a young boy asks whether we want to fly with him to the moon, we do not call NASA. Bateson argues that all organisms that play (human or not) have adapted signals that allow us to know when an action is intended to be real or not. Dogs that are play fighting wag their tails so that playmates will know that their nips are not bites. Humans develop both verbal and nonverbal signals to communicate their intent. "[P]lay, could only occur if the participant organisms were capable of some degree of metacommunication, *i.e.*, of exchanging signals which would carry the message 'this is play' " (Bateson, 1955/2000, p. 179).

Bateson's argument about play signals has evolutionary, philosophical, cognitive, and social aspects. In terms of human evolution, play allowed us to decontextualize our communications. In our ancient history, before humans played, we were limited to interpersonal signals about what was present—typically, our moods. With the onset of play, we were able to begin to communicate about the nonpresent (i.e., what was or what will be, rather than what is; what is happening elsewhere). This evolutionary leap in communications allowed our minds to evolve, creating cognitive processes for dealing with the nonliteral or imaginary; we became capable of thinking about things other than what we were doing. Such thinking leads to abstraction and the ability to theorize. As humans evolved, we needed to develop social communications so that others would be aware of the difference between the here and now and the abstract or non-present. Play is important because it allows us to act both in and out of context and to know the difference; play is a tool for decontextualization. This is a form of the rhetoric of the Imaginary (Sutton-Smith, 1997, 1999).

The key to Bateson's theory is his notion of the **play frame**. The frame is that which we signal, when we indicate to others that we want to shift from reality to imaginary. For Bateson, the imaginary is a map and reality is the terrain, which can be mapped. When we play house, our table-setting and baby-dressing actions are the map, and real-life housekeeping is the terrain; when we play the computer game, Sim City, the computer screen images are our map, and city planning is our terrain. The frame might be seen as knowledge, or scripts (Bretherton, 1989; Goffman, 1974; Nelson, 1989). What makes the frame important is that it is not real, not present, which means that effort must be made to indicate that it is being created and what it is to be. Anna and Zoe agree on play about pumpkins (a "Halloween picture"), witches, and ghosts, all of which relate to Halloween. It is perhaps no surprise that many frames that children select as they play relate to events in their worlds. Bateson gives us a way of beginning to relate those worldly experiences to what children negotiate in their play; Halloween means (at least) pumpkins, witches, and ghosts for these girls. Thus, signals and elaborated communications are necessary for human play to take place.

Socially, it becomes important to take roles and to learn to make use of signals. To be in the same frame, players must agree to be in the same imaginary world and they must know what to do there. Childhood play allows children to develop role flexibility, so they can move in and out of the many roles they will eventually take in life. Perhaps our adult ability to take many roles (e.g., spouse, parent, employee, neighbor) is based on the way we took roles as players. For Bateson, particular roles matter less than the facility to move in and out of roles; we do not play cowboys when we are children in order to grow up to become cowboys. And cognitively, the ways we explore the nonliteral worlds within frames may allow our minds to move beyond the here and now, to worlds of theory and abstraction.

Clearly, we can see that most humans have evolved to the point where we play and communicate, but variation in human play may explain variation in adult actions. At the extreme end of adult maladaption (e.g., schizophrenia), the frame between real and not real is lost, and communication lacks meaning to those of us for whom the frames are clear. Whether play could ever remedy such problems is questionable. Cultural differences in play may be a function of the roles and frames that are legitimate within a culture (see Chapter 7). Within the realm of typical humans, research has revealed a number of useful communicative signals theorized by Bateson, Catherine Garvey has done much to document the language of play communication, as described next.

Garvey on Play Talk

As a psychologist interested in language of children, Garvey (1993) has done a number of studies describing transitions into and out of pretend play frames. Her observations and analyses of preschoolers (primarily girls) as they pretend have revealed the sorts of communicative efforts that Bateson predicted, with spoken language serving as a vehicle for indicating the play frame and its meanings. When most young children (especially girls) engage with one another, they use the types of talk that Garvey identified (see Figure 2–1).

When observing and listening to children play, it is apparent that children are signaling one another as the theory suggests. They frequently invite others to "pretend," and they often indicate exactly what frame is relevant to the play. Anna did so

FIGURE 2–1 Garvey's Language Tools for Social Play

Preparatory Talk ("Let's play"; "These dolls are mine")

Explicit Directions for Pretend
- Transformation of self ("Pretend I'm a doctor")
- Transformation of other ("You be a patient")
- Transformation of joint roles ("Let's be nurses")
- Transformation of action for self ("I need to make some medicine")
- Transformation of action for other ("Pretend you broke your leg")
- Transformation of joint actions ("Let's pretend we're saving lives")
- Transformation of object ("This clay can be our medicine")
- Transformation of environment ("Under the table can be our hospital")
- Transformation of nothing to something (Child holds up empty hand while approaching another child and says, "This is a needle so I can give you a shot")

Within Pretend Talk (enactment talk)
- "Take all your medicine."
- "Let the nurse give you your shot."

Negation of Pretend
- "I don't want a shot. I'm leaving."
- "I don't want to play anymore."

Play Signals
- Altered tone of voice (e.g., high-pitched when speaking like a baby)
- Giggles while acting or speaking
- Winks

Source: Adapted from Garvey (1993).

when she said, "I'm makin' pumpkin", and Zoe signaled, "Me, too." They elaborate their Halloween frame by signaling that "I am a witch", and that, as a witch, Anna has transformed her paint into "purple stew" (probably a witch's brew). We can also hear Anna and Zoe make use of enactment talk, when they talk as the witches they are pretending to be: "Hehehehe. We are witches." When listening for Garvey's types of play talk, we can hear the children negotiate and refine their play frame, then move into the frame to enact it. When the frame becomes boring or threatening, they may terminate it or alter it, as Zoe did when Julie criticized her painted pumpkin; Anna explicitly alters the frame when she says, "I have another idea that we can do" and suggests the ghost peek-a-boo game. Many students have been able to replicate Garvey's framework for pretend play, especially for girls (who tend to be more verbal in general than boys). The decontextualized language that is implied by Garvey's framework has proved to be useful as a way of understanding the foundations of literacy (Christie et al., 1997; Reifel, 1995).

Garvey's version of Bateson's theory is clearly useful, but there are still areas where research has not followed this theory. It gives us lenses for understanding play through the types of play language signals that children use when they pretend. Those lenses are less helpful for understanding nonverbal play, games, and some aspects of pretend. For example, boys play just as much as girls do, but without as many of the language signals that girls use (Scales & Cook-Gumperz, 1993). What signals are the boys using? How do boys come to know that a certain gesture or sound indicates that it is time to be a superhero? This code has not yet been cracked. And the frames that children elect to pretend have not been studied, in spite of our culture's efforts to promote particular frames for play. We could know much more about gender stereotypes implied by certain frames. Bateson's idea that fantasy contributes to role

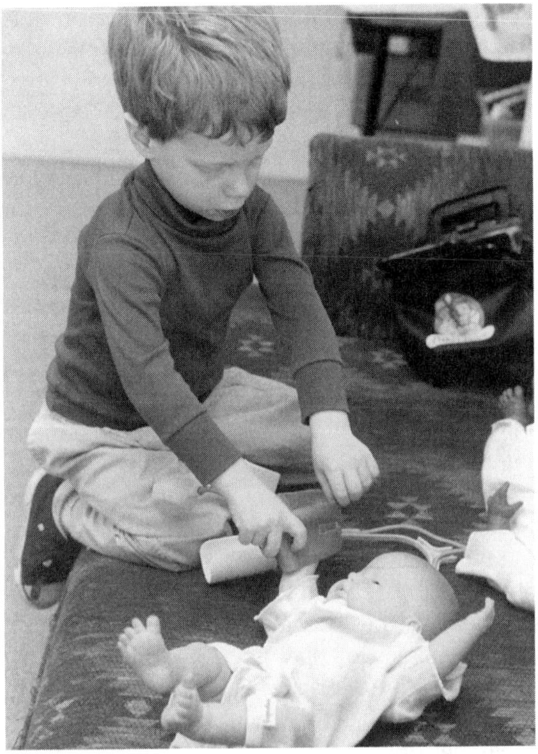

The social roles that children take as they play can be understood in terms of any number of theories.

flexibility also deserves further attention. In any case, we have naturally evolved the propensity to communicate in different ways by means of play, as Anna and Zoe show us with their signals about what they are playing. This refines the rhetoric of the Imaginary (Sutton-Smith, 1997, 1999). How culture nourishes such play and communication is fully described in Chapter 7.

Cognitive Views

Vygotsky on Play as a Zone of Proximal Development

Lev Semenovich Vygotsky (1896–1934) was a Russian student of psychology, philosophy, linguistics, social sciences, and the arts. His systematic work in psychology, education, and psychopathology, begun in 1924, was cut short by his untimely death of tuberculosis at the age of 38. The Western world did not have ready access to his work until the mid-1950s, for it was suppressed by Soviet guardians of "proper Marxian interpretation" (Bruner in Vygotsky, 1962). As a researcher interested in materialist influences on psychology, he advanced an approach to social constructivism that has become influential in many Western countries.

With respect to the role of play in the development of young children, Vygotsky (1966) was concerned with two fundamental issues: first, the origin and genesis of play and how it develops and, second, whether play is the predominant activity of young children. He concluded that play is not the predominant activity during the preschool years but it is the leading source of development. As Vygotsky (1978, pp. 96–97) says, "The child sees one thing but acts differently in relation to what he sees. Thus, a condition is reached in which the child begins to act independently of what he sees." Play frees the child's thinking from concrete experience, allowing for higher levels of thinking. Play is therefore a form of Progress (Sutton-Smith, 1997, 1999).

Vygotsky was critical of the usual definitions of play. He rejected the view that play could be defined on the basis of the pleasure it gives to the child. Many activities give the child keener pleasure than play does, and some games do not afford pleasure at all, particularly organized games (athletic sports) with unpleasant outcomes. (This, of course, begs the question currently debated among play professionals: are organized games play?) Vygotsky was inclined to focus on broader, more general meanings of play—namely, the child's needs, inclinations, incentives, and motives to act or play.

In *Mind and Society* (Vygotsky, 1978), a chapter on "The Role of Play in Development" sketches some of the key elements of play as a contributor to mental development. Play, primarily pretend play, serves a key developmental function for mental development for a number of reasons. As play develops, a conscious realization of purpose emerges, as when Anna and Zoe agree on what it means to play Halloween. Play is purposeful, as seen in games in which children can win or lose and the purpose decides the winner. The intent or object of winning is recognized in advance of playing the game; and the more demanding the rules ("Well, a pumpkin doesn't look like that"), the more intense the play becomes. As children develop, play without purpose or rules results in increasingly dull, unappealing activity. For school-age children, the separation of play and work (i.e., compulsory activity based on rules) is possible, and play is increasingly of the athletic type. As development evolves from imaginary play to games and work, play permeates reality and is continued in school instruction and work. Play evolves but does not die.

For the young child, special needs and incentives arise that are spontaneously expressed in play. The child desires immediate gratification but many needs cannot be immediately realized (e.g., no young child wants to wait a few days for a birthday party). "[P]lay is invented at the point when unrealizable tendencies appear in development" (Vygotsky, 1966, p. 7). Indeed, if all needs could be gratified immediately, there would be no play. Therefore, the explanation of why children play is the "imaginary, illusory realization of unrealizable desires" (p. 7).

In explaining play or distinguishing it from other forms of activity, Vygotsky (1966) proposes that in play the child creates an imaginary situation that is, in fact, rule-based play. There is no such thing as play without rules laid down in advance by real-life behavior. For example, if the child is "nurturing" a child, she is obeying the rules of maternal behavior—rules that are not noticed by the child in real life. In imaginary play, there are rules that govern roles the child will play so the child's play is free, but this is an illusory freedom. Here, Vygotsky conflicts with those, including Piaget, who propose that rules emerge after the preschool period, primarily in organized games or games with rules. Vygotsky goes further to propose that all games with rules contain imaginary situations (play), just as all imaginary play contains rules.

Vygotsky (1978) maintains that it is impossible for a child under three to play with an imaginary situation. The child must be liberated from situational or concrete constraints (e.g., playing with real or concrete objects) in order to play with an imaginary situation. Play objects (i.e., toys, or **pivots** in Vygotsky's language) are one key factor in liberating children from the concrete; orange, green, and purple paint and brushes are pivots that create opportunities for Halloween play for Anna and Zoe. The preschool child (3–5) begins to separate thought from objects during play, and so a stick becomes a gun or a rag becomes a doll. Play serves as a transitional stage for disconnecting thought from objects. At the point when the rag becomes a doll, meaning begins to dominate the object. Play becomes the context for acquiring culturally sanctioned meanings (like Halloween for Anna and Zoe), by way of the pivots for meaning that children encounter.

At school age, play is converted to internal processes: internal speech, logical memory, and abstract thought. The child can now play with meanings derived from objects. The meaning of rag can be transferred to a doll, and the child can act as though the rag is a doll. He is no longer constrained to concrete situations. Anna and Zoe have enough internalized ideas about Halloween that they can play the peek-a-boo ghost game without having any objects that suggest ghosts (although the presence of the easel may suggest peek-a-boo in general). Play is connected to pleasure, so children subject themselves to rules for they promise greater gratification than acting on impulses does. The inner self-restraint and self-determination established through obeying rules help shape the child's standards of action and morality in later years. However, Vygotsky warns that the real world is not a play world, and one cannot live in search of pleasure (as in play) or subordinate oneself to the kind of rules existing in play.

Vygotsky (1966) proposes that a **zone of proximal development (ZPD)** exists—a range of tasks between those the child can handle independently and those at the highest level she can master through play or with the help of adults or more competent **peers**. Thus, three factors are seen as creating levels of the ZPD above the normal independent or lower levels. Play is a source of development and creates a ZPD. In play, the child performs above his usual behavior, as though he were a "head taller" than himself (Vygotsky, 1978, p. 102). The upper levels of the ZPD are also promoted by social interactions with adults and more competent peers who create situations that challenge or require the child to think and act beyond her independent level. Adults and competent peers can effectively **scaffold** the child's learning, helping her achieve ever-higher levels of development of thought and action. The play-development relationship is similar to the instruction-development relationship, but the activities and consequences of play are much broader than those provided by peers and adults, making it the "highest level of preschool development" (1966, p. 16). No one was present to assist Zoe as she tried to paint a pumpkin, but Julie's criticism of her painting may begin to create a ZPD wherein Zoe will attempt to improve her painting.

The lens on play Vygotsky provides has only recently been studied. Many find his argument that play is a developmental zone, in which the child can do more than she can under normal circumstances, to be persuasive and supportive of play as an educational activity (Bodrova & Leong, 1995, 1998; Berk & Winsler, 1995; Gregory, Kim, & Whiren, 2003). Critical aspects of his theory, in particular the pivotal roles of objects and culture for preschool play, are currently under investigation (Chin & Reifel, 2000; Lin & Reifel, 1999; Reifel & Yeatman, 1993).

Piaget on Play as Assimilation

Jean Piaget (1896–1980) was a Swiss scholar who has variously been described as a psychologist, logician, biologist, or genetic espistemologist (Elkind, 1968). Piaget's interests in **cognition** took shape based on philosophical foundations (an assumption that innate mental structures were an inevitable result of experience, a post-Kantian structuralism, Piaget, 1970) and on observations of his three children, who were subjects for his early studies of the development of intelligent behavior. The child as knowledge constructor approaches the environment in terms of the mental structures already developed. These are incorporated into existing schemata or patterns of behavior through assimilation and accommodation. **Assimilation** is the action of the child on surrounding objects, while the converse action, **accommodation**, is the action of the environment (objects) on the child (Piaget, 1966). Adaptation is the equilibrium between assimilation and accommodation. Play is essentially assimilation (action on objects) or the primacy of assimilation over accommodation. A continuation of accommodation for its own sake is described as imitation (repeating actions already learned) (Piaget, 1962).

Play, Dreams and Imitation in Childhood (Piaget, 1962) is perhaps the most incisive and thorough analysis of linkages between play and intellectual development; certainly it is Piaget's seminal work on play. It is this work that has allowed researchers and educators to argue that play has a central role in children's cognitive development. However, in this volume, he describes play as essentially assimilation:

> In every act of intelligence is an equilibrium between assimilation and accommodation, while imitation is a continuation of accommodation for its own sake, it may be said conversely that play is essentially assimilation, or the primacy of assimilation over accommodation (1962, p. 87).

Play, then, follows development rather than causing it (Sutton-Smith, 1970). All activities during the first months of life, except feeding and **emotions** (fear, anger, etc.,) are play, which Piaget calls "practice" or "functional play." When the child repeats actions or operations previously learned (grasping for the sake of grasping; shaking hanging toys repeatedly), she is performing actions that are ends in themselves and have no external aim. Symbolic play, like Anna and Zoe's pretend, occurs during the preoperational period, when construction and dramatic play symbolically reflect the thoughts the child is developing. As the child enters the concrete operational period of thought, games with rules, like Anna and Zoe's peek-a-boo ghost game, become the play form that reflects level of cognition (see Figure 2–2).

Piaget drew close linkages between forms or types of play and stages of development. Contemporary research indicates that with respect to drawing accurate conclusions about the nature and development of play, these links are questionable and perhaps inaccurate. He proposed that the only form of play occurring during the **sensorimotor period** is functional or practice play. Zoe's finger painting could be seen as a form of practice play. Practice play begins after the child has learned (i.e., developed schemata) for grasping, swinging, throwing, and so forth, and repeats her behavior for the mere joy of mastery and feelings of power in subduing reality. The child initially modifies existing mental structures (accommodation) to develop swinging or throwing schemata and later advances to the level of subordinating (repeating and mastering) the behavior (assimilation). From then on, practice play, accompanied by "functional pleasure," occurs. At any stage of development, it is probably the case that we will see a predominant form of play, as outlined by Piaget, but any child at any age may be able to play at any of the levels he describes (VanHoorn, Scales, Nourot, & Alward, 1999); we see Anna and Zoe pretending, constructing with paint, manipulating the paint with their senses, and playing a game with rules, but at their ages we are most likely to see repetitive pretend and construction. The arc of Piaget's thinking has been influential in any number of studies describing the cognitive progression that can be seen in a child's play (e.g., Fein, 1975; Nicholich, 1977; Watson & Fisher, 1977; Watson & Jackowitz, 1984). It is probably incorrect to associate a particular play activity with a particular age, but we can typically see a progression in the complexity of most children's play as they develop. (See Figure 2–3 for a descriptive progression in symbolic pretend play based on research inspired by Piaget.) Piaget helps us see the mental transformations associated with Anna and Zoe's play desires, including their role transformations of themselves ("I'm a witch." "My name is Black Cat.") and the object transformations they need for their play ("I am makin' pumpkin." "I make purple stew.").

FIGURE 2–2 Piaget's Concept of Play as Cognitively Assimilating Experience

Stage 1:	Functional (exploratory, sensorimotor) activity (e.g., grasping a rattle; repeatedly dropping a toy on the ground)
Stage 2:	Symbolic play (representing experience)
	Construction (a special category, between sensorimotor and symbolic games; e.g., building with blocks, modeling clay)
	Sociodramatic play (e.g., pretending to feed a doll; role playing in a pretend doctor's office)
Stage 3:	Games with rules (e.g., marbles; tag)

Given the current critical examination of the accuracy and relevance of Piagetian theory for early childhood education (Smolucha & Smolucha, 1998), certain cautions and clarifications are needed. Piaget warned that the age at which intellectual abilities appear is approximate and varies with individual children. The fact that he attached approximate ages to stages of development led to misunderstanding about his intent regarding individual differences in children. The stage theory that Piaget articulated provides a set of lenses for identifying types of play with particular age groups, and perhaps his greatest weakness was proposing that children cannot progress beyond the stage within which they are operating. This view has been challenged by theorists from around the world. Another weakness in his approach is his view of

FIGURE 2–3 Pretend: The First Eight Years

Single pretend transformation toward self (with toys that resemble real objects; e.g., the child hugs a toy doll or toy animal; the child pretends to eat toy food.)

Other object is pretend agent (object is treated as if it acts, with toys that resemble real objects; e.g., the child has a toy doll or toy animal act as if it is eating toy food.)

Single pretend transformation (with toys that have no resemblance to real objects; e.g., the child creates a bed out of building blocks; the child forms a pancake from Play-Doh®.)

Pretend role (with toys associated with a role that resemble real objects; e.g., a child pretends to be a cook with toy food; a child pretends to be a firefighter with a toy fire hat and a toy truck.)

Multiple pretend role transformations (with toys that resemble real-world objects; e.g., a child takes roles such as doctor, patient, and nurse while playing with dolls or toy animals.)

Pretend role (without the support of toys that resemble real objects; with blocks or Play-Doh®, a child creates a pretend setting by constructing the objects needed; e.g., children pretend to be farmers by building a farm from blocks and forming animals with Play-Doh®.)

Multiple pretend roles (with toys that resemble real-world objects; a group of children negotiates roles such as a doctor, patient, and nurse in the presence of doctor's office toys.)

Multiple pretend roles (without toys that resemble real objects; e.g., children create a pretend setting with blocks or Play-Doh® and designate pretend roles to enact.)

Sources: Adapted from Fein (1975), Nicholich (1977), Watson and Fischer (1977), and Watson and Jackowitz (1984).

the individual child at play; Piaget analyzes individual cognitive development as reflected in play, while much play is social, requiring an analysis of what occurs in a group context (Reifel & Yeatman, 1993). We will revisit these criticisms later.

Bruner on Problem Solving

In *Play: Its Role in Development and Evolution*, Jerome Bruner, Alison Jolly, and Kathy Sylva (1976) collected landmark articles on many aspects of play, including Bruner's own classic survey on "The Nature and Uses of Immaturity" (1972). Sections in the book included "The Evolutionary Context," "Play and the World of Objects and Tools," "Play and the Social World," and "Play and the World of Symbols." By bringing together diverse writings on play in this one volume, Bruner was able to demonstrate the predominant themes in play research and the theories associated with them. The overriding theme was that play allows development to occur in many domains, including **problem solving**, cooperative and competitive social interactions, sex roles, cultural acquisition, language, and **creativity**. His interest in play, as a developmental foundation for problem solving and thinking, was represented by his own work on cognitive and social play. For example, Anna and Zoe painting at the easel creates opportunities for solving problems about depiction, relating socially, and dealing with criticism.

Bruner (1972) values play as an immature activity that allows children to explore and master abilities that they will need in their adult worlds. Play allows children to act in ways that minimize consequences, allowing errors to be made before there are real consequences. It also allows actions to be combined in ways that might never occur under normal circumstances; we can learn to relate subroutines to larger tasks by means of play. Play is a context for using objects as tools to solve problems, and when adults are involved, there is potential for teaching social conventions and symbols. The skills acquired in play also require decontextualization, or the transition from "knowing how" to "knowing that"; like Bateson (1955/2000) and Vygotsky (1978), Bruner sees play as a transition from action (which reflects knowing how) to meaning (which reflects knowing that). Play requires that we psychologically separate actions from the contexts in which they normally take place, and that psychological separation makes the mind operate in new ways; the Halloween play of Anna and Zoe takes ideas about the holiday out of context where they are practiced into the context of peer play. Bruner places play in the realm of nature (what he calls "biologically rooted modes") that is shaped by culture (i.e., rituals, like Halloween). Play is a way we have evolved to learn to use tools to problem solve, and play is the setting where social meanings are constructed; for Anna and Zoe, they are constructing meanings about Halloween as well as about social relations such as friendship and disagreement. Play is clearly one way of understanding evolutionary and developmental Progress (Sutton-Smith, 1997, 1999).

By 1990 in *Acts of Meaning*, Bruner had placed much of this thinking in the service of narrative. Human efforts, including play, are directed toward creating meaning. Narrative is one form that meaning can take. While Bruner has not elaborated his current theoretical position with the earlier work on play, it may be fair to infer that one of the social problems that gets solved by means of play is how we come to understand our experiences. This strand of theory, while based on cultural and cognitive rather than biological assumptions, appears to mirror the lens of psychoanalytic thought about play.

Social Play

Many people automatically assume that play is a social activity, something one does with friends, like painting at an easel. This common assumption persists in spite of the fact that we have abundant evidence that a good deal of childhood play time is spent alone, with a child engaged in solitary pretend, computer games, television viewing, or other activities that could be done with others but, as often as not, are done solo. Our theoretical picture of play as a social activity may be biased by the fact that much research is done in classrooms, where group play is more likely to occur. Only recently have studies of children's play at home and outside of schools reemerged as a source of understanding about children's lives (e.g., Haight & Miller, 1995; Kelly-Byrne, 1989).

Interest in social play has increased, not only in terms of how peers play with each other but also regarding other social influences on play (e.g., Smilansky, 1968). The roles of adults in children's play has reemerged as a theoretical concern, whether the adults are parents, teachers, play facilitators, or therapists. Beyond questions of social interaction influences on play, there are questions of the social meaning for media (computers, television, cinema) and children's culture for play. The meaning of social play today differs from earlier versions of the topic. To understand these various social lenses on play, we will look at traditional theory (Parten's developmental stages) about play relationships and then review current thinking on play culture and social constructivism (Corsaro, 1985; Meckley, 1995; Opie & Opie, 1959, 1969, 1997).

Parten on Social Participation

Mildred Parten (1932) conducted a classic study on the development of social relationships in group settings for children. Her interest was in the genetic sociology of the classroom, or what transitions children make as they become social participants in group activities. Her assumptions appear to fall on the nature end of the nature-nurture continuum, with a belief that social relations are more innate or genetic than shaped by the environment. While her framework for observing children as they interact is frequently equated by researchers with play in its various forms (see Howes, 1987, 1992; Rubin, Fein, & Vandenberg, 1983), her theory applies to all social contacts that might occur in groups, including eating snacks, washing hands, or participating in any event where children might enter and leave a group. Her main point is that for any child, we see a developmental progression in the type of social involvement that child exhibits, and the onset of each type is roughly linked with age. The developmental progression is presented in Figure 2–4.

The sweep of Parten's theory suggests that from age two on, children make the transition from being nonsocial (uninvolved), to socially aware (onlooker observes others; solitary acts like others while not near them), to close proximity (acts in parallel with others, as Anna and Zoe demonstrate when they both paint pumpkins on their separate sides of the easel), and finally to interactive (associates with others while not sharing a joint purpose, then sharing a joint purpose, as when Anna and Zoe decide to play witches, or when they play peek-a-boo). We see the child developing from pre- or asocial, toward a stage when an experience is socially shared. This change typically occurs in the preschool years, so that children will be cooperative with peers by age 5 or 6.

It is worth remembering that these stages are useful for describing play and any other social event. We might see onlooker (Julie observing Zoe), parallel activity (Anna and Zoe painting on opposite sides of the easel), or cooperative interactions at the snack table, as well as when children pretend to play house or build with blocks. Parten's stages are not just play stages, but because much of what young children do is play, many associate her stages primarily with play. Parten did not equate play and social participation.

It is also worth noting that the validity of Parten's stages has been confirmed by numerous researchers. Current research has demonstrated the developmental progression that she described, although some studies have indicated that today's children, who have been entering group care in the form of childcare at earlier ages, may be progressing through these stages at an earlier pace; we might see parallel or cooperative interactions with 2- or 3-year-olds, if those children have been in child care since they were babies (Howes, 1987). It is also true that children who as preschoolers may not have been exposed to groups of peers demonstrate the same developmental progression at the time when they first encounter peers, but they may go through the stages more quickly.

Parten did not try to account for individual differences in her social theory. She did not attempt to deal with the idea that some children may prefer to play alone, even if they have the skills to play cooperatively (Takhvar & Smith, 1990). So the developmental progression that Parten's theory sets forth provides a general framework for considering how children interact with peers, including those times when they are playing. Her theory does not provide a lens for understanding individual children's reasons for wanting to play, or not, with others in their groups. How the social environment might nurture or support social relations is beyond the scope of her theory.

Peer Culture and Play

Parten and her work represent more the biological influences on social play theory; social play naturally emerges as the child grows. Contrasting

FIGURE 2–4 Parten's Genetic Sociology of Social Participation

Uninvolved:	The child is active and mobile but seemingly aimless; there is no sense of others' play.
Onlooker:	The child attends to others' play, may speak with players, but does not participate.
Solitary:	The child plays alone, with own toys; typical of 2- to 3-year-olds.
Parallel:	The child plays beside or near others, but not with them—no sharing, including play goals.
Associative:	The child plays with others, conversing, but purposes of play may not be similar.
Cooperative:	Goals of play are shared and negotiated; tasks and roles relate to play's purpose; group sense is marked by turn-taking, common goal, product, or game.

Source: Adapted from Parten (1932).

cultural influences are well represented by writers who come from anthropologic, sociologic, and folkloric traditions (e.g., Corsaro, 1985; Opie, 1993; Opie & Opie, 1969, 1997; Schwartzman, 1978). These theorists question the biological inevitability of social play, arguing that play is a context in which social relations and meanings (i.e., culture) are constructed. Growth in this realm of thought about play has been dramatic over the past 10 years. In some cases, researchers build on classical social science theory (e.g., Bateson, 1955/2000; Goffman, 1974; Mead, 1934), while in other cases, theory emerges from empirical findings (e.g., Corsaro, 1985; Opie, 1993; Opie & Opie, 1969, 1997).

There are many notions of **peer culture**, but most seem to assume that children, as they interact, create communities of participants who share common **values**, interests, and rituals. These communities are most frequently formed based on play activities, in which participants learn who shares their interests (such as in Halloween or in other cultural events), who has skills (like who can paint well), and who can be counted on to make the "right" things happen (who criticizes whom, and who does not). Some of the earliest efforts to document and describe this phenomenon were the Opies' studies of *The Lore and Language of Schoolchildren* (1959) and *Children's Games in the Street and Playground* (1969). The Opies revealed that play exists in an astonishing range of forms, most of which serve children's social purposes. (See Figure 2–5.) Those purposes include fun but also function to create cohesive social systems that operate with rules that are meaningful to children themselves. Children will use games and chants to keep others in line or to exclude them from the group. Adults are outsiders, if not anathema, to these forms of play; adults might ruin it.

Such peer cultures will develop on streets and playgrounds and may lead to activity of which the larger culture disapproves (i.e., gang activity). Cultures also develop under adults' noses, in preschool and elementary classrooms (Corsaro, 1985; Meckley, 1995; Miller, Fernie, & Kantor, 1992; Reifel, 1986; Scales, 1996). Children pretend or play games in ways that most adults ignore (as long as there is no disruption to adult-sanctioned activity), establishing shared meanings that create in-groups, out-groups, and hierarchies of influence in classrooms. In some cases, we choose to see such play as the basis for forming friendships (Corsaro, 1985; Howes, 1992). In most cases, such play is overlooked entirely. Sutton-Smith (1984) has noted that this play can be cruel to those who are excluded or scapegoated.

Corsaro (1985) has formalized one understanding of peer culture with his sociolinguistic analysis of talk during play. He theorizes that language during play serves social functions for creating play groups, including children's efforts to exclude others from play. Like Garvey (1993) has done for pretend communications, Corsaro identifies types of talk that can be heard during play, talk that leads to hierarchical group formation (see Figure 2–6).

Patterns of **play talk** reveal who has power in the group and what is the relative **social status** of players, such as Zoe's relative subordinate status with peers. Zoe is informed by Julie that the painted pumpkin does not look like a pumpkin, and Zoe answers Anna at a very high rate. Instead of reflecting social status, play is seen as the context where social status, social power, and shared values are created. These creations may be adaptive for humans who must learn to work together, but they may be maladaptive for those who are excluded from play. The long-term effects of such exclusion have been studied by developmentalists for decades (e.g., Moore, 1967; Kemple, 1991).

As a part of children's culture, play becomes an activity with significance in its own right. Instead of being an activity in which we can witness individual children's various forms of development, it is seen as an activity that creates development. The trouble with peer culture theory is that it begins to raise questions about the values inherent in play (Sutton-Smith, 1997). Play per se is no longer just a benign activity that

FIGURE 2–5 Types of Peer Culture Play

Wit and Repartee/Nonsense

Kindergartener girl

I'm gonna tell on you,
That you put ants in my pants
And made me do a boogie dance.

Kindergartener

Look left;
Look right;
Look everywhere.
Na Na Na Na Na Na!
Your pants are falling down.

2nd Grader

Look up, look down. Look all around.
Your pants are falling down.

Kindergartener

Skunk in the barnyard: P.U.!
Somebody ate it: that's you!

Kindergartener group

Bubble gum, bubble gum, in a dish.
How many pieces do you wish?
One, two, three, four

Guile

2nd Grader

Are you a P.T.?
If yes: Then you're a pregnant teacher.
If no: Then you are not a pretty teacher.

Are you an S.K.?
If yes: Then you're a stupid kid.
If no: Then you are not a smart kid.

Jeers and Torments

2nd Grader

Say I.
I
Your mommie had a baby at the FBI.
Whoever looks at _____ is a nerd [has cooties, etc.]

Riddles

2nd Grader

What's green and flies through the air?
Super pickle.

3rd Grader

Why do you salute the refrigerator?
Because it's General Electric.

Kindergartener

What goes up white and comes down yellow?
An egg.

2nd Grader

What's green and red and goes 30 miles an hour?
A frog in a blender.

2nd Grader

Knock! Knock!
Who's there?
Banana.
Banana who?
Knock! Knock!
Who's there?
Banana.
Banana who?
Knock! Knock!
Who's there?
Orange.
Orange who?
Orange you glad I didn't say banana?

Pranks

2nd Grader

Child left his seat to get something. Prankster ran quickly to the vacant seat, took the lunch tray, and moved it to a new location. The returning child missed the tray and had to search for it.

Pretend

Kindergartener boys

Sneak Matchbox® cars into cafeteria and pretend to race during lunch.

2nd Grader

Blow bubbles through a straw into chocolate milk, to make a "milkshake."

All ages

Make little "pills" out of wads of white bread, then take "medicine."

2nd Grader

Chew around the edges of graham crackers to form toy "guns" that they shoot at one another.

Kindergartener boys

Use bananas from lunchboxes as "phones" to have conversation.

3rd Grader group

When a cafeteria monitor limited to 3 the number of boys at each table, one of the boys asked, "How do girls eat?" All the children began to eat their lunches "the way girls do," lifting little fingers as they brought food to their mouths, taking delicate little bites, and raising the pitch of their voices and giggling. Then they all pretended to be boys.

Source: Opie & Opie (1959, 1969), from Reifel, 1986.

FIGURE 2–6 Corsaro on Social Play Talk

Imperatives: commands, warnings (make play happen; common from superordinate player to subordinate)
Informative statements: acknowledge or provide information (clarify what is going on; common with all players, but more so for subordinate to superordinate and from one superordinate to another)
Request for permission: ask to engage (from subordinate to superordinate)
Request for joint action: refer to another speaker's suggestion (from superordinate to superordinate)
Answers: respond to a directive (more common from subordinates)
Information requests: ask for clarification (more common from superordinates)
Directive questions: give indirect orders
Tag questions: make statement with "OK?" or "Right?" (from superordinate to superordinate)
Greetings: say "Hi" (most common among children of the same status)
Baby talk: human or animal forms (more subordinates)

may contribute to Progress; it can now be seen as a context for creation of both good (social cohesion, role exploration, sense-making, exploration of meanings) and bad (social rejection, prejudice, bullying). The meaning of play activities, however defined, takes on new significance when we think about the cumulative meaning of play, filtered through a theory of child culture.

One way of seeing this theoretical perspective in practice is through the work of Alice Meckley. Meckley (1995) observed preschoolers at play over a 5-month period and documented their pretend actions, playmates, social status, and other features of what they did during play time. The same play would repeat itself from day to day, but with different players taking roles. She found that play ideas (themes, topics) seemed to transfer over time from more popular to less popular children and that less popular children took desirable roles after popular children were done with them. All children were creating social meanings as they played, but what they played (and when) was influenced by the status of players in the classroom peer culture. We have a picture of play that is very much shaped by the social environment.

Creativity in Play

The assumption that play is linked with the arts, aesthetics, and creativity emerged hundreds of years ago with Enlightenment scholars such as Schiller (1965) (see Chapter 1). Current researchers have pursued that assumption by studying the relationship of childhood play to different aspects of creativity. Just as play has been defined in different ways by different theorists, so has creativity. Researchers in this tradition have considered creativity in terms of originality and fluidity (after Guilford, 1957), flow experience (after Csikszentmihalyi, 1977, 1979; Csikszentmihalyi & Csikszentmihalyi, 1988), intelligence (after Gardner, 1983; Gardner & Hatch, 1989), or educational programming (after Reggio Emilia; Edwards, Gandini, & Forman, 1997). Clearly, the Imaginary is central to much of this scholarship (Sutton-Smith, 1997, 1999).

Creativity can take many forms, which means that play can be associated with any number of variables. Theories such as Guilford's assume that creativity takes the form of individuals finding original solutions to problems or challenges, acting in a fluid and flexible manner; Anna and Zoe find lots of ways to use the paint and the easel to create different forms of play. A child who uses a towel to create a roof for a block building might be considered creative from this point of view. Others, such as Csikszentmihalyi, consider the subjective experience of the individual; if an activity, such as playing computer games, psychologically transports the player to a state where time and the environment are irrelevant, then the player might be engaged in creative flow.

Anna and Zoe can be seen in creative flow when they pretend to be witches and when they play their peek-a-boo game. Creativity can also be understood theoretically as a form of intelligence, as Gardner has done; in addition to traditional forms of intelligence (language, math), other creative activities such as musical and visual expression may be part of an individual's potential.

Some educational programs, such as the Reggio Emilia School in Italy, may build their entire curriculum around creativity. The arts and other forms of expression are encouraged, although a particular theory of creativity is not identified within the program. The play of children, as guided by teachers and the environment, is assumed to be creative. This sort of expressiveness is valued in that program, as it is by many educators in other parts of the world (e.g., Isenberg & Jalongo, 1997).

EMERGING THEORIES OF PLAY

Over the past decade, a number of new theories related to play, or combinations of theories, have appeared in the literature. These theories have attempted to explain some aspect of human development, social relations, or play in particular contexts. For example, Fromberg (1997, 1999) and others (e.g., VanderVen, 1998, in press) have begun to apply complexity or **chaos theory** and hermeneutics to group play. Working from principles that have been applied to geology, physics, psychology, and many other branches of science (e.g., Waldrop, 1992), these authors are attempting to understand the various contributors to play equilibrium, or play's oscillating balance. One thing triggers another, through the lens of chaos theory, and regular patterns emerge from the interplay of social relationships, ideas, materials, and guidance in the play setting. At this point, complexity theory has not been fully tested.

Theory of mind has been linked with play since Leslie's 1987 article, in which he argues that pretend play provides the context in which children begin to understand that others have thoughts, beliefs (true and false), and desires. Play requires children to acquire this **theory of mind**, from which they become aware of the internal mental states of themselves and others (Lillard, 1993, 1998a, 1998b, 2000; Woolley, 1995). The concerns of this theory are how aspects of play, such as communications about the "as if" of play, are linked to mental representations about social relationships. Most of the work with this theory has been done in laboratory settings, but it deals with issues encountered in many play contexts, including imaginary companions (Taylor, Carlson, & Gerow, 2000) and gestural meanings (Suddendorf, 2000).

Older concerns are reappearing in new theories about play. The centrality of emotion for play is no longer associated only with psychoanalytic theories. Greta Fein (1989; Fein & Kinney, 1994) has directed her thinking to the feelings that are expressed in play and how those feelings organize play for children. Communication, metacommunication, and creativity during play were analyzed by Sawyer (1997, 2003), going beyond the work of Bateson, Garvey, and Corsaro. Sawyer argues that play is a form of improvisation, subject to the same rules of social interplay that apply to all generative encounters. He uses sociolinguistic theory to show how early childhood pretend play is not only metacommunicative but also metapragmatic. Children are not just signaling others about what they are playing; they are signaling each other about relationships. Both Fein and Sawyer's ideas rework long-standing views of play with their contemporary lenses.

Emerging theories of children's play do not reflect only abstract ideas and concerns. Many new theories are tied to play as it is practiced in classrooms and homes and on playgrounds. Several attempts to make the prerational into something rational (Spariosu, 1989) begin with children's play activities and seek theory to aid understanding. A number of these efforts combine existing theories to interpret children's actions. For example, Meckley (1995) draws on Vygotsky, Mead, and other social theorists to make sense of the roles and rules of children's play. Reifel and Yeatman (1993; Yeatman & Reifel, 1997) combine the theories of Bateson and Vygotsky to create a model for understanding children's creation of meanings around pivots in classroom play. As teacher-scholars such as Scales (1996), Reynolds and Jones (1997), and Paley (1981) provide more description of play with their thoughtful theoretical analyses, we are left with new combinations of lenses to enhance our understanding.

PLAY THROUGH DIFFERENT LENSES

Play has theoretical significance from the point of view of any number of disciplines and scholars (Sutton-Smith, 1997, 1999; Rubin et al, 1998). In previous sections, we have demonstrated how a number of theoretical perspectives provide us with different lenses for understanding play. Psychoanalysis gives us a view of play as critical for balancing the conflicting pressures that result when our biological drives meet social constraints. The emotions of players motivate them and are treated by means of play therapy. Communications theory marks play as crucial for establishing signal systems, frames of reference, and all those social and cognitive skills that are required for communications. Cognitive theory gives us a number of alternative lenses: play reflects developing cognition (Piaget), play is a tool for problem solving (Bruner), or play is a zone to promote mental development (Vygotsky). The biological and environmental are given varying weights in these cognitive views. Socially, we can see play as an innate, unfolding process (Parten) or as a context for generating **social structure** and meaning (in peer culture). Play can also be linked to creativity in its many theoretical forms, reflecting a belief that goes back hundreds of years. Each of these lenses can show us a different perspective on Anne and Zoe's play, including their relationships, how they are communicating, their thinking, what they are thinking about, and how they are relating to the world around them. Each of these theoretical views points to the importance of play, but they do not share common assumptions about the role or function of play. As Figure 2–7 illustrates, important thinkers attribute slightly different meanings to play, whether it deals with play's functions (personality integration, problem solving, abstract thought, social group formation), as a reflection of or contributor to development, as a process within an individual or a group, or related to ideas or relationships. They tell us to look at play, but they tell us to look for different things (or to listen for different things) when we see play. It is as if we were using a different lens to see what is there, and each lens allows us to see something different in the same activity.

BELIEFS AND PHILOSOPHY

How do we resolve this theoretical heterogeneity? How do we know whether play is biologically determined, based on a child's drives, or culturally determined, leading to social power for some players and inferiority for others? One way to deal with this theoretical heterogeneity is to reflect on the reasons why we are engaging with children as they play. Scholars seldom attempt to resolve the differing perspectives that are reflected in the theories presented earlier; research often tends to reduce play to one domain or another, leaving it to the reader to draw implications for what happens in day-to-day play. People who deal with play on a daily basis must create their own ways of thinking about play, possibly based on scholarly theories (Gross, 2003). Are you a parent, hoping for the happiness and stimulation of your child? Are you a teacher, aiming to educate young children? Are you a therapist, hoping to help a child master psychological challenges? Each of these aims is associated with different adult roles and assumptions about what children are experiencing when they play. It is likely that particular theories may be more or less relevant as each of those questions is answered. In the following sections, we will make sense of play

FIGURE 2–7 Key Theoretical Statements on Play

Psychoanalysis: Emotional Motives for Play
"In Mary's case, her play disruption and her play satiation, if seen in the framework of all the known circumstances, strongly suggest that a variety of past and future, real and imagined events had been incorporated into a system of mutually aggravating dangers." (Erikson, 1950/1963, p. 232)

Communications and Play

Bateson on Play Frames
"'This is play' looks something like this: 'These actions in which we now engage do not denote what those actions *for which they stand* would denote.'" (Bateson, 1955/2000, p. 180)

Cognitive Views of Play

Vygotsky on Play as a Zone of Proximal Development
"In play thought is separated from objects and action arises from ideas rather than from things: a piece of wood begins to be a doll and a stick becomes a horse. Action according to rules begins to be determined by ideas and not by objects themselves." (Vygotsky, 1978, p. 97)

Piaget on Play as Assimilation
"Symbolic play, then, is only one form of thought, linked to all the others by its mechanism, but having as its sole aim satisfaction of the ego, i.e., individual truth as opposed to collective and impersonal truth." (Piaget, 1962, p. 167)

Bruner on Problem Solving
"Play appears to serve several centrally important functions. First, it is a means of minimizing the consequences of one's actions and of learning, therefore, in a less risky situation." (Bruner, 1972/1976, p. 38)

Social Play
"'First-years against second-years, OK?' 'I know, let's play Om Pom [hide and seek].' Two girls approached a third and said with almost oriental politeness, 'Melanie, may we play Stuck in the Mud, please?'" (Opie, 1993, p. 21)

theories based on who we are and how we will use them.

A Model of Classroom Play

At the beginning of this chapter, we suggested that one way that educators, parents, or other professionals will relate to play is in terms of their principles and beliefs, as well as any theories they may have learned. One trouble with this point is that our beliefs are complex and, at times, conflicting (Bennett, Wood, & Rogers, 1997). Sorting out beliefs can be confusing when they may blend with ways of thinking about children and (for example) education. To value play as a means of forming meaning, for instance, has implications for the theories we turn to in order to make sense of play and the research findings we look to as validation for our practices. Parents, on the other hand, may have more of an interest in their children's play as a basis for exploring family interests and recreation. Therapists have a commitment to healing their patients, so their theoretical view will take that fact into account. These are all ways we as concerned adults relate to play, and we are not yet detailing the complexities of children's play itself.

To put theory (or theories) into practical context, we will explore how it plays a role in a particular context—the early childhood classroom. We will present a model of classroom play that combines theory, beliefs, values, and practice. This model should have implications for others engaging children in play, whether at home, in hospitals, or in any other play space.

Figure 2–8 attempts to elaborate more fully how educators may relate to play. We see that beliefs are part of this figure, but there are many more ways we can relate to play as an educational activity. Theories, or scientific ideas about play, are important, as they give us the frameworks we need to make sense of those things we believe. Research findings are also a consideration, in so much as they provide examples of what theories might look like in practice. And the details of practice can show up in any number of ways to which we need to relate, including the play materials we include in our classrooms, how they are arranged, and the real-world experiences we provide with the intent of stimulating play (Reifel & Yeatman, 1993).

FIGURE 2–8 A Model of Classroom Play

Beliefs in the Importance of Certain Values
- Creativity
- Freedom
- Social skills
- Meaning/understanding
- Expression
- Fun

Theories
- Vygotsky (1986)
- Guilford (1957)

Research
- Reifel & Yeatman (1993)
- Parten (1932)

Environment
- Materials
  - Markers
  - Paints
  - Books
  - Blocks

Social Relations

Real-world Experiences
- Field trips
- Family activities

Time (i.e., duration)

Note: Examples are provided here; alternatives may be substituted to create a particular model based on local needs.

In addition to this model, we must specify actions. What do we do if everyone in the class wants to play with blocks? What do we do if all children's ideas for play come from television cartoons? What do we do when some children are rejected by play groups? It is apparent that we have additional ways to relate to play, in terms of our actions—how we guide and participate in play. These questions bring us closer to the experiential practice of daily classroom play to be discussed in later chapters. Selecting from among the theories presented here may help make decisions (Bennett et al., 1997), but finding the place for those theories in a philosophy is necessary.

To manage some of this complexity, it is helpful to delimit the range of issues being considered. Principles, or the basic beliefs that guide us, are one place to begin. Among the many beliefs that one could have, core beliefs, as shown in Figure 2–9, might include the valuing of a free society (Cuffaro, 1995; Dewey, 1916); people should participate in activities of their own choice, within which mistakes can be made, rules generated, and conflicts resolved.

A second core belief might be that we learn (or understand) what we do from our own efforts. Any meaningful activity becomes meaningful by virtue of what we bring to it. We do construct our knowledge, based on our participation in the experiences of life (Dewey, 1938; Vygotsky, 1978). In Chapter 1, we reviewed some of John Dewey's (1896/1972) educational and psychological writing on play. The quotes we cited there address the nursery school child's experience and the centrality of play for helping the child make ideas her own: "The child does

FIGURE 2–9 Teaching in a Model of Classroom Play

Teacher Guidance
- Shaping social interactions
- Shaping communications
- Shaping meanings

Teacher Participation
- Commenting on play
- Pretending with children

not get hold of any impression or any idea until he has *done* it" (p. 195). "He acts the idea *out* before he takes it *in*" (p. 196). When children choose their classroom play activities, they create a sense of ownership for their actions. As they communicate about those actions with others, they become more clear about what they are doing and how they are relating to others. The social laboratory of play allows children to create and refine their interests by acting, through play, in a community of learners.

A related belief that ties together the two core principles thus far is the importance of expression. It is only through expression, whether saying, drawing, building, enacting, or representing by any other means, that we can truly construct knowledge. We can freely participate in any number of experiences, but it is only in our efforts to communicate those experiences to others (i.e., to express) that our meanings can take shape. Without communication, we can have no clarification, correction, or elaboration.

An additional core belief that helps focus thinking about play is that cultural context is essential for giving meaning to experience. Our cultures give us the physical and social environments that we experience. They also give us beliefs and customs that provide essential meanings for life. Culture also gives us our language(s) for socially sharing experience. Our cultures, including our own backgrounds, as well as those of children and their families, become critical sources for meaningful experiences.

How do these principles help us delimit the complexity of play? First, these beliefs point to a model of the sorts of activities we will want to encourage in the classroom—activities in which children are free to choose and free to express themselves; interactive activities in which conflicts emerge and are resolved; activities in which cultural meanings are elaborated. We can further delimit our complexity by acknowledging that the play that we are considering is classroom play, and not the play of home or neighborhood. We are thinking about expressive, freely chosen social activity in a cultural setting (school) where society's values (as reflected by teacher and parent beliefs) are furthered. What are other possible beliefs that could serve as principles? We could add an appreciation for literacy, inquiry, diversity, fairness, or any number of other values that speak to our society. For example, in the area of early writing, Dyson (1997) argues that imaginary topics created by friends during play are important bases for early composition. Depending on how those values are featured in the model, we will need to select theoretical lenses to focus on them.

The unique educational purposes of classroom play, as opposed to children's play at home or in their neighborhoods, requires specialized play theory. Context must be understood if we are to understand classroom play. For example, a contextual model including the play theories of Bateson (1955/2000, on the play frame) and Vygotsky (1978, on meaningful play pivots to create zones of proximal development) might call our attention to the play materials and what the children are playing with those materials. No matter what her beliefs are, the early childhood teacher will be selecting meaningful play materials (i.e., pivots) with which children will create meaningful pretend frames. Particular beliefs will constrain teacher choices: culture and consensus will lead us to include certain meaningful materials for play (e.g., play houses for domestic play, phone books for literacy play, blocks and paint for creative symbolic play); more or less time will be allotted to play (e.g., to explore in depth whatever meanings are to be developed); social relations will be encouraged based on values (e.g., who chooses playmates; how many can play with particular materials; who resolves disputes); and how play relates to other curricular decisions (e.g., field trips that provide ideas for classroom play).

Vygotsky's and Bateson's theories may be ways to understand meaningful educational play. But we also need other theories to provide the lenses that allow us to relate to play through our observations. It seems necessary to understand about communication during play and social decision making. The writings of Garvey (1993) and

Corsaro (1985), among others, provide necessary dimensions that we must consider as we observe communicative play interactions. To understand more about the expressive qualities of play, post-Piagetian researchers, such as Fein (1975) and Watson and Jackowitz (1984), are informative; they describe the development of expressive transformations that children make with the pivots we provide them. Again, theoretical writing gives us the lenses with which we can see what is happening during play.

What we are constructing is a model of classroom play, as an ideal representation of the educational play we believe is good for children and that we want to think about and make sense of as we are teaching. Theory will be one important part of that model. In the next paragraphs are a number of points about what such a model will do to clarify teaching in a playful classroom, acknowledgment that no one model will be appropriate for everyone, ideas for reflecting on how everyone can participate in creating their own models, and implications for research.

Creating a Playful Classroom

When we plan to include play in our classrooms, we do so with reasons. Based on some of the values articulated earlier in this section, some of the reasons we might have for classroom play might be (a) learning to make choices and dealing with the ramifications of those choices and (b) communicating and expressing ideas. How can we know that children are having playful experiences related to these reasons? Teachers need to keep in mind the dimensions of their models, to assess, for example, whether children are making responsible choices and expressing themselves. Having such a theory-based model helps focus on important, valued beliefs and directs us to observe these features of play that are most relevant to our purposes. The model is useful, to the degree that it tells us what to look for in play, and directs us away from those aspects of play that we value less, so that we will not focus so much, for example, on gender differences in cognitive development.

Embracing Flexibility

There are many possible differing configurations of elements that can vary from school to school and community to community. How might the model of play look different, for example, if literacy were the core belief underlying the educator's thinking? First, a different set of theories and research may guide our thinking (e.g., Christie, 1994; Christie, Enz & Vukelich, 1997; Dyson, 1997; Miller, Fernie, & Kantor, 1992; Vygotsky, 1978). Second, the environment might look very different, with more books, play materials for words and writing, and props such as phone books, menus, and magazines in dramatic play centers. Also, we would expect that time would be spent exploring these materials, including guiding and questioning children about their use during play. Clearly, a teacher relates to play very differently when literacy is a core value, and relationships to play vary when different values predominate.

It is fair to ask, What if values about play change? Values do change, and such changes may be part of a vital curriculum. If teachers observe that children are exploring certain meanings, as Cox (1996) did when she tracked children's explorations of the idea of bridges, then there would seem to be reason to value children's interests and make sense of ways to expand their understandings. The same argument could be made when there is reason to consider emotions (Fein, 1989), spatial understanding (Golbeck, 1995; Reifel, 1984), creativity (Isenberg & Jalongo, 1997), or any other phenomenon that we might elevate to high value. Children's interests, experiences in communities, or societal priorities might contribute to such changes. A teacher's perceived needs of her class might also suggest different needs. Not to acknowledge shifts in basic values toward play is unrealistic and may lead to a rigid, prescriptive play curriculum.

For any model of classroom play to function, in any of its variations, a teacher must be willing to revisit her thinking about play, observe children carefully, relate observations to research-based constructs, and, when research does not tell us all it could about what occurs in classrooms, be willing to become an action researcher to expand our database (Chafel & Reifel, 1996; Williams, 1996). It is through reflection that the teacher has numerous ways to relate to play theory.

Research Implications: Teacher Beliefs

In their recent study of teacher thinking about play, Bennett et al. (1997) found that when asked to reflect on their own classroom play practices, a range of teachers, from novice to experienced, had dynamic theories of what play is and what roles it might have in the classroom (see Figure 2–10). When those teachers viewed a video segment of play in their own classrooms, it stimulated reflection on what play means. Without the impetus of the video, teachers were satisfied to assume that they knew what children were doing when they played, and they were frequently mistaken: materials did not stimulate the expected exploration or pretense, children did not make expected play choices, materials did not generate meanings desired by the teacher, and the pleasures of play were not what they were expected to be. What the teachers thought was going on during play was not in fact happening. The point here is not that teachers can be mistaken about play but that they do immediately think about play when they pay attention to it. Observing is important, and filtering observations through our own thinking, including beliefs and theory, is necessary.

What can serve as a template for our observations and thinking about play? Our knowledge base about play is a key framework for guiding such observations and interpretations. Seeing girls painting pumpkins at the easel (Reifel & Yeatman, 1993), for example, can be seen as a Piagetian construction play form (Piaget, 1962), a symbolic transformation by means of low-resemblance materials (Watson & Jackowitz, 1984), an associative social play form (Parten, 1932), a part of a Halloween script (Bretherton, 1989; Nelson & Seidman, 1984), or a meaningful pivot for generating pretense (Vygotsky, 1978). Can one play act be all these things? Yes. The question is, Which theories and databases are most consistent with the values of the educational program? We must know the various theories that provide us with ways of choosing what to look for and with ways of making sense of what we see. Theories of play become our lenses for observation and reflection.

FIGURE 2–10 Key Ideas Teachers Have about Play

Nature and Benefits of Play
- Distinct from "formal" work
- Build confidence
- Learning medium

Planning Learning Intentions and Outcomes
- Play is how children would learn if left to themselves
- Inevitability of learning
- Planned environment

Assessing Children Through Play
- Social development
- Observe/try to understand what is going on in their heads

Constraints
- Demand of national curriculum
- Environment (buildings, available space)
- Lack of teacher experience

Teacher's Role
- Demonstrate techniques
- Teacher in supporting role
- Extend the activity and the learning by making suggestions directing explorations

Note: Examples are from Bennett et al. (1997).

ISSUES SHAPING PLAY THEORY

From our basic definition of theory to the survey of theories as they inform us of children's play, it is clear that ideas about play are central to our understanding of children and how children grow. There are different perspectives on these matters, but most practitioners, if not most researchers, are eclectic in the way they draw on theory to understand play. As we look at play more closely, to help us in our work with children and to further our research, we find that several issues may shape future views or rhetorics of play.

The Need for Theory About Unique Contexts

We are finding that some forms of play (social relationships) are more likely to be seen and understood in particular settings (neighborhoods, where children can freely select playmates, as opposed to in school, where choices may be limited). Some cognitive forms of play may be best studied in unique settings, such as computer worlds. The context of play is becoming a consideration for our theory of play. What makes play activities meaningful, for participants and observers, may be the context itself. Theories that recognize context are being developed (e.g., Fromberg, 1997; Meckley, 1995; Reifel & Yeatman, 1993).

Interdisciplinarity

Following on Sutton-Smith (1997, 1999) and his argument that play can be understood in terms of disciplinary rhetorics, it appears that multidisciplinary views of play may be necessary. Any one discipline may inadvertently remove a play activity from its context, thereby stripping it of its meaning. We may need to link theories or generate new theories to acknowledge the social, aesthetic, physical, meaningful, virtual qualities of play, as several researchers have done (e.g., Reifel, 1999; Sawyer, 1997; Scales, 1996).

Teachers' Thinking About Play

Much children's play is context-specific, and as more play is taking place in settings that have been designed for play and supervised by adults, it may be that adult perceptions of play will be a growing area of play theory. How do participants make sense of play? How are the multiple perspectives of participants resolved, so that activity becomes and remains meaningful? Contextual theory, perhaps building on some of the theories presented earlier, is needed (Bennett et al., 1997; Kontos & Dunn, 1993; Stremmel, Fu, Patet, & Shah, 1995).

SUMMARY

Theory helps us think about what we experience. It is a tool for understanding, and it can serve as a lens for viewing the world and making sense of it. Theories of children's play provide diverse lenses that are shaped by the many disciplines that have contributed to our knowledge of play. Those theories, and the beliefs and assumptions associated with them, form different rhetorics of play (Sutton-Smith, 1997, 1999). Much theory about children's play can be described in terms of a rhetoric of Progress, the assumption that play is a contributing factor to human development.

Any number of contemporary theories provide lenses for our understanding of play. Those theories may emphasize the nature or the nurture of play (i.e., the biological, cultural, or interactive influences of play on development). Psychoanalytic theory emphasizes the emotional, motivational aspects of play and how play allows children to express their feelings. Scholars such as Freud, Erikson, and Peller have refined psychoanalytic theoretical lenses. Bateson and Garvey have given us ways to view play in terms of communications. Children signal one another when they play, and those verbal and nonverbal signals provide theoretical lenses for understanding children's play talk and the pretend frames they create. Cognitive theorists, such as Piaget, Bruner, and Vygotsky, tell us that play links theoretically with our minds. Play may be a way of assimilating knowledge (as Piaget tells us), problem solving (in Bruner's sense), or creating knowledge within a zone of proximal development (in Vygotsky's terms). Depending on the cognitive lens we select, we can see different aspects of thinking in the developing child's play.

Play is often understood to be social. Theorists have provided a number of rational frameworks for understanding the social features of play. Play may be a setting for increasing social participation, as Parten tells us. Or it may be the setting for creation of social structures, where social status is established. Corsaro and social status researchers provide a number of lenses for seeing (and hearing) how play relationships benefit players differently, making some popular and others less so. Others show us how play is a foundation for children's own culture. Other scholars see play as a creative activity, in which children find original solutions to their problems and explore novelty and the arts. Different theories are needed for all these views of play, and each view provides us with unique lenses for observing and understanding children's play.

Given the selection of contemporary play theories that exist, how do we decide which is true or even useful for us? As the play example presented in this chapter suggests, we can see many theoretical ideas about play in one play event. We argue that children's play theories may be more or less appropriate, depending on the role you will be taking with children. Parents may have one set of concerns about their children's play, but those concerns will probably differ from a play therapist's interests. The special needs of teachers, as planners and observers of play, are explored. A model of classroom play is presented, in which competing values and beliefs help determine which theories will be most relevant for planning the environment, guiding children, and assessing their play. Different theoretical lenses are needed to understand children's play if a teacher is more interested in a particular aspect—social relationships, literacy, or problem solving. The challenge for the teacher is to become familiar with theories, in order to make sound decisions about classroom play. Teachers may also add to theory, with their own research on play in their classrooms. The lenses we need to view play are changing, as we create new contexts for play, as the composition of the players changes, and as new research becomes available to us.

KEY TERMS

Adaptation
Assimilation/
accommodation
Beliefs
Chaos theory
Cognition
Communication
Creativity
Emotion/feeling
Frame
Motivation
Peer culture
Peers
Pivot
Play
Play talk
Problem solving
Psychoanalysis
Rhetoric
Imaginary
Progress
Self
Scaffold
Sensorimotor period
Signals
Social status
Social structure
Theory
Theory of mind
Values
Zone of proximal
development (ZPD)

STUDY QUESTIONS

1. What is a theory? What is a theory of play?
2. What beliefs about play do you have? Which of those beliefs do you share with others?
3. What discipline are you studying? What rhetoric of play is most likely to be associated with that discipline?
4. In a small group, see whether you can identify examples of children's play that correspond with each of the seven rhetorics of play.
5. With a number of classmates, observe children's play. Try on a number of theoretical lenses as you observe. How does the play look different if you are wearing psychodynamic lenses versus cognitive lenses? (Try thinking of Bruner's ideas about play, then consider Vygotsky's.) Cognitive lenses versus communication lenses? (Try thinking of Garvey's forms of talk, then consider Corsaro's.)
6. Compare observations of children that you make with Parten's social participation lens to observations those made with Corsaro's social structure lens. What differences do they tell you about the children you see?
7. In a small group, list your beliefs and values about what is good for children. Identify play theories that are most closely associated with those beliefs and values. Why are some values higher on your list?
8. Which theory (or theories) seem most reasonable to you? How does that theory align with the beliefs you stated in question 2?
9. In a small group, identify your basic beliefs, values, and theories. What play objects and settings are necessary for your view of play to be put into practice?
10. What play have you seen that does not seem to be described by any of the theories presented in this chapter? What research might help you understand that play better?

Chapter 3

Neuroscience, Play Deprivation, and Pay-for-Play

ZAP: neurons in the brain's amygdala send pulses of electricity through the circuits that control emotion. You hold him on your lap and talk, and neurons from his ears start hardwiring connections to the auditory cortex. And you thought you were just playing with your kid.

(Begley, 1996, p. 55)

Rapidly expanding research on the brain is showing that play plays a far more important role in development than previously assumed, even by scientists. Although the research is far from definitive, the findings are sufficiently compelling to warrant careful study. Drawing conclusions for child development and education is a subject of growing controversy, with some calling for educational programs based on brain research and others declaring it is far too early for such optimism. Brain research to date has not demonstrated conclusively that specific educational practices are warranted. Consequently, the reader should beware of claims that a specific "brain-based" curriculum or program should be followed.

In this chapter, we examine research in historical perspective, focusing on brain and play, and suggest implications for early child development that we expect to be modified with time and further study.

There is good (enabling or constructive) play and bad (disabling or destructive) play. Good play promotes healthy development; bad play or deprivation of play may restrict or damage development. This chapter illustrates the nature and scope of neuroscience research, explains how children are being deprived of rich, healthy play opportunities and contexts, and describes trends toward substitution of **pay-for-play** entertainment and other **pseudoplay** forms for traditional, spontaneous play. Research and experience lead us to conclude that such deprivation of spontaneous, creative play, whatever the cause, may result in stunted or aberrant development and behavior. The growing trend toward substituting high-tech entertainment and structured activity for play in homes, schools, and communities is a critical health issue that will be intensely debated by professionals from various disciplines. Brain research is a promising avenue for helping to resolve such educational/developmental concerns.

NEUROSCIENCE, PLAY, AND CHILD DEVELOPMENT

With the aid of high-tech brain-imaging technology, scientists around the world are making unprecedented inroads into understanding the role of experience in human development. As early as 1996, the United States had more than 3,000 brain researchers with research resources of over $1 billion, and the Japanese had drafted a plan to invest $18 billion in brain science over the next two decades and about $1 billion in a state-of-the-art nuclear magnetic resonance (NMR) center for structural biology (Barker, 1996). Because of this unprecedented interest in neuroscience, the 1990s are now called the "decade of the brain." **Neuroscience** appears to be the new frontier for revolutionary research into the structure and function of the brain, the prevention and treatment of neurological disorders, and virtual replication or mimicking the brain's information processing functions.

Neuroscientists are seeing both planned and unanticipated results that are relevant to education and child development. Play, the seemingly frivolous, unimportant behavior with no apparent purpose, has earned new respect as biologists, neuroscientists, psychologists, and others see that it is indeed serious business and is perhaps equally important as other basic drives like sleep, sex, and food. In the scientific community, if not in social institutions, play and the people who study it are not seen as strange and immature. One would hope that this unprecedented explosion of information about the importance of play for brain growth and child development will influence families, schools, and other social and corporate institutions to rearrange their attitudes and priorities about play, recess, physical education, music, games, art, and rich, personal interactions between caregivers and children.

Emergence of Neuroscience

Research in neuroscience is confirming theoretical positions held for several decades—which have already been implemented in early childhood programs. Studies of the role of the human brain in child development gained considerable momentum during the 1960s. A number of professionals (Frost, 1968, 1975; Hess & Bear, 1968; Hunt, 1961) concluded from both animal and human studies that infancy and early childhood were optimum periods for development and that the brain is most plastic during these periods and highly influenced by environmental stimulation. Animals (dogs) raised in isolation from birth were unable to avoid pain (Melzack & Scott, 1957), acquire normal social interactions (Melzack & Thompson, 1956), or perform well on problem-solving tasks (Thompson & Heron, 1954). Similarly, children raised in orphanages with minimal ongoing stimulation suffered emotional deprivation resulting in apathetic, immature behavior during adolescence (Goldfarb, 1953), and in cases of most severe deprivation, 2- to 4-year-olds could not sit alone or walk alone (Dennis, 1960).

In his classic work *Intelligence and Experience*, J. McVicker Hunt, as early as 1961, garnered extensive evidence to conclude that the concept of fixed intelligence was no longer tenable. He viewed intelligence as problem-solving capacity based on hierarchical organization of symbolic representations and information-processing strategies of the brain, derived to a considerable degree from past experiences. He believed that the child's intelligence quotient (IQ) may vary as much as 20 to 40 points as a result of environmental stimulation or lack thereof.

Although Piaget's work has been questioned regarding its authenticity and currency, the serious scholar must acknowledge his brilliant insights into cognition, play, early development, and, in a more remote sense, brain science. Analysis of Piaget's (1945/1951, 1936/1952) work on cognitive structures, which he called **schemata**, reveals a number of principles relevant to this context. First, the formation of schemata depends on opportunities for use of action sequences. Second, there is continuous development of schemata through use and stimulation. Third, accommodation by the child depends on a proper match between existing mental structure and objects and events encountered. Fourth, the greater the variety of situations to which the child must accommodate his behavioral structures, the more differentiated they become, and the more rapid his rate of intellectual development. Fifth, the rate of development appears to be the result of a variety of stimulation during infancy and early childhood.

Research of the 1960s and earlier established the early years as optimum times for intervention and supported a plastic view as opposed to a fixed view of the brain and cognitive development. The early observational studies were sufficiently compelling to influence the development of a range of federally sponsored early childhood intervention programs such as Operation Head Start and the High Scope Project.

The plasticity of the infant brain (**infant plasticity**) does not appear to be an advantage in all situations. In 1974, the President's Committee on Mental Retardation sponsored the National Conference on Early Intervention with High Risk Infants and Young Children at the University of North Carolina in Chapel Hill (Frost, 1975; Tjossem, 1976). Here, early plasticity theories were documented with physical evidence. A relatively small amount of damage to the infant brain was found to result in a reduction in volume of the entire hemisphere by more than 30%, while similar damage to the adult brain resulted in a reduction of only 20% to 30% (Isaacson, 1974).

Albert Einstein College of Medicine physicians presented evidence at the North Carolina conference that there can be too much stimulation—or too little. Lipton (1974) believes that no stimulation leads to no elaboration of neurological structure and processes, while pushing brain maturation (over-stimulation) leads to over-development and later deficits in behavior. In other words, either under-stimulation or over-stimulation seems to result in damage to the child. However, the range of normal stimulation conducive to healthy growth is broad. The implications of such findings are now being examined critically, using brain-imaging technology that provides visible, concrete, quantifiable evidence that is clearer and more convincing than earlier evidence.

High-Tech Brain Imaging

Sylwester (1995) and Thatcher, Lyon, Rumsey, and Krasnegor (1996) describe the new brain-imaging technology in detail. The technology focuses on three elements of brain organization and operation: (a) chemical composition, (b) electrical transmission and magnetic fields, and (c) distribution of blood through the brain.

Two types of imaging technology are used to study chemical composition: **computerized axial tomography** (CAT scan) and **magnetic resonance imaging** (MRI). These create graphic, three-dimensional images of the anatomy of the brain (or other body parts). The CAT scan uses multiple X-rays that respond to the density of areas scanned—dark gray for denser elements (e.g., bones, tumors, and dense tissue) and lighter shades of gray for soft tissue. The MRI provides an image of the chemical composition of the brain by focusing on chemical differences in soft tissue. Fast MRI allows researchers to observe brain activity on television during a subject's cognitive activity.

Positron emission tomography (PET) traces sequential changes in brain energy by monitoring chemical functions, including blood flow, through the brain and other body organs (Chugani, 1994; Sylwester, 1995). This noninvasive technique allows the tracing of brain energy as parts of the brain are activated.

Organization of the Brain

The function of the brain is based on activities of several billion brain cells, or **neurons**, and trillions of connections, or **synapses**, that transmit (receive and send) electrochemical signals (messages). Each single neuron has an **axon** that sends electrochemical signals to other neurons and contains many small, hair-like structures, or **dendrites**, that receive the signals. When the axon of one neuron connects with the dendrite of another neuron, a synapse is formed. Electrochemical transmission across these structures requires **neurotransmitters** (chemical catalysts) such as dopamine, serotonin, or endorphins. Neural development, then, is (includes) the proliferation or growth of these key brain elements. For elaboration, see Begley (1996), Healy (1997), Shore (1997), Thompson (1997), and Hirsh-Pasek, et al. (2003).

Before a baby is born, considerably more neurons and synapses are developed than the child will need, but most of the surplus neurons have disappeared by the time of birth. As neurons expand, the brain grows in volume and weight. Although the number of synapses increases at a remarkable rate during the first 3 years, the number of neurons remains stable (Shore, 1997). Normal early development is so rapid that the PET scan of a 1-year-old more closely resembles an adult's brain than a newborn's. By age 2, the number of synapses reaches adult levels. By age 3, the child's brain has about 1 quadrillion (1,000 trillion) synapses, or twice the number of an adult's brain, and is two and a half times more active (Shore, 1997). The density of synapses remains supersaturated through the first decade of life, followed by a decline in density. By late adolescence, about half of the brain's synapses have been discarded.

This discarding of synapses is a lifelong process of refining or **pruning** to eliminate those that are not used in favor of those that are used through everyday experiences. The early experiences of children play a critical role in determining the wiring of the brain and, it is hypothesized, the range and quality of the child's intellectual abilities. As the child grows, a complex system of synapses or neural pathways is formed. The pathways that are repeatedly activated or used are protected and retained into adulthood.

Effects of Deprivation on Brain Development

When a child is born, her brain is a mass of neurons, ready to be wired or programmed through use and experience. Some hard-wiring is already present to produce breathing and reflexes, regulate body temperature, and control heartbeat. Billions of other neurons are ready to be connected to other neurons, but they must be used in order for connections to be made and circuitry to be formed. Unused neurons do not survive; the potential synapses or connections are not formed, and the child may never reach her potential. Brain development is truly a "use it or lose it" process. (However, under therapeutic conditions, many at-risk children manage to thrive). Early experiences determine which neurons are to be used and which are to die and, consequently, whether the child will be brilliant or dull, confident or fearful, articulate or tongue-tied (Begley, 1996).

Much of the violence in the United States may be related to the lack of appropriate attachments of young children to adults. Inappropriate attachments associated with neglect and traumatic stress result in overdevelopment of the brainstem and midbrain, areas that are primitive, hardwired, and not very susceptible to external influence (Perry, 1996). The long-term research of Stroufe and his colleagues (Renken, Egeland, Marvinney, Mangelsdorf, & Stroufe 1989; Stroufe, in press) confirms the link between attachment and violence. Children with primary caregivers who are emotionally unavailable during the early years are often more aggressive in later childhood and adolescence. Even lingering depression of mothers has adverse effects on young children, particularly those 6 to 18 months old, when mothers fail to provide cognitive stimulation that promotes healthy brain growth (Ounce of Prevention Fund, 1996).

Genetics and experience work together to form the child's intelligence. The effects of sensory and motor experience on brain development begin before birth. The neurons that develop in utero begin driving the infant's limbs as early as 7 weeks of gestation (Shore, 1997). Brain development is adversely influenced by environmental influences on the mother—drugs, stress, malnutrition, illness, trauma, abuse—that are passed on to the fetus. Trauma and abuse in the fetus and during infancy continue to have a devastating effect on brain development throughout childhood. Neglect by parents, social deprivation, stressful living conditions, and lack of appropriate stimulation jeopardize early brain development and may result in immature social and emotional behavior, impulsivity, violence, and dramatic reduction in capacity for later learning. These negative influences are often associated with living in poverty (Ramey & Ramey, 1996) and living in institutions such as orphanages (Frank, Klass, Earls, & Eisenberg, 1996).

In the orphanages of Romania, about 100,000 children live under cruel and debilitating conditions (ABC News, 1996). According to ABC News, these conditions resulted from one dictator's plan to double the Romanian population. He outlawed birth control and demanded that women have children, resulting in thousands being placed in institutions. The children were reared under conditions of almost total neglect—some penned in cages; others confined to cribs with little or no stimulation from caretakers. Between 1960 and 1996, more than 3,000 were adopted by Americans.

Many (not all) of these adopted children, particularly those confined to orphanages over extended periods, failed to develop emotionally and intellectually. Some were so severely damaged that one mother described hers as the "child from hell." Some never learned to talk, read, accept love, or even feel pain. Some were violent. After several years of pain and frustration, a support group of American parents of these orphans organized and sought specialized assistance. Scientists at the Denver Children's

Hospital conducted PET scans and learned that the children's brains were remarkably different from those of normal children. Although measurable progress resulted from therapy, including **play therapy**, they never developed like normal children. For many, the therapy came too late. The window of opportunity is open during infancy, but appears to narrow for some children with each passing year and to close for some between ages 8 and 10.

An interview between the author and the adoptive parents of a Romanian orphan in 2003 revealed that their child (now school age) was developing at a relatively normal rate. They attributed this to their intensive interaction with the child from the beginning and the use of specialized help as needed. Their experience with other families of such children led them to believe that not all parents were able, sufficiently skilled, or inclined to provide such intensive interaction.

Neuroscience and Play: Connections

What are the linkages between brain development and play during the early childhood years? Let us begin with a few fundamental principles that have considerable support from both neuroscientists and play scholars.

First, *all healthy young mammals play*. Beginning shortly after birth, using built-in neural mechanisms, infant animals and humans engage in their first playful games. Animal infants tend to initiate the early games. Early frivolity is encouraged and mediated by adults, usually the parents or other primary caregivers. Since the human infant's period of helplessness and motor immaturity is relatively long, parents of human infants "must both initiate and give structure and direction to play. . . . That structure acts as a scaffolding for development" (Fagen in Angier 1992, p. B-8).

Second, *the range and complexity of play quickly increase as neurons start hardwiring connections at a remarkable rate*. Simply put, play programs neural structures, and the resulting, increasingly complex, neural structures influence ever more complex play. "[A]n animal plays most vigorously at precisely the time when its brain cells are frenetically forming synaptic connections, creating a dense array of neural links that can pass on electrochemical messages from one neighborhood of the brain to the next" (Angier, 1992, p. B-8).

Third, *the early games and frivolity of animals and humans equip them for the skills they will need in later life*. Angier (1992) and Brownlee (1997) describe these games. Games are "tailor made" to fit the very different tasks animals and humans will face. Animals practice those skills that assist survival in a dangerous world. Prey animals play escape games, such as mock flight and carnivores play stalking, pouncing, and capturing games. In so doing, they learn flexibility, inventiveness, and versatility (Brown, 1994). Human infants and young children practice motor, language, and negotiation skills. Across cultures, boys and girls play differently. Boys are more likely to engage in rough-and-tumble and organized games of physical contact and war using miniature war figures and toy weapons. Girls tend to engage in such games us chase, tag, jump rope, and hopscotch and rehearse motherhood and housekeeping roles with dolls and utensils. Both boys and girls engage in socially and culturally mediated task analysis, problem solving, negotiation, and discourse during their play (Frost, 1992; see Chapter 7).

Fourth, *play is essential for healthy development*. Early childhood experiences exert a dramatic, precise impact on the wiring of the neural circuits and the formation and selecting out (pruning) of synapses coincides with the emergence of various developmental abilities (Begley, 1997). During the first years of life, playful activity makes a positive difference in brain development and subsequent human functioning. Direct instruction, seclusion, deprivation, and abuse have negative consequences (Nash, 1997). Play deprivation resulting from deletion of recess in schools and increased time with computer games and television, is a growing factor leading to negative developmental consequences for American children (Frost & Jacobs, 1995; Frost,

2003). Reports from research at Baylor College of Medicine indicate that children who don't play much or are rarely touched develop brains 20% to 30% smaller than normal for their age (Frost, 2003, p. 51).

Neuroscience and Cognitive Development

Brain development and cognitive achievements of very young children are well disguised in the seemingly innocuous cloak of play (Sylwester, 1995). Essentially, only neuroscientists see physical evidence (brain scans) that reveal the relative consequences of environmental stimulation or neglect. The casual observer does not grasp the profound relationships between achievement and the endless games that the very young play—the patty-cake, peek-a-boo, and sing-song rhythms that are in reality storehouses or machines for programming the brain for language, art, music, math, science, kinesthetic, and interpersonal abilities and intelligence.

Many key brain areas are formed and dedicated before birth to general problem-solving areas. Although these systems are interrelated, a distinct brain area is dedicated to processing each function. Gardner (1993) proposes that seven distinct forms or systems of intelligence exist: linguistic, musical, logical-mathematical, spatial, bodily-kinesthetic, intrapersonal, and interpersonal. An individual can perform exceptionally in one system and poorly in another, depending on complex interactions between genetics and experience. The implications of **multiple intelligences** are profound. Should we focus on optimizing strengths or remediating weaknesses? Should we value social, cooperative behavior or solitary, competitive behavior? What are the proper roles of parents, teachers, and social institutions in optimizing intelligence?

Neuroscience and Language Development

Language learning begins long before babies are able to speak first words. As early as 6 months, infants develop "**language magnets**" that attune their ears to the sounds of their native language (Kuhl in Education Commission of the States, 1996); they have learned the basic phonetic elements of their native language (Blakeslee, 1997). As early as 11 months, infants are losing the ability to distinguish between phonetic sounds not spoken in their presence (Long, 1997).

A growing body of evidence indicates that languages should be taught in preschool or in families before entry in to school. Vocabulary development is strongly correlated with parents talking with their babies. Through reciprocal talk (parents talking, babies listening and making primitive reactions), parents strengthen the neural pathways essential to language development.

Some researchers at the 1997 White House Conference on Early Child Development concluded that "the number of words an infant hears each day is the single most important predictor of later intelligence, school success and social competence" (Blakeslee, 1997, p. A-14). However, recent brain research supports earlier studies concluding that there can be too much stimulation and too little stimulation. Merely filling the child with information or scheduling too many activities may lead to overstimulation. Live language in a warm, emotional context with a caring adult, not endless, mindless television, video games, or drilling for high-stakes testing boosts language development (Frost, 2003). Information received in an emotional context is more powerful in stimulating neural development than information alone. Even the tone of voice makes a difference.

Neuroscience and Social Development

Before the availability of high-tech, brain-imaging research, the importance of young children's socialization with adults and older children was highlighted by the work of Vygotsky (1933/1976), who proposed that play, and consequently the higher mental functions, evolve from interactions between the child and her caregiver and socialization with older children. Interaction or socialization with others is essential for healthy development. "[T]he single best childhood predictor of adult adaptation is not IQ, not school grades, and not classroom behavior but, rather the adequacy with which the child gets along with other children" (Hartup, 1992).

Children and animals learn social skills through socialization. Animals learn to interpret signals and actions of other animals and to respond appropriately (Brownlee, 1997). Through negotiation during play, they develop mental and emotional mastery and learn cooperation and leadership skills. Children's imaginative or make-believe play is a powerful medium for socialization, allowing them to simplify a complicated world and make otherwise complex and frightening events manageable and comprehensible. Such play also assists the development of cooperation, sharing, negotiating, and problem-solving skills and helps the child get along in an increasingly complex world.

Neuroscience and Emotional Development

New brain-imaging technologies "have made visible for the first time in human history what has always been a source of deep mystery: exactly how this intricate mass of cells (brain) operates while we think and feel, imagine and dream. . . . This flood of neurobiological data lets us understand . . . the brain's centers for emotion" (Goleman, 1994, p. xi).

The basic wiring that controls emotions develops before birth. After birth, parents play a significant role by playing back the child's emotions—his squeals of delight—with hugs and supporting words. Such experiences reinforce the brain's chemical and electrical signals and "wire the brain's calm down circuit" (Begley, 1996, 58). Stress also has its effects. Extreme or continuous trauma floods the brain's circuits with neurochemicals such as cortisol, and the more frequently they are stimulated, the easier it is for the circuits to react. Indeed, repeated stress changes the structure of the brain (Begley, 1997). Merely thinking about traumatic experiences or seeing signs related to an incident (e.g., abuse by a parent, a natural disaster) can trigger the flood of neurochemicals and condition the brain to a pattern of high alert.

Texas children who experienced a devastating tornado that killed many relatives and friends and destroyed dozens of homes in 1997 still slept in their clothes, without blankets, one year later so they could be ready to seek cover. Their drawings and paintings still reflected those harrowing experiences, and the mere memory or reminder (clouds and wind) of a storm induced fear. Calm, soothing touch and language by an adult calms these emotions and appears to allow emotion and reason to connect.

Play is the language of children. While adults talk out their fears and traumatic experiences, children play theirs out. They may lack the words or the cognitive abilities to understand what has happened to them or to resolve their conflicts, but play has therapeutic qualities that allows children to play out their conflicts and to deal with them. "Play gives concrete form and expression to children's inner world. . . . A major function of play is the changing of what may be unmanageable in reality to manageable situations through symbolic representation" (Landreth, 1991, pp. 9–10).

Neuroscience and Physical Development

At birth, infants are awkward and have little control over their limbs. They cannot sit, stand, crawl, or walk and rely on primitive reflexes such as sucking and grasping. These reflexes are rapidly replaced by increasingly complex neural pathways as various regions of the brain develop to accommodate different abilities. Intense sensory and physical stimulation is critical to the growth of synapses in the **cerebellum**, a region that regulates coordination and muscle control (Angier, 1992). The development of **fine-** and **gross-motor skills** develop independently, but both require the formation and **myelination** (nerve cell coating that insulates against loss of electrical signals) of synapses. The neural circuits that connect the motor cortex of the brain and the muscles are strengthened by repeated motor activities.

If the child's **motor neurons** are not trained early for a particular athletic skill, there is little chance that the child will be outstanding in that skill. "No world champion skater or golfer took up the sport after 12" (Underwood & Plagens, 1997, p. 15). Tiger Woods, for example, started playing with a golf club at 10 months. Adult neurons do not appear to be plastic enough to allow the required wiring. However, related factors are influential in achieving high levels of motor ability, such as toughness, concentration, motivation, and ambition. Practicing related skills also appears to carry over to developing new skills. The great football player Walter Payton was in ballet classes as a child; skills learned there encompassing strength, flexibility, and grace may have helped him become a record-holding running back. "Sometimes it is not the obvious experiences that sculpt performance" (Underwood & Plagens, 1997, p. 15). The bottom line is that adults must provide experiences that program the neural structures for the skills to be achieved, and they must do so in a caring, supportive context.

NEUROSCIENCE AND EDUCATIONAL PRACTICE: BRIDGING THE GAP

Whenever scientific breakthroughs occur, critics, quite appropriately, question their validity and warn against overgeneralization and speculation. Bruer (1997), for example, proposes, "Neuroscience has discovered a great deal about neurons and synapses, but not nearly enough to guide educational practice" (p. 15). Scientists at the Bridging the Gap between Neuroscience and Education workshop, sponsored by the Education Commission of the States (1996), urged the educators in attendance "not to attempt to apply new research findings until further studies confirm and expand them" (p. vi). Such cautions should, of course, be carefully considered. It is far too early to reshape American education around brain science. "The danger with much of the brain-based education literature is that it becomes exceedingly difficult to separate the science from the speculation" (Bruer, 1999, p. 650).

Although researchers themselves are often reluctant to draw implications for the appropriate roles of adults in stimulating healthy development, the collective historical evidence about effects of experience on brain development and behavior is sufficiently compelling to warrant the formulation of tentative implications for child development. Open-mindedness and attention to future research are essential. Just as medicine is now beginning to reap practical benefits from neuroscience, professionals should also study brain research for practical applications in child development and education. For current examples see <http://serendip.brynmawr.edu/sci_edu/education/brain.html>.

The Committee on Developments in the Science of Learning, sponsored by the National Research Council and the U.S. Department of Education and composed of prominent scientists, conducted a 2-year evaluation (Bransford, Brown, & Cocking, 1999) of new developments in the science of learning and made the following conclusions:

1. The organization of the brain depends on experience.
2. Instruction and learning are very important in brain development.
3. Different parts of the brain are ready for learning at different times.
4. Development is a biologically driven unfolding process and also an active process of deriving information from experience.
5. Some experiences have the most effect on development during the sensitive periods, but others affect the brain over an extended period.
6. The issue of which research findings have implications for education is still very much open. For example, which experiences and

learnings are tied to critical periods and for which is timing less critical?

This landmark document was followed by a second (Donovan, Bransford, & Pellegrino, 1999) that synthesized research on how people learn to draw implications for classroom practice. In this document, Wolfe and Brandt (2000) hold that "educators should help direct the search to better understand how the brain learns" (p. 28). Bergen and Coscia (2001) reviewed an extensive array of research on brain and childhood education to conclude that many current educational practices likely have some effect on brain structures and functions, but none of these practices are validated by current brain research. The reader should be cautious about adopting curricula ostensibly based on brain research. The present chapter does not attend to the classroom practice issue but rather to the implications of neuroscience for early development.

Neuroscientists are only beginning to learn which experiences wire the brain in which ways, so drawing conclusions from brain research for education and child development is not exact. However, some general conclusions emerging from laboratories across the nation are gaining support. The resulting patterns of intervention are remarkably consistent with what "good" parents have always known and done. The following conclusions address parents but may be considered by all adults responsible for the care of children.

BRAIN RESEARCH AND CHILD DEVELOPMENT

What follows is a summary list of some of the conclusions we feel are reasonable to make between brain research and child development:

- Start early. The proper starting time for stimulating healthy brain development is conception, involving two healthy adults. If you wait until your child is in preschool or Head Start to begin, you have already missed the most formative period for some aspects of brain development.
- Spend lots of time playing with children. They need secure attachment or bonding with their parents. Disavow the misguided contention that a little "quality time" compensates for extended parental absence. Healthy brain development does not take vacations or keep a calendar. There is no downtime. Both dads and moms are needed.
- Be positive, playful, warm, and nurturing. Activity is essential, but there is good activity and bad activity. Good activity supports healthy brain development. Bad activity programs unhealthy brain development, resulting in ability deficits and behavioral aberrations.
- Pay attention to children's moral development. Even simple games carry moral overtones such as taking turns, sharing objects, and listening to others. Meeting children's physical and emotional needs does not mean catering to their every whim. Parents, caretakers, and teachers should have clear moral expectations from the beginning, and these should be modeled and enforced. Ensure that toddlers have opportunities to play with other toddlers. This is important for developing social skills—friendships, sharing, negotiating, problem solving, concern for others—and morals. Some moral bases may be hardwired at birth, but patterns of brain chemistry, emerging in early childhood, appear to influence later moral behavior.

  Scientists who study **neurotheology** are now seeing connections between spirituality and brain structures and activity. "Spiritual experiences are so consistent across cultures, across time and across faiths that it suggests a common core that is likely a reflection of structures and processes in the human brain (Begley, 2001, p. 53).
- Challenge children, but not beyond their range of abilities. Adults' expectations should be difficult but do-able. Infants and toddlers are far more capable than commonly realized, and adults, especially parents, are far more important in their

development than generally acknowledged, even by leading professional groups.

- Hug children. Touching has health and therapeutic results. Touch, caress, pat, and cuddle infants. Gently rock them back and forth. People never outgrow their need for physical contact, including hugs. As children develop, engage in gentle wrestling, tugging, tossing, and chasing games. Such activities are essential in programming motor abilities and emotional behavior and in reinforcing related thinking abilities. Adults should be cautious not to shake infants' or toddlers' heads vigorously, for shaken-baby syndrome may include brain damage, developmental delays, or other injury.
- Talk to children. Respond to infants' cooing and babbling. Use "parentese" (baby talk) with babies. Expand your vocabulary as children develop. Listen to children. Early language must be personal—between child and adult—and related to ongoing activity to best stimulate neural development. For positive results, language needs to be used in a positive emotional context.
- Introduce music, art, and dance early. Play soft, soothing music. Introduce children to sing-song games during infancy. Introduce musical instruments. Make simple art materials and simple tools available. Cultivate art through simple manipulative activities, and expand to art appreciation activities.
- Substitute play, art, music, family outings, and field trips for television. Control television viewing. Select programs wisely. Do not use television as a baby sitter, as a substitute for family interaction at home, or as a "time filler" at the child care center or school. Play, art, and music may produce long-term changes in neural structures that influence thinking and reasoning abilities.
- Make homes, child care centers, and schools drug-free. Model drug-free behavior for children. Drugs, including tobacco, alcohol, and misuse of prescription drugs, can have a devastating effect on children's development, in utero and later.
- Provide blocks, beads, sand, water, simple tools, pots and pans, dress-up clothes, and other simple and raw materials at age-appropriate times. No child care setting need be devoid of stimulating materials, for the very young child does not discriminate between simple, inexpensive, natural materials and toys and manufactured, expensive ones. Free, cheap, and natural are good enough, assuming the toys are safe.
- Protect young children from stress and trauma, including extreme scolding, loud persistent noise, isolation, and physical and emotional abuse. The brain is acutely vulnerable to stress and trauma, and the consequences of extended exposure on brain development may be permanent.
- Don't overstimulate children with too many toys, too much meaningless talk, too much noise, or too much activity. Provide plenty of time and interesting, safe places and materials to explore. Special toys or high-tech materials are unlikely to be more effective than talking with the child and making simple toys available. Very young children don't need flash card drills, incessant babbling by a parent, or constant noise to get adequate stimulation for development. Indeed, overstimulation and trauma appear to have negative effects on brain development (Lipton, 1974; Shore, 1997).
- Read to children, sing with children, and play simple games with children. Do this every day.
- Extend your interest in healthy development to wherever children are present. Ensure that your children have good nutrition at home, child care centers, and schools. Be wary of high-stakes testing leading to overemphasis of test skills over developmental based curricula. Don't accept the growing pattern of deleting recess, physical education, art, and music (the frills) from the

school day. Consider another school for your child if such conditions exist.

- If a child has a birth defect or developmental disorder or has suffered a disabling injury, don't give up. The human brain has an amazing capacity to compensate and, to some degree, regenerate, given proper care and therapy. This has been demonstrated in studies of Romanian orphans adopted by American parents.
- Children are primed by biology to acquire certain basic skills of language and thinking that are intricately wired in early childhood. This wiring is the basis for later, complex, technical problem solving (e.g., mathematics, computer sciences) that will depend on strong cultural and social support for realization. The earliest years (0–3) may be a critical period for ensuring later success in a technological society.

At the time of this writing, new research is modifying and extending knowledge in neuroscience. Begley (2000) reports that contrary to the notion that the brain is fully developed before puberty, maturation continues into the teens and 20s. For example, the frontal lobes of the brain, responsible for numerous functions such as planning, judgment, and emotional regulation, grow rapidly around puberty, followed by pruning into the 20s. In other words, just as there is a period of rapid neural development during infancy, followed by pruning, such phenomena also exist during the preteen and teen years.

Different regions of the brain develop on different timetables. The neural network isn't completely installed in most people until they are in their early 20s. Among the last parts to mature are those that make sound judgments and calm unruly emotions (Brownlee, 1999, p. 46). Crenson (2001, p. A20) explains: The immature brain development of adolescents appears to help explain why they are vulnerable to risk taking, traumatic experiences, and unhealthy influences. The prefrontal cortex, not yet fully developed, is responsible for goal and priority setting, planning, organizing, and impulse inhibition. Possible consequences of immature brain development include a number of profound statistics: Accidents are the leading cause of death among adolescents. They are the group most likely to become crime victims. The large majority of smokers start as teens and a quarter of all people with HIV contract it during their teen years.

EFFECTS OF PLAY DEPRIVATION ON CHILD DEVELOPMENT

Anecdotal evidence about the effects of **play deprivation** on child development (Brown, 1994; Frost, 1999; Frost & Jacobs, 1997) continues to mount and is supported by the findings of recent brain research. Stuart Brown, a physician, psychiatrist, and play researcher, has presented some of the most compelling studies (Brown, 1994) to date about the effects of play and play deprivation. Having long studied the development of abused children who became violent adults, he was charged by Governor John Connally of Texas to investigate the behavioral characteristics of Charles Whitman, who in 1966 barricaded himself on top of the University of Texas's 27-story tower and shot 44 people.

Brown found that Whitman had a history of violence and brutality at the hands of his father and did not engage in normal play as a child. He secluded himself on the playground and was allowed no time to play at home. Following this investigation, Brown helped conduct a study of 26 convicted Texas murderers. He found that 90% showed either the absence of childhood play or abnormal play such as bullying, sadism, cruelty to animals, or extreme teasing. In yet another study of mostly drunk drivers who killed themselves or others while driving, Brown found that 75% had play abnormalities.

The growing view that spontaneous play has declined or is disappearing is frequently debated among proponents of play. Some writers contend that modern activities such as sports at an early age and television viewing are displacing **spontaneous play** (Devereux, 1976; Eifermann, 1971; Postman, 1982). Indeed, Pee Wee, Bantam, and Little League sports (baseball, football, soccer) are increasingly involving children as young as 5 to 8 years old, and in some instances even younger. The evidence of extensive television viewing is reasonably clear. Children spend more time watching television than they spend in classrooms (Medrich, Roizen, Rubin, & Buckley, 1982). Presently, the growing popularity of video games and Internet activities, ranging from violent games, to chat rooms, to adult-style **gambling**, has directed more of children's time away from spontaneous, traditional play. Yet another factor implicated in the apparent decline of play is the loss of places to play. Once-rural landscapes and wilderness areas are now covered with buildings and populated with vehicles, ever smaller backyards are devoted to adult interests (pools, tennis courts, barbecue areas), and high-rise apartments offer few play places.

Children are not merely losing opportunities for spontaneous play but are being deprived of the richest forms of play, that is play that transcends, that is very intense, characterized by risk, obsession, complete absorption, ecstasy, and heightened mental states—**transcendental play** (Frost, 2003, 2004).

"My earliest recollection of transcendental play dates to the primary school with a small stream running out of the nearby woods and across the schoolyard, gaining vigor and intrigue following the rain. Pulling off shoes and rolling up pants, we waded in and built dams of mud to capture large expanses of water. A rival group, catching the excitement, built a dam upstream and eventually let the water loose in torrents to wash out our downstream dam. This led to frantic activity and collaborative schemes to ultimately build a dam from rocks and limbs that could not be washed out by our competition. We even selected a resourceful third grader to direct the operation! Through trial and error we discovered the value of dense, heavy materials to withstand pressure and of spillways to divert water from our masterpiece of construction" (Frost, 2004).

Drawing from the work of Australian writers, Evans (1992) raised the relevant issue as to whether today's children play less or merely play differently from their predecessors. Factor (1988) argues that adult-inspired activities (e.g., sports) have not obliterated children's traditional play; Palmer (1986) believes that children use television in many creative ways; and Roberts (1980) concludes that the play of children, though ongoing, is not always seen by adults. Also offered are the arguments that children will struggle to play, even under terrible conditions (Factor, 1993). It appears that the nature and extent of children's play may indeed differ from country to country, and such factors must be taken into account when assessing the issue of play deprivation.

Children do struggle to play, even in war-torn areas. Hughes (1998), a play worker in the United Kingdom and director of a project to explore relationships between sectarianism and play in strife-torn Northern Ireland, found that not only does the sectarian conflict have shattering effects on the population as a whole, but is especially traumatic for children. The carnage and disruption have reduced ranging behavior and the natural diversity of play, creating fear, withdrawal, and manipulation and repression of the outcomes of play. Yes, children struggle to play, even under adverse conditions. However, such play may be radically different from normal play, and the results may be either negative or therapeutic.

There is **rational play** and **irrational play** (Sutton-Smith, 1985), normal and abnormal play (Gitlin-Weiner,1998), or, from the perspectives of healthy child development, good play and bad play (enabling or **constructive play** and disabling or **destructive play**) (Frost, 1987). In adolescence, **rough-and-tumble play** "is used primarily by bullies victimizing their weaker peers. . . . This form of play is not all good for all children" (Pellegrini, 1998, 406). Therapists commonly encounter children whose play is characterized by inflexibility, concreteness, constrictedness, impulsivity, irrationality, unreliability, inability to sustain play, and inability to distance oneself from previously experienced negative or painful emotions (Gitlin-Weiner, 1998, p. 77). The power of imagination has both destructive and creative impulses (Tuan, 1998). One impulse opens up experiences, broadens possibilities, extends thought and action, generates ideas and diversity, and promotes positive social behavior. The other (addictive, bullying, violence, sadism, animalistic, deviant) narrows possibilities, limits thought and action, and leads to antisocial behavior, channels, and patterns. In sum, good (enabling or constructive) play is creative and promotes positive social behavior; bad (disabling or destructive) play is narrow, unimaginative, uninspired, and cruel (Frost, 1987, p. 166). Play encompasses a broad band of behaviors from the dark, messy, and barbaric (Sutton-Smith, 1981) or irrational play to the rational dimensions of play seen in child care centers (Sutton-Smith, 1985). From a scholarly perspective, one must study the full range of playful activities—rational/irrational, normal/abnormal, good/bad, constructive/destructive, enabling/disabling—to gain an expansive view of the nature and consequences of play.

Hughes's (1998) employs such distinctions in his analysis of children's play in strife-torn Ireland. Children in extreme conflict situations, e.g., racial or sectarian conflicts cannot avoid the absorption of that conflict into their play behavior. . . . They imitate the actual physical conflicts, adopt the visual identity of their side, sing the songs, tell the jokes, express the insults and demonize the target of their hatred in much the same way as their extreme adult counterparts (p. 74).

Play prompted by natural disasters such as floods and tornadoes, terrorism, and war, as well as planned play therapy for domestic abuse, appears to be therapeutic and allows children to play out destructive experiences in order to understand and deal with them. Adults should use caution in distinguishing the motives for children's play but must draw the line against allowing children to victimize others or to engage in extreme mental or physical abuse in their play.

Although American children are not directly involved in the kind of extremely violent sectarian conflict seen in Ireland, their constant exposure to violence on television appears to have detrimental effects on their play behavior and, consequently, their ability to relate to others in constructive ways. The National Coalition on Television Violence (1985) concluded from 850 studies in 20 nations, including the United States, that viewing television violence increases violence and aggression in children. The American Psychiatric Association, the National Parent-Teacher Association, the U.S. Surgeon General, and the National Institute of Mental Health have reached similar conclusions. Teens themselves say that television is a bad influence (Elias, 1995).

ALTERNATIVES TO TRADITIONAL SPONTANEOUS PLAY

The natural forms of children's spontaneous play emerge with time and experience. Across cultures and geographic areas, healthy children engage in similar forms of play. A conference of leading theorists ended their deliberations with the conclusion that "studying nuclear physics is child's play compared to studying child's play" (Sutton-Smith, 1979, p. 294). Each discipline represented at the conference held differing views of the nature and purposes of play, approaching the phenomenon from cultural, sociological, psychological, anthropological, linguistic, and developmental perspectives. However, conference participants generally agreed that there are different forms of play across the age spans, childhood to adulthood, ranging from the relatively simplistic peek-a-boo play of infants and mothers; across the symbolic, pretend play of early childhood; the organized games of later childhood, the culture of sports; the technology games; the "irrational" (Sutton-Smith, 1985) adult games of gambling, war, and sex; and even "irreverent games" (Sutton-Smith, 1997) of gossip. Almost any human activity can have playful qualities, even those typically classified as entertainment, diversion, work, recreation, or leisure.

Features of traditional, spontaneous play may be present in a wide range of activities that only marginally resemble play. As children develop and gain experience, the orientation of their play changes. For example, sports are sufficiently different from symbolic and constructive play to warrant special and distinct explanations, especially for the organized sports of juveniles and adults. We should also explore the relationships between play and **leisure**, play and **entertainment**, play and **recreation**, and play and **work**, for it appears that a factor now depriving children of traditional, spontaneous play is adult misunderstanding about the commonalities and distinctions between these related activities.

Play and Organized Sports

There is a **sport culture** that emphasizes extrinsic rewards, competition, elitism, and skills specialization (Beal, 1998; Lincoln, 1989; Szala-Meneok, 1994). In addition, formal rules, coaches or referees, and organized contests, all imposed from outside the activity, are usually present. Play may be described as an "inversion of sport." **Symbolic inversion** has been used to analyze different forms of play and is defined as "any act of expressive behavior which inverts, contradicts, abrogates, or in some fashion presents an alternative to commonly held cultural codes, values, and norms" (Beal, 1998, p. 209; see also Babcock, 1978). Spontaneous child play has many similarities to sports but is commonly different in several key components—namely, intrinsic motivation, lack of imposed rules and authority figures, the option of starting and stopping when desired, and noncompetitiveness.

Beal (1998) uses playful (not competitive) skateboarding as an example of symbolic inversion of sport. Skateboarding, of course, is subject to the rigid rules of competitive sports, but the usual skateboarding activity has no rules, coach, or referee. The players create their own tricks and games; determine how long they will play; contribute their own language, style, and dress; and do not anticipate any extrinsic rewards. In such a play environment, usually in streets, on sidewalks, along concrete canals, or other "found" places, the players are free to control their own activity, create their own styles and games, and they tend to help and encourage one another. The emphasis is on cooperation and the activity or process itself rather than the outcome. This noncompetitive environment means that there are no losers.

A central variable in distinguishing spontaneous play and sports is the creative element. For example, the **make-believe play** of early childhood, compared to organized sports, is freer, more open-ended, more subject to ongoing modification, more dynamic, less bound by rules—in sum, more creative. Traditional games such as chase and tag are valuable activities for children's cognitive, social, and motor development. Games can stimulate positive socialization and creativity when children are allowed to plan, create, and manage their own games. The consequences of adult pressure from outside the game on children's organized games, including sports, are well known.

Play and Leisure

Perhaps the most prevalent notion of leisure is free time—free from work, free from imposed constraints and responsibilities, free to do what one pleases. But leisure is more than free time. "It is the experience associated with intrinsically enjoyable activities initiated by the individual" (Kleiber & Barnett, 1980, p. 47). To the extent that the experience is governed or directed by others, it is no longer leisure. Freedom of choice and lack of outside restraints sustain leisure (Kelly, 1976). Leisure is a context in which play, entertainment, and "messing around" can take place.

Two decades ago, sociologists were predicting an era of leisure, but the reality is that a growing number of overscheduled, two-income households are experiencing what some call "the death of leisure." A 1998 study of the diaries of families of 3,600 children by the University of Michigan's Institute for Social Research (Vobejda, 1998) found that free, unstructured time left after school, eating, and sleeping has decreased from 40% of a child's time in 1981 to 25% in 1997. With the demise of leisure comes the demise of free, unfettered, spontaneous play.

There is something innate about the spontaneous play of the child—the motivation, tension and joy, the unfettered, creative expression. All healthy children in all cultures play from infancy, though their playthings differ. Contrast such play with that of a typical, lone, adult fisherman, casting resolutely for fish. His playthings are expensive and specialized: a high-powered motorboat, comfortable swivel chair, two ice chests (one for drinks, one for food), proper clothing (cap with colorful flies embedded, picture of big bass on front of shirt, white deck shoes), and high-tech sonar for locating fishing places. What a difference in the motivation, structure, thought, and content of this highly planned and organized yet freely chosen activity and the play of a 5-year-old in a simple mud-hole. The adult fisherman has, at least to some degree, become a creature of expectation. His toys dictate what he can do. Experience and skill restrict his behavior to whatever produces results. Opportunities for creativity and growth have narrowed, for he has learned how to do it. He is indeed doing what he wants to do, taking whatever time he desires, and gaining freedom from work. The child playing in mud has no expectations for results. Her playthings are natural and malleable. The focus of her play has no limits. Leisure—time that is free of responsibilities—makes both activities possible. Which activity has greater potential for growth?

Play and Entertainment

To be entertained is to be amused, pleased, and diverted from other activities. For the most part, entertainment is more sedentary than play and may require less involvement. Someone else can make the efforts to entertain you, but this is not true of pure, unfettered play. In spontaneous play, the child is involved, making decisions and generating opportunities. The very popular **theme parks, video arcades, vacation retreats**, and many other **pay-for-play** places across America do indeed amuse or entertain, but most are inferior to the best playgrounds, botanical gardens, **children's museums**, and a growing number of creative pay-for-play places in promoting imagination, exploration, invention, creativity, and constructive socialization among children. Even Froebel understood that people who think that children are only seeking amusement when they play are committing a grave error, for he proposed that play is the first means of development of the human mind (Baker, 1937, p. 5). Many modern children grow so accustomed to being "entertained" that they become social misfits, incapable of intelligent, warm human interaction and creative industry.

We wish to stress that there are creative designers in the entertainment industry that put the needs of children first. Some design/production firms speak about the evolution of next-generation "edutainment centers" that feature no rides, and no technological gimmicks or virtual reality. Rather, they are based on actual reality and are high-touch, offering children a place with the tools to create their own magical worlds and develop their minds, souls, and bodies—A place where kids can just be kids.

Play and Work

Csikszentmihalyi (1975, 1990) explains play (see Chapter 13) as the experience of **flow** in a voluntary, autotelic context in which there is no concern for outcomes or real-life applications. In his studies of adults at play and work, Csikszentmihalyi followed Huizinga (1938/1950) and Callois (1961) in proposing that a **spirit of play** prevails during play. However, he extended this proposal and agreed with John Dewey (1916/1966) and other contemporaries in concluding that the dichotomy between play and work is largely artificial and that flow and **peak experiences** characteristic of play can and may be present in work. In many work roles, flow is defeated by boredom and drudgery.

The significance of Csikszentmihalyi's work is the elimination of a hard and fast distinction between play and work and the potential of extending the spiritual, joyful, flow qualities of play, so prevalent in childhood, to the work and games of adults. Of special significance is the potential to re-create sterile, structured, hazardous play and work environments, as in many playgrounds, **gambling casinos**, factories, and offices, to incorporate the spiritual, joyful, growth-inducing, creative flow qualities of play.

A growing number of corporations are scheduling recess and building playgrounds for their adult employees (Joyce, 1998). Workers bent on making profits for the company engage in hula hoop contests, hopscotch, foosball, darts, table tennis, boating, and four-square. They walk and bike through parklike settings or simply relax and hang out. Workplace researchers say that this transformation from "hierarchical stuffiness to worker environments" help stimulate creativity, teamwork, and employee loyalty and job satisfaction (Joyce, 1998).

Obviously, we have not made hard and fast distinctions between play and related behaviors. Perhaps it is less important that we have a precise definition than the fact that most people, including children, know when work and play are happening. Our interactions with third grade students demonstrated that children know the difference between play and work. They concluded that play is fun—you have a choice, it is not planned, and one is free to do what one wants, free to imagine and create, to construct something—that play can lead to a product or a job, and that sometimes work can be play. Research supports these conclusions (Garza, Briley, & Reifel, 1985).

In a study of kindergarten and first- and second-grade children, Wing (1995) found that children have fairly consistent criteria in distinguishing work and play. The single most distinguishing element was whether the activity was obligatory. One must work. One can play. Other factors included whether the activity was designed and directed by teachers or supervisors, whether there was a specific product, whether someone evaluated the activity, whether the activity required "finishing" or one could merely "quit," whether it was necessary to extend effort and be neat, and whether the activity was easy or hard. The children characterized some activities as "in between"—that is, part play and part work. Overall, children seem to be quite clear about what is play and what is work. The old adage "Play is the work of the child" is clearly misleading. Some contemporary early childhood program developers understand the relationships between play and work and have developed programs that merge play/work activities. Among the best are the High Scope Curriculum (Hohmann & Weikart, 1995) and the program at Reggio Emilia, Italy (Katz, 1994).

IMPEDIMENTS TO SPONTANEOUS PLAY

American children, and, increasingly, the children of other industrialized nations, are losing the freedom to play when and where they choose. Their lives are controlled by the relentless schedules of parents and their own daylight-to-dark schedules, and creative play is displaced by television and pay-for-play entertainment. The current revolution in playground development is resulting in more and better playgrounds (though they are still mainly uninspiring), but these are not compensating for deprivation of spontaneous play, resulting from urbanization, inaccessibility to natural play places, growing violence, addiction to television (and bad television generally), and fractured families (Frost & Jacobs, 1995). American children are increasingly deprived of free recess play because of the national emphasis on **high-stakes testing** and the widespread belief that play is irrelevant or unimportant in the educative process (Frost, 2003).

High-stakes testing is now implemented throughout America's public schools and is affecting children beginning in Head Start (Brandon, 2002; *USA Today*, 2003) despite the fact that a growing number of research studies and professional organizations conclude that such emphasis on testing is harmful, illogical, damages morale, and fails to result in better educated students (Frost, 2003; Amrein & Berliner, 2002; Popham, 2002; National Association for the Education of Young Children, 1988; Association for Childhood Education International, 1991).

Play is made possible and takes place within defined contexts, both physical (as in playgrounds) and symbolic (as in make-believe play)—in the physical or concrete settings and the symbolic playgrounds of the mind. Contemporary research and the brilliant views of Vygotsky and Piaget show that it isn't enough merely to let children play. They need to learn to use tools and create with materials. Given the disappearance of natural play places in urban settings, they need creative playgrounds that feature the lost opportunities. Some of the best urban play environments are "compact countrysides."

The growing availability of pay-for-play places in shopping malls, theme parks, casinos, and vacation destinations gives the false illusion that concern for children's play is alive and well in America. In fact, most of these places substitute high-tech entertainment, pseudo- or actual gambling, junk food, sexual and violent video games, and sedentary activity for spontaneous, vigorous, creative activity and further deprive children of close, intensive, personal interaction with parents, nature, simple tools, and opportunities for positive, imaginative play.

The substitution of entertainment for creative play and quality interaction with adults in homes and communities is deeply implicated in the growing problems of our society. American children rank last among children of industrialized countries on tests of physical fitness. They are the most violent, use more drugs, engage in sex at earlier ages, and, thanks to overdoses of sedentary television viewing and junk food, are growing more obese and developing early symptoms of risk for later cardiovascular disease (Center for the Future of Children, 1996; Children's Defense Fund, 1996; Deitz & Gortmaker, 1985; Dennison et al., 1988; Elias, 1995; Frost, 1986; Ross & Gilbert, 1985; Winston, 1984, Sutterby & Frost, 2002; Frost, 2003). As outlined earlier, recent brain research is further demonstrating the positive effects of spontaneous play and the negative effects of play deprivation.

Common but misguided conceptions in America are that good parenting is "Disney Dads" showing up occasionally to spend a little "**quality time**" with their kids, and that infants and toddlers can be reared just as well by strangers as by parents. Harris (1998) contends that parents do not affect their children's behavior, self-worth, personality, intelligence, mental health, or relationships. Leading child development and psychology researchers label her thesis absurd, extreme, wrong, embarrassing, and a disservice to the profession of psychology (Begley, 1998). Fortunately, there are signs that attitudes of parents may be changing to reflect the growing awareness of the importance of parents in child rearing and, consequently, the need to spend time with their children. The May 12, 1997, article in *Newsweek*, "The Myth of Quality Time"; its special spring/summer 1997 issue on children; and the May 12, 1997, article in *U.S. News and World Report*, "The Lies Parents Tell about Work, Kids, Money, Day Care, and Ambition," illustrate the growing willingness of popular media to discuss the state of parenting in America and highlight the growing body of evidence that parents should spend a lot of constructive time with their kids.

The myth of quality time is especially pernicious, for a little scheduled "quality" time has never adequately substituted for genuine, continuous quality time. We cannot merely pencil in time for kids on calendars and expect them to thrive. Kids don't do meetings (Shapiro, 1997), they require lots of time and attention, and their need for close, extensive interaction with parents never goes away. As they enter the teen years, their needs become even more intense. They face a growing array of pressures—sex, drugs, peer influences at a time when their brain development has not caught up with their need to make decisions—and the need for monitoring and guidance grows.

PAY-FOR-PLAY AND TECHNOLOGY

Healthy children will play anywhere they find themselves, but the growing array of impediments and alternatives to creative play is channeling children away from play and toward entertainment, sports, and other leisure activities. Chapter 10 describes how traditional, creative, spontaneous play places can be made available for children. This section focuses on technology and pay-for-play places that are growing in popularity.

Governments throughout the world now view technology as a means for improving their country's educational processes and bolstering their political and economic stature (Swaminathan & Yelland, 2003). Yet, the impact of computers, video games, the Internet, and virtual reality on children's brain development has yet to be thoroughly explored. A growing body of neurobiological research concludes that computers, television and other technological media are changing the way children's brains develop (Healy, 1998; Walsh, 2003; Hirsh-Pasek, et al., 2003). Over time, electronic images are internalized, permanently changing the way children think and behave.

In April 2003, U. S. Senator Sam Brownback chaired a hearing on "Neurobiological Research and the Impact of Media," in the Senate Subcommittee on Science, Technology, and Space (Brownback, 2003). The prominent researchers in attendance presented studies supporting earlier research on the probable negative effects of violent and sexual content on children's development. Research conducted at the University of Michigan concluded that exposure to violence during childhood directly predicts young adult aggressive behavior for both males and females, regardless of social standing, intellectual capability, or family conditions. Other studies reported at the conference concluded that pretend violence affects brain development the same way that real violence does, registering in those areas of the brain that store long-term memories of traumatic events.

Aside from the desire of parents and educators to protect children at play from crime and violence and to focus their energies on academic pursuits, the high-tech boom is a central factor attracting children's time and energy. Homes are sprouting every imaginable "technologically smart" innovation: home theaters, media rooms, audio systems, computer networking systems, intercom systems, cable TV systems, satellite systems, remote control appliances, security systems, humidity control systems. Both parents and children tote cellular phones and pagers to allow instant, continuous communication. Not to be left in the dust, designers and builders are now integrating smart technology into apartment complexes. Leaving no alternative untouched, automobile manufacturers are filling the drive-time gap with devices to give drivers and passengers constant access to E-mail, the **World Wide Web**, on-demand satellite audio and video systems, global positioning systems, and a growing volume of entertainment, safety, and educational systems.

The smart technology of the future will likely make cars, like homes, immune from such interferences as books, one-on-one conversation, spontaneous games, and close, warm human relations. Indeed, scientists are designing smart robot systems that within two decades may be able to do all the driving (Supple, 1997). The **robot revolution** is not only transforming the way we work, by taking on the menial, repetitive, hazardous work, but is also changing the nature of children's toys and entertainment and, consequently, their spontaneous play.

Children's rooms are becoming high-tech havens and retreats for nonstop entertainment and communication with peers via computers, faxes, and phones. Kids keep calendars for their dawn-to-dusk schedules but find hours—evenings, weekends, vacations—to engage in endless hours of movies, television programs, computer chat rooms, and video games. Even the high-tech devices originally designed for adults are quickly modified to make kiddie versions available to children spending their allowances. For example, the sophisticated digital cameras used by sales personnel, originally selling for over $1,000, were modified to allow children to purchase a version for $49.95 (less from mail-order houses) so they, too, could take digital pictures, download them into their computers, play with them, and store them for later use. Such activity may produce either educational benefits or educational damage.

Electronic Play

Television. Watching television is more accurately described as entertainment than play but it is in reality a tool for both. Watching programs is one side of the picture, using the equipment for video games is another. Whatever the purpose, American children watch television an average 3 to 5 hours per day (Spencer, 2003).

The effects of television viewing on children has been widely researched. As early as 1985, the National Coalition on Television Violence (1985) identified more than 850 studies and reports of 120,000 people of all ages, in 20 nations, showing the harm of viewing television violence. The most common effects were increases in anger and irritability, loss of temper, increased verbal aggression, increased fear and anxiety, and a desensitization toward violence. The studies also documented increases in fighting, distrust and dishonesty, decreases in sharing and cooperation, increases in depression, willingness to rape, and actual criminal behavior.

By 2003, the U. S. Department of Education Educational Resources Information Center Clearinghouse on Elementary and Early Childhood Education (ERIC, 2003) reported research demonstrating these and additional negative effects of television viewing including violent or overly aggressive behavior, precocious sexuality, obesity, and the use of drugs or alcohol. The ERIC system also reported studies showing that television negatively affects creativity, language skills, children's learning and school achievement. The effects of television violence may also result in immunity to the horror of violence, acceptance of violence as a way to solve problems, imitation of television violence, and identifying with characters, victims and/or victimizers (American Academy of Child and Adolescent Psychiatry 1999).

Taking television research into account, the American Pediatric Association, in 1990, recommended that children's television viewing be limited to 10 hours per week. In 2001 the American Academy of Pediatrics recommended that children under two should not watch TV at all and that no child should have a TV in the bedroom (Meltz, 2003). These recommendations seem reasonable if accompanied by responsible adult roles in planning and evaluating with children and in providing a range of alternate, developmentally relevant activities.

These activities should include:

- Limiting television viewing time to one to two hours per day.
- Suggesting and participating in alternate activities.
- Planning television viewing with children to ensure that the children have a role in decision making and that the adult remains in control.
- Monitoring the child's television viewing habits to ensure that acceptable programs are watched and that time constraints are followed.
- Watching with the child and discussing programs to help her learn to critically evaluate what she is watching.
- Helping children to develop alternate solutions to problems seen on television.
- Keeping objectionable programs out by installing filters, deleting channels, and setting a good model by refusing to watch objectionable programs.

- Helping children understand the difference in make-believe and real life—that characters on television are not hurt in violent scenes, but the same actions would inflict pain and suffering in real life.
- Discussing violence and sex openly so that children know where adults stand on the issues. Let them know your values and watch programs consistent with your values.
- Talking with other adults to help ensure that children are not exposed to objectionable programs away from home.
- Turning off objectionable programs and explaining why to children.

Computer Play. Computers, the Internet, video games, and electronic toys are the new **electronic playgrounds** for children, combining three forms of games: practice, symbolic, and rule governed. They require a great deal of practice to gain mastery for advancement. They allow players to engage in the "as-if" quality of fantasy worlds. They present a set of rules that must be discovered and mastered to win the game. The convergence of these three forms of game playing sets video games apart from traditional toys and this combination of features may help explain the appeal that video games hold for children (Kafai, 1998). Malone and Lepper (1987) identified fantasy, challenge, curiosity, and control as major features attracting children.

Issues about appropriateness of computers and video games for preschool children are passionately debated. There is little question that preschool children can use appropriate computer programs (Clements & Nastasi, 1992). The critical issues are how and to what extent they should use them and what role computer use will play in their lives.

When computers are used appropriately in the context of complementary resources, they can have positive effects on self-esteem (Clements, Nastasi, & Swaminathan, 1993), intelligence (Haugland, 1992), creativity (Haugland, 1992; Reimer, 1985), literacy (Fein, 1987), independent learning (Walker, 1983), problem-solving skills (Clements, 1986), exploration (Escobedo, 1992), use of tools in playful ways (Henniger, 1994), and provision of microworlds for children's learning (Baird & Silvern, 1990).

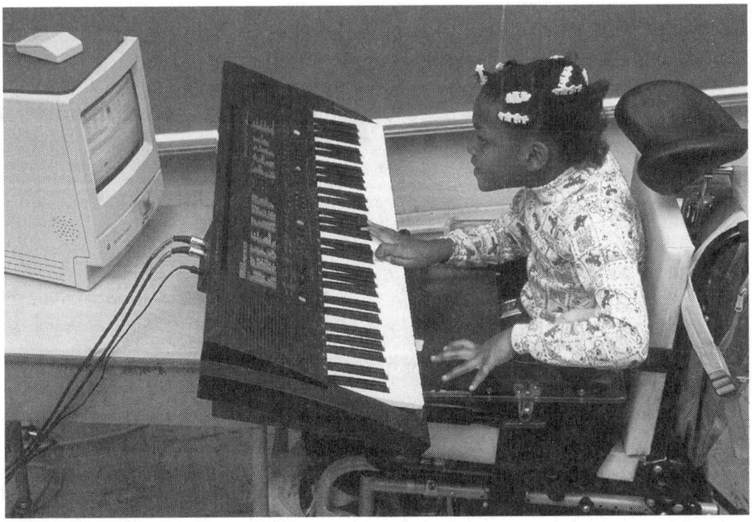

Issues about computer and video game play for young children are passionately debated.

Despite the evidence of positive results from computer access and use, the Alliance for Childhood (2000) published a critical analysis of computers in education, and called for a moratorium on further introduction of computers in early childhood and elementary education. It claimed that computers pose serious health problems for children including eyestrain, obesity, repetitive stress injuries, and possible physical, emotional, and intellectual damage. Additional side effects include taking time from play, physical activity, and bonding with adults. The Alliance position focuses on the need for children to develop imaginative thinking, critical skills, personal interactions with adults, and engaging their hearts, minds, bodies, and hands in personal interactions not commonly received in computer activities. Too much of their computer interaction is with inappropriate adult content, aggressive advertising, and trivial games.

In opposition to the Alliance for Childhood report, the Software and Information Industry Association (SIIA, 2000) released a report profiling many studies showing a positive relationship between computer use and student achievement (SIIA, 2000). The studies reviewed show benefits in student achievement, motivation, self-confidence, self-concept, and individualized learning. SIIA proposes that common sense, not a moratorium, is needed in considering children's computer use.

Yet another group, the David and Lucile Packard Foundation (2001) examined both sides of the issue and concluded that the growing use of computers raises both the promise of enriched learning and the risk of possible harm. Children in low socio-economic area schools and homes generally have more limited access to equipment and fewer opportunities to use computers than more privileged children. A major problem in schools is the lack of computer training for teachers. They also warn against possible hampered social development, depression, loneliness, obesity due to inactivity, and repetitive motion injuries. They do not believe that sufficient research is available to predict the long-term effects on children's social, physical, and cognitive development.

Technology is obviously a two-edged sword, offering both advantages and disadvantages (Silvern, 1998; Ginsburg, 2001). Computers can exert pressure on young children and detract from them valuable life experiences such as free play, art, music, and social interaction (Barnes & Hill, 1983; Brady & Hill, 1984; Elkind, 1981, 1985). Elkind also warns that computers should not be allowed to replace traditional play activities, time for interaction with teachers, or give false impressions about children's thinking abilities.

The developmental appropriateness of software is a key element in children's appropriate use of computers. Children exposed to developmental software make significant gains in intelligence and self-esteem, while those exposed to nondevelopmentally based software have significant losses in creativity Haugland (1992). The Children's On-Line Privacy Protection Act of 1998 prohibits Web sites from collecting personal information from children under age 13. A law of a similar name, the 1998 Child On-Line Protection Act, is intended to shield children from commercial pornography. However, such laws have limited effectiveness, for unsupervised children can merely plug into sites for adults when child sites are filtered out.

Haugland and Shade (1988), Dodge, et al, (2002) and Fischer & Gillespie, 2003) offer guidelines for selecting **computer programs** that are congruent with the National Association for the Education of Young Children's (NAEYC) Developmentally Appropriate Practices (Bredekamp & Copple, 1997).

Software. Developmentally appropriate software:

- Contains simple and spoken directions.
- Allows independent exploration and discovery.
- Is open-ended and allows children to maintain control.
- Provides many opportunities for problem solving.
- Allows children to impact the program through a variety of responses.

- Emphasizes the process of discovery.
- Teaches cause-and-effect relationships.

In addition, the NAEYC (1996) Position Statement on Technology and Young Children recommends:

- That violent themes be avoided; and
- That content reflect diverse cultures, ages, abilities, and family styles.

Parents, teachers, and other adults must assume responsibility for guiding children in their use of computers. Guidelines are available from a number of sources including the American Library Association, the American Academy of Pediatrics, the ERIC Clearinghouses on Early Childhood, Elementary and Secondary Education (2000), and the National Association for the Education of Young Children (2001).

Guidelines for adults include:

- Stay involved in children's computer activities including Web sites, chat rooms, and computer games.
- Complement computer time with other developmentally appropriate activities, including physical activity.
- Place computers in areas that adults frequent regularly.
- Monitor and discuss the content of Web sites with children and help them understand the limits imposed.
- Use **filtering hardware** to help ensure that objectionable material is not viewed by children.
- Seek help in selecting appropriate content for children.
- Pay attention to the food that children eat during computer use. Replace junk food with nutritious snacks.
- Pay attention to the emotions of children engaged in computer use. Look for signs of fatigue, eyestrain, etc.
- Place limits on the amount of time that children use computers.

The Internet. The guidelines for use of computers and software noted above apply generally to the selection and use of the **Internet**. Fortunately, research on use patterns is expanding and guidelines are becoming more reliable. The Internet itself is the best, quickest source of research about the Internet with unlimited resources available to assist people of all ages in securing information on virtually any topic.

There are potential risks for children going online, including exposure to sex and violence, pornographic peddlers, commercialism, and excessive isolation. Despite such risks, the Internet can be a useful tool in developing social, cognitive, and literacy skills (NAEYC, 1998), in increasing family and public involvement in the schools, and in meeting the educational needs of diverse groups of students (National School Boards Foundation, 2002).

A national survey of 1,735 households nationwide (National School Boards Foundation, 2002) revealed a mostly positive picture of Internet usage by children ages 9 to 17. In about half of the households, one or more children were online, with the percentage growing to three of four teenagers. Parents and children told the researchers that:

- Families buy computers for education.
- The Internet does not disrupt healthy activities.
- The Internet does not isolate children.
- Girls and boys use the Internet equally but in different ways.
- Parents trust their children's use of the Internet.
- Most view the Internet as a valuable new tool.

The reader should bear in mind that these conclusions reflect responses from households to a survey and do not include direct observations of children's Internet usage. All adults involved in children's education, especially parents and teachers should focus on positive, constructive ways to use the Internet while remaining vigilant to possible misuse.

- Know what children are watching.
- Keep computers in open spaces where adults will be present on a regular basis.
- Discuss Internet content with children and help them develop educational projects which include Internet use.
- Balance Internet use with a range of activities that involve books, hands-on projects, and projects that require physical activity.
- Help children sort out fact from fiction in what they see on the Internet.
- Learn Internet skills so you can assist beginners and participate in some of their projects.
- Install filtering hardware to shield children from objectionable content.
- Help children learn to shield their identity when using the Internet.
- Know about the "friends" your children are communicating with on the Internet.
- Develop plans for interaction between schools and homes on Internet usage. Open up communication via Internet as well as through direct, person-to-person contacts between parents and teachers.
- Involve children in setting policies for using the Internet at home and school.
- Help develop training classes for unskilled and minimally skilled parents and teachers.

Video Games. The phenomenal growth of the video game industry is leading to a major new international industry. Nearly 200 colleges worldwide now offer coursework in videogame development and about two dozen offer comprehensive programs (Mclure, 2003). Computer games do not stop at the "antiseptic, socially acceptable environment" of the classroom where trained adults are present, but extend to "darker, more aggressive simulations" (Silvern, 1998, p. 530). Consider the popularity of the video game industry, the content of video games, the time devoted to video games, and the context in which they are played. The most devout players start early as children and continue their fascination into adulthood, devoting countless hours in their bedrooms, on their couches, and at friends' houses.

Adult computer game addicts say that the games give them the same feeling they get when on amphetamines—feeling euphoric, craving more and more games, feeling unable to stop, neglecting family and friends, lying about game playing, experiencing stress disorders and sleep disturbances, feeling empty and depressed, and having school and job problems (Marriott, 1998).

Video games are generally considered to be solitary activities, but a group culture is springing up involving movies, fan clubs, video contests, and machines are being programmed to accommodate two or more players, supporting the appealing cooperation/competition aspect of games (Malone & Lepper, 1987). The video game culture involves mainly boys (Provenzo, 1991; Walsh, 2002), explained in part by the violent themes and gender stereotypes (Kinder, 1991). However, gender differences in spatial skills (favoring boys) required for success in video game play may disappear after extensive practice (Subrahmanyan & Greenfield, 1994).

The best-selling games glorify and reward extreme violence and sex, particularly toward women and girls. For example, in *Grand Theft Auto III,* a top seller in 2001, the player is rewarded for murdering a prostitute after having sex with her. The latest edition, *Grand Theft Auto: Vice City*, released in 2002, is predicted to become the top-selling video game ever, with sales of over 5 million copies (Walsh, 2002). Sales of a hit video game title can rival the box office take of a hit movie (*Austin American–Statesman, 1998,* p. E–12).

A growing number of studies conclude that watching sexual violence tends to desensitize viewers to it (Mullin & Linz, 1995; Strasburger & Wilson, 2002). Gentile, et al (2002) found that 8th and 9th grade students exposed to more violent video games were more likely to get into fights and received lower grades in school. Twenty percent of the players said they felt addicted to the games. Buchanan, et al (2002) concluded that 3rd to 5th grade students who played more violent video games were more likely to be described by their peers as mean and rude. Both these studies indicate that both amount and content of video games are important considerations for parents.

Brain research at the University of Indiana Medical School, reported by Walsh (2002), concluded that playing video games resulted in reduced activity in the section of the brain controlling emotional impulses. This is consistent with the research reported earlier in this chapter concluding that the emotional areas of the brain of teens are still developing and adds further credence to the view that exposure to violence increases violence among adolescents.

In addition to research conclusions, there are theoretical, perspectives on the effects of playing video games. Griffiths (2003) hypothesizes that playing video games would have two major effects based on either social learning theory or catharsis theory. He hypothesizes that social learning supports the view that playing aggressive video games stimulates aggressive behavior. Catharsis theory, on the other hand, supports the view that playing aggressive video games has a relaxing effect by channelling latent aggression and would have a positive effect on the child's behavior. However, catharsis theory as applied to video games has much to learn from long-term experience and research in play therapy. Exposing the child repeatedly to the offending element (e.g., violent video games) is the cause, not the catharsis (therapeutic activity). In play therapy, the child is removed from the abuse or offending element and supported in her creative playing out of personal emotions related to that abuse or offending element. Catharsis is a purging phenomenon, not a process of repeating punishment over and over.

The challenge to parents, teachers, child development professionals, and the video game industry is to limit violence, monitor game selection to ensure availability of prosocial, educational games, monitor the viewing habits of children and youth, and provide healthy alternatives. They must also push for ratings enforcement and enforcement of bans on renting and selling violent video games to children. Millions of children are entertaining themselves every day with games that glamorize violence, denigrate women and reduce time for creative, developmentally appropriate activities. In 2003, the State of Washington passed legislation prohibiting the sale of violent video games to children under the age of 17.

The **video game junkie** pursues his compulsion to video game arcades at shopping malls, vacation resorts, and an assortment of pay-for-play places. The worst video arcades and pay-for-play places are dark, dirty, loud, boisterous, crowded, chaotic, and attract people of all ages, from preschoolers to adults. Many spend money needed for basic living expenses on games focused on noise, violence, brilliant colors, sex, and competition with machines. Many pay-for-play places rent facilities for parties featuring junk food and sometimes "live" entertainment. A relatively few pay-for-play places feature dress-up dramatic play areas, art areas, computer coves for selected children's games, construction zones supplied with building materials, high-tech places for creating and reviewing TV programs, science and nature areas, and snack bars with nutritious foods.

Immersive Reality and Theme Parks

Computer technology makes it possible to create entertainment devices that give the participant the illusion of reality, an illusion so virtually real that it is difficult for the human mind to perceive the difference between fake reality and real reality. The potential positive applications are remarkable, promising to bring worlds that most can never visit into every home and classroom.

These devices are rapidly finding their way into theme parks and video arcades around the country which are patterned after blockbuster action and horror movies such as *Jurassic Park, Star Trek, Terminator, Godzilla, Twister,* and *King Kong*. Theme parks are drawing over 324 million visitors each year and reaping revenues of 9.9 billion (International Association of Assessment Parks and Attractions, 2003). Universal Studios' mammoth theme park, near Orlando, Florida, features five huge islands with virtual reality experiences focused around popular superheroes or selected movies. The paying participants are part of the action and experience sensations similar or equivalent to the real thing. Not far away in the Orlando area, Walt Disney World spreads over 7,000 acres and offers over 40 major adventures.

The designers of **immersive reality** theme parks and video arcades work with several goals: to leave the participant with a satisfied feeling of having accomplished something, to feel alive, to control danger, to exhilarate, to terrify, and to experience fear and anxiety. Naturally, these emotions are accompanied by a rush of chemicals in the brain, especially adrenaline, that create profound physiological changes in the players. The pulse rate quickens, the hands sweat, the pupils dilate, breathing quickens, and the mouth becomes dry. This is especially true for the super–roller coasters that team with immersive reality entertainment to attract thrill seekers to theme parks.

Super rides closely simulate the sensations felt by jet fighter pilots and astronauts, manipulating inertia and G-forces to give the greatest possible thrill. Some exceed 100 miles per hour and exert G-forces rivaling that of the space shuttle. A growing number of reports show possible brain damage resulting from the extreme G-forces (Rosenberg, 2002, p. 49). As immersive technology advances, these experiences, with barely perceptible differences in sensation from the real thing, can be available in shopping center arcades. The effects on children are yet to be thoroughly explored.

Lest the reader be left to believe that all theme parks showcase violence, sex, and terror, we must consider those that emphasize wholesome entertainment, exploration, discovery, history, family interaction, and imaginative play. For example, Silver Dollar City in Branson, Missouri, has been named one of the top three theme parks in the world by the International Association of Amusement Parks and Attractions and was named in 1998 the top theme park in America. The park is a friendly 1890s village surrounded by nature's beauty, featuring more than 100 traditional craftspeople, fast, fun (but no "suicidal") rides, 50 family-friendly shows daily, the world's largest tree house, interactive geographic adventures created by the Smithsonian Institution and the National Geographic Society, shows and games designed after Nickelodeon's television programs, special features for toddlers, and hands-on Imagination Station featuring Lego bricks for creative construction. The emphasis is on interactive learning opportunities that are fun and exciting and that combine education, entertainment, and play.

CHILDREN'S MUSEUMS

Fortunately, there are other counters to the influences of poorly conceived and often abused play and entertainment venues. The best children's museums are exemplars for re-creating natural and scientific wonders and transforming them into tools for creativity, exploration, discovery, and intrigue. Children's museums are the fastest growing type of cultural institution, with more than 100 opening between 1990 and 2003. During this period attendance tripled, reaching 24 million in 2002 (Association of Children's Museums, 2003). Here, the child sees and feels the richness of raw materials for construction and art, bends and shapes her mind while exploring and discovering properties and functions, and sharpens reflexes and technical skills by manipulating simple tools and technology. A growing number of children's museums are expanding into the outdoors to complement indoor activities. These are further enriched by the growing availability of children's gardens sponsored by various urban agencies.

Contemporary children's museums are places where adults and children can engage in interactive exploration, adventure, and learning together, quite unlike the staid activity of observing exhibits in traditional museums. The best exhibits are hands-on, participatory, and interesting, with certain common features (Forman, 1998). First, children in the age range for which the exhibit is designed can quickly discern its purpose. Second, children can control the events within the exhibit. Third, these changes are within the difficulty levels of the age group designations. Fourth, the exhibit requires more than a single reaction to a simple act. Finally, the exhibit leads children to solve interesting problems.

Shine and Acosta (1999) studied parent-child interactions in a grocery store exhibit at a children's museum and developed a model of the influence of the physical and social environment on child and parent behaviors. The major dimensions of this model were physical context, message set, social context, parent and child play behaviors, and parent-child interactions.

Children's museum exhibits are designed to send four messages: explore materials, engage in pretend play, explore concepts, and self-regulate. Parents and children follow different paths. Children choose to explore the materials and engage in pretend play. Adults engage in attempts to explore materials and concepts with their children and to guide them toward self-regulation of social behaviors. Adult actions appropriate for very young children may not be congruent with older children's interests. Children tend to prize autonomy and approach pretend play with intensity, persistence, and through interaction with coplayers. Consequently, parent-child interactions may be brief and sporadic as children resist interference in their play.

Shine and Acosta suggest several positive roles for adults; as organizers of experiences, they may frame pretend play scenarios (e.g., suggest roles), guide the sequence of events, probe knowledge of concepts, interpret museum artifacts and protocol, and scaffold (pace learning) experiences in exhibits. Too much or inappropriate intervention by adults can inhibit pretend play, so exhibits may be designed to allow unobtrusive adult supervision.

SUMMARY

Thanks to high-tech brain imaging equipment, neuroscientists are making unprecedented inroads into understanding the role of experience in brain development. Neuroscience carries profound implications for a range of professions, from medicine to criminology, and promises to become the new frontier in understanding child development and education. Among the emerging results of neuroscience are deeper insights into nature and nurture, infant plasticity, effects of play and play deprivation, consequences of neglect, emotionality, socialization, language and cognitive development, and motor functions. The implications for practitioners are profound.

Research in neuroscience demonstrates the power of play and the consequences of play deprivation. This research is buttressed by studies of neglected and abused children and studies of criminals. Children struggle to play even under distressing conditions, yet a growing number are deprived of creative, spontaneous play by loss of recess, emphasis on academics, out-of-control schedules, absence of parents, fear of crime, substitution of organized sports, and high-tech play including video games, computer play, and pay-for-play places. This is having detrimental effects on children's health, physical fitness, and emotional adjustment.

Play may be both constructive and destructive, rational and irrational. The emerging and rapidly growing alternatives to traditional spontaneous play have both positive and negative consequences. High-stakes testing in schools, computer chat rooms, carnival and theme park play, and a wide range of pay-for-play places offer obstacles to healthy development that must be reconsidered and managed by parents and teachers and by policy makers and sponsors. Recess, well-designed playgrounds, adapted to the wide range of children's developmental play needs, various computer related activities, selected theme parks and pay-for-play places, and children's museums are acceptable counters to these emerging negative play places and forms.

KEY TERMS

Axon
Cerebellum
Children's museums
Computer programs
Computerized axial tomography
Constructive play
Dendrites
Destructive play
Electronic playgrounds
Entertainment
Filtering hardware
Fine-motor skills
Flow
Gambling
Gambling casinos
Gross-motor skills
High-stakes testing
Immersive reality
Infant plasticity
Internet
Irrational play
Language magnets
Leisure
Magnetic resonance imaging
Make-believe play
Motor neurons
Multiple intelligences
Myelination
Neuroscience
Neurons
Neurothealogy
Neurotransmitters
Pay-for-play
Peak experiences
Play deprivation
Play therapy
Positron emission tomography
Pruning
Pseudoplay
Quality time
Rational play
Recreation
Robot revolution
Rough-and-tumble play
Schemata
Spirit of play
Spontaneous play
Sport culture
Symbolic inversion
Synapses
Theme parks
Transcendental play
Vacation retreats
Video arcades
Video game junkie
Work
World Wide Web

STUDY QUESTIONS

1. How has neuroscience contributed to understanding child development? What are the linkages between neural development and physical development, cognitive development, language development, and social development?
2. Explain the basic functions of the brain that lead to neural development. What is the role of early experience on brain development?
3. What are the effects of early sensory deprivation on child development? Give examples.
4. What are the connections between neuroscience and play? Prepare a defense of the role of play in neural development.
5. What recommendations would you offer to parents on child rearing and to teachers on teaching, based on contemporary knowledge of neuroscience?
6. What is play deprivation? What are the principal contributing factors? How can policy makers help remedy play deprivation?
7. Play has been dichotomized as rational versus irrational, constructive versus destructive, normal versus abnormal, good versus bad. Should children be allowed to engage in irrational, abnormal play? Why or why not?
8. Distinguish among spontaneous play, organized sports, leisure, entertainment, and work. What are the advantages and disadvantages of each for promoting spontaneous play?
9. What are the major impediments to spontaneous play? How can parents and teachers help ensure opportunities for children to engage in spontaneous play?
10. Is technology promoting or restricting healthy play? Defend your answer. What do children learn through electronic play?
11. What advice would you give to an elementary school PTA about children's video games and Internet chat rooms?
12. What advantages and problems for child rearing do you anticipate for immersive reality play?
13. What are the pros and cons of high-stakes testing? What are the alternatives for ensuring quality and accountability?
14. How do children's museums differ from theme parks? Which are more likely to promote creativity, language development, social development, and academic knowledge?

Chapter 4

Play

Infants and Toddlers

> *AT 0, (10) J. put her nose close to her mother's and then pressed against it, which forced her to breathe much more loudly. This phenomenon at once interested her, but instead of merely repeating it or varying it so as to investigate it, she quickly screwed up her nose, sniffed and breathed out very hard (as if she were blowing her nose), then again thrust her nose against her mother's cheek, laughing heartily. These actions were repeated at least once a day for more than a month as a ritual.*
>
> (Piaget, 1951, p. 94)

In Chapter 2, Jean Piaget's theory of play included his position that infants engage in activities that have the character of play. In the quotation just cited, Piaget observed an early form of play in his daughter Jacqueline at 10 months. In this chapter, we will describe the relationship between development and play in infants and toddlers. The nature and evolution of motor, cognitive, language, and social development will be discussed, as well as examples of variations in development. The relationship between development and play in each developmental domain will be explained with relevant examples of infant and toddler play.

After presenting information on development and play, we will discuss the characteristics of infant and toddler play. It is important to understand the integrated nature of play; that is, developmental advances in each separate domain affect the characteristics of play in the other domains.

Although infants and toddlers initiate their own play activities, their ability to play benefits from play experiences with others. Adults, especially parents, facilitate play development in very young children. Adults provide toys, materials, and interactions that foster play in infants and toddlers. These interactions change as the child develops. As a result, play interactions with infants are different from those with toddlers.

Peers and siblings also have a role in infant and toddler play. Older siblings include younger brothers and sisters in their play activities. They, too, are able to promote play in siblings who are infants and toddlers.

The final part of the chapter will address how adults facilitate play with infants and toddlers. Toys and materials that are appropriate for play will be included.

PHYSICAL AND MOTOR DEVELOPMENT

Characteristics of Physical Development

The first 2 years are the most rapid period of development in children. In their first 2 years, infants and toddlers achieve more physical growth and development than in any other period of their childhood. By the end of the 1st year, the infant has tripled its weight and increased its length by 75%. Growth occurs in spurts, with periods of no development followed by a period of rapid change (Berk, 1996). Growth proceeds at a slower rate in the 2nd year. Body proportions change. At birth, infants' heads are one-fourth of their length. Gradually, growth in the trunk and legs pick up speed. Physical development is termed **cephalocaudal**, as development emerges from the top of the body down to the legs. Another growth pattern moves from the center of the body outward, known as **proximodistal development**. The head, chest, and trunk grow first, followed by the arms and legs, and finally the hands and feet (Berger, 2000; Santrock, 2000).

An important characteristic of physical development is the growth of the brain. At birth, the brain has achieved one-fourth of its adult weight and will develop to three-fourths of its adult weight by age 2. Skill growth is also rapid as a result of the increase in brain size (Nash, 1997). The appearance of teeth is another physical characteristic. The average age of appearance of first teeth is 6 months.

Characteristics of Motor Development

Perhaps the most significant changes in the first 2 years are in the area of motor development. The newborn infant's motor abilities are described as **reflexes**. By the age of 2 years, the toddler has achieved full mobility and is able to climb stairs and run outdoors. Cephalocaudal and proximodistal development have resulted in development of gross- and fine-motor skills.

Gross-Motor Skills

Gross-motor skills involve large body movements that begin to emerge early. Berk (2002) describes motor development as a system because separate abilities in motor skills work together to produce more advanced abilities. Berk explains:

> During infancy new systems of action emerge constantly. For example control of the head and upper

> chest are combined into sitting with support. Kicking, rocking on all fours, and reaching are gradually put together into crawling. Then crawling, standing, and stepping are united into walking alone. (p. 184)

When the child is able to walk without assistance, at about 12 months, the period of infancy is completed and toddlerhood begins. In the 2nd year of life, mobility expands rapidly as the toddler tries new motor actions. Figure 4–1 shows the sequence of motor achievements during the first 2 years.

Fine-Motor Skills

Control of the arms and hands result in the development of fine-motor skills. Because fine-motor skills require coordination of emerging abilities, they also require a system approach to development (Berk, 2002). The first skill developed is the ability to grasp an object, which requires coordination of the eyes and hands. This skill is mastered at about 6 months, followed by exploration and practice in grasping objects in the environment. Other fine-motor skills developed during the first 2 years include transferring an object from one hand to the other, holding an object in each hand, clapping hands, and scribbling.

FIGURE 4–1 Gross-Motor Achievements from Birth to 2 Years

Gross-motor achievements during the first 2 years follow a predictable sequence as listed below:

- Lifts head and holds erect and steady
- Rolls over
- Sits propped up
- Sits without support
- Stands holding on
- Walks holding on
- Stands momentarily
- Stands alone well
- Walks well
- Walks backward
- Walks up steps with help
- Jumps in place
- Kicks a ball

Source: Adapted from Frankenburg, Frandel, Sciarillo, and Burgess (1981).

Variations in Physical and Motor Development

Although physical and motor development occurs in the same sequence in infants and toddlers, much variation can be due to normal ranges in acquisition of skills. Some differences in physical development are the result of gender, ethnicity, and nutrition. Girls are slightly shorter than boys in infancy. African American infants tend to be larger and more advanced physically, while Japanese infants tend to be smaller than American norms (Brown et al., 1986; Super, 1981; Tanner, 1990).

Physical development is affected by inappropriate nutrition. Children who experience prenatal malnutrition and malnutrition after birth grow to be smaller in physical dimensions. Brain development is also affected. Mental delay can result from institutionalization during infancy or living in harsh, unresponsive environments (Kagan, Kearsley, & Zelazo, 1978; see Chapter 3). Deprivation and malnutrition can also result in delays in acquisition of physical abilities. Dennis (1960) found that infants raised in very deprived institutions in Iran did not move about on their own until after they were 2 years of age.

Cultural differences affect motor development. In Uganda and Jamaica, it is believed that infants in the Baganda Community and West Indian populations are advanced in motor development because their mothers train them to sit up early. They experience a formal handling routine according to the traditions of their cultures and the belief that the babies will grow up to be strong and healthy. It is believed that infant care practices among the Kipsigis of Kenya and other African groups give them an advantage over Western infants. Unlike Western infants, who spend large amounts of time in a crib, African babies are held next to the adult's body all day as the adult works. Thus, the baby is able to practice movement while in an upright position and experience the adult's physical movements, which promote early motor development (Berger, 2000). The Zinacanteco Indians of southern Mexico, on the other hand, discourage progress in motor development. Because their environment is dangerous, mothers discourage the infants from acquiring crawling and walking skills (Berk, 2002; Hopkins & Westra, 1988).

Play and Motor Development

Infants are able to engage in physical play shortly after birth. Very young infants use their senses for play. During the first months of life, infants use visual observation and other senses to engage in practice play.

As soon as young infants are able to grasp objects, their emerging physical abilities support their efforts at play. During the 1st year, much of the infants' first play is with their bodies. Infants play with their own fingers and toes and then use kicking and grasping to initiate play with objects. This first stage of physical play is **manipulative play**.

Between 1 and 4 months of age, play involves watching and practicing body actions (Garner, 1998). Infants watch their own body movements and enjoy bright colors and interesting sounds (McCall, 1979). By 4 months of age, infants learn to grasp and play with objects. Infants first explore the objects and then play with them. A first step in exploration is to bring the object to the mouth to explore it actively with the teeth and tongue. Exploration can also involve looking at the object. Banging the object might be the next step in exploratory behavior (McCune, 1986). Later, the infant can hold two objects and bang them together.

With the ability to sit, infants use visual assistance to grasp and explore objects. Between 4 and 12 months, they can bring their hands to midline to explore objects; and between 7 and 12 months they can use both hands independently. Between 9 and 16 months, they are capable of making inferences about toys after very short periods of exploration (Garner, 1998).

As the infant develops motor skills, the world of play enlarges. Each new physical skill such as crawling, standing, and walking is practiced until mastered. Garner (1998) reports that with lessened use of playpens, the age of onset of walking has decreased. After mastery has been completed, the baby is able to play using the new skill. As explained by Piaget (1976, p. 167), "In a word, he repeats his behaviour not in any further effort to learn or to investigate, but for the mere joy of mastering it and showing off to himself his own power of subduing reality."

Next, infants and toddlers try out physical actions with toys. They learn to push, pull, and punch toys. They enjoy toys that have buttons to push and knobs to twirl. Emerging fine- and gross-motor skills are complemented as they fill and dump objects out of containers and experiment with new ways to play with common household objects (Rogers & Sawyers, 1988). They enjoy poking their fingers in holes and become interested in materials that make marks (Garner, 1998).

Exploration or Play?

In previous sections of this chapter, exploratory behaviors of infants and toddlers have been included within descriptions of play. Some play scholars differentiate between exploration and play, stating that not until the infant has completed exploration of an object or toy does play begin. Much of this separation between the two can be traced back to the work of Hutt. She explains the difference:

> Consideration has primarily been given to specific exploration of a novel object and its habituation as well as those responses which might be termed play. By restricting myself to these responses directed towards the same stimulus object, I have tried to draw some distinction between exploration and play. These behaviours can be differentiated on a number of grounds. Investigative, inquisitive or specific exploration is directional, i.e. It is elicited by or oriented towards certain environmental changes. . . . The goal is "getting to know the properties," and the particular responses

> of investigation are determined by the nature of the object.
>
> Play, on the other hand, only occurs in a known environment, and when the animal or child feels he knows the properties of the object in that environment; this is apparent in the gradual relaxation of mood, evidenced not only by changes in facial expression, but in a greater diversity and variability of activities. In play the emphasis changes from the question of "what does this *object* do?" to "what can *I* do with this object?" (Hutt, 1976, p. 211)

Other scholars have extended and refined Hutt's definition. Athey (1984, p. 11), describes exploratory behavior as including, "looking, touching, grasping, experimenting with parts of the body, vocalizing, and so forth." For Athey, the repetition of movements leads to playful repetition of the skill and establishes the neural pathways that make the movement readily accessible.

Wohlwill (1984, p. 143) cites Weisler and McCall's (1976) definition of exploration. "Exploratory behavior consists of a relatively stereotyped perceptual-motor examination of an object, situation, or event the function of which is to reduce subjective uncertainty (i.e. acquire information)." Wohlwill (1984) then defines play

> as spontaneous activity, not directed at some externally imposed goal or serving some ulterior purpose, which involves manipulation of or other actions directed at an object or set of objects, resulting in some transformation of their location, arrangement, shape, etc., or of their meaning for the child (pretend play). (p. 144)

Wohlwill describes a sequence from exploration to play. It is when the child can transform the object and use pretense that exploration transitions into play. Exploration and play serve different purposes. Furthermore, the child's affect is different for the two behaviors. During exploration, the affect, is neutral or mildly negative, while during play, the affect is marked by smiling, laughter, and other expressions of pleasure.

Infants and toddlers practice motor skills until they are mastered.

Whether or not researchers distinguish between exploration and play, it is clear that one leads to the other. The child explores the object prior to playing with it. If Wohlwill's definition is correct, play with objects begins when cognitive development permits pretend play and transformation of objects. More on the topic of pretend and symbolic play will be discussed later under "Play and Cognitive Development."

Adult Roles in Motor Play

Parents and caregivers can encourage motor development by arranging the environment to provide support for emerging gross- and fine-motor skills. They can also interact with the child to encourage play and assist her to play just beyond her current abilities.

Play with toys is enhanced by interaction and encouragement from adults. The adult can talk about what the baby is doing and provide assistance when needed. Deiner (1997) provides a framework for how adults can enrich infant play with increasing complexity. Figure 4–2 shows this model for infant-adult interaction with toys

WHAT PARENTS AND CAREGIVERS CAN DO TO PROMOTE MOTOR PLAY

1. Attempt to get young infants to look at, reach for, and kick at objects.
2. Encourage young infants to hold, mouth, bang together, and examine rattles and other safe objects.
3. Try to arrange toys for infants to see and to manipulate with fingers, hands, or feet when they are in a quiet state.
4. Use a variety of objects and toys as playthings for exploration and manipulation; check to be certain that manipulatives are childproof.
5. Encourage rolling over, sitting, and creeping, providing both a safe, nonrestrictive area for practice and physical support and verbal encouragement.
6. Arrange soft, sturdy objects so that older babies can practice standing and pulling up to stand; encourage the children.
7. Provide tiny, soft food objects to facilitate use of fingers and promote self-feeding by older babies.
8. Use chairs, hassocks, or pushcarts, as well as abundant praise and encouragement with toddlers learning to walk independently.
9. Demonstrate to toddlers and assist them in undressing skills.

Source: C. Z. Cataldo (1983), *Infant and toddler programs: A guide to very early childhood education* (pp. 81–82). Reading, MA: Addison-Wesley.

that can be particularly effective for caregivers in infant rooms.

Motor development alone does not totally account for the child's ability to play. Cognitive development facilitates play activities, as will be demonstrated in the next section.

COGNITIVE DEVELOPMENT

Characteristics of Cognitive Development

Cognitive development, like physical development, proceeds at a rapid pace in infants and toddlers. Piaget (1936/1952) proposed that infant thinking is quite different than that of older children and adults. He believed that intelligence in infancy was dependent on the senses and physical abilities, or in his terms, a **sensorimotor period.**

Infants are able to see, hear, taste, and smell from birth. They can use their senses to perceive the environment around them. Infant perception supports cognitive development. For example, Bower's (1989) research demonstrates that infants perceive the graspability of objects before they are able to grasp successfully. Infants also understand very early which objects can be sucked, can be made to move, or will make a noise. For example, the infant perceives differences in sucking the breast, a nipple on a bottle, and a pacifier. Later, as more mobility and cognitive development are accomplished, the infant acquires perception of depth and constancy of objects. The individual infant's perception is dependent on past experiences, cognitive awareness, and current use

FIGURE 4–2 Adult-Infant Interactions with Play Materials

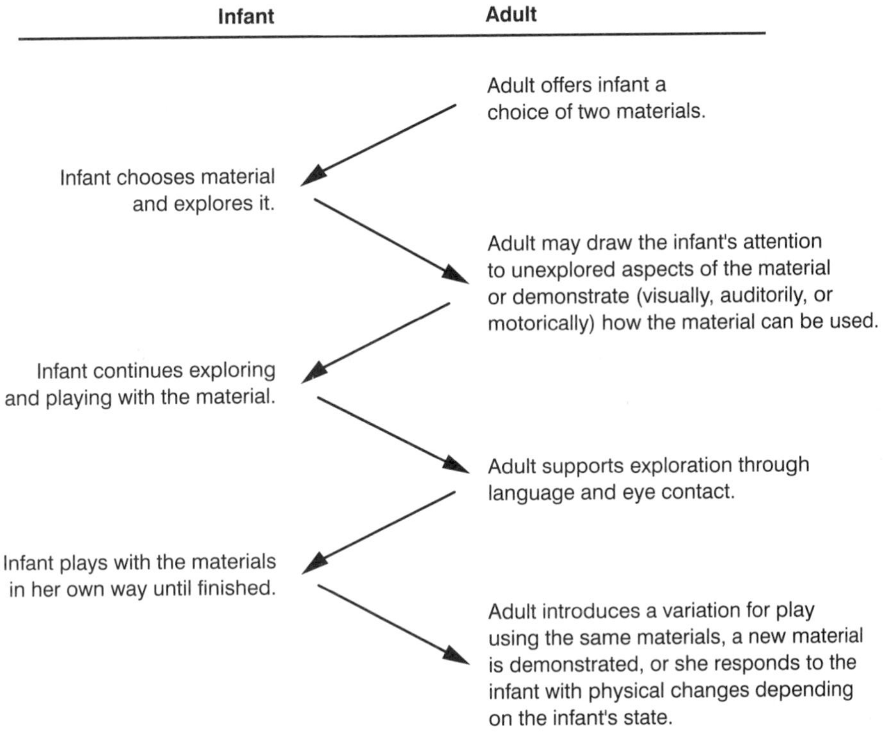

Source: From *Infants and Toddlers: Development and Program Planning* (p. 376) by P. L. Deiner, 1998, Pacifio Grove, CA: Thompson Learning Global Rights Group. Copyright 1998 by Harcourt Brace. Reprinted with permission of Wadsworth, a division of Thompson Learning Global Rights Group.

of the senses (Berger & Thompson, 1996). Infants do not merely absorb the sensory information they encounter; in addition, they interpret and integrate it with their existing experiences.

Sensorimotor intelligence, then, results from infants behaving as active learners. The infant uses emerging physical abilities to grasp, bang, taste, shake, and otherwise interact with people and objects to extend her sensory abilities and to aid cognitive growth. Piaget (1936/1952) believed that infants actively use their senses and motor abilities to comprehend their world. The sensorimotor period of development is described in six substages. Intelligence becomes more advanced in each substage. Figure 4–3 describes each of these stages.

Variations in Cognitive Development

Piaget's observations of infant development have been found to be quite accurate by researchers who have tested his theories. Multicultural scholars have confirmed that Piaget's view of cognitive development is culturally neutral (Hale-Benson, 1986). Infants follow Piaget's views of mental functioning that focus on universal thought processes. Kagan (1977) found that infants in Guatemala followed the same sequence in achieving object permanence as middle-class Euro-American children, although the Guatemalan children were slightly delayed in learning some skills. These kinds of research findings support Piaget's theory that cognitive development proceeds in predictable, invariant steps.

FIGURE 4–3 Substages of the Sensorimotor Period

Stage 1: Reflexes. In this first stage between birth and 1 month, the infant uses reflexes to learn. Newborns use the sensorimotor activities of sucking, looking and listening, and grasping. They exercise and refine and organize these reflexes.

Stage 2: Primary circular reactions. Infants between 1 and 4 months begin to adapt their reflexes as they interact with the environment. Sucking is adapted to specific objects such as nipples and pacifiers. Objects are sucked for nutrients or for pleasure. Other actions involving the child's own body are repeated because the infant finds them to be interesting. For example, the infant kicks his legs or stares at his hand. These actions are repeated over and over in a circular reactions of actions and response.

Stage 3: Secondary circular reactions. Between 4 and 8 months, the infant repeats actions that involves objects, toys, clothing, or another person. The infant performs an action that elicits a pleasing response from a parent and repeats the action to extend the reaction. The infant might also kick repeatedly to activate a crib toy or shake a rattle to hear the sound again and again. Vocalizations are included in the actions taken by the infant to get a response from another person.

Stage 4: Coordination of secondary circular reactions. The infant between 8 and 12 months can coordinate several behaviors. Piaget identified infants as capable of true intelligence because their behavior is goal directed. The infant might try to reach a forbidden object or use different vocalizations to hear the sounds made. Emerging motor skills enable the child to incorporate more of the environment in her activities. As part of the emergence of intentional behaviors, infants achieve object permanence. Infants can retrieve hidden objects, demonstrating that they understand that an object still exists when it is out of sight. They can anticipate events such as the departure of a parent or preparation of a meal.

Stage 5: Tertiary circular reactions. Toddlers between the age of 12 to 18 months now become creative and experiment with new behaviors. A toddler might try different ways to drop food from a highchair or to throw a toy. The toddler does not repeat the same behaviors but tries variations on the original behavior. Toddlers' inventive behaviors can be very trying for parents and caregivers. One of my children enjoyed emptying kitchen cupboards and experimenting with new ways to roll canned goods and open containers, and banging different combinations of cooking pans and lids on the kitchen floor.

Stage 6: Mental combinations. True problem solving emerges between 18 and 24 months. The toddler can mentally consider solutions to problems before taking any action. Rather than using trial and error, the child can anticipate what might happen if certain behaviors are used. In this stage, toddlers develop a more advanced understanding of object permanence. They understand that objects can be moved when they are out of sight and look in different locations to find a toy. They are able to represent mentally something that is not present. For example, a toddler can pretend to be sleeping. The toddler is leaving the sensorimotor period of development and moving toward the preoperational period of thinking.

Nevertheless, some researchers have found that infants have greater cognitive capacity than Piaget described. Habituation-dishabituation studies have supported evidence of earlier understanding of object permanence as early as 3½ months of age (Ballargeon & DeVos, 1991; Berk, 2002).

Recent brain research has found remarkable evidence that environmental conditions early in life affect the course of cognitive development. Nourishment, care, stimulation, and environment all affect brain development. During the first 3 years of life, the vast majority of synapses and cells in the child's brain are produced. The number of synapses increases with astonishing rapidity during the first 3 years, and the number remains for the first decade of life. After the first decade, the synapses that are not used are eliminated (Blakeslee, 1997; Greenspan, 2000; Shore, 1997).

There is great variation in brain development during the first 3 years depending on the types of experiences available to the young child. How the child develops and learns during the first 3 years depends on the interplay between the child's genetic endowment and the experiences or nurture in the child's life; moreover, availability of playful activities affects not only the course of development but also the size of the brain (Begley, 1997; Greenspan, 2000; Nash, 1997). Availability of verbal language is also significant. Children under the age of two who hear rich adult language achieve more gains in cognitive development (Blakeslee, 1997).

The brain has the capacity to change; moreover, there are optimal periods when the brain is primed for specific types of learning (Begley, 1997; Shore, 1997). While appropriate stimulation, nutrition, and support can enhance brain development and learning (Poussaint & Linn, 1997), negative factors in the environment can have adverse effects on cognitive development. Infants and toddlers of depressed mothers can have cognitive delay because of lack of appropriate stimulation. Neglect by parents, stressful living conditions, social deprivation, and other factors, including living in poverty, can result in a dramatic reduction in a child's capacity for later learning (Frost, 1998; Lott, 1998).

The brain is extremely plastic during the infant and toddler period of development. Infants and toddlers who have strong attachments and a secure, supportive environment will have optimal opportunity for brain development and learning. Infants and toddlers who experience serious stress, neglect, and trauma can recover if they are given sustained help. These young children need quick and intense intervention if they are to overcome developmental problems that can decrease their ability to learn (Lott, 1998; Shore, 1997).

Play and Cognitive Development

In the section on motor play, how the infant's first play activities are limited to the senses and controlled by the ability to grasp an object was discussed. Once grasping skills have been developed and some mobility has been achieved, the infant's domain for play expands. Play is at first described in terms of the infant's sensory and motor modalities, but during the second half of the 1st and 2nd year of development, cognitive development adds new dimensions to the young child's play activities.

Between the ages of 8 to 12 months, the infant is in Piaget's stage called *coordination of secondary circular reactions*. The infant is achieving the ability to walk and can coordinate several behaviors, such as playing with two objects and using true verbalizations. But, most important, memory has developed as demonstrated by the emergence of **object permanence**. With the development of memory, **symbolic play** or pretend play begins. Early pretend play is a solitary activity. Later social pretend play emerges after 12 months of age (Howes & Matheson, 1992). The complexity of symbolic play has its own sequence of development. When the child is between 18 and 24 months and is able to represent objects mentally and engage in pretend actions in the stage of mental combinations, symbolic play reflects planning on the toddler's part.

Piaget described the development of cognitive play in three stages—practice play, symbolic play, and games with rules—that parallel his stages of cognitive development. Practice or **functional play** appears during the sensorimotor period and continues in later periods of development. This first level of play involves the practice of some behavior that is repetitive. The action is pleasurable, and the child repeats actions that have been mastered (Buhler, 1937; Gottlieb, 1983). Practice play can be mental, such as repeatedly asking questions or making vocalizations such as **babbling** or singing for pleasure (Rogers & Sawyers, 1988).

Symbolic play also appears in the later months of the sensorimotor period and continues through the preoperational period. It is also described as pretend play and emerges when an absent object is represented by another object. McCune (1986) describes stages in symbolic play with levels of play within each stage that develop between 10 and 24 months. In the first stage, the Sensorimotor Period, the infant engages in presymbolic play that lacks the characteristics of true pretend play. The child then is able to engage in pretend play that involves the child's own body or action with a toy.

The second stage, Symbolic Stage I, has three levels of sophistication in pretend play. Within the three levels, the child moves beyond her own actions to including other people or objects. These efforts at symbolic play combine more elements until the most advanced stage of 2 years, when the toddler can use language to describe the pretend action and demonstrate that the pretending has been planned. The sequence of symbolic play in toddlers appears in Figure 4–4.

Adult Roles in Cognitive Play

Knowledge of emerging cognitive development can also provide guidelines for supporting infant and toddler play. Wilson (1990) outlined Piagetian substages of development with toys and materials and caregiver strategies that will facilitate cognitive play. Table 4–1 shows Wilson's suggestions for supporting cognitive development and play.

Adults also have a role in encouraging pretend play. Although not all mothers actively engage in pretend play, they can have an indirect role. Parents who provide opportunities for play and engage in discussion and storytelling provide an environment and structure for pretend play. They can nurture pretend play by providing toys and materials that facilitate pretending (Garner, 1998).

Infant attachment to significant adults indirectly affects pretend play. Infants and toddlers who are securely attached are more likely to engage in peer interactions and engage in more complex and sustained symbolic play (Pepler & Ross, 1981).

Sibling play encourages pretend play. In an investigation of pretend play with a mother and with an older sibling, more pretend relationships were found between the infant and a sibling than with the infant and the mother. The infants also engaged in more role play with the older sibling than with the mother (Youngblade & Dunn, 1995).

At the end of the 2nd year, the toddler is combining play with objects, symbolic play, and emerging language skills to enrich play episodes. In the next main section, language development and how play with language emerges will be addressed.

Cultural Differences in Parent-Child Pretend Play

Parents from different parts of the world engage in pretend play differently (see Chapter 7). Haight, Parke, and Black (1997) describe these variations:

> Available cross-cultural research suggests a relation between variation in parental beliefs about play, and their support of play. Turkish and Chinese parents generally view themselves as appropriate play partners for their children. In contrast, Mexican, Italian, Mayan, and Indonesian parents typically do not view play as particularly significant to children's development, and/or adult participation as appropriate. Consistent with these beliefs, naturalistic observations reveal that Turkish and Chinese parents typically participate in pretend play with their young children, whereas Mayan, Mexican, Italian, and Indonesian parents engage in relatively little or no parent–child pretending. (p. 271)

LANGUAGE DEVELOPMENT

Characteristics of Language Development

How early does language development begin? It begins in the womb when the fetus hears her mother's voice and language in the environment. Babies who are 4 days old can distinguish between languages. Newborns show their preference for the language that is familiar by

TABLE 4–1 Cognitive Development and Play: Piaget's Substages

Piagetian Substage	Materials	Examples of Caregiver Strategies
Substage 1: Simple reflexes (birth to 1 month)	Visually attractive crib and walls to crib, objects near crib; occasional music, singing, talking, chimes	Provide nonrestrictive clothes, uncluttered crib to allow freedom of movement; provide environment that commands attention during the infant's periods of alertness.
Substage 2: First habits and primary circular reactions (1–4 months)	Face and voice, musical toys, musical mobile; rattle; objects infant can grasp and are safe to go in the infant's mouth; objects the infant can grasp and lift.	Provide change in infant's environment; carry infant around, hold infant, place infant in crib; observe, discuss, record changes in the infant; turn on musical toys and place where the infant can see them; place objects in the infant's hands or within the infant's reach; provide clothes that allow freedom of movement; provide time and space for repetition of behaviors.
Substage 3: Secondary circular reactions (4–8 months)	Objects that attract attention (of contrasting colors, that change in sounds, have a variety of textures or designs); toys; balls	Watch movements the infant repeats as when a waving arm hits the crib gym and then this action is repeated; provide materials that facilitate such repetitions (new items on the crib gym, for example); place blocks, dolls, ball, and other toys near the infant so they can be reached; initiate action, wait for the infant to imitate it, then repeat the action (smile, open mouth, for example)
Substage 4: Coordination of secondary circular reactions (8–12 months)	Toys, visually attractive objects	Place objects near the infant; play hide-the-doll-under-the-blanket; place the block behind you; verbalize your own actions; such as "I put the ball behind me," introduce new copy game; allow time and space for the infant to play.
Substage 5: Tertiary circular reactions, novelty, and curiosity (12–18 months)	Blanket, paper, toys, dolls, spoon, interesting objects; water toys water basin, narrow-neck milk carton and different sizes and shapes of objects.	Play game of hide-the-object with infant—hide the object while the infant watches, let infant watch you move the object to a different place under the blanket, and ask, "Where is it?" "Can you find it?"; observe and allow infant to find the object, praise infant for good watching and thinking; allow infant to play with water and toys to discover different actions of water and of the objects in the water; provide time and materials that stimulate infant to think and try out new ideas; ask questions but do not tell answers or show infant; encourage infant to pretend—to drink from pretend bottle like baby Gwen, to march like Pearl, to pick up toys; allow infant to repeat own play and develop own preferences.
Substage 6: Internalization of schemes (18–24 months)		Allow toddler time to figure out solutions; allow toddler time to think and search for objects; observe toddler's representations and identify the ideas that seem important to the toddler, allow the toddler to act out conflict in play with toys and materials, observe toddler's play and identify consistent themes; provide clothes and materials that help the toddler pretend to be someone else.

Source: From *Infants and Toddlers: Curriculum and Teaching* (2nd ed.) by L. C. Wilson, 1990 p. 16. Albany, NY: Delmar. Copyright 1990 by Thomson Learning Learning Global Rights Group. Reprinted by permission.

FIGURE 4–4 Pretend Play from 10 to 24 Months

	Levels and criteria	Examples
Sensorimotor Period	**Level 1 Presymbolic scheme**: The child shows understanding of object use or meaning by brief recognitory gestures. No pretending. Properties of present object are the stimulus. Child appears serious rather than playful.	The child picks up a comb, touches it to his or her hair, drops it. The child picks up the telephone receiver, puts it to the ritual conversation position, sets it aside. The child gives the mop a swish on the floor.
Sensorimotor Period	**Level 2 Auto-symbolic scheme**: The child pretends at self-related activities. Pretending. Symbolism is directly involved with the child's body. Child appears playful, seems aware of pretending.	The child simulates drinking from a toy baby bottle. The child eats from an empty spoon. The child closes her or his eyes, pretending to sleep.
Symbolic Stage I	**Level 3 Single scheme symbolic games**: Child extends symbolism beyond her or his own actions by: **Level 3.1** Including other actors or receivers of action, such as a doll. **Level 3.2** Pretending at activities of other people or objects such as dogs, trucks, and trains.	Child feeds mother or doll. Child grooms mother or doll. Child pretends to read a book. Child pretends to mop floor. Child moves a block or toy car with appropriate sounds of vehicle.

Source: From "Symbolic Development in Normal and Atypical Infants" (p. 49) by L. McCune, 1986, in G. Fein and M. Rivkin (Eds.), *The Young Child at Play: Reviews of Research* (Vol. 4), Washington, DC: National Association for the Education of Young Children. Copyright 1986 by NAEYC. Reprinted by permission.

sucking more vigorously on a nipple when they hear it as compared to an unfamiliar language (Cowley, 1997).

Like cognitive development, acquisition of language during the first 2 years is an impressive achievement. Between birth and 2 years, infants and toddlers learn enough about their language to speak and develop a vocabulary ranging from 50 to 200 words (Berk, 2000). Children of every culture and country learn the language of their community. Italian babies, for example, understand names of different kinds of pasta quite early in life (Traywick-Smith, 1997). Children from bilingual families learn words from both languages before 18 months.

Theories of Language Development

How do theorists explain language development? Three major theories have informed our understanding of how language develops. The **behaviorist theory** of language development was led by B. F. Skinner (1957). Skinner proposed that language is acquired through operant conditioning; that is, parents reinforced the baby's efforts at language. Subsequently, they reinforced the most correct forms of efforts to say words. Behaviorists

	Levels and criteria	Examples
Symbolic Stage I	**Level 4 Combinatorial symbolic games**: **Level 4.1** Single Scheme Combinations: One pretend scheme is related to several actors or receivers of action.	Child combs own, then mother's hair. Child drinks from bottle, feeds doll from bottle. Child puts an empty cup to mother's mouth, then experimenter, and self.
	Level 4.2 Multi-scheme combinations: Several schemes are related to one another in sequence.	Child holds phone to ear, dials. Child kisses doll, puts it to bed, puts spoon to mouth. Child stirs pot, feeds doll, pours food into dish.
	Level 5 Planned symbolic games: Child indicates verbally or nonverbally that pretends acts are planned ahead.	
	Level 5.1 Planned single scheme symbolic acts—Transitional type: Activities from Levels 2 and 3 that are planned. Type A—Symbolic identification of one object with another. Type B—Symbolic identification of the child's body with some other person or object	Child finds the iron, sets it down, searches for the cloth, tossing aside several objects. When cloth is found, she or he irons it. Child picks up play screwdriver, says "toothbrush" and makes the motions of toothbrushing.
	Level 5.2 Combinations with planned elements: These are constructed of activities from Levels 2 to 5.1, but always include some planned element. They tend toward realistic scenes.	Child picks up the bottle, says "baby," then feeds the doll and covers it with a cloth. Child puts play foods in a pot, stirs them. Then says "soup" or "Mommy" before feeding the mother. She or he waits, then says "more?"offering the spoon to the mother.

also propose that the child learns language through imitation. The adult conditions the child to use correct language forms by rewarding efforts to imitate adult language.

Noam Chomsky (1957) understood that even very young children take charge of learning language. His theory was labeled as **nativist** because he believed that children have an innate ability to acquire language. He proposed that all children have a biologically based innate system for learning language that he called a **language acquisition device (LAD)**. Chomsky believed that the LAD contains a set of rules common to all languages that children use to understand the rules of their language.

A more recent theoretical approach, termed **interactionist**, is based on the fact that language is not acquired without socialization. Language cannot be acquired without a social context. Infants and toddlers have an innate capability to learn language that is facilitated by adult caregivers (Berger & Thompson, 1996; Berk, 1996). Vygotsky (1984) proposed that language is learned in a social context. Language is centered in the sociocultural history of a population. The child as a member of the group learns the language to communicate in her community.

Sequence of Language Development

All children learn language in the same sequence. Although the timing may vary for different languages, the developmental sequence is the same. From the moment of birth, the neonate uses cries and facial expressions to express her needs. She can distinguish her mother's voice from other voices and can discriminate among many different speech sounds (Berger & Thompson, 1996). Thereafter, steps toward speech and the use of language develop at regular intervals. Figure 4–5 traces these steps between birth and 24 months.

Variations in Language Development

There are wide variations in how rapidly language development occurs. Some variation can be very normal and based on differences in language style. Other variations can be a cause for concern, indicating a delay that warrants intervention.

A normal type of variation in language development and usage is language style. Berk (1996) describes these differences as **referential style** and **expressive style**. Toddlers who use a referential style use words to refer to objects; those who use an expressive style use more pronouns and social words. The vocabulary of toddlers who use a referential function for language grows more rapidly than those who use an expressive style because languages have more objects than social expressions.

Language differences are due to cultural and ethnic diversity. In addition, young children may be bilingual or speakers of another dialect or language. Any of these cultural differences can result in standard English language acquisition that appears to be at a different rate than native English speakers; however, Traywick-Smith (1997) cautions that these children should not be labeled as language delayed because they have a culturally derived communicative style or language difference. For example, American mothers label objects more often than Japanese mothers, while Japanese mothers engage their toddlers in social routines more often than American mothers. The nature of language development will be different in children from these cultures (Fernald & Morikawa, 1993).

FIGURE 4–5 Sequence of Language Development: Birth to 2 Years

- **2 months:** The infant is developing a range of meaningful noises that can be discriminated by the mother. Cooing, fussing, and crying as well as laughing are used.
- **3–6 months:** New sounds such as squeals, croons, and vowel sounds are added. Parents direct their attention to what the baby is looking at and often verbally label what is seen.
- **6–10 months:** Utterances begin to include repetition of syllables known as babbling. Gestures such as pointing are also used to communicate. Babbling begins to incorporate the sounds of the infant's language community. Deaf babies babble with their hands. (Berk, 1996)
- **10–12 months:** The infant comprehends simple words. Utterances sound more like adult words in intonation. Deaf babies communicate by expressing a sign.
- **13 months:** First words are spoken. Vocabulary increases steadily. Holophrastic speech is used. The infant uses a single word to express a complete thought. The child has a larger receptive than expressive vocabulary, meaning that the child understands more than she can express or verbalize.
- **13–18 months:** Continued growth of vocabulary using one-word utterances.
- **18 months:** Spurt in vocabulary development.
- **21 months:** Begins to combine two words in an utterance. Described as telegraphic speech because the child focuses on high-content words as in a telegram. Vocabulary expands rapidly. The toddler is beginning to understand rules of grammar.
- **24 months:** The toddler has a vocabulary of up to 200 words.

If a child is still having great difficulty in understanding and speaking language at age 2, she may have a serious language disorder (Kalb & Namuth, 1997). Language delay can be caused by a hearing impairment, Down syndrome, or a general language delay. A child with general language delay might have minor damage to the brain or other factors such as poor health, poverty, or family stress. There are multiple causes for language delay, and interventions must be planned for individual children (Traywick-Smith, 1997).

The Role of Adults in Language Development

Adults have a major role in infant and toddler language development, as was demonstrated in how parents of different cultures use language with their very young children. Although children have an innate ability to acquire language, their social interaction with adults is also a major factor in language acquisition.

Adults begin speaking to their babies during the first days of life. Moreover, they adjust their style of talking to fit the infant's stage of development. This type of baby talk is termed **parentese**. Parentese is higher in pitch, simpler in vocabulary, and shorter in sentence length. It uses more questions and commands and fewer complex sentences than adult talk.

Parentese is used by people of all ages. Siblings are natural users of baby talk. At first all of the talking is done by the parent or other person. The infant is the interested recipient. The parent might engage in both sides of a conversation. The infant signals its responsiveness with smiling, gestures, and physical actions. Once the child begins to use **holophrastic speech,** the parent interprets and clarifies the child's speech and meaning in the conversation. The toddler is trying to communicate in all efforts and speaking. The adults use labeling, expansion of the child's speech and nonverbal smiling to support the child's development of language (Berger, 2000).

The language interaction between adults and infants has been described as a dance. The individual characteristics of the parent and child affect the nature of the dance. Parents who talk extensively to the child will have more of an influence in the child's development of language than parents who use restricted language in their communications with the child.

The nature of the child's interaction also affects the interactive relationship. The responsiveness of the parent can be affected by the child. The infant's temperament or intelligence might affect how responsive the infant is to the mother. This in turn can affect the level of the mother's responsiveness to the child (Stevenson, 1989). In sum, in the interactive relationship or dance between mother and child, both partners affect the richness and extent of language that takes place. Both partners affect the other. The mother initiates the language relationship, but the child's responses can affect how much the mother continues the language conversations.

Play and Language Development

Infants and toddlers play with language at a very early age. Before talking begins, the infant plays with babbling sounds. Garvey (1977) documented infants producing a variety of such sounds between 6 and 10 months. At 1 year of age, the child engaged in long periods of vocalizations of single vowels. Weir (1976) described these episodes of sound play as the child's monologues.

During the 2nd year, the toddler uses sounds to enhance pretend play. Frost (1992, p. 41) describes this private speech as allowing the child "to identify events and actions of self, others, and objects such as the telephone, dog, and automobile horn." The child is using play with sounds to accompany pretend play with objects.

The toddler uses play with language after words appear and combinations of words begin. Weir (1976) describes language play using

WHAT PARENTS AND CAREGIVERS CAN DO TO PROMOTE LANGUAGE PLAY

1. Understand the need to be an active conversational partner. Initiate conversational episodes with the infant frequently during the day. Use caregiving episodes to talk to the baby.
2. Talk to the infant as if she understands. Use parentese strategies such as raising the pitch of your voice and speaking in an enthusiastic tone when engaging the infant in "conversations."
3. Be sure to respond to the infant's efforts to communicate. React as if the infant did speak to you, and reward with a smile and other physical forms of encouragement.
4. Continue to initiate conversations with toddlers. Listen to them carefully; give them time to express themselves.
5. Do not be concerned with the inaccuracy of the toddler's use of language. Expand, repeat, and respond positively to the toddler's attempts to use language forms.
6. Make your toddler feel that she is understood when she has difficulty pronouncing words. Support all efforts.

telegraphic speech with a grammatical pattern and substitution of nouns as follows:

What color
What color blanket
What color mop
What color glass (p. 611)

Adult Roles in Language Play

Language play is also a social activity in the infant and toddler years. The role of the parent, sibling, or other caregiver in using parentese with the child teaches the child the game of taking turns in speech. At first the mother takes the turn for both, but soon the infant engages in the play with cooing, babbling, and attempting vocalization. Play with language is extended with the first mother-infant games involving motor activities, such as peek-a-boo and patty-cake. The infant imitates the physical movements and gestures used by the mother and enjoys the gestures that accompany the games. Object permanence in cognitive development permits the child to enjoy the disappearance and reappearance of the play partner in peek-a-boo.

Parents and caregivers also follow the lead of the child in communicative language play. When the infant initiates the play with babbling, the adult responds by imitating the infant's vocalizations. The game continues with infant and adult taking turns making new vocalizations.

Toddlers use emerging vocabulary to engage in symbolic play. McCune (1986) describes a child using a play screwdriver for a toothbrush by first labeling it in the example of planned symbolic games in Figure 4–4. This anticipates the more advanced play with language that will emerge in the early childhood years when social development makes it possible for young children to interact in play activities.

BEGINNING STEPS IN LITERACY DEVELOPMENT

All of the language experiences in which infants and toddlers engage are essential for language development. Further, these experiences are also building foundations for literacy. Familiar songs and rhymes and mother-infant games are first steps in acquiring literacy.

Toddlers also learn that pictures can stand for real things and symbolize things in the world. Symbols in the environment give clues about

WHAT PARENTS AND CAREGIVERS CAN DO TO PROMOTE LITERACY

1. Read often to infants and toddlers.
2. Show enthusiasm as you share books with the child.
3. Make the experience pleasurable.
4. Talk to the child about the book by pointing to pictures and talking about what is happening.
5. Name objects in picture books. (Armbruster, Lehr, & Osborn, 2002).

things and places. For example, an 18-month-old toddler traveling with her mother and grandmother recognized signs along the highway—the McDonald's golden arches—and pointed to them as they passed, exclaiming, "McDonos!" Toddlers recognize packaging of favorite foods in the grocery store and can name some familiar food items. Often they are able to make these first connections through sibling and adult encouragement (Durkin, 1966; International Reading Association & National Association for the Education of Young Children, 2000).

The single most important activity that establishes foundations for literacy is reading aloud to infants and toddlers. The best oportunities for these experiences are when youngest children feel emotionally secure and are active participants in the activity.

SOCIAL DEVELOPMENT

Characteristics of Social Development

Infants have a need to be social beings. There is evidence of all the basic emotions very early in life. Infants vary greatly in temperament, which is influenced by both heredity and environment (Kagan, 1994). During the first 2 years, infants and toddlers develop an attachment to their caregivers that is affected by the circumstances in their environment. An important achievement during the first 2 years is the development of a sense of self that includes self-recognition and self-control.

Theories of Social and Emotional Development

Several theories inform our understanding of social development (see Chapter 2). Erik Erikson's (1950) psychosocial theory is based on Freud's psychoanalytic theory, while Mahler's separation-individuation theory focuses on the development of self that occurs during the 2nd year of life.

Erikson believed that emotional development occurs throughout the life span as the individual resolves life stages positively or negatively. During the first 2 years, the infant and toddler experiences the stages of **trust versus mistrust** and **autonomy versus shame and doubt**.

In the first stage of social development, trust versus mistrust, the infant learns whether the world is a secure place. The infant develops a sense of trust if her basic needs are met with consistency and continuity. On the other hand, if the mother lacks sensitivity to the infant's needs and cannot be depended on to respond when the infant is hungry or uncomfortable, the infant will develop a sense of mistrust.

During the 2nd year, the toddler encounters the conflict of autonomy versus shame and doubt. Toddlers seek to become autonomous and independent. If the toddler encounters support and firmness as she seeks to control her own actions and body, autonomy will be the result. If, on the other hand, the adult is very restrictive and overcontrolling, the toddler will develop a sense of shame and will doubt her ability to act competently.

Margaret Mahler (Mahler, Pine, & Bergman, 1975) perceived social development to be based on an awareness of self that develops during the 2nd year. This awareness develops in two phases: **symbiosis** and **separation-individuation**.

According to Mahler, symbiosis begins during the 2nd month, when the infant is more alert and aware of events around her. The infant is fused with the mother and does not realize that people and events exist outside of herself. The infant's symbiotic relationship to the mother affects social development. If the infant experiences prompt and positive responses from the mother, development can proceed to the next phase. If the infant is handled harshly, and inconsistently, she will have difficulty in moving away from the mother in the next phase.

In the separation-individuation phase, self-awareness is triggered. This phase begins at about 4 to 5 months, when the infant begins to separate from the mother. As toddlers become more mobile, they increasingly develop the capacity to initiate their movement away from the mother. Between 2 and 3 years of age, toddlers emerge with a positive sense of self if their experiences with adults have been supportive and gratifying. Toddlers who remain insecure have more difficulty in accepting themselves as separate people and in enjoying independence (Berk, 2002).

Sequence of Emotional Development

The first emotion expressed by newborn infants is distress. Brief smiles also emerge during the first days of life. A social smile that responds to a human voice or face occurs at about 6 weeks. Other emotions that can be identified in very young infants are joy, surprise, fear, anger, disgust, sadness, and interest (Izard, 1991).

During the second half of the 1st year, infants experience new emotions labeled **stranger anxiety** and **separation anxiety**. Stranger anxiety is expressed through fear of strangers that can emerge as early as 6 months. Response to a stranger also depends on temperament and the proximity of the stranger and the mother (Berger, 2000). Separation anxiety is fear of being left by the mother or other adult. A factor in separation anxiety is the development of memory, and it is expressed with anger.

Variations in Social and Emotional Development

Infants and toddlers are beginning to form the personality that they will have as adults during the first 2 years of development. Individual differences in emotional reactions are known as **temperament** and can be identified in young infants. Differences in temperament have been described by Thomas and Chess (1992). Three basic temperaments as developed by Thomas and Chess are the **easy child**, the **difficult child**, and the **slow-to-warm-up** child. The easy child is generally cheerful, establishes regular routines as an infant, and adapts to new experiences easily. The difficult child, to the contrary, finds it difficult to establish routines and also has difficulty with new experiences. The slow-to-warm-up child reacts slowly to new experiences. This type of child exhibits lower reactions to stimuli from the environment and is generally inactive and negative in mood. Some children do not fit any of the patterns; rather, they are a blend of temperament characteristics. In addition, temperament can change over developmental periods. Although there are genetic influences in temperament, environment makes a contribution.

Sex and ethnic variations are also apparent in temperament and emotional development. For example, Chinese and Japanese babies are more easily soothed when they are upset, but they tend to be less active and more irritable. Male babies tend to be more active, which persists into childhood. Female children tend to be more anxious and timid (Berk, 2002).

The Role of Adults in Social and Emotional Development

Parenting styles affect the development of temperament in their infants and toddlers. As we discussed in the previous section, there are ethnic differences in how parents approach child rearing. American mothers work for their babies to become autonomous, while Japanese mothers teach their babies to become dependent on them. Parents perceive male infants to be better coordinated and strong, encouraging them to be physically active. Female infants are regarded as being weaker and more delicate. They are encouraged to be dependent and close to the parents.

An important element of the parental role in emotional development is the development of **attachment**. Attachment is the emotional connection between the infant and adult caregiver. It is hoped that the infant will achieve a **secure attachment** in which she will become close to the caregiver and develop confidence in exploring the environment. Unfortunately, some infants experience an **insecure attachment** that is troubled. The infant exhibits fear and anger toward the caregiver and has less confidence. These children were not readily comforted by the parents as infants and can exhibit lack of interest in the parent or overdependence (Berger, 2000; Lott, 1998).

The relationship between parents and infants and toddlers can be described as a partnership. Temperament, attachment, and parenting styles interact in the developing relationship. The social partnership develops during the first months of infancy. By the age of 2 months, the infant is able to respond to the parent. Smiling and cooing in response to the parents deepen the attachment process. As face-to-face interactions proceed, the mother and infant are able to synchronize the relationship, thus deepening the social partnership. Both partners initiate and respond to the social behaviors of the other. They also adapt to repairing the synchrony when social interactions are not successful (Honig, 2002; Tronick, 1989). The evolving social interactions between caregiver and infant become play episodes that will be discussed in the next section.

Play and Social Development

Social play begins when the newborn infant is able to use a social smile in response to a caregiver's presence. Smiling to another expands into babbling and cooing as the communicative repertoire expands. The first and most important play partner for infants and toddlers is the caregiver, whether it be a parent, sibling, or other adult. As has been discussed previously, the adult takes the initiative in engaging the infant in early social interactions. The infant in turn uses physical movement, facial expressions, and vocalizations to engage in socialization (Kid's Health, 2001).

Infants and toddlers learn and practice social rules through early social games. They learn turn taking, role repetition, and mutual involvement through adult-infant play (Bruner & Sherwood, 1976; Power, 1985). The adult-infant games of peek-a-boo and patty-cake incorporate these rules.

The Effects of Adult-Child Attachment and Play

The strength of adult-child attachment in infant and toddler years can be seen in the later social competence and play of preschool children. Attachment studies have indicated that secure attachment in infancy predicts more positive affect and greater peer acceptance in play in the preschool years. Secure attachment is also predictive of more positive social engagement and more elaborate play styles (Waters, Wippman, & Sroufe, 1979).

Peer Play

Infants are aware of their peers at an early age. In fact, they have unique reactions to another infant's presence, including looking intently, leaning

THE GAME

The Game is NOT important to the infant because people play it, but rather people become important to the infant because they play "The Game."

Source: J. Watson (1976), Smiling, cooing, and "The Game." In J. S. Bruner, A. Jolly, and K. Sylva (Eds.), *Play: Its role in development and evolution* (p. 275). New York: Basic Books.

Peekaboo surely must rank as one of the most universal forms of play between adults and infants. It is rich indeed in the mechanisms it exhibits. For, in point of fact, the game depends upon the infant's capacity to integrate a surprisingly wide range of phenomena. For one, the very playing of the game depends upon the child having some degree of mastery of object permanence, the capacity to recognize the continued existence of an object when it is out of sight. . . . The successful playing of the game is dependent in some measure on the child being able to keep track of the location in which a face has disappeared, the child showing more persistent effects when the reappearance of a face varies unexpectedly with respect to its prior position.

Source: J. S. Bruner & V. Sherwood (1976), Peekaboo and the learning of rule structures. In J. S. Bruner, A. Jolly, & K. Sylva (Eds.), *Play: Its role in development and evolution* (p. 278). New York: Basic Books.

Adults support infant play.

forward, and making excited movements with their arms and legs (Fogel, 1979). Investigations of peer interaction during the 1st year have shown that more interaction occurs under 1 year when there are no objects in the environment (Garner, 1998). In the 2nd year, they can exchange smiles and vocalizing while playing together (Howes, Unger, & Seidner, 1989).

Toddlers are able to engage in limited forms of play with other children. Objects become more important for peer interactions and are used in early play encounters (Garner, 1998). Toddlers approach another child or adult to engage them in play. Toys serve as the mediators for play (Johnson, Christie, & Yawkey, 1999). The emergence of pretend play provides a vehicle for toddlers to engage in play together. They engage in identical pretend activities, such as pushing doll carriages and smiling at each other (Howes et al., 1989). They also participate in run-and-chase activities (Howes, 1987).

Temperament Differences and Peer Play

Temperament variations in young children have been studied in terms of inhibited and uninhibited children (Kagan, Reznick, & Snidman, 1983). Inhibited 2-year-olds are more likely to be reticent in play with peers at age 4. Likewise, preschool children who have poor self-regulation of emotions seem to have anxiety during peer play when compared with children who have developed appropriate self-regulation (Rubin, Coplan, Fox, & Calkins, 1995).

Adult and Sibling Roles in Social Play

Adults serve in a support role in infant and toddler social play. Parents and caregivers encourage pretend play by providing materials and setting the stage for pretending. They might model pretend play using toys and objects. These supporting activities are called **scaffolding** in that parents are eliciting play skills rather than directing them (Bruner & Sherwood, 1976; Power, 1985).

Adults are able to sustain the child's interest in play activities. The scaffolding that they do in structuring play events results in more complex play on the child's part. Mothers adapt play activities for the developmental needs of their child and vary their own behaviors and new materials in response to the child's changing interests or emotional reaction (Escalona, 1968). Other studies have supported that infant and toddler play are more sophisticated in children who have access to adult partners (Ross & Kay, 1980). Parents select games and enable the infant to play the game. They model the steps in the game and position the infant so that he will focus on the game. Clues are given as to the infant's role in the game, and the game changes as the infant matures and understands how to play the game (Beckwith, 1986).

Siblings tend to have a different role than parents in infant-toddler social play. While parents serve as social partners who support advances in social play, siblings help the infants use the play skills that they have developed. They do not participate as social partners but play alongside the younger child (Dunn, 1983).

Each child is unique in social development as she is in language development. Adults want to establish a secure and trusting environment for infants and toddlers. In addition, they can support or scaffold social play.

CHARACTERISTICS OF INFANT AND TODDLER PLAY

Four basic characteristics in infant-toddler play have been introduced in this chapter: motor play, object play, social play, and symbolic play. Each of these types of play will be reviewed, followed by information on how domains of development are integrated in play. In addition,

HOW PARENTS AND CAREGIVERS CAN PROMOTE SOCIAL PLAY

Cataldo (1983) suggests that adults can interact with infants and toddlers for social and emotional development and play in the following ways:

1. Regularly providing babies with moderately stimulating experiences, such as comforting, talking, playing music, and moving mobiles, even though very young infants may respond little
2. Attempting to achieve smiling and cooing in young infants with animated and frequent face-to-face interactions
3. Paying attention to infants when they actively seek attention or comfort
4. Engaging babies in frolic and imitation play, such as rattle shaking, patting, arm waving, tickling, and laughing
5. Playing cooperative interaction games, such as peek-a-boo and patty-cake
6. Responding positively to toddlers' requests for help and guidance with toys, games, and play involvement with other children, even when problematic
7. Handling frequent management or discipline problems in toddlers with consistency, affection, and a view toward learning from conflict and challenge
8. Demonstrating realistic expectations and flexibility regarding toddlers' beginning skills in taking turns, sharing, and waiting for assistance

Source: C. Z. Cataldo (1983), *Infant and toddler programs: A guide to very early childhood education* (p. 81). Reading, MA: Addison-Wesley.

gender differences in play emerge in toddlers. These differences will also be discussed.

Motor Play

Infants first engage in motor play as they gain control of their body. Initially, they play by themselves with body parts. One of the first manifestations of motor play is playing with fingers and toes. As they are able to sit, stand, and walk, they are able to use new motor skills to include objects and the environment in their play. Fine-motor development enables them to grasp and explore toys, while gross-motor development permits them to reach new places and explore new things. Climbing and running are accomplished by toddlers who use furniture or climbing equipment in their motor play repertoire. Push and pull toys and riding toys now become important (Garner, 1998; Johnson et al., 1999).

Object Play

Interest in objects first emerges at about 4 months. First activities with objects include mouthing, shaking, and banging of all objects. Later, infants differentiate which behaviors are appropriate for individual objects. For example, rattles are shaken, while food and bottles are mouthed (Uzgiris & Hunt, 1973). At between 7 and 12 months, infants develop the ability to use both hands independently in object play. One hand can stabilize a toy, while the other manipulates the object (Kimmerle, Mick, & Michel, 1995).

During the 2nd year, mouthing decreases as the toddler moves from exploration to play. Toddlers enjoy action toys such as a jack-in-the-box or toys that respond with music or words when a string is pulled or a button pushed. By the end of the 2nd year, object play has expanded to include books, dolls, stuffed animals, and toys for water play (Garner, 1998).

Social Play

Adults, particularly mothers and fathers, are the first play partners of infants and toddlers in many cultures (see Chapter 7). Social play begins in the first months as adults initiate play with simple exchanges of vocalizations. Tickle games become popular, but by 8 months begin to decrease as patty-cake and peek-a-boo games increase. By the end of the 1st year, give-and-take games and point-and-name games have emerged (Lockman & McHale, 1989).

Social play includes the unexpected. The infant responds to the playfulness of the parent with positive expressions that include gleeful vocalizations. The parent who varies the game of peek-a-boo elicits laughing responses. The element of surprise in rolling a ball differently intensifies the child's positive reaction (Johnson et al., 1999).

Play with objects is a major factor in social play. Toys facilitate social interactions between peers in play as toys are offered and accepted. Objects mediate interactions when they are used to move children from parallel play to interactive play (Johnson et al., 1999). At about 14 months, objects contribute in lengthening the time in interactive play (Jacobson, 1981). By the end of the 2nd year, children in group settings begin to show a preference for certain play partners, and first friendships are formed (Howes, 1987; Howes & Matheson, 1992).

Symbolic Play

Symbolic play emerges at approximately 1 year of age. First examples of symbolic play include actions by the infant on herself. The infant pretends to drink a bottle or eat. These activities are at first solitary, which later broaden to include eye contact with a peer. By age 2, toddlers engage in the same type of symbolic play alongside each other and then later exchange vocalizations and smiles as they play (Garner, 1998).

Combinations of symbolic actions begin to be used when the child pretends to feed the doll and then washes its face. Pretense with objects and inclusion of peers in pretend play are expanded as toddlers begin to play roles such as pretending to cook while a peer holds a doll or rocks it. In these examples, social play and object play support symbolic play. Finally, language play also facilitates

Toys facilitate social play between peers.

other categories of play. Emerging abilities in language enable toddlers to engage in social and symbolic play activities with their peers. Objects, real or imagined, support their play.

Gender Differences in Play

A child's gender identity emerges early in life, and when gender identity is established, the nature of play changes. Children's identification of whether they are boys or are girls will result in playing more with other children of their gender (Fagot, 1994; Fagot & Leve, 1998). Once children engage in gender-specific play, they tend to play more with same-gender peers and play less with opposite-gender peers. This tendency increases as the children grow older in the preschool years (Maccoby, 1988).

One source of gender segregation is culture. In some cultures, boys are separated from girls at a very early age. In others, there is little concern for sex segregation, particularly in Western Europe. When these children attend nursery schools, however, they play in same-sex groups (Fagot, 1994).

Family and parenting are a factor in gender differences in play. It has been proposed that parents interact differently with sons than daughters. Moreover, these differences extend to differences in how mothers or fathers interact with sons and daughters. Research on this topic has resulted in disparate results partly because differing research methods have affected findings, studies have resulted in conflicting results, and differences in children's personalities and behaviors affect parent interactions (Lindsey, Mize, & Pettit, 1997).

Sex-types play choices can be seen at about 2 years. Boys spend more time playing with blocks, transportation toys, guns, and manipulative objects, while girls spend more time playing with dolls, stuffed animals, and art materials (Fagot & Leve, 1998; also see Chapter 7).

Creativity and Play

What is the role of creativity in toddler play? How do toddlers express creativity in their play?

For toddlers, creative activities are a part of exploratory play. When they engage in pretend play, they are using their imaginations to create or replicate a role. When they explore in the mud or make marks on a piece of paper, they are becoming aware that they can make something that is theirs alone. Toddlers can engage in art, music, dramatic play, and aesthetic appreciation in their expressions of creativity.

Creativity and Art

Toddlers begin to become artists as they learn to explore with pencils, crayons, markers, and finger paint. They can explore with play dough and shaving cream, and they enjoy using glue and scrap materials to construct their art.

Creativity and Music

Infants begin to appreciate music before they are born. In infancy they respond to music using the physical and verbal abilities that are available to them. Quiet music induces sleep, while bouncy music can encourage them to engage in creative movement. They can follow the leader to marching music and enjoy classical music during meals. They can learn simple songs and songs with finger plays.

Creativity and Dramatic Play

Once a toddler has engaged in symbolic play, experiences with dramatic play expand possibilities for pretending. In a group setting, dramatic play areas can facilitate the opportunities for dramatic play and permit children to express their feelings in a familiar housekeeping, store, or other thematic dramatic setup.

Aesthetic Appreciation

Whenever infants and toddlers are able to experience expressive arts, they are developing aesthetic appreciation. Sensory activities, experiences with books, engaging in listening to music and singing songs, and experiencing natural elements in the environment all foster a sense of beauty in the world. Fish, colorful plants, flowers, and interesting smells and sounds both indoors and outdoors help toddlers appreciate their surroundings.

The Integrated Nature of Play

As has just been described, the emergence of play in infants and toddlers depends on development in social-emotional, physical, and cognitive domains. Higher, more complex levels of play result from advances in development that are mutually supportive. Advances in a domain of development result in changes in play in that domain. Garner (1998) describes these advances as follows:

> Changes in physical development, for example, result in changes in coordinated motor play. As children acquire gross motor skills that allow mobility, they can expand their exploration of the environment, and advanced fine motor skill promotes exploration through greater manipulation of objects. (p. 137)

Categories of play are integrated or overlap. Again, Garner (1998) explains the process:

> Children engaged in exploratory play, for example, may be practicing newly acquired motor skills in the presence of familiar peers. Similarly, when children imitate each other's motor behaviors, the activity may be either practice play or social play, and when infants are practicing emerging motor skills, the activity may be play, exploration, or work. Because infants are not able to label their play, it may be especially difficult to identify pretense when observing certain motor actions. (p. 137)

Table 4–2 provides examples of how exploratory play is integrated with cognitive and social development. Although cognitive development in mathematics is the focus, these play activities integrate social and physical development as well.

We can extend our understanding of the interdevelopmental nature of play if we look at individual children.

MARTA: 3 MONTHS

Marta is the youngest of three children. At 3 months she smiles and coos when her older siblings talk to her in her crib. She enjoys looking at crib toys and uses vigorous kicking and waving of her arms in her efforts to get the toys to move. She likes to scratch the surface of her crib mattress. Although Marta's play is not yet characterized as true play, she has found her hands and enjoys watching her fingers move. When Marta's mother hands her a rattle, she enjoys looking at it as well. She makes attempts at rattling it but tends to drop it instead.

JONAH: 6 MONTHS

Jonah, an only child, knows how to play with a rattle. He can reach for it, grasp it, look at it, and shake it. Jonah has also benefited from his social environment. Jonah is in child care during the day. His caregiver at the center, Loisa, talks to him and he enjoys playing games with her. They engage in mutual gazing, cooing, talking, and tickling games. When Jonah is at home with his parents, he enjoys playing the same games with them. In

---

GEORGE AND WATER PLAY

When he reaches the deck, George sets the bottle on the deck and then uses both hands to pull himself up. Standing, he holds the bottle in his right hand and goes up the stairs, one foot leading, stepping up so that both feet are together. He turns toward the right-hand deck and also climbs those two steps carefully. At times he stumbles and puts out his hand to correct his balance. Jacinta and Clarrisa are in the wooden tunnel, and George bends forward slightly to peek in and smile. He then turns to the vertical ladder, stands on top and tips the water down and watches the water fall. When he sees me watching him from below, he gives me a huge grin.

Source: Stephenson, A. (2002). What George taught me about toddlers and water. *Young Children*, *57*, p.11.

TABLE 4–2 Examples of Integrated Exploratory Play

What Children Might Do	How the Behavior Relates to Mathematics	What Teachers Can Do
Dump blocks out of a bucket and put all of the blue ones in a pile.	Infants and toddlers look for exact matches because that is the level of classifying they can handle. They cannot understand that things can be the same and different at the same time (e.g., round and blue vs. square and blue). Classification skills will one day be used for the math content areas of measurement, patterning/ algebra, and geometry/spatial.	Provide plenty of blocks and other toys and items of different shapes, colors, and sizes. Play with children, notice what they do, and record observations. Use words that describe attributes such as size, shape, and color: "You made a big pile of blue blocks."
Beat on a drum, shake a tambourine, or play another musical instrument.	Infants and toddlers are slowly constructing number sense (e.g., realizing that numbers have meaning), concepts of quantity, and other ideas through their interaction with the environment. These beginning concepts of number will eventually lead to understanding one-to-one correspondence and quantification.	Provide plenty of sound makers (e.g., wrist bells, pots and wooden spoons, rhythm instruments) so children can experiment and experience rhythm and beat. Encourage children to play and move along with recorded music. Talk with children and describe what they are doing: "Shake, shake—shake, shake, shake. You made your own music."

Source: Geist, E. (2003) (p.10) Infants and toddlers exploring mathematics. *Young Children, 58*, 10–13.

addition, Jonah's dad sometimes swings him around like an airplane. Jonah can be encouraged to laugh out loud when he gently moves through the air.

HUANG: 13 MONTHS

Huang has one brother who is 10 years old. Huang is a very busy little person. He has learned how to crawl up the stairs, and a fence has been installed so that this activity can be limited to times when he can be supervised. Huang tries to crawl up on everything—chairs, the coffee table, the back of the sofa, and especially his mother's favorite rocking chair. Huang has learned the meaning of "no" and hears it frequently.

Huang's brother is usually out with his friends. When he is home, he sometimes plays chase with Huang. They take turns being chased and being the chaser. Huang loves this game and shrieks with pleasure. When the game becomes too rowdy, Huang's mother or father tells his brother to stop. A quieter game that Huang enjoys is rolling or throwing a ball. He plays this with both his brother and father. Huang loves to bang toys together. He has a favorite pull toy train that he pulls around the house and makes chugging sounds as he moves along. If he is lucky, his brother will bring out some of his model cars and let him push them around and makes noises like an engine. Another favorite game is tearing up an old magazine or newspaper.

Huang's mother works at night, so Huang's father prepares his supper and cares for him in the evening. Huang's father lets him ride on his back while he crawls around the house or ride on his shoulders. He also lets him ride up and down on his leg. Before bedtime, he and his dad look at picture books. Huang can name some of the pictures of toys or animals when his dad points to them. His favorite story is *Good Night, Moon*; his favorite word is "more."

MARY AND MINTA: 20 MONTHS

Mary and Minta are fraternal twins. Minta is larger than Mary, and they have different temperaments. Mary is easy-going, while Minta is described as "stubborn." Minta is the leader and talks more. Mary is content to follow her lead and is happy and secure with their relationship. Both of their parents work, and Minta and Mary are in the care of a nanny. Their nanny takes them to a park to play and also takes them to a nursery school program two mornings a week.

The twins' favorite toys are their baby dolls. Their grandparents gave them a play stove and plastic dishes. They enjoy playing with their dolls, feeding them, and putting them to bed. Recently Mary and Minta started calling each other "Maya." They also have some other conversations that even their sisters can't understand. Minta tends to speak for Mary and to communicate her wants. Family friends have expressed concern that Mary speaks very little, but their mother is a teacher and realizes that Mary understands more than she speaks and will express herself eventually. She spends time talking to Mary by herself to encourage her to depend less on Minta. She also realizes that she needs to spend time alone with Minta as well as with the older sisters. This is difficult because she works long hours and often has evening meetings.

The twins mostly play by themselves. Their older sisters have their own friends and rarely include Mary and Minta in their play activities. The nanny plays with them some, but they usually are left alone. Their father talks to them but has not shown an interest in engaging in their play. When they are upset, they get into the big rocking chair together in the living room and rock until they stop crying.

The twins enjoy nursery school. They can sing parts of songs and look at the books at school. They participate in school activities and usually choose the rocking boat when the class goes outdoors. They make little attempt to interact with other children and spend most of their time playing alongside each other in the play centers.

JEREMY: 2 YEARS

Jeremy just had his second birthday; his parents gave him a tricycle for a present. He has a new baby sister who spends most of her time crying and sleeping. Jeremy's mother works in a doctor's office, and his father is a computer specialist.

Jeremy goes to a child development center for child care every day. He practices riding the tricycles at school. He also enjoys playing with blocks, wooden vehicles, simple puzzles, and in the play house in his classroom. Jeremy occasionally chooses to make pictures in the art center and would rather use the big paint brushes or finger paint than use the crayons.

Jeremy is a big talker. He asks questions about everything both at home and at school. He has favorite storybooks that he wants his parents to read over and over. He asks his parents to play with him when he is at home and sometimes wishes his little sister would disappear. He enjoys pretend play with his stuffed animals and still enjoys putting objects into a large container and taking them back out. He talks to himself as he plays and does a

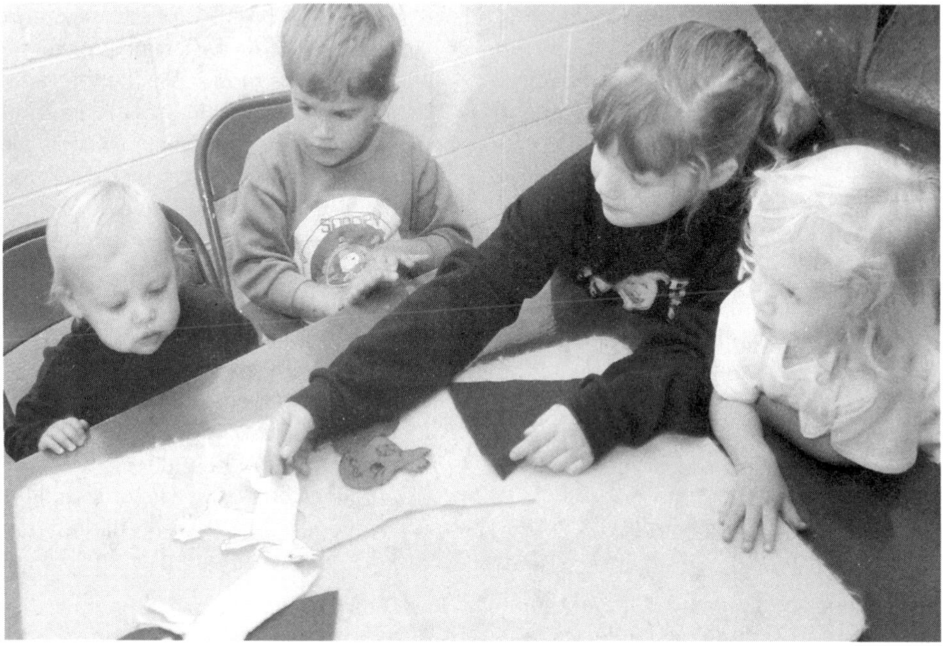

Older children scaffold play for younger children.

lot of pretend playing both at home and at school. He sometimes plays with friends at school but only can play successfully for a few minutes at a time. There are occasional arguments about toys, but Jeremy can usually play with a classmate playing nearby.

Jeremy's favorite toys at school are the play farm and play space station. He likes making the little people and animals do things. He also likes to play with his many small vehicles when he is at home. But his favorite plaything is his tricycle. He is learning to make it go backward and forward and turn. He spends much of his time outdoors at home riding his tricycle in the driveway.

ADULT ROLES IN INFANT AND TODDLER PLAY

Throughout this chapter, we have described how parents, other adults, and siblings contribute to infant and toddler play and development. In the examples of developmental play provided in terms of infants and toddlers of different ages in the previous section, play interactions of different types were discussed. Play interactions vary depending on the child's temperament, family environment, and play styles of both children and adults. Since a high percentage of infants and toddlers are placed in caregiving settings during the day, caregivers play a major role in adult-child play. We have already noted how cultural differences affect how parents play with their babies. In this section, we will consider how mothers and fathers play differently with their very young children. Then we will discuss caregiver roles in infant-toddler play in child care settings.

Parenting styles are changing. Until recent decades, research on parent-infant interactions were almost exclusively focused on the mother as the play partner. However, with the advent of working mothers and the evolution of different roles for both parents, fathers are taking increasingly important roles in the care and nurture of their children. Research into this phenomenon has revealed that mothers and fathers play differently with infant and toddlers.

In spite of the fact that more mothers are working, they still tend to take the major responsibility for caregiving. Although fathers help in the evenings and on weekends, mothers still have the major responsibility for caring for the child (Thompson & Walker, 1989).

Although fathers might provide less of the care of babies, they do play with infants. In the first months of life, fathers might move the infant's arms and legs, zoom her through the air, or tickle her stomach. From the very beginning fathers play more physically and more noisily with their infant.

Mothers, on the other hand, are more likely to blend play activities with caregiving routines. They talk or sing to the infant in a soothing manner (Parke & Tinsley, 1981). Their play is more verbal and instructive in nature.

When parents play with toddlers, differences in play activities persist. Mothers help their toddlers play with toys, read to them, or play traditional games such as patty cake and peek-a-boo. Fathers, on the other hand, engage in increasing amounts of physical play. They play chase and crawling games or wrestle with them. As a result, some researchers have found that toddlers are more responsive to their fathers than to their mothers (Clarke-Stewart, 1978).

Caregivers in child care settings have a different type of support role for infant-toddler play. Because they are responsible for the care of a group of infants or toddlers, their play interactions are more likely to be brief. They interact with infants while other babies in their care are asleep. They might engage in talking with infants while they are changing them or while alternately feeding two or more infants.

Caregivers also have a more structured environment for infants and toddlers. They provide cognitive stimulation by providing toys that are appropriate for developmental levels. Like parents, they talk to the children about their play and encourage them to try new toys. Toddlers spend 50% of their time interacting with a caregiver in a child care setting, 23% in social play, and 23% in object play (Howes & Unger, 1989).

Social play is enhanced in group care. Toddlers have a group of potential playmates and an environment that encourages play both indoors and outdoors. Caregivers can assist toddlers in playing in the group setting and introduce opportunities for social interactions as they engage in a variety of play activities. Peer interactions can also take negative forms such as aggressive encounters or running that is out of control (Howes & Unger, 1989).

TOYS AND MATERIALS FOR INFANT AND TODDLER PLAY

Parents and caregivers benefit from knowing about appropriate toys for infants and toddlers. Toys appropriate for infants who are not yet able to grasp might become dangerous once the infant can put them in her mouth. Parents should consider the following guidelines when selecting toys for their infants and toddlers:

- *Toys should be appropriate for the child's development.* Parents should select toys that are interesting and with which the child can play with successfully. They should be bright and colorful.
- *Toys should be safe and durable*. Toys should be able to withstand being mouthed, banged, and thrown. They should be free of small parts that can come off and be swallowed or cause the infant to choke.
- *Toys should complement the child's ability to grasp and manipulate*. Parents should consider the size, weight, and stability of the toy.
- *Toys should appeal to the child's senses*. Soft toys are desirable, as are toys that make a noise and/or can be acted upon (poke, turn knobs, pull strings to initiate noises, etc.) (Bronson, 1995; Deiner, 1998).

Caregivers who serve infants and toddlers in group settings will want to provide toys of different categories that will provide variety for very young children. Selection of toys should include a balance of the following categories (Deiner, 1998, p. 377):

- Materials that encourage awareness of self and others: toys with mirrors, dolls, and puppets
- Materials with varied textures: textured rattles and blocks and fuzzy puppets
- Materials that make noise: musical toys, rattles, squeaky toys
- Materials that reflect ethnic diversity
- Materials for cuddling: soft stuffed dolls, animals, toys, and other huggables

Bronson (1995) has developed lists of toys that are specific for different ages and developmental levels of infants and toddlers. Figure 4–6 lists toys for infants from birth to 6 months and from 7 to 12 months; Figure 4–7 lists toys and materials for toddlers 1 to 2 years old.

FIGURE 4–6 Play Materials for Children from Birth to 12 Months

Infants: birth through 6 months
Basic play materials for young infants:

- unbreakable mirrors that can be attached to a crib, changing table, or other play area
- one or two special items, such as dolls and stuffed animals, that may be brought from home as comfort items for individual children (for hygienic reasons, not to be used by other infants)
- a variety of mobiles/visuals that can be changed and rotated among infants
- a variety of toys that infants can bat or kick, mouth, grasp, and manipulate
- rattles and bells (with a handle or for the wrist or ankle) that make interesting sounds when manipulated.

Infants: 7 through 12 months
Basic play materials for older infants:

- large, unbreakable mirror(s) placed so that children can see themselves move
- a few soft, washable dolls and stuffed or other play animals
- a small selection of soft, lightweight blocks
- a variety of grasping toys that require different types of manipulation
- a varied selection of skill-development materials, including nesting and stacking materials, activity boxes, and containers to be filled and emptied
- a variety of small cloth, plastic, or cardboard books for children to handle, and additional books for adults to read
- a few varied bells and rattles that produce interesting sounds
- several types of one-piece push toys (cars, animals) for children who can crawl
- a variety of balls, including some with interesting special effects
- a climbing platform for crawlers

Source: From *The Right Stuff for Children: Birth to 8* (pp. 26 and 42) by M. B. Bronson, 1995, Washington, DC: National Association for the Education of Young Children. Copyright 1995 by the National Association for the Education of Young Children. Reprinted by permission.

FIGURE 4–7 Play Materials for Toddlers

Toddlers: 1 year old

Basic play materials for young toddlers:

- a sturdy, unbreakable, full-length mirror
- a few simple, washable dolls
- a few small wood or sturdy plastic people and animal figures
- simple dress-ups (kept very clean), and a doll bed and carriage that a toddler can fit into
- several lightweight transportation toys (cars, trucks)
- simple sand and water play materials (from about 18 months)
- a beginning set of small, lightweight blocks and simple, press-together bricks
- a variety of 3- to 5-piece puzzles with knobs
- a number of large, colored pop beads or stringing beads (after about 18 months)
- a variety of specific skill-development materials, including shape-sorters, stacking and nesting materials, pop-up and activity boxes, and simple matching materials
- foam/wood/plastic pegboard(s) with large, blunt-ended pegs
- a variety of sturdy books for children to handle and additional books for adults to read
- a supply of sturdy paper and large, nontoxic crayons in bright, primary colors
- a beginning set of simple musical instruments (from about 15 months)
- recorded music and a record, CD, or tape player
- a variety of push and pull toys
- several types and sizes of balls
- a few stable ride-on toys with four wheels or casters and no steering mechanism or pedals
- low, soft, climbing platform(s) and tunnel for crawing through

Toddlers: 2 years old

Basic play materials for older toddlers:

- a sturdy, full-length, unbreakable mirror
- dolls with simple garments and caretaking accessories
- role-play materials, including a selection of dress-ups, large, sturdy doll bed; child-sized stove and refrigerator; simple pots and pans; and a cleaning set
- a variety of wood, plastic, rubber, or vinyl people and animal figures to use with blocks
- vehicles (cars, trucks) to be used with blocks; a few large ride-on trucks (if cost permits)
- sand/water table(s) with containers and simple pretend materials
- a set of unit blocks and other materials, such as plastic bricks and large plastic nuts and bolts
- an assortment of fit-in puzzles
- pegboards with large pegs
- large beads for stringing; lacing shoes or cards with large holes; and materials to practice buttoning, snapping, buckling, etc.

(*continued*)

Source: From *The Right Stuff for Children: Birth to 8* (pp. 63 and 81) by M. B. Bronson, 1995, Washington, DC: National Association for the Education of Young Children. Copyright 1995 by the National Association for the Education of Young Children. Reprinted by permission.

FIGURE 4–7 *(continued)*

- simple matching and sorting materials; graduated nesting, stacking, and ordering materials; simple lock boxes; and sensory materials, such as "feel bags"
- simple lotto games and giant dominoes
- a variety of sturdy books
- a supply of crayons, paints, paintbrushes, markers, clay or dough, scissors, chalkboard, chalk, paint and colored paper, and adjustable easel
- a standard rhythm instrument set
- recorded music and a record, CD, or tape player
- push toys that support pretend play (vacuum cleaner, baby carriage)
- large ball(s) to kick, throw, and catch
- stable ride-on materials pushed by feet
- a low climbing structure and slide

SUMMARY

The first 2 years of life are important for development and play. Neonates use emerging senses to engage in playlike activity. This engagement in pleasurable activities increases as new abilities in physical, cognitive, and social development widen possibilities for play.

Gross- and fine-motor skills development enable the infant and toddler to achieve mobility and to grasp and explore objects. Play using available sensory and motor abilities become more sophisticated as gross- and fine-motor skills are mastered. Play with body parts expands to play with toys as the infant can move about and manipulate objects. Adults facilitate in motor play by providing toys that complement the baby's development and encourage the infant to engage in play activities.

Cognitive development proceeds at a rapid pace. Cognitive development in stages and substages as described by Piaget help explain how infant and toddler intellectual development promote cognitive play. The substages in the sensorimotor stage of development explain how emerging physical and intellectual skills work together to extend infant and toddler play. While early stages of play are limited to sensory and physical play, toddlers in the 2nd year are able to engage in pretend play in increasingly sophisticated ways.

Language development follows a predictable sequence in all children. During the first 2 years, language development is impressive as very young children are able to communicate with a rapidly growing vocabulary. Adults play a major role in language development, initiating language encounters with infants and clarifying and extending toddler language through the use of parentese. Infants and toddlers also engage in play with language following their own initiatives. Infants play with babbling sounds, and toddlers use developing grammatical patterns to engage in language play.

Social and emotional development depend on the parenting styles and emotional environment of the family. Cognitive development in the early months affects the expression of emotions and first experiences with fear and anxiety. The temperament of the infant and toddler affect their interactions with the adults in their lives and vice versa. The security experienced by the infant affects development of attachment with parents and caregivers.

Social play requires interactions with adults. Parents engage infants in social games and conversations that nurture attachment and confidence to explore and play. Although infants are aware and interested in their peers, social peer play emerges gradually in the 2nd year as toddlers exchange toys, smile at playmates, and play alongside peers in the same activity.

Emerging development in social, physical, language, and cognitive domains interact in infant and toddler play. Developmental advances in individual domains support development in other domains that support advances and sophistication in abilities to play.

KEY TERMS

Attachment
Autonomy versus shame and doubt
Babbling
Behaviorist theory
Cephalocaudal development
Difficult child
Easy child
Expressive style
Functional play
Holophrastic speech
Insecure attachment
Interactionist theory
Language acquisition device (LAD)
Manipulative play
Nativist theory
Object permanence
Parentese
Proximodistal development
Referential style
Reflexes
Scaffolding
Secure attachment
Sensorimotor period
Separation anxiety
Separation-individuation
Slow-to-warm-up child
Stranger anxiety
Symbiosis
Symbolic play
Telegraphic speech
Temperament
Trust versus mistrust

STUDY QUESTIONS

1. How do cephalocaudal and proximodistal development explain the nature of growth in motor skills? Explain these patterns of development.
2. Describe three causes of differences in physical development.
3. Trace how emerging physical development affects how infants and toddlers play. Show the steps in the development of motor skills and play activities that can result from the new skills.
4. Explain cognitive development in terms of the sensorimotor period. How do children from different cultures vary in sensorimotor development?
5. Define symbolic or pretend play. How do toddlers engage in more sophisticated forms of symbolic play?
6. How do adults facilitate symbolic play?
7. Explain three theories of language development. How do they support an eclectic theory of language development?
8. How can cultural and ethnic differences affect language development?
9. How do adults support language through parentese? Explain how parentese facilitates language play.
10. How do the home environment and parenting practices affect social development?
11. What do theories of emotional development imply are needed for optimal emotional development?
12. How do temperament and attachment affect emotional development?
13. Explain how social games teach infants and toddlers how to play with others. Give examples.
14. What roles can adults play in supporting peer play? Why are peer play activities important for toddlers?

Chapter 5 Play in the Preschool Years

IN SPEAKING of play and its role in the preschooler's development, we are concerned with two fundamental questions; first, how play itself arises in development—its origin and genesis; second, the role of this developmental activity that we call play, as a form of development in the child of preschool age. Is play the leading form of activity for a child of this age, or is it simply the predominant form?

It seems to me that from the point of view of development, play is not the predominant form of activity, but it is in a sense, the leading source of development in the pre-school years.

(Vygotsky, 1976, p. 53)

In addition to Vygotsky's observation that play is the leading source of development in the years between the ages of 2 and 6, play characterizes the preschool years, according to Berger (2000). These authors call the preschool years "the play years."

> [t]he years of early childhood are the most playful of all, for young children spend most of their waking hours at play, acquiring the skills, ideas, and values that are crucial for growing up. They chase each other and dare themselves to attempt new tasks, developing their bodies; they play with words and ideas, developing their minds; they invent games and dramatize fantasies, learning social skills and moral rules. (p. 293)

This chapter continues the relationship between development and play as described within motor, cognitive, language, and social domains of development. Milestones in development will be noted as well as how play affects and reflects development in each domain.

Characteristics of preschool play and gender differences in play will be described, followed by the role adults have to nurture and facilitate play. This will include the nature of play in group settings. Finally, the last section of the chapter will discuss influences on children's play and how developmentally appropriate toys and materials are selected.

PHYSICAL DEVELOPMENT

The preschool years are the period when young children acquire basic motor skills. The skills fall into two categories described in Chapter 4: fine-motor and gross-motor. The reader will recall that fine-motor skills involve use of the hands and fingers, while gross-motor skills are the movements that allow the individual to become mobile and engage in skills requiring body movement. Perceptual-motor development will also be discussed in terms of the relationship between movement and the environment.

Gallahue (1993) proposes that children move through a developmental progression in the acquisition of motor skills. This progression includes the **reflexive movement phase**, the **rudimentary movement phase**, the **fundamental movement phase**, and the **specialized movement phase**. The sequence of the appearance of these phases is universal, while rate of acquisition of motor skills varies from child to child.

The reflexive movement phase ranges from birth to about 1 year of age. In this phase the infant engages in reflexive movements, as described in Chapter 4.

The rudimentary movement phase includes the basic motor skills acquired in infancy: reaching, grasping and releasing objects, sitting, standing, and walking. The skills of the rudimentary movement phase that are acquired during the first 2 years form the foundation for the fundamental phase.

The fundamental movement phase occurs during the preschool years ranging from ages 2 to 3 to ages 6 and 7. During this phase, children gain increased control over their gross- and fine-motor movements. They are involved in developing and refining motor skills such as running, jumping, throwing, and catching. Control of each skill progresses through initial and elementary stages before reaching a mature stage. Children in this phase first learn skills in isolation from one another and then are able to combine them with other skills as coordinated movement.

The specialized movement phase begins at about 7 years of age and continues through the teenage years and into adulthood.

Gallahue cautions that maturity and physical activity alone do not ensure that children will acquire fundamental movement skills in the preschool years. Children who do not master these skills are frustrated and experience failure later in recreational and sports activities. Knowledge of the process of fundamental motor skills can help early childhood educators to design appropriate curriculum and activities for children.

Characteristics of Motor Development

Gross-Motor Skills

Whereas toddlers are gaining control over basic movement skills and mobility, preschoolers refine mobility skills through a range of motor activities involving the entire body. **Gross-motor development** includes (a) locomotor dexterity, which requires balance and movement, and (b) upper-body and arm skills.

Locomotor skills are those movements that permit the child to move about in some manner, such as jumping, hopping, running, and climbing. Jambor (1990) extended this basic list to include the following types of locomotion: rolling, creeping, crawling, climbing, stepping up and down, jumping, bouncing, hurdling, hopping, pumping a swing, and pushing or pulling a wagon. Marked-time climbing, or climbing up one step at a time, is mastered by toddlers, but preschoolers can use alternating feet to climb stairs. At the latter stages of locomotor development during the preschool years, children are able to add galloping and skipping to running and jumping. They advance from riding a tricycle to a bicycle, and some older preschoolers are able to roller-skate and kick a soccer ball (Johnson, 1998; Mullen, 1984; Schickedanz et al., 1993). Two basic upper-body and arm skills that are practiced during the preschool years are throwing and catching a ball (Johnson, 1998).

Fine-Motor Skills

Preschool children gain more precision in **fine-motor development**, or the use of the hands and fingers, between the ages of 3 and 5. They acquire more control of finger movement, which allows them to become proficient in using small materials that require grasping and control. In preschool classrooms, children learn to work with puzzles; cut with scissors; use brushes, pencils, pens, and markers; and manipulate small blocks, counters, and modeling clay. They refine self-help skills used in dressing themselves by learning to button, use zippers and snaps, and tie shoelaces (Johnson, 1998; Wortham, 1996).

Perceptual-Motor Skills

Perceptual-motor development refers to the child's developing ability to interact with the environment, combining use of the senses and motor skills. The developmental process of use of perceptual or sensory skills and motor skills is viewed as a combined process. Perceptual-motor development results from the interaction between sensory perception and motor actions in increasingly complex and skillful behaviors (Jambor, 1990; Mullen, 1984). More specifically, visual, auditory, and tactile sensory abilities are combined with emerging motor skills to develop perceptual-motor abilities.

Perceptual-motor skills include body awareness, spatial awareness, directional awareness, and temporal awareness. **Body awareness** means the child's developing capacity to understand body parts, what the body parts can do, and how to make the body more efficient. **Spatial awareness** refers to knowledge of how much space the body occupies and how to use the body in space. **Directional awareness** includes understanding of location and direction of the body in space, which extends to understanding directionality and objects in space. **Temporal awareness** is the development of awareness of the relationship between movement and time. Skills involving temporal awareness include rhythm and sequence. The sequence of events using a form of rhythm or pattern reflects temporal awareness (Frost, 1992; Gallahue, 1989; Jambor, 1990).

Play and Physical Development

Play, especially outdoor play, is most commonly associated with physical exercise. Parents and teachers appreciate the child's need for opportunities for active physical activities. They may not, however, distinguish among free play, teacher-directed motor skills activities, and adult-directed sports. While each type of activity provides opportunities for physical exercise, play is different in that it is initiated by the child.

Children today are more sedentary than they were 20 years ago (Helm & Boos, 1996). Inappropriate nutrition has resulted in an increase in obesity and poor physical condition, and young children with elevated blood pressure and cholesterol (Frost, 1992; Mullen, 1984; Santrock, 2002). The increased number of both parents and single parents working outside the home has resulted in large numbers of latchkey children and children in after-school care (Frost, 1992; Helm & Boos, 1996). If today's children are to develop motor skills in the preschool years, they must be engaged in physical exercise through both directed physical education programs and opportunities for free play in preschool and other group settings (Mullen, 1984).

Directed Physical Play

Organized sports for preschool children are gaining in popularity. Four- and 5-year-old boys and girls often have the choice of participating on a soccer or T-ball team. Six-year-olds can join a football team. Gymnastic lessons frequently are offered for children as young as 3 years. Children enjoy these group activities and sports, are proud of their uniforms, and look forward to the games and performances. If handled correctly by adults, sports can have a positive effect, including the social experiences of being a part of a group. Nevertheless, sports activities are structured and adult led, and physical activities are limited to those related to the sport.

Motor skills activities likewise are directed by an adult. They play an important role in gross-motor development because the teacher can work with children in a variety of activities that ensure that the child will develop the desired physical movements. Children's physical development can be evaluated and attention given to correct inappropriate movements that can be an impediment to the child in later years when participating in sports and recreational physical activities (Gallahue, 1993; Mullen, 1984; Pica, 1997).

Because increasing numbers of preschool children spend much of their day in group settings, either child care or preschool classrooms in public schools, there is a growing awareness of the need for directed motor skills programs (Gabbard, 1995; Helm & Boos, 1996). Programs need to be developmental, in that they reflect activities that are appropriate for the developmental needs of preschool children (Sanders, 2002). Evidence indicates that quality programs can have positive results for motor development (Bohren & Vlahov, 1989). These developmental motor skills programs should not be confused with perceptual skills programs originally designed to help students with academic difficulties. Perceptual-motor programs have been used widely in preschool programs despite research that indicates that they are not effective in remediation of learning disabilities or appropriate for preschool classrooms (Campbell, 1997; Frost, 1992; Gallahue, 1993). A comprehensive preschool program should include locomotor skills to include walking, running, hopping, throwing, catching, and other motor skills described earlier in this chapter (Gallahue, 1993; Sanders, 2002). Fine-motor activities such as block construction, sand play, and art activities should be included in the overall program (Frost, 1992; Pica, 1995).

Few physical educators in public schools are trained to provide appropriate motor development programs for preschool children. Likewise, child care staff are not likely to have training in motor skill development. Collaborative planning between early childhood educators and physical education educators is needed if programs are to be developmentally appropriate for young children (Gabbard, 1979, 1995; Helm & Boos, 1996). Helpful information on movement programs can be found in *Active for Life* (Sanders, 2002).

Free Play

Motor skills can also be developed in free play on a playground that is equipped appropriately. Play environments with play apparatus that includes opportunities for upper-body exercise contribute to increased muscular endurance (Frost, 1992; Gabbard, 1979). Myers (1985) compared motor behaviors of kindergarten children who participated in a physical education class with children who participated on a well-developed playground during free play. She found that the children in free play engaged in significantly more motor behaviors in free play than in the structured physical education classes. Nevertheless, Frost (1992) suggests that the most effective teacher might be the one who provides a balance between directed and free-play activities.

Although a full range of motor skills can be nurtured through adult-directed activities, the opportunity for children to engage in physical movements related to spontaneous, natural play is needed as well. Young children particularly need to be outdoors where there is space for all kinds of physical movement as they engage in play activities alone or with their friends. Moreover, they need time and opportunity to participate in the social, sociodramatic, and cognitive elements possible in physical play. Since many parents feel a need to restrict children's play because of the dangers in contemporary urban and suburban environments and since sports activities may limit time for outdoor play in a neighborhood setting, schools and other preschool centers should be aware of their responsibility in maintaining time for play both indoors and outdoors for the child's physical development (Wortham, 1996).

Adult Roles in Physical Play

In an era when children spend large amounts of time watching television or video games rather than engaging in physical play, adults have a major responsibility in being diligent in including outdoor playtime for preschool children. Parents need to understand the need for free play at home or in a nearby public park. Teachers need to become knowledgeable about motor skill development and how they can develop structured activities that will include modeling of motor skills (Campbell, 1997; Sanders, 2002). They also need to include outdoor free play or similar play in an indoor physical play space. Teachers in public schools where recess has been eliminated or limited to structured activities need to become advocates for time for free physical play.

WHAT PARENTS, CAREGIVERS, AND TEACHERS CAN DO TO PROMOTE PHYSICAL PLAY

1. Adults can ensure that preschool children are given daily opportunities to engage in motor play.
2. Adults can make sure that the outdoor play environment contains play equipment that include opportunities to exercise all types of motor skills.
3. Adults can become advocates for outdoor play. Parents should find out the status of free-play opportunities in their child's preschool center and insist that it be a part of the daily schedule (see Chapter 11).
4. Caregivers and teachers of preschool children should learn how to lead activities for the development of motor skills.
5. Caregivers in after-school programs for preschool programs should include opportunities for free physical play and limit television viewing when children are in their care.
6. Caregivers and preschool teachers can develop their schedule to alternate between quiet and more active play experiences.
7. Parents can be intentional in taking children to areas for physical play if there are no spaces at home.
8. Parents can limit television viewing and encourage children to engage in physical play instead.
9. Parents and caregivers can accept gender differences in play and support play behaviors of both males and females. (See the discussion of gender differences in play discussed later in this chapter and in Chapter 7.)

COGNITIVE DEVELOPMENT

Children make major strides in cognitive development in the preschool years. These are years when children have more opportunities to explore the environment and learn new information. In this part of the chapter, we will discuss how changes in thinking skills broaden children's knowledge about their world.

Characteristics of Cognitive Development

Preschool children are characterized by preoperational thought. They have moved from the limitations of a sensorimotor approach to understanding their world to one of symbolism and intuitive thinking, as described in the next subsection.

Cognitive-Developmental Theory: Preoperational Thought

Children between the ages of 2 and 7 are in Piaget's (1936/1952) **preoperational stage** of development. In this stage, children are able to represent objects and events mentally, thus permitting more complex symbolism. However, they are controlled by their perception; that is, they understand concepts in terms of what they can see.

Preoperational children are described as **egocentric.** The child is concerned with her own thoughts and ideas and cannot consider the point of view of others. These characteristics of the preoperational period develop within two substages, the symbolic function substage and the intuitive thought substage.

The **symbolic function substage** occurs between the ages of 2 and 4. Symbolic thought allows the child to picture things mentally that are not present. Young children who have achieved symbolic function can use art experiences, especially scribbling, to represent things in their environment such as houses, trees, flowers, and people. Symbolism also allows them to engage in pretend play.

Egocentrism in this substage results in the child's inability to distinguish between her own perspective and the perspective of another child or adult. In play, the child assumes that other children share her feelings and thoughts. She believes that other children share her feelings and may have difficulty relating to another child's ideas or emotions that are different from her own.

Piaget also characterized preoperational thinking as animistic in young children who may believe that inanimate objects are alive and can take action on their own. For example, he asked children about the movement of clouds and found that they believed that clouds propel themselves in the sky.

Between the ages of 4 and 7, the preoperational child enters the **intuitive thought substage,** when primitive reasoning begins. The child's thought process is changing from one of symbolic thinking to intuitive, or inner, thinking. The child can organize objects into primitive collections but is unable to group objects in a consistent manner. This primitive system of organization is caused by centration. The child tends to center, or focus, on one characteristic or attribute. Two attributes cannot be considered at one time. As a result, the child may change from attribute to another when trying to organize a group of objects. If the child is asked to put a collection of shapes of different color into groups with the same characteristic, he can organize them by shape or by color, or he might change from one to the other during the activity. Once the child is able to move beyond centering, developmental characteristics of the concrete operational stage can emerge that include **classification** and **conservation** (Piaget, 1936, 1952).

Conservation is the ability to understand that the physical attributes of material remain consistent, even altered or rearranged. For example, a child who can conserve understands that a ball of clay has the same amount when the shape is changed or that the number of coins in a row is the same whether spaced close together or farther apart.

The ability to classify permits the child to consider the characteristics of objects (color, size, shape, texture, etc.) and to organize them into groups using a scheme for establishing the groups.

Now the child can take the group of shapes used in the example above and decide to group them by color while ignoring their shape or organize them by shape while ignoring their different colors.

Recent Research and Preoperational Thought

Many studies have reexamined Piaget's perception of thought in the preoperational stage of development. Do young children have animistic beliefs, and are they egocentric? Familiarity with the environment seems to be a factor in the nature of how preoperational children think. Gelman (1972) found that children can conserve number when the task includes three or four items instead of six or seven. Likewise, children can form global categories of familiar objects denoting that the capacity to classify hierarchically is present in the preschool years (Mandler, Bauer, & McDonough, 1991; Mervis & Crisafi, 1982; Ricco, 1989). Children's ability to adapt their conversations to fit the listener, such as a younger child, contradicts the notion that they are egocentric (Gelman & Shatz, 1978).

Research studies have revealed that familiarity with objects affects animistic thinking. Researchers in this characteristic believe that Piaget asked children about objects with which they had little experience. When questioned about more familiar objects, such as crayons, children know that they are not alive. They make errors about vehicles because they appear to move on their own, but they err because of incomplete knowledge rather than the belief that inanimate objects are alive (Dolgin & Behrend, 1984).

Magical thinking (when children believe something magical or supernatural makes something happen) is also related to familiarity. Children believe that fairies and witches have supernatural powers, but people and objects related to their everyday experiences don't. They think magic is related to events that they cannot explain, but as they gain more experience, their beliefs in magic decline (Phelps & Woolley, 1994; Subbotsky, 1994).

Flavell and his colleagues (Flavell, Green, & Flavell, 1987) studied whether children are bound by perception. They found that young children were easily tricked by appearance versus reality. It was not until they were 6 or 7 years old that they could do well on appearance versus reality tasks. Make-believe play helps children master this concept. Children can differentiate between pretend and real experiences. Pretending helps children identify what is real versus what is unreal (Woolley & Wellman, 1990).

Play and Cognitive Development

Benefits of Play on Cognitive Development

Play is considered necessary for cognitive development and learning (Ellis, 1973; Piaget, 1962). Researchers have found that preschoolers who spend more time engaged in sociodramatic play are advanced in intellectual development. In addition, children who enjoy pretending score higher on tests of imagination and creativity. Novel play with objects may enhance children's ability to think inventively (Freyberg, 1973; Pepler & Ross, 1981).

Two essential ingredients of play are the involvement of the thinking processes and repetition of social interactions. Play is the foundation of academic learning. Pretend play fosters young children's ability to reason and assists children in separating meanings from objects and thus manipulate the meanings themselves (Berk & Winsler, 1995; Yawkey & Diantoniis, 1984; Vygotsky, 1976).

Theoretical Views of Play and Cognitive Development

There are variations on how cognitive play develops in the young child. Piaget described levels of cognitive play that built on the work of Karl Buhler (1937). Smilansky (Smilansky & Shefatya, 1990) gave a different interpretation to levels of play in cognitive development. Vygotsky (1976) perceived that play permitted the child to function at a cognitive level higher than exhibited in other types of activities. Each of these theoretical approaches to developing hierarchical categories in cognitive play will be described, followed by more recent perceptions of developmental characteristics of cognitive play.

Piaget's Levels of Cognitive Play. Piaget's two levels of play, practice play and symbolic play, have been discussed in Chapter 4. Practice or functional play appear during the sensorimotor period, while symbolic play first appears in the sensorimotor period and develops into dramatic play in the preoperational period. Games with rules characterize the concrete operations period and continue in the formal operations period (Frost, 1992; Piaget, 1962; Rogers & Sawyers, 1988).

During the years from 4 through 7, dramatic or symbolic play is characterized as imitation of reality. Piaget described preschool dramatic play as including the features of orderliness, exact imitation of reality, and collective symbolism of play roles (Piaget, 1962; Rogers & Sawyers, 1988). In dramatic play, children develop play themes and carry them out by playing different roles. Dramatic play enables children to use pretend or fantasy in their play in a more organized fashion as they engage in pretend play in more complex forms.

Piaget's highest category of play is games with rules, which emerges between the ages of 7 and 12. During these years, symbolic play declines and becomes rule governed. Children play games such as marbles with set rules. They are interested in competitive games. Children are becoming socialized as reflected in the ability to engage in activities in which rules must be followed.

Smilansky's Levels of Cognitive Play. Although Piaget did not describe collective dramatic play in terms of sociodramatic play, Smilansky (1968) included this category in stages of play development. She also included construction play as a category. She did not organize categories by levels of cognitive development but proposed that children from the age of 3 to school age alternate between the different types of play at different levels of complexity (Smilansky & Shefatya, 1990).

Smilansky described functional play as the first form to appear and continues in the early childhood years. It is based on the child's need for physical activity. The child uses repetition in physical actions, language, and manipulation of toys.

Constructive play first appears in early childhood and continues into adulthood. Sensorimotor activity is combined with a preconceived plan and creativity. The child has moved from handling objects and materials to constructing or building something.

Although Piaget described games with rules as the most complex form of play that emerges in the concrete operations period, Smilansky described this type of play as more elaborate. The child must be able to accept and adjust to prearranged rules. Social interactions are required including the ability to control behavior and actions within rules. Games with rules also continue into adult life.

Dramatic play or pretend play first emerges during the 2nd year in the form of pretend behavior. Dramatic play, for Smilansky, permits the child to imitate human relationships through symbolic representations. However, the symbolic representations are person oriented rather than object related, as found in symbolic play of younger children. When children can engage in person-oriented play with other children in various roles, dramatic play has achieved its most complex form, sociodramatic play (Smilansky & Shefatya, 1990), which will be further described under "Social Development."

Vygotsky's Perceptions of the Functions of Play. Vygotsky (1976) focused on representational play and fantasy play rather than on stages of play. He described representational or make-believe play that emerges at the end of toddlerhood, develops in the early childhood years, and evolves into games with rules.

Representational play has specific functions. First, it permits the child to deal with "unrealizable desires" (Berk & Winsler, 1995). Fantasy play appears when toddlers must learn to follow approved behaviors and delay gratification. As the child matures, more rules and routines are expected, fantasy play expands. The child engages in imaginary play that is governed by rules.

Representational play, as described in Chapter 2, also allows children to separate objects and meaning. When the child substitutes one object for another, the representation helps the child separate an object's real meaning to a pretend meaning. Pretend play, then, represented in separating meaning from objects, serves as preparation for later abstract thinking and use of symbols for literacy (Berk & Winsler, 1995; Vygotsky, 1976).

For Vygotsky, the essential feature of play is self-restraint. In play the child subordinates momentary desires to play roles. Moreover, the child willingly follows set rules for imaginary play that enable the child to follow rules in real life. Vygotsky (1976) believed that young children are able to follow such games with rules much younger than the age characterized in Piaget's stage of games with rules. He felt that observance of rules in fantasy play in the early childhood years leads to game play in the middle childhood years.

Characteristics of Cognitive Play

Current Views of Categories of Cognitive Play

The work of Piaget, Vygotsky, and Smilansky provide a sound framework for understanding the role of play in cognitive play and vice versa. When the views of these theorists are combined, a more comprehensive picture emerges. Categories still guide our understanding of cognitive development and play:

Functional Play (Piaget, Smilansky)

Constructive Play (Smilansky, Vygotsky)

Symbolic/Representational/Dramatic Play (Piaget, Smilansky, Vygotsky)

Games with Rules (Piaget, Smilansky, Vygotsky)

Recent researchers caution against viewing play in terms of levels of performance or hierarchies (Johnson, 1998; Takhvar & Smith, 1990; Tegano & Burdette, 1991). Some researchers propose that children's play is complex and exceeds classification into categories. Children can be engaged in several categories of play simultaneously (Takhvar & Smith, 1991). Moreover, not only do play episodes include multiple categories that go beyond cognitive categories of play, but, "there is a need for additional modifiers to capture something about play tempo, intensity, style, and other important qualifiers. There is also the need to note information about the play setting and context" (Johnson, 1998,p. 146). The work of current researchers thus characterizes cognitive play as overlapping in both developmental levels and categories of play.

Functional play begins with practice play and play with objects in infancy. In early childhood, object play becomes more complex and goal oriented and incorporates construction play. Preschoolers use increasingly complex constructions that are elaborated by 5- and 6-year-olds through social interactions (Johnson, 1998; Rubin, Fein, & Vandenberg, 1983).

Representational or symbolic play also emerges prior to the early childhood years. Symbolic play begins with substitution or representation of one object for another (Piaget, 1936/1952; Vygotsky, 1976) and becomes more complex in dramatic play that includes imitating, imagining, dramatizing and role play in the early childhood years. Again, social interactions impact dramatic play, as do language and motor development. The interaction of domains of development on play with be addressed later in the chapter.

Finally, games with rules begin early in life, particularly in the early childhood years for Vygotsky (Berk & Winsler, 1995; Vygotsky, 1976). Piaget and Smilansky placed games with rules in the school-age years. Johnson (1998) clarifies this process by reporting that preschool children can observe the rules in simple games such as lotto, matching games, and games with spinners and dice. More sophisticated games with rules become possible when children achieve concrete operations.

As researchers continue to investigate cognitive play, they reinforce the understanding that the role of play on cognitive development is complex. Definitions of categories and levels of play are affected by many variables. For example, Tegano and Burdette (1991) found that length of time in play facilitated transformation of functional play to constructive play, while Takhvar and Smith (1990) found that Smilansky's categories of play are parallel rather than hierarchical.

Adult Roles in Cognitive Play

If children are to benefit from cognitive play, adults have a role in providing play activities that will lead to thinking and problem solving. Vygotsky (1978) proposed that more competent cognitive activities occur when the environment includes rich and varied materials. However, it is the adults who enhance the activities through social interactions. In addition, if adults provide emotional security, children have a secure base for exploration of the environment (Howes & Smith, 1995).

Teacher and caregivers can further encourage cognitive and problem solving by teaching children to use their senses. Through modeling playful behaviors and problem solving through guided imagery using intervention lessons with senses, teachers can help young children to be more playful in their free-play interactions with their peers (Boyer, 1997a, 1997b).

Adults must distinguish between play as manipulation and play that is active education if they are to facilitate cognition through play. When children are merely manipulating materials without using cognitive processes, they are not constructing understanding. An example of play as manipulation can be found on many preschool playgrounds. Many climbing structures designed within the last 15 years contain tic-tac-toe games in the form of cubes that can be rotated. Because most preschool children have little or no knowledge of the game, they turn the cubes to see the Xs and Os rotate rather than manipulate them to play the game. However, what initially appears as manipulative play can, in fact, be rich cognitive play. Teachers in a preschool classroom were concerned that new flexible wheel blocks were only used for constructing wheels that could be rolled. Extended observation revealed that the construction and play with the wheels included the use of various types of mathematical and other concepts (Seo, 2003).

When children are engaged in active education, interest, play, experimentation, and cooperation are brought to the activity. For example, when children challenge themselves in practice play with jump ropes by trying to jump longer or jump with two ropes, they exhibit some intent to learn. Likewise, experimentation is used when children construct props for dramatic play or use cooperative negotiation when planning a dramatic play event (Chaille & Silvern, 1996). Again, the types of materials and play opportunities teachers provide make a difference in cognitive development through play (Gmitrova & Gmitrov, 2003).

WHAT PARENTS, CAREGIVERS, AND TEACHERS CAN DO TO PROMOTE COGNITIVE PLAY

1. Ensure that toys and materials provided children are open-ended and promote problem solving.
2. Provide opportunities for children to engage in dramatic play that encourages cooperation and negotiation.
3. Make available materials that encourage representation through construction.
4. Provide art materials that encourage expression of ideas through art experiences.
5. Offer simple games that include rules that preschool children can follow.
6. Provide learning activities that accentuate the senses and playfulness that can be incorporated into play.
7. Engage children in simple games and cognitive activities that can later be played independently.
8. Make sure that construction and art materials are available in both the indoor and outdoor play environments.
9. Ensure that there are dramatic play materials in both the indoor and outdoor play environments.

LANGUAGE AND LITERACY DEVELOPMENT

Characteristics of Language Development

The preschool years are significant for language development in young children. Between the years of 2 and 6, children learn about 10,000 words. Language development is related to advances in cognitive development, follows rules of language, and is characterized by development in vocabulary, grammar, and pragmatics (Berk, 2002).

Rule Systems

Concurrent with acquisition of a remarkable number of words, children in the preschool years learn the rules of their language; that is, they learn **morphology rules, syntax rules,** and **semantic rules.** Morphology and syntax rules relate to understanding of the sounds and grammar of language, while semantic rules explain vocabulary and meaning development.

Grammatical Development. By the age of 2, toddlers typically speak in two-word utterances mostly composed of nouns and verbs with some adjectives and adverbs. As they develop longer statements, typical sentences contain four and five words by age 5. As children become able to express themselves using longer sentences, they demonstrate that they know rules of morphology, or the use of plurals, possession, and tense in nouns and verbs. For example, they are able to use the word *cats* when they are talking about more than one cat and can use prepositions to denote location such as *in* and *on*.

Complexity and length of verbal strings or utterances also reveal that the children are learning the syntactical rules or how words should be ordered in a sentence. They learn to ask questions and to make negative statements (Santrock, 2000).

The third system of rules in language development is semantic rules, or the knowledge of meanings of words. Understanding of semantic rules is demonstrated through the children's use of an expanding vocabulary in the preschool years.

Vocabulary Development. Young preschool children acquire vocabulary at the astonishing rate of an average of five words per day (Berk, 2002). Words are added daily in groups and make some basic assumptions about a word's meaning. Thereafter, children refine understanding of the meaning of the word as it is heard again and used in different contexts. Children also develop understanding of the meaning of words by contrasting them with words they already know (Berk, 2002).

Pragmatic Development. Preschool children also learn the rules of conversation. The **pragmatics of language** are the rules of carrying on a conversation. Children must be able to learn to communicate with others in their language community. They must be able to listen to the statements made by others, ask questions, and interpret language functions required in conversations.

The ability to participate in a conversation develops at a very early age and is extended and refined as the child expands language abilities and has experiences in conversations. By the age of 4, preschool children have some understanding of the culturally accepted ways to carry on a conversation in their culture (Berk, 2002).

Characteristics of Literacy Development

Literacy development is directly related to language development. Literacy is defined as the ability to read and write. Although much communication is accomplished through oral language, the ability to read and write extends possibilities for transmitting and receiving information. As researchers learn more about how children become literate, it is clear that literacy, like oral language, begins in infancy; nevertheless, rapid advances are made in the development of literacy in the preschool years.

Although very young children are unable to interpret words in print and to write using adult forms of the alphabet and standard spelling, they become aware of books and written language at a very young age. Like acquisition of oral language, literacy occurs through interaction within the child's language and literacy community. The uses of literacy that are experienced by the child through day-to-day living are the forces that influence the child's enculturation into reading and writing. The literacy activities within the child's language and cultural community will affect that child's understanding of the purposes and functions of literacy (Dyson & Genishi, 1993; Wortham, 1996).

Building on oral language development with books and environmental print, preschool children develop strategies for becoming literate. As a result of their experiences, children gradually come to understand that print, not just pictures, gives meaning to books. They come to recognize print, as well as the spacing between words, and learn that individual letters are used to form words (Fields & Spangler, 1995; Roskos & Christie, 2002; Roskos, Christie, & Richgels, 2003).

Young children also develop literacy through writing efforts. They use scribbles, mock letters, letter reversals, and other print efforts as part of their natural growth toward literacy. Preschool children use trial and error and hypothesis testing in their efforts to understand reading and writing, just as they do in acquiring oral language (Morrow, 1997; Roskos & Christie, 2002; Roskos, Christie, & Richgels, 2003).

Variations in Language and Literacy Development

Although all children learn the language of their culture and achieve major milestones in language development by the age of 6, differences occur in language achievement. When children enter kindergarten, language differences can be great.

There are differences in families and cultures as to how much and what type of language is used. As a result, differences in language acquisition can be documented. First, girls tend to be more proficient than boys, and middle-class children are more advanced in language than lower-income children. Single-born children are more proficient than twins, and triplets are less proficient than twins (Berk, 2002).

Researchers who have studied familial and cultural differences in the language children hear have found that mothers talk more to daughters than to sons. Middle-class parents use more elaborated language with their children, while parents in all groups talk more to first-born children than to later-born children and multiple-birth children. Some adults use strategies that foster language development such as encouraging the child to talk and providing specific responses to the child's comments. Using Vygotsky's ideas on scaffolding, some parents provide new topics for discussion through experiences such as looking at and conversing about picture books and taking excursions to new places in the community (Genishi & Dyson, 1984).

Play and Language and Literacy Development

When the relationship between language development and play is described, play can be discussed in two categories: how children play with language and how language is used in play. In the following sections, children's play with language will be explained followed by the role of play in language development and in literacy development.

Play with Language

In Chapter 4, very young children's play with language was described as sound play by infants and play with speech within a grammatical pattern by toddlers. This process continues in the preschool child as part of a system of play with language. Pellegrini (1984, p. 46) describes speech play as "[a] mode whereby young children explore and manipulate the many aspects of their language system." The play process includes play with the phonological, semantic, and pragmatic aspects of language in which the process of the play is more important than communication. Cazden (1974) proposes that children explore the elements of language and develop a metalinguistic awareness or understanding of the rule system through play with language.

Cazden also explains that there is a hierarchy in how children play with language. Play with phonological sounds occurs first in the infant followed by syntactical play when toddlers are able to use two-word utterances in telegraphic speech. Semantic play involves play with word meanings that later advances to the use of narratives and rhymes (Opie & Opie, 1959). Cazden warns that the categories do not develop independently, nor do they imply that one precedes the other. For example, Pellegrini (1984) cites Bruner's (1974, 1975) research in which infants conveyed meaning to caregivers through gestures rather than sounds. Likewise, McCune (1985) considers the use of an object in pretend play to be the equivalent of using a word to label the imagined object.

Davidson (1998) provides many examples of children's play with language. She describes the phonological play of a toddler who had completed building with blocks as follows:

> Now it's don un un
>
> Done un un un un. (Garvey, 1990, p. 62, cited in Davidson, 1998)

Examples of more purposeful play are children's use of jokes such as knock-knock jokes or inappropriate use of words. Thus, a 2-year-old says "meow" as the sound for a dog in a farmyard picture and a 4-year-old calls her doll "Poopy-head" (Davidson, 1998).

Play and Language Development

Beginning efforts to play with language are solitary activities as infants babble and play with language sounds. Older children collaborate in play with language in telling jokes and using chants and parodies of rhymes. When language is used in play, it is necessarily a social event. It is used as a tool in their play, especially pretend or dramatic play (Davidson, 1998). Language is used to plan play episodes, carry out roles, and talk about play events.

When planning for play, children must use persuasive language if they are to prevail in the play event that follows. During dramatic play, the child must use tone of voice and expressions that are representative of the role or character that is being played. The language children use when playing pretend is similar to the language they have heard from books. The language they use is like a story when they play a character or narrate their play with small figures (Davidson, 1998).

Children demonstrate metalinguistic awareness when they talk about the language they will use in pretend play. They might give instructions to each other as to what should be said and how the children should express their part of the dialogue or conversation in play. An example is when one child tells another, "You need to yell at me to clean, 'cause you're the mean stepsister" (Davidson, 1998, p. 181).

Play and Literacy Development

Pretend play also has a role in the development of literacy in preschool children. The ability to use pretend talk and symbolism is related to literacy. The storylike language used by children in role play described earlier and the explicit and elaborated language used in dramatic play episodes can be related to later literacy (Roskos, 1990). Symbolic transformations used by 3-year-olds in play predicts their writing status at age 5, and their use of oral language in dramatic play predicts later reading achievement (Roskos & Neuman, 1998).

Dramatic play that involves role play and make-believe supports the development of literate oral language because children are motivated to generate explicit and elaborated language in their play. Engaging in sociodramatic play leads to the later ability to encode information in words (Pellegrini, 1984).

Children who experience opportunities for dramatic play that include information about literacy are more directly informed about components of literacy. Teachers in preschool settings and parents can provide literacy experiences that promote literacy development through play

WHAT PARENTS, CAREGIVERS, AND TEACHERS CAN DO TO PROMOTE LANGUAGE AND LITERACY PLAY

1. Promote language play by engaging in play experiences with children and by modeling expanded language, language in dramatic play roles, and suggestions for how language can be used in play events.
2. Promote literacy play by providing props and materials for dramatic play that encourages the incorporation of literacy behaviors.
3. Encourage literacy play by showing approval when children incorporate literacy materials in play.
4. Facilitate literacy play by joining in play and modeling the use of literacy materials.
5. Promote literacy by planning theme centers that focus on literacy activities.

(Neuman & Roskos, 1993; Roskos & Neuman, 1993, 1998; Roskos & Christie, 2002).

Adult Roles in Language and Literacy Play

Adults make a difference in the development of language and literacy through play. It has already been established that the use of expanded language with children results in a higher level of language development than the use of restricted language (Wilcox-Herzog & Kontos, 1998).

Adult support and participation in children's play also can promote the development of language and literacy. Children play at higher levels, stay on-task, and solve more problems when teachers make suggestions, ask open-ended questions, and use elaborated language (Klenk, 2001; Pellegrini, 1984; Roskos & Christie, 2002).

Literacy can also be promoted through adult support and participation in play. Through play, children engage in social routines and skills that are related to reading and writing (Roskos & Neuman, 1993). Adults can facilitate literacy development by providing materials such as writing pads and pencils for center play (Christie, 1994; Vukelich, 1989). Theme centers such as an office or a topic that entails reading and writing can enhance children's interest in using developmental literacy skills (Klenk, 2001).

Teachers and caregivers can engage in children's literacy play by observing and encouraging the use of literacy activities in play, joining play that includes the use of books and writing materials, or providing literacy objects as children participate in a play event (Roskos & Neuman, 1993). The teacher can take a leadership role by introducing specific literacy props and modeling how children can incorporate literacy activities into their play (Roskos & Christie, 2002; Roskos & Neuman, 1993; Vukelich, 1989).

SOCIAL DEVELOPMENT

Characteristics of Social-Emotional Development

During the preschool years, children increasingly understand themselves as individuals; in addition, they understand themselves as part of a social world. They are becoming more autonomous, and their cognitive abilities permit them to understand how they fit into their family and a group of friends. Important characterizations of social and emotional development are **self-concept, self-esteem**, and **self-regulation of emotions**. Relationships with others are exhibited through the development of **empathy** and

social competence. The nature and direction of social-emotional development are affected by relationships with their parents, siblings, and peers. They are in Erikson's stage of initiative versus guilt described in Chapter 4. If they can become secure about separating from their parents and feel competent in their abilities, they can develop autonomy and eagerly participate in new tasks and experiences.

Self-Concept

A major social accomplishment between the ages of 3 and 6 is the development of self-concept. Young children develop a firm awareness that they are separate from others and have individual characteristics. Their self-concept is partially defined by physical characteristics but more significantly by mastery of skills and competencies (Berger 2000; Berk, 2002).

Self-Esteem

Preschoolers begin the task of making judgments about their own worth and competencies. They tend to overestimate their mastery of new skills and underestimate how hard new tasks are. They feel that they are liked or disliked depending on how well they can do things and are easily influenced by parental approval or disapproval. They are rapidly acquiring new skills and translating these accomplishments into positive or negative feelings about themselves (Harter, 1990).

Self-Regulation of Emotions

Children develop an awareness and understanding of their feelings in the preschool years. As a result of their greater understanding of the causes of emotions in themselves and others, they are able to initiate behaviors that permit them to cope. Children pick up strategies for coping with emotions from their parents. Those whose parents have difficulty controlling anger and hostility have similar problems (Gottman & Katz, 1989). Children who have difficulties in controlling negative emotions also tend to get along poorly with peers (Berk, 2002; Eisenberg et al., 1993).

Empathy

A significant characteristic of the preschool years is the development of empathy—the ability to understand and respond to the feelings of others. Preschoolers can provide comfort and support for a peer, sibling, or parent. Expanding language development enables them to use words as well as gestures to console another. They can explain another child's emotions as well as the causes. Children who exhibit empathy are more likely to be able to use positive social behavior (Berger, 2000; Eisenberg & Miller, 1987).

Parent-Child Relationships

Social-emotional development is affected by the relationships children have with their parents and other adults as well as with other children. Perhaps the most significant relationship is the one with parents and caregivers because of their influence in guiding the child's development. Factors that affect the parent-child relationship include parenting style, the child's temperament, and the type of discipline that is used. The dynamic nature of the interaction of these three factors is complex, and social development occurs within the tension among them. Parents can have authoritarian, authoritative, and permissive parenting styles, with many variations. The child's temperament in turn influences the parenting style the parent adopts. A child who is compliant makes it easy for a parent to be authoritative, while a difficult child's behaviors make it more likely that authoritarian parenting strategies will be felt to be necessary (Dix, 1991). A positive fit between the parenting style and the child's personality have more positive results on the child's social and emotional development than a poor fit between the two (Kochanska, 1993).

Sibling Relationships

A preschool child's social-emotional development is also impacted by the relationship with siblings in the family. Siblings have a strong but different relationship than parents and children.

There is a wide variation in sibling relationships that is affected by the personalities of the children, birth order, and parent-child relationships. In addition, parent-child relationships are different for each child. The influence that siblings have on a preschool child's social and emotional development can be nurturing and supporting or full of conflict (Berger, 2000).

Peer Relationships

Peer relationships also affect the social-emotional development of preschool children. Social development is affected by the opportunities the child has to engage in activities with other children. Preschool children who attend day care or a preschool program have more opportunity to interact socially; however, the quality of the program can affect whether the child becomes more socially competent or, instead, more assertive and aggressive (Hayes, Palmer, & Zaslow, 1990; Zigler & Lang, 1990).

Social Competence

Progress in the characteristics of social development in the preschool years leads to social competence. Indeed, social competence is the overarching characteristic of positive social development.

A definition of social competence is difficult to describe because it is understood differently by researchers. Creasey, Jarvis, and Berk (1998, p. 118) have synthesized diverse descriptors and definitions to the following: "socially competent children exhibit a positive demeanor around or toward others, have accurate social information processing abilities, and display social behaviors that lead them to be well liked by others."

Various factors can affect the child's development of social competence. Infants with insecure attachment can be predicted to be more dependent and less curious and have less positive affect during social interactions, leading to less optimal relationships with peers during the preschool years (Creasey et al., 1998). Later interactions with parents and siblings affect social competence. The child's social network of parents and siblings provides opportunities to observe and practice social skills that can be introduced into emerging peer relationships (MacDonald & Parke, 1984). Parents and caregivers also influence social competence by arranging social interactions and coaching young children on how to interact appropriately in social interactions.

Quality of attachment to preschool teachers and quality of caregiving settings has an impact on social competence. Children who are enrolled in poor-quality day care have more problems with social competence than children enrolled in high-quality day care (Howes & Stewart, 1987; Howes & Matheson, 1992). As a result, factors external to family influences can "support, compensate for, or even undermine the influence of the family context" (Creasey et al., 1998, p. 120).

Play and Social-Emotional Development

Earlier in the chapter, we characterized the preschool years as the play years. This description is particularly apt for social development because much of the progress occurs through play. In this part of the chapter, we will review the relationship of theory to social play as well as current perspectives on the developmental progression of social play. With this theoretical foundation in place, characteristics of social play will be discussed to include play and social competence, sociodramatic play, and variations in the development of social play.

Theoretical Views of Play and Social Development

Piaget's cognitive-developmental theory, Erickson's psychosocial theory, and Vygotsky's sociocultural theory have significant contributions for understanding the relationship between play and social development. In addition, Sutton-Smith has advocated that play can also be viewed from an evolutionary perspective.

Although Piaget (1962) felt that play has a primary role in the child's development, he placed little emphasis on play as a factor in the child's responses to the social environment. Nevertheless, he saw a role for peer interactions within play for social-cognitive development. More specifically, play interactions helped children understand that other players have perspectives different than their own. Play, for Piaget, provides children with opportunities to develop social competence through ongoing interactions.

Erikson (1950) maintained that there is a relationship between make-believe play and wider society. Make-believe permits children to learn about their social world and to try out new social skills. Moreover, play facilitates the understanding of cultural roles and to integrate accepted social norms into their own personalities. For Erikson, like Piaget, play promotes a child who is socially competent (Creasey et al., 1998).

Vygotsky's sociocultural theory has a significant role for play in that he proposed that make-believe play in the preschool years is vital for the acquisition of social and cognitive competence. Vygotsky suggested that make-believe play required children to initiate an imaginary situation and follow a set of rules to play out the situation; the child is able to act separately from reality. This type of play helps children choose between courses of action (Creasey et al., 1998). Make-believe play also forces young children to control their impulses and subject themselves to the rules of play; moreover, Vygotsky believed that all imaginary situations devised by young children follow social rules. Through make-believe play, children develop an understanding of social norms and try to uphold those social expectations (Berk, 1994).

Sutton-Smith (1976) and others maintain that there is a relationship between play and evolution. Much of children's social play resembles that of primates and is necessary for survival. For example, rough-and-tumble play, in which both children and primates engage, offers a survival benefit in that it provides experiences in being dominant that later promote self-confidence in social interactions. It must be noted that more recently Sutton-Smith (1997) has embraced a wider understanding of play. He suggests that the usual psychological theories of play present a sanitized, middle-class perspective of play (Vandenberg, 1985). The negative social attributes of play, such as violence and aggression, are given less importance. In addition, he believes that too much stress has been placed on the function of play to promote development and progress and to describe what is done by immature organisms (Sutton-Smith, 1997). Sutton-Smith currently is expanding his understanding and definition of play described within seven rhetorics of play (Sutton-Smith, 1997, undated).

Characteristics of Social Play

Social development in the preschool years permits young children to include others in their pretend and dramatic play. While infants and toddlers use their ability to symbolize in solitary play, preschoolers use their expanded cognitive and social abilities to play with their peers (Bretherton, 1986). In this section, some aspects of social play that contribute to social development and vice versa will be discussed. The characteristics include understanding the developmental levels of social play, play and social competence, the expression of emotions or feelings through play, and sociodramatic play.

Developmental Levels of Social Play

We are indebted to the work of Parten (1932) in observing and describing how social play develops in preschool children. In her studies of young children, Parten observed that social play increases with age. As introduced in Chapter 2, she described development of social play into six categories: unoccupied behavior, onlooker behavior, solitary play, parallel play, associative play, and cooperative play. The first two categories are considered to be nonplay behavior, and the last three categories are indicators of social participation (Berk, 2002; Caster, 1984; Frost, 1992). Frost (1992) defines the six categories as follows:

Unoccupied Behavior. The child is not playing but occupies herself with watching anything that happens to be of momentary interest. When there is nothing exciting taking place, she plays with her own body, gets on and off chairs, just stands around, follows the teacher, or sits in one spot glancing around the room (playground).

Onlooker Behavior. The child spends most of her time watching the other children play. She often talks to the children being observed, asks questions or give suggestions, but does not overtly enter into the play. This type differs from unoccupied in that the onlooker is definitely observing particular groups of children rather than anything that happens to be exciting. The child stands or sits within speaking distance from other children.

Solitary Play. The child plays alone and independently with toys that are different from those used by the children within speaking distance and makes no effort to get close to other children. She pursues her own activity without reference to what others are doing.

Parallel Play. The child plays independently, but the activity chosen naturally brings her among other children. She plays with toys that are like those the children around her are using but she plays with the toys as she sees fit, and does not try to influence or modify the activity of the children near her. She plays beside rather than with the other children.

Associative Play. The child plays with other children. The communication concerns the common activity; there is borrowing and loaning of play materials; following one another with trains or wagons; mild attempts to control which children may or may not play in the group. All the members engage in similar activity, there is no division of labor, and no organization of the activity around materials, goal, or product. The children do not subordinate their individual interests to that of the group.

Cooperative Play. The child plays in a group that is organized for the purpose of making some material product, striving to attain some competitive goal, dramatizing situations of adult and group life, or playing formal games. (pp. 85–86)

Parten's categories of developmental levels of social play provided the first guidelines for understanding how young children progress from playing by themselves to becoming social players. Researchers have continued to refine and redefine Parten's categories in the light of their own observations of social play. Two areas of research have focused on the definition of solitary play and frequency of play in the six categories.

In Parten's classification, the child's movement from solitary play to more social categories of play is a positive developmental step. While Parten believed solitary play was the least mature form of play, subsequent research defined other more mature roles for solitary play. Kenneth H. Rubin and others have found different indicators for the role of solitary play. In what he defines as nonsocial play, Rubin (1982) found that socially competent 4-year-olds who were popular with their peers engaged in solitary or parallel play activities such as artwork and block construction. From their own work, Moore, Evertson, and Brophy (1974) found that almost half of the solitary play they observed consisted of goal-directed activities and educational play. The findings from these and other similar studies indicate that solitary play might not be the result of social immaturity but rather a desirable form of play (Moore et al., 1974; Rubin, 1982; Rubin, Maioni, & Hornung, 1976).

Another area of research has been the percentages of children who engage in the six categories of social play. Researchers have differed in their findings as to what percentages of children engage in parallel, associative, and cooperative play (Bakeman & Brownlee, 1980; Barnes, 1971; Rubin et al., 1976) when compared to Parten's findings in 1932. Two conclusions have surfaced from these studies and others: today's preschoolers are less skilled in the higher levels of social play (Frost, 1992), and social class can have a bearing on levels of social play (Rubin et al., 1976; Smilansky, 1968). In addition, the context of the child's play has a bearing on the maturity demonstrated in solitary play.

Rubin and his colleagues and others have continued to develop their understanding of the progression of social play (Coplan, Rubin, Fox, Calkins, & Stewart, 1994; Rubin & Coplan, 1998; Rubin et al., 1983). Rubin and Coplan (1998) report that Piaget's structural components of play and Smilansky's stages of play can be utilized to better understand progress in social play. To understand children's social participation, observers need to view play content within the context of the play (Rubin et al., 1976). The Play Observation Scale (see Figure 5–1) developed to achieve this purpose demonstrates how a broader exploration of social play indicators was achieved (Rubin, 1986; Rubin & Coplan, 1998).

FIGURE 5–1 Play Observation Scale

	Time Sample					
	1	**2**	**3**	**4**	**5**	**6**
Transitional						
Unoccupied						
Onlooker						
Solitary:						
Constructive						
Exploratory						
Functional						
Dramatic						
Games						
Parallel:						
Constructive						
Exploratory						
Functional						
Dramatic						
Games						
Group:						
Constructive						
Exploratory						
Functional						
Dramatic						
Games						
Peer Conversation						
Double Coded Behaviors:						
Anxious behaviors						
Hovering						
Aggression						
Rough-and-Tumble						

Source: Reprinted by permission from *Multiple Perspectives on Play in Early Childhood Education* edited by Olivia N. Saracho and Bernard Spodek, the State University of New York Press.

In their continued work, researchers have made the following conclusions about levels of social play:

1. Social play becomes more prominent during the preschool years to include an increase in the frequency of social contacts, longer social episodes, and more varied social episodes (Jones, 1972; Holmberg, 1980; Rubin et al., 1978).
2. Although preschoolers tend to spend more time playing alone or near others, they play with a wider range of peers (Howes, 1983).
3. The major developmental change in preschool play is due to cognitive-developmental maturity within the categories rather than change in the amount of play in the categories. The frequency of play in the categories remains the same during the preschool years, while the significant changes come in sociodramatic play and games with rules (Rubin et al., 1978).

Sociodramatic Play

Sociodramatic play is the most advanced form of social and symbolic play. In sociodramatic play, children carry out imitation and drama and fantasy play together. Sociodramatic play involves role playing in which children imitate real-life people and experiences that they have had themselves. Make-believe is also a component because it serves as an aid to imitation. It allows the children to represent real-life events and include their imaginations in carrying out their roles. The child's abilities in sociodramatic play improve with experience, and, as she plays with different children, play becomes more varied to include new interpretations and ideas (Smilansky & Shefatya, 1990).

Smilansky (1968) characterizes six criteria of dramatic play that evolve into sociodramatic play. She defines the first four criteria as dramatic play and the last two as sociodramatic play as follows (Smilansky & Shefatya, 1990):

- *Imitative role play.* The child undertakes a make-believe role and expresses it in imitative action and/or verbalization.
- *Make-believe with regard to objects.* Movements or verbal declarations and/or materials or toys that are not replicas of the object itself are substituted for real objects.
- *Verbal make-believe with regard to actions and situations.* Verbal descriptions or declarations are substituted for actions and situations.
- *Persistence in role-play.* The child continues within a role or play theme for a period of time at least 10 minutes long.
- *Interaction.* At least two players interact within the context of a play episode.
- *Verbal communication.* There is some verbal interaction related to the play episode. (p. 24)

Smilansky and Shefatya prefer the terms *make-believe* and *pretend play* to *symbolic play* and feel that role play is too narrow a description of what children are doing when they are engaged in sociodramatic play. They prefer the term *sociodramatic play* because "[i]t involves not only representation and pretense, but also reality orientation, organizational skills, reasoning and argumentation, social skills, etc." (Smilansky & Shefatya, 1990, p. 27).

Sociodramatic play is the vehicle whereby young children use all of their developmental attributes. Children combine physical, cognitive, language, and social play in carrying out a play theme or event. Observation of sociodramatic play provides snapshots of a child's development.

Play as Expression of Feelings

Unlike adults, preschool children are not able to verbalize how they feel. They experience the same feelings and express them through play. Because they feel safe in play, and because play is a primary activity in the preschool years, young children exhibit the full range of their feelings in play activities (Landreth & Hohmeyer, 1998).

Freud (1935) proposed that play can be cathartic. Children use play to reduce anxiety and understand traumatic experiences. They may recreate an unpleasant experience over and over to assimilate it and diminish the intensity of feelings (Frost, 1992; Schaefer, 1993).

Children also use play to express positive feelings such as joy and contentment as well as aggressive feelings. As they externalize these feelings through play, they develop a sense of mastery and control. After they express negative feelings, such as fear and aggression, they can move on to express more positive feelings. When negative feelings have been resolved, children can move to other types of expression in their play (Landreth & Hohmeyer, 1998).

Although expression of emotions can be exhibited in solitary play, sociodramatic play has a major function in emotional development. As they take roles in dramatic play, young children can act out relationships and experience the feelings of the person in the role they are playing. By engaging in different roles, they can express emotional responses to the roles, which leads them to understand differences in feelings and develop problem-solving skills (Cohen & Stern, 1983). Sociodramatic play promotes emotional development and feelings that results in a greater feeling of power, sense of happiness, and positive feelings of self (Piers & Landau, 1980; Singer & Singer, 1977).

Variations in Social Competence and Play

Developmental changes in social development lead to progress in social play in preschool children; however, there are individual differences in social play just as there are differences in social development. These differences in sociability are generally consistent or stable over time. Children who are less competent in peer interactions in early childhood might be at risk for later problems that can include school dropout, depression, and aggression. Some of the factors that can affect individual differences have been widely researched. These include genetic differences, parenting style and effectiveness in child rearing, and effective peer relations (Rubin & Coplan, 1998).

Genetic Differences

Genetic factors manifest in ways such as differences in twins and gifted preschool children. Identical twins are more similar in sociability than fraternal twins. Shyness that can be identified in younger fraternal twins can be seen later in school-age children (Plomin & Daniels, 1986; Scarr, 1968). Gifted children, to the contrary, can find play to be a valuable activity. Although children studied by Wright (1990) engaged extensively in solitary and nonplay activities, they were highly social and deliberately used strategies that would bring them in contact with their peers.

Parenting Style and Effectiveness in Child Rearing

Evidence indicates that parenting style affects sociability in children. Parents who are authoritative have children who tend to be socially responsible and are friendly and cooperative in peer interactions. Children of authoritative parents have been found to have positive self-esteem and be prosocial. On the other hand, parents who are authoritarian or permissive tend to have children who are socially withdrawn and incompetent and aggressive (Baumrind, 1991; Roopnarine, 1987).

Parents who are effective in child rearing have children who are competent in social play. Effective parents show their infants and young children how to engage in more sophisticated symbolic play and make-believe themes, model play, support social-linguistic skills, and encourage pretend play. They arrange play activities for their young children; as a result, their children tend to be able to initiate peer contacts and display prosocial behaviors with their playmates. Caregivers in child care settings can also affect socially competent play (Creasey et al., 1998; Howes & Stewart, 1987; Ladd & Hart, 1992; Rubin, Maioni, & Hornung, 1976).

On the other hand, there is a lack of complex social play interactions in low-quality child care centers. Families who do not provide mentoring and social play opportunities for their preschool children have children who do not have the background for advanced social play (Howes & Stewart, 1987; Rubin et al., 1976; Smilansky, 1968). Family social class was found to be a factor in competent social play by these researchers.

Effective Peer Relations

Children who are socially competent are able to engage in successful peer play. They are able to use proactive methods to join a group and use advanced social skills to recruit play partners. During the preschool years, socially competent children become more skilled in understanding the play cues exhibited by peers and improve in negotiating play themes (Goncu, 1993; Howes, 1987). Moreover, children who are skilled in peer interactions are more likely to engage in high levels of fantasy play (Creasey et al., 1998).

Variations in Sociodramatic Play

Preschool children's differences in social play have been documented in the previous sections. These differences provide a logical sequence into understanding differences in sociodramatic play. Again, Smilansky's work (1968; Smilansky & Shefatya, 1990) provides the leadership in understanding these differences.

Smilansky conducted extensive research on sociodramatic play that resulted in three conclusions: lower-class children engage in less and poorer-quality sociodramatic play than middle-class children, children who have deficits in sociodramatic play are the result of parents' child-rearing attitudes and practices regarding their child's sociodramatic play, and training in sociodramatic play can ameliorate the deficits described (McLoyd, 1986).

Smilansky's early work led to much research on differences in sociodramatic play. The findings of these studies did not always agree. Most researchers confirmed Smilansky's findings that middle-class preschoolers participate in sociodramatic play more often than lower-class preschoolers (Fein & Stork, 1981; Rosen, 1974). Some studies, however, found no difference (Rubin et al., 1976), and one study (Eifermann, 1971) noted differences that favored lower-class children.

Research on individual differences in sociodramatic play continue. In addition to socioeconomic differences, researchers also study such factors as the effects of the environment (Frost, 1992) and the sociodramatic play of mixed-age groups (Stone & Christie, 1996). Socioeconomic differences will be discussed in more detail under Socioeconomic Status and Cultural Differences in Play later in this chapter.

Adult Roles in Social Play

If adults are to support social play in preschool children, they need to understand and value both social and sociodramatic play. First and foremost, adults need to believe in the importance of social play for preschool children. Both parents and teachers must be advocates for daily social play opportunities, and their roles are different.

Parents are significant role models for social play. Parenting styles affect how socially competent their children will be. In addition, parents can coach their children on prosocial behaviors and model how their children can develop friendships. They can provide play partners for their children by arranging play dates with peers. They can also widen friendships by inviting a variety of children to play.

Parents, teachers, and caregivers can encourage both social and sociodramatic play. Daily opportunities for free play are important in preschool classrooms. In addition, the props and materials that teachers provide can stimulate sociodramatic play. Teachers can model role playing by entering into children's sociodramatic play episodes or making suggestions for dramatic play themes. Frequent changes of toys and materials enrich sociodramatic play, as do props to support specific play themes.

It is helpful if adults can appreciate the positive characteristics of rough-and-tumble play, superhero play, and chase games. Although caregivers and teachers express concern about violent themes and possible injuries in superhero and rough-and-tumble play, they can take a broader view and try to see the benefits of these types of sociodramatic play for young children.

Teachers and caregivers also support social competence through play. They can support positive social interactions and provide support and intervention for children who are not socially successful.

WHAT PARENTS, CAREGIVERS, AND TEACHERS CAN DO TO PROMOTE SOCIAL AND SOCIODRAMATIC PLAY

1. Make provisions for preschool children to engage in social play both at home and in group settings.
2. Facilitate play with a wide group of peers to encourage child-initiated relationships.
3. Guide children in developing prosocial skills that will help them be successful members in play groups.
4. Engage in children's play to model social skills and appropriate play behaviors.
5. Provide props and materials for sociodramatic play.
6. Supply props that are specific for play themes.
7. Suggest or model roles in sociodramatic play.
8. Offer intervention and redirecting strategies for children who express aggression in play to help them use more positive social behaviors.

CHARACTERISTICS OF PRESCHOOL PLAY

The Integrated Nature of Play

In earlier sections, characteristics of play were discussed within each domain of development. The relationships between development and play in the preschool years were drawn for motor, cognitive, language, and social-emotional development. In this section, we will discuss play in terms of overall development.

All domains of development are engaged in preschool children's play. Moreover, the level of development in each domain affects the child's ability to use other developmental domains in play. Children who are socially mature are able to bring their social skills into leadership roles in sociodramatic play. Ability in expressive language affects a child's social interactions and level of participation in sociodramatic play. Motor skills impact how preschool children use physical movement in fantasy or thematic play.

The next section describes factors that impact individual differences in play. This will be followed by a discussion of the types of play that characterize the play years in preschool children. These include games entailing gender differences, rough-and-tumble play, superhero play, and chase games.

Variations in Development and Play

Individual children vary in their development and play. In the discussion of social development and play individual variations were discussed in terms of parenting practices, and differences in temperament, social competence, and effectiveness in peer relations. Now looking at differences in play as an integrated process, individual variations will be discussed in terms of cultural and socioeconomic status, and gender differences.

Socioeconomic Status and Cultural Differences in Play

In the earlier section on sociodramatic play, we discussed the work of Smilansky (1968), which investigated socioeconomic differences in play with children from different cultures. Because much of the research that has been conducted has included both socioeconomic and cultural factors, these two are discussed together to explain play differences in preschool children.

Low income or poverty can have negative effects on child play. Children from homes with limited income may not have access to high-quality play environments, expensive toys and equipment, and experiences outside their immediate home environment (Johnson, 1998). When quality of play is affected as a consequence, children engage in lower forms of play such as exploration and functional play instead of higher forms of play such as constructive and sociodramatic play (Pellegrini & Boyd, 1993; Smilansky, 1990).

When cultural factors interact with socioeconomic factors, variations in play are more complex. Although some elements of play such as sociality of play and imagination are similar across cultures, expressive or recreational play, especially play themes, are more likely to reflect specific cultures (Johnson, 1998).

Differences in the amount and types of play have been observed in different cultures. In some cultures, children are observed engaging in complex and elaborate games. Games are more simple in other cultures and nonexistent in some cultures (Frost, 1992; Hughes, 1995; see Chapter 7). In addition, some researchers have proposed that children from cultures where work comes early in childhood engage in limited forms of play. However, research has demonstrated that children who engage in adult work or are from poverty-level homes do engage in dramatic play with other children. Their play does not depend on having toys or materials for pretense play, nor are same-age peers a crucial element (Johnson, Christie, & Yawkey, 1999; Schwartzman, 1978).

Gender Differences in Play

The ability to label gender affects the emergence of gender-segregated play, as introduced at the beginning of this section. Children who can label gender are more likely to play with same-gender children, more likely to select gender-identified toys, and girls who label gender early are less likely to engage in aggressive play than other children (Fagot & Leve, 1998).

Smilansky's (1968) play categories can be used to identify gender difference in play. There is little difference in functional play; however, boys are more likely to engage in constructive play (Rubin, Watson, & Jambor, 1978). In dramatic play, boys and girls take on different roles. Girls are more likely to engage in social roles, while boys engage in mock battles (Johnson & Roopnarine, 1983). Girls engage in feminine or housekeeping roles in fantasy play, while boys

Children of all cultures play.

engage in superhero and adventure themes (Johnson et al., 1999; Sutton-Smith, 1979).

In addition to the differences just cited, many characteristics of preschool play are gender-specific. Girls use verbal interactions and suggestions while playing in a novel manner with toys. In physical play, boys engage in more rough-and-tumble play than girls. In social play, girls play in small groups, while boys play in larger, more organized groups (Ausch, 1994; Fagot & Leve, 1998; Neppl & Murray, 1997).

There are differences in how boys and girls play games. Girls play games that involve taking turns and avoid addressing conflicts. Boys, on the other hand, engage in games that have unspecific rules. They enjoy negotiation and disagreements because it makes the game more interesting (Ausch, 1994). In other types of social interactions, girls seek help from others in the environment, whereas boys tend to play independently.

Boys engage in more aggressive play than girls, which increases between infancy and school age. Although there are cultural differences in aggression in play, the predominance of aggression in boy's play rather than girl's play persists. It is significant to note that in the United States, a list of sex-role stereotyped toys for boys includes guns, knives, and other fighting tools (Fagot & Leve, 1998).

The information provided about differences in play related to gender are but a fraction of the research that has been conducted on the topic; several other characteristics of preschool play can also be explored. In the sections that follow, rough-and-tumble play, superhero play, and chase games will be discussed. Although they will be discussed as separate kinds of play, in reality they are frequently combined as children engage in dramatic play.

Rough-and-Tumble Play

Rough-and-tumble play has been characterized as "friendly chasing and playfighting" (Berk, 1996, p. 414). It also may entail hitting and wrestling, but it is significantly different from real fighting. Although rough-and-tumble play is more prevalent in the primary grades (Pellegrini & Boyd, 1993), Jones (1976) first witnessed this type of play when observing nursery school children. He describes seven movement patterns that tended to occur in this type of play: "These are running, chasing, and fleeing; wrestling; jumping up and down with both feet together . . .; beating at each other with an object but not hitting; laughing" (p. 355). A major difference between real fighting and rough-and-tumble play is the fact that children are laughing and smiling as they play.

What is the nature of rough-and-tumble play in the preschool years? It is typified by reciprocal role-taking. Several children are engaged in the activity and take turns in roles such as "bad guys" and "good guys" (Johnson, et al., 1999; Pellegrini & Boyd, 1993). The children might be engaged in a play theme that also includes running and chasing and play fighting. They might change roles during the play episode and replay the scenario. Jones (1976) gives the examples of tag and "cowboys and Indians." Today, play themes might include *Star Wars* themes and reenactment of favorite television shows such as "Power Rangers."

While preschool children engage in rough-and-tumble play, 5% of the time in free play, it increases to 10% to 17% of play in primary grade years (Johnson, 1998). More about rough and tumble play will be discussed in Chapter 6.

Superhero Play

Rough-and-tumble play and **superhero play** are closely related. Indeed, teachers often fail to notice any difference between the two because superhero play is often a part of rough-and-tumble play. There is a difference, however, in that rough-and-tumble play can occur without superhero play.

Superhero play is a result of television programming for young children. As children reflect their favorite programs in their dramatic play, superhero play results. Boyd (1997, p. 23) defines superhero play as follows: "superhero play refers to the active, physical play of children pretending to be media characters imbued with extraordinary abilities, including superhuman strength or the ability to transform themselves into superhuman entities."

Rough-and-tumble play is playful aggression.

Superhero play appeals particularly to boys for several reasons. First, it permits young boys to engage in running, wrestling, jumping, and shouting that are characteristic of rough-and-tumble play. Second, superheroes possess powers children wish they had; they can feel that they are strong and powerful when they engage in superhero roles. Third, preschool boys are attracted to superhero play because they can pit good against evil and play roles that are always "good" (Bauer & Dettore, 1997).

As is the case with rough-and-tumble play, teachers commonly ban superhero play in their classrooms and on the playground. They might be concerned about the violent content, viewing it as aggressive and frightening as well as bizarre (Carlsson-Paige & Levin, 1995). As in the case of rough-and-tumble play, they are concerned that children can get hurt when the play gets out of control and because it can escalate into noisy and chaotic play (Bauer & Dettore, 1997).

Part of the concern about superhero play is the perception that it is escalating. There is little concrete evidence, however, that this is so. Boyd (1997) asserts that much of the data used to support the increase is based on anecdotal reports and may include a lack of objectivity on the part of teachers. Furthermore, teachers characterize superhero play as characterized by fighting, martial arts moves, and kicking. These play behaviors are reportedly the main source of teachers' concerns (Bergen, 1994; Carlsson-Paige & Levin, 1991, 1995). Teachers also make a connection between preschool play and later membership in adolescent gangs (Boyd, 1997).

Superhero play actually offers benefits, again similar to benefits of rough-and-tumble play. First, superhero play is engaged in by friends, thus promoting friendships between children. Second, children can use superhero play to elevate their status within the group. They select players similar in strength or choose a slightly stronger partner (Smith & Boulton, 1990).

Banning superhero play can have negative results. Undesirable behaviors that can result when teachers ban superhero play include children feeling guilty about engaging in superhero play or learning to be deceptive when in engaging in superhero play. They can fear talking to adults about their interests in superhero play (Carlsson-Paige & Levin, 1990). Teachers send the message that such play is wrong for them, as is being interested in some of the values such as good and evil that are part of superhero themes (Boyd, 1997). Teachers also lose opportunities to incorporate superhero characters as a positive influence in children's development and learning (Bauer & Dettore, 1997). Carlsson-Paige and Levin (1995) suggest to teachers that superheroes can be used to instill positive behaviors in children if they are used as a motivational tool.

Chase Games

Running and chasing are a part of rough-and-tumble play, as described earlier. Now **chase games** will be discussed as a separate type of play that emerges in the preschool years and continues to expand and develop after children enter school. Although many writers on the subject prefer to discuss chasing as a subelement of rough-and-tumble play (Humphreys & Smith, 1984; Pellegrini, 1995), we support the premise that chase games are worthy of discussion as a separate category.

How are chase games defined as a separate category? Chase games involve physical skill, strategy, and possibly also tagging and hiding (Clarke, 1999). Chasing can include cross-gender play as well as same-gender play (Thorne, 1995). There can be a sequence in the chasing game: initiation with a provocation such as a taunt or poke; the chasing; the end when the chaser is outdistanced, the chased is caught and perhaps wrestled to the ground, or the chased reaches a "safety zone" (Thorne, 1995).

Both boys and girls engage in chase games, although boys participate more frequently than girls (Pellegrini, 1995). Chase games are found in many cultures, with cultural differences. Four common types of cultural differences are variations on individual and group chases: an individual chases a group; a group chases an individual; an individual chases an individual; and a group chases a group (Clarke, 1999; Opie & Opie, 1969; Sutton-Smith, 1972).

Gender differences in chase games are apparent as well. When same-gender chasing occurs, the chasing between boys frequently ends in wrestling or play fighting (supporting the connection with rough-and-tumble play). Girls, on the other hand, are less physical. They might flee for a safety zone where they can stop and then reenter the game.

Cross-gender chasing is frequently labeled such as "girls chase the boys" or "catch and kiss" (Thorne, 1995, p. 68). Cross-gender chasing is also characterized by discussions and retellings of the chase episode. Individuals may call for help or offer to assist one of the groups involved in the chase.

Chase games may have a developmental sequence beginning with reciprocal mother-child interactions in infancy. The beginnings of this type of play can have their origin with mother-child social games such as peek-a-boo and "I'm going to get you" (Humphreys & Smith, 1984). Chasing episodes emerge at about age 2, when toddlers play fleeing games with adults and then engage in chase games with their peers (Clarke, 1999). By age 3, they use language to initiate games, as either the chaser or the one who is chased (Frost, 1992). By 5 years of age, chase games include strategies, plans, incorporation of themes, and deliberate rules (Clarke, 1999; Schneider, 1997). Clarke and Schneider have described this developmental sequence into seven stages for preschool children, as pictured in Table 5–1. When children enter school, chase games continue and become more complex. Chase games in the elementary grades will be discussed again in Chapter 6.

Creativity and Play

Preschoolers engage in all types of creativity in their play. Their emerging abilities in cognition, language, fine-motor skills, and social development make it possible to weave creativity into their everyday play activities. They are creative with speech, sociodramatic play themes, classroom materials that include art and music materials, and the constructions that they make with

TABLE 5–1 Stages in Chase Games

Stage*	Age	What actions are indicative of chase?	What is the outcome or consequence of the action?	What is the distinguishing factor of this stage?
1	Birth to age two	"Peek-a-boo" is like a stationary "hide-and-seek" game. The child's face is covered and the adult has to "find" them. The child learns to hide self.	The child laughs in surprise. The child learns to hide self and then learns to find the hidden adult.	There is not a clear chase involved.
2	Birth to age two	The adult is engaging the child in a stationary game initially. Then, when the child can crawl or cruise, they play chase. The adult verbally or non verbally initiates the game.	The actions most often end in an embrace with hugging, tickling, laughing.	This begins as a stationary game and evolves into a chase game when the child can crawl.
3	Birth to age two	The child moves away by crawling, cruising, or toddling and the adult pursues. Action is occasionally reciprocated with the child pursuing the adult.	Again, the action ends in embracing, hugging, tickling, and/or laughing. If the child is the chaser, there is not always a clear consequence.	Adult and child begin initiating the chase games. As children begin toddling, the game is not only played with the parents, but with peers.
4	Age 2–3	Children pursue or run away from one another in a reciprocal and random fashion.	There is no clear consequence. Children often run into each other and get hurt at this stage.	The reciprocity of the game. The game is still random, but the children will chase one another.
5	Age 2–3	The game begins when one child moves toward or away from another child. A push toy may be used to pursue or an animal may be used to chase another child.	There is again no clear consequence. When one child nears or contacts the other child, the roles are often reversed.	There are clear intentions of chasing for the fun of it. Toys or animals are often used to initiate and play the game.

6	Ages 4–5	The actions include pursuit by running after, or away from, another child. The chase game may involve a prop.	The game ends with a touch or capture of the other child. It may also end in a hug, tickle, tackle, rough-and-tumble, and possibly hitting.	The initiator is not only the chaser, but the chasee.
7	Ages 4–5	Themes and fantasy play guide the chase game at this stage. Rules may be decided upon and role reversal is not random, but deliberate.	Outcomes vary according to theme (i.e. jail, tapped by a monster, mommy and her babies).	Chase games become a plan of action and themes are often involved.
8	Ages 6–11	The chase games are now organized games with rules. Still, the rules can be changed to suit the players.	Consequences depend upon the game. At this stage, arguments over rules often occur.	The chase games are now organized games with rules.
9	Age 12 through adulthood	There is an offensive player being chased by an defensive player. The games have definite rules that are not changed (basketball, soccer).	If the defensive player is successful, the offensive player does not score. The ultimate consequence is winning and losing.	Not only are the games organized with rules, but there are winners and losers.

*Stages 1–3 parallel Piaget's sensorimotor stage; stages 4–7 parallel the preoperational stage; stage 8 parallels the concrete stage; and stage 9 parallels the formal operational stage.

Source: From "Development Reflected in Chase Games" (pp. 78–79) by L. J. Clarke in S. Reifel (Ed.), *Play and Culture Studies* (Vol. 2), Stamford, CT: Ablex Publishing. Copyright 1999 by Ablex Publishing. Used by permission.

large blocks and small manipulative materials. Their world can be rich with opportunities for creative expression.

Young children's creativity has three unique characteristics. First, creative children can be sensitive to internal and external stimuli. Second, they demonstrate a lack of inhibition, becoming completely absorbed in the creative activity. In addition, they have a unique ability to use imagination and fantasy in their play (Isenberg & Jalongo, 1997).

The relationship between play and creativity has generated great interest. Lieberman (1965) studied the relationship between playfulness traits and divergent thinking. She found that children who were the most playful were also the most creative. Smilansky (1968) observed a relationship between creativity and sociodramatic play. She found that children with higher levels of pretend play or sociodramatic play had more success with achievement later in school. She also described how children with lower levels of sociodramatic play could be guided to use more creative thinking and extension of play themes.

Johnson (1976) also found a relationship between fantasy play styles and creativity. He was able to describe a relationship between social fantasy play and divergent thinking tasks. He suggested that this relationship leads to the ability to generate a variety of ideas. Pepler and Ross (1981) also found that children who had divergent play experiences used more imagination in responding to divergent thinking tasks. Their study also indicated that play with unstructured materials rather than structured materials leads to creativity. Likewise, social play is more beneficial for creativity than nonsocial dramatic play (Johnson, 1976). Finally, the availability of an enriched and flexible play environment with less intrusive adult intervention facilitates creativity in play (Pepler, 1979).

In previous sections, we have discussed many of the characteristics of children's play. Now, let's look at characteristics of preschool play using examples of some individual children.

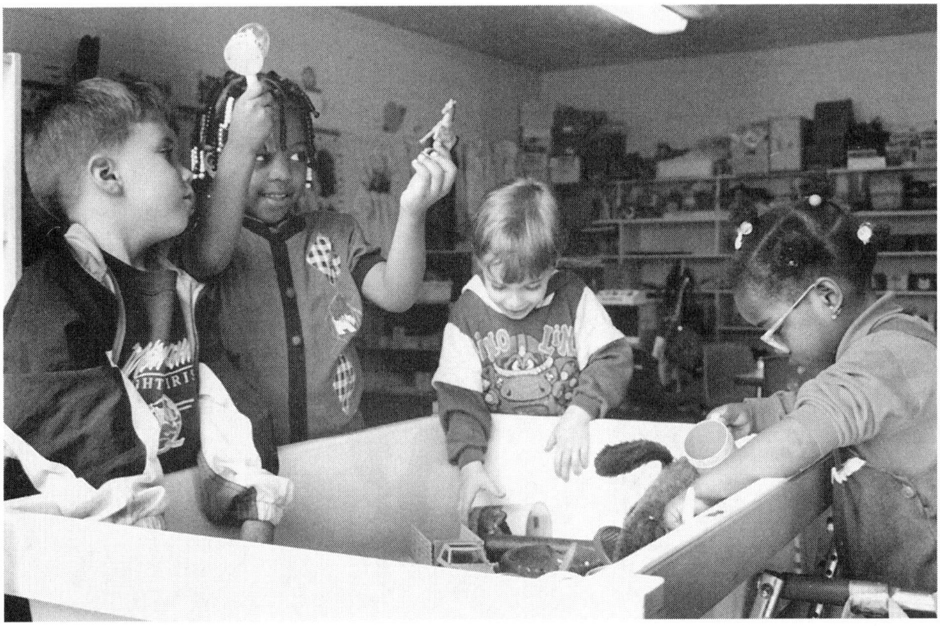

In sociodramatic play, children combine physical, cognitive, language, and social play in carrying out a play theme.

CARL AND LOLO

Carl and Lolo attend a child care center adjacent to a low-income housing development in the inner city. Some of the housing units near the center are being demolished and have been the focus of much of the children's play time. Carl and Lolo call to several other boys to come and play like they are workers tearing down houses. The boys pull some wooden blocks and boards together and "build" a house. Carl decides to be the one in charge and tells the others, "When I say 'Go,' knock the house down." He gives the signal, and Lolo and the other boys knock down the blocks and boards. Their teacher, Miss Reynolds, walks over and tells the boys that their play is dangerous and they should go and play on the swings. Carl and Lolo move to the sandbox and fill trucks with sand.

TATA

Tata is 3 years old and attends a Mother's Day Out program. Her favorite play activity is to role-play mommies and daddies. Today she invites Marcy and Anna to play house with her. They move to the playhouse that is located in a small building on the playground. They decide that they will make pancakes. Tata takes a plastic container to the sandbox and fills it with wet sand. The other girls take dishes and put them on the table. There is some argument about who will be the mother and cook. After some discussion, Tata says, "Let's play McDonald's and we can all cook." Marcy and Anna agree, and now the girls use the stove to make sand hamburgers and milkshakes.

LARRY, JOSEPH, AND PERRY

Larry, Joseph, and Perry are in public school kindergarten. They are finishing their work pasting collages and getting ready to go outside to play. As they line up, they discuss what they will play when they get outside. Larry suggests that they play "races." This is a game they have invented in which they race across the playground to see who can run the fastest. After they have run some races, they get a drink of water. They see some of the girls talking under a tree. "Let's chase the girls!" shouts Perry. Perry calls to the girls, "Let's see if we can catch you!" The girls shriek and start running with the boys in pursuit.

LORI

Samantha and Julia are visiting at Lori's house. The girls have decided to play Old Maid. After they have played two hands of the game, Lori has been the Old Maid both times. Lori suggests they play something else, but Samantha and Julia are enjoying the game. As they finish another hand, Samantha is left with the Old Maid. "I'm tired," she announces. "Let's play school." Lori agrees, and the conversation turns to who will get to be the teacher.

ADULT ROLES IN PRESCHOOL PLAY

Parents, caregivers, and teachers have important roles in preschool children's play. They serve as facilitators, models, supervisors, and participants in children's play. In this section, we will take a look at adult roles in sex-typed behavior, aggressive play, and involvement in play activities.

Earlier in the chapter, we discussed how preschool children begin to engage in gender play and how this process is refined as children get older. The trend in recent decades has been away from gender differences in play. With the advent of higher percentages of working mothers, fathers taking responsibility for tasks in the home, and fathers spending more time playing with their children, preschool children exhibit less gender-based play. As a couple of examples, girls now engage in more sports that were once thought to be a male form of play, and preschool boys are more likely to role-play fathers in nurturing roles in dramatic play.

At one time there was an effort on the part of teachers to advocate cross-gender play and to focus on eliminating stereotypical gender play. However, we are cautioned to be aware of ethnic and cultural groups who oppose moving away from traditional gender roles in children's play (Johnson et al., 1999). In some circumstances, however, parents and teachers can foster play that is gender-neutral. Parents can treat their children's play in an equitable manner. Equal time should be spent with children of either gender and equal emphasis placed on toys and activities. Fathers and mothers should include girls in traditional male games and engage their sons in cooking and other activities in the home once thought to be females' territory.

Another adult role in preschool play is as supervisor. Caregivers and teachers working in group settings supervise larger numbers of children at play. They must make decisions about whether play activities are appropriate and safe. Children who play aggressively are a concern. Supervisors can limit aggression and redirect children who are aggressive or violent (Kuykendall, 1996). This type of play behavior is distinct from rough-and-tumble and superhero play, which can pose no threat when play episodes are carried out in a positive manner. Teachers also are concerned about playground safety (see Chapter 11).

Teachers can provide opportunities for children to broaden their play by arranging the indoor and outdoor environments with activities for both genders. Many kindergarten teachers have had a majority of "female"-type activities because of their concern for noise and safety. Large wooden blocks, work benches, and dramatic play themes that focus on male roles rather than female roles can provide opportunities for children to engage in these roles.

How much should adults become involved in children's play? Throughout the chapter, we have made suggestions as to how parents, caregivers, and teachers can promote play in individual developmental domains. But the question of too much adult involvement in children's play is valid. For example, when parents or teachers get too involved in children's play, they tend to take over the play episode or become too directive. When this happens, children play at a lower level or lose interest in the activity. Research study results have shown that adult involvement is most effective when the adult becomes a coplayer or provides suggestions and materials to enrich play. Adults are least effective when they are uninvolved or merely observe play. At the other extreme, they are equally ineffective when they become instructors or directors of play (Johnson et al., 1999; Roskos & Neuman, 1993).

TOYS AND MATERIALS FOR PRESCHOOL PLAY

Young children are strongly influenced by toys that are marketed on television. Many of these toys are related to cartoon shows, current children's movies, or children's television programs that feature violence and action figures. Unfortunately, these toys have little play value and can be related to aggressive play (Frost, 1992). They do not stimulate the imagination, dramatic play, or creativity.

More appropriate choices are toys that are unstructured, diverse in playability, and simple in design. Frost (1992) provides points for toy selection that would meet these criteria for appropriate toys (see Figure 5–2).

Parents, teachers, and caregivers can also consider play in developmental domains in their choices of toys and materials for preschool children. They will want to include a balance of toys for different types of play, as suggested in the following list:

Gross-Motor Play

Large blocks

Transportation toys

Climbing equipment

Tricycles, wagons, Big Wheels®, and so forth

Woodworking equipment and materials (child-sized hammers, workbench, vise, screwdrivers, scrap lumber, etc.)

Fine-Motor Play

Clay

Puzzles

Art supplies (finger and water paints, brushes, markers, crayons, scissors, etc.)

Beads for stringing

Construction materials (small blocks, Legos®, Lincoln Logs®, etc.)

Language and Literacy

Books

Writing materials (notepads, individual chalkboard, pens, pencils, old typewriters, sand trays, etc.)

Thematic props (teddy bears for "Goldilocks," puppets, etc.)

Cognitive Play

Materials for water play (buckets, squirt guns, sieves, etc.)

Simple board games

Simple card games

Materials for science experiments (balance scales, eye droppers, animal cages, aquariums, terrariums, etc.)

Objects from nature (leaves, bird's nest, feathers, etc.)

Sociodramatic Play

Dolls and stuffed animals

Props for dramatic play (hats, neckties, child stethoscope, lensless eyeglasses, etc.)

Miniature life figures

Housekeeping equipment and props (child-sized broom, dishware, table and chairs, etc.)

FIGURE 5–2 Suggestions for Selecting Toys

- Select multi-purpose toys (a gun can be used for one purpose only).
- Select materials that allow children to make their own toys (tools, blocks, erector sets).
- Combine toys with natural materials (sand, water, etc.) and in natural settings (backyards, etc.)
- Select toys that expand discovery—seeds, soil, magnifying glass, etc.
- Select safe toys. Look for sharp edges, parts that can break off, parts that can cause choking, parts that can puncture or cut.
- Select toys that are durable—expect heavy use, abuse.
- Consider ages of children—select toys that can be used in different ways at different levels of development.
- Balance your selection—promote physical, intellectual-emotional, language, creative development.
- Match toys to developing interests (music, pets, board games).
- Avoid bombarding children with too many toys.
- Avoid toys that encourage violent fantasy or games that encourage physical risk.
- Discuss toy selections with children.
- Limit the number and variety of "bought" toys, especially theme-specific toys. Encourage children to make or adapt toys.
- Consider involving children in donating toys to charitable organizations as they are outgrown and more appropriate ones are purchased.
- Ensure that toys reflect ethnic/culture balance.

Source: From *Play and Playscapes* (p. 73) by J. L. Frost, 1992, Albany, NY: Delmar.

SUMMARY

Children make major progress in development during the preschool years that is reflected in their play. In motor development, their gross-motor skills include acquisition of fundamental movement skills and perceptual-motor development. Progress in fine-motor skills results in the ability to use art and writing materials and work puzzles and small construction toys. Play occurs both at home and in preschool group settings. Although preschool children engage in free play, they also enjoy teacher-directed activities in group settings. Although physical development specialists suggest that motor development programs should be a part of preschool curriculum, few early childhood educators are trained to provide a quality program.

Children are in the preoperational stage in cognitive development when primitive reasoning begins. Play promotes cognitive development. For example, sociodramatic play promotes intellectual development to include imagination and creativity. Children move through stages of play that have been described in various ways by various theorists to include Piaget, Vygotsky, and Smilansky. The stages reflect the child's cognitive progress and ability to use cognitive advances in play.

Development in language and literacy permit preschool children to communicate with others. During the years between 3 and 6, children acquire the major components of their language to include morphology rules, syntax rules, and semantic rules. Their vocabulary increases dramatically. They also learn rules of conversation and the nature of literacy. Through experiences with books, stories, and writing activities, young children learn about written language and take initial steps in acquiring literacy. These emerging interests in language and literacy are reflected in their play, particularly sociodramatic play.

Social development provides young children with the ability to understand themselves and others. They continue to develop social relationships with adults and peers and establish friendships through play. Social competence is a factor in successful play relationships.

Social development is reflected in social and sociodramatic play. Children reflect their social development in stages of social play that begin with individual play and move to collaboration in group play. Sociodramatic play includes pretend play and role play. Children make-believe in carrying out play themes within a group of children. Sociodramatic play incorporates all domains of development and facilitates the expression of feelings. The types and levels of sociodramatic play engaged in by young children reflects differences in gender, temperament, and parenting styles and effectiveness. Although there are cultural and socioeconomic differences in sociodramatic play, all children engage in such play, even in cultures where children participate in work early in their lives.

Unique forms of play in the preschool years include rough-and-tumble play, superhero play, and chase games. Although some teachers are wary of these types of play activities, they are particularly a part of boys' sociodramatic play. Girls also engage in rough-and-tumble play and chase games, but differently than boys.

Adults assume a major role in children's play. The time and type of play engaged in by parents and other adults affect the quality of preschool play. They provide materials, ideas, and serve as coplayers with children. However, there are extremes of adult involvement that are not conducive to enriched play. When adults are disinterested or merely watch play, their lack of involvement has a negative effect. Likewise, when they are overinvolved or too directive, the child's interest and play level are diminished.

KEY TERMS

Body awareness
Chase games
Classification
Conservation
Directional awareness
Egocentric
Empathy
Fine-motor development
Fundamental movement phase
Gross-motor development
Intuitive thought substage
Locomotor skills
Morphology rules
Perceptual-motor development
Pragmatics of language
Preoperational stage
Reflexive movement phase
Rough-and-tumble play
Rudimentary movement phase
Self-concept
Self-esteem
Self-regulation of emotions
Semantic rules
Social competence
Sociodramatic play
Spatial awareness
Specialized movement phase
Superhero play
Symbolic function substage
Syntax rules
Temporal awareness

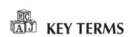

STUDY QUESTIONS

1. How does play support motor development in the preschool years?
2. Why do some educators advocate that motor development programs are needed in preschool settings?
3. Why is it important for parents to provide times for preschool children's play?
4. How does cognitive development in the preschool years affect how children play?
5. How can cognitive play in the preschool years predict later academic success?
6. Define and describe current thinking on hierarchical categories in cognitive development and play.
7. Why do some theorists question that there is a hierarchy in cognitive categories in play?
8. Describe how adults can promote cognition through play in an appropriate manner.
9. How can play promote literacy development? Give examples.
10. Why are there variations in language development? What are some factors that affect language development?
11. Explain how children play with language in the preschool language.
12. How do preschool children use language to support their play?
13. How do parents affect language and literacy development?
14. How does social competence predict success in sociodramatic play?
15. Describe some of the relationships in the preschool child's life that affect social competence.
16. How does pretend play help preschool children develop social skills?
17. Why do some children develop positive social skills and others do not?
18. Explain how social play proceeds through stages and why some researchers question those stages.
19. Explain factors that can result in variations in social competence and play.
20. Why is Smilansky's work on sociodramatic play significant in understanding variations in levels of sociodramatic play?
21. What evidence do we have that boys and girls play differently in the preschool years? Give examples of differences.
22. Explain rough-and-tumble play, superhero play, and chase games. How are these types of play related?
23. What do preschool children need from their parents to maximize their play?
24. Explain different adult roles that can promote and broaden preschool play.

Chapter 6 Play and the School-Age Child

IT WAS on the afternoon of the day of Christmas Eve, and I was in Mrs. Prothero's garden waiting for cats, with her son Jim. It was snowing. It was always snowing at Christmas. December, in my memory, is white as Lapland, though there were no reindeers. But there were cats. Patient, cold and callous, our hands wrapped in socks, we waited to snowball the cats. Sleek and long as jaguars and horrible-whiskered, spitting and snarling, they would slink and sidle over the white back-garden walls, and the lynx-eyed hunters, Jim and I, fur-capped and moccasined trappers from Hudson Bay, off Mumbles Road, would hurl our deadly snowballs at the green of their eyes. The wise cats never appeared. We were so still, Eskimo-footed arctic marksmen in the muffling silence of the eternal snows—eternal, ever since Wednesday—that we never heard Mrs. Prothero's first cry from her igloo at the bottom of the garden. Or, if we heard it at all, it was to us, like the far-off challenge of our enemy and prey, the neighbor's polar cat. But soon the voice grew louder. "Fire!" cried Mrs. Prothero, and she beat the dinner-gong.

(Thomas, 1954, n.p.)

As Dylan Thomas recalled about his own childhood, children in elementary school have not lost their interest in play. Dramatic play continues as do other types of play first observed in preschool children such as rough-and-tumble play and chase games. Accomplishments in cognitive, physical, and social development add new dimensions to how children play.

There is, however, a definite difference in opportunities for play and social expectations for sports activities that can preclude opportunities for school-age children to hang out and engage in free play. One of the issues to be discussed in this chapter is the lack of play opportunities at schools, especially the elimination of recess in the interest of improvement of student achievement. While the preschool years were described as play years in Chapter 5, once children enter elementary school, parents and teachers seem to place little value on free play and fail to understand its benefits (Manning, 1993, 1998). Some forms of play are available to school-age children, as will be described under sections on physical, cognitive, language, and social development. We will also discuss general characteristics of play as well as adult roles in providing play both within and outside the school environment.

PHYSICAL DEVELOPMENT

During the school years, children's physical development in more refined gross- and fine-motor skills are manifested in the emergence of new forms of play. School-age children are more skilled in skipping, hopping, climbing, and chasing. They learn to ride bicycles and improve their ability to draw, color, and use a computer keyboard. Later, they are able to construct model planes and other more complex constructions (Johnson, 1998).

Gallahue (1993) describes the elementary school years as the specialized movement phase introduced in Chapter 4. During this period, children continue in the development of mature movement skills that will carry on until adulthood. Differences in fundamental movement abilities also become more varied. Although children may have the potential to develop fundamental movements to their most mature stage, differences in opportunities and the effectiveness of development in the early childhood years have influenced their skill levels. Children vary widely in their abilities, and problems have become evident in many children that affect their successful participation in group play and sports. As is true for younger children, a quality motor and movement development program is needed to correct problems and maximize opportunity for children to develop mature levels of skills.

Various factors affect physical development during the elementary years. At one extreme, many children lack a balanced diet and suffer from malnutrition that affects motor development and later learning. At the other extreme, obesity has become a problem in affluent nations such as the United States. Obese children develop high blood pressure and cholesterol levels that used to be limited to adult health issues (Unger, Kruger, & Christoffel, 1990; Zeisel, 1986). School-age children experience higher rates of illness during the first 2 years of elementary school. Many children, particularly those from low-income homes, tend to develop chronic health problems. Asthma, cystic fibrosis, cancer, and acquired immune deficiency syndrome (AIDS) are illnesses that affect school-age children's development and learning (Berk, 2002).

Injuries are another cause of differences in physical development. Although the incidence of injuries begins to rise in early childhood, the frequency increases steadily during the years of middle childhood and into adolescence. Boys have a higher injury rate than girls, and auto and bicycle collisions account for a majority of the injuries (Brooks & Roberts, 1990).

Characteristics of Motor Development

Growth is slower and more regular during elementary school years. Between the ages of 6 to 8, boys are taller and heavier. This trend changes by the age of 10, when girls experience more dramatic physical growth. Large motor development focuses on the legs, which lengthen more than the upper body. There is more diversity in individual growth that can be attributed to genetics, nutrition, and other environmental factors (Berk, 2002).

Gross-Motor Skills

Improved motor skills in school-age children is reflected in flexibility, balance, and agility. There is more flexibility in swinging a bat or engaging in tumbling. Improved balance supports participation in sports, and agility can be seen when children jump rope, play tag, soccer, and hopscotch. Six- and 7-year-old children are still inaccurate in batting and are more successful at T-ball. Older school-age children can also throw and kick a ball with greater force. They are also able to participate in handball, tennis, basketball, and football (Berk, 2002; Cratty, 1986; Thomas, 1984).

Fine-Motor Skills

Refinement in fine-motor skills is exhibited in many of the activities of school-age children. Children's writing and drawing skills continue to develop throughout elementary school. First grade children, age 6, can generally write their name, the letters of the alphabet, and numbers. Their writing is large until they can move from using the entire arm to using the wrist and fingers. Older school-age children form letters more accurately and use letters of uniform height and spacing. By third grade, refinements in writing skills prepare them to move into cursive writing.

Children's drawings also reflect their progress in fine-motor skills. They become able to use more detail and organization in their drawings. Older school-age children can represent depth in their drawings as they master linear perspective. This skill begins to emerge at about age 9 or 10 (Berk, 2002).

Fine-motor development is reflected in the types of activities school-age children select. In addition to building model airplanes or engaging in computer activities, working with puzzles and practicing yo-yo skills are popular activities.

Variations in Motor Skill Development

Variations in motor skills during elementary school years can be attributed to social class and sex differences. Students who come from affluent families are more likely to have gymnastic, tennis, skating, swimming, and dancing lessons than children from less affluent homes. These children also have more opportunities to engage in team sports.

Significant differences in skills development are gender based. Girls continue to be more advanced in fine-motor skills, while boys gain an advantage in gross-motor skills. Girls are better at handwriting and drawing, while boys outperform girls in throwing and kicking (Cratty, 1986).

These differences seem to be environmental rather than derive from variations in physical development. Parents have higher expectations in physical abilities for boys than for girls. In addition, children view sports as more important for boys. Girls perceive that they have less talent in sports than their male peers (Coakly, 1990; Eccles & Harold, 1991). In recent years, this trend has begun to change. More girls are participating in organized sports in the elementary grades, and parental expectations for girls to excel in sports has increased accordingly. It should be noted, however, that there is a concern for the role of organized sports for both genders in the primary grades because developmental limitations make it difficult for children to master the skills needed for these sports (Berger, 2000).

Play and Physical Development

Outdoor Play

Physical play in the elementary school years is increasingly influenced by peers. Children, particularly boys, engage in outdoor play with their peers on playgrounds, ballfields, and recreation centers where there are facilities and equipment that can be accessed for games and sports. Not only does such play provide vigorous physical activity for school-age children, but socialization is also a benefit (Johnson, 1998). Although children of this age seek to be away from direct adult supervision in their play, this type of opportunity is not always readily available because some working parents require that their children remain at home after school for safety reasons, and because school schedules have decreased opportunities for outdoor play in the interest of academic achievement and concern for inappropriate outdoor play behaviors (Blatchford, 1996; Manning, 1998; Pellegrini & Bjorklund, 1996). Elementary school teachers vary in the value they place on play. Teachers in rural schools are more likely to provide more time for play than urban teachers. Moreover, teachers' attitudes affect play time. Teachers who have a positive attitude toward play are more likely to provide play opportunities than those with less positive attitudes toward play (Newman, Brody, & Beauchamp, 1996).

There is also a concern for the safety of outdoor play. The urbanization of America has made it difficult for elementary school children to play outdoors. Public play spaces are victims of drug traffickers, homeless transients, and vagrants. The gun epidemic has increased incidents of violence on the streets where children might play (Edelman, 1994). The concern for lawsuits has resulted in inaccessibility of vacant property and schoolyards where children might gather to play. Although many urban children have found ways to continue outdoor play by being creative in using their environment (Dargan & Zeitlin, 1998), a majority of children living in cities and smaller urban communities find themselves transported from one location to another by public or private transportation and engage in physical play in basement playrooms, rooftop play areas, and within their family home or apartment (Rivkin, 1998).

Risk Taking in Play

One characteristic of school-age play is the desire for physical challenge and risk taking. Children seek to test their physical skills in their play to find out what they can and cannot do. They challenge themselves by trying new skills and learn through trial and error what their capabilities and limitations are (Jambor, 1998). An example is the game of tag. Individual players take physical risks in running, jumping, and performing other motor skills to avoid being caught. In more structured playground environments they challenge themselves in mazes, physical exercise equipment, and complex climbing structures.

A concern for adults is whether to permit risk-taking activities because of the danger of injury. Another concern is when more capable players lead children who are less physically developed to challenges they cannot handle. The availability of appropriate equipment that provide challenges for school-age children is a primary factor in whether children will be exposed to excess danger. Inappropriate equipment that does not include levels of challenge will lead to dangerous risk-taking behaviors as children seek to make the play equipment more interesting. An example is children climbing to the top of swinging equipment or climbing structures. Another example is young children playing on equipment designed for older children.

The need for challenge is a natural part of motor development for school-age children. They learn to understand their developing capabilities and extend their challenges. Because adults are rightfully concerned about dangerous risk taking, they need to provide environments where challenges are provided, but within reasonably safe limits. Playgrounds that eliminate all challenges are sterile and uninteresting to children. On the other hand, play environments that have dangerous risk factors can provide too high a level of challenge that can encourage children into inappropriate risk-taking activities (Jambor, 1998; Wallach, 1992).

Directed Play

When children enter elementary school, their daily or weekly schedules include periods for physical education. The physical education teacher engages the children in activities for motor skill development that include games and sports. Can these activities be described as play?

School-age children engage in vigorous outdoor play and organized games.

Hopper (1996) promotes the idea of the physical education lesson as play. He believes that games and playful aspects of physical education activities are similar to the criteria given for free play. He urges physical education teachers to reinterpret the meaning and importance of play and to incorporate it into directed play activities in the physical education program. Others believe that because students enjoy directed game activities and engage in behaviors such as running, chasing, and fleeing found in free-play chase games, such behaviors in directed tag games qualify them as play (Belka, 1998). Furthermore, attempts to teach children how to be inclusive in selection of play partners in directed game activities also can be described as a form of play. A program to teach fairness in play during recess, labeled "Play Fair," may be used to teach students to eliminate bullying on the playground and to include all students as players in games. Although the activities are teacher-directed during a recess period, the intent is for students to become fair in their free play (Chuoke & Eyman, 1997).

Participation in organized sports also increases in importance during the school-age years. While there is justifiable concern about the adult dominance of sports and adult-imposed rules rather than child-initiated and child-dominated play, increasing numbers of school-age children participate in one or more sports. Supporters of sports as a form of play suggest that sports also contain many of the elements used to describe play. They compare the purposes for involvement in informal games such as the opportunity to be with friends a similar purpose for involvement in sports. Although children engaged in sports are concerned for winning as an important goal, they also engage in playful pranks, verbal banter, and trading insults. Another side effect of participation is enjoying playful behavior in addition to playing baseball, basketball, or football (Hilliard, 1998).

Free Play

Earlier in this section on physical development and play, the description of the play of school-age children included outdoor play as an important element. The need for outdoor play was discussed as well as factors that limit outdoor play in the larger community where children live. Recess is another source for free play; however, at the beginning of the chapter limitations or elimination of recess as a current trend in elementary schools was introduced as an important variable in the opportunities school-age children have to play. The issue of whether recess or "break time," as it labeled in Great Britain, is needed by school-age children and should be a relevant part of the curriculum in elementary schools is a controversial topic.

One subtopic of the issue is whether school-age children need time for recess and unstructured play. Many schools that have eliminated recess employ educators who believe physical education periods are sufficient for the physical needs of elementary school children. Opponents of recess voice concerns about aggressive play, playground bullies, and the loss of time from academic activities (O. Brian, 2003; Smith, 1998).

Proponents of recess express concern that many children do not have opportunities for free outdoor play outside school hours, either, because they are in scheduled activities or organized sports most school days. If they live in an urban area, safe areas may not be available for outdoor play. Furthermore, working parents might forbid outdoor play when they are away from home.

Proponents of recess periods also propose that social as well as physical benefits can result during recess; moreover, as a respite from attention to classroom tasks, outdoor play can help bring about academic benefits. Although the long-term benefits of recess are not currently available, evidence indicates that children's attention wanes when they are expected to work for sustained periods. Recess provides the break that allows them to give maximum attention to their work once again (O'Brien, 2003; Pellegrini & Bjorklund, 1996). Researchers caution, however, that there is little research to support the role of play for academic success in the elementary grades (Glickman, 1984). Recess is also an opportunity for aggression, as many teachers point out and, without proper supervision, can be a negative factor in the school experience (Pellegrini & Smith, 1993).

Although proponents of recess suggest that vigorous physical play occurs when children are provided with regular outdoor play periods, many children in fact select quiet, passive play activities, and some children prefer to use their play period in indoor activities. A study of recess activities of school-age children at different ages revealed that the type of activities engaged in changed over time (Blatchford, 1996). Seven-year-olds reported spending their time running around and playing games. Ball games and chasing games were most popular. By 11 years, girls preferred pretending and skipping games, while football dominated the boys' play.

The issue of whether recess should be retained in the elementary school continues. Glickman (1984) proposes that definitive research is needed linking achievement with outdoor play before elementary schools will see recess as a priority. The implication seems to be that elementary educators do not perceive the value of physical play as a reason for scheduling recess. Only overwhelming evidence that there is a positive connection between free play periods in the school day and increased achievement will change the trends to reduce or eliminate recess periods.

Adult Roles in Physical Play

The discussion in Chapter 5 indicated that directed play might be found in preschool settings, but structured motor development programs are not commonly found in programs for children under the age of 6. Once children enter elementary schools, however, physical education classes are the rule rather than the exception. Trained physical educators work with students on a regular basis and seek to refine motor skills and teach the basics of sports and games. While motor development is the primary purpose for physical

WHAT PARENTS, CAREGIVERS, AND TEACHERS CAN DO TO PROMOTE PHYSICAL PLAY

1. Adults can work to ensure that school-age children have time and opportunities for free play both at school and outside school hours.
2. Adults can ensure that there are quality outdoor play environments available for school-age children both at school and in the larger community.
3. Parents can work to influence their children to have a balance between physical activities and sedentary activities when they are at home.
4. Parents can encourage their children to be selective in sports participation so that they also have opportunities for child-initiated play in addition to adult-directed physical play.
5. Parents can encourage children of both genders to participate in sports and physical play, while accepting gender differences in play selections.
6. Parents can encourage and support their children's interests for play.

education programs, a playful and enjoyable experience is also advocated for directed programs (Hilliard, 1998; Hopper, 1996).

Classroom teachers should also have a role in provisions for physical play. Although teachers might believe that they have no responsibility because the physical education teacher conducts the program for physical development, they, too, should become advocates for opportunities for physical play beyond directed activities. This advocacy would include time for free play and maintenance of quality outdoor play environments that provide challenge as well as a safe place to play. Both physical education and regular classroom teachers can work together to achieve this goal on behalf of the physical development of school-age children.

Parents definitely have a role in the physical play of their children. Because research shows that parental influence and expectation affect the physical play and participation in sports of their children (Coakly, 1990; Eccles & Harold, 1991), parents should be sensitive to how they can affect participation in physical play. Parents also can be sensitive to providing opportunities for school-age children to engage in free play. Understanding the limitations of environment, safety issues, and time for free play, they can encourage their children to have a balance of activities during after school hours and weekends. A balance is particularly needed between sports and free play and sedentary activities such as watching television and engaging in video and computer games and free play.

COGNITIVE DEVELOPMENT

School-age children think differently than preschool children. Cognitive changes make it possible for them to plan using cognitive resources, remember important information using thinking strategies, and solve problems using thinking and reasoning skills. Children become aware of their intellectual abilities and can recognize their strengths and weaknesses. They understand how to think and are aware when they are using "good thinking" (Berger, 2000).

Unlike preschool children, school-age children can focus on the task at hand. They are able to screen out distractions and concentrate on their work. Moreover, they know when they need to use selective thinking and where they should focus their attention.

The cognitive competencies of school-age children develop rapidly during the school-age years. Whereas preschool children are intuitive thinkers who center on one characteristic at a time, school-age children use deliberate thinking strategies and mental planning to accomplish tasks in learning. In Piaget's (1936/1952) cognitive developmental theory, school-age children use mental abilities that are within the **concrete operational stage**. New thinking abilities can also be attributed to the information processing approach to mental development. These new abilities characterize their cognitive development.

Characteristics of Cognitive Development

Concrete Operational Thought

Children's thinking in the concrete operational stage is more logical and organized than in the preoperational period. The word *operations* is relevant because children use mental actions or mental operations in a logical manner. This mental ability is evidenced when a child **decenters**, or focuses, on more than one aspect of a task or uses **reversibility**, or mentally works through a series of mental actions and then reverses the process. School-age children can learn subtraction, multiplication, and division, because they are able to understand that subtraction is the reverse process of addition and division reverses multiplication.

Children who have achieved concrete operations can use classes and subclasses to classify objects. School-age children enjoy collecting objects and can classify them by more than one characteristic. Berk (2002) provides the example of a child who sorts his collection of baseball cards by first one attribute such as team membership, and then by another attribute such as playing position.

Other characteristics of concrete operational thinking are **seriation**, or the ability to order items by some dimension such as length or diameter, and **spatial reasoning**, an understanding of space that permits children to give directions on how to get from one point to another. They can combine distance with speed and understand that the faster the speed, the shorter the time to reach a distant point or location (Acredolo, Adams, & Schmid, 1984).

A limitation of concrete operational thinking is that it depends on the child's concrete experiences. Children can use logical thinking when it deals with concrete information they can perceive (Berk, 2002). This ability cannot yet be applied in abstract contexts. In addition, the ability to use concrete operational thinking is a gradual process. School-age children cannot readily use logical thinking in a familiar context and transfer it in a more general application to less familiar concepts. For example, the child who can classify baseball cards might not be able to classify trees by some given category without experiences to become familiar with the trees and categories.

Thinking Strategies

Cognitive changes in the school-age child can also be explained by looking at how information is processed. Some characteristics of mental strategies that can be attributed to this approach are selective attention, the use of memory strategies, and knowledge growth.

School-age children are able to focus on a task or use **selective attention** in their learning. Whereas preschool children are easily distracted when working on a learning activity, school-age children are able to screen out distractions and focus on information that is relevant to their task. They use selective attention for both memorizing and problem solving. In problem solving, the child can focus on the information that pertains to finding a solution. To remember important information, the child focuses on relevant strategies that will assist in retaining the material (Flavell, Miller, & Miller, 1993; Miller, 1993).

Children can use specific strategies to memorize information. They use *organization* strategies to place the material into a logical order, *rehearsal* strategies to repeat the information to be remembered, and *retrieval* strategies to be able to recall the information when needed. These strategies for remembering information are called **mnemonics**, or memory aids (Berger, 2000).

The more advanced thinking skills developed during the school-age years lead to significant cognitive growth. The more information the child is able to acquire, the more substantial the growth. In other words, the more connections that are made in the brain from input and storage of new information, the more competent the child becomes. As the amount of information increases, the child is able to also increase the rapidity of thinking and to develop metacognition, an awareness of the cognitive processes being used (Flavell et al., 1993).

Variations in Cognitive Development

Concrete operational thinking is not achieved uniformly by all children. There appear to be cultural and environmental differences. Children who have extensive interest and exposure to a type of information will achieve concrete operational thinking in that topic. For example, the child with extensive experience in computers can apply concrete operational thinking and information-processing skills to challenges encountered in using the computer. On the other hand, children in cultures where there is no formal schooling are delayed in understanding conservation tasks compared to children who attend school from the age of 6 or 7. Some researchers thus believe that acquisition of concrete operational thinking is not spontaneous but socially generated. The practical activities in specific cultures lead to the logic required in Piagetian tasks (Berk, 2002; Flavell et al., 1993).

Another cognitive variation is in intelligence. Variations in intelligence become more obvious in school-age children. One approach to comparing intelligence is to use intelligence quotient (IQ). Children range in IQ as measured on standardized intelligence tests.

A different approach to understanding variations in intelligence has been described by Howard Gardner (1983). Gardner believes that there are seven types of intelligence: linguistic, logicomathematical, musical, spatial, kinesthetic, interpersonal, and intrapersonal skills. Each type of intelligence involves cognitive skills, and variations occur in children in each type of intelligence. Children will be stronger in some types of intelligence and weaker in others.

Regardless of individual and cultural differences, children in all cultures gain in their ability to use thought in learning. Whether one looks at information processing as the source for advancement in thinking, the cognitive developmental theory, or Gardner's intelligences, school-age children use logic and mental strategies in their learning. The ability to develop memory strategies and to organize information within more than one characteristic is applied to their cognitive play.

Play and Cognitive Development

In Chapter 5, levels of cognitive play were discussed based on the theories of Piaget and Smilansky. Although they disagreed on the developmental level needed to engage in the highest form of play, both agreed that games with rules followed lower levels of play such as practice play and symbolic play. Games with rules require concrete operational thinking, motor skills, and social competence. In the following section, games with rules will be discussed as well as advances in pretend play and technological play.

Characteristics of Cognitive Play

Games with Rules

Johnson (1998) describes how preschool children can engage in simple games such as lotto and board games with spinners. It is not until children have achieved concrete operations that they can engage in a wide array of different types of games with rules. When they are capable of designing and implementing a plan or strategy and playing in both competition and cooperation with other players, they are able to participate in all types of games with consistent and complex rules.

Between the ages of 8 and 12, games are very popular with school-age children. Some of the games are constant, such as tag; others are cyclical or seasonal, such as marbles or hopscotch

(Manning, 1998). These games require cooperation among players as well as the ability to remain engaged in play activities for a longer period of time. But, most important, players must be able to submit to the rules and exercise self-control as a game player.

Games with rules that are child initiated evolve from practice and symbolic play. Like the ability to use concrete operational thinking, the transformation into games with rules can be gradual and specific to familiar play activities. Practice play where children engage in practicing a motor skill such as jumping can evolve into a game with rules when children agree on rules for jumping that can result in a winner (DeVries, 1998).

The ability to devise games with rules can evolve in stages. DeVries and Fernie (1990) were able to trace the stages in developing rules for the game tic-tac-toe by watching children move from putting pieces in squares without waiting turns to taking turns and using blocking strategies to defeat another player.

When children invent games, they understand that they have to develop rules to play the game as well as rules for social functioning. Opportunities to design games within the classroom help children learn to work cooperatively and have autonomy as part of the group of classmates. By creating rules, students feel ownership and responsibility for how they participate in games (Castle, 1998; DeVries & Zan, 1994).

Piaget (1932/1965) was able to observe stages in playing marbles from exploring the ability to shoot a marble in preschool children to the development of complex and consistent rules in older children. Teachers also teach and use games with rules in the classroom. Once children have acquired the ability to participate in rule-governed activities, teachers can use games as instructional tools and to introduce a playful atmosphere into the classroom. Games have been incorporated into science, mathematics, and reading as well as physical education (Barta & Schaelling, 1998; DeVries & Kohlberg, 1990; Hewitt, 1997; Jarrett, 1997; Kamii & DeVries, 1980; Owens & Sanders, 1998).

Pretend Play

School-age children do not engage in pretend play as much once they have entered the elementary grades. However, they continue this type of play away from school building forts and tree houses and also use miniature figures in fantasy play. Older children engage in giving plays (Manning, 1998). Many girls enjoy using Barbie dolls in pretend play, while boys frequently spend many hours playing with miniature vehicles of various types.

Technological Play

Computers and video games are a popular form of play for school-age children. While some children enjoy the challenges of finding information on the Web, others prefer to play games. Some of the games require little more than dexterity in manipulating figures in the game, while others demand more sophisticated thinking and problem solving.

More and more software is becoming available that fits the definition of play. There are games that permit children to play with digital dolls within software or engage in creative activities with three-dimensional media that becomes animated when completed (Yelland, 1999). Electronic games that mimic board games involve the application of educational concepts in literacy and mathematics.

Interactive toys with embedded computer programs permit the child to converse with the toy or play games and watch television simultaneously. Some newer interactive toys allow the child to react to particular television shows or videos. While there is much that a young child can learn from interactive toys and electronic games and software, there is the usual caution about the quality of play that these technological activities afford (Brooker, 2003). The limitations of technological play still exist as well as new avenues for play that provide exciting opportunities for play that are unavailable in other play materials (Oravic, 2000/01). More about technology play will be discussed in Chapter 9.

WHAT PARENTS, CAREGIVERS, AND TEACHERS CAN DO TO PROMOTE COGNITIVE PLAY

1. Adults can provide children with games that permit experience with games with rules to develop.
2. Adults can provide free play periods that will give children opportunities to develop their own games with rules.
3. Teachers can incorporate a playful environment in the classroom that will foster cognitive play.
4. Teachers can incorporate games into classroom learning experiences that will help students develop a playful approach to learning.
5. Teachers can use learning activities that will promote concrete operational thinking and information processing skills in classroom games.
6. Adults can play games with children that will foster the use of planning and mental strategies.

LANGUAGE AND LITERACY DEVELOPMENT

If language development is characterized as an explosion during the preschool years, school-age language development can be described as more subtle but equally important. Changes in language development are consistent during school-age years although they are less dramatic than in preschool years. Vocabulary, grammar, and pragmatics continue to be expanded and refined. In addition, school-age children develop an awareness of language. Their emerging thinking skills permit them to think about language and plan how they will express themselves. The interrelationship between cognitive development and language development is reflected in literacy development as the child develops new skills in writing and reading.

Characteristics of Language Development

Vocabulary Development

On average, school-age children learn about 20 new words a day. Many words are picked up in the context of reading. In addition, they are able to analyze words to derive their meaning. The ability to think about words enhances vocabulary development in addition to understanding that some words have multiple meanings. The grasp of multiple meanings enables children to engage in humor as they tell riddles and jokes (Berk, 2002; Waggoner & Palermo, 1989).

Grammatical Development

Preschool children have essentially mastered the grammar of their language; however, school-age children improve in more complex grammatical constructions. Cognitive development enables children to learn more subtle elements of grammar, such as the use of passive voice and infinitive phrases (Chomsky, 1969; Romaine, 1984).

Pragmatic Development

Although preschoolers begin to understand the use of pragmatics, school-age children steadily improve in their communication skills. Through their ability to listen carefully, understand what others will think is funny, and remember how to tell a joke, school-age children use their growing ability to use pragmatics in conversations using humor. They also learn the functions of polite speech and are able to use it—for example, when making a request (Berger, 2000).

Code Switching

School-age children understand different language codes and can move from one to another.

They know they can use swearing with their friends, but not with their parents or teachers. They are aware of a formal language code that is used in the classroom as compared with a more restricted or colloquial code (slang) with friends in the lunchroom or on the playground (Romaine, 1984).

Bilingualism and Nonstandard English

School-age children become aware of the use of nonstandard English or dialects. All language cultures have an informal language that can be dialectical. Children from different regions of the United States speak in different dialects, as do children from unique cultures within a region (Berger & Thompson, 1996).

Many children speak more than one language. As they enter elementary school, children who speak a language other than English will learn English as a second language. Children who continue to use a language other than English are **bilingual**, or capable of speaking two languages (Diaz, 1985).

Children who are bilingual, and children who speak a dialect benefit from daily interaction with speakers of standard English. This is true whether the interaction is with peers or adults. At the same time, teachers accept the child's language while guiding expansion and refinement using standard English. There is currently controversy as to how bilingual school-age children should be taught. For decades, there have been bilingual programs where children are taught or supported in their home language while learning English. More recently, English only, or an immersion process in English is preferred in some states.

The school environment that has children who speak several different languages affords opportunities for children and challenges for teachers. Appreciation for other languages can be learned by the children. At the same time, teachers can use language differences to enrich the understanding of the role of language. Assisting children who speak other languages is complex when the teacher seeks to meet individual language development and needs.

Characteristics of Literacy Development

School-age children continue the journey into literacy begun in the preschool years. For many children, entry into first grade is anticipated as the time they will learn to read and write. In emergent literacy-based primary classrooms, children use emergent writing and reading skills as they individually acquire more advanced levels of literacy. Children are taught phonics and word identification skills as they are encountered in their writing efforts and reading activities. Some classrooms focus on instruction in reading and writing skills, while others are a blend of various approaches to literacy (Bradley & Pottle, 2001). Moreover, children can benefit from frequent experiences with varied forms of literacy, including informational texts (Walker, Kragler, Martin, & Arnett, 2003).

The beginning stages of reading are followed by refinement in reading and writing in each subsequent grade. By the end of elementary school, children have moved from learning to read and write to using reading and writing to learn. Play with literacy enhances the process, as does using literacy in play activities. Playful literacy, or using playful activities in literacy instruction, can be valuable experiences in literacy development (Scully & Roberts, 2002).

Language and Literacy Development and Play

Infants begin play with language by playing with the sounds of language. Preschoolers begin to use language in their sociodramatic play, both within the play and in a metalinguistic capacity as they talk about their play. School-age children also use language in a supportive role as an element of their play but are more subtle in incorporating language into their play activities.

Play with Language

Although younger children are able to tell simple jokes, such as knock-knock jokes, older children use jokes and riddles in a broader perspective.

School-age children were described earlier as understanding that words can have more than one meaning. This double-meaning of words is used in jokes and riddles. Jokes and riddles are collected and used as social rituals with friends and new acquaintances.

Jokes can be used to try out off-color language and humorous insults. Older elementary school children try out playful insults on each other, and the ensuing dialogue can become a contest as they try to outdo each other in trading insults (Davidson, 1998).

Language and Pretend Play

We have mentioned that school-age children tend to use pretend play outside of the school environment. Another characteristic of pretend play is that language is now substituted for the more physical enactments of play in preschool children. Pretend play takes on the character of a story and is planned carefully before its enactment. It can focus on toys, such as Barbie dolls with the creation of a story line for the dolls, or be more abstract, with only a dialogue to support the pretend story. Boys might play out a sports event such as football or reenact a movie with language to support the plot. Davidson suggests that the difference between pretend play and storytelling becomes blurred in school-age children because they are simultaneously creating a story and using language to support pretend play.

Language and Social Play

In the discussion about motor development and play, jump rope was described as a favorite game for school-age girls. They now combine their enjoyment of jump rope with that of rhymes, so that these games then become a socialization activity in play. Children learn traditional jump rope rhymes and invent new ones.

Language is also used for social rituals. School-age children organize "clubs" with secret passwords and special phrases that outsiders cannot understand. Pig Latin is an example of the special language that can accompany membership in a social club. This and other language variations invented by children require an understanding of how words are composed and the development of new rules for the invented language (Davidson, 1998).

Adult Roles in Language and Literacy Play

In much of the play that occurs in preschool settings, teachers play a facilitative role in encouraging play. They might engage in play with the children to encourage higher forms of play, but the children tend to initiate most of the play activities.

As children enter elementary school, play becomes more teacher directed. As was seen earlier in motor play and cognitive play, the teacher either directs the activity, as in the case of the physical education teacher, or designs the activity, such as cognitive games in different subject areas.

In the case of language and literacy play, especially literacy play, there is some discussion in the literature as to what the teacher's role should be. Emergent literacy is seen as developing within the child with reading and writing evolving through opportunities to engage in literacy activities through sociodramatic play. As children enter a more teacher-directed learning environment in first grade, there is some concern that these opportunities can become lost (Seally & Roberts, 2002).

Some researchers regard symbolic play as essential for literacy. They propose that language and literacy learning occur naturally in symbolic play contexts. The teacher serves as a facilitator in setting up play environments that incorporate literacy activities. Likewise, the teacher scaffolds or supports language and literacy development by modeling literacy during play activities (Chang & Yawkey, 1998; Morrow & Rand, 1991; Pickett, 1998; Vygotsky, 1978).

Primary grade teachers, especially first grade teachers, might not perceive the use of play centers as important for the acquisition of literacy skills. Even if they would like to use play centers for

WHAT PARENTS, CAREGIVERS, AND TEACHERS CAN DO TO PROMOTE LANGUAGE AND LITERACY PLAY

1. Teachers can incorporate literacy and sociodramatic centers into primary grade classrooms to support student-initiated activities with literacy.
2. Adults can provide opportunities for children to have time for play where conversation can be incorporated into play.
3. Adults can encourage children in learning rhymes and chants as well as developing their own.
4. Adults can engage children in games such as Scrabble where literacy skills can be practiced in a playful mode.
5. Teachers can design and encourage students to design board games that incorporate literacy skills.

literacy, they might not include them because of pressures for children to read and write using more formal approaches (Patton & Mercer, 1996). In an effort to help primary grade teachers continue a more facilitative role using play to promote literacy, suggestions have been offered as to how centers can be incorporated into the classroom that can accomplish the desired literacy objectives. Block play (Pickett, 1998), symbolic play (Chang & Yawkey, 1998), and sociodramatic play (Patton & Mercer, 1996; Stone & Christie, 1996) are proposed as avenues for primary grade teachers to use to facilitate and model literacy skills. Although such teaching approaches might seem inappropriate to some primary grade teachers, there is evidence that literacy and symbolic and sociodramatic play are natural partners in a continuum of literacy development that begins in preschool and continues into school-age classrooms (Chang & Yawkey, 1998; Pellegrini & Galda, 1990).

SOCIAL AND EMOTIONAL DEVELOPMENT

As children move through the elementary school grades, they undergo major personality changes and experience many factors that affect their social and emotional development. Although their family remains an important influence, peer relationships and success in school are also significant to the success of their development. They continue in the progress of development in self-concept and self-esteem, but emerging cognitive skills permit taking perspective and developing morals. This period of social development was labeled **industry versus inferiority** by Erikson (1950).

The emotional tasks faced by school-age children, according to Erikson, is whether they will develop confidence and competence in useful skills and tasks or whether they will feel inferior and unable to be successful. If children are able to meet the challenges of this period of development, they become industrious and seek mastery over their learning. If they are unable to meet the challenges, they become sad and pessimistic, feeling that they are unable to succeed and be good at anything (Berk, 2002). As they work alongside their peers in school, children become aware of their own abilities as well as those of their peers. They are able to evaluate their strengths and weaknesses and compare themselves with their classmates. Their social development permits them to have lasting relationships with peers and friends. Social and emotional development interact in characteristics of social development.

Characteristics of Social and Emotional Development

Self-Concept

Children continue in their development of **self-concept** in the school-age years. In comparing themselves with others, they are able to make social comparisons. They compare their appearance, abilities, and accomplishments with those of their classmates. Their interactions with others include the emerging ability to use perspective taking in their social relationships, which enables them to understand what others are thinking or to take the other person's viewpoint into account. They interpret what others think about them into their concept about themselves (Rosenberg, 1979).

Self-Esteem

Because school-age children are more aware of their own successes and failures, they have much more information about their performance than they did as preschoolers. They use feedback from their own evaluation of performance plus feedback from others to assess their self-esteem in terms of their physical, academic, and social abilities. They are able to describe their overall feeling of self-worth by combining their achievements in these three categories. While they are able to be fairly realistic in appraising their own characteristics, they tend to give themselves lower ratings than they did as overly optimistic preschoolers.

Students who see themselves as successful in social development, or have a **positive self-esteem**, believe that their successes are due to their ability—they become success oriented. On the negative side, children who see themselves as failures and unable to succeed develop **learned helplessness**. They feel that their failures are due to bad luck and cannot be changed by hard work. They give up on trying to succeed in school and social tasks and depend on others to help them (Dweck & Leggett, 1988).

Perspective Taking

When children are able to imagine what others are thinking and feeling, it affects how they react in social situations. **Perspective taking** helps them get along with others. Children go through stages of perspective taking (Selman, 1976) and develop individual abilities. Children who are good perspective takers are more likely to express empathy and compassion. They are better at social problem solving in that they are able to find solutions to difficult social situations. Children with very poor social skills lack an awareness of others' thoughts and points of view. They exhibit angry and aggressive behaviors and are likely to mistreat their peers (Berk, 2002).

Moral Development

A parallel characteristic of perspective taking is **moral development**. Children's moral understanding advances in the school-age years through their increasing understanding of others' perspectives. They are developing ideas of fairness and merit. They also can recognize that special consideration should be given to their peers who are at a disadvantage. Their developing ideas of fairness are supported by social interactions and adult encouragement and advice (Damon, 1990).

Peer Relationships

Elementary school children are able to organize into peer groups that consist of leaders and followers. These peer groups become a **peer culture** that is expressed in uniform dress and ritual activities. Children who are accepted into a group or club acquire a sense of group identity. Through their experiences in the peer group, children learn about participation in social organizations and acquire social skills.

In addition to their own social groups, school-age children enjoy more structured organizational groups such as 4-H groups and Boy and Girl Scouts. With adult guidance, children grow in moral and social understanding through community service and group projects.

Some children make friends and are accepted into social groups more easily than others. Children who are accepted by their peers are more likely to have later positive social adjustment. Children who are rejected, on the other hand, develop a low sense of self-esteem and are likely to have emotional and social problems as well as poor school performance (Ollendick, Weist, Borden, & Greene, 1992).

Parent-Child Relationships

Parent-child relationships change in school-age years; however, the quality of parent-child interactions plays a major role in the child's social development.

School-age children's parents spend less time with them than they did when they were preschoolers, and they find that their children are easier to manage. A major task for parents is to promote responsible behavior in their children and how to deal with school problems. Some parents are uncertain about how to relate to the school and how much they should become involved in the child's homework. Effective parents are able to include the child in some of the decisions that must be made. They can develop a cooperative relationship with their child and appeal to the child's ability to think logically in problem-solving situations.

There are also negative influences on parent-child relationships. Many American children experience divorce in their family, and new family relationships can cause disturbed relationships over a period of at least 2 years. Divorce and remarriage can result in children having to adapt to new stepparents and blended families (Lutz, 1983).

Sibling Relationships

Siblings can provide support and companionship during school-age years. However, they also experience rivalry and conflict. Children who receive less parental support and attention are more likely to express resentment toward a sibling that they perceive to get more approval and attention. Siblings who are close in age are more likely to engage in quarreling and antagonism. Birth order has an effect as well as older children receive more pressure to behave maturely and succeed in school. Younger siblings tend to be more popular with age mates, perhaps as a result of learning to get along with the older sibling (Berk, 2002).

Play and Social-Emotional Development

Chapter 5 presented an extended discussion of how young children develop social competence that is reflected in their play. The role of parenting in children's social competence was described, as well as how children engage in social play and sociodramatic play. In this chapter, the direction of social competence developed in the preschool years is described as predictive of successful social interactions in school-age years. Characteristics of social play in school-age children are similar to those in preschool years; however, peer relationships are more important to successful social play than parenting roles.

Theoretical Views of Social Play

The theories of Piaget (1962), Vygotsky (Creasey, Jarvis, & Berk, 1998), Parten (1932), and Smilansky (1968) helped define development in social play in the preschool years. In school-age children, two approaches now describe social play. Earlier in the chapter under "Cognitive Development," children's play was characterized as dominated by games with rules. Piaget and Smilansky both believed that games with rules comprise the highest level of social play. Games with rules bring together social, physical, and cognitive development in children as they engage in games and sports in elementary school.

Social play of school-age children also fits Parten's (1932) highest category of play, cooperative play. Children's cognitive development permits them to understand the ideas and thoughts of others, while social development makes it possible for children to interact with children in social play by appreciating the needs of others

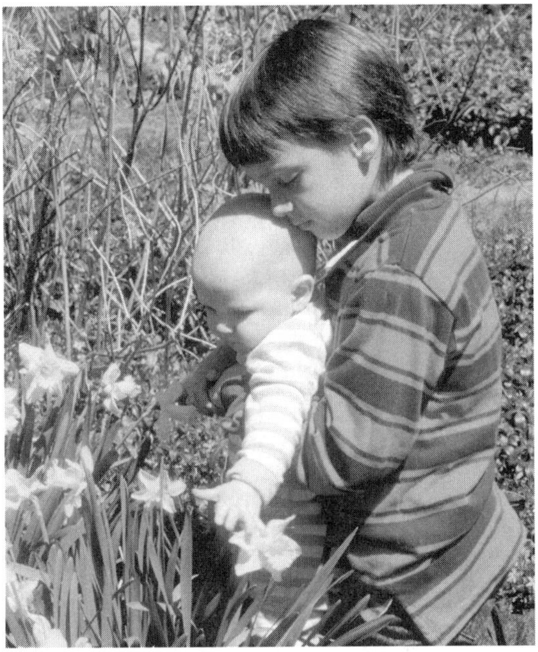

Siblings provide support and companionship.

and using problem-solving skills to work through difficulties in social play. Keeping in mind that games with rules, cooperative play, social competence, and peer influence and relationships are the primary factors in school-age play, we will next look at the characteristics of social play in school-age children.

Characteristics of Social Play

Rubin and his colleagues have conducted longitudinal studies of social play (Coplan & Rubin, 1998) and have found that social play is relatively stable when preschool play is compared with school-age play. In their observations of social play, they found that peer-rated social competence at age 7 could predict either higher self-regard or self-reported loneliness in later childhood (Rubin, Chen, McDougall, Bowker, & McKinnon, 1995). Social play competence in preschool years could be traced to peer-rated social competence or peer rejection in school-age children. However, these researchers cautioned that frequent social play in itself was not predictive of later social competence and not all preschoolers who engaged in a high frequency of social play grew up to be well-adjusted teenagers (Coplan & Rubin, 1998).

Manning (1998) summarizes the characteristics of social play in school-age children when their physical, cognitive, language, and social skills support each other as follows:

> Ten- to 12-year-old children, in particular develop the social skills necessary to participate in complex, cooperative forms of play. The complexity and flexibility of their verbal as well as nonverbal communication contribute to this cooperative potential. They are also able to make friends, interact competently and confidently in social situations, and build on their increasing social skills (Manning, 1993). These enhanced social skills allow children to see others' perspectives and allow them to realize the benefits of playing socially and cooperatively. Actual play, which requires social skills, might consist of games, team sports, and organized activities. (p. 157)

Manning's description includes how the ability to cooperate enhances social play, as such play encourages cooperation and fosters the development of social skills. The trend at the current time, however, is away from cooperation and toward more competition. Educators seem not to understand that child-initiated social play is important for the development of social skills. Some encourage competition in physical education classes and sports activities, which removes opportunities for social development through play (Manning, 1998).

Variations in Social Competence and Play

Effective Peer Relations

We can see from the discussion about characteristics of social play in school-age children that social competence is not uniform in children, especially after they enter elementary grades. Children vary in how they are accepted by their peers, and acceptance or rejection affects how successful children are in engaging in all types of play activities. Children who develop social competence in the preschool years are more likely to be accepted into peer group play. Rejected children are likely to be left out of group play activities, ending up feeling lonely and unworthy.

School personnel are attempting to address the problems of rejected children on public school playgrounds. One cause of rejection is children's play behaviors. Some children have problems in understanding how to enter a play group (Dodge, Coie, Pettit, & Price, 1990), and teachers can help them learn these skills so that they can enjoy playing with peers.

Educators in school settings are also trying to ameliorate the plight of children who are excluded from play or teased. Researchers developed a project that initiated a policy of play inclusion in which the rule is "You can't say you can't play" (Sapon-Shevin, Dobbelaere, Corrigan, Goodman, & Mastin, 1998). In the project classroom, teachers used the rule with their children and followed through with guidance to see that all children were included in classroom and outdoor play. Teachers experimented with different ways to use the rule with their classes. Many issues were raised by older elementary school students, who questioned whether students should be made to include all children into their play groups. They also questioned whether there were situations when group size was limited, thus forcing some children to be left out.

Aggression and Bullying in Play

Two negative behaviors related to social play are **aggression** in play and **bullying** (Shantz, 1986). Although boys are responsible for the majority of incidents of aggression, girls, too, can be described as aggressive. However, the type of aggression exhibited is different for the two genders. Boys tend to be physically aggressive, while girls are verbally aggressive (Shantz, 1986).

Researchers have looked at both the causes and the outcomes of aggression. The assumption has been that aggressive children are rejected by the peers, but studies have found mixed results. On the one hand, Cairns, Cairns, Neckerman, Gest, and Gairepy (1988) found that aggressive children had their own social networks that included children who were also aggressive. They were picked as best friends as frequently as nonaggressive peers. Moreover, bullies often feel powerful, superior, and justified in their aggressive behaviors (Bullock, 2002).

A different type of information was found in a study of 8- and 9-year-old boys. Aggressive boys were found to spend more time alone without being involved in play activities. They changed the peers they played with more often and showed and received more negative behaviors than a control group. This study determined that aggressive boys misinterpret play invitations, which leads them to fights rather than play. They are more self-centered and not as interested in the reactions of peers in play. They have poor social skills and have had negative experiences in play relationships with others, which has become a spiraling problem leading to more aggression (Willner, 1991).

Bullying is a form of aggressive play. Olweus (1993) defines bullying as "exposure, repeatedly and over time, to negative actions (words, physical contact, making faces, gesturing), or intentional exclusion from a group on the part of one or more other students" (p. 9). Boys are more likely to be bullies, but girls and boys are equally likely to become recipients of bullying (Froschl & Sprung, 1999). Although bullying begins in the early childhood years, it is most significant in later grades. Children who learn patterns of bullying in the early years may develop a pattern of violence in later life (Baumeister, 2001).

The role of teachers in reacting to bullying affects the frequency of the behavior. Researchers have found that teachers do relatively little to stop bullying, either because they are unaware that it is occurring or because they want the children to work out their own problems. When teachers do not intervene, children believe that they condone the behavior (Bullock, 2002). Children may also perceive that boys are being given permission to tease and bully (Olweus, 1993, 1994).

There seem to be behavioral characteristics of children who are the victims of aggression and bullying. Aggressive children did not expect their victims to fight back. In addition, the victims were quick to show their pain and stress to the aggressors. The victimized children were likely to be rejected, and students expected that no punishment would result from attacking them (Perry, Williard, & Perry, 1990). Children who were bullied were younger and weaker, and appeared anxious and insecure. They often reacted by crying and withdrawing (Bullock, 2002).

In spite of the common belief that nothing can be done to stop bullying, efforts can be made to prevent this type of aggressive behavior. One approach is to address the issue of bullying with younger children before it becomes serious during school-age years. Preschool teachers can use intervention and teaching strategies to help children understand more positive play behaviors. Parents, too, must be part of the solution by being kept apprised of bullying behavior and being involved in helping their own children avoid bullying of their peers (Froschl & Sprung, 1999).

School intervention policies can address the problem of bullying. The school, including teachers and children can develop policies and strategies for appropriate behavior and sanctions against bullies (Lickona, 2000; Olweus, 1997). Such a project was developed to reduce bullying by older children directed at younger children on the playground. Sessions conducted by a counselor and school resource officer raised sensitivity to the problem, while student-teacher partnerships fostered positive interactions and provided protection from possible bullies on the playground (Youngerman, 1998).

From Sociodramatic Play to Structured Dramatics

Sociodramatic play permeates the social play of preschool children. In Chapter 5, we considered the importance and evolution of sociodramatic play, especially as it related to the work of Smilansky (Smilansky & Shefatya, 1990). This emphasis on children's sociodramatic play drops substantially in the school-age years. It is not necessarily that children's interest in sociodramatic play has declined but that opportunities for and approval of sociodramatic play are lost in school during the primary grades. Instead, older children can engage in this type of play only in the home environment (Dunn, 1998).

Creative dramatics becomes the accepted form of dramatic play in school in the primary years and can extend through all elementary school grades. Definitions of creative drama include "improvised drama [that] exists primarily for the enjoyment and benefit of the players" (Mellou, 1994, p. 126). This type of play is characterized as appropriate for children from the age of 5 or 6 and older, and the teacher has a role in guiding and facilitating dramatic enactment. A theatrical presentation is not the goal of creative dramatics; moreover, improvisation is part of the process. The dramatization can change and expand as the children use their imagination and play in pretending (Johnson, 1998).

Creative dramatics is also seen as preparation for a dramatic performance by teachers. Although the children are engaged in inventing or developing the "play," the teacher has more of a directive role in structuring the performance and guiding the children in perfecting the production (Schooley, 1995). In addition, the creative drama presentation may include making costumes and other props (Soefje, 1998).

It may be asked at what point does creative dramatics eliminate the child's dramatic play? Is there a need to understand a difference between creative dramatics and dramatic productions? Do children need to continue in sociodramatic play within the school setting in the school-age years? It is clear that the pattern is toward more structure and teacher direction and less emphasis on children's natural creations in dramatic play. Is there room for both in elementary classrooms? Are there benefits in sociodramatic play as described in the preschool years that continue to be important for school-age children? There are definite differences in untutored dramatic play and tutored creative drama (Mellou, 1994). Teachers need to understand the differences as well as benefits of both types of dramatic play and creative drama.

Adult Roles in Social and Sociodramatic Play

It is during the elementary school years that social competence and acceptance in play groups become most apparent. Positive play behaviors include development of friendships and acceptance into peer groups. Negative play behaviors are obvious in children who become playground bullies and those who are isolated and lonely because they are rejected.

Parents and teachers can play significant roles in intervening in helping children use positive social skills in their group interactions and play. Efforts to reduce exclusion from play were described earlier; however, there is evidence that teachers do not necessarily see it as their responsibility to intervene when bullies prevail or when children are isolated from social groups on the playground. Parents need to be aware whether their child is aggressive or a bully so that they can work with the teacher in eliminating inappropriate behaviors. Likewise, parents and teachers need to work together in assisting children who are socially rejected and excluded from opportunities to play with their peers.

Adults also need to understand the role of sociodramatic play in school-age children. Parents can support and encourage sociodramatic play when children are playing together in the home environment. Teachers need to understand the role of sociodramatic play in school-age children and provide for this type of play as well as creative dramatics in the curriculum.

WHAT PARENTS, CAREGIVERS, AND TEACHERS CAN DO TO PROMOTE SOCIAL AND SOCIODRAMATIC PLAY

1. Adults can observe social behaviors and intervene to encourage positive social behaviors.
2. Adults can work with individual children who are rejected socially or use inappropriate bullying or aggressive play behaviors.
3. Adults can facilitate opportunities for rejected children to be included in peer play groups.
4. Adults can help popular children be accepting of children who have difficulty being accepted socially.
5. Adults can facilitate sociodramatic play in school-age children. Teachers can accomplish this goal by including theme-related dramatic play centers that include appropriate props related to classroom curriculum.
6. Teachers can include opportunities for creative dramatics and dramatic productions within the classroom curriculum.

CHARACTERISTICS OF SCHOOL-AGE PLAY

The Integrated Nature of Play

School-age children use all of their capabilities in their play. The types of play engaged in reflect their abilities and interests as well as how well developed they are in a particular domain. Children who are physically competent are more likely to enjoy participating in physical games and sports, while students who are more adept socially are more likely to use their social skills in play. While language, cognitive, motor, and social skills are all required for play, definite differences in ability and motivation have appeared by the time children enter school. Opportunity for participation also affects how skilled children become in sports and other activities such as ballet and music.

Gender Differences in Play

Earlier in the chapter, gender differences in play was partially attributed to parental expectations, particularly in the case of physical play. These differences are also affected by social expectations; however, currently there is more of an emphasis on gender-equitable play with more equal opportunities provided for boys and girls. Gender differences persist, though, in school-age children in all types of play, as will be discussed in the following sections.

Gender Differences in Physical Play

In the school-age years, boys tend to play outdoors more than girls. Boys play in larger groups than girls and tend to play more in same-age groups (Vaughter, Sadh, & Vozzola, 1994). Both boys and girls tend to play at or near their homes. Boys spend more of their time in ball games, while girls spend their play time in conversations, apparatus play, and games that require taking turns (Tracy, 1987).

In mixed-school settings girls tend to stay closer to an adult than boys; however, when in an all-girl group, girls are willing to go farther from an adult (Maccoby, 1990). Both boys and girls prefer to play with same gender peers rather than in mixed groups (Maccoby, 1988).

Gender Differences in Social Play

School-age children demonstrate gender differences in their social play. Boys engage in play that is less mature than girls' play. They are occupied more often in solitary-functional play and rough-and-tumble play. Girls, on the other hand, spend more time in quiet activities such as peer conversations and parallel and constructive play (Rubin, Fein, & Vandenberg, 1983).

Gender differences can be noted by grade level. One study found that boys in fourth grade engage in more group play than girls. This is reflected in a high frequency of rough-and-tumble play by boys. Contrasted with this boisterous play is the predominance of conversational activities on the part of fourth grade girls (Moller, Hymel, & Rubin, 1992).

Gender Differences in Electronic Game Play

Boys spend more time playing electronic games than girls do; moreover, the most popular games present stereotyped characterizations of men and women: men are pictured as aggressors; women are portrayed as victims. It is possible that girls are not attracted to electronic games because women have secondary, negative roles in the games (Provenzo, 1991). A study of preferences showed that both boys and girls preferred games that were violent in nature. However, boys preferred realistic violence, while girls preferred fantasy violence (Buchman & Funk, 1996).

Boys seem to enjoy playing electronic games more than girls, which thus explains the more extensive time they engage in these games. Evidence indicates that some children are at risk from playing these games when preexisting adjustment problems are affected or new problems are precipitated (Funk & Buchman, 1996).

Gender Differences in Rough-and-Tumble Play

We will discuss gender differences in rough-and-tumble play more comprehensively in the next section; for now, we will point out a few of them. First, boys engage in rough-and-tumble play more than girls. Second, cultural differences affect this type of play. For example, according to Garvey (1990), boys engage in more rowdy play than girls among the Mixtecans of Mexico and Taira of Okinawa. However, among the Pilaga Indians, girls also participate in rough play (Manning, 1998). Finally, boys are most likely to select boys for rough-and-tumble play. To the contrary, when girls engage in this sort of play, they select both boys and girls (Pellegrini, 1998).

Rough-and-Tumble Play

Rough-and-tumble play reaches a peak during the elementary school years. It accounts for about 5% of the play of preschool children but up to 17% of school-age play. It declines again in middle school.

Since aggression and aggressive play are important factors in school-age children's play, it would follow that the comparison of play fighting and aggression would be a part of the understanding of rough-and-tumble play among elementary school children. In discussing the topic in the preschool years in Chapter 5, we made a comparison between the behaviors in play fighting and real fighting. Also discussed was the reality that teachers did not recognize the differences between play fighting and real fighting. This type of comparison continues when discussing school-age children. Teachers in primary grades also reported difficulty in differentiating between the two in a primary school study (Schafer & Smith, 1996). Nevertheless, there are other significant differences in play fighting or rough-and-tumble play that are related to the play of rejected children and bullies and the play of children who are socially skilled and accepted by their peers.

Rough-and-tumble play is characterized by running, chasing, fleeing, and wrestling behaviors. When engaged in this play, children often remain together when the episode has ended and move on to other activities (Pellegrini, 1988). In rough-and-tumble play, children often exchange roles or discuss roles (Burns & Brainerd, 1979). In aggressive play, to the contrary, children do not play together after an incidence of fighting with aggression, nor do they exchange roles. The perpetrator of the aggression does not trade roles with the victim (Pellegrini, 1998). Moreover, in a review of studies of aggression, researchers found that boys were more aggressive than girls in 67% of the studies (Maccoby & Jacklin, 1974).

Rough-and-tumble play reaches a peak during the elementary school years.

Definite differences appear in rough-and-tumble play by boys who are accepted socially and those who are rejected socially. Boys who are rejected engage in the same levels of rough-and-tumble play; however, their play is likely to end in true aggression (Pellegrini, 1988). While rough-and-tumble play declines during adolescence in socially accepted boys, rejected and aggressive boys continue in this type of play; moreover, they select weaker boys as their play partners and victims (Fagen, 1981). Socially popular boys use sports and academics for peer relationships in early adolescence, while bullies use physical aggression for peer status. They use rough-and-tumble play as a pretext for victimizing other, weaker boys.

There are differences also in the perception of rough-and-tumble play by socially adjusted boys and boys who are peer rejected. Children who are well adjusted can differentiate between aggression and rough-and-tumble play, while rejected children tend to see this play as aggression (Dodge & Frame, 1982).

Chase Games

Rough-and-tumble play includes chasing; however, in Chapter 4, chasing was discussed as a type of play in itself. Chase games were described as involving physical skill, strategy, and tagging and hiding (Clarke, 1999). Although chase games begin in the preschool years, they extend into the school-age years.

By the age of 5, chase games are incorporated into sociodramatic play. Between ages 5 and 7, chasing continues to initiate thematic play. Children are not only creating their own organized chase games but are also learning traditional chase games such as hide and seek. Clarke (1999) and Schneider (1997) have designated the period from age 4 to 5 as stage 6 in the developmental sequence of chase games and stage 7 for development between ages 5 and 7.

The last stage of chase games, stage 8, occurs from ages 7 to 11. Chasing occurs primarily within the context of organized games. There are predetermined rules for the game and social consequences for those who break a rule. Thus, chase games complement other cognitive and social categories of development in each stage and complement advances in development in other domains. Table 5-1 in Chapter 5 shows stages 5, 6, 7, and 8 in the development of chase games into school-age years.

School-age children play chase games differently than preschool children. One theme of chase games is the threat of kissing, particularly in the primary grades. This type of cross-gender chasing is accepted in primary grade children but stops in intermediate grade children, especially if wrestling or other types of rough-and-tumble play is involved (Thorne, 1995). Other chase games involve giving and getting "cooties" or some other type of contamination. Called "pollution games," chase games in this context might involve rejected children or children who are considered unequal, such as children of different ethnic groups. This included girls by the boys in a playground study who considered girls to be inferior (Thorne, 1995).

Chase games can be initiated by interrupting an ongoing activity, such as boys invading a group of girls playing jump rope or girls interfering with a football game, thus inviting the other group to chase them. This is sometimes not perceived as play by the group who is invaded, who might be respond by complaining to a teacher instead of starting the chase. Girls are more likely to complain than boys, and adult supervisors show more concern when boys interrupt girl activities (Thorne, 1995).

War Toys

Play with **war toys** has been associated with aggression by teachers. Although preschool children like to engage in fantasy play with guns and other weapons, this type of play persists into elementary schools, where it is generally banned. Play with war toys is primarily of interest to boys, who use guns and weapons to carry out fantasy play. It seems that boys label the play as play fighting or part of rough-and-tumble play, while adults characterize it as violent play causing aggression. Prohibition of war toys themselves does not discourage war play. Children use other substitutes for weapons (Wegener-Spohring, 1989).

It is not clear that the war toys themselves cause aggressive play. In a study of research on the relationship between war toys and aggressive play, Sutton-Smith (1988) found unclear results. Play fighting supported with war toys is generally sociodramatic play in which children carry out movie or television roles. Thus, the toys may not be the only or most significant influence toward aggression.

War toys can be used for many purposes. One possibility is when they are transformed in pretend play into something else (Bagley & Chaille, 1996). Goldstein (1995) cites 25 possible reasons that children play with war toys from his study of the literature on this topic. Although some of the reasons are directly or indirectly related to aggression and violence, some purposes can lead to nonviolent play. Figure 6–1 shows the biological,

FIGURE 6–1 Reasons for Play with War Toys

Biological/Physiological

1. Achieve a pleasing level of arousal/stimulation/excitement.
2. Expand energy, engage in intense physical activity.
3. Hormonal influences.

Psychological

4. Achieve a desired emotional state.
5. Prime cognitive salience of aggression.
6. Try to understand violence, war, death.
7. Feel in control of aggression.
8. Allay anxiety about violence, war, guns.
9. Engage in fantasy/imaginative play.
10. Experience an "altered state of consciousness/flow."
11. Practice strategic planning, problem solving.
12. Set goals and determine effective means for accomplishing them.
13. Gain a sense of mastery.

Social

14. Belong to a positive reference group.
15. Experience intimacy.
16. Direct modeling by peers or family.
17. Indirect modeling: Influences of media, marketing.
18. Rewards and encouragement for such play.
19. Salience within a culture of war, fighting.
20. Learn to control and resolve conflict and aggression.
21. Wield power; to affect others.
22. Exclude oneself from a (negative reference) group (e.g. parents, girls, boys who disapprove of these games).
23. Elicit a predictable reaction from parents/teachers.
24. Sample a variety of adult roles.
25. Role-play.
26. Reflect cultural values, themes (If a culture values dominance, aggression, and assertion, this will appear in children's play and recreation).

Source: From "Aggressive Toy Play" (p. 140) by J. Goldstein in A. D. Pellegrini (Ed.), *The Future of Play Theory,* 1995, Albany: State University of New York Press.

psychological, and social reasons that Goldstein offers as to why children play with war toys.

Adult views of war toy play are at odds with the perception of the players and researchers. Adults view play fighting in this context as violent and aggressive (Conner, 1989; Kuykendall, 1996). Furthermore, although research does not support the premise that war toys cause aggressive play (Conner, 1989), teachers believe that war toy play will lead to more serious forms of aggression and should be eliminated from the school environment (Kuykendall, 1996).

Creativity and Play

When young children enter the school years, their capabilities to be creative are full of possibility. They can use painting, photography, musical performance, drama composition and performance, computer programming, and dance as some of the venues for creativity and expression. School-age children are eager inventors and artists who demonstrate confidence and competence in their creative endeavors.

However, the same negative attitudes toward time for play that limit recess in elementary grades are also reflected in lack of time for creative activities (Manning, 1998). Unfortunately, the push for increased academic achievement has taken a toll on opportunities for creativity. Moreover, the school environment is accused of suppressing creativity in the elementary grades through a lack of understanding of the nature of creativity or a focus on convergent rather than divergent thinking. The enthusiasm for being creators in the preschool years is replaced with being passive spectators. Elementary school children often become more cautious and less innovative (Isenberg & Jalongo, 1997). Some of the characteristics of schools that discourage creativity are strict time limits for activities, an emphasis on memorization and convergent tasks, and an overemphasis on valuing conformity and following directions. Schools that nurture creativity, to the contrary, have the following practices (Isenberg & Jalongo, 1997, pp. 23–25):

1. School personnel strive to reduce stress and anxiety in children and in themselves.
2. Process is valued over product.
3. Time limits are removed from activities in which children are deeply involved.
4. A free, open atmosphere is established where self-expression is encouraged and valued.
5. The children are encouraged to share ideas, not only with the teacher but also with one another.
6. Competition and external rewards are minimized.

Contemporary school cultures commonly mitigate against creativity; nevertheless, many teachers naturally incorporate creativity into classroom activities without impinging on the stress on academic achievement. Teachers who understand creativity know the difference between predesigned art activities and opportunities for individual expression. They understand the difference between teacher-designed games and student efforts to create games to play with their peers. They understand the difference between developing ideas for classroom projects and nurturing students' ability to plan and implement curriculum activities. Creativity will emerge in the classroom where innovative thinking is valued and encouraged. If the classroom is truly supportive of student ideas and efforts to use creative expression, students will use their individual interests and talents to participate in classroom activities.

School-age play can be characterized through adult memories. Following are a few accounts of how adults remember their play as children.

SUSAN

> Tommy or Bob or Lon glided under water toward us, often in twos or threes, as though they needed support. We girls pretended not to notice them coming until they spouted to the top, with loud shouts, and pounced on us to dunk us. . . . Being shoved under water was

recognized as a sign that a boy had noticed you. He had at least taken the trouble to push you down. We certainly never complained, though I sometimes swallowed water and came up coughing. At other times the boys would ignore us and engage in their own elaborate games, diving for pennies or playing tag. We girls hung to the side, hanging onto the gutters and watched. (Thorne, 1995, pp. 81–82)

RICHARD

When I was a kid, I had a lab. It wasn't a laboratory in the sense that I would measure, or do important experiments. Instead, I would play: I'd make a motor, I'd make a gadget that would go off when something passed a photocell, I'd play around with selenium; I was piddling around all the time. (Feynman, 1985, pp. 74–75)

ANNIE

Some boys taught me to play football. This was a fine sport. You thought up a new strategy for every play and whispered it to the others. You went out for a pass, fooling everyone. Best, you got to throw yourself mightily at someone's running legs. Either you brought him down or you hit the ground flat out on your chin, with your arms empty before you. It was all or nothing. If you hesitated in fear, you would miss and get hurt: you would take a hard fall while the kid got away, or you would get kicked in the face while the kid got away. But if you flung yourself wholeheartedly at the back of his knees—if you gathered and joined body and soul and pointed them diving fearlessly—then you likely wouldn't get hurt, and you'd stop the ball. Your fate, and your team's score, depended on your concentration and courage. Nothing girls did could compare with it. (Dillard, 1987, p. 45)

ADULT ROLES IN SCHOOL-AGE PLAY

Adults have different roles in children's play when they enter the elementary school. Partly due to a different perspective of the value of play and partly due to the classroom environment being more teacher directed than in the preschool years, adult roles are more directed in play. Teachers who use play for learning experiences in the classroom engage children in games, perhaps in designing games. Children might participate in creative dramatics, but this, too, is more likely to have quite a bit of teacher direction. Opportunities to facilitate child-initiated play and to encourage exploratory play are not as common as in the preschool classroom.

Physical education teachers also engage in adult-directed activities with students. They teach games and sports during structured class times. Students have opportunities to engage in play, but they have been planned by the teacher and are supervised by the teacher.

If there is a time for free play outdoors, teachers play a supervisory role for the most part. They do not engage in play activities with the children, and sometimes offer little supervision, as noted in the section on rough-and-tumble play.

Parents also teach their children how to play sports. Fathers, particularly, work with their sons and daughters to learn baseball, basketball, soccer, and other sports. Fathers, and occasionally mothers, serve as coaches in Little League teams or other recreational clubs such as Boy and Girl Scouts and church youth groups.

A major role of parents is to provide transportation to organized play activities. It might be of an informal nature, as when parents take their child to play with a friend at the friend's house. More time is spent taking children to practice for a team. Parents with several children spend many hours after school and on Saturdays transporting their children to practice and games. A parallel role in these activities is to attend the games and support the child's team.

TABLE 6–1 Toys and Materials for School-Age Children

Overview of Play Materials for Primary-School Children—6 through 8 Years

Social and Fantasy Play Materials	Exploration and Mastery Play Materials
Mirrors Same as for adult use	**Construction materials** Large number of varied materials for detailed construction and for creating models (can use metal parts and tiny nuts and bolts)
Dolls Washable, rubber/vinyl baby dolls (with culturally relevant features and skin tones) (for younger children—age 6) Accessories (culturally relevant) for caretaking—feeding, diapering, and sleeping (for younger children—age 6) Smaller people figures for use with blocks or construction materials (for fantasy scenes and models)	**Puzzles** Three-dimensional puzzles Jigsaw puzzles (50 to 100 pieces)
Role-play materials Materials for creating and practicing real-life activities—play money with correct denominations, book- and letter-creating materials	**Pattern-making materials** Mosaic tiles, geometric puzzles Materials for creating permanent designs (art and craft materials)
Puppets Puppets that represent familiar and fantasy figures for acting out stories (children can create their own) Simple puppet theater—children can construct own (children can creats props and scenery)	**Dressing, lacing, stringing, materials** Bead-stringing, braiding, weaving, apool-knitting, and sewing materials now used in arts and crafts
Stuffed toys/play animals Realistic rubber, wood, or vinyl animals to incorporate into scenes and models or that show characteristics of animals being studied (such as reptiles and dinosaurs)	**Specific skill-development materials** Printing materials, typewriters, materials for making books Math manipulatives, fraction and geometrical materials Measuring materials—balance scales, rulers, graded cups for liquids, etc. Science materials—prism, magnifying materials, stethoscope Natural materials to examine and classify Plants and animals to study and care for Computer programs for language arts, number, and concept development and for problem-solving activities
Play scenes Small people/animal figures and supporting materials with which to construct fantasy scenes or models related to curriculum themes	**Games** Simple card and board games Word games, reading and spelling games Guessing games Memory games (Concentration) Number and counting games (dominoes, Parcheesi) Beginning strategy games (checkers, Chinese checkers)
Transportation toys Small, exact (metal) replicas preferred by children of this age range are not usually used in school settings, but more generic small models are useful Construction or workbench materials for children to use to make models of forms of transportation	**Books** Books at a variety of difficulty levels for children to read Storybooks for reading aloud Poetry, rhymes, humorous books, adventure books, myths Books made by children

(continued)

TABLE 6–1 *(continued)*

Overview of Play Materials for Primary-School Children—6 through 8 Years

Music, Art, and Movement Play Materials	Gross-Motor Play Materials
Art and craft materials Large variety of crayons, markers, colored pencils, art chalks, and pastels (many colors) Paintbrushes of various sizes A variety of paints, including watercolors A variety of art papers for drawing, tracing, painting Regular scissors Pastes and glues (nontoxic) Collage materials Clay that hardens Tools (including pottery wheel) More complex printing equipment Craft materials, such as simple looms, leather for sewing and braiding, paper-maché, plaster of paris, small beads for jewelry making, etc. Workbench with more tools and wood for projects (with careful supervision)	**Balls and sports equipment** Youth- or standard-size balls and equipment for beginning team play (kickball, baseball, etc.) Materials for target activities (to practice skills) **Ride-on equipment** (Children may be very interested in riding bicycles, but this is no longer included as a school activity) **Outdoor and gym equipment** Complex climbing structures, such as those appropriate for age 5 (including ropes, ladders, hanging bars, rings)
Musical instruments Real instruments, such as recorders (sometimes used for group lessons in school settings) A wider range of instruments for children to explore (borrowed or brought in by parents or special guests)	
Audiovisual materials Music for singing Music for movement, including dancing (folk dancing by age 8) Music, singing, rhymes, and stories for listening Audiovisual materials that children can use independently	

Note: Although the four categories provide a useful classification, play materials can typically be used in more than one way and could be listed under more than one of the categories.

Source: From *The Right Stuff for Children Birth to 8* (pp. 120–121) by M. B. Bronson, 1995, Washington, DC: National Association for the Education of Young Children.

Parents also engage in quieter forms of play in the home as the family plays card and board games. This practice has declined with the advent of video games and computer games, which are more likely to be solitary forms of play. Some parents, however, do participate in video games that have more than one player.

Overall, parents spend less time in participating in children's play in the school-age years. This is offset by the increased amount of time spent in the car transporting children to organized sports lessons and activities.

TOYS AND MATERIALS FOR SCHOOL-AGE PLAY

The nature of toys and materials shifts in the elementary grades to complement children's abilities and interests in play. Bronson (1995) has outlined play materials that are appropriate for school-age children. Although they are described as being appropriate for primary grade children, most are also appropriate for older children in elementary grades. Table 6–1 shows the variety of materials that can be used.

SUMMARY

Play takes on different dimensions in the school-age child. Peer play becomes very important as do games and sports. Advances in physical, cognitive, and social development combine to enable children to enjoy play activities with their peers.

Physical development enters a period when gross- and fine-motor abilities are refined and strengthened. Through practice, children are able to engage in many more activities; however, there are variations in the opportunities available to children to engage in physical activities. Poor nutrition, illness, and injuries can affect motor development, as can the lack of opportunities to participate in group sports and instruction in sports such as tennis and swimming.

Gender differences in physical development can be due to parental and societal expectations that are different for boys and girls. The interests of boys and girls are also a factor in their selection of activities.

School-age children have fewer opportunities for free play partly because schools are placing more emphasis on academic instruction and partly because fears persist that students will injure themselves on the school playground. Parents who are unavailable after school also might expect children to remain indoors until they return from work. Although there are many proponents of making free play available at school through recess periods, current trends are for less free play rather than more.

Children enter the concrete operational period in cognitive development, which enables them to use logical and organized thinking. These advances in cognition help explain children's interests in games and sports since they are able to participate in games with rules. Children can follow rules for a game as well as develop rules for their own games. While games with rules becomes more popular, pretend play declines.

Developments in language and literacy also extend possibilities for participation in play. Children play with language as they tell jokes and engage in social rituals. They trade playful insults with their friends and use special language with peers in their social groups.

Social development also enters a significant period as children face challenges in becoming competent learners and members of social groups. They become aware of their abilities and weaknesses and are able to evaluate themselves in comparison with their peers. Self-concept and self-esteem are part of their social development. If they see themselves as successful in school and with their peers, they become success-oriented. Unfortunately, many see themselves as failures or realize that they are rejected in social and play situations.

Success in social development is reflected in success or rejection in social play. Although school personnel may attempt to help rejected children, many children find themselves in a lonely situation or victimized by others.

Aggression and bullying are common factors in children's play. Although teachers are aware of these aspects of school-age play, they might not see it as their responsibility to intervene. Fortunately, a few structured programs are available to help all children be included in play.

School-age play is characterized by an interest in sports and games and play with a group of peers. There are gender differences in play. Boys are most likely to engage in rough play and play outdoors, while girls are more likely to engage in conversations and engage in play that requires taking turns. Boys play electronic games more than girls, and both genders participate in chase games.

Adults have a more directive role in school-age play. Both in the classroom and on the playground, adults engage in directed play opportunities to the limitation or exclusion of child-initiated or free play. Physical education teachers conduct structured classes rather than encourage free play. Classroom teachers place less emphasis on exploration through play and more on classroom games and teacher-directed activities such as creative dramatics. Parents spend less time with their children in play activities, but they support their children's participation in sports and lessons for individual sports and games. Parents do teach their children games with rules and spend time transporting their children to organized activities.

KEY TERMS

Aggression
Bilingual
Bullying
Concrete operational stage
Decenter
Industry versus inferiority
Learned helplessness
Mnemonics
Moral development
Peer culture
Perspective taking
Positive self-esteem
Reversibility
Selective attention
Self-concept
Seriation
Spatial reasoning
War toys

STUDY QUESTIONS

1. Why is free play less of a priority for adults for school-age children?
2. How does physical development facilitate more sophisticated forms of play in school-age children?
3. Why do some children gain more in motor skills than others? Describe several factors that can affect physical development.
4. Describe some reasons that outdoor play environments might be less available to elementary school children today?
5. Why do school-age children like to take risks in play? How can this interest be helpful for development, and how can it be dangerous?
6. Some people are proponents of recess; some are opposed to recess. Discuss both sides of the issue.
7. What roles should classroom teachers have in physical play? How can they advocate for children's development through play?
8. How does cognitive development in school-age children facilitate participation in games with rules. Describe cognitive characteristics that enable participation in games and sports.
9. How does information processing help explain cognitive development?
10. How does the ability to play games with rules evolve? Explain how cognitive advances help children play games more effectively?
11. How do code switching and other language differences become important in school-age children? Give examples of how children use more than one code in language.
12. Describe how language development advances socialization in school-age children.
13. How do teachers interpret their role in social play in the classroom? How is social play reflected in elementary school curriculum?
14. How does social development determine social acceptance in school-age children? Describe some factors that affect acceptance or rejection into peer social groups?
15. How do self-concept and self-esteem help explain social development in school-age children?
16. Are peer relationships the most important element of school-age social development? Explain why or why not.
17. Cooperative play is seen as most important for social development while our society emphasizes competition. How do these factors conflict in promoting children's play?
18. How does aggression characterize social play? Explain the differences between play fighting and aggression.
19. What should be the teacher's role regarding aggression and bullying? What can teachers do to reduce bullying?
20. What is the difference between sociodramatic play, creative dramatics, and dramatic productions? Are all essential for elementary school classrooms?
21. How do boys and girls play differently in the school-age years? Give examples.
22. How do accepted and rejected children engage in play fighting differently in elementary school? Why do rejected children engage in play fighting longer than their more popular peers?
23. How is school-age play in chase games different than preschool play? Describe how school-age children expand in how they participate in chase games.
24. Are war toys good or bad for children? Give arguments for both positions.
25. What role should parents have in organized sports? How can they determine how much their children should participate in sports?

Chapter 7 Culture and Gender in Play

THE MASANSA *or children's villages have been infrequently described in the ethnographic literature for this area [Zaire].* Masansa *are built during the dry season, when the weather is good and food is not in short supply and children have few economic duties to perform. Younger and older children participate in this activity, each with a role to play as they set about to re-create elaborately the life of the village. . . . According to Centner, missionaries in this region have discouraged the* masansa *practice because they believe that it encourages children to engage in sex play. However, she reported that such behavior occurs only infrequently and is discouraged and punished by parents.*

(Schwartzman, 1978, pp. 170–172)

WHEN THEY DID use the [play] house area in conventional ways, they did not verbally identify what role each child was performing. . . . Tetsu and other [playing] boys left home for work (as police officers), and Toshi stayed home to do household duties. While he waited alone, he cooked a meal. When the boys came home, they performed the Banshaku *ritual (alcohol drinking ritual before supper) common among Japanese men, and Toshi served them a meal.*

(Suito & Reifel, 1993, p. 37)

Girls and boys all around the world play, in some ways that we recognize and in other ways that are not so familiar to us. While play exists worldwide as a human activity, research has informed us only to varying degrees about what play is and what that play means to children in different parts of the world. What we know about play is shaped by the differing research agendas of scholars, including anthropologists, ethnographers, developmentalists, and other cross-cultural social scientists. Those scholars, cumulatively, provide a fractured picture of play in children's lives. One reason for the fractures in the picture is the difference in research agendas; scholars do not share common definitions of play, interests in children, or conceptions of the play's role in human life. Therefore, play may appear as either a central or a marginal topic for scholars, allowing them to see more or less play in their investigations. Neither are scholars of one mind when they study **culture** or ethnicity. Scholars who study peoples from different parts of the world, from different language groups, or with unique **customs** and beliefs may have diverse understandings of what culture may mean. Play may or may not be central to their work.

Despite the lack of a concentrated effort to understand play in different cultures, we have amassed an incredible number of findings about children's play around the world. These findings point to play as a common feature of children's lives; children everywhere play. (See Roopnarine, Johnson, & Hooper, 1994, for a collection of studies on children's play in various parts of the world; a number of those studies are reviewed in this chapter.) Research also tells us that the conditions of children's play vary a great deal, depending on the **values,** beliefs, practices, **institutions,** and **tools** that surround them; culture does contribute to children's play. To understand more fully the play that we see and support in our culture, whether it be pretend games, jumping rope, or computer games, we would do well to understand children's play in other cultures. As our already diverse culture becomes increasingly multicultural, we will need the lenses of cross-cultural studies to understand the confluence of meanings about play that are forming in American play settings.

Lancy (2002) indicates multiple ways that cultures vary in the degree to which children's play is supported or constrained, with clear constraints noted in a number of studies. He cites evidence that in different cultures, children are limited by safety in where and how they can play; girls may play less because they have more chores; gender appropriate play may be imposed; appropriate scripts for play may be imposed; cooperation, rather than competition, may be supported; community size may create play options; and lack of a "benign environment" may inhibit play. The things we take for granted when we play or think about play may not be shared by other cultural groups.

As mentioned earlier, the social sciences are not of one voice when researchers study the diverse manifestations of human behavior, including play. Scholars have created concepts of culture, ethnicity, geography, race, linguistics, custom, and other conceptual frameworks to explain why people in one area act the same way or differently than people in another area. Many of these concepts were first articulated by E. B. Tyler (1871), who saw culture as including man's habits or capabilities that are acquired through our social interactions, including customs, beliefs, morals, law, art, and knowledge; Tyler was an early student of games (Schwartzman, 1978). More current views of culture vary only slightly from Tyler's, to include tools, practices, values, beliefs, and institutions (e.g., Whiting, 1980; Whiting & Edwards, 1988; Whiting & Whiting, 1975). For this chapter, we will not appropriate a particular view or definition of culture. We will assume that there are unique features (like those listed earlier) associated with any self-identified group of people and that those features can be called aspects of culture. These features may be associated with play within a culture, the way the Banshaku ritual appears in Japanese preschool boys' play (and not in the play of Japanese girls or in the play of children in any other culture).

We will see that tools (i.e., toys), customs (e.g., rituals), beliefs (about how play contributes to a culture), and institutions (informal or organized settings for play) all contribute to cultural variations in play, including **gender** differences.

A unique contribution of cultural or anthropological research is its methodology, which emphasizes but is not limited to ethnography. **Ethnography** is the description of a group, based on intensive observation and interviews of people as they engage in their habitual activities. This method allows anthropologists to describe customs that are meaningful, in one way or another, for participants. Students of culture look at what people ordinarily do, not at how they behave in laboratory or contrived situations. Such an approach allows people to express those patterns of behavior that give meaning to their lives over the course of their lives. The ethnographer's challenge is to describe those patterns, discern what they mean to participants, then relate the patterns and meanings to larger conceptions of human development. How is African *masansa* role play like or unlike Japanese Banshaku role play, as a pattern of role play, as a meaningful activity for the players, as a meaningful activity for their respective cultures, and as a contributor to children's **socialization** to their societies? Ethnography requires a detailed description and interpretation of play in its **context;** it is not enough for ethnographers to say that children in each of these settings are demonstrating a type of play that we all call role play. The methods of cultural study demand a rich, sometimes called "thick," narrative description and analysis that reflects actions and meanings in their context. Such description frequently requires extensive narrative presentation of play events.

In Chapter 1 on the history of play, the work of Johan Huizinga (1938) was introduced. In his argument that play forms culture and civilization, Huizinga drew on documented evidence of play practices from many sources and many cultures. Some of those sources will be presented here. However, many of the pieces of evidence that he presented were fragmented observations—anecdotes taken from myriad reports of practices from different cultures. Huizinga's work drew on anthropological and other forms of inquiry and related to issues of culture and civilization, but it was historical work, not ethnographic. As this chapter will illustrate, Huizinga's historical argument touches on cultural issues related to play, but scholars of culture have attended to matters that go well beyond his work.

This chapter will describe research on play and culture, including thinking about the relationship between children's play and gender. Traditional anthropological research on children and play is reviewed, including contemporary work that points to the importance of migration, diversity, and play in multicultural contexts. Family and peer contributions to play figure in this discussion, and lead to questions about how play can be best understood. The play literature on gender differences builds on the cultural literature, pointing to and detailing the differences in boys' and girls' play relationships, their preferences and activities, and the kinds of play texts they enact.

THE ROOTS OF CULTURAL PLAY RESEARCH

Masses of existing research on culture, gender, and play have accumulated over decades. Two earlier publications provide thorough reviews of cultural research. Schwartzman (1978) extensively treats cross-cultural research that focuses on or addresses some aspect of play. Slaughter and Dombrowski (1989) update Schwartzman's review, raising critical questions about current trends in play research. Both of those publications will be reviewed and made current in this chapter, followed by a presentation of cross-cultural and gender play research that has appeared since 1989. Readers are encouraged to read Schwartzman (1978) and Slaughter and Dombrowski (1989) for comprehensive, detailed presentations of the research that serves as background for what follows in this chapter.

The Work of Helen Schwartzman

Helen Schwartzman was one of the first scholars to integrate research on children's play from an anthropological perspective. Her 1978 book, *Transformations: The Anthropology of Children's Play,* serves as a landmark for researchers on children's play. It provides an extensive review of research and thinking that shaped scholarship to that date. Schwartzman does a number of things in this book. First, she situates play in the context of culture. Second, she distinguishes between the study of play in general from the study of children's play in particular. Third, she explores the ideologies and metaphors that have shaped cultural perspectives on play. Fourth, she identifies predominant theoretical views that give researchers the questions that they attempt to answer with their research. Finally, she presents an argument and data for considering children's play as a significant text that relates to its cultural context; play is a culturally meaningful activity, that can be "read" (described and interpreted) by group members (Reifel, Hoke, Pape, & Wisneski, 2004). Given the pivotal importance of *Transformations* for our understanding of connections between children's play and culture, we will look at a number of Schwartzman's points and elaborate on them with more current material.

From an anthropological perspective, with its concern for the customs, beliefs, institutions, and values of a culture, children's play can be seen to serve any number of purposes. Children's play, like adult recreation, may express a culture's values, or it may create the cohesive bonds that allow culture to maintain itself. While considerable variation is evident in the amount and kind of play that children and adults display in different cultures, there has been some consensus that children's play differs from adult play in the sense that it provides children with some form of socialization into their cultures. Part of this socialization can be understood in terms of child development, but students of culture show us that efforts to develop children can be understood only in terms of the culture in which they are growing. Children's play functions to bind children to their societies in ways that are uniquely meaningful to each society.

How have anthropologists described this socialization process? Schwartzman identifies a number of metaphors that anthropologists have used in their interpretations of children's play. These metaphors typify children in their play activity as being primitive, copycat, personality trainee, monkey, or critic. Some of these metaphors (e.g., copycat, monkey) suggest an imitative view of play; play allows children to practice those things they see adults doing and they will be doing themselves when they grow up. Interpretations like these echo theories like Groos's (1901) on practice play (see Chapter 1). Other metaphors (e.g., personality trainee) suggest that children are acquiring a sense of how to act and who they are as actors in their culture, building on theories such as Freud's psychodynamics (see Chapter 2). All of the metaphors address some aspect of the nature-nurture debate, with its questions about how much of human behavior is biologically determined and how much is shaped by **environment;** much of the anthropological agenda has tended to favor environmental (i.e., cultural) explanations.

The bulk of *Transformations* is Schwartzman's impressive integration of the anthropological play literature. In a series of chapters, she shows how play can be further understood in terms of data on game diffusion, **play functions,** projecting personality, communication, and subjectively meaningful events. Her review of these topics leads her to raise questions about definitions of play, which she does in her final chapters. Some of these topics have only historical interest for us, while others tell us a great deal about development. In either case, patterns of data show us the commonalities of play, its diversity, and a variety of ways we can make sense of play.

Game Diffusion

The notion of cultural diffusion is not as prevalent as it was a century, or even a half century, ago, although it continues to echo in the form of debates about the relative statuses and values of different cultures, diversity, and multiculturalism. If one begins with the assumption that some cultures are "superior" to others and that more advanced customs transfer from "superior" to "lesser" cultures, then it should be possible to follow the trail as customs (e.g., games) from "civilized" cultures begin to appear in so-called "primitive" societies. Some anthropologists set out to demonstrate this spread, or diffusion, of higher culture to primitive groups by looking at the emergence of any number of (typically, but not always European) customs, including children's games, toys, songs and rhymes, in (typically) underdeveloped countries. For example, Tyler (1879/1971) argued that the similarities between the Mexican *patolli* game and Hindu *pachisi* (both games are precursors of backgammon) could not be due to chance; the game, like all of the other high achievements of ancient Mexican cultures, must have migrated to Mexico from Asia. Other anthropologists, who opposed the notion of any culture being superior or lesser, set out to show that every culture had indigenous children's play customs that were every bit as sophisticated as the customs that were coming from other lands. For example, Roth (1902) cataloged hundreds of Australian aboriginal games, including more than 70 string games that reflected animal and human symbolism.

Today we tend to see questions such as these as representative of ethnocentric or racist thinking. Beyond these concerns, we still have from this group of studies a grand collection of observations of different forms of play from diverse cultures around the world. Some of the observations are fragmentary, while others are systematic and extensive. We can see the universality of certain forms of play (e.g., chase games, ball games, imitative games), as well as how they appear within their cultures (e.g., among boys or girls, when chores are done, with or without adults). What we cannot see is those instances or forms of play that the ethnographers overlooked or missed as they attempted to answer their questions about diffusion. And, since those earlier researchers were working without the benefit of contemporary play theories, we are left with a stunningly wide range of play types (e.g., games of dexterity, games of pursuit, "little girl" game—summer) that may not make sense to us now.

The tradition of creating typologies of games and play, begun during the earliest years of diffusion studies, continues today. Contemporary studies, like those conducted by Opie and Opie (1997) on games, continue to organize analysis according to types, such as Chucking and Fetching, Marbles, and Skipping. Other scholars, such as Van Rheenan (2000), emulate some of the diffusion methodology by looking at the game of hopscotch as it transforms as a gender-linked activity over time and geography.

Play Functions

A second anthropological approach to the study of play, as described by Schwartzman, deals with questions of function. This approach is more familiar to child development students, in that it assumes that play has a developmental influence on children. The ways children play are associated with socialization into their societies, including the acquisition of **gender roles,** values, and understandings about social institutions. Children during play may also begin to acquire a sense of power relations and acceptable roles in their society. Again, play patterns are documented by ethnographic description over time.

For example, Schwartzman uses Salter's (1974) study to illustrate how Australian aboriginal children's play prepares them for political, economic, "worldview" (i.e., spiritual), and "normative" customs in their culture. Salter describes how games like hide-and-seek and mud-ball fights prepare children for political relationships. Economic preparation comes through tree climbing and playing with miniature canoes, both of which are key to economic survival. Children acquire the group's worldview by means of playing string games and singing. Pretend families and doll play are a foundation for normative participation in the culture. Play is described as a functional set of activities that take the children from childhood and prepare them for what they will do later.

Much of the cultural research on the functions of play shares the developmental assumption, or rhetoric, about how play serves human development (Sutton-Smith, 1997). This cultural approach to children's play differs from noncultural views in a number of ways. First, it links particular descriptions of play to the culture in which they take place. Play activity is described in a manner that makes it unique to the setting in which it occurs. Related to this point is the assumption that the same play activity, seen in a different culture, might have a very different function. A behavioral pattern in one culture may not have the same meaning as the same behavior in another culture. We will return to this point in our summary comments on Schwartzman.

Functional approaches to ethnographic children's play research continue to inform us about children and play. In his study of a Kpelle town in the African country of Liberia, Lancy (1996) features descriptions of play as central to children's daily life and socialization. While children must participate in the work of the town, as an economic necessity, there are rich opportunities for play of many sorts. Lancy describes make-believe role-play activities (called *nee'-pele* in that culture) that allow children to acquire skills in farming, weaving, providing for the family, and harvesting palm nuts. Make-believe of this form is an opportunity to practice adult roles and for adults to teach children about those roles. As they get older, children will participate in games such as *sua-kpe'* and *kpasa* (hunting and fighting games for boys), hiding games (*loo-pele* for both girls and boys, including *sua-iseler,* a wild animal game), drawing play (*pelin-pele* for both girls and boys), stone-tossing games, and many others. These games require that children learn how to play (rules, as described by Piaget (1965)), as well as "showing sense." Having sense is highly valued by the Kpelle, for whom a sensible response to their environment is necessary for survival. Lancy also describes children's play including songs, dance, stories, and other activities that promote the acquisition of values. Play, as described by adult informants and seen by Lancy, prepares children functionally for roles, customs, beliefs, and values that they will practice as adult Kpelle.

Projecting Personality

Schwartzman gives credit to Sigmund Freud and his contributions to anthropological studies of children's play in her discussion of play as projecting. The unique function of play as a reflection of personality or character is demonstrated in a number of ways. Children's play is credited as the setting where nature and nurture create a socialized community member, where psychological imperatives meet each culture's socializing influences. Play reflects, or projects, those imperatives in ways that are unique for each culture.

The 1953 study by Whiting and Child (and related publications, such as the Whitings' (1975) book) serves as a case in point. These authors studied six field sites around the world, consisting of communities in India, the Philippines, Okinawa, Kenya, Mexico, and the United States. Long-term, detailed descriptions of growing up in these communities allowed the Whitings to create a model of personality development that revealed itself in each community in terms of child rearing practices, the community's ecology, and resulting adult behavior, cultural products, and child behavior. Play, in the form of games, fantasy, and other forms of recreation, was seen as the outcome of this model, reflecting the influences of the other factors. Instead of functioning to define who the child is within a culture, play functions to express who the child is as an individual.

This projective approach to play studies continues in the work of Kelly-Byrne (1989). In her ethnography of play with Helen, Kelly-Byrne describes home play sessions with the 6- to 7-year-old daughter of a dual-career American family. The analysis deals both with Helen's patterns of play (her imaginary play themes about self, good and evil, relationships, female power, intellect, parenting, and gender; and the stages she went through during the course of play) and Helen's play relationship with Kelly-Byrne (recognizing the child's needs, adult power, and how their relationship changes over time). The author shows how play is an expression of the child's ways of dealing with her experiences growing up in her family and society, as well as how play allows her to grow. Kelly-Byrne offers evidence and insight into the unique opportunities of social play, as well as the complex challenges for adults as they try to enter child's play.

Communication

The issue of communication as part of play is of particular interest to Schwartzman, as it served as a framework for her own empirical study of preschoolers' play. A necessary and unique feature of pretend play is the communication that must occur for it to happen. As Bateson (1955/2000) argues, play is a "framed" activity whereby we begin to act "as if" something else were real. When we play space monsters, we are not really space monsters, but we act and communicate as if we were. Bateson calls attention to the layers of meaning in actions and to the communications we must use to make those layers apparent to playmates. Part of that communication is about the frame (when we stop being children and begin being space monsters, and when we return), which takes the form of signals, indicating "This is play." We are supposed to know that the actions that follow are not intended to be interpreted as real. The communications of pretend play are seen as an important developmental foundation for later social and cognitive functioning. We need these decontextualizing experiences (taking actions out of a real context and putting them into play) so we can better take roles, think about experience while not in that experience (i.e., speculate, theorize), and correctly interpret others' signals (e.g., do words and actions signal romance or something else). Culture operates with webs of social agreement about shared experience, shared beliefs, and our abilities to communicate about them (see Chapter 2).

The complexity of communications during play and the meanings that communications can signal are described by Schwartzman (1978) in a range of studies. She recounts Geertz's classic 1972 study of cockfighting in Bali, where the very real interpersonal hostilities of the Balinese are shown in the violent contest of their fighting birds; the play frame (it is "only" a fighting game) sets the players apart from reality, where they are not allowed to express their antipathies, into a play setting where their emotions can be given expression. She also details the child play communication strategies identified by Garvey (1995), as described in Chapter 2.

The communicative aspects of play have been explored in more current studies in English-speaking and other countries. Lin and Reifel (1999) document a range of communications and framed meanings in Taiwanese kindergarten play. In their analysis of the influences of physical and social context on children's use of play materials, space, time, incorporation of experiences from outside school into play, classroom culture, social relations, and social custom, these authors identify culturally characteristic pretense, such as making sugar cane out of clay and peeling it before pretending to sell it; negation of pretense after the teacher signaled the end of play time (". . . then we got married and the end"; p. 163); and explicit instructions to a playmate about how to accept an object respectfully (within this culture) while pretending to play doctor's office ("Use both hands to receive it"; p. 172). Lin and Reifel argue that the frames about which children communicate when they play will reflect unique cultural meanings. These unique meanings in Taiwan's cultural context appeared irrespective of school program structure (Chang, 2003).

Subjectively Meaningful Events

Schwartzman also acknowledges that children's play has an element of cognitive meaning for players, which she calls "minding play." Children think when they play, and they learn. Constructing meaning has been studied by anthropologists and others in a number of ways, including explorations of the thinking of players and their use of language in play. Schwartzman reviews the work of Piaget, Vygotsky, and Bruner to demonstrate the ways that play engages the mind (see Chapter 2). She also looks at research on language use to see how children's play is the setting for the development of narrative. Kirshenblatt-Gimlett's (1976) review of *Speech Play* provides ample evidence for ways that children's minds are engaged by playing with sounds, rhymes, other sound patterns, and ultimately, jokes. From the ethnographer's point of view, these examples of children's speech play are important samplings of what children do in the everyday context of their lives. Relevant examples of humor (e.g., Wolfenstein, 1954), secret languages (e.g., Opie & Opie, 1959), verbal contests (e.g., Abrahams, 1962; Dundes, Leach & Ozkok, 1970; Gossen, 1976), and games (e.g., Brewster, 1939; Goldstein, 1971) demonstrate the diverse use of "thoughtful" language around the world.

More recent studies have looked at the stories children tell when they are playing. Building on Paley's (1981) approach to documenting children's classroom play narratives, Scales and Cook-Gumperz (1993; Nicolopoulou, Scales, & Weintraub, 1994) analyzed 582 stories told by 28 preschool children over the course of a school year. Their analysis of these spontaneously generated stories revealed that girls' stories reflected an orderly, domestic world of family relationships, while boys' stories were active, violent, and fragmented. Girls' narratives were far more likely to center on idealized characters (princesses and princes), while boys' more often created stories about monsters and bad guys. Scales and Cook-Gumperz argue that these stories "provided vivid evidence of the social significance of gender distinctions in the lives of young children" (p. 182).

Definitions of Play

In her final chapters, Schwartzman (1978) analyzes the nonethnographic play literature to understand how other social scientists make use of children's play. She reviews classic ecological (e.g., Barker & Wright, 1966), ethological (e.g., Blurton Jones, 1972), and experimental studies (e.g., Hutt, 1970) to see how play is treated in these studies. While the ecological and ethological studies conform to the naturalistic principles of ethnography, they fail to relate observed behaviors to any cultural meaning system. Experimental studies seldom pretend to reflect naturalistic circumstances that the participants might experience in ordinary play. These differing approaches lead to lack of definition about what play is and what it means to participants in their cultures.

As a solution to this problem, Schwartzman suggests that play cannot be defined simply in terms of the environments where it takes place (after all, those environments vary a great deal from culture to culture) or of specific behaviors (which may mean something entirely different in another culture). The ethnographic point of view requires that play be seen as a "text in context," a described set of naturally occurring actions that are connected with the larger society in which they occur. We cannot read the text of play without knowing about the society in which it takes place, in general and in particular. Schwartzman (1986) later modified this view, by arguing the play needed to be seen as "text in context, and context in text." It is not enough to relate what we see of play to the larger culture, but we must also see how that culture and the players' individual experiences bring culture to their play text. Play does not only reflect experience; play also shapes experience.

In *Transformations,* Schwartzman (1978) addresses any number of topics that are of interest to students of child development, including the cognitive, social, and emotional functions of play for development. She also deals with subjects that are of less interest to traditional developmentalists, such as game diffusion. Much of the evidence that she presents tends to support the idea that play is an adaptive activity for all humans, but an activity that is nurtured in many different ways by the unique aspects of cultures. That perspective is echoed by more recent scholars who are concerned with the cultural and economic diversity of the United States and its children.

The Work of Slaughter and Dombrowski

Diversity in American culture, as well as a general trend toward migration in many parts of the world, has increased interest in the likely role of culture in human development (Greenfield & Cocking, 1994). Play scholars are among the forefront of social scientists who are taking diversity to heart in their attempts to understand more about children as they grow. Slaughter and Dombrowski, in their 1989 review and research agenda, build on Schwartzman's arguments by using her view of "play in context" to call attention to issues of ethnic and socioeconomic diversity in development. Their interests are primarily psychological, but they recognize that psychological processes are very much shaped by the contexts in which they operate.

A unique and useful contribution of this argument is the authors' recognition that "culture should be expanded to include a focus on intergenerational transmission of behavior in both culturally continuous and discontinuous contexts" (p. 285). Aspects of culture are important within their original settings, but they also have weight when they migrate to a new setting, as when people move to a setting where different aspects of culture exist. Families carry beliefs and traditions with them when they move, but in new settings they may have different meanings. Slaughter and Dombrowski argue that children should be studied both in continuous contexts, where their cultures have remained in place for generations, and in "discontinuous" contexts, where due to migration they may be encountering multiple cultural influences. This argument also applies to studies of groups that may have subgroups that exist at different socioeconomic levels, where the culture of poverty or affluence may contribute to developmental processes such as play. The research agenda suggested by this argument has not been fulfilled.

Slaughter and Dombrowski challenge views of beneficial play development, citing a number of debates and other evidence to question the cross-cultural and cross-social class generality of classic, normative descriptions. For example, are there cultural and economic differences associated with differences in play that may predict later deficits in social and cognitive functioning? If we subscribe to classic descriptions of play, based on Western cultural norms, then any differences we see in the play of non-Western children could mistakenly be associated with other developmental deficits (e.g., school achievement) (Sutton-Smith, 1983) unless we situate differences in play within their larger cultural and social ecology (McLoyd, 1983). Traditional descriptions of play and its correlates may be perfectly valid within the societies where it has been studied, but expressions of play will vary. As Slaughter and Dombrowski (1989, p. 290) state, "children's social and pretend play appear to be biologically based, sustained as an evolutionary contribution to human psychological growth and development," but "cultural transmission regulates the expression (i.e., the amount, content, breadth or range, mood, meaning) of this play. Further, over time it is probable that the play itself reciprocally impacts culture" (p. 304).

Adults in different cultures may support play or engage in play with their children to varying degrees.

TABLE 7–1 Culturally Significant Play Findings from Slaughter and Dombrowski (1989)

Study	Culture	Findings
Continuous Contexts		
Bloch (1984, 1989)	Senegal & America	Time spent crafting toys; play with those toys; infant–age 6 gross-motor, rough-and-tumble, constructive, music and art play; boys (ages 5–6) decrease pretend play; younger children more functional play; Americans did more play of all types, mostly gross-motor and television viewing
Udwin & Shmukler (1981)	Israel & South Africa	Similar amounts of pretend with lower-SES preschoolers in both cultures; relatively less pretend time for South African middle SES, compared to Israeli middle SES
Al-Shatti & Johnson (1982)	Kuwait & America	No statistical differences between cultures or genders; descriptive differences: Kuwaiti girls more sociodramatic play than Kuwaiti boys; American girls less sociodramatic play than American boys; American girls more functional play than American boys
Yawkey & Alverez-Dominques (1984)	Puerto Rico & America	Hispanic girls more reality-oriented play than Anglo girls; Hispanic boys more functional play than American boys; Anglo boys more fantasy play than Hispanic boys; American girls more functional play than American boys; American boys and girls more functional and fantasy than reality oriented; Hispanic girls more reality than functional, and vice versa for Hispanic boys
Bower, Ilgaz-Carden, & Nori (1982)	Turkey & Iran	No SES differences in Turkey in play space used; Iranian middle SES more toys and space for play
Hrncir, Speller, & West (1983)	Bermuda & America	Bermudans at 12 months at play level behind Americans

These authors give full weight to nature and nurture as sources for human play. The challenging aspect of their argument is to begin to identify those expressions of play that are different from those that appear in the traditional literature and from our own culturally limited experiences. Slaughter and Dombrowski assist with their review of play in socially continuous, discontinuous, and sub-cultural contexts. Those studies are summarized in Table 7–1.

Based on a review of these studies, Slaughter and Dombrowski (1989) argue that few studies have accounted adequately both for play and its development and for cultural influences. Children's play must be understood in the "cultural ecology" (p. 304), or social context, in which it is meaningful. This is true for children who are growing up in a social setting that has remained constant for generations, in a setting to which their parents have migrated, or in settings with a representation of multiple cultures. Socioeconomic status is a dimension of culture that should always be considered. Understanding the perspectives of participants, including their

TABLE 7–1 *(continued)*

Study	Culture	Findings
Discontinuous Contexts		
Christman (1979)	Mexican American	Sociodramatic play lower for boys than girls at age 3, but equal at age 4
Robinson (1978)	Vietnamese refugees (America)	Boys (ages 9–12) more competitive and aggressive; girls more accommodating and passive; differ from American in relation strengthening and rule clarifying
Young (1985)	Canada (various origins)	Non-Anglos gained social status from skilled soccer play
Child (1983)	East Asian (England)	Less pretend than English children (preschool); Muslim and Sikhs less play, less often, less playfulness; English initiated more play; Asians more likely to play alone
Ariel & Sever (1980)	Arab & Israeli	Rural Arabs (ages 5–6) less pretend, interaction, fewer modes; less talk
Subcultures		
Nevius (1982; Nevius, Filgo, Soldier, & Simmons-Rains, 1983)	Multicultural (African American, Mexican American, Anglo)	Incidence of play too low to compare groups
McLoyd (1980)	African American	African American preschool pretend utterances were like Anglo pretend, but girls did more transformations of social roles
Lefever (1981)	African American	Relates ritualized language play to self-protection in low-SES groups
Montare & Boone (1980)	Puerto Rican, Anglo	Puerto Rican boys (ages 9–13) showed more aggression in team play sessions, as did Anglos with absent fathers

customs, beliefs, and values, is necessary for understanding children's play. Slaughter and Dombrowski's view seems to be consistent with some of the basic tenets of ethnography.

Context: Expanding on Developmental Views

The scholarship reviewed thus far, framed broadly within frameworks articulated by Schwartzman (1978) and Slaughter and Dombrowski (1989), provides a challenge to traditional developmental views of play, without dismissing them. There can be no doubt that there is some sort of common strand of children's play that cuts across cultures; play is in our nature. These cultural studies of play raise serious questions about what aspects of play are shared and how we can communicate about similarities and differences. Slaughter and Dombrowski and others raise questions about the norms of play development, but that does not mean that play development does not exist. Cultural studies of play provide us with a larger repertoire of children's play to consider, as well as more understanding of what play means to them and their families. By putting play in cultural context, we begin to ask additional questions about what we might look for as children play (e.g., novel forms of language play, expression of customs that are foreign to us), as well as how we talk about play with people from cultures other than our own (e.g., if we call activities play, will others dismiss our words as meaningless?). It is also fair to consider historical context for play activities; what may be culturally sanctioned play for boys in one era may become sanctioned for girls during another era (Van Rheenan, 2001). We will return to these questions after reviewing three current strands of research that are informing us about the diversity of play.

CULTURAL INFLUENCES ON CHILDREN'S PLAY

What does culture contribute to children's play? What features of culture create opportunities for play in some contexts, but apparently not in others? What are universal commonalities to play, and what are play's subtle variations across cultures? Although we do not yet have answers to these questions for every group of people around the world, we do know partial answers to each. In the following sections, we will explore these topics and others, based on research that has appeared since 1989. Patterns of findings will be presented according to these themes that reflect different aspects of culture and play: family influences on play and differences in group play. Issues and findings related to gender and play will be presented, then discussed in a section of their own.

The complexity of issues related to culture, gender and play are reflected in current research. Chang and Reifel (2003) report an experiment conducted in Taiwan, where children's dolls are typically Caucasian in appearance (blue eyes, blonde, fair skin), reflecting the power of Western toy markets on toy availability. Urban and rural boys and girls were given either a Caucasian or an Asian doll for home play, then assessed in terms of racial attitudes and self-concept. Girls more than boys preferred the Caucasian doll and were biased toward the Caucasian race, more so for urban children who are exposed to more Western media and culture. Positive attitudes toward the Caucasian dolls were the norm. Few studies look at the relationships of toy markets to culture, gender, and developmental factors.

Family Influences on Play

Play is often described in terms of its socialization functions. By means of play, society shapes children to become participants in the larger group. These perspectives on play, heavily influenced by developmental theories, reflect beliefs that play, at least in certain forms, contributes to meaningful social interactions that become adaptive for individuals in their social groups (see Chapter 2). We can see such views expressed in many ways, including assertions about play: children learn to get along with one another; they learn to become team members; they learn their place; they learn to take different roles; they learn social rules, or morality; they learn to communicate; they learn to think out loud; and so on. Many of these assertions are made about peers playing with one another, but they also apply to play within the social group we call the family. Over the past decade, we have seen growth in the number of studies done of play in family settings here and abroad.

Parental influences on play have been of particular interest to a number of scholars. In the United States, Haight (1998; Haight, Masiello, Dickson, Huckeby, & Black, 1994; Haight & Miller, 1992, 1993; Haight, Parke & Black, 1997; Haight & Sachs, 1995) has conducted any number of observational studies of mother-child play in the home, as well as interview studies with mothers and fathers about their play with their children. These studies show how American mothers (typically) facilitate play through direct and indirect means. Direct means include, for example, teaching children to pretend by introducing the play frame to infants, prompting pretend, and elaborating children's expressions. American parents might use indirect means of promoting play by arranging the home environment, especially with replica toys, and inspiring play by expressing positive affect (Haight, 1998). While there is clearly a range of things that middle-class American parents might do to promote children's play, it seems that play for children is generally valued in American culture.

What about play within families in other cultures? We know that children play in different ways, but how do parents and other family members participate in the play lives of children? A number of studies from various places around the world reveal diversity in terms of play participation and apparent attitudes toward play. For example, Lancy's (1996) study of the Kpelle in Africa indicates that parents believe that play does contribute to children's future roles and common sense but that play (especially pretend) is viewed with "mild tolerance" by adults (p. 91). Most adults are so engaged with work that they do not have time to play with their children, which is a common pattern in subsistence cultures (Bloch, 1989; Bloch & Adler, 1994; Schwartzman, 1978). In other, nonsubsistence cultures, adults may pay attention to play in different ways.

While play was not the primary focus of Rogoff et al.'s (1993) monograph on learning and development, those authors provided cross-cultural description of mother-child interactions that support cognition (see also Goncu & Mosier, 1991). American mothers described themselves as and acted like playmates more often than did Guatemalan mothers, while tribal Indian mothers facilitate, more than participate, in play. Turkish mothers appear to play with their children as much as American mothers do. Attitudes about play, as well as engagement in labor, appear to contribute to maternal participation in play. These analyses were limited to mother-child observations, so there is no evidence whether other adults or relatives play with those children.

Farver (1993; Farver & Howes, 1993) has conducted a number of studies comparing the play of American and Mexican families. In her observations and interviews, she has found that Mexican mothers do not believe play to be important for children's development; in fact, they do not play with their children. Children within this culture do have older play partners, in siblings and other family members. A similar set of findings are reported by New (1994) for Italian families. Mothers of young children do not see their role to include play, leaving that activity to older siblings and neighbors. Italian mothers appear to believe that whatever play is appropriate for children will be provided by others. These apparent low levels of parental involvement in child play are in contrast to American parental involvement, but these studies suggest that other family members and neighbors engage young children in play, probably providing the same developmental benefits that American children obtain. And, as we will see in the discussion of differences in group play that follows, there are also differences in peer relationships in Italian preschool peer play.

Research done in Asian countries reveals different, sometimes conflicting, patterns of mother-child play. Chinese parents view play as beneficial for children and see themselves as play partners, much as American mothers do (Haight, Wang, Fung, Williams, & Mintz, 1995). Chin and Reifel (2000) found Taiwanese mothers to be highly engaged in their preschoolers' play, although the specificity of their involvement was a good deal more differentiated than the pattern provided by Haight and her colleagues (1998; Haight & Miller, 1992, 1993). In a laboratory-like setting in an urban Taipei neighborhood, they found that mothers provided developmentally nuanced support for pretend play. Contingent statements clarified 2-year-olds' pretend actions and attributed meanings to them, while they added details to the play of 3-year-olds and elaborated roles for 4-year-olds. As children grew older, mothers provided increasing challenges during pretend, requiring more events in play scripts, demonstrating toy use to enhance pretend, and progressing from factual questions to reasoning questions about enacted events. Mothers verbally connected pretend actions for 3-year-olds and converted playful accidents into pretend themes for 4-year-olds. Older children got more coaching from their mothers about toy use and how to elaborate events. Mothers of children at all ages verbally interpreted what they saw, showed compliance to children's play themes, and challenged children to include additional elements in their play. Mothers taught what their children needed to know to make pretense meaningful, whether how to use a stethoscope to act like a doctor or where to store toy vegetables when they are not being "cooked." The nuanced scaffolding that these mothers provided reflects a complex, intuitive sense of components of play (action related to object, then related to meaning; meanings related to roles; roles as part of scripts). These findings were confirmed in Kim and Frost's (2003) analysis of Korean mother-child play, in pretend, puzzle solving, and story telling contexts. The value of play for children's learning and development is apparent.

As Haight (1998) suggests, parents may have indirect influence on their children's play by means of the settings they arrange for play. Some evidence exists on cultural variation on these influences. Tudge, Lee, and Putman (1998) observed play in American and South Korean middle- and working-class homes. The value of play in these cultures is apparent in the high incidence of play at home, as opposed to school work, other work, or conversation. Pretend and academic play (i.e., with academic objects and information) were common forms of play in both cultures, but Korean middle-class children showed significantly more academic play. Middle-class girls in both cultures were more apt to engage in academic play. Children in both cultures were more likely to play alone or with peers than with parents, but when parents did play with children, it was far more likely to be the mother (significantly so in Korea). Home settings in these cultures had different effects on play.

The low level of parental involvement in Korean and Korean-American children's play is echoed in the work of Farver, Kim, and Lee (1995). These authors argue that Korean culture values academic goals for children and that play at home is not believed to contribute to that goal. Parents and teachers with Korean backgrounds were less likely to play with their children, and as a result the children engaged in more parallel and less pretend play than did Anglo-American children.

Parents from different cultures may or may not play with their children, and if they do play with their children, they may do so to varying degrees. If parents do not play with children, suggestive findings tell us that others in that culture will engage children in play. In some cases, parents may not become playmates for their children for clear reasons. For example, if parents must work at a subsistence level, then there is no time or energy for play. It may be that attitudes and beliefs follow such subsistence needs, so that parents who are working hard just to get by will value play less and downplay the importance of play for their children. Or, beliefs about play may not relate to socioeconomic status. Parents who believe in play may simply decide to play more with their children, as Indonesian mothers and fathers do with their toddlers (Farver & Wimbarti, 1995). Likewise, parents with more resources may have more time and energy to play, and they may have attitudes and beliefs that reflect their practices. Or, as the Italian data suggest, parents may assume that children will naturally get whatever play they need (New, 1994).

Irrespective of the links between adult participation in children's play and prevailing values, the patterns of diversity that exist among cultures provide challenges to practitioners. If adults value play and think that children should be playing, then supporting play in schools and neighborhoods is not a problem. If adults, for cultural or personal reasons, do not value play, it is more difficult to describe its benefits and argue that children should be engaging in it. This may be especially true if the forms of play that adults see are alien to their cultural or gender-linked experiences; those adults may not have a way of relating to the play or of valuing it (Holmes, 1999). These challenges become especially problematic in diverse communities, where teachers, parents, and other community members may come from differing backgrounds.

Cultural differences in adult-child relationships during play may add to confusion for children in diverse play settings. If children come from a culture where adults are not part of child play, they may have difficulty understanding why a teacher or play leader would be trying to engage them in play; adults would not be expected to do such a thing. Children who are familiar with adults as playmates may have different expectations for adult support during play. Diverse classrooms may bring together these practices and require sensitive responses to the needs of children.

Differences in Group Play

Adults can have significant roles in contributing to children's play, depending on the culture where we look. Likewise, the role of peers in play can vary a great deal, depending on culture. Peer interactions, whether within families, neighborhoods, or classrooms, should have a distinctive caste by virtue of the culture associated with that play. The examples reported earlier from Lin and Reifel (1999) and Suito and Reifel (1993) speak to this point; culturally unique customs appear in children's dramatic play, as do desired social roles. Sometimes the aspects of culture that appear in play are fleeting but significant. Woods (1995), in the ethnographic fieldwork that supports her analysis of continuities and discontinuities between Mexican-American Head Start children's home and school experiences, notes many instances of play. One telling example is an older brother who interrupted his play with a friend to correct his sister. Even though his sister was younger, the boy made use of the formal pronoun *usted* to address his sister, reflecting the respect associated with family relationships in this culture. The subtleties of culture can appear in many ways in children's play.

One dimension of play for which there are demonstrable cultural differences is playfulness. Playfulness is an aspect of play that was first elaborated by Lieberman (1965), and it has to do with the humor, joy, and spontaneity of activities. In a series of studies, Rogers and her colleagues assessed young children's playfulness in America and Japan (Rogers et al., 1998; Taylor, Rogers, & Kaiser, 1999). Children were rated by teachers with a 31-item instrument that reflects six traditional dispositions of play (from Rubin, Fein, & Vandenberg, 1983). American children were found to be significantly more playful by their teachers than were the Japanese children. Factor analysis revealed that dimensions of playfulness were different in these cultures. Japanese playfulness is associated with 17 of 28 items, with "Finds unusual things to do" and "Uses toys/objects in unusual ways" appearing high in the factor loadings, and "Active Involvement" ("Gets very involved/forgets what is going on") appearing as a significant factor. American playfulness is associated with 21 of the 28 items, with "Invents new games" and "Is imaginative" having high load factors, and "Externality" ("Looks to others to tell him/her what to do") as a significant factor. Playfulness characterizes peer school play in both cultures, but in very different ways.

Some of the reasons for the cultural differences in classroom play in Japan and American may be explained by Takeuchi's (1994) survey of Japanese play. This study found that forms of play are similar there as in other Western and Asian countries. Leisure time for children in Japan is filled with television, comics, games, sports, and video games. Play for young children is integrated into the school curriculum, where it is assumed that play influences development. Teachers are taught to consider play in terms of health, human relations, environment, language, and creative expressions, but these dimensions are interpreted in terms of inclusiveness (playing with others) rather than emphasizing individual expressiveness. Playing to be part of the group, learning a group ethos, is emphasized more than developing individuality and uniqueness, as is done in American schools (Lewis, 1994; Tobin, Wu, & Davidson, 1989).

Beliefs about play and playfulness vary, as does how Japanese and American preschoolers structure their classroom role play. Suito and Reifel (1993) analyzed preschool children in both countries based on tape recordings made during free play. Communications about play were described and analyzed, in terms of deciding about roles to play, actually playing those roles (Garvey, 1977), and gender differences. Girls in both cultures were more likely to identify play roles, especially family kinship roles. Japanese girls were much more likely to argue about who will take what role, valuing the role of mother most of all; mother was seen as an authority role in both cultures. Japanese boys were more likely to play house unaffiliated with other players, and American boys were the only ones seen to take the baby role. Gender stereotypes appeared in both cultures, with mothers doing housekeeping and fathers leaving for work outside the home. Boys in both groups, when playing in single-sex groups, would enact meal preparation and serving, but their roles were never identified. American children were far more likely to play nonfamily roles (e.g., pilot, cashier, Superman) in the housekeeping play area than were the Japanese; the range of legitimate play roles for Japanese children, especially boys, was far more restricted. This study suggests that culture may contribute to play by providing a set of roles (particularly gender-linked roles) that can be played during pretend. An implication is that children from different cultures who play together in diverse settings may not share a common repertoire of acceptable roles.

Another thing that children from diverse cultural backgrounds may not share is the facility to communicate about playing with one another. Scales (1996; Van Hoorn et al., 1999) reports on the difficulties of a troubled African American boy who appeared unhappy and secluded during play time in a preschool. This boy's efforts to play with others were rejected consistently. Systematic observation of his play efforts, making use of Corsaro's framework for understanding ritualized patterns to access play (1979, 1985), showed that his typical entry efforts were with African-American speech style, which were not familiar to potential playmates. Teachers did note that this child had, on one occasion, used an entry ritual in the style of a television superhero and had been successful. Teachers encouraged his use of this style, which was very familiar to other children in the classroom. The African-American boy used this approach to enter play and found common ground for continuing peer play.

Other cross-cultural studies of preschool play provide additional differences to consider when observing social play. Corsaro (Corsaro & Rizzo, 1988; Corsaro & Schwarz, 1991) documents a range of social play actions, some of which have their parallels in American and other cultures. Italian children "make do" when they are not provided play materials that suit their pretend interests, such as when they convert sticks to guns and swords to play fight; we see similar things in American settings. Italian children are more often left to their own devices for resolving conflicts, but when teachers do intervene, they help children think of social rules; this pattern also does not seem foreign to us. What may seem more strange is the lack of emphasis on the individual in Italian play settings. Children are expected to play in groups, discuss in groups, and consider the welfare of the entire group rather than individual interests. Play is not a matter of personal expression; players must recognize the interests of everyone in the community.

Cultures adapt to their physical settings, and play activities reflect those cultures and settings. Nwokah and Ikekeonwu (1998) compared the games of rural Nigeria, the Igbo people, with those of rural America (Indiana), the Hoosiers. Children in both cultures were engaged in spontaneous neighborhood play, not organized events. Children in both groups averaged age 8, although the Igbo included significantly younger children in their play groups (age 5, as opposed to age 6 for the Americans). Games lasted varying lengths of time for both groups. Environment played a key role in play, with the Igbo playing far more outdoors in the morning when it was cooler, and the Hoosiers playing more in the afternoon; about 25% of games were played in the evening in both cultures. A higher proportion of Igbo games were mixed gender. The objects that children used as they played were typically man-made for the Hoosiers (paper bags, string, pen tops) and natural materials for the Igbo (banana leaves, water, seeds). Games were rule bound in both cultures, but the Igbo adhered to the rules, while the Hoosiers argued about and changed rules. There was more gross-motor physical movement in Igbo games, although some high-level activity occurred in both groups. Traditional games were evident in both cultures—for example, checkers, tag, and red rover for the Hoosiers; hopscotch (swehi), throw seeds (*itu okwe*), and leopard and sheep (*agu na aturu*) for the Igbo. The Igbo had more mild and harsh penalties for infractions of rules than did the Hoosiers. Environment and culture—in these cases, the play objects and customs of these groups—were reflected in documented games. Both help socialize children to cultural concerns.

With an increase in diversity within American schools, we are more aware of the blending of groups of children within classrooms. Howes and Wu (1990) studied the play of diverse children in primary grades. They found that kindergarten children were less likely to play with children from other ethnic groups, while third graders engaged in much more cross-ethnic play. We have no indication that any efforts were made to facilitate this grade-linked increase in cultural mixing. Younger children may not have had appropriate communication skills to establish and maintain play with peers, while older children had learned those adaptive play skills. Studies of preschool children indicate that language differences tend to segregate players, at least initially in their school experiences (Clawson, 2002; Sutterby, 2001). In diverse settings where multiple languages are present, children gravitate toward those with whom they can communicate while they play.

Current research has affirmed the existence of unique play activities in a range of cultures. Eskimo girls make "storyknives" on which they carve symbols relevant to their culture (deMarrais, Nelson, & Baker, 1994). Chinese and Taiwanese children have holiday festivals, when they celebrate with fireworks, lanterns, or kites (Pan, 1994). Maori children in New Zealand walk on stilts that they make (Best, 1925). Polynesians have *keu tictoc,* a chase game where children hold hands to form a swinging line (Martini, 1994). The consensus is that these unique forms of play reflect particular cultural values and are given differing meaning within their cultures. There may be more or less time for play, more or fewer resources given to play, more or less adult support for play, but the universality of play is apparent.

What children play with, their approach to play, the roles they take, and how they communicate about their play will all vary with cultural influences. Each culture may have its own unique play forms, but each form makes sense within the culture for its own reasons. Japanese children do not like to pretend to be a baby in the family, because babies have low status in their culture. Italian mothers do not play much with their children, because they believe that others in the family will. Mexican mothers do not play with their children because the mothers must work; older siblings do

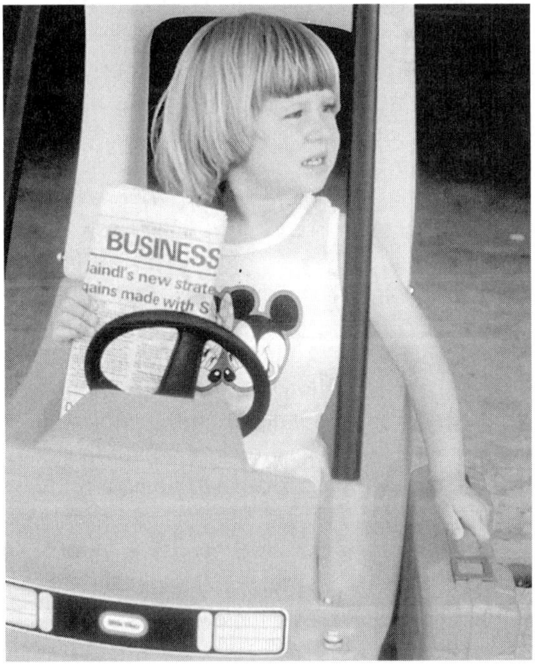

Cultures vary in the degree to which traditional gender roles are allowed expression by means of play.

play with children. Peer play is valued in Nigeria for developing common sense, while in America it is the basis for social skill, moral reasoning, and social cognition; in Korea peer play is less valued. American child developmentalists and Japanese educators agree that play supports learning and development in the early childhood classroom, but they differ about what play is; Korean adults see no value in educational play. These findings, as well as the others presented here, require that we take customs, values, and beliefs into account when we observe children from diverse backgrounds as they play.

Gender and Play

The differences between the play of boys and girls are noted in research findings around the world. Scholars who look at play and gender are well aware of pronounced differences between boys and girls in the roles that children play, the tendency of boys and girls to segregate themselves into same-gender play groups, patterns of play and toy preferences, how parents respond to the play of girls and boys, and many other issues. Findings from these studies are complicated by different theoretical and rhetorical perspectives. Some researchers are interested in seeing how play functions in children's gender socialization (e.g., Fagot & Kronsberg, 1982; Fagot & Leve, 1998; Geary, 1998; Maccoby, 1990; Ruble & Martin, 1998), while others may look at issues of identity formation or cultural replication (Schwartzman, 1977; Sutton-Smith, 1997). The underlying issue—the interplay of nature (a biological basis for gender) and nurture (how contexts participate in gender formation)—suggests that research must be evaluated along a number of dimensions that authors do not always address.

The nature of play and gender is noted by those who point to male/female differences in primate play (e.g., Biben, 1989; Cheney, 1978; O'Neill-Wagner, Bolig, & Price, 2002). There is a long history of research that documents male/female differences in non-human primate infants and juveniles. Monkeys, chimpanzees, baboons, and other primates tend to play in gender-segregated groups. O'Neill-Wagner et al. (2002) describe the onset of this gender socialization from infancy in rhesus monkeys, and how males and females grow up playing with age-cohort, same-gender mates. This early socialization contributes to troop social structure, including social hierarchy and gender roles. Easily recognizable patterns of play for males and females across species suggest that there may be a genetic and adaptive basis connecting gender and play.

Differences between boys' and girls' play have been explained by a number of theories. It may be that both boys and girls prefer certain toys and gravitate to others who share those interests, or it may be that as children acquire a beginning conceptual understanding of sex differences, they find playmates like themselves (Kohlberg, 1966). Others have argued that gender segregation may be due to preferences for compatible play interactions; one finds playmates who act like oneself (Maccoby, 1990; Moller & Serbin, 1996). From a social constructionist perspective, one may argue that play is a setting for expressing aspects of gender roles that are being explored by the players; boys and girls explore and express different perceptions of who they are in the world (Scales & Cook-Gumperz, 1993). All of these theories recognize the nature of play; children are biologically gendered and bring that fact with them. Distinctions among these theories seem to lie in the degree of nurture that occurs during play. We know boys like boy toys, but what makes adults give boys those toys? We know that boys are more active than girls and that girls are more verbal, but do we as a culture provide play opportunities to enhance or diminish those differences? Do we direct children to forms of expression that highlight rather than reduce differences in play?

Play as an avenue for nurturing children toward their expected gender roles is noted (Lindsey & Mize, 2001). Boys and girls are treated differently from their birth, if not before. As soon as pregnancy is acknowledged, for many families the first question asked is, "Is it a boy or a girl?"

Toy selection for newborns, room decoration, and interactive play are different for girls and boys. The context of play as a socializing influence on gender development is pronounced, and surely varies from culture to culture. Families, media, and peer relations (as a vector for culture) all contribute to how we see gender differences in play.

Social Relationship Differences

A number of the studies reported so far include findings about differences in girls' and boys' play. Nigerian rural children play more mixed-gender games than do American children (Nwokah & Ikekeonwu, 1998). Kuwaiti preschool girls pretend play more than boys (Al-Shatti & Johnson, 1982). Vietnamese immigrant school-age boys are more competitive and aggressive, while girls are more accommodating and passive (Robinson, 1978). Hispanic preschool girls play more reality-based pretend than functional games, while the reverse is true for boys (Yawkey & Alverez-Dominques, 1984). Japanese preschool girls have a wider range of possible pretend roles than do boys, but neither has as many as American preschoolers (Suito & Reifel, 1993). Preschool boys create more fragmented play narratives about monsters and superheroes, while girls create cohesive play texts about domestic relationships (Scales & Cook-Gumperz, 1993). These and many other findings point to the importance of gender when we talk about play and development.

The range of findings about play and gender in Western societies has been well reviewed by a number of scholars who specialize in this field of research (see Fagot & Leve, 1998; Ramsey, 1998). Gender segregation during play early in life is a common Western observation, as are different styles of play for boys and girls (Sutton-Smith, 1997). Boys' play is typified by competition, aggression, rules, and relatively low levels of talk; girls' play is relational, inclusive, and highly verbal. As some of the studies reported indicate, these generalizations are far from universal; in some cultures play-linked gender segregation may appear much later (Bloch, 1989) or simply be less prevalent (Nwokah & Ikekeonwu, 1998). In this section, we will briefly review a number of theories and related data dealing with issues of gender, culture, and play.

While there are many studies of play and gender in other cultures, much of the discourse about the topic is dominated by studies done in Western settings and using Western developmental norms for play (e.g., Fagot & Leve, 1999; Leaper, 1994; Moller & Serbin, 1996; Ruble & Martin, 1998). Differences in boys' and girls' play are described in terms of gender identity, in which children's knowledge of their gender predicts how they play in group settings (e.g., Fagot, Leinbach, & Hagan, 1986) or at home (e.g., Fagot & Leinbach, 1989). Such knowledge may lead to greater cooperation in segregated play groups (Jarrett, et al., 2001; Serbin & Sprafkin, 1986). Preferences for gender segregation may also relate to the type of play as well as sex of playmate, with younger children (aged $2\frac{1}{2}$) of both sexes opting for same-sex partners, and older girls (aged 4–5) opting for cooperative play and boys choosing boy playmates (Tietz & Shine, 2000). In most of these studies, the roles of cultural and parental expectations are not considered. Neither do we learn about the contexts or texts of the play that children create in these studies (Schwartzman, 1986).

Differences in Play Preferences and Activities

There is a longstanding tradition in child development to describe the different play preferences and activities of girls and boys. Some of the earliest developmental research (e.g., Bott, 1928; Farwell, 1930; Van Alstyne, 1932) pointed to gender differences in play. Using interviews and observations of children in laboratories, those researchers describe familiar patterns of play. Girls prefer to paint, draw, model with clay, look at books, and play with dolls; girls play tends to be more sedentary. Boys like to build with blocks, play with cars and trucks, ride toy vehicles, and overall tend to be more active.

Such differences in preferences continue to present day, with gender-typed play activities noted in a broad review of research (Ruble & Martin, 1998). Boys are still observed to be more physical, including physical contact (e.g., chasing, rough-and-tumble,) during play, with girls being more social-skills oriented and precise in their physical activities (e.g., clapping games, jacks) (Ramsey, 1998). Jarrett and colleagues (2001) conducted a number of studies describing the play preferences of ethnically diverse elementary students (up to grade 5), and found activity level differences between boys and girls, with boys involved in more ball games, while girls tended to play synchronized or traditional games (e.g., Red Rover).

Differences in Play Texts

A number of recent efforts have explored the gendered construction of play in childhood, looking in particular at our assumptions about what toys and play mean to us culturally, and how our gender understandings may bias us toward replication of stereotypical gender expectations. In a number of analyses, MacNaughton (1999, Hughes & MacNaughton, 2001) has looked at girls' play, in particular, as it relates to play materials provided for girls. She has looked at Barbie doll play as well as additional girl pretense to see how play might construct identity. The pronounced influence of commercial culture on play creates discourses that have particular meanings for children. Hughes and MacNaughton (2001) conclude that there is a balance between "children's active creation of identities within the discourses that they have acquired as a result of their specific social and material circumstances," and "the increasing ability of major corporations to influence the availability of particular discourses of identity" (p. 127). Toys, media, families, and peers all provide specific, particular contributions to play.

As noted above, boys' play tends to be more "active"; boys tend to move more quickly, use louder voices, and move about the play space (perhaps on vehicles) with little regard to ongoing activities. There has been some note of the "active", if not violent, role play characters that boys opt for (Carlson-Paige & Levin, 1990, 1995), as opposed to the quieter, more domestic doll play of girls. There has been growing interest in the characteristically male form of play called rough-and-tumble (R&T). R&T is often seen as play fighting, although many teachers have difficulty distinguishing play fighting from real fighting, thereby missing the play element in R&T (Pellegrini; & Smith, 1998; Smith et al., 2002). It is difficult for many adults to identify the "text" of R&T, as it does not often fit into a recognizable narrative of pretend. But many boys participate freely and happily in R&T, laughing as they roll around together on the ground or shove one another, to establish dominance and maintain social status. Pellegrini (1988, 1995, 2002; Pellegrini & Smith, 1998) has identified a number of signals that boys use to indicate that their R&T actions are play: positive affect, minimal physical contact, reciprocity, and continued affiliation. While pleasurable for the players, this male play text evokes ambivalence in many (Smith, et al., 2002), and needs further study.

More of the texts and context of gender-linked play appear in the writings of Paley (1981, 1984, 1992). She recounts her teaching efforts in a kindergarten classroom where children's relations become subject matter for research and practice. The stories that children create while they play become part of the curriculum, and reflect differences between the texts of boys and girls (Paley, 1981, 1984). The rules that boys and girls make about their play (e.g., "No superheroes in the doll corner"; Paley, 1984) reveal much about the text of gender relationships during play. The ownership of play by children is affirmed when Paley (1992) attempts to impose her rules on what children chose to do when they play. These accounts reveal how children come to make sense of issues such as gender in the course of their play.

Studies of gender and play conducted in Western settings, like those reported in the previous paragraphs, point to dimensions of play that may vary for boys and girls. They provide particulars about play that make sense in terms of theories of gender identity. What they do not do is relate those particulars to the cultural context in which these children are developing. Play provides one avenue for children to explore and express gender, but, as Slaughter and Dombrowski (1989) point out, at some point play may contribute to culture. The children's play we support is nurturing gender development as much as it is allowing for exploration. The range of expressions of gender and play that are revealed from cross-cultural research suggest different ways that play is associated with culturally sanctioned gender development.

SUMMARY

The vast body of literature on culture and play that has been sampled and reported here tends to support the universality of children's play as a natural human activity that is nurtured quite differently in various cultures. Depending on a culture's environment and economic conditions, play may take certain forms. Beliefs about play and the value it is given by members of a culture will influence the degree to which adults engage and support children. How they play, and what meaning that play has for them, will be dependent on the culture of which they are a member. These conditions will affect the amount of play, customs reflected in play, gender roles associated with play, and objects considered appropriate for play. Irrespective of any of these conditions, children will play.

As cultures come together, by means of migration and a global economy, we are seeing more settings where children from diverse backgrounds are meeting. Play is typically part of these settings, but, as this chapter illustrates, there might not be universal agreement about what play is. Games that are known in one part of the world are unfamiliar in another. Rituals for initiating play might not be shared. Participation by adults with children in their play might be a source of confusion. The subtleties of play might interrupt its performance, when something as simple as playing house becomes an event where legitimate and valued gender roles are ambiguous and where scripts for household rituals are not shared. This chapter points to the importance of knowing diverse cultures, to better understand the particular features of children's play. We have described some of the features of play that may be relevant. A number of recent publications have provided sensitive guidance for professionals (Dockett & Fleer, 1999; MacNaughton, 1997; Ramsey, 1998; Roopnarine, Johnson, & Hooper, 1994; Van Hoorn, Scales, Nourot, & Alward, 1999).

Questions of culture and play are described in this chapter in terms of the ways different groups of people nurture play to support the maintenance of the group. The customs, beliefs, values, and institutions of a culture are tied to play, whether in the form of play activities that socialize children into the group, adult efforts to engage in or support play, or activities that reflect the environment of the culture. The field of **anthropology** has provided much of this work, and ethnography, the primary methodology of anthropology, offers detailed description of play in the settings where it is meaningful. The classic works of Schwartzman (1978) and Slaughter and Dombrowski (1989) discuss culturally relevant aspects of play that frame our review of the literature. Those aspects include game diffusion, play functions, projecting personality, communication, subjectively meaningful events, continuous and discontinuous culture, and subcultures (including migrants and socioeconomic status). Review of these literatures reveals that children's play is a multifaceted human activity that is difficult to understand from any one perspective. It also shows that much of children's play around the world can be understood in terms of how play contributes to child socialization within a culture, as well as how culture shapes play (Lancy, 2002).

Recent research continues these themes, pointing to the particular meanings of play within different cultures. The diversity of play activities is demonstrated through reviews on family influences on play and differences in group play in various cultures around the world. Parental values and beliefs about play vary a great deal, as does the degree to which parents play with their children. Cultural support for play may be pronounced or not. Peer play is equally diverse in different cultures, with unique forms of play still appearing in local cultures. Subtle but significant influences of culture appear in peer play, in the form of variations in games, roles taken (or not), play communications, and size and range of play groups. Gender differences in play are also a source of variation in a number of senses. Boys and girls play differently all around the world, but the ways they play differently appear to be influenced to some degree by values and beliefs. Differences between the play of boys and girls in different cultural settings reveal that play is to a great degree nurtured. It is important to note the particular cultural, material, and social contexts for play that girls and boys experience.

Issues of understanding and working with diversity are raised by these reviews. As children from different cultural backgrounds come together, due to migration and the world economy, opportunities for peer relationships must be filtered through an understanding of play as a part of culture. Knowing that play reflects particular customs, values, and beliefs that may be different than our own should be a first step toward engaging diverse children in meaningful play.

KEY TERMS

Anthropology
Context
Culture
Customs
  Institutions
  Tools
  Values
Diversity
Environment
Ethnography
Gender
  Gender roles
Play functions
Socialization

STUDY QUESTIONS

1. Identify your own cultural heritage. Ask your parents and grandparents (or other older relatives) how they played as children. What did they pretend, and what games did they play? What did it mean for them to play? How is their play characteristic of your cultural heritage?
2. Ask your family members how they played with you when you were an infant and toddler. What games did they play with you? What were their reasons for playing with you? What do you think you gained from such play?
3. With a group of friends, discuss the play and games you remember from childhood. Try to include friends who come from a different region of the country or from a different country. What play is the same, and what differences are there? How does your immediate environment (setting, objects, playmates) shape childhood play, and what aspects of play seem common to all?
4. Select one play activity (e.g., pretend house play, a chase game) and find a description of that activity in two different cultures. How are those activities alike in both cultures, and how are they different? How does each play activity have particular meaning for its culture?
5. With a group of men and women, discuss the play and games you remember from childhood. What play is the same, and what differences are there? What do group members think they gained from childhood play? Why was play fun?
6. You are a teacher of a kindergarten class that includes immigrant children from Mexico, Taiwan, and Italy. What might you ask parents of these children about their past experiences? What aspects of play might you observe as these children play in your classroom?
7. Select a game familiar to you. What functions might this game be promoting? How might the game shape or reflect personality? How are players being socialized by this game?
8. Interview boys and girls about pretend play. What roles do they take when they play? What roles will they not take? Ask them, "Why?"
9. Children communicate with each other as they play. List the ways that they communicate, and identify similarities and differences between cultural groups.

Chapter 8 Play and the Curriculum

By Jeffrey Trawick-Smith
Eastern Connecticut State University

WITHOUT SOME adult intervention, play ability does not develop. . . . The natural processes of child growth and the nondirective enriched environment in preschool and kindergarten are not enough to give children the necessary boost. Without some degree of positive play intervention by teachers, children will lack the requirements essential to develop.

(Smilanksy, 1984, p. 39)

OUR VERY SERIOUSNESS and sobermindedness as adults have led us away from the study of play itself. We keep using play to achieve intellectual growth or emotional development. . . . This is not to argue that there are not many uses that play has, including cognitive. It is to argue against our adult-centric tendency to reduce the structure of play to other structures of development. . . . We wouldn't do it to music, why must we do it to play?

(Sutton-Smith, 1984, p. 24)

UH-OH, HERE COMES Mrs. R. Now she's going to ask us, "What are you playing?" and then you have to answer, and then she just talks and talks and talks, and we can never finish the castle for Queen Wonder.

(A 4-year-old child in a dramatic play center, warning a peer about an approaching teacher)

The contributions of play to children's development have been described in previous chapters. Research conducted over many decades has consistently shown a strong relationship between play in its many forms and social, physical, and intellectual development. Newer studies have revealed connections between certain types of play and competence in traditional academic subjects, particularly literacy (Christie, 1994; Levy, Wolfgang, & Koorland, 1992; Roskos & Neuman, 1998). Based on this research, many teachers, educational theorists, textbook authors, and leaders of professional organizations now advocate "play-based programs" or a "play-oriented curriculum," especially for young children (Bredekamp & Copple, 1997; Isenberg & Jalongo, 2000; Van Hoorn, Scales, Nourot, & Alward, 2002). For example, in the position statement on developmentally appropriate practice of the National Association for the Education of Young Children (NAEYC), play is described as "a vehicle for children's social, emotional, and cognitive development" and "an opportunity to understand the world, interact with others in social ways, express and control emotions, and develop their symbolic capabilities" (Bredekamp & Copple, 1997, p. 14). Among the classroom practices recommended in this document are "extended periods of time (at least one hour at a time) for children to engage in play" (p. 126).

Authors of state and national academic standards, which are currently guiding curriculum reform in the United States, also acknowledge the importance of play. For example, the Head Start Child Outcomes Framework (U.S. Department of Health and Human Services, 2002) includes the following important indicator of early learning: "Participates in a variety of dramatic play activities that become more extended and complex." The newly-adopted early childhood standards of many states include items related to play—e.g., "Plays cooperatively with others" and "Engages in pretend play with other children" (Connecticut State Department of Education, 1999). The joint position statement of NAEYC and International Reading Association on early literacy, includes a standard that "children will incorporate literacy into their play" (Neuman, Copple, & Bredekamp, 1999, p. 7).

So, play should be a fundamental part of every school curriculum. What could be more clear? In fact, the issue of play in the classroom is unclear—exceedingly murky, in fact. Questions abound: What *is* play, exactly? *Which* play activities are most useful to children? *How much time* should be devoted to play in the classroom? To what degree do play activities promote the many state and national standards that are now the focus of American schools? What should teachers do while children are playing? Confusion over these questions has led DeVries and her colleagues (DeVries, Hildebrandt, & Zan, 2002) to lament that there is a "problem with play"—a general bewilderment over what comprises high-quality play experience. Such confusion, they contend, leads to contradictory classroom practices and to poor outcomes for children.

Play-based classrooms often appear to be quite similar. They may include similar materials; play spaces may be arranged in a similar fashion. Daily schedules often resemble one another, each offering extended periods of time for free play. However, careful examination of these programs reveals significant differences in regard to how play is defined and how it is included in the curriculum. In this chapter, common elements of play programs and major differences among these will be examined.

COMMON ELEMENTS OF PLAY-BASED CURRICULA

Most play models examined in this chapter share common features—a certain type of classroom arrangement, the provision of special kinds of play materials, careful attention to safety, and a daily schedule that allows active child involvement.

Indoor Play Space: Centers and Their Arrangement

Many play-oriented programs are arranged into clearly defined **play centers** (or *learning* *centers*). Types of centers that are typically found in play-based classrooms are presented in Table 8–1.

These centers are often constructed and organized in special ways to enhance play. In an extensive review of research on indoor classroom space, three play center design features that promote play development and learning have been identified (Trawick-Smith, 1992): (a) logical arrangement of space and materials, (b) a modified open plan design, and (c) stimulus shelters.

TABLE 8–1 Common Classroom Play Centers

Play Center	Sample Materials
Dramatic play center	Dress-up clothes Dolls Housekeeping props (dishes, mirror, plastic tools, etc.) Thematic props (post office props, grocery store props, etc.) Literacy props (checkbooks, grocery lists, envelopes, etc.)
Block area	Set of hardwood blocks Set of large hollow blocks Set of smaller table blocks Replica play sets (farm sets, parking garage sets, train sets) Replica play toys (plastic people, toy cars, dinosaurs, etc.)
Art center	Paint (tempera, watercolor sets, block printing paints, etc.) Paper (construction, butcher, posterboard, cardboard, etc.) Drawing implements (markers, crayons, chalk, pens, etc.) Collage media (buttons, seeds, beans, cut-and-paste materials) Sculpting materials (clay, sand, plaster, wire, papier-mâché)
Music center	Recorded music and tape recorders with headphones Stringed instruments (autoharp, child-made guitars, etc.) Percussion instruments (drums, rhythm sticks and blocks) Shakers (maracas, child-made rain sticks, etc.) Materials for reading and composing music (song charts, music writing materials, sheet music, etc.)
Book center	Collection of high-quality children's literature Big books Child-made books Puppets of characters from children's books Comfortable sites for reading (bean bags, carpet squares, couches, etc.)
Writing center	Writing implements (pens, computer, moveable alphabet) Child journals Blank books Clipboards Stationery and envelopes
Manipulatives center	Legos Puzzles Bristle blocks Lacing boards Peg boards

(*continued*)

TABLE 8–1 *(continued)*

Play Center	Sample Materials
Math/science/ cognitive center	Geoboards Ordering and categorization games Card and dice games Scientific tools (magnifying glasses, balances, thermometers, etc.) Live animals for observation and care
Water/textural center	Water table with measuring and floating materials Toy ships, fish, and people for water play Sand Beans, rice, and other textural materials Funnels, tubes, and other tools for pouring experiments
Motor play (indoors)	Riding toys Small climber/play house Balls Obstacle courses Jump ropes
Motor play (outdoors)	Riding toys Large playscape with slides, swinging tires, lofts, and climbing nets Sand boxes Hills for climbing and rolling Large parachutes and balls

Logical Arrangement of Space and Materials

A **logical arrangement** of centers has been found to increase play frequency and quality and to promote learning. Such an arrangement is one in which compatible materials are positioned near one another and far away from incompatible ones. In most play-based classrooms, for example, blocks, dramatic play, or motor play centers are placed together and far away from quieter centers, such as book and science areas. In logically organized classrooms, messy areas, such as those for art or water play, are situated over washable floor surfaces and near a source of water. Less active, more intimate activities are positioned far away from louder ones on softer surfaces, such as carpeting. Comfortable cushions or couches may be provided for these quieter play experiences.

Related to logical arrangement is the principle of clear organization of materials within centers. Golbeck, Rand, and Soundy (1986) found higher scores on measures of general cognition for children enrolled in classrooms where the materials themselves were ordered in clear and logical ways within each play area. For example, materials of like function might be stored in the same place in the dramatic play area (e.g., cooking and eating materials on one shelf, dolls and doll clothes on another, and plastic tools, work boots, and hard hats on another). In the block center, blocks might be stored on shelves based on shape. Within shelves, smaller blocks might be placed on upper shelves, larger blocks on lower ones. Clean-up time then becomes an elaborate categorization task.

Modified Open Plan Design

One effective way that play centers can be defined is through the use of visual partitions—bookshelves, bulletin boards, and other dividers that separate one area from another. In his classic research on play space, Moore (Moore, 1987; Moore & Marans, 1997) discovered that a **modified open plan design**—one in which centers are divided on two or three sides, but left open on at least one side for easy access—were superior to other arrangements in promoting play persistence and quality. In a more recent investigation in one child care program, visual partitioning was found to double the rate of children's engagement in play tasks (Trawick-Smith & Landry-Fitzsimmons, 1992).

Stimulus Shelters

A final design concept that has been found to contribute to development is the provision of a **stimulus shelter**—a space for children to be alone and to enjoy a brief respite from active classroom life. Cozy spaces for just one or two children that are separated from the rest of the classroom have been found to contribute to feelings of comfort and security in school (Wachs, 1979). A small loft filled with pillows, dolls, and puppets is an example.

Balance of Play Materials

Most play-based programs include similar kinds of materials; examples of these are presented in Table 8–1. A **balance of play materials** has been found to be most critical to the quality of children's play. Prescott (1987) has found that a good balance between complex versus simple materials and open-ended versus closed ones was associated with greater play involvement and a "smoother" day in child care centers. She defines *complex materials* as those with many uses (e.g., sculpting clay), whereas *simple materials* have only one or a few (e.g., a book). She describes *open-ended materials* as those with which children are able to express themselves freely and creatively (e.g., hardwood blocks) and *closed materials* as those with only a single use (e.g., an ordering game in which objects are arranged by size). Prescott's research suggests that children benefit from an optimal mix of these various types of toys, games, and art media.

Prescott notes that balance among activities can be achieved within a single play center. To create more open-ended opportunities within a science area, for example, blank scientific journals and art materials can be added for sketching and writing. To add closed, convergent experiences to the block center, photos of buildings in the neighborhood can be posted for children to replicate. Copy play cards can be included—cards with sketches of block structures of varying degrees for complexity that children may choose to build.

Other researchers have discovered that nonrealistic materials—nondescript objects, such as boxes, cardboard pieces, or rubber shapes—contribute to play quality, particularly in the dramatic play center (McLoyd, 1986a). In one study of play materials, it was discovered that the optimal balance between nonrealistic and realistic play objects was related to age (Trawick-Smith, 1993). For 2- and 3-year-olds, a center with only realistic props—toy kitchen equipment or dolls, for example—elicited more language and symbolic play. For 4-year-olds, a center with a blend of realistic and nonrealistic props was most effective. Five- and 6-year-olds engaged in more language and make-believe in a center with only nonrealistic props. It appears that with development children become less dependent on toy realism and can even perform highly sophisticated enactments without any toys at all.

Divergent Activities and Creative Expression

Most play-based curricula focus on creative process—the imaginative expression of ideas and open-ended experimentation—rather than on end products. Activities that require divergent thinking are most common. For example, a play-oriented program is more likely to include a wide range of open-ended art materials (e.g., paint, markers, and sculpting clay) than an art project with a single intended outcome (e.g., making clown faces that all turn out the same). In a typical play-based curriculum, mathematics problems are more likely to have multiple solutions and multiple answers (e.g., constructing triangles in different ways with geoboards). Right answer-oriented math worksheets are less prevalent. This emphasis on creative process is based on several important research findings on play and divergent thinking:

1. Open-ended play activities have been found to be related to **ideational fluency**—an ability to generate many and varied ideas in writing, language interactions, and art (Fisher, 1992).

2. Play has been found to lead to more effective problem solving because play experiences enable children to generate more solutions to challenging problems (Pepler, 1986).

Based on this research, Johnson, Christie, and Yawkey (1999) recommend three broad categories of divergent play that enhance creativity: microworlds and narratives (including sociodramatic play, replica play with miniature figures, and computer game play that involves imaginary settings and situations), art (especially creative representation with raw materials), and musical expression (including spontaneous singing and movement).

Safety

Play can be active and even rough. Common to all play programs is an overriding concern about safety. Not only does a safe space protect children—which is paramount—but it also allows for greater independence (NAEYC, 1998). Children can explore and express themselves more freely when adults do not need to intervene constantly for safety reasons.

Table 8–2 presents several major safety concerns and how materials and space can be planned to address them.

Regardless of how well play spaces are planned, however, there is no substitute for vigilant supervision. Adequate numbers of adults are needed in a classroom to keep children safe. NAEYC (1998) recommends an adult to child ratio of from 1:3 to 1:5 for infants and toddlers, with at least two adults always present. For preschool children, a ratio of from 1:4 to 1:10 is recommended, with no fewer than 2 adults supervising. A 1:10 ratio is encouraged for children older than this.

The mere presence of adults is not adequate to ensure that play will be safe. In a survey conducted by Peterson, Ewigman, and Kivlahan (1993), consensus was found among child development specialists and parents about how much supervision is needed: for children under five, constant supervision is required. That is, very young children should never be out of sight of an adult. According to the survey, children of age 6 and older should not play on their own for more than 5 minutes without an adult checking on them. These recommendations are based on the assumption that children are playing in safe spaces. Nearly all of those interviewed agreed that when children are playing in high-risk areas—where there are unsafe surfaces and materials or nearby traffic, for example—constant supervision is required at any age.

Schedule of the Day

Most teachers in play-based programs follow a daily schedule that allows adequate time for play and a balance between active and quiet experiences. At least an hour of uninterrupted free play time is recommended for younger children (Bredekamp & Copple, 1997; Johnson et al., 1999). Even this time period may not be adequate. Several authors have reported that some children spend 45 minutes to an hour planning their play—designing play sets, negotiating roles, and discussing themes (Enz & Christie, 1997; Trawick-Smith, 1994b). At the end of an hour, some children may just be preparing to begin actual play!

A **quiet-active-quiet schedule** is illustrated most clearly in the well-known **High/Scope program**, to be examined in a later section (Schweinhart & Weikart, 1996). In this model, children follow a **plan-do-review structure**: they begin each day with a reflective, teacher-directed group time in which they plan their play activities. Next comes a period of active playing. Another quiet period follows this play time, in which children review and evaluate their accomplishments. In this model, child-directed free play and teacher-guided small-group activities are also alternated. Even the most ardent play enthusiasts believe that active periods should be occasionally broken up by short rest times.

VARIATIONS IN APPROACHES TO PLAY

Although most play-based classrooms share these common elements, they also have fundamental

TABLE 8–2 Safety Concerns and Ways to Address Them

Safety Concern	Protecting Children in the Classroom
Falling	Lofts, climbers, and other climbing equipment should have protective, 38-inch railings and should not be higher than several inches above children's reach. Impact-absorbing surfaces should extend at least four feet beyond the "fall zone" under climbing equipment (National Program for Playground Safety, 1999).
	Surfacing material should be 6 inches deep under moderately high climbers (5 feet or less) and up to 12 inches deep for higher equipment (NAEYC, 1998).
	Unsafe equipment, such as slides without platform railings, trampolines, and unstable or imbalanced riding toys, should be avoided and children should wear impact-absorbing helmets when riding on tricycles, wagons, or bicycles (Sayre & Gallagher, 2001).
	For infants, cribs should have railings that are at least $^{3}/_{4}$ of a child's height (Kendrick, Kaufmann, & Messenger, 1991) and walkers should be avoided (Sayre & Gallagher, 2001).
	Indoor play surfaces should be made of a non-slip material and should be free of water or unmarked obstacles.
Traffic Accidents	All play spaces should be fenced and active play should take place far away from vehicular traffic.
Cuts, Scrapes, Pinches, and Splinters	All toys and equipment should be free of sharp or protruding areas, wood splinters, rough areas, chipping paint, and rust. Areas that can pinch or crush fingers, such as the bottoms of see-saws or merry-go-rounds, should be completely enclosed (Sayre & Gallagher, 2001). Play surfaces should be kept free of glass and other sharp objects.
Entrapment and Suffocation	Any opening in play equipment must be smaller than the width and length of a child's head—between $3^{1}/_{2}$ and 9 inches (Sayre & Gallagher, 2001). The distance between crib slats should be no more than $2^{3}/_{4}$ inches (Kendrick et al., 1991). Shades, drapes, and blinds should be tied out of reach and children's clothing should be free of strings, hooks, or buttons that might get caught in equipment (Sayre & Gallagher, 2001).
	Toys and materials smaller than $1^{1}/_{4}$ inches in diameter should be avoided; Styrofoam plates and cups and plastic utensils should not be used (Sayre & Gallagher, 2001).
Poisoning	Medications should be dated, appropriately administered, and stored out of reach. Only safe, nontoxic houseplants—such as jade plants, coleus, hen-and-chickens, rubber plants, and dracaena—should be displayed (Kendrick et al., 1991).
	Art supplies should be avoided that may contain toxic materials or that are easily inhaled, such as powdered clay or tempera paint, lead-based glazes and paints, paints that require solvents to clean, commercial dyes, permanent markers, instant papier-mâché, instant or solvent-based glues, and aerosol sprays (Kendrick et al., 1991).

differences. With this point in mind, the classroom interactions of four different teachers are presented in this section. They illustrate the diversity of approaches to play found in modern schools and centers.

APPROACH 1

A 6-year-old sits at a table with three peers writing answers to math problems in a workbook. At a certain moment, she pauses in her work and performs a make-believe action with her pencil. "Shooom," she sings, moving the pencil along through the air like a rocket ship. "Going into light speed," she mutters. The teacher quickly approaches and places a blue, plastic chip in front the child sitting just to her right. "Samantha, I like how you're working so quietly," she says. "I'm going to give you a token that you can use during play time." Quickly, the girl ends her pretend play and returns to her work, hoping that she, too, will earn a token.

Later, during a brief play time, the girl watches her peers play with blocks. She is unable to join them, however, because she has not earned enough tokens to do so.

This teacher would argue that she is using play in the classroom—but as a *reward* for completing more important work. From her view, play is a frivolous but highly enjoyable activity that can serve as a motivation for completing more taxing and less interesting learning activities. In this teacher's view, play contributes to the achievement of state and national academic standards by serving as an incentive—the pay-off for learning to read or do math. Some early childhood educators still adhere to this view; in fact, this approach is enjoying something of a revival in some parts of the country (Chedekel, 1999).

Many questions can be raised about this kind of a curriculum. Is a message being imparted to children that learning and play are distinct and mutually exclusive—that learning is tedious work that is performed only so that rewards of play can be earned at some later time? Do children in such classrooms have enough time for play, so that positive social and emotional development occur? (The child in this example appears to have not had sufficient play time, for she performs what has been called **illicit play** during a work period (Fein & Wiltz, 1998). Will children experience stress and anxiety—those deleterious emotions that play is believed to reduce—in such didactic classrooms (Hart et al., 1998)?

APPROACH 2

A kindergarten classroom is arranged into seven distinct learning centers. Two children have chosen to play in one of these: the dramatic play area, which has been arranged into an elaborate, make-believe hospital. As the children discuss their play theme, select imaginary roles, and then enact these, their teacher observes from a distance. He makes note of their language and social behavior and studies their emotional responses to the hospital play theme. Do the children show concern or upset over medical props or play enactments? Are both able to "play out" anxieties about medical encounters and gain mastery over them?

Recognizing that the two children are engaged in rich and meaningful play, he chooses not to intervene in any way and allows them to continue with their pretend theme for over an hour, even postponing snack time so that they are able to reach a satisfying conclusion.

In sharp contrast to teacher 1, this teacher provides many opportunities for open-ended play during much of the school day. To him, in fact, play *is* the curriculum. He has adopted a **hands-off play approach**, adhering to a traditional belief that unrestricted, self-directed activity is essential for positive development. Like Dewey (1913), he believes that children should be allowed to pursue their own play interests; he shows great faith that children, in free play, will naturally select those experiences that are most meaningful and useful to them. His approach also has a psychoanalytic flavor (Axline, 1947; Freud, 1961); he appears to view play as a way for children to bring anxieties to the surface and to discharge them. A primary purpose of play, from his perspective, is to assist children in gaining mastery over negative experiences and to resolve emotional conflicts in a healthy manner.

Teacher 2 adopts a hands-off play approach because he believes that adult interference might interrupt the process of resolving inner conflicts or pursuing self-felt needs. He views play as having an important, though indirect, influence on learning in academic areas. Children cannot achieve important academic standards, he believes, if they are anxious, depressed, or doubt their self-worth or abilities. Through play, children gain the emotional well-being to learn effectively.

His approach is shared by many teachers in the field. In a study of preschool play interactions, File (1994) found that teachers spent only about 15% of class time interacting with children in play. Some prominent play theorists also hold the view that adults should not interfere in children's activities. Sutton-Smith (1990) has argued that adults cannot be trusted to intervene in childhood pursuits, because they too quickly lapse into "didactic play bumblings" (p. 5).

Many questions arise about this approach to play. What happens if some children do not engage in useful forms of play? What if some are unable to play at all, because of social or cognitive limitations or other special needs? How can a teacher be certain that playing will help students learn to read or to do math or to meet other state and national academic standards? Is a hands-off approach to play really just an example of laissez-faire teaching?

APPROACH 3

A kindergarten classroom is arranged into learning centers. The teacher provides materials and activities and encourages children to play independently. Occasionally, he enters the dramatic play area to intervene. Two 5-year-olds are now sitting rather passively in this center. One child rocks in a small rocking chair, holding a doll; the other repetitively stirs a spoon in a small pan on top of a pretend stove. Neither child speaks to the other. After observing for a few minutes, the teacher moves over to them. "Mmmm," he purrs, sitting down at a small table. "Something smells so good. I'm hungry. Is it almost dinner time?"

"What?" the child at the stove asks.

"Will dinner be ready soon?" the teacher repeats.

"Oh, yes," the child says and begins to set dishes on the table in front of him. "We have spaghetti today."

"Spaghetti. Yum," the teacher says, then, turning to the child in the rocker, he asks, "I'll bet your baby is hungry, too. Is she old enough to eat spaghetti?"

This child quickly joins the child and teacher at the table. "Yes. Babies can eat spaghetti. I can feed her."

"Great," the teacher answers. "Why don't we all eat now? Let's say we're a family."

"Yeah, and I'll be the mother," one child responds.

"And I'll be the other mother," her peer adds.

The interactions of teacher 3 exemplify a **narrowly focused play intervention**. He is striving to enhance specific play abilities—make-believe actions and role playing, for example. His assumption is that enhancing these aspects of children's play leads to higher-quality play interactions over time. These interactions will, in turn, contribute to positive development in the long run (Trawick-Smith, 1994a).

A distinct feature of teacher 3's interactions is his focus on just one particular type of play. In this example, he is striving to enhance sociodramatic play, following a framework recommended by Sara Smilansky (Smilansky & Shefatya, 1990). Many teachers and play theorists advocate such focused sociodramatic play interventions, based on two interrelated assumptions: (a) certain types of play—sociodramatic play, construction play, and **games with rules**, in particular—are more developmentally useful; and (b) children can be taught to play in these ways in order to enhance cognitive and social development. If children can be guided in inventing more elaborate make-believe situations, transforming themselves into complex make-believe characters, or persisting at roles for longer periods, from this view, they will enjoy a range of developmental benefits (Smilansky & Shefatya, 1990).

Teacher 3 believes that play influences academic learning indirectly. As children play, they acquire specific play abilities that, in turn, contribute to reading or math skill. Children who engage in high-quality dramatic play, for example, learn how to invent and structure stories. Eventually, they will become more competent writers (Trawick-Smith, 2001). Children who play board games acquire specific game-playing skills, such as counting the number of spaces one moves or reading numerals on a spinner. In time, these children will excel in math abilities (Cutler, Gilkerson, Parrott, & Bowne, 2002).

Concerns have been raised about such an approach to play. One worry is that adult involvement will inhibit creative expression and imagination (Trawick-Smith, 1994a). Are children really playing when they are being guided in pretense by an adult (Sutton-Smith, 1998)? Multicultural scholars have posed other questions. Are these specific play forms—say, sociodramatic play—important and equally valued in all cultures? When we enhance make-believe, are we not really teaching all children to play in ways that are most common and appreciated in Western societies (Trawick-Smith, 1998)?

APPROACH 4

In a preschool classroom, children spend most of their morning playing in centers. One 4-year-old is building with blocks. A teacher watches as he constructs a farm, which includes a block enclosure—a corral—into which he has placed plastic farm animals. At a certain point the teacher approaches and says, "Tell me about what you're building."

"A farm," the child answers. "See? The animals are in the farm."

"Yes, I see," responds the teacher enthusiastically. She pauses, then asks, "Are these pigs inside or outside the fence?"

"Um. . . ." The child studies his structure and animals a moment. "Inside."

"*Inside* the fence. I see," the teacher reiterates. She moves away for a time and allows the child to play independently.

She now approaches two other children who are painting. She studies their work a moment then, asks, "Tell me about what you're doing."

"This is the castle where the queen lives," one child answers, pointing to her painting.

"Me, too," the other child says.

"You're making two castles," the teacher comments.

"Right. One, two," one child counts.

"How are your castles different?" the teacher asks.

"Oh, well, mine's really big," a child responds. "See? It's big."

"Your castle is *bigger* than Sara's? How else are your castles different?"

"I know," the other child says. "There's more green. More green in mine."

"You have more *green* in yours, I see. And Sara has more blue," the teacher summarizes. She watches the children a minute more and then quietly leaves the art center.

Teacher 4 has adopted a **broadly focused developmental approach** to play. Like teachers 2 and 3, she provides many play opportunities in her classroom. However, she intervenes regularly and vigorously to promote a broad range of concepts and skills. Her assumption is that adult intervention in all types of play assures positive development. As shown in the preceding description, such interventions are often responsive and spontaneous. The teacher usually makes a decision, on the spot, about which concept or skill—cognitive, social, or physical—to enhance (Trawick-Smith, 1994a). Play, from this teacher's view, is an enjoyable medium through which she can enhance certain areas of development. It is a context in which teaching and learning can be made fun.

This teacher uses play to address state and national academic standards more directly. She teaches reading by including books or writing materials within play centers and guiding children in using them. Prompting children to write signs for their block city is an example. She asks questions about size, amount, or spatial relationships as children play with blocks to enhance math skills.

Questions can be raised about this approach as well. Play enthusiasts might ask, Do these interventions—queries about relational concepts, for example—interrupt creative expression and make-believe? Can a child's activity even be considered play once a teacher has interceded? Advocates of more **didactic programs** might ask a different set of questions. Is play intervention the most efficient way to promote cognitive or social growth? Wouldn't learning be somewhat haphazard using this approach? Would a child be distracted from learning by other stimuli in an active play environment? Wouldn't a quiet, teacher-directed lesson on size or color be more effective?

All four of the teachers described here would claim that they are using play to achieve positive outcomes in the classroom. In fact, they would likely argue that their own approach to play is most effective in meeting critical state and national standards in literacy, mathematics, and other academic areas that are receiving emphasis in schools. Yet their strategies are quite different. These four approaches are contrasted in Table 8–3.

TABLE 8–3 Approaches to Play

Approach to Play	Key Theorists	Underlying Assumptions	Examples
Hands-off play approach	Axline (1947); Freud (1961)	Children benefit most from self-guided play with open-ended play materials. Adult intervention interferes with self-expression.	A kindergarten teacher provides a traditional "housekeeping corner," equipped with home-related play props. He observes children playing themes or issues of concern or interest but does not intervene.
Nonplay approach	Bereiter & Engelmann (1966); Skinner (1966)	Play is distinct from and less important than learning or work. Because it is enjoyable, play can serve as a reward for working hard in school.	A teacher assigns work-book activities to first grade children. If they finish their work quickly and carefully, she allows them to play games for several minutes.
Narrowly focused play intervention	DeVries et al. (in press); Isenberg & Jalongo (1997); Neuman & Roskos (1997); Piaget (1962); Smilanksy (1968)	Certain types of play are most useful to children, especially sociodramatic play, block play, and games with rules. Adults can intervene in play to promote skill in these specific areas.	A preschool teacher sets up a dramatic play center as a pretend restaurant. As children play there, she intervenes to encourage more make believe, verbalization, social interaction, and persistence.
Broad-based developmental approach	Biber (1977); Bodrova & Leong (1998); Gandini (1997); Hohman & Weikart (1995); Trawick-Smith (1994a, 1994b)	All types of play activities are useful to children. As children play, they acquire a broad range of cognitive, social and play skills. Teachers can intervene to promote all areas of development.	A second grade teacher moves over to a group of children who are arguing about the outcome of a card game. He asks questions that guide children in quantifying and conflict resolution.

In the following sections, common curriculum models that reflect these four teaching approaches will be analyzed critically in regard to the play opportunities they afford and the obstacles they create.

APPROACH 1: NONPLAY CURRICULUM MODELS

Before examining true play approaches, it is important to consider a variety of **nonplay curriculum models** that are growing more prevalent in American schools. Some teachers, such as the one in approach 1, offer play opportunities only infrequently, if at all. When they do allow play in their classrooms, it is often used as a reward to encourage nonplay work. Two assumptions underlie nonplay approaches: (a) play and learning are distinct and mutually exclusive, and (b) learning is more important than play and should be the ultimate goal of education.

Behaviorist Models

During the 1960s and 1970s, a period of great experimentation with curriculum models for preschool and primary education, a variety of nonplay **behaviorist models** were developed and studied. Grounded in the work of B. F. Skinner (1966), these models included direct adult instruction, programmed workbooks, and tangible rewards for appropriate behavior and learning. Play was deemphasized or even prohibited. One such program, the Behavior Analysis Follow Through model (Bushell, 1970) for children from preschool to grade 3, provided extended instructional periods in which children would be rewarded with tokens for appropriate behavior. These tokens could later be redeemed for play activities during short free periods. Play activities were only allowed during these special play periods and only for those children who had earned enough tokens to "purchase" them.

Another behaviorist early childhood program developed in the 1960s, the **Direct Instruction model** (Bereiter & Engelmann, 1966), included no play whatsoever. Every minute of the school day was devoted to intensive, adult instruction in academic skills. Children were induced to persevere in rather austere learning tasks with rewards and adult praise. Some of the developers of this model created a companion language program, **Distar**, in which teachers taught oral and written language directly. Words and sentences were presented, and children were rewarded for restating or rereading these aloud (Bereiter & Engelmann, 1966).

Such behaviorist programs have fallen out of favor with most educators (especially play advocates, for obvious reasons!). Although research has shown that the narrow academic goals of such programs can be achieved (Bushell, Wrobel, & Michaelis, 1968), these outcomes are generally short-lived; most benefits to children have been found to disappear by grade 3 or 4 (Miller & Bizzell, 1989; Schweinhart & Weikart, 1996). Furthermore, studies that have examined responses of individual children to such approaches (rather than aggregate data on large subject samples) show that not all children enjoy these gains, even in the short run (Betancourt & Zeiler, 1971). Finally, although short-term achievement outcomes are sometimes reported, these tend to be less pronounced than those for children enrolled in less didactic, play-based models (Burts et al., 1993).

A frequent criticism of behaviorist programs is that they fail to address important nonacademic areas of development. For example, such models have been found to be less effective than play-based programs in promoting social development and creativity (Miller & Bizzell, 1989). Schweinhart and Weikart (1996) found, in fact, that by adolescence, children who attended a direct instructional preschool (Distar) engaged in twice as many delinquent acts—including violence against persons and property—participated less often in school activities, sought less help from others in coping with personal problems, and had less positive relationships with their families than those who attended a play-oriented program (High/Scope, to be examined in a later section).

In a longitudinal program comparison study, children in more didactic, less playful programs were found to exhibit twice the frequency of stress behaviors as those in "developmentally appropriate" classrooms (Hart et al., 1998). This finding was particularly pronounced for males and children from low socioeconomic backgrounds. In response to these findings, Schweinhart, Weikart, and Larner (1986) ask whether the short-run intellectual gains of direct instructional programs are "purchased at the price of deficits in social behavior" (p. 42).

Didactic Elementary School Programs

Many elementary school teachers are committed to providing daily play experiences for their students. In some public and private elementary schools, however, play has been abandoned in favor of behaviorist approaches, described earlier. One school district, in Hartford, Connecticut, serves as an example of the revival of direct instruction in early childhood education (Chedekel, 1999). In response to declines in test scores of academic skills in this urban school system, the superintendent has mandated a direct instruction model—from preschool to high school. Reading and reading readiness instruction have been particularly emphasized. In the primary grades, for example, a "power hour" of reading lessons has been added to the existing time period allotted for reading. How do teachers create such large blocks of time for direct teaching? They eliminate child-centered activities—that is, play—and even reduce recess time. To "get through the material," some teachers have resorted to inappropriate time-saving practices, such as not allowing children to ask questions or talk to each other (Chedekel, 1999).

The trend of replacing play time with direct instruction is not found only in large cities or public schools, however. In some states, recess has been almost eliminated from the elementary school day. Academically-oriented private schools are common. In a small town in New England, a first grade teacher voices concern about his school district's views on play:

> Our school has been making a big deal out of increasing our "instructional time." They've added minutes to our school day and days to our school year. Several weeks ago, I received notification that outdoor time would no longer be considered instructional time. The memo read, "Since recess cannot be counted in the determination of instructional minutes, outdoor free time must be reduced or eliminated, or the school day lengthened."
>
> I argued to my principal, "What do they mean recess isn't instructional time? In my view, there is no greater learning period in the day. Aren't board members concerned about play and social interaction? Aren't they concerned about mental and physical health? Don't they understand the connections between the body and the mind? Better they give up math time than recess!" My principal smiled and nodded, but has yet to take any action on my concerns. (Trawick-Smith, 2000, p. 344)

Reductions of play time are not always so extreme. Even in play-friendly schools, however, the following common practices threaten play opportunities for some children:

- Children are not allowed to use play centers until after their abstract "seat work" is completed.
- Children who do not finish workbook pages or dittos are not allowed go out for recess.
- Children are required to play very quietly.
- The number of children allowed in a given center is restricted to two or three.
- Children are not provided with adequate space or a long enough block of time to engage in meaningful play.

Sadly, research suggests that academic gains from nonplay approaches will be short-lived (Miller & Bizzell, 1989; Schweinhart & Weikart, 1996), may increase the stress level among at-risk students (Hart et al., 1998), and will not effectively promote social skills (e.g., conflict resolution), which are so crucial in urban neighborhoods (Schweinhart & Weikart, 1996).

APPROACH 2: THE "HANDS-OFF" PLAY CURRICULUM

Many teachers include much play in the classroom. Some still approach play as teacher 2 has done: providing rich materials and ample space and encouraging children to play completely independently. Perhaps the best example of this approach may be found in descriptions of the early nursery schools that opened in the 1920s in this country—the Teachers College Nursery School of Columbia University and the University of Iowa Child Welfare Research Station, for example. These were the first and perhaps the purest of the play-based programs; their influence on later classroom practice in early childhood education has been long-lasting.

Though these programs did not comprise a curriculum model per se (they varied markedly in a variety of ways), they were uniform in an adherence to a psychoanalytic theory. Their overall goals were to promote social development and mental health. Based on Freud's (1961) view of play, classrooms were designed so that children could spend the majority of their time expressing themselves in open-ended ways with toys and art media. Children engaged in make-believe, built with blocks, sculpted, and painted. The role of the teacher was primarily to serve as an attachment figure who would respond with warmth and interest when children needed attention, reassurance, or assistance. Teachers were also informal therapists, who helped children talk out or play out conflicts and anxieties (Katz, 1970). Teachers in these early nursery schools were keen observers and recorders of behavior; they carefully documented the social and emotional growth of their students.

Research on the outcomes of these early programs is scant; those studies that have been conducted are inconclusive. In an early review of investigations of "free-play nursery programs," Sears and Dowley (1963) conclude that "attendance, in and of itself, does not radically alter personalities of children, but. . .certain social participation skills are enhanced and can be observed several years later" (p. 850).

Traditional, psychoanalytic free-play nursery school classrooms were included in the well-known High/Scope longitudinal comparison study of program models (Schweinhart & Weikart, 1996). In a series of follow-up investigations over more than 20 years, children who attended these programs did not differ significantly in intellectual or achievement measures from those who attended either a direct instructional preschool (Distar) or one with adult play intervention (High/Scope). Subjects in this free-play preschool group did fare better than the Distar group on social development measures (including a lower frequency of violent behavior in adolescence) but slightly less well than those attending High/Scope preschools (Schweinhart & Weikart, 1996).

More recent child care quality research has given pause to hands-off-play proponents, however (Howes, Ritchie, & Bowman, 2002). In one investigation, the frequency of adult engagement in children's play was found to be related both to attachment to caregivers and to the intellectual quality of children's activities (Howes & Smith, 1995). In another study, the nature and amount of adult-child interaction was found to be a fundamental indicator of overall quality in child care (Howes, Phillips, & Whitebrook, 1992).

What can be concluded about a hands-off play approach? Most play theorists and researchers now advocate some type of adult involvement in children's play activities, yet in many community-based preschools and child care centers, this involvement is still relatively infrequent (Johnson et al., 1999).

APPROACH 3: NARROWLY FOCUSED PLAY INTERVENTIONS

A number of play models have been designed to enhance specific types of play. In most cases, these models are administered in typical play-based classrooms, not unlike those described

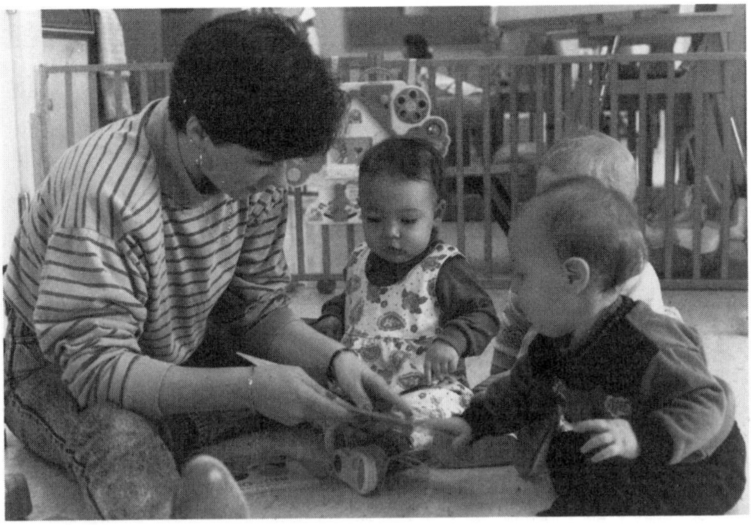

Adult play interactions should enrich what children are currently doing.

under approach 2. A full complement of play activities and centers are usually included. What sets these more focused programs apart is that they emphasize one play form—say, sociodramatic play—more than others. A special play space may be created for this featured type of play; special interventions are planned for enhancing it. Among the programs considered in this section are those focusing on sociodramatic play, creative dramatics, literacy play, and games with rules.

Smilansky's Sociodramatic Play Intervention

Smilansky (1968) developed an intervention program designed to enhance **sociodramatic play**—that is, make-believe role playing in which children assume the pretend roles of other persons, animals, or even objects, and play out imaginative situations that hold personal meaning. Developed for use with low-income immigrant children in Israel, Smilansky's model is based on four key assumptions:

1. Sociodramatic play is related to social and cognitive development and school success.
2. Not all children engage in sociodramatic play; some who do perform play enactments that are less social, imaginative, verbal, or organized.
3. Absence of sociodramatic play abilities among children of low socioeconomic status may explain their academic difficulties in later childhood.
4. Adult intervention can increase the quantity and quality of sociodramatic play and enhance overall cognitive development.

Smilansky's strategy includes four steps, each of which is described in Table 8–4.

Children are first provided with rich experiences (e.g., field trips, stories) on which they may later base play in the sociodramatic play center. This is an important step, Smilansky (1968) argues, because sociodramatic play is primarily *assimilative* (Piaget, 1962); that is, it involves the reenactment of previously acquired experiences. Children who lack rich experience may not be able to pretend at all (Smilansky & Shefatya, 1990). Next, a special play area, equipped with props related to these field trips or experiences, is created within the sociodramatic play center of the classroom. After a trip to the grocery, for example, a make-believe store with empty cans and boxes, plastic produce, and a cash register might be provided.

TABLE 8–4 Steps in Smilansky's (Smilansky & Shefatya, 1990) Sociodramatic Play Intervention Program

Steps	Examples
Step 1: Provide unique experiences for children to re-create in play.	A kindergarten teacher takes his class on a field trip to a pediatrician's office.
Step 2: Create a special play center with thematic props that relate to these unique experiences.	A make-believe doctor's office, including medical props, a cot to resemble an examining table, and a waiting area are created in the dramatic play center of the kindergarten.
Step 3: Observe children's play, and note play strengths and deficits. Identify children who need special support in play.	A teacher notices that one child only watches others play in the pediatrician's office and rarely engages in make-believe.
Step 4: Intervene in children's sociodramatic play, either from within or outside the play theme, to address play deficits.	A teacher pretends to be a patient who has a cough and asks a child who only watches if she would listen to his lungs with a stethoscope. When another child shows interest, he facilitates play between this withdrawn child and her peer.

A third step in the program involves observation of children's play and the identification of individuals who show play deficits. Some children do not interact with peers, for example; others rarely assume the roles of make-believe characters. Some are unable to transform real objects or events into pretend ones. Others quickly switch from one role to another without developing elaborate themes or enactments. Such children are targeted for intervention.

In the final step, teachers play along with children to address these observed play deficits, following specific guidelines: they observe first before entering a play setting, so that they fully understand children's play in progress. They intervene in sociodramatic play only if it is determined that children need support. Teachers can enter play from inside the role-playing theme by taking a role themselves. For example, a teacher might enter children's restaurant play by pretending to be a customer who is ordering lunch. At other times the teacher might intervene from outside the role playing, merely asking interesting questions or offering new props. A teacher might ask a group of children who are playing "gas station," "What will you use for a hose to pump the gas?" Teachers must not force themselves on children as they play, Smilansky urges, and should honor their students' wishes to be left alone.

In Smilansky's model, all interventions are aimed at preserving and enhancing the ongoing sociodramatic play theme. Interactions that significantly interfere with activities in progress are inappropriate. One important guideline in Smilansky's approach is that teachers should only intervene for a short time to enhance one or two play skills; after this, they should withdraw. The goal of Smilansky's program is to enrich self-directed play, not to provide continuous adult-guided make-believe.

Which specific behaviors do teachers facilitate as they play with children? Smilansky (1968) has identified six sociodramatic play quality elements that are significant to children's development: imitative role playing, make-believe with regard to objects, make-believe with regard to actions and situations, persistence in role playing, social interaction, and verbal communication (see Chapter 4). In the following classroom example, a teacher uses an inside-of-play intervention to enhance several of these play quality elements: make-believe in regard to actions and situations, verbal communication, and social interaction.

Child A sits alone in the dramatic play center dressing and undressing a doll. She doesn't look at or interact with the other children who play near her. A teacher observes her for a few minutes, then intervenes.

Teacher: Is your baby hungry? We could make her some dinner.

Child A: (Says nothing, continues dressing the doll)

Teacher: If she's hungry let me know. We could make her a big meal in the kitchen (Moves over to the kitchen and begins to pull out pans and dishes, playing along parallel to Child A)

Child A: (Moves over to the teacher) My baby's hungry.

Teacher: Okay. Let's see. What should we make her?

Child A: Baby food.

Child B: (Moving over to the teacher) Here, I'll make the food.

Teacher: Why don't you and Celeste work together. I'll rock the baby. (Rocks the doll)

Child C: Can I play?

Child B: No. We're making the supper, right, Celeste?

Child A: (Nods, says nothing)

Teacher: Why don't you cut vegetables, Sara?

Child C: Okay. Celeste, can I have a knife?

Child A: I'm using it. (Hands Child C another plastic knife) Here.

Child B: What's your baby named, Celeste?

Child A: Lawanda.

Child B: Okay, Lawanda, your supper's ready.

All three children and the teacher sit down to eat. Children B and C direct questions and conversation to both the teacher and Child A. Child A nods or gives single-word responses. After a few minutes the teacher leaves the table. Child A plays with her peers for many minutes until clean-up time. (Trawick-Smith, 1994a, p. 61)

Smilansky's (1968) own research has demonstrated that her approach enhances the frequency and complexity of play. Others have found that her interventions (or those similar to hers) can promote general cognition (Christie, 1983; Saltz, Dixon, & Johnson, 1977), language (Levy, Wolfgang, & Koorland, 1992), school achievement (Smilansky & Shefatya, 1990), and social interaction (Smith, Dalgleish, & Herzmark, 1981; Udwin, 1983).

Multicultural scholars however, have challenged the notion that sociodramatic play has universal benefit. McLoyd (1986b) suggests that children of historically underrepresented groups may engage in this type of play less often or may embed their dramatic role playing in other pastimes, such as motor activity on the playground. Rough-and-tumble play, music play, or even teasing may be more socially organized and symbolic for some children. According to McLoyd, teachers do not always appreciate the developmental value of such play forms. Because children of color do not play in a specified way, their activities are often judged to be deficient.

A number of studies of children from non-Western cultures have supported McLoyd's argument. In an investigation in Senegal, children were found to engage in **work-play**, in which make-believe and games were embedded in family chores (Bloch & Adler, 1994). A child might pretend to be a mother while helping her own mother with household duties. Such actions are not always appreciated or even recognized as play. In a recent study in Puerto Rico, 5-year-olds were found to rarely play in the dramatic play area of their classrooms (Trawick-Smith, 1998a). However, they performed rich make-believe within their active motor play on the playground and in music play in the music center. Such research raises questions about whether classroom interventions should focus so narrowly on just one type of play. Sociodramatic play may be just one of many valuable pastimes for children across cultures.

Isenberg and Jalongo's Creative Drama for the Primary Grades

Isenberg and Jalongo (2000) have proposed a program to enhance **creative drama**—a more organized and elaborate "cousin" of sociodramatic play. In their approach, primary grade children are guided informally in dramatizing stories—their own or others'—or reenacting experiences or events of the classroom. It is important to draw a distinction between their recommended drama activities and formal, scripted performances in front of large audiences. Isenberg and Jalongo argue that these latter experiences are stressful and generally inappropriate for children through the primary years.

This approach resembles that of Smilansky's in that children are encouraged to engage in make-believe. In fact, one of the six play activities these authors include in their program is spontaneous sociodramatic play. The Isenberg and Jalongo model is distinct, however, in its emphasis on planning and social collaboration. In all recommended activities, children are encouraged to plan with peers in small or large groups. They decide collectively about the stories or experiences to be dramatized and negotiate role assignments and scripts. They collaborate on set design and the creation of props. Following Isenberg and Jalongo's method, a single dramatization can comprise an ongoing play project that lasts for a week or more.

These authors recommend six different types of drama for primary grade children. These are presented in Table 8–5.

Like Smilansky, these authors propose a thematic sociodramatic play center in which props are provided that relate to particular stories or themes. Children are encouraged to select from these during free play periods. Another recommended play type is **story play**, based on the work of Paley (1981). In story play, children—individually or in groups—write or dictate to a teacher their own imaginative stories. When these stories are completed, children dramatize them, assigning roles and making props. The following is an example of story play in a third grade classroom:

> A third grade teacher has planned a unit on African folktales. She reads many different types of traditional stories to children and provides

TABLE 8–5 Isenberg and Jalongo's (1997) Creative Drama Model

Type of Drama	Description
Sociodramatic play	Children are provided with thematic and/or literacy props and a special play center and are encouraged to engage in spontaneous make believe.
Story play	Children write their own original stories or dictate these to a teacher. They plan out a dramatization of their stories, creating props, assigning roles, and even writing scripts.
Pantomime	Children select a work of children's literature to enact. They plan out a silent re-creation of the story. They may perform all or part of their pantomime for others, asking their audience to guess what actions are taking place.
Puppetry	Children select a work of children's literature and use puppets to reenact it. They plan out their performance, assigning roles, decorating a puppet stage, and making the puppets themselves. They perform the puppet show in front of a mirror to observe their own puppetry actions.
Story drama	Children select a work of children's literature and spontaneously retell it in a dramatic fashion. They assign roles to enact the story and often identify one child to be a narrator.
Readers theater	Children plan a dramatic reading of a favorite work of children's literature. Children plan who will read which parts, which interesting voices will be used for the dialogue, and when choral reading or choreographed movements will be used.

additional books for them to read independently. As a culmination of this study, she guides small groups of children in writing and dramatizing their own African folktales.

The teacher now moves over to a group of students struggling with the dramatization of their original story, "How the Tigers got Their Roars Back."

Child A: (To the teacher) We can't do this, 'cause we don't have enough people. Our story has all these tigers and there aren't enough people. Only one, two, three, four. Not enough.

Teacher: How many characters are in the story you wrote?

Child B: Well, there's four tigers and two people.

Child C: (Corrects Child B) They're *villagers*. And there's an elephant, too, so we don't have enough people.

Teacher: What could you do about that?

Child B: We could take out some of the tigers.

Teacher: That's one idea. What do you all think?

Child A: No, 'cause then we'd have to change the whole tale! All the tigers need to roar! That's the story!

Teacher: Could some of you play two different characters?

Child C: Like I could play a tiger and villager?

Teacher: Would that work?

Child B: Wait. Let me see something. (Studies the written story.) OK. We could be tigers, and we could be villagers.

Child C: Or a tiger and the elephant.

The children all agree to this solution and resume their planning, each choosing two separate roles to play. The teacher quietly moves on to another group.

Pantomime activities—also included in Isenberg and Jalongo's (2000) model—are proposed as particularly useful play alternatives for less verbal children with special needs and those who do not speak English as a preferred language. Although a goal is to help children learn to pantomime stories independently and with peers, Isenberg and Jalongo recommend several preliminary, teacher-guided activities to help them get started. One such activity involves teacher modeling. At group time, teachers might conduct pantomime games in which they silently perform actions and ask children to guess what they are doing.

A fourth type of creative drama proposed by Isenberg and Jalongo (2000) is **puppetry**. They include this type of play because they view it as less threatening than conventional role playing for children with limited language or social competence. Among the specific classroom strategies they recommend are providing mirrors or "silhouette puppets" and an illuminated screen so that children can study their own puppet actions. Older children are encouraged to plan out puppetry dramatizations and to construct the puppets themselves.

Another type of play in Isenberg and Jalongo's (2000) model is **story drama**, a "teacher-led group experience with children creating scenes from familiar literature that use both dialogue and movement" (p. 191). This type of play resembles the classic **thematic fantasy play training** developed by play pioneers Eli Saltz and James Johnson (1974). In this activity, groups of children select a story, then reinterpret it dramatically. The role of teachers in story drama is to facilitate children's planning, role assignments, and dramatization by asking key questions. To help a child explore the dimensions of a particular character, for example, a teacher might ask, "How do you suppose the bears felt when they came home and saw their porridge, chairs, and Goldilocks sleeping in their bed?" (p. 192).

A final type of play included in the Isenberg and Jalongo (2000) model—**readers theater**—represents a transition between the spontaneous symbolic play activities of young children and more conventional reading in later childhood. In readers theater, children select a book and plan an elaborate, dramatic rereading of it.

This enactment involves few props; the focus is on reading expression and gesture. As children plan, they must decide: Who will read which parts? Will there be a narrator? What types of dramatic voices will be used? Will there be choral readings? What gestures or movements will be choreographed?

A number of questions can be raised about the Isenberg and Jalongo (2000) model. What precise teaching strategies are used to facilitate these various forms of play? Although these authors briefly describe teachers as "coparticipants," the exact nature of the their role is not fully articulated. Lack of clarity about adult intervention leads to a larger concern: Are such teacher-directed, -planned, and -organized activities even true play?

Research suggests that Isenberg and Jalongo's (2000) model, in fact, addresses quite well the unique play interests and thinking of primary grade children. Several studies have shown that, between the ages 6 and 8, children's play naturally becomes more planful, socially organized, rule governed, skill oriented, and reality based (Hughes, 1998; Trawick-Smith, 1994b). Children of this age are drawn to make-believe roles and enactments that resemble real-life theater. They wish to exercise sophisticated skills in art, drama, reading, and writing. Often they spend an inordinate amount of their free time in joint preparation and planning for play. Isenberg and Jalongo's play activities include all of these newly acquired play elements.

The Isenberg and Jalongo (2000) model has not been empirically tested. However, early studies of similar, teacher-guided play programs have shown positive and lasting effects on intelligence quotient and other measures of general cognition (Christie, 1983; Saltz & Johnson, 1974; Saltz et al., 1977; Smith et al., 1981). Studies on story reenactment have found that children who dramatize favorite books show greater comprehension and story recall and an increased ability to retell stories (Galda, 1982, 2000). Isenberg and Jalongo provide rich anecdotal evidence of the value of each type of play—particularly in relation to literacy (McCaslin, 1990; Paley, 1981; Tompkins & Hoskisson, 1995).

Roskos and Neuman's Literacy Play Model

A play intervention model that focuses specifically on literacy has been proposed by Roskos and Neuman (1998). This approach is based on the assumption that in sociodramatic play, children regularly engage in **literacy routines**—reading and writing actions that they have observed adults perform in real life. A child in a make-believe grocery store may write a grocery list, just as she has seen her father do. Another child, in a library play theme, may read and check out books as he has observed at his local library. Thus, sociodramatic play is an ideal context for children to practice **functional uses of print** (Neuman & Roskos, 1997).

In this approach, teachers create special sociodramatic play centers that include an inordinate number of literacy props—pens and markers, pads of paper, stationery and envelopes, books, and signs. Often these props are related to specific play themes. If the sociodramatic play area is organized as a grocery store, for example, shopping lists, coupons, sale advertisements, checkbook stubs, and product labels are provided. Merely offering such props may not be sufficient to promote literacy play, these authors contend. Interactions with other children are often necessary. A child with more print experience can support the reading and writing of a less competent peer (Neuman & Roskos, 1991; Stone & Christie, 1996). Play experiences within mixed-ability peer groups are an important feature of this model.

Teachers can enhance literacy play, as well, through thoughtful play interventions. Adult modeling of functional uses of print is especially emphasized (Enz & Christie, 1997; Roskos & Neuman, 1998). A child who does not play with literacy props in a pretend restaurant center may be prompted to do so through a nonobtrusive teacher demonstration: "I think I'll look at the menu and see what I can order."

The following is another example of a teacher facilitating literacy play:

> Two 4-year-olds are playing in a pretend post office that has been created in the dramatic play area. They mail envelopes in a mail box that has been provided. A teacher moves into the center.
>
> *Teacher:* (Speaks to no one in particular) I haven't written to my mother in so long. I think I'll jot her a note. (Places stationery, envelopes, and markers on the table; begins to write) Let's see. I think I'll write, "Dear Mom."
>
> *Child A:* (Approaches the teacher) Can I write one?
>
> *Teacher:* Sure. Who will you write to?
>
> *Child A:* (In a pretend, adultlike voice) Well, I need to write to my daughter. She has moved away and I need to write her. Come on, Maria. Let's write to our daughters, okay?
>
> *Teacher:* You have daughters? How old are they?
>
> *Child A:* Let's say they're teenagers.
>
> *Child B:* Okay. We can write 'em and mail 'em. (Points to the make-believe post office)
>
> The two children write and discuss their letters. The teacher continues to write with them. Finally, the children place their letters in envelopes, address these in "scribble writing," and mail them at the post office.
>
> *Child A:* Let's say I'm the daughter now and I get your letter, okay? (Takes an envelope from the mailbox and now assumes a different voice) Oh. A letter! What does this say? (Shows the letter to the teacher)
>
> *Teacher:* You should ask Maria. (Points to Child B)
>
> *Child B:* (Takes the letter from Child A; runs her fingers along the scribbles) "Dear Daughter. Please come home now. Aren't you scared by yourself? Love, Mommy."
>
> The children continue to play mother and daughter, writing more letters and mailing them. The teacher eventually leaves the play area. (Trawick-Smith, 1994a, p. 73)

The teacher in this example facilitates literacy by providing props and modeling their use. When one child has trouble reading another's letter, the teacher encourages peer interaction. Research has shown that this approach can increase the frequency of literacy activity and foster print awareness (Morrow & Rand, 1991; Neuman & Roskos, 1991; Vukelich, 1991). A concern raised about this model, however, is whether a literacy-enriched dramatic play center is still a play center and whether literacy play is still real play (Trawick-Smith, 1994a; Trawick-Smith & Picard, 2003). When a child pauses in library play to read a book, has she suspended her make-believe? When a child stops to write a letter in the pretend post office, is he still pretending? Can literacy routines disrupt an ongoing play frame? As with all interventions described in this chapter, great care must be taken not to turn play into something else—into those "didactic bumblings," for example, that Sutton-Smith (1990) warns against.

Kamii and DeVries's Group Games

A very different approach to play has been articulated by Kamii and DeVries (1980). Their work can be distinguished from previous models in several ways. First, their recommendations do not comprise a model per se but a theoretical orientation. They postulate a **constructivist** perspective on learning and teaching that can guide professionals in making their own classroom decisions. Their work may be further differentiated by its broad focus on all areas of development and the interrelationships among these. They do not consider play to be a distinct and independent psychological process; they would, in fact, be troubled by their inclusion here under the category of narrowly focused play interventions. From their view, development is global; feelings, thinking, and social interactions all influence each other and cannot be teased apart. Furthermore, they might not wish to have their work characterized as a play theory at all; they prefer to use the term *constructivist activities* instead of *play,* so that developmentally meaningful experiences can be clearly distinguished from more traditional and less useful classroom activities (DeVries et al., 2002).

Why, then, is the work of these authors included in this section of this chapter? They have provided the most elaborate and well-articulated theory on games with rules that exists in the literature. They have written extensively and specifically on the value of games and the role of adults in facilitating game playing. Their ideas on just this one type of play will be considered in this section.

Influenced by Piaget's theory of play and development, Kamii and DeVries (1980) advocate the use of traditional childhood games in the curriculum. They argue that games are especially challenging—cognitively and socially—because children must think about and adhere to rules and take the perspectives of peers as they play. Games are an enjoyable and nonliteral context for making moral decisions based on social contracts and agreements. In board games, for example, children must set aside an immediate ego need—a desire to win—and conform to agreed-on conventions (e.g., moving only the number of spaces shown on the dice). Failing to abide by rules interferes with game playing and may destroy the game altogether.

Children regularly contemplate the feelings and motives of their peers and anticipate their future actions as they play games (DeVries et al., 2002). In a game of checkers, for example, a child makes a move based on predictions about an opponent's thoughts and intentions. A child who wants to avoid going back to "start" after landing on a certain space in a board game might try to persuade an opponent to suspend the rules, based on an understanding of this peer's thinking or disposition. Additionally, many games encourage children to acquire specific concepts of number (e.g., scorekeeping or board games with dice), space (e.g., checkers), literacy (e.g., a game with written rules), and decentration (e.g., an "I'm thinking of something" game).

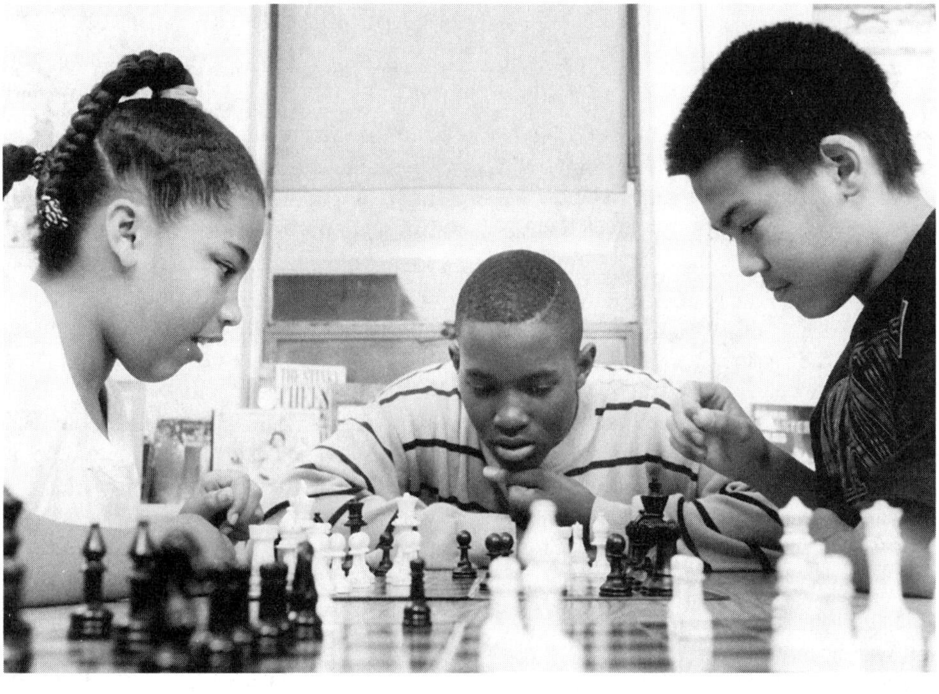

In games, children think about and adhere to rules and take the perspective of peers.

Some teachers raise concerns about competition. Do children suffer stress in game playing? Do games nurture competitive, noncooperative interactions? Kamii and DeVries (1980) argue that the competitive nature of games actually fosters sociomoral development. The tension between an immediate need to win and a need to adhere to rules so that play will continue leads children away from pure egocentrism toward more social and rule-governed thought and action. In most cases, games are relaxed and nonliteral, so children find it easier to suspend their own desires and to follow rules.

These authors do acknowledge that intense competition can be problematic. To reduce this intensity, they propose that teachers respond to winning in a casual way ("Well, Brenna won that time. What shall we play next?") and avoid such practices as giving prizes or eliminating "losers" as a game progresses (e.g., in the traditional version of musical chairs). In spite of these efforts, some children may be unable to cope with the stress of competition. Kamii and DeVries (1980) propose that, in these cases, children be given an option to play in a noncompetitive way. In a game of Concentration, for example, all the players might pool their matching pairs, so that they "win" together when all matches are found. Kamii and DeVries (1980) provide detailed guidelines for teaching interactions during group games. The role of an adult is to ask interesting questions, guide children's problem solving, or facilitate the clashes of opinion that inevitably arise. The teacher can prompt children to set up the game and negotiate rules. In a game of musical chairs, a teacher might ask, "Can you get enough chairs so that we all have one?" A teacher might settle a dispute about rules by asking, "Do you want to say that you don't have to go all the way back to the start when you land on that space? How many spaces back should you go if you land on it?"

Teachers can guide children in distributing materials (e.g., "Can you pass out the cards so everyone has the same amount?"). Playing along with children, the teacher might ask questions that guide their thinking (e.g., "Who has won the most cards so far? How do you know?"). When arguments arise, teachers can mediate ("Cheryl's angry. She says you moved too many spaces. What should we do about that?"). Even when putting a game away, children's thinking can be challenged (e.g., "Did we put away all the markers? Are there any missing? How do you know?").

All interventions are designed to facilitate the game playing itself and related intellectual and social processes. DeVries and Kohlberg (1990) emphasize that teachers should build on what children are doing, rather than interrupt them. The following narrative illustrates this approach:

> Three 5-year-olds have just completed a traditional game of Concentration. "I won!" one young player announces.
>
> A teacher approaches and asks, "How did you figure out that you won the most cards?"
>
> "Well, because," exclaims the child, holding a mass of cards in one hand and then placing them next to a classmate's pile in comparison. "See? I've got more!"
>
> "Does everyone agree?" the teacher asks.
>
> "Wait a minute!" another child protests. "Let me look at something." He spreads his cards end to end in a line on the floor. This line contains so many cards that it extends from the math area out into the center of the classroom. He makes similar lines, next to his own, with each of his playmate's cards.
>
> The teacher, observing this, asks, "Well, what do you think?"
>
> "Look. See?" he answers. "*My* line is longer. *I* won."
>
> "Does everyone agree with that?" the teacher asks the group. "Are there any other ways to figure out who won?"
>
> With the teacher's encouragement, the group continues to try solutions to the problem until snack time.

Kamii and DeVries (1980) present an elaborate, theoretical justification for game playing, generally, and for many traditional childhood games, specifically. They have conducted qualitative investigations of game playing in which spatial reasoning, quantification, perspective taking, and other social-cognitive processes have been described (DeVries et al., 2002; Kamii & DeClark, 1985).

Beyond the competition concern, some educators may raise questions about the practical application of Kamii and DeVries's (1980) work in modern schools. How can teachers—lone adults in classrooms of 25 or more children—spend such extensive periods of time in group game playing? Can disputes and upset about losing always be so smoothly resolved by teachers? In spite of these reservations, the Kamii and DeVries games strategy is one of the most unique and well-conceptualized play approaches reviewed in this chapter.

APPROACH 4: BROADLY FOCUSED DEVELOPMENTAL MODELS

In many curriculum models, play and development are more broadly addressed. Teachers in these programs, such as the teacher in approach 4 at the beginning of the chapter, provide materials and intervene in children's play to enhance a wide range of concepts and skills—not just play, but math abilities, language, or social competencies as well.

The Bank Street Approach

The **Bank Street** program—designed for children from preschool through the primary grades—is one of the most well-known and fully elaborated play-based approaches in early childhood education. It was developed by luminaries in the field: Harriet Johnson (1928), Lucy Sprague Mitchell (1950), Caroline Pratt (1948), and Barbara Biber (1977). Influenced initially by psychoanalytic thought, this method, in its earliest design, resembled a hands-off play approach. Expressed goals were the nurturance of ego development and overall mental health; the vehicle for achieving these was play in all its forms (Biber, 1977).

Play activities that are found in most preschool and child care programs today—pretend play, sand and water play, blocks, puzzles, clay, painting, swings, and riding toys—have their origins in the Bank Street approach. These activities are arranged into well-defined "interest centers" that are logically organized yet flexible. Spatial arrangement is regularly modified to meet the specific needs of children (e.g., a new animal care center might be added in response to children's interests, or the dramatic play center may be expanded to accommodate a more active group). The schedule of the day in the Bank Street classroom—which is also flexible—includes individual, small-group, and large-group play and learning. Passive, teacher-directed lessons are deemphasized.

During the 1960s and 1970s, as a greater focus was placed on early cognitive development, the program evolved to more fully address intellectual goals. A modern Bank Street classroom includes centers for all major academic subjects. Language and literacy are especially emphasized. A library is always available that provides child-made as well as published books, magazines, reading kits, and newsletters. A separate writing center contains journals, blank books, moveable alphabets, and spelling cards. A listening center, where children can hear recorded books or even record their own stories, is offered. Elaborate, cognitively oriented projects—cooking, woodworking, or caring for plants and animals—are often included. Separate math and science areas provide both found and commercial materials for child-directed experimentation and problem solving. All play centers are embellished with much print—written labels, teacher messages, and job charts.

Over the past few decades, Bank Street authors have more clearly defined the role for teachers in children's play. Although there remains a primary focus on facilitating trust and autonomy—Eriksonian concepts related to social and emotional development—a new emphasis has been placed on guiding the development of "cognitive proficiency" (Biber, Shapiro, & Wickens, 1971, p. 4). In a Bank Street classroom, teachers engage in four teaching strategies, as they interact with children in play: (a) observe and assess levels of thinking; (b) "verbally respond, amplify, rephrase, and correct children's comments, confusions, and actions" (Biber et al., 1971, p. 4); (c) foster higher levels of thinking; and (d) pose challenging problems for children to solve. Verbal elaboration on children's activities is particularly emphasized; it is through conversation with children in play that higher levels of thinking are stimulated (Biber et al., 1971).

The following is an example of a typical Bank Street teacher-child play interaction in a classroom art center:

> A child is painting at an easel; a teacher studies her activities a moment and then asks, "Tell me about what you're painting."
>
> "Red flower," the child mutters.
>
> "I see. You're painting red flowers—one, two, three of them."
>
> "Yeah," the child answers proudly.
>
> "Are you going to paint a whole garden?" the teacher asks.
>
> "What?"
>
> "Will you paint a whole garden, with lots of flowers?"
>
> "Oh. Yes," the child responds.
>
> "Will your flowers be of all different colors?" the teacher asks.
>
> "Yes. I'm going to use yellow, I think," the child says.
>
> "And blue and green?" the teacher asks.
>
> "Yeah, and brown. A whole garden." The child says, selecting a new color and resuming her painting.

Here the teacher is attempting to use play to facilitate a variety of cognitive and language abilities. By elaborating on the child's original utterance (from "Red flower" to "You're painting red flowers"), the teacher is trying to extend language and thinking. When asking whether the child will paint a full garden, the teacher is introducing a new concept and posing a challenging problem for the child to solve. Although the interaction is not highly intrusive, its focus is obviously on elaborating on the child's thinking in a purposeful way. Note that the aim is not to enhance the play, itself—in this case painting development—but to promote broader cognitive and verbal abilities.

There is a paucity of research on outcomes of the Bank Street approach. Most empirical evaluations of the program have been aimed at describing classroom interactions or verifying that the model has been properly implemented (Zimiles, 1986). In one investigation, children in Bank Street classrooms were found to interact more often with peers, to express more high-order cognitive statements and questions, and to show more autonomy in thought and action than those attending more traditional kindergarten to grade 3 classrooms (Ross & Zimiles, 1976). In a program comparison study, subjects who attended Bank Street programs were found to perform less well on traditional achievement tests but more competently on group problem-solving tasks than those from typical elementary schools (Minuchin, Biber, Shapiro, & Zimiles, 1969).

DeVries and Kohlberg (1990) raise concerns about the role of adults in Bank Street play activities. They argue that the efforts of Bank Street teachers to modify language and to extend children's thinking can amount to correction. In such interchanges, they contend, children may inadvertently receive messages that their ideas are not well expressed or that problems are not solved correctly—messages that could "operate against the encouragement of thinking" (p. 315). In spite of these criticisms, DeVries and Kohlberg view the Bank Street approach as closely aligned with other "child-centered" or "child development" approaches.

High/Scope

High/Scope is one of the most prevalent play-based early childhood curricula in the United States. It has been widely adopted as a model for both public and private preschool and kindergarten programs, in part because of the astounding and headline-grabbing results of a longitudinal study on its outcomes (Schweinhart & Weikart, 1996). Positive social benefits for children who have attended the program (for as little as 1 year at age 4!) have been found to persist through age 23.

The High/Scope classroom includes extended periods of free play in carefully designed centers. The earliest High/Scope programs contained four major play areas: dramatic play, blocks, quiet activities (e.g., puzzles, lotto games, books), and art. In later years, more literacy activities and a computer have been added to the model. Centers contain high-interest and concrete play materials that children may use in a variety of ways. These are carefully organized. Blocks may be ordered by shape and size; plastic tools in the dramatic play center may be arranged from longest to shortest. Cleanup time, then, becomes a lesson in ordering or classification.

A well-known feature of High/Scope is its plan-do-review schedule, described in an earlier section. In an initial planning session, children decide which play activities they will pursue during an upcoming free-choice period. Their plans are often presented verbally in a group discussion; teachers comment on and guide this planning process. In some kindergartens, children are encouraged to record their plans in writing by making marks next to pictures of centers they plan to visit or actually writing out their planned activities on a special planning form.

The "do" portion of the schedule involves actual play in centers. Some children follow their plans exactly; others deviate from these during the course of day. In a "review" session—another group time—children recall the activities they have completed. They revisit their plans and compare intended activities with actual accomplishments. After this plan-do-review routine, small-group, teacher-guided projects are conducted. A final circle time experience completes the schedule.

The model includes very specific guidelines for adult intervention in these play activities (Schweinhart & Weikart, 1996). As with the Bank Street model, these interventions are aimed at teaching concepts and enhancing skills. What sets this model apart, however, is that a specific set of cognitive abilities are targeted in intervention. Whereas Bank Street goals for teaching are rather open-ended and general (in fact, limitless cognitive and language processes may be enhanced), the High/Scope model focuses on just a few. Its authors have selected "key experiences of cognitive development"—"Piagetian skills," based on Piaget's theory of cognitive development—to be fostered as children play (Hohman & Weikart, 1995). These include such mental abilities as classification, seriation, spatial relations, time, and number, which have been drawn directly from Piaget's work. The teacher's role is to ask questions related to these specific areas as children engage in free play.

The description of teacher 4 at the beginning of this chapter serves as a good illustration of the High/Scope method of play intervention. The following is another example:

> A 5-year-old is constructing two buildings with blocks. As he works on his structures, the teacher moves into the area and says, "You're making two buildings! Great! How are these two buildings different?"
>
> "Different?" the child responds. "This one's bigger."
>
> "Bigger?" the teacher repeats.
>
> "Yeah, see?" the child touches the top of one of his block structures.
>
> "Right, it's taller. This building's taller than that building," the teacher replies, pointing to each structure.
>
> "Yeah."
>
> "How else are they different?" the teacher continues to query.
>
> "Well. . .this one has more," the child answers.
>
> "More blocks?" the teacher asks.
>
> "Of course, silly," the child answers. "I used more."

In this interaction, the teacher is using play to teach about comparisons. As in the Bank Street approach, he is using play as a vehicle for promoting a cognitive skill; he is not enhancing the block play itself. Unlike a Bank Street interaction, however, here the teacher has approached the play setting with a very specific skill already in mind—one of only a finite set of cognitive abilities that are taught during such interactions.

Although research shows long-term benefits of the High/Scope model, criticisms are prevalent in the literature, particularly from those who oppose heavy-handed interventions. Kohlberg and DeVries (1990) argue that High/Scope teacher questions are often delivered completely outside the child's intended play goals or interests. Such intrusions, they argue, "result in a lost opportunity to build on a child's purpose" (p. 68). Others have suggested that such strategies can completely shatter a **play frame**—a complex, nonliteral world of ideas, feelings, and imaginings that a child has created with great effort in play (Trawick-Smith, 1994a). From this view, a teacher not only has briefly interrupted a behavior by asking these questions but has disturbed an intricate, underlying state of mind.

Vygotskian Play Models

Several authors (Bodrova & Leong, 1998; Trawick-Smith, 1994a, 1998b) have proposed models of play that are based on the work of Lev Vygotsky (1977). These approaches are similar to those of other play-based programs in a number of respects. Like Bank Street and High/Scope, these models include extensive play experience in the preschool and primary grade classroom. In these approaches, as in Bank Street and High/Scope, play is viewed as a context for acquiring general cognitive processes, not just narrow play skills. For example, play is considered to be a primary mechanism for the acquisition of symbolic thought (Bodrova & Leong, 1998). It is viewed as a fundamental way that children acquire logico-mathematical reasoning (Trawick-Smith, 1994a).

Vygotskian models differ from each other in some ways. In one such approach, the Bodrova and Leong (1998) model, play is defined quite narrowly to include only make-believe and games. These are activities to which Vygotsky assigned special developmental significance. In another approach, the Trawick-Smith (1994a) model, play is defined more broadly, to encompass almost any self-chosen and self-expressive activity. From this view, even conducting scientific experiments, writing stories, or solving math problems may be viewed as instances of play if these are freely-chosen, pleasurable, and process-oriented. In contrast, seemingly playful activities such as block building or make believe are not considered play if these have been assigned or directed by an adult (Trawick-Smith, 1994a, p. 4).

These two Vygotskian models share three features, however, that distinguish them from other approaches. First, they both place great value on child-directed play and discourage its disruption. In Vygotskian models, adult involvement "may only be necessary for specific children or groups of children who are having trouble sustaining their interactions" (Bodrova & Leong, 1998, p. 281). Furthermore, teachers are encouraged to adhere to a **nonobtrusion rule** (Trawick-Smith, 1994a, p. 49), which limits adult interactions to those that enhance the play, itself—that is, the pretending, representing, thinking, conversing, or negotiating *that are already in progress*. The goal is to enrich what children are currently doing, not to promote other, extraneous modes of thinking and learning.

A second distinctive feature of Vygotskian models is the importance they place on peer interactions. When "expert" players interact with novice players, they enhance play quality and related advancements in thinking.

A final characteristic of Vygotskian models is a clearly articulated strategy for adult intervention. As children play, teachers are encouraged to **scaffold** children's activities, based on the level of support that is needed within a given context. As they observe children in play, teachers might determine that interactions are rich and meaningful and require no intervention whatsoever. Thus, a hands-off response is often prescribed. On the other hand, teachers may sometimes discover that children in play are confronted with insurmountable challenges—both intellectual and social. A child may be unable to proceed with a puzzle that has too many pieces; another may be unable to dress a doll because of motor limitations. Two children may have lapsed into a screaming match in which there can be no positive resolution without adult assistance. In these cases, the teacher intervenes in a relatively straightforward manner, perhaps even directly offering a solution.

Often, children are faced with problems that they can solve on their own with only a little assistance from an adult. This is a situation—within what Vygotsky called the **zone of proximal development** (see Chapter 2)—in which most learning and development can occur. When such situations arise in a classroom, teachers can offer gentle guidance—interesting questions, hints, encouragements—that assist children in solving problems independently. A teacher might ask, "Which of these [collage materials] would stick best to your paper, do you think?" or "You don't have anything to put out the fire? What would be something we could use as a pretend fire hose?" Note that such interventions are responsive; they are offered only when a need arises in play. Note, too, that they are intended only to enhance play—to support make-believe, artistic expression, social interaction, and other playful processes. An underlying assumption of this model is that enhancing play itself will, in turn, promote important areas of development.

The following is an example of such a teacher intervention:

> Two 5-year-olds play in the music center. One strums on an autoharp, while the other attempts to compose lyrics to go along with his chords.
>
> *Child A:* (Singing) The man fell . . . um . . . down a tree, down a tree . . . I don't know. . . .
>
> *Child B:* (Playing chords) Come on! Sing the song!
>
> *Child A:* No.
>
> *Child B:* (Still strumming the autoharp) Come on! The song's almost over! Sing!
>
> *Child A:* But I can't think of the rest.
>
> A teacher, who has been observing, enters the play area.
>
> *Teacher:* I like that first part. "A man fell down a tree." That's a good start to a song.
>
> *Child A:* Yeah, but I don't know any more words to sing.
>
> *Teacher:* Well, what else could the man do besides fall down a tree?
>
> *Child B:* (Stops playing the autoharp) I know. He could go up the tree. (Laughs)
>
> *Child A:* Okay. Play it. (Sings along to Child B's strumming) A man fell down the tree, up the tree, up the tree. A man fell up and down and up and down . . . and . . . (Stops singing) Wait. What can he do next?
>
> *Teacher:* Maybe you could sing what happens to him when he falls down.
>
> *Child A:* Oh. (Finishes the verse) A man fell up and down and up and down and fell to the dirty floor.
>
> *Teacher:* Wonderful. Now what will be your second verse?
>
> The teacher listens as the two compose a new verse, then quietly withdraws from the center. (Trawick-Smith, 1994a, p. 232)

In this interchange, the teacher has scaffolded children's musical play interactions within the zone of proximal development. When a problem of what to sing arises, she asks questions and gives hints that guide their independent problem solving. She does not solve the problem for them. The focus is not on drawing extraneous learnings from the interaction; the teacher is not trying to extend language directly or offer a lesson in mathematical thinking. She enhances the play itself—in this case, musical representation.

Although the outcomes of Vygotskian play programs have not been examined empirically, a number of researchers have demonstrated the impact of a scaffolding strategy on development, generally (Berk & Winsler, 1995). This method of guiding children's thinking and behavior within the zone of proximal development has been reported to enhance problem solving in classrooms (Bodrova & Leong, 1996; Rogoff, 1994) and at home (Freund, 1989; Rogoff, Mistry, Goncu, & Mosler, 1993).

Music enhances creativity, language, and cognitive processes.

Reggio Emilia Programs

A final play model to be considered in this section is the **Reggio Emilia approach**, which has been implemented for decades in infant, toddler, and preschool classrooms in a region in northern Italy. As in other broad-based developmental models, Reggio Emilia classrooms are designed to enhance all areas of development, not just play. Group experiences and projects, field trips, and other adult-guided experiences—activities not always considered play—are prevalent. The traditional play opportunities that are provided—dramatic play, blocks, and art—are varied and designed to achieve complex and global developmental outcomes (Edwards, Gandini, & Forman, 1998). A major goal of most Reggio Emilia activities is intellectual adaptation. Children's expressive experiences are intended to provide new understandings, not just opportunities for creative representation of existing concepts. For example, children may be guided in an artistic activity related to clouds and weather so that they can learn more about these phenomena (Gandini, 1997).

Many Reggio Emilia experiences include one particular kind of play: artistic representation. Although traditional play theorists have rarely considered art a play form, a growing number of researchers have demonstrated its playful elements (Reifel & Yeatman, 1993). Art may be a more prevalent play form in communities outside the mainland United States. In a study in Puerto Rico, it was discovered that the visual and musical arts were the most common types of spontaneous play among 4- and 5-year-olds (Trawick-Smith, 1998a).

It is important to note that teachers in Reggio Emilia prefer the term *symbolic representation* to *art,* to emphasize the integrated nature of expressive activities within the curriculum (Gandini, 1997). However, the model does specifically stress the creative uses of visual art media.

The Reggio Emilia approach includes several key components that distinguish it from American preschools. Children spend much time in small and even large groups, collaborating on projects and play activities. One group of children may gather to work on a papier-mâché sculpture of a lion, while another may use markers, paint, and photographs to represent the findings of a scientific experiment. Play experiences are most often collaborative, then; individual autonomy is less emphasized than it is in typical American programs.

In-depth, ongoing, emergent investigations are another feature of Reggio classrooms. Children select issues and topics to explore, plan field trips and individual research activities around these, and then represent their findings with artistic media. Some of the resulting artistic representations are organized on elaborate panels, which are displayed throughout the classroom. This latter step is called **documentation**; teachers and children use art media to document their thinking and learning. These projects can last for several months and usually include numerous drafts or revisions of artistic efforts (Gandini, 1997). The remarkable sophistication of the artistic works of Reggio Emilia children—displayed in the traveling exhibit "The Hundred Languages of Children"—has been attributed to this emphasis on revision and ongoing reflection.

The schedule of the day in Reggio Emilia classrooms is flexible and open-ended, emerging from the children's needs and interests. Students can choose to work and play alone or in groups and persist at tasks for as long as the tasks remain meaningful. As one researcher notes, "Time is not set by a clock. . . . Children's own sense of time and their personal rhythm are considered in planning and carrying out activities and projects" (Gandini, 1997, p. 17).

What is the teacher's role in children's play? Two types of professionals work in Reggio Emilia classrooms: the regular teacher, who plans and implements the day-to-day curriculum, and the *atelierista,* an individual who is trained in the visual arts. In collaboration, these adults intervene vigorously in children's activities, asking questions, providing materials, and assisting in the planning of research projects. They suggest and demonstrate the uses of various art media that are available in the *atelier*—a fully equipped art studio in each school. In addition, they encourage children to study their artistic works and to add to or revise these based on new understandings. For example, children might be guided in creating several drafts of self portraits over time. Eventually, they might be encouraged to use these portraits to sculpt their own faces in clay.

The following is an example of this teaching role. It is based on a story told by an elementary school teacher who implemented a Reggio Emilia approach in an American first grade classroom (Tarini, 1997, pp. 56–59):

DAY 1

A child approaches a teacher and says, "Know what? I'm going to make a butterfly."

"Wonderful. You're going to draw it?" the teacher responds.

"Yeah. With crayons and markers, maybe," the child replies.

"You know, I have a beautiful book with photographs of many different types of butterflies," the teacher informs the child. "You could look at it, if you want. It might give you some ideas."

"OK," the child answers, enthusiastically. After studying the teacher's book, she draws a first draft of a butterfly. Her work has captured the attention of two other children who join her at the art center. Each of them studies the book and also creates a draft.

DAY 2

The teacher sits with the three children who have drawn butterflies and talks with them about photographs in the book and their drawings. "You've made very interesting first drafts of your drawings," she says.

"Drafts?" one of the children asks.

"Yes. Artists sometimes draw something, then look at it later, and draw it again. Each time they draw it, it's called a draft. Sometimes they draw the same thing many times before they're done."

"OK," another child says excitedly. "I'm drawing another one."

"I will, too!" a peer responds.

"Let me show you something first," the teacher says, opening the butterfly book. "Did you notice that real butterflies don't have faces and smiles like people do? See? No faces." She points to a photograph. "Also, look at this. See how the wings go out like this?" She notes the angle of a line on the butterfly's wing. "Can you see how the wings go out?"

"OK!" responds one child. All three draw new, more accurate drafts of butterflies. One child draws *two* additional drafts.

DAY 3

The teacher sits with the three children again and suggests they use paint to add color to their butterfly drawings. One child immediately begins painting her final draft. Another, however, says, "Can I take a break from my butterfly today?" The third child indicates he wants to make a larger butterfly. The teacher guides him by offering a transparency and setting up an overhead projector. "You could trace your butterfly on this," she suggests, showing the transparency. "Then you can show it up on the screen."

"OK, but I'm going to make a new butterfly first," the child responds, completing a final draft before tracing and projecting it.

All three children end up with different final works—all are significantly more sophisticated than what these children had produced up to this point in the class.

It is obvious from this example that the Reggio Emilia approach assigns a more active and complex role to adults in play and art. This teacher's interactions contrast markedly with the hands-off play approach described earlier or the purely child-directed art experiences recommended by traditional art educators (Lowenfeld, 1947).

Because the Reggio Emilia approach was conceived of and first implemented by practitioners, evidence of its outcomes has been in the form of rich narratives about children's classroom activities. The remarkable artistic and intellectual achievements of children from Reggio Emilia have been described and analyzed by teachers from Italy (Malaguzzi, 1993) and by theorists and researchers from the United States (Edwards, Gandini, & Forman, 1998; New, 1993). A number of American educators have implemented aspects of the approach in their classrooms and have described positive experiences and outcomes for students (Breig-Allen & Dillon, 1997; Haigh, 1997; Saltz, 1997).

There are detractors of the approach. Superintendents and principals in modern American schools often thirst for hard data to support Reggio Emilia techniques. Do activities and interventions in this model, they ask, lead to significant gains on traditional measures of achievement? Will academic standards be met? More concern has been expressed about the portability of the model from one culture to another. Can a Reggio Emilia approach be implemented in communities with fewer resources, smaller and less innovative classroom spaces, single-aged classroom groupings, and less enthusiastic community support for the arts (Katz, 1997)? A growing body of anecdotal evidence indicates that the model can be successfully implemented—with adaptations—even in American public elementary schools (Tarini, 1997).

BORROWING THE BEST FROM EACH APPROACH

Which approach to play is most effective? Which strategy or strategies reviewed in this chapter should be adopted in classrooms? A teacher might wish to borrow key concepts from *each* approach—particularly those ideas that have been supported by research or well-formulated theory. Based on the perspectives of hands-off play theorists, teachers might increase time for child-directed free play and might more fully utilize these play periods for observing and assessing of the social and emotional development of their students. They might select more open-ended play materials that allow the expression of and mastery over anxieties or social problems. The hands-off play tradition provides, perhaps, the most convincing rationale for including play in the classroom: it is the most enjoyable and therapeutic activity of childhood.

Researchers who have developed and studied narrowly focused play intervention programs also have much to offer the classroom teacher. Their work suggests that teachers should sometimes enhance *specific types* of play—sociodramatic play, drama, literacy, and games. Emphasizing just one of these forms of play, however, is ill advised. Also, care must be taken to include alternative types of play—rough-and-tumble play, motor activity, or music—that are more meaningful to some families and cultures.

Those advocating broadly focused developmental models contribute another useful perspective on classroom practice. Borrowing from this approach, teachers might provide classroom space and materials to promote many different kinds of play and those play activities that best enhance other areas of cognitive and social development. They might intervene more regularly in play to facilitate higher levels of thinking, language, and human understanding within play contexts. A child-guided science experiment, for example, might be an ideal context for prompting categorization or ordering. A card game might be a useful setting for extending language. The sociodramatic play area might be a good place to extend symbolic thinking. So long as such interventions are not done too often or too obtrusively, they can enhance students' general development.

What practical guidance do advocates of nonplay models offer to teachers? Perhaps the most important idea from the behaviorist, direct-instruction tradition is this: that play is not *all* that children need. Carefully planned, small- and large-group lessons that include presentations, demonstrations, and opportunities to discuss concepts are very appropriate for children. Adults *can* teach children things directly. Care must be taken, however, not to become too didactic, to impart knowledge when children could construct their own, or to give the message that play and work are separate, mutually exclusive activities. Sociodramatic play, storytelling, puppetry, music, construction, art, and games can be integrated with adult instruction to assure optimal learning and development.

KEY TERMS

Balance of play materials
Bank Street
Behaviorist models
Broadly focused developmental approach
Constructivist
Creative drama
Didactic programs
Direct instruction model
Distar
Documentation
Functional uses of print
Games with rules
Hands-off play approaches
High/Scope program
Ideational fluency
Illicit play
Literacy routines
Logical arrangement
Modified open plan design
Narrowly focused play interventions
Nonobtrusion rule
Nonplay curriculum models
Pantomime
Plan-do-review structure
Play centers
Play frame
Play-based classrooms
Puppetry
Quiet-active-quiet schedule
Readers theater
Reggio Emilia approach
Scaffold
Sociodramatic play
Sociodramatic play intervention
Stimulus shelter
Story drama
Story play
Thematic fantasy play training
Work-play
Zone of proximal development

STUDY QUESTIONS

1. Why do educators disagree about the best ways to include play in the classroom?
2. What are three fundamental ideas for arranging play centers that have been supported by research on play-based classrooms?
3. What is a modified open plan design, and how does it contribute to children's development?
4. Research has suggested that a balance of play materials promotes play development. Which types of play materials should be balanced?
5. What is a common pattern of classroom scheduling in most play-based programs and why is it important?
6. What are four major approaches to including play in the classroom? How do they differ in regard to assumptions about play and development?
7. What are the fundamental assumptions about learning and play that underlie a behaviorist classroom model?
8. What does research show about the outcomes of a behaviorist, nonplay approach?
9. What are current trends in some public schools that threaten play development?
10. What fundamental beliefs about play are expressed by hands-off play advocates?
11. What does research suggest about the effects of a hands-off play approach?

12. How does the modern Bank Street classroom differ from a traditional, hands-off play nursery school?
13. What are the major criticisms of the High/Scope program's approach to play?
14. What is a play frame, and why is it sometimes threatened by play intervention?
15. What is the nonobtrusion rule in play intervention?
16. What is an example of an adult scaffolding strategy in a play-based classroom?
17. Which specific elements of play are enhanced in Smilansky's sociodramatic play intervention model?
18. What concerns are raised by multicultural scholars about sociodramatic play intervention?
19. How is creative drama in the primary grades similar to and different from spontaneous sociodramatic play in the preschool years?
20. In what ways does readers theater meet the unique developmental needs and interests of primary grade children?
21. A teacher creates a pretend grocery store in the dramatic play center. Describe three different literacy props that can be included to enhance reading and writing. What role should the teacher play to promote literacy?
22. In what ways can games with rules and competition enhance sociomoral development?
23. How do teachers applying the Reggio Emilia model differ from traditional educators in their interactions with children in the art center?
24. What are key ideas from *each* approach to play that are useful to teachers?
25. Which approach to play best reflects your own beliefs about child development and education?

Chapter 9 Play and Children with Disabilities

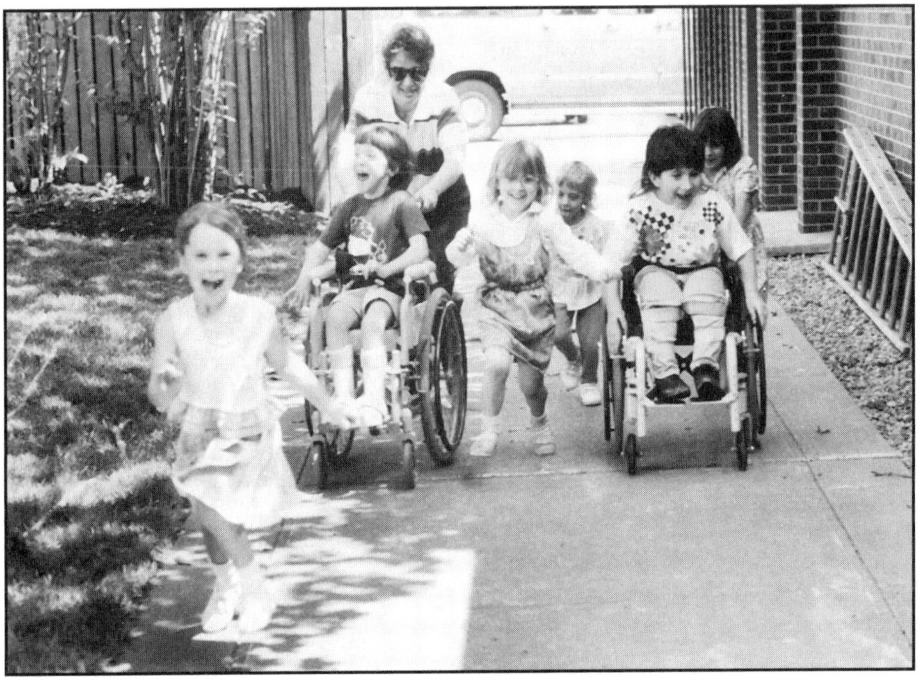

ALTHOUGH ADULTS may permit non-handicapped children to engage in play that does not lead directly to learning goals, they may not believe that the handicapped child has time to "just play." If play is to be used appropriately in early intervention, it must be evaluated not only in terms of its effectiveness in meeting intervention goals but also in relation to its role in helping children to feel in control of their lives, use their preferred modes of interactions, and freely imagine a wide range of possibilities. While this may be more difficult for the handicapped child to do, it is also crucial to the development of their self-worth and their competence.

(Bergen, 1991, p. 20)

All children engage in play. Children with disabilities may engage in play differently than their peers without disabilities; nonetheless, play is an important element in their overall development and learning.

The nature of play for children with disabilities depends on the disability or combination of disabling factors, the opportunities for play, the accessibility of toys and a modified play environment, and the presence of peers and adults to facilitate and encourage play.

In this chapter, we will explore how children with disabilities play, why play is important, and how we can maximize their opportunities for play. First the types of disabilities that are present in children will be reviewed, followed by a discussion of how families and programs use early intervention through play to enhance children's developmental potential. Next we will discuss different types of disabling conditions and how they affect a child's play.

The variables that influence the play of children with disabilities that include the play environment and assistive technology will be studied next. The role of adults in expanding children's play will be described as well as the influence of acceptance by peers in inclusion settings during preschool and school-age years.

The play of children with disabilities is a significant factor in assessment and diagnosis of a child's disabilities. A discussion of play-based assessment will explain how the child's play provides a window into developmental differences and clues as to how adults can use play with children with disabilities to enhance development and higher levels of play behaviors.

THE NATURE OF DISABILITIES

When determining how to discuss different types of disabilities children experience that can affect ability to play and benefit from play, several organizational patterns can be used. One approach is to classify disabilities in terms of **intellectual impairments**, **physical disabilities**, and **emotional disorders** (Rubin, Fein, & Vandenberg, 1983). Another possibility is to use development and **developmental delay** as a category or **children at risk** for development as a focus for children who might become disabled without intervention. Because many children have multiple disabilities, they might have disabling conditions in more than one type of category. In the discussion to follow, disabilities will be described within physical disabilities, children at risk for various reasons, developmental delay, and emotional and behavioral disorders.

Physical Disabilities

Children with physical disabilities have impairments that affect their ability to use their senses or their physical mobility. Specifically, they can have **hearing impairments, visual impairments**, or **motor impairments**. Each of these disabilities is discussed in the sections that follow.

Hearing Impairments

Children with hearing impairments are not able to hear sounds normally because of a malfunction of the ear or associated nerves. The degree of impairment varies from mild to severe and can be temporary or permanent. Conductive hearing losses prevent sound waves from reaching the brain through nerve fibers. Sensory-neural losses result from damage to nerve fibers and are hereditary or result from medical causes. While conductive hearing losses can be repaired through surgery, sensory-neural losses are irreversible.

Visual Impairments

A visual impairment can be slight or severe enough to be categorized as blindness. It can be caused by premature birth, injury, or from a medical cause. Mild visual impairments can be corrected with glasses, but little or no vision can be restored in children who are legally blind.

Motor Impairments

Children with motor impairments have physical restrictions that affect use of their limbs, hands, trunk, control, mobility, and strength. Motor impairments are caused by **spina bifida**, **cerebral** palsy, or **muscular dystrophy** during childhood. Accidents, such as automobile accidents, can also result in motor impairment. Because mobility is affected, many children must use wheelchairs or other orthopedic appliances such as crutches and walkers.

Spina Bifida. Spina bifida develops when the spinal cord is not fully developed and has an opening that affects protection of the cord. There are three types of spina bifida that vary in how much physical impairment is involved. With significant impairment, loss of bowel and bladder control, bone deformities, motor impairment, paralysis, and hydrocephalus can result. **Hydrocephalus** is a collection of spinal fluid in the brain. If left untreated it can result in retardation and seizures. Surgical implantation of a tube into the brain allows the fluid to drain and blood to circulate properly.

Cerebral Palsy. This disability is one of the most common orthopedic impairments that is the result of injury to the brain before or during birth. A neuromuscular disability, it can cause mild to severe impairment of motor skills. Children with mild to moderate cases are able to walk and use other motor movements with some awkwardness. Children who have severe involvement often have other disabilities, such as mental retardation, and have little or no mobility.

Muscular Dystrophy. This condition is a progressive disease that results in progressive degeneration of the voluntary muscles of the arms and legs. It causes increasing muscular weakness and coordination problems as children grow older. It is genetic in origin, and symptoms can appear in children as young as 3 years old. Symptoms can include an appearance of awkwardness, walking on tiptoes, severe curvature of the spine, and other postural abnormalities. There can be periods of remission; however, children gradually lose the ability to walk, and early death usually results during adolescence or the early 20s.

At-Risk Children

The term *at risk* is used to indicate that an infant or very young child may have biological or environmental life factors that can result in developmental delay or disabilities. Older children can be at risk because of chronic health conditions that cause them to be medically fragile.

Biological Risk Factors

Children with **biological risk** factors have a biological history that can result in later developmental problems. Premature babies are at risk, as are children born to mothers who have German measles while pregnant or complications during labor. Babies with a low birth weight and children who accidentally ingest toxic substances during infancy or the toddler years are also at risk.

Environmental Risk Factors

Children can be at risk because of the environment in which they lived before and after birth. Several of the risk factors result from the mother living in substandard or deprived environments. A major factor in environmental risk is low income. Low-income children are less likely to have an appropriate play environment, books, developmental toys, and life experiences that foster language and conceptual development. **Environmental risks** are many: parents who ingest drugs, physical and mental abuse, poor nutrition, or mothers who drink heavily during pregnancy. Refugee children can be at significant risk from escaping civil war in their homeland, or having their home and community destroyed by famine, flood, or war (Waniganayake, 2001). Early identification and treatment can reduce the possibility of negative outcomes from physical and environmental factors that can affect development and later learning.

Health Conditions

A variety of **health impairments** can affect a child's ability to engage in normal activities. Some of the health conditions are genetic in origin; others have been caused by environmental factors. Each of the conditions impair the child's ability to participate with other children because of limitations of strength and stamina. Health impairments that can limit children's activities include **heart conditions**, **bronchial asthma**,

diabetes, **rheumatic fever**, **hemophilia**, **lead poisoning**, and **cystic fibrosis**.

Developmental Delays

It can become evident quite early in life that some infants and toddlers are not developing normally. Their development is atypical, and these children are at risk for continuing developmental delays. At-risk children can develop delays in development after birth, but delays can also be traced to genetic factors. Three types of developmental delay are **cognitive delay**, **language delay**, and **attention deficit hyperactivity disorder (ADHD)**.

Language Delay

Delay in language development can result from environmental or medical causes. A child with language delay can have a limited ability to communicate characterized by immature use of language and limited vocabulary. A communication disorder might be characterized by difficulty in articulating or expressing things through language. There might be speech deficits that limit verbalization, such as stuttering or inability to utter sounds correctly. Regardless of the type of delay or disorder, the child experiences a delay in ability to communicate with others that can affect social interactions.

Cognitive Delay

Another type of atypical development is cognitive delay. Like language delay, cognitive delay can be traced to genetic or environmental causes. Ingestion of lead paint or exposure to alcohol during prenatal development can lead to cognitive delay. A child with **Down syndrome** experiences cognitive delay that results in **mental retardation**. A child with cognitive delay or mental retardation is unable to use thinking skills to the level that is characteristic of normal development. Social and language skills can also be involved.

Attention Deficit Hyperactivity Disorder

Children with ADHD experience a delay in their ability to lengthen attention span, resist distractions, and focus on learning tasks. They can be impulsive and hyperactive in their behavior but do not have a mental disorder. They may have difficulties with social interactions and adjusting to group settings. ADHD is difficult to categorize because different types of behaviors can be manifested in a child who is diagnosed as having ADHD.

Emotional and Behavioral Disorders

Children with **emotional** or **behavioral disorders** have atypical social development. They exhibit deviations from age-appropriate behavior that can cause them to be very aggressive or very withdrawn. The behavior problems that result can include aggression, anxiety, academic disability, and depression (Luebke, Epstein, & Cullinan, 1987). Behavioral deviations can be caused by psychological, environmental, and physiological causes. Psychological causes can include bereavement due to loss of a parent through divorce or death. Parenting methods of child management and teacher management strategies are environmental factors. Physiological factors can include genetic predispositions. Children with ADHD discussed in the previous section can also have behavior problems. Two types of behavior problems to be discussed here are children with **autism** and **abused children**. Autism has a physiological cause, while inappropriate parenting can lead to abused and neglected children.

Autism

Children with autism experience severe emotional disturbance. Autism is first noticeable at about $2^1/_2$ years of age and is more common in boys than girls. Behaviors exhibited by autistic children include head banging, echolalia speech, extremely delayed expressive language, and stereotypical body movements. It is thought that autism is a biological problem that occurs during prenatal or perinatal stages of development. Children with autism can seem to be insensitive to sounds and events around them and have difficulty in interacting with others socially. They apparently fail to recognize that the outside world is different from the self (Atlas & Lapidus, 1987). Children with autism often experience mental retardation as well.

Abused and Neglected Children

Children can be abused emotionally, physically, or sexually, or be neglected. Frequently, children who are abused experience more than one form of abuse. Although many abused children are aggressive and use inappropriate social behaviors, they are equally likely to be withdrawn and passive. Aggressive children can be disruptive and antisocial, while withdrawn children might make no attempts to interact with other children. Children who have been sexually abused might use inappropriate sexual behaviors in social interactions with their peers. Physically abused children might wear clothing that is seasonally inappropriate to cover physical signs of abuse, while neglected children might be dressed inappropriately or in dirty clothing because they have received minimal care and supervision.

Children with Multiple Disabilities

Unfortunately, children with disabilities frequently have a combination of conditions. For example, children with visual impairments can also have hearing impairments. Mental retardation can accompany visual and hearing impairments. As was mentioned earlier, children with cognitive delay or mental retardation can also have language delay and communication disorders. Children with behavior disorders can also experience language abnormalities or cognitive delay. Children with ADHD can experience cognitive difficulties, although they typically have normal intelligence.

It is important to understand the nature of disabilities if we are to understand how these conditions and variations from normal development affect how children play. It is easier to understand the limitations children with physical disabilities face and how their play is affected compared to children with behavioral or mental disabilities. When a combination of conditions is present, providing play opportunities is even more challenging. In the next section, we will discuss how the play of children with disabilities, as well as current research to find methods that will improve settings and conditions for play.

CHILDREN WITH EXCEPTIONAL ABILITIES

Gifted children have a high level of development for their chronological age. These children are characterized by high intelligence and/or high creativity. Some children have a specialized talent that may be expressed in sports, the arts, mathematics, or the sciences. Gifted and talented children are inquisitive, persistent, and highly motivated to pursue their interests.

DISABILITIES AND PLAY

It is difficult to study the play of children with disabilities. First, because handicapping conditions can involve a wide range of disabilities, it can be difficult to determine the cause of [differences in play]. Moreover, many studies are flawed and fail to separate developmental differences from differences caused by a disabling condition (Quinn & Rubin, 1984). In addition, depending on the nature of the disability, research on the play of children with disabilities can be conducted by researchers from different professions. Thus, researchers in medicine, mental health professionals, and educational psychologists might be studying play for different purposes and with different results. Some research studies are conducted with individual children and do not consider the effect of peer relationships or behaviors in a group setting (Hughes, 1998; Quinn & Rubin, 1984).

Regardless of these limitations, there is a growing body of information on the play of children with disabilities with implications for practice. In the following sections we will discuss how play is affected by different disabilities. The role of adults in the child's play will also be described, particularly in regard to how adults can expand the play of children with disabilities.

Children with Visual Impairments

Characteristics of Play

There are significant differences between the play of sighted children and that of blind children. Troster and Bambring (1994) have summarized the research on these differences:

> [I]t has been found that, in comparison to sighted children, blind children do the following:
>
> 1. Explore their surroundings and the objects in their surroundings less often (Fraiberg, 1977; Olson, 1981, 1983; Sandler & Wills, 1965; Troster & Bambring, 1992, 1993; Wills, 1972).
> 2. As infants and preschoolers, frequently engage in solitary play that is repetitive and stereotyped (Freeman et al., 1989; Parsons, 1986; Sandler, 1963; Warren, 1984; Wills, 1972).
> 3. Exhibit less spontaneous play; far more than sighted children, they have to be taught how to play (Burlingham, 1961, 1967, 1972, 1975; Rothschild, 1960; Sandler, 1963; Sandler & Wills, 1965; Tait, 1972c; Wills, 1965, 1968, 1970).
> 4. Do not or only rarely imitate the routine activities of the caregivers (Fraiberg, 1977; Sandler & Wills, 1965).
> 5. Play less frequently with stuffed animals and dolls and rarely engage in animism (Warren, 1984; Wills, 1979).
> 6. Play less frequently with peers and usually direct their play toward adults (Schneekloth, 1989; Tait, 1972a, 1972b; Wills, 1968, 1970).
> 7. Exhibit clear delays in the development of symbolic play and role play (Fraiberg & Adelson, 1973; Sandler & Wills, 1965; Tait, 1972a, 1972b; Wills, 1968, 1970).
> 8. Engage in play that contains fewer aggressive elements (Burlingham, 1961, 1965; Fraiberg, 1968; Wills, 1970, 1981). (pp. 421–422)

These characteristics of the play of blind children as compared to sighted children can be explained further. Children with visual impairments often have developmental delays in other domains of development that could easily affect their play skills (Warren, 1984). Moreover, overprotection by adults or fear of dangers might result in limited attempts to engage in play (Rettig, 1994; Schneekloth, 1989).

Although sighted children spend most of their play time interacting with other children, children with visual impairments spend 56% of their time playing alone (Schneekloth, 1989).

Because visual impairment makes it difficult for these children to orient themselves to space and time and to separate reality from nonreality, they need more time to adapt themselves to a play environment (Frost, 1992; Frost & Klein, 1979; Hughes, 1998). Moreover, because of these limitations, the child who is blind or has limited vision is unable to respond to the quick and perhaps unpredictable movements of sighted children and responds less quickly to different activities. Changes in play activities thus may also be more difficult for children with visual impairment who also have difficulty in moving from the known to the unknown (Rettig, 1994).

Children with visual impairments may also experience language delay and have been found to use language differently from their sighted peers. Children with visual impairments are slower to develop a sense of self and delay in using I as a pronoun. This is related to a delay in symbolic play (Fraiberg & Adelson, 1973). Blind children tend to ask more questions of adults in an effort to further their understanding of the environment, while sighted children use language to relate to objects or to refer to past experiences (Erin, 1990). An additional problem is that children with visual impairments have obstacles to interpreting nonverbal communication that can impede interacting with sighted children.

There are differences in the cognitive play of children who are visually impaired and their peers with normal sight. In object play, sighted children use their eyes to explore objects, while children with visual impairments use eyes, hands, feet, and other parts of their body to explore objects (Hughes, Dote-Kwan, & Dolendo,

1998; Preisler & Palmer, 1989). Moreover, their lack of interest in exploring toys in the environment might be due to a lack of experiences and the tendency to be more interested in their bodies than the environment. Preisler and Palmer (1989) found them to be more interested in environmental elements that opened and closed, such as doors, than toys. Unsurprisingly, the materials and equipment provided in the environment also affect the amount of exploratory play as much as the visual capacity of young children (Skellenger, Rosenblum, & Jager, 1997).

The Role of Adults

When discussing the role of adults in the play of children with disabilities, a major purpose is to intervene and help the child develop play skills. Five intervention strategies that can be used to enhance the play skills of children with visual impairments are as follows (Rettig, 1994):

1. Specific instruction in play skills
2. Manipulating toys and playthings
3. Adapting the setting
4. The use of peers without disabilities
5. The role of adults (pp. 413–414)

The involvement of adults in play activities is crucial in the acquisition of play skills. Adults must not only be involved in play activities but also systematically incorporate play into the curriculum in group settings.

Children with visual impairments may need intervention in how to play with toys or peers. Adults should provide a variety of real objects for play and assist children in the symbolic use of the objects. Exploration can include household items and objects such as doorknobs, locks and keys, plastic bowls, wooden spoons, and pots and pans (Recchia, 1987; Schneekloth, 1989). Toys should be selected to encourage symbolic representation. Dolls are a good example as are wooden trucks (Rettig, 1994). Adults can provide experiences with objects that sighted children acquire automatically. One example is learning to pour from a pitcher into a cup (Skellinger & Hill, 1994).

Adults can support play by providing opportunity to explore in a safe, familiar environment. Partially sighted children need opportunities for motor play so that they can develop the same abilities as their sighted peers (Schneekloth, 1989). Schneekloth suggests that visually impaired children needed guided exploration experiences to understand their surroundings. The environment should also include a soft area where visually impaired children can move about freely without fear of injury.

Children should be assisted in becoming autonomous and independent in play. Adults should assist children in developing social interactions with other children. If they are using stereotyped behaviors, they can be guided in using more imagination and fantasy so that their play with sighted peers can be enhanced. To encourage play interactions between sighted and visually impaired children, the adult should start with one sighted playmate and then gradually increase the number of sighted children in the group (Recchia, 1987). Sighted children need to understand the nature of a visual impairment. The teacher should help them acquire information about what it means to be blind or have low vision and encourage them to play with children who are visually impaired (Rettig, 1994).

Children with Hearing Impairments

Characteristics of Play

Children with hearing impairments are less affected in their play than children with visual impairments. The most significant factor is delay in language, which results in less interest in make-believe play or fantasy play than their hearing peers have. They engage less often in sociodramatic play and use less symbolism of objects than children with normal hearing ability (Esposito & Koorland, 1989; Hughes, 1998).

Social interactions with hearing children can be facilitated if signing is used in a group setting or if hearing children are given information on how to communicate with children who are learning to lip read. Children with hearing impairments who are placed in self-contained classes for children are likely to play in a less sophisticated manner than children who are placed in integrated settings with hearing children. Parten's (1932) level of parallel play was observed more often in the self-contained setting for hearing impaired children, while associative play was more common in the integrated setting in a study conducted by Esposito and Koorland (1989).

The Role of Adults

Because children with hearing impairments can engage in all forms of play, adults do not have to teach them how to play with objects or guide them in the use of materials and equipment. Acting as a facilitator of communication between children who have hearing impairments and children who hear normally is an important role. Modeling and engaging in pretend play is also helpful in expanding children's use of sociodramatic play and symbolic play.

One of the authors designed a playscape for a preschool for children with hearing impairments. The school was integrated in that children with normal hearing were also enrolled at the school. In discussing how children used the play environment, particularly the outdoor environment, the teachers saw their major responsibility as finding lost hearing aids. The children's favorite play activity was to roll down a long, grassy hill under large shade trees. Children invariably lost their hearing aids on the way down the hill, and the teachers were constantly on the alert to locate the aids.

The playscape also had an outdoor center for sociodramatic play. The teachers planned for rotating props and materials to be located in the center and encouraged children to engage in sociodramatic play by playing alongside them when necessary.

Children with Motor Impairments

Characteristics of Play

Describing the play of children with motor impairments is complex because there are so many kinds of motor impairments, and the severity of the impairment varies. Obviously, the most significant limitation is in play that involves physical activity. Indoor play is the least affected because some of the activities do not require gross-motor skills. With modifications in classroom space to accommodate wheelchairs and other physical assistance devices, children with mobility problems can be included in games and other play activities with a minimum of adaptation. Unless the child has other disabling conditions, social interactions are affected only to the extent that children without disabilities are guided in accepting the child's limitations and can modify their play to include the child.

A factor in the ability of a child with severe physical limitations to play is the use of positioning equipment. **Positioning equipment** is equipment that provides support and proper positioning that permits children to carry out daily self-care activities and engage in play (e.g., toilet seats, car seats, prone standers, strollers, and crawlers). This equipment not only permits a child with weak muscle support to be placed in a sitting position but can also provide mobility for some children. At a minimum, the positioning equipment makes it possible for children to use their hands to play with objects (O'Brien et al., 1998).

Outdoor play is more of a concern. Lack of mobility or limitations in mobility make it difficult for the child to participate in physical play with peers who are not disabled. Access to play equipment on the playground is a major issue in making it possible for children with physical limitations to engage in play. The issue of making the environment accessible to children with motor impairments will be discussed later in the chapter.

Inclusion in sports is an issue for older children. All children would like to be included in sports to the extent that they are able to participate. The popularity of Special Olympics programs for citizens who are mentally retarded testifies to the need for availability of sports activities for children with all types of disabilities, but especially for children with motor impairments.

An issue in school settings is inclusion of children with motor impairments in sports and other physical activities with their peers who are not disabled. Including students with motor impairments in physical education classes and school teams for sports can be seen as a serious problem. This becomes even more of an issue after children with motor and other impairments leave elementary school (Burkour, 1998; Kozub & Porretta, 1996; Moucha et al., 1997).

The Role of Adults

The Americans with Disabilities Act (ADA) ensures the rights of people with disabilities to have access to all aspects of community life, including participation in physical activities and integrated settings. For children with motor impairments, this means that settings and activities must be adapted to their individual needs. Teachers, physical education coaches, and sports leaders must find ways to adapt and accommodate to provide support on an individual basis. The goal is to remove barriers to participation in physical activities.

Burkour (1998) suggests the following to include children with disabilities in youth sports:

- *Skill assessments/task analysis*. Clearly identifying all of the physical, sensory, learning, communication, and socialization skills needed to be successful. This can be done by looking at the child's participation in an activity from beginning to end.
- *Focus on maximizing abilities*. Utilizing individual strengths. Not everyone has to do every aspect of every sport independently to be successful.
- *Ask everyone for accommodation ideas*. The child, family, teachers, recreation therapists, physical therapists, and particularly other children. These children will come up with the most unobtrusive adaptations that will not get in the way of the "fun!" (p. 73)

Burkour (1998) further believes that "adaptations can be made by making adjustments in leading/teaching/communication, placement in positions on the field/court, performance expectations, and rules of the game" (p. 73). For example, a child in a wheelchair can have a "pusher" to run the bases in baseball. Another example is the use of a brightly colored basketball for a child with a visual impairment.

Children at Risk for Developmental Delay or a Disability

As discussed earlier, children can be diagnosed as being at risk for normal development because of biological factors or environmental factors. They might also have a condition that has been diagnosed as a handicap or disability. The main focus for at-risk children is prevention of delay or to minimize the effects of a disability. Early intervention programs are used to maximize potential of at-risk children; moreover, characteristics of play are used in diagnostic assessment to determine the child's status and needs. In the following sections on developmental delay, the characteristics of play described for at-risk children will be developed more fully. More emphasis will be placed on the role of adults in using play for intervention purposes.

Characteristics of Play

The play of at-risk children can be described in terms of sensorimotor/practice play, symbolic play, and social play. The sensorimotor play of at-risk children develops similarly to that of nonrisk children; however, if play indicates differences, it can give early indications of a possible delay or handicapping conditions. For example, children who exhibit a narrower range of sensorimotor activities might be found to be visually impaired or autistic or to have a motor impairment.

The level of symbolic play with play objects is affected in sensory-impaired, mentally retarded, and autistic children who show less ability to use complex object transformations in their play. Down syndrome and autistic children tend to use more repetitive play with objects, as do infants and toddlers exposed prenatally to PCP and/or cocaine (Bergen, 1991; Hughes, 1998).

Preterm infants might also present delay and limitations in play with objects that might be more related to a shorter period of development than can be explained by the difference between chronological age and gestational age (Hughes, 1998; Ruff, Lawson, Parinello, & Weissberg, 1990). Children who have attention deficit disorders (ADD) may have difficulty in focusing their play. They may begin several activities without completing any of them (Gitlin-Weiner, 1998).

At-risk children are particularly vulnerable to delays in social play. Interactive adult-child social play routines can be impaired in children with visual, motor, cognitive, or emotional impairments. Social interactions between mothers and children are influenced by the responsiveness of the other. Children born to teenage mothers can have delays in social play because the mothers may have fewer social support systems, are less knowledgeable about parenting, and are especially sensitive to babies who seem to be unresponsive (Fewell & Wheeden, 1998; Helm, Comfort, Bailey, & Simeonsson, 1990). Children who develop poor social interactions with adults may also experience delay and distortions in social play interactions with peers (Bergen, 1991).

The Role of Adults

Infants, toddlers, and preschool children who are found to be at risk for development or a disability are generally served through interventions to enhance development and minimize the risk or handicapping condition. Services might be provided directly to the child, indirectly through parents and other adult caregivers, or both. Thus, both the adults who interact with the child and specialists who provide assistance in the intervention are engaged in improving conditions for the at-risk child (Gitlin-Weiner, 1998).

Play has a significant role in development for at-risk children. Providers of intervention services in settings outside the home include play in the curriculum for children at risk for delay as well as for children with diagnosed disabilities. Parents and other caregivers in the home need to know how to use play and how to enhance the child's ability to play. Bergen (1991) expresses concern that play be used appropriately for intervention purposes. Although the adult plays a major role in helping children learn to play, a child's need to play and purposes for play should be the major focus of play activities. It is very easy for adults to use play activities within intervention services to advance their own agenda rather than the child's play agenda. Because of their concern for helping the child, play activities can become work activities. Bergen cautions that play for at-risk children should have the same purposes as for children who are not at risk and do not have a disability. In addition, it is possible that under conditions of environmental risk, the parent may not have the desire or ability to provide appropriate social play interactions. In any case, a distinction should be made between appropriate play interactions and activities that are directive rather than playful.

Children whose normal development is at risk need assistance in using appropriate play behaviors. Play activities provide opportunities for adults to help children compensate for their risk status. Children with biological risk factors, environmental risk factors, and health impairments may have common or unique needs for play activities. It is important for adults to observe children's play to determine the successes and needs of each child.

A primary cause of delayed play behavior is serious emotional and social impairments. Adults should guide these children in natural play activities. They might demonstrate appropriate social behavior or redirect the child to use a different social behavior. This might be particularly evident in children who have lived with environmental risk factors. Children who experienced environments that are insecure, unsafe, or without adequate nurture need adult support that will help them develop emotionally. Improvement in social and emotional development will be observed in subsequent play behaviors.

Children with health impairments might have limitations in play because they lack the strength to engage in vigorous physical activities. Adults can provide quieter play alternatives that permit the child to engage in play that is less physically demanding. These activities can be embedded within other activities so that all children might find them to be an attractive play choice.

Children who have difficulty in persisting or following through with play choices need help focusing and in completing play activities. Whether children have ADD or simply too few opportunities to play, they can be encouraged to select a play activity that is highly motivating and praised for engaging in the activity and finishing it. Children can also be teamed with other children who can provide leadership and direction in play.

Children with Cognitive Delay and Mental Retardation

Characteristics of Play

Literature describing the play of children with cognitive delay is limited when compared to the information available for other types of disabilities. There are multiple causes for this lack of data. First, much of the research has been done with individual children and is limited to the study of their play with objects. Second, a lot of the research has been medical in nature. Study of play has been for diagnostic purposes and to determine skill levels rather than to understand the child's ability to play (Gleason, 1990; Rubin & Quinn, 1984). Third, research results have been inaccurate in that the researchers seemed to be unaware of the nature of early development that includes individual differences in rate of development in children without developmental delays (Rubin & Quinn, 1984). Even more significant was the assumption for many decades in the 20th century that children with cognitive delay are not interested in play or have to be taught to play (Bergen, 1991; Hughes, 1998). The error of this assumption was documented in the play of two institutionalized males with severe developmental disabilities who were able to initiate play with toy lawnmowers (Gleason, 1990). When comparing the recorded abilities of the males in clinical training with the motor and social skills used in the play episode, it was found that the abilities in play were much more advanced than the abilities used in structured play therapy sessions.

It is not surprising, given the limitations in research just cited, that information gained from research on cognitive delay and play is unclear. Some researchers have concluded from their work that the play of children with cognitive delay is less sophisticated and more functional than the play of children without cognitive delay, and requires more structure (Beckman & Kohl, 1987; Mindes, 1982; Weiner, Tilton, & Ottinger, 1969). Other findings support the approach that the play of children with cognitive delay is similar to that of children without cognitive delay and is developmentally appropriate (Switzky, Ludwig, & Haywood, 1979; Weiner & Weiner, 1974). Differences in findings might be attributed to lack of control for toy familiarity (whether the child was familiar with the toy) in some studies and the differences in context for the studies (Malone & Stoneman, 1990; Rubin & Quinn, 1984).

The conclusion seems to be that when equated for mental age, retarded children do not differ from children with normal development in some characteristics of play. Nor do they differ in their preferences for unstructured activities versus structured activities. They prefer child-centered or child-initiated activities to adult-directed activities (Hupp, Boat, & Alpert, 1992; Quinn & Rubin, 1984).

The Role of Adults

Adults can use play as an assessment tool to identify specific delays that need intervention, as a skill that can be taught to parents of infants who are at risk for delay, and as a strategy that can be used in intervention programs (Bergen, 1991). This is a new direction from earlier methods of intervention that were based on behaviorist theory that focused on shaping behavior using adult reinforcement strategies. The new direction of using play with at-risk children for parent intervention is derived from the literature on early social play routines of normally developing infants and toddlers. The value of social play between adults and infants or toddlers is also valuable for children with cognitive delay or mental retardation.

However, techniques used with children with cognitive delay are adapted to use a range of directive to playful strategies. These strategies are taught to parents and used by caregivers in intervention programs. Parents and adults involved in intervention are taught to be playful and responsive to their children.

Intervention specialists also use play in their individual intervention goals for young children, especially to increase symbolic play. Modeling by adults is used to demonstrate symbolic play roles, with more structured coaching used for children who are severely impaired.

A balance between free play and guided play should prevail in play intervention programs for toddlers and preschool children. Nevertheless, it is natural for adults to be more directive in play with children with cognitive delay than with nondelayed peers. Integration of skills teaching into play routines can improved play and development. Free play can also facilitate development, especially when adapted toys and play environments facilitate social interaction between children.

Some question whether a balance between guided play and free play can be achieved in intervention programs. When adult educators become focused on achieving the goals of intervention, do the activities cease to be play? If the child loses the opportunity for internal motivation and control and is not given the opportunity to decide what to play and who to play with, the play activity becomes "nonplay" (Bergen, 1991).

The challenge for adult providers of intervention for children with cognitive delay or mental retardation is to affirm the child's ability and interest in engaging in play. They need to remind themselves constantly that these children also have the right to free play, and that adult-directed play is different from child-initiated play. The child with cognitive delay needs both, as do children with other types of disabilities.

Children with Language Delay and Communication Disorders

Characteristics of Play

The focus of research on the play of children with language delay or a communication disorder has been in two primary areas: symbolic play and social relationships with peers. The interest in symbolic play stems from the relationship between the development of speech and the development of symbolic functioning. The two types of development have a parallel course, with major advances emerging in the second year (Fenson, 1986). The question has been, if a child is delayed in language development, will she also experience symbolic play deficits? Although a number of researchers have found a relationship between language delay and symbolic play deficits, the correlation does not necessarily indicate that children with delayed speech will have deficits in symbolic play (Lombardino, Stein, Kricos, & Wolf, 1986; Tamis-LeMonda & Bornstein, 1991). In many studies, children with speech impairments did engage in make-believe play, but it occurred less often and was of a less mature level than the play of children whose speech was not delayed (Quinn & Rubin, 1984; Rubin, Fein, & Vandenberg, 1983). Moreover, children with good expressive language are at an advantage in verbal-symbolic play (Rescorla & Goossens, 1992).

In the case of symbolic play with objects, children with language impairments are capable of engaging in object substitutions and object transformations. Again, they exhibit this form of play less frequently than their peers with typical language development (Casby, 1997). This difference is more significant in older children. At younger ages, language delay is not as important because language plays a more limited role in symbolic play. The difference seems to emerge at about age 4 or 5, when language-impaired children use less complexity in their play activities (Lovell, Hoyle, & Siddall, 1968; Terrell & Schwartz, 1988).

Less research has been conducted on peer relations of children with communication disorders

(Guralnick, Conner, Hammond, & Kinnish, 1996). Because much variation occurs in language development in normally developing children, the differences in play for children with language disorders can be very similar to those for children with normal language development. Nevertheless, some characteristics indicate the presence of peer interaction problems. In group settings, children with communication disorders interact more with adults than with peers, are less likely to respond to peer initiations for play, and tend to be ignored more often by peers (Guralnick et al., 1996; Hadley & Rice, 1991).

The social setting can make a difference in peer relationships. The comparative ages of the children as well as whether children with language delays play in settings with peers with typical language development is thought to affect the level of symbolic play. However, studies comparing mainstreamed children with children in self-contained classrooms have found no difference in the level of play for children with language disorders (Guralnick et al., 1996).

The Role of Adults

Although children with language impairments may lag behind their peers in object play and sociodramatic play, they benefit from playing in integrated settings (Hughes, 1998). Children who have normal language development do experience obstacles in communication when playing with children who have difficulty expressing themselves; however, children without communication difficulties adjust their verbal interactions to the developmental characteristics of children with communication disorders (Shatz & Gelman, 1973). Children in classrooms with children who have language delay or a communication disorder can learn how to communicate and interact with these children.

Adults who work with children with language delays and language disorders need to be skilled in providing language intervention within play. The adult can serve as a facilitator of communication between children at play without directing the play activity. They can encourage the child with language delay to use verbalizations and model appropriate language. Modeling of language in sociodramatic play can also guide the child with language delay in how to engage in more sophisticated play.

Children with Autism

Characteristics of Play

Some children with developmental delay or disabilities also experience delay in some characteristics of play. Children with autism have a pattern of development that is distorted (Quinn & Rubin, 1984). Play patterns of autistic children are also different from children with other types of delay and disabilities.

One characteristic is in symbolic play. Autistic children do not generally engage in symbolic play. This seems to be true regardless of the intelligence of the child. Children with severe mental retardation do engage in symbolic play, while highly intelligent autistic children do not (Hill & McCune-Nicolich, 1981; Hughes, 1998; Sigman & Sena, 1993). One explanation for the lack of make-believe in their play is that autistic children lack basic representational skills (Baron-Cohen, Leslie, & Frith, 1985). That is, autistic children are unable to have one object represent another or to represent to themselves the mental states of dolls or roles that they might play (Hughes, 1998).

Other researchers believe that autistic children do have the ability to represent or symbolize. They believe that the lack of symbolic play is due to lack of motivation. This position was supported by Lewis and Boucher (1988), who were able to elicit make-believe play in autistic children through adult instructions about toys. However, the children did not display this type of activity in spontaneous play. It is also projected that poor social contact and level of receptive language skills might also influence an absence of symbolic play (Rutter, 1983; Wing, Gould, Yeates, & Brierly, 1977). Because they lack peer interactions in play, their play can be rigid and unimaginative (Wolfberg & Schuler, 1993). Even when autistic children have opportunities to play with peers, unless they receive support, they are likely to remain in isolation outside nearby group play.

Autistic children tend to engage in repetitive and stereotyped manipulation in toy and object play. They are less likely to use toys appropriately or to engage in complex toy play (Tilton & Ottinger, 1964). Nevertheless, not all autistic children display stereotyped play behaviors; many play similarly to mentally retarded children and normal children (Quinn & Rubin, 1984).

The Role of Adults

Historically, autistic children have been taught play skills through behaviorist methods that include rewards for using appropriate play behaviors. Difficulties with this approach are that the play is highly structured and adult led; moreover, the desired play behaviors do not generalize in unstructured play situations (Rubin, Fein, & Vandenberg, 1983; Stahmer & Schreibman, 1992; Wolfberg & Schuler, 1993). Alternatives to adult-directed intervention strategies are more child initiated and focus on planned environments and opportunities to play with peers in groups. In an approach titled the Integrated Play Group Model (Wolfberg & Schuler, 1993), the play opportunities have eight components:

- *Natural integrated settings*. Children engage in play with other children. Play partners are socially competent and peer-mediated approaches are used to encourage social interaction.
- *Well-designed play spaces*. The spaces include consideration of spatial density and size, organization of materials, spatial arrangements, and accessibility.
- *Selection of play materials*. Play materials are selected for their influence on the play and social behavior of children with autism. The toys include constructive and sociodramatic toys that can be used by children of different abilities.
- *A consistent schedule and routine*. Children with autism respond to predictability and consistency. The play environment includes a consistent play group schedule and ongoing routines.
- *Balanced play groups*. Play groups include familiar peers who are limited in number. They meet to play on a consistent basis and include peers of different ages and developmental status.
- *Focus on child competence*. Children with autism are evaluated for their individual competencies in play. Play support is provided to match the child's "zone of proximal development" (Vygotsky, 1978; see Chapter 2).
- *Guided participation*. The adult's interactive role is to guide the children in participating in increasing social and sophisticated levels play. Adult-imposed structure is avoided and adult support is gradually decreased and removed to encourage the child to demonstrate increasing competence.
- *Full immersion in play*. Children are engaged in the whole play experience rather than having play taught as discrete tasks. Children are encouraged to take roles in play with more advanced children. Adults use support and collaboration to encourage more sophisticated object and sociodramatic play.

Wolfberg and Schuler (1993) report rather dramatic gains in a study they conducted using the model. However, as in many research studies conducted with children with autism and other disabling conditions, only three children were included. Limited play research with children with autism indicates that the strategies used in the model are a promising alternative to structured teaching of play skills. However, much more research is needed to confirm success in enhancing play skills.

Abused and Neglected Children

Characteristics of Play

There are some indicators that abused and neglected children play differently from their peers who have not experienced abuse. In addition, the type of abuse can affect play behaviors differently.

A study comparing abused children with a control group (Alessandri, 1991) found the following differences (Hughes, 1998):

> Abused children played in less mature ways, both socially and cognitively, than did the children in the control group, engaged in less play overall, involved themselves less often in group and parallel play, and used the play materials in less imaginative and more stereotyped ways. Their fantasy themes were more imitative and less creative. They repeatedly played out domestic scenes, for example, whereas the control group also played the roles of fantasy characters, such as monsters or superheroes. (p. 182)

The type of abuse affects the play behaviors of young children. Sexually abused children had an absence of fantasy play suggesting a need to occupy the present. Play themes were essentially domestic, as Alessandri (1991) reported, as were repetition of play themes (Harper, 1991). Sexually abused children have been found to be more passive than children who have not been abused, but they are not necessarily antisocial or negative. They usually play quietly by themselves (Fagot, Hagan, Youngblade, & Potter, 1989). Some researchers have found sexually abused children to be more focused on the sexual features of anatomically correct dolls than children who have not been sexually abused (August & Forman, 1989; Jampole & Weber, 1987). However, Cohn (1991) found that children who have not experienced abuse are equally likely to engage in sexual types of play with dolls.

Play themes of physically abused children were more action oriented to include fights, wars, and sudden disasters. Physically abused children tend to be disruptive and uncommunicative. Unlike sexually abused children, they are antisocial (Fagot et al., 1989). Harper (1991) characterized their play as fantasy, aggressive, and chaotic. There was more variety in their play themes in Harper's study, and one child continually played themes that ended in loss.

One must use caution in generalizing the behaviors found in two studies to describe abused children in general. Very little research has regarded the play of abused children, and the samples in the studies cited was very small; nevertheless, they provide some indicators of how the play of abused children can reflect negative experiences in their lives.

The Role of Adults

The abused children discussed in the previous section were included in studies comparing the play of children who have been abused with children who have not been abused. Teachers of children in preschool and school-age settings who have children who have experienced abuse will also have children who have not experienced abuse. The play behaviors of abused children may not appear to be all that different from play behaviors of other children. Aggressive and antisocial play can have many causes. Repetitive theme play and passive play can characterize children other than children who have been sexually abused. The teacher's role would seem to be to guide children in ways to play appropriately and expanding sociodramatic play to include many types of themes. Children who use aggression in play all need to have alternatives introduced or avenues to express frustration and anger. However, it would seem important that the teacher be aware of the differences in play behaviors and be alert to the possibility that the child has been experiencing abuse.

THE ROLE OF THE ENVIRONMENT

A focus of research on the play of children with disabilities thus far has been on how their play compares with the play of children without disabilities. Although many studies cited in earlier sections were conducted in laboratory classrooms where children were selected and grouped for the length of the study, many others were conducted with children in existing classrooms. The classrooms were exemplifying **inclusion** or **integrated classrooms**, in keeping with the practice of placing children with disabilities in classrooms with children who have typical development.

In this section, we will direct attention away from comparing children with disabilities with peers to looking at how effective inclusive classrooms have been in socially integrating children with disabilities with their peers. Since social interaction occurs primarily through play, the interest is in how children with disabilities benefit from engaging in play in integrated settings. Part of the effectiveness of play in these settings depends on teacher behaviors and how teachers affect children's play. Available research on teacher interactions with children's play will also be discussed.

Influences of Inclusion Classrooms on Children's Play

A major goal of intervention programs is to help children with disabilities develop social competence. A concern about inclusion has been whether children with disabilities are socially integrated with peers who do not have disabilities or whether they are merely integrated in a physical sense (Guralnick, 1990). Therefore, study of peer play in integrated settings is seen as a vehicle to determine whether children with disabilities are benefiting from the opportunity to interact socially with peers of normal development. Social interaction is seen as a way for children with disabilities to overcome language delay and to acquire developmental skills. Social play is also perceived to benefit children who involve themselves with less complex forms of play as a result of a disability (Kontos, Moore, & Giorgetti, 1998).

Study of children's play in integrated programs shows that children with disabilities are not isolated; however, they are not as involved or accepted as children who are developing typically. Children with disabilities initiate and receive opportunities for social play less often and have fewer reciprocal friendships. They are less involved in higher levels of social play (associative, cooperative) than their peers with typical development, and generally lag behind them in social development (File, 1994; Guralnick & Groom, 1987, 1988; Guralnick & Weinhouse, 1984; Kontos et al., 1998).

Nonetheless, children with typical development have been found to have positive attitudes toward children with disabilities (Hess & Sexton, 2002). In programs where children were placed in play groups, social skills groups, and cooperative learning groups, children with normal development expressed personal interest in and a desire to be friends with children with disabilities (Kamps, Lopez, Kemmerer, Potucek, & Harrell, 1998). Peer-mediated activities in inclusion classrooms were found to increase peer interactions, and children with disabilities benefited both academically and socially. Nevertheless, a 2-year study of students served in an inclusion setting found that the sociometric status of students with disabilities was lower than that of typically developing peers. Students with disabilities received fewer nominations for "most liked" and more nominations for "least liked" than peers with typical development (Sale & Carey, 1995). In another study, first graders reported in interviews that children with disabilities did not really belong to the group (Schnorr, 1990).

Children with disabilities can benefit from inclusion in mixed-age classrooms. Children with disabilities placed in a classroom with children of different ages achieved a sophistication in play with toys that was not achieved in a classroom with peers of the same age. The researchers proposed that the children with disabilities were influenced by the sophistication of play demonstrated by the older children who were developing normally in the play setting. Nevertheless, social mastery was not improved for children with disabilities. As in other studies, children without disabilities were more likely to engage in social mastery than children with disabilities (Blasco, Bailey, & Burchinal, 1993).

The teacher plays an important role in inclusion classrooms. The teacher's attitude toward inclusion can have an effect of successful social relationships. Teachers with a positive attitude toward inclusion have a positive effect on paraprofessional time, direct time with children with disabilities, and the social competence of children with disabilities (Janney, Snell, Beers, & Raynes, 1995; Kamps et al., 1998; Wolery, Werts, Caldwell, Snyder, & Lisowski, 1995).

Studies of teacher's interactions in inclusive classrooms indicate that teachers interact in a more directive manner with children with disabilities when compared with interactions with children who develop typically (Brophy & Hancock, 1985; Stipek & Sanborn, 1985). However, File (1994) observed that interactional frequencies between the two groups of children and their teachers were very similar.

Teacher training can be a factor, as can specific teaching behaviors that are supportive of play. Teachers with more training in early childhood education are more involved in supporting cognitive and social play (Arnett, 1989; File & Kontos, 1993; Whitebrook, Howes, & Phillips, 1990). However, teachers were found to be more likely to support cognitive skills rather than social skills (Clarke-Stewart, 1987).

Other factors can affect how effectively inclusion benefits children with disabilities. The number of children in the classroom can be significant. Teachers with fewer children tend to be more involved in the social and cognitive play of children with disabilities (File & Kontos, 1993; Sontag, 1997). The number of children in the play group can also be a factor (Belsky, 1984, 1990; Kontos & Fiene, 1987).

Adapted Play Environments

Designing play environments for inclusion of children with disabilities is a challenge for playground developers. Each disability presents unique considerations, while environments that serve large numbers of children must include modifications for all types of disabilities (Doctoroff, 2001). Children with hydrocephalus need protective head gear, and those with spina bifida need special mobile equipment and consideration for urine bags used for incontinence. Blind or partially sighted children need time to explore the environment to become familiar with its features. The environment needs to be predictable so that they can play with confidence. Children with cerebral palsy are best served when they can have the playground to themselves to prevent abnormal reflex patterns of movement. They might also need physical assistance until they can relax and enjoy both the environment and the play actions of their playmates with normal physical development (London Handicapped Adventure Playground Association, 1978, as cited in Frost, 1992).

In the United States, there has been an interest for several decades in developing play environments that can serve children with disabilities. In 1976, the New York City Department of Planning and U.S. Department of Housing and Urban Development conducted a design competition to encourage play environments that would include children with disabilities. Suggestions were given for meeting that goal (Frost, 1992). In 1986, Play and Learning in Adaptable Environments (PLAE) conducted a series of sessions at Stanford University to develop guidelines for playgrounds that would address the needs of children with disabilities, after a series of workshops were held in which disabled adults and children dialogued about play and made suggestions about appropriate play environments. A variety of professionals involved in children's play met to discuss an initial draft of the guidelines. Those present included playground designers, university professors, and child care specialists representing almost 200 agencies and institutions. The work of this group culminated in the publication of *Play for All Guidelines: Planning Design and Management of Outdoor Play Settings for All Children* (Moore, Goltsman, & Iacofano, 1987). This document was the first comprehensive guide to the development of outdoor play environments that would serve all children, including those with disabilities (Frost, 1992).

In 1990, play environment development to include children with disabilities gained further momentum with the passage of ADA, which aims to "ensure that people with disabilities have access to employment, public accommodations, commercial facilities, government services, transportation, and telecommunications" (Lindemann, 1992, p. 48). Covered in this law are institutions serving children, including play environments. The Architectural and Transportation Barriers Compliance Board (Access Board) was made responsible for developing accessibility guidelines relevant to ADA, to include the construction of new facilities. Part of their responsibilities are the development of guidelines of sports facilities; places of amusement; play settings; golf, boating, and fishing facilities; and outdoor recreation facilities (Recreation Access Advisory Committee, 1994).

The Play Settings Subcommittee of the Access Board developed preliminary accessibility guidelines for play areas that the committee defined as

> [a] designated play and learning environment with a range of settings carefully layered on the site. A play area may be inside or outside and contains one or more of the following elements: entrances, pathways, fences and enclosures, signage, play equipment, game areas, landforms and topography, trees and vegetation, gardens, animal habitats, water play, sand play, loose parts, gathering places, stage areas, storage, and ground covering and surfacing. (Recreation Access Advisory Committee, 1994, p. 89)

Subsequently, in 1997 the Regulatory Negotiation Committee on Accessibility Guidelines for Play Facilities, also a subgroup of the Architectural and Transportation Barriers Compliance Board, issued a final report relative to play environments that include children with disabilities. The guidelines provide suggested accessibility standards for play facilities addressed by ADA, Titles II and III (Americans with Disabilities Act Accessibility Guidelines [ADAAG], 1991). The committee included representatives of 17 organizations and agencies with interests and expertise in children with disabilities and play environments. While the guidelines lack the force of law, they provide an interpretation of the intent of ADAAG for children's play environments. They are consistent with the ASTM Public Playground Equipment Standard F 1487-95 issued in 1995 and revised in 1998 (American Society for Testing and Materials, 1998). The expectation is that children with disabilities will play in the same environment as children without disabilities and that modifications will permit all children to enjoy play experiences together.

The Regulatory Negotiation Committee on Accessibility Guidelines for Play Facilities members included persons with disabilities, representatives of state and local governments, designers, manufacturers, owners and operators of play areas, and voluntary standards groups. They based their approach to reaching consensus on guidelines on the following principles (Regulatory Negotiation Committee on Accessibility Guidelines for Play Facilities; see Architectural and Transportation Barriers Compliance Board, 1997, p. 3):

- Be based on children's anthropometric dimensions and other resource information.
- Be based on children with disabilities using a variety of assistive devices.
- Provide opportunity for use by children who have a variety of abilities.
- Support social interaction and encourage integration.
- Create challenge, not barriers.
- Provide advisory information to assist designers, operators, and owners, to effectively incorporate access into their designs. Information should be in an understandable format.
- Maintain safety consistent with ASTM requirements.
- Be reasonable in terms of cost relative to benefit.
- Address access for parents and caregivers.
- Provide access to elevated structures. Additional ground-level accessible play components may be required, depending on the type of vertical access provided to elevated structures.

The guidelines focus on accessibility to various components of the play environment. Specifically, they address ground-level play components, elevated play components, and accessible routes to play components.

Ground-Level Play Components

Ground-level play components are the different types of play components that can be entered and exited at ground level (e.g., swings, climbers, spring rockers, natural features). The recommendation for this category is that children with disabilities have a choice of at least one of each of the different types of play components. In addition, there should be ground components equal to 50% of the total number of elevated play components. So, if 10 elevated play components are provided, there should be 5 ground-level play components also.

Elevated Play Components

Elevated play components are part of a composite play structure and are entered above or below grade. Slides, climbers, and activity panels that are part of a composite play structure are categorized as elevated play components. The recommended guideline for these components is that at least 50% of all elevated play components be accessible to children with disabilities. This guideline allows for integration of play for all children. While children with disabilities would not be able to access all components of a composite play structure, they would be able to play on at least half of the play components.

Accessible Routes

Children who use a wheelchair, crutches, or other assistive equipment for mobility have special needs to be able to access the playground as well as the play components within the play area (Doctoroff, 2001). The guidelines require that pathways be constructed of a material that is suitable for wheelchairs and other mobility aids. Guidelines recommend that at least one **accessible route** be provided within the boundary of the playground. In addition, "the accessible route is required to connect accessible play components, including entry and exit points" (Regulatory Negotiation Committee on Accessibility Guidelines for Play Facilities; see Architectural and Transportation Barriers Compliance Board, 1997, p. 6). Entry and exit points can be at ground level or elevated. When accessibility is provided for elevated play components, ramps and transfer systems provide accessibility. Expectations for accessible routes for small composite play structures (fewer than 20 play components) are less than for larger structures (20 or more play components).

Ramps, Decks, and Stationary Bridges

Access to elevated play components is provided for children with physical disabilities through the use of ramps, decks, and stationary bridges. Landings where wheelchairs can be parked are also needed so that children can leave the wheelchair to use the play components. ADAAG recommendations for ramp width are 60 inches or greater. Minimum criteria are as follows:

a. Minimum width of 36".
b. Cross slope not to exceed 1:50.
c. Running slope not to exceed 1:12.
d. Ramp run or length not to exceed 12'.
e. Landings at bottom and top of ramp run shall be a minimum of 60" in diameter (Recreation Access Advisory Committee, 1994, p. 93)

Additional guidelines specify recommendations for handrails and transfer points where children can transfer themselves onto play equipment or be assisted by an adult to make the transfer. Figure 9–1 shows specifications for ramps, landings, and parking spaces; Figure 9–2 provides information for turning spaces for wheelchairs.

Access also needs to be provided to sand and water play areas and other play opportunities that might be provided. Although elevated sand, water play, and gardening components may be provided through elevated equipment that can accommodate a wheelchair space underneath, ground-level components are preferable, with transfer points providing access. Figure 9–3 shows possibilities for both raised and ground-level sand play areas.

FIGURE 9–1 Playscape Wheelchair Ramp

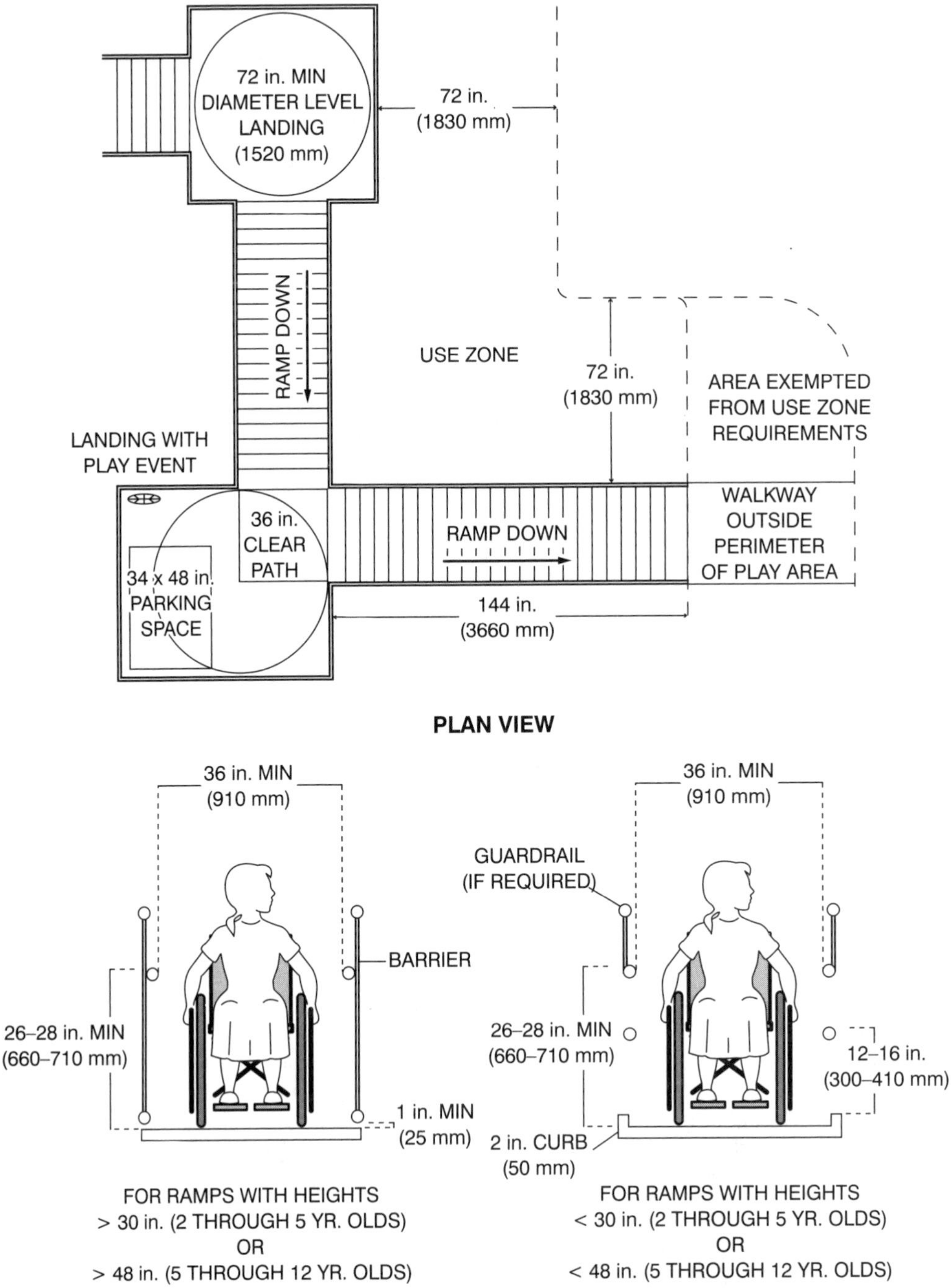

Source: From *Standard Consumer Safety Performance Specifications for Playground Equipment for Public Use* (p. 47) by American Society for Testing and Materials (ASTM), 1998, West Conshohocken, PA: ASTM. Reprinted by permission.

FIGURE 9–2 Platform Wheelchair Transfer Point

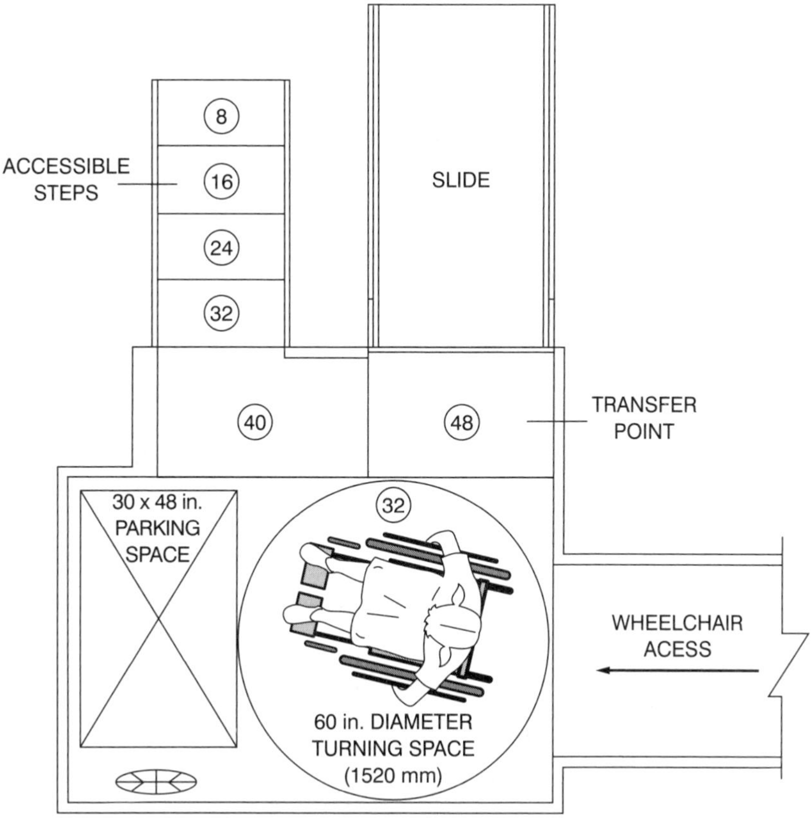

Note 1—Turning space and parking space may not overlap.
Note 2—⊗ denotes the height of the designated play surface in inches.

Source: From *Standard Consumer Safety Performance Specifications for Playground Equipment for Public Use* (p. 49) by American Society for Testing and Materials (ASTM), 1998, West Conshohocken, PA: ASTM. Reprinted by permission.

Children with disabilities need to have the same types of play experiences as children without disabilities. The ADA guidelines (ADAAG Standards) and ASTM Safety Performance Specifications provide guidance in how playgrounds can be adapted to include both safety and appropriate play features. Schools, child care centers, and other settings that plan playgrounds to serve all children need to follow the example of the PLAE organization and involve adults and children with disabilities as well as parents, playground specialists, and representatives of local and state organizations and agencies when preparing for design. Planners are urged to consult the following resources before beginning the planning process:

Regulatory Negotiation Committee on Accessibility Guidelines for Play Facilities: Final Report
U.S. Architectural and Transportation Barriers Compliance Board
1331 F Street, NW, Suite 1000
Washington, DC 20004-1111

Standard Consumer Safety Performance Specification for Playground Equipment for Public Use
American Society for Testing and Materials
100 Barr Harbor Dr.
West Conshohocken, PA 19428

FIGURE 9–3 Raised Play Landscapes

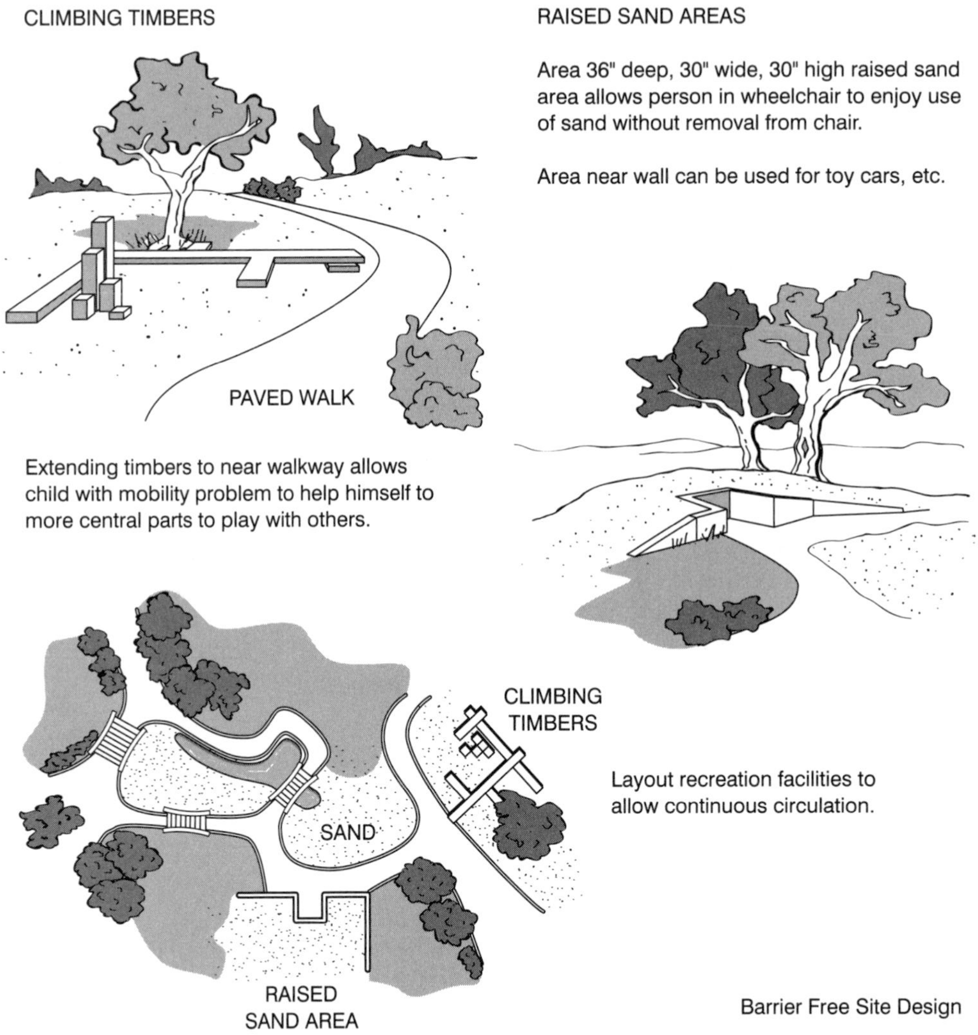

CLIMBING TIMBERS
PAVED WALK
Extending timbers to near walkway allows child with mobility problem to help himself to more central parts to play with others.
RAISED SAND AREAS
Area 36" deep, 30" wide, 30" high raised sand area allows person in wheelchair to enjoy use of sand without removal from chair.
Area near wall can be used for toy cars, etc.
CLIMBING TIMBERS
SAND
Layout recreation facilities to allow continuous circulation.
RAISED SAND AREA
Barrier Free Site Design

Source: From *Play and Playscapes* (p. 10) by J. L. Frost, 1992, Pacific Grove, CA: Thompson Learning Global Rights Group. Reprinted by permission.

Recommendations for Accessibility Guidelines: Recreational Facilities and Outdoor Developed Areas
Recreation Access Advisory Committee
U.S. Architectural and Transportation Barriers Compliance Board
1331 F Street, NW, Suite 1000
Washington, DC 20004-1111

THE ROLE OF TECHNOLOGY

Assistive Technology

Technological advances in recent years have enhanced possibilities for children with disabilities to be able to communicate, participate, and engage in play with their peers. The Individuals

Children with disabilities need the same types of experiences as children without disabilities.

with Disabilities Education Act Amendments of 1991 (IDEA) require school districts to provide assistive technology services to children who need them. These assistive services can be as simple as a drinking straw or as complex as adaptations to computers so that they can be used for both communication and learning. The assistive devices are provided as the result of an evaluation of the technological needs of individual children and selection of the most appropriate devices that can be acquired or devised.

Assistive technology, then, can involve low or high technology and can be described in 10 categories (Parette & Murdick, 1998):

> a. Mobility (e.g., wheelchairs and scooters);
>
> b. Electronic communication (i.e., devices which produce artificial or real life speech for talking with others);
>
> c. Visual (e.g., magnification devices for reading tasks;
>
> d. Assistive listening (e.g., hearing aids);
>
> e. Environmental access (e.g., infrared control unit for manipulating a TV or stereo);
>
> f. Computers (e.g. game software enabling cooperative play with others);
>
> g. Leisure/recreation (e.g., hand-held electronic toys used for independent play);
>
> h. Independent living (e.g., buttoning or reaching devices for children with physical disabilities);
>
> i. Positioning (e.g., vinyl-covered rolls and bolsters used to maintain proper body alignment);
>
> j. Adaptive toys (e.g., battery-powered toys which are switch-controlled by the child). (p. 194)

While some of the devices listed affect the play of children with disabilities indirectly, many of them have a direct impact on the child's ability to play. Although the term *technology* generally brings to mind the use of computers, in reality assistive technology includes a broad range of devices that are also simple to complex. Parette and Murdick (1998) have designed a chart to demonstrate the varying degrees of complexity found in assistive devices, ranging from Velcro to computers. Figure 9–4 shows examples of such devices.

FIGURE 9–4 Continuum of Technology Assistive Devices

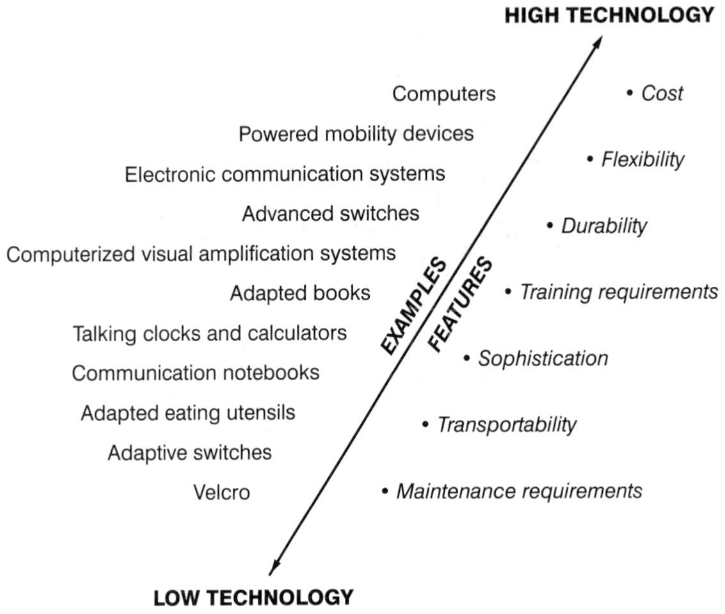

Source: From "Assistive Technology and IEPS for Young Children with Disabilities" (p. 194) by H. P. Parette and N. L. Murdick, 1998, *Early Childhood Education Journal, 25,* 193–197. Reprinted by permission.

Adapted Toys

Assistive technology can be used to adapt toys for children with disabilities. Specially designed switches, control units, battery device adapters, and mounting systems can be used with available toys to make toys interesting and accessible. Battery-powered toys can be adapted for external switch control so that the child can control the on and off operation of the toy. Switch control adaptations can be used for battery-powered kitchen appliances, action toys such as train sets, and cassette players (Locke & Levin, 1998).

Games can also be adapted with a control switch. The action of rolling dice can be simulated using a switch and special overlay. The child with disabilities can then actively participate in such games as "Chutes and Ladders," "Monopoly," and "Clue" (Locke & Levin, 1998).

The St. Agnes Hospital Children's Rehabilitation Center in White Plains, New York, uses adapted toys for children being treated for spina bifida, cerebral palsy, and other physical disabilities. Engineers, technicians, and occupational therapists study available toys to determine how they can be adapted for children who have impairments. They use a variety of types of switches and sip-and-puff devices to activate toys (Anonymous, 1997).

Stone and Sagstetter (1998) have specific suggestions for how adapted toys can be used for play. Children with disabilities can engage in bubble play with a battery-operated bubble maker with a battery device adapter and switch attached. Likewise, children can blow streamers or a mobile by using an adapted battery-operated fan.

Interactive Video

Research has been conducted to determine whether interactive video can benefit children with special education needs. Interactive video combines interactive video machines with computers as an adapted learning tool. Blisset and Adkins (1993) have found benefits to low-ability learners. In addition, reality-based interactive games can be used to change the learning environment. Using interactive video machines with keyboards and a mouse as input devices for mathematics problems, Chambers (1997) found that interactive video can help raise self-esteem, provide equal opportunities for learning, and support collaborative learning. Reduction of anxiety, language development, and a sense of ownership that result from the use of interactive video can be translated into enhanced play activities using the same medium and strategies.

Computer Technology

Like interactive video, computer skills permit children with disabilities to engage in socialization that may not be available to them in other classroom and play activities. Some activities described as play by researchers in this area were computer learning games. Students also engaged in free-play activities. Usually children were paired with another student without disabilities. In a study of preschool children's problem-solving activities using the computer, Muller and Perlmutter (1995) found that they engaged in more social interaction than when working on a jigsaw puzzle. Toddlers and preschoolers with disabilities exhibited more positive, interactive social behaviors when engaged in computer-based activities (Howard, Greyrose, Kehr, Espinosa, & Beckwith, 1996). Children without disabilities who had developed friendships with children with disabilities displayed increased interactions with their friends when engaged in computer activities. Moreover, children with disabilities used turn-taking skills and increased socialization when engaged in free-play activities on the computer (Goodman, 1981; Zippiroli, Bayer, & Mistrett, 1988).

Assistive technology is commonly needed by children with disabilities to participate in computer activities. A touch screen, attached to the front of the computer monitor, is activated by the touch of a finger. Expanded keyboards and trackballs also permit access for children with limited physical abilities (Dell & Newton, 1998). Students with sight limitations and other disabilities might need to use Soundproof software that reads what is entered from a keyboard and vocalizes it back to the writer (Beigel, 1996).

Adaptive communication refers to the application of computer technology to permit disabled children who are unable to speak or write to communicate with others. A portable computer equipped with speech output can be used by a nonspeaking child to "talk" with others. The child can type or press on the screen to express the desired communication. Likewise, children who cannot use their hands can use the computer for writing or drawing. Both strategies enhance interactions with teachers and peers and facilitate social and language development. Blind children can use large print or Braille key labels for writing purposes (Burgstahler, 1998).

Although software for creative and play activities is limited, several types are recommended for preschool and primary-grade children. Among them are "Kaleidoscope" (SEMERC), "Kid Pix Studio Deluxe" (Broderbund Software, Inc.), "IntelliTools Coloring Books" (IntelliTools), and "Blocks in Motion" (Don Jonston Incorporated). The following Web sites can provide additional information and resources for computers:

National Association for the Education of Young Children: *www.naeyc.org/*

Alliance for Technology Access: *www.ataccess.org/*

National Center to Improve Practice in Special Education through Technology, Media, & Materials (NCIP): *www.edc.org/FSC/NCIP*

CREATIVITY AND PLAY

Assistive technology makes it possible for children with some types of disabilities to engage in creative activities, as we discussed in the previous section. Other types of adaptations make it possible for children with disabilities to enjoy creative play. If children have the ability to hold crayons and other art materials, they can engage in creative art activities. Children with mental retardation can participate at their own developmental level. Those with hearing impairments can also participate in expressive arts activities.

However, children with severe hearing disabilities find it difficult to enjoy music. They can be taught to feel the beat of music through vibrations in the floor. They might need to learn to sign or be able to lip-read to enjoy books. They can engage in dramatic play when guided and assisted by adults and peers.

Children with visual impairments can enjoy finger painting and other art activities that permit them to use the sense of feel to express themselves. They enjoy hearing stories, especially if sensory materials are used to help them experience the content of the story. They readily engage in sociodramatic play when the environment is arranged so that they can find their way around in the dramatic play center.

With careful planning, children with disabilities can be encouraged to engage in creative activities. Many of the materials are the same, but adults must determine what kinds of adaptations need to be made so that individual children can participate.

PLAY-BASED ASSESSMENT

Much attention was given in earlier sections to the differences children with disabilities display in play when compared to peers without disabilities. Each disability can be unique in the play differences and behaviors that affected children use. While understanding play variations resulting from disabling conditions can be helpful in understanding their needs for intervention, the appearance of or a delay in the play behaviors can also be used to assess children. Information in this section focuses on the use of play to assess children for possible delays and disabilities and to plan intervention programs when needed. A background of how play assessment came to be used will be discussed, followed by why and how it is applied with young children with disabilities. Research efforts to determine the efficacy of play-based assessment will also be reported.

The use of observation of a child's play for assessment is not new. Teachers and caregivers have observed play to determine young children's developmental progress for many decades. In addition, the use of play as an intervention strategy was promoted in the 1960s and 1970s to prevent developmental delay for children who were at environmental risk. Nevertheless, the use of play-based assessment for children with disabilities has gained in popularity only recently. Identification of children with delay or disabilities traditionally has been conducted primarily through standardized assessments. Instruments such as the *Bayley Scales of Infant Development* (Bayley, 1969) and *Stanford-Binet Intelligence Scale* (Thorndike, Hagen, & Sattler, 1986) have been commonly used to assess young children.

Why Play-Based Assessment Is Being Used

A growing concern about the limitations of standardized tests has led psychologists and special educators to look for alternative methods that will be more effective (Linder, 1990, 1994). Limitations of standardized tests include the examiner's inability to modify items with the result that they are biased against young children with some disabilities, particularly children with language deficits (Bailey, 1989; Brooks-Gunn & Lewis, 1981). Other limitations in standardized tests are that they do not provide information about learning styles, problem-solving strategies, and contextual skills at school and home (Bailey, 1989). Finally, tests assess developmental skills as separate domains, while children use the skills in combination in their environment (Fewell & Rich, 1987).

Assessment of play activities, then, provides information about domains of development that are correlated with other domains—specifically, cognitive, social, and language development (Belsky & Most, 1981; Fenson, 1986; Linder, 1998). Play assessment is nonthreatening and can be done unobtrusively (Fewell & Kaminski, 1988). Other information that can be observed through children's play includes the ability to initiate and carry out play schemes, as well as what a child can do with play materials (Fewell & Rich, 1987). Segal and Webber (1996) list nine benefits of play observation as contrasted with standardized assessments:

- Play observations provide an opportunity to assess the functional behavior of a young child who either cannot or will not perform in a formal testing situation.
- Because of the flexibility and spontaneity of a play situation, infants and toddlers may achieve a level of object or symbolic play that they did not demonstrate on a standardized assessment.
- Play observations can provide important insights into temperamental variables.
- Play observations can reveal aspects of the parent-child relationship that help explain the behavior of the child.
- Play observations can provide insights into numerous domains of development.
- Play observations provide clinicians with special opportunities to learn effective play strategies from a child's parent.
- Play observations suggest ways of helping parents modify play strategies that are not fully effective.
- Play observations implemented within a home can identify strengths, coping skills, and risk factors that impact a diagnosis and may be useful for designing a treatment plan.
- Play observations can enhance the parent-professional partnership. (pp. 215–224)

How Play-Based Assessments Are Conducted

People disagree on how play-based assessments should be conducted. Three approaches to play observations are being used: nonstructured assessments, structured assessments, and transdisciplinary assessments.

Nonstructured assessments have as their purpose to identify all behaviors that occur during a play session, whereas structured assessments focus on a previously designed set of play behaviors. In structured play observations, procedures are established, as are the toys to be used and techniques employed by adults to initiate the play activities. Spontaneous play is observed in nonstructured play assessments, and play may be initiated by either the child or the caregiver (Segal & Webber, 1996).

Transdisciplinary play-based assessment includes a team of evaluators who observe the child at play concurrently. Each member of the team observes a different domain of development or for a different purpose. These play observations are generally structured and may include planned adult interactions (Bergen, 1991; Linder, 1998).

The transdisciplinary team observes how the interplay of domains in child development as well as individual differences in development characteristics are revealed in play opportunities. The makeup of the the team, to include parents, is based on the nature of the assessment, the needs of the child, and the purposes of the intervention plan. Structured observations include the presentation of selected tasks and play materials to elicit demonstration of higher skills than are present in free-play activities (Linder, 1998).

Research and Play-Based Assessment

Because the use of play observations for assessment are relatively new, research evidence on how valid they are for screening children with developmental delay and making diagnoses for intervention programs is scarce (Eisert & Lamorey, 1996; Myers, McBride, & Peterson, 1996). Studies have been conducted to measure play-based assessment as compared to assessment using standardized tests. Myers et al. (1996) used transdisciplinary assessment to determine whether this type of observation can supply information that is useful for intervention purposes. The researchers also sought information on the efficiency of the method and to find out whether professionals and parents are satisfied with play-based assessment results.

Play-based assessment has been used to determine play differences between children with ADHD and children with both mental retardation and ADHD. Structured play observations were conducted to determine the quality of play, the amount of time the two groups were able to play, appropriateness of conduct during play, and impulsivity. Although the results of behaviors used by the two groups were inconclusive, these types of play observations might help in discriminating between children with mental retardation who have or do not have ADHD (Handen, McAuliffe, Janosky, Feldman, & Breaux, 1998).

SUMMARY

Children can experience a variety and/or combination of disabilities that can affect their ability to play. Disabilities can be physical, intellectual, or emotional and can range in severity from mild to profound; nevertheless, all of these children have some capacity to engage in play. Their play abilities will be different and of a lower sophistication than those of their peers without disabilities, but with adaptations provided by adults and interventions to help them experience a broader range of play activities, they can benefit from opportunities to play.

It is difficult to categorize the play needs of children with disabilities because the nature of the disability and the abilities of children are unique to each individual. Children with multiple disabilities present more challenges because the interaction of disabilities impacts different developmental domains in play.

Adults play an important role in facilitating play for children with disabilities. They need to be aware of the challenges faced by each child with a disability and know how to adapt the environment and encourage the child to explore the possibilities for play. In addition, they must ensure that the child has opportunities to self-initiate play, even though adult modeling and guidance may be required before the child is able to play independently or with peers. Children without disabilities can become helpful play partners when they are knowledgeable about the nature of their friends' disabilities and how to interact with them. With the advent of inclusion or integrated classrooms, children are more likely to have a child with disabilities in their classroom and accept them as play partners. However, they, too, might need adult guidance in how to include a child with disabilities in their play activities.

The environment plays an important role in accessibility to play for children with disabilities. The indoor environment needs to be modified to accommodate children with different disabilities. Especially important are modifications of space and accessible location of materials for children using wheelchairs and other mobility aids.

More extensive adaptations must be made in outdoor environments. In the last two decades, much progress has been made in determining the best adaptations to the outdoor environment to provide access to play components and maintain safety at the same time. While there are no standards with the force of law, guidance for designing playscapes have been provided by the U.S. Architectural and Transportation Barriers Compliance Board and American Society for Testing and Materials.

Assistive technology has made it possible for children with disabilities to engage in play. Through the use of different levels of technology, ranging from wheelchairs to infrared control units, children with disabilities are able to access physical environments and technological devices such as computers and interactive videos. Toys can be adapted through switches and adaptations so that children can activate them when their manual dexterity is severely limited, thus enabling them to participate with their peers with typical development.

In recent decades, professionals who diagnose and plan intervention programs have been using play-based assessment to determine the abilities and needs of children with disabilities. The common method of assessment has been the administration of standardized tests; however, these instruments have limitations when applied to individual children with varying types of disabilities. Moreover, play-based assessment provides a more integrated perspective of developmental domains rather than the assessment of skills in isolation. Because children can display more advanced skill development in play activities than in clinical testing, play-based assessment is being researched for its usefulness for diagnosis and intervention.

Play is important for all children. In the past, the perception has been that children with disabilities, especially children with cognitive delay, are not interested in play. Although play research on children with disabilities is lacking in some areas, much has been learned about how children with disabilities play and how their play possibilities can be expanded. As more is learned and newer advances are made in all types of play environments, more opportunities will be possible for children with disabilities to participate in childhood play.

KEY TERMS

Abused children
Accessible route
Attention deficit hyperactivity disorder (ADHD)
Autism
Behavioral disorders
Biological risk
Bronchial asthma
Cerebral palsy
Children at risk
Cognitive delay
Cystic fibrosis
Developmental delay
Diabetes
Down syndrome
Elevated play components
Emotional disorders
Environmental risk
Ground-level play components
Health impairments
Hearing impairments
Heart conditions
Hemophilia
Hydrocephalus
Inclusion
Integrated classrooms
Intellectual impairments
Language delay
Lead poisoning
Mental retardation
Motor impairments
Muscular dystrophy
Physical disabilities
Positioning equipment
Rheumatic fever
Spina bifida
Visual impairments

STUDY QUESTIONS

1. Why is it important to understand an individual child's disability or disabilities when planning for play?
2. Explain how play might be affected for children with visual impairments, motor impairments, and emotional disorders.
3. Children can be at risk for developmental delay because of biological or environmental factors. Explain how these life factors can affect children.
4. What is a medically fragile child? What health conditions can cause a child to be medically fragile?
5. What are some causes of behavioral disorders?
6. Compare the play behaviors of children who have been sexually abused with children who have been physically abused.
7. Why is language an important component of play with peers? How does language delay affect social play?
8. Why do autistic children fail to engage in symbolic play? Explain.
9. How do inclusion classrooms generally benefit play behaviors in children with disabilities? Give examples.
10. Explain what is meant by ground-level components, elevated play components, and accessible routes in outdoor playscapes. How do these components provide access for children with disabilities?
11. Why are ramps, decks, and stationary bridges important for children who use wheelchairs?
12. What is a transfer point? Where are they needed on adapted playgrounds?
13. Define assistive technology. Describe some examples of assistive technology.
14. How do adapted computers facilitate play between peers with disabilities and those without disabilities?
15. Why is play-based assessment beneficial for diagnosis and plans for intervention? Describe some advantages of using play-based assessment.

Chapter 10

Introduction to Play Therapy

PLATO IN HIS Republic, *which is considered so stern teaches the children only through festivals, games, songs, and amusements. It seems as if he had accomplished his purpose when he had taught them to be happy.*

(Rousseau, 1911, p. 71)

PLAY THERAPY is the systematic use of a theoretical model to establish an interpersonal process wherein trained play therapists use the therapeutic powers of play to help clients prevent or resolve psychosocial difficulties and achieve optimal growth and development.

(Board of Directors of the Association for Play Therapy, 1997, p. 14)

The belief that play is therapeutic and healing is fundamental to understanding the delicate dance among child, playthings, and therapist in the play therapy relationship. Throughout the 20th century, child developmentalists, psychologists, and other behavioral scientists recognized the therapeutic power of play for young children (Adler, 1927; Axline, 1947b; Erikson, 1950; Freud, 1928, 1946, 1961, 1965; Kottman, 2001, 2003; Landreth, 1991, 2001; O'Connor, 2000; Rogers, 1942; Schaefer, 1993; Webb, 1991). Play therapy is now a rapidly growing and respected profession, applicable to a wide range of children's problems. The establishment of the International Association for Play Therapy in 1982 marked play therapy's acceptance as a specialized field within the mental health profession.

The growing interest in play therapy coincided with the acceleration of fragmented parenting, divorce, school and neighborhood violence, media violence, child abuse, and drug abuse during the latter quarter of the 20th century (Frost, 1986). These and other factors, including natural disasters, accidental injuries, and physical, mental, and emotional disabilities, create an ever-growing need for therapeutic intervention.

Principles of play therapy can serve as both a specialized process for helping alleviate the consequences of trauma and as a guide for parents, teachers, and other significant adults for preventing children's emotional trauma. Psychoanalysis should be conducted only by highly skilled professional therapists. Untrained parents, teachers, and other adults should not attempt to conduct play therapy with disturbed or traumatized children.

Scientists have now demonstrated that extreme stress or trauma floods the brain with neurochemicals, which over time can change the nature of the brain, sometimes permanently (Begley, 1996, 1997; Frost, 1998; Shore, 1997; see also Chapter 3). Prolonged stress, neglect, or abuse disrupt **bonding** between child and caregivers (DeAngelis, 1997), damage memory and learning, and negatively impact the functioning of affect, empathy, and emotions (Lowenthal, 1999; Nash, 1997; Neuberger, 1997).

Play therapy is a supportive relationship between a child and a therapist who allows the child to play out or express her feelings and emotions in a context of supportive play materials and positive relationships. Play is the child's natural medium of expression. In play therapy the child "plays out" her feelings and problems just as in certain therapeutic contexts, adults "talk out" or express themselves through language (Axline, 1949). Play therapy can be *directive,* in which the therapist guides and interprets, or it may be *nondirective,* in which responsibility and direction are left to the child. Play therapy may also be individual (i.e., between a therapist and a child in a play setting), or it may be in a group, in which a child plays with other children and must consider the reactions and feelings of others in the group. Children may not fully understand the source of their problems leading to play therapy and may not have the language to express problems, frustrations, hurts, or abuses. Play is children's language and has therapeutic powers that allow children to play out their problems and, potentially, to heal.

Play is the major therapeutic approach for individual and group therapy with children for several reasons:

- Play is the child's natural medium for self-expression, experimentation, and learning.
- The child can readily relate to toys and play out concerns with them because she feels at home in a play setting.
- Play facilitates the child's communication and expression.
- Play allows for a cathartic release of feelings and frustrations.
- Experiencing play is renewing, wholesome, and constructive in the child's life.
- Observing the child at play allows the adult therapist to understand the child's world.
- The therapist can more readily relate to the child through play activities than through verbal discussion. (Schaefer, 1985, pp. 106–107)

The primary focus in this chapter will be on the origins, development, and approaches of client-centered or child-centered play therapy, with lesser emphasis on the more structured approaches. How did we arrive at a child-centered approach to therapy for children? How has play therapy been used to treat maladjusted children? What is the appropriate context and process for play therapy? How successful is play therapy? This chapter will introduce play therapy by tracing its history across various approaches, theorists, and practitioners; explaining how play acts as a therapeutic agent; describing the nature and importance of play therapy; and reviewing research on effectiveness of play therapy.

HISTORY AND THEORIES OF PLAY THERAPY

Psychoanalysis: Roots of Play Therapy

The following brief discussion will serve to introduce a sampling of the rudimentary elements of psychoanalysis. Traditional psychoanalysis per se was not conducted in a play setting. However, play therapy has foundations in psychoanalysis and modern approaches to play therapy, especially structured approaches, still rely on psychoanalytic traditions.

Sigmund Freud

Modern play therapy is rooted in the **psychoanalytical method** pioneered by Sigmund Freud and associates during the early 1900s. Although Freud is widely credited with founding **psychotherapy,** the approach was developed and refined by a number of scientists. Freud (1938, p. 933) himself stated in a public lecture that "it was not I who brought psychoanalysis into existence," crediting Josef Breuer for doing so while Freud was still a student. However, Freud's associates declared that Breuer's "cathartic procedure" was a mere preliminary to psychoanalysis that began when Freud rejected the hypnotic technique (some people cannot be hypnotized) and introduced **free association.** Freud (1938) himself declared that the history of psychoanalysis started with the "technical innovation of the rejection of hypnosis" and stated that "the theory of repression is the pillar upon which the edifice of psychoanalysis rests" (p. 939) Repression theory held that typical neuroses are developmental disturbances due to repression of infantile sexual impulses made unconscious and appearing mainly in dreams.

Freud's repression technique depended on the expression of experiences that could be observed by the therapist during analysis. Freud traced back the morbid symptoms of neurotic people to sources in their life history by uncovering unconscious experiences and explaining **transference** and **resistance** demonstrated by the patient.

Transference refers to attitudes transferred by the client to the therapist that were originally transferred to the parent or other significant person. In transference, the patient perceives the therapist as the representative of his original repressed reactions. The patient creates, in relationship to the therapist, new editions of early conflicts during which the patient behaves as he originally behaved.

Resistance is the defensive striving against painful memories or experiences that can lead to forgetting and keeping experiences repressed and out of consciousness. It is the unconscious process of rejecting or attempting to discard unwelcome impulses or unconscious neuroses.

The basic concepts underlying Freudian psychoanalysis are broad and complex, some requiring a book in themselves for explanation. The unconscious is that highly active self within us of which we are essentially unaware. The **id,** the **ego,** and the **superego** can be broadly understood as, respectively, the unconscious, the conscious, and the "conscience" functions of the self. Freud's **Oedipus complex** refers to the feelings surrounding the natural impulse of children to crave exclusive love, usually from the parent of the opposite sex (Freud, 1946, pp. v, vi).

Freud attempted to explain and confirm his discoveries by observation and analysis of very young children, focusing on infantile sexuality, which he believed was the ultimate source of neurotic symptoms. He later developed techniques for interpreting dreams, integrated dream interpretation into his practice of psychoanalysis, and even conducted an analysis of his own dreams that "led me through all the happenings of my childhood years" (1938, p. 942). Jung (1954, pp. 23–24) later declared that Freud's interpretation of dreams was the decisive step that made modern psychotherapy a method of individual treatment.

Carl Jung

By 1911, psychoanalysis was championed and carried out in several countries. In 1908, the first private congress of psychoanalysts was held, with Sigmund Freud presiding. In 1909, Freud and Carl Jung, a Swiss psychiatrist, were invited to North America by Clark University President Stanley Hall to give lectures at that institution. Freud soon transferred leadership of the congress of psychoanalysts to Jung, and the International Psychoanalytic Association was formed in 1910, with Jung the elected president, and the first American group was formed under the name of "The New York Psychoanalytic Society." By this time Freud had become disappointed with Jung's leadership and believed that the theories of both Jung and Alfred Adler, another rising star in psychoanalysis, were rife with contradictions and misconceptions. Freud (1938) stated, "Any analysis carried out in accordance with the rules [Freud's rules] . . . repudiates the new interpretations of Adler's and Jung's systems" (p. 976).

Since individuality is unique and unpredictable, Jung (1954) proposed that the therapist must abandon preconceptions about psychotherapy and engage in a dialectical procedure. In such, the therapist is no longer the agent of treatment but a fellow participant in the therapeutic process, entering into the relationship as both questioner and answerer. He is no longer the superior or judge as in traditional psychotherapy but a fellow participant who is as deeply involved as the patient.

Jung's break with Freudian therapy was not complete. He continued to rely on interpretation of dreams but emphasized that the patient should learn to understand his own dreams—to go his own way. He continued to focus on examining the unconscious but attempted to articulate the unconscious with the conscious mind. He considered it the prime task of psychotherapy to pursue the goal of individual development, to bring life to its fullest fruition.

Jung also proposed that the cause of mental illness or neurosis was related to suppression of the symptom that was a marker for the cause of the illness. These causes were to be brought to consciousness through therapy. And he, like Freud, claimed that all clear cases of neuroses deal with misdevelopment rooted in childhood, yet he declared that the main emphasis in therapy should be on the attitude of the patient rather than "chasing after infantile memories" (Jung, 1954, p. 31). Jung credited Freud and Adler with developing the major viewpoints of psychotherapy but maintained that his own "deviationist views" were equally relative.

Psychoanalytic Play Therapy

Freud was not credited with developing play therapy for children, but his description of work with "Little Hans and The Rat Man" (Freud, 1909/1955) was the first published case describing a psychological approach to working with a child. He believed that play had a cathartic effect, allowing children to purge themselves of negative feelings associated with traumatic events. Play rids the child of the constraints and sanctions of reality and provides a sanctuary for venting unacceptable or aggressive impulses. In play, the child can assume the role of the punisher and transfer negative feelings to a substitute object (doll, puppet) or person (sibling, classmate).

Hermine Hug-Hellmuth (1921) was among the first therapists to propose that play was central in child analysis and to use play materials for play expression, but Melanie Klein (1932) and Anna Freud (1946) built on the psychoanalytic tradition to construct approaches to play therapy. Both continued the tradition of seeking to uncover past experiences of the child and strengthening the ego.

Melanie Klein

Melanie Klein (1932) gained access to the minds of young children and developed play therapy procedures by applying Freud's findings and procedures. She concluded that the criteria of psychoanalysis for adults could be applied to children and lead to the same results. However, for children she substituted play for Freud's free verbal association. She believed that children suffer from more acute degrees of anxiety than adults do, so it was important to establish therapy quickly and gain access to their anxieties and guilt as early as possible. To Klein, children lived through and worked out their anxieties and phobias when the therapist treated those anxieties and phobias as transference situations (making connections between original experiences or fantasized ones and the actual situation). In response to continued interpretation by the therapist of the meaning of a child's play, the scope of play widened and the child's inhibitions were reduced.

Through uncovering the child's infantile experiences, Klein's analysis ostensibly corrected "errors of development" (1932, p. 18) and resolved fixations. She saw symbolic sexual meanings, frequently involving sexual behaviors of the mother or father, in virtually all play episodes and interpreted these for the child.

Ruth (4 years old) exhibited excessive reliance on her mother, disliked strangers, and could not make friends with the children—all leading to anxiety attacks and other neurotic symptoms. Ruth drew a picture of a tumbler with several small round balls inside and a lid on top. She stated that the lid was to keep the balls from rolling out. She had previously shut a purse and a bag tightly to keep items from falling out.

The therapist [Klein] immediately sought to bring about a positive transference by interpreting these actions. She explained (interpreted) to Ruth that the balls in the tumbler and the items in the purse and bag "all meant children in her Mummy's inside, and that she (Ruth) wanted to keep them safely shut up so as not to have any more brothers and sisters." Whereupon [Klein wrote], "The effect of my interpretation was astonishing. For the first time Ruth turned her attention to me and began to play in a different, less constrained, way" (Klein, 1932, pp. 26–27).

Despite her apparent excessive reliance on the significance of infantile sexual anxieties, Klein advanced the practice of play therapy well beyond its earlier state. Her therapy setting was simple, containing a low table holding a number of small, simple toys—carts, trains, animals, bricks and houses, carriages, little wooden men and women, paper, scissors, and pencils. The child soon began to play freely with these toys, offering the therapist insight into her complexes by the manner of play and attitude toward the toys. Interpretation followed promptly during the first session, carrying the negative transference back to its roots in reality, reducing the child's resistance, and eventually resulting in diminished anxieties.

Anna Freud

Anna Freud, a contemporary of Klein's and Sigmund's daughter, disagreed with Klein on several major points regarding play therapy. She maintained that Klein's play method was almost indispensable with small children who are not capable of verbal self-expression or free association as adults are in psychotherapy (Freud, 1946). But while Klein saw underlying symbolic meanings in virtually all play, Anna Freud believed that instead of a particular play activity being invested with symbolic meaning, there may be a simple, harmless explanation. For example, the child who shuts a bag or purse tightly is not necessarily symbolically shutting up her mother's womb to ensure she will have no new brothers or sisters, but may merely be playing out some previous experience with such objects.

Unlike Klein, who followed the procedures of adult analysis strictly, Anna Freud sought to develop positive emotional relationships and positive transference from the child to the therapist and to avoid negative relationships and negative transference. She believed that a child will only believe a loved person. Negative impulses or transference toward the therapist should be dealt with promptly, for the really fruitful work takes place in the context of positive attachments and transference.

In spite of the difficulties in child therapy, Anna Freud identified several advantages of child therapy over adult therapy. The neuroses of the child must be traced only a short distance in time to arrive at normal behavior; in child therapy one deals with living, usually accessible people; and the child's needs are simpler and easier to fulfill or oversee, because the therapist can deal with the child's actual environment rather than relying on an adult's memories of times long past.

Anna Freud extended her knowledge of play therapy by observing children's play and interviewing their parents. She used play and art to form alliances with children, then proceeded to interpret the child's unconscious motivations. Having developed positive emotional relations with a child (the "wooing period"), she encouraged the child to verbalize fantasies and daydreams or to sit quietly and "see pictures." She also pioneered storytelling in the therapeutic setting. As the child verbalized, she helped her understand her feelings, and the emphasis shifted from play to verbal interaction.

Structured Play Therapy

Several **structured play therapy** approaches grew out of the psychoanalytic school. The basic tenets of psychotherapy were retained, but major differences in therapeutic procedures emerged. In general, the structuralists assumed the major role in therapy, believing that the therapist is more aware than the child of the child's needs. Consequently, the therapist designs the activity, selects the medium, and makes the rules.

David Levy

During the 1930s, David Levy (1939) formulated **release therapy,** a structured approach for children ages 2 to 10. In release therapy Levy determined the cause of a child's difficulty by studying his case history, then controlled the play by providing selected toys expected to assist in working out the child's problem. If, for example, the child was experiencing nightmares or night terrors about monsters, the therapist provided toy monsters for play. The therapist then asks questions about the child's feelings and thoughts and observes the child's verbal and nonverbal behaviors during play. At times the therapist plays with the child or even models play for the child.

Three forms of release therapy were developed: (a) release of aggressive behaviors by throwing objects or bursting balloons; (b) release of feelings in a common setting that would simulate sibling rivalry, such as presenting a baby doll at a mother's breast; and (c) release of feelings by presenting in play the child's stressful experiences.

An example of Levy's release therapy is the case of a 2-year-old girl who suffered from night terrors resulting from a fish merchant holding her up to see a fish in his display. A clay fish was introduced during therapy, and the therapist asked the child why she was afraid of the fish. The child replied that the fish would go "in here," pointing to her eye, ears, and vagina. The fish was introduced in various parts of a 10-session play therapy experience in which the chief process was facilitating the child's own types of play. Fear of the fish left after the third or fourth session, and improvement was judged to be maintained 7 months later (Levy, 1939, p. 720).

Gove Hambridge

Structured play therapy was further developed by Gove Hambridge (1955). He developed a thorough history of the child from parents and observations of the child at play, developed hypotheses about the sources of her stress, then recreated the stressful situation through dramatic play. He disapproved of the common practice of "flooding" or pushing the child to release strong, massive negative feelings. Rather, he started slowly with less threatening materials and progressed to more threatening materials. He stressed that parents should be assisted in learning to help structure the child's recovery process.

Hambridge advocated the development of strong, positive supportive relationships between the therapist and the child. He identified repetition as the most important factor in structured or release therapy. Repetition of a stressful event allows release of tension and assists the child in assimilating and mastering stressful feelings and experiences. This basic repetition, **catharsis,** or "emotional purging" approach was not unique to 20th-century therapists, but was discovered by Josef Breuer over a century ago when found to be effective with mental patients (Schaefer, 1985, p. 100). A major advantage of release therapy is that it increases specificity of treatment, saving hours of time by avoiding diffuse and haphazard therapy (Schaefer, 1985).

Nondirective Therapy

Carl Rogers

The work of **relationship therapists** (Allen, 1942; Taft, 1933) was synthesized and expanded by Carl Rogers (1942) as **nondirective therapy,** later called **client-centered therapy** (Rogers, 1951). Rogers's and Virginia Axline's works were influential in modifying relationship play therapy (Moustakas, 1953) and establishing group play therapy (Ginott, 1961) and **child-centered play therapy** (Landreth, 1991; Moustakas, 1953).

According to Rogers (1951), therapy is "a process, a thing-in-itself, an experience, a relationship, a dynamic . . . therapy is the essence of life" (pp. ix, x). Such descriptive conceptual underpinnings are light-years apart from the structured conceptions of psychoanalysis and place virtually unlimited faith in the striving of all individuals to seek **self-actualization** or self-fulfillment—to become the best they can become (Rogers, 1962). The emphasis is on the well person rather than the sick person.

Rogers broke with the tradition of promoting therapy primarily for adults and adolescents. He recognized that Axline's play therapy for problem children was effective and that client-centered play therapy was appropriate for a wide variety of people, problems, and contexts, including the military, industry, and schools.

According to Rogers, the client-centered therapist should give up subtle directiveness and concentrate on understanding the client. If the therapist can help the client understand the way the client seems to himself, he can do the rest. The therapist must give up his preoccupations with professional evaluations, diagnoses, and prognoses and concentrate on one purpose: help the client understand and accept conscious attitudes held at that moment while exploring the dangerous areas denied to consciousness.

The setting for therapy must be one of safety and acceptance in which the client is free to explore without guilt the hostile meanings and purposes of his behavior. The client is able to do this because another person, the therapist, has adopted his frame of reference and perceives his problems with acceptance and respect. The client must come to be loved—that is, deeply understood and accepted. Such outcomes do not depend merely on verbal exchange but on the experiences in the relationship. Unlike psychotherapists, Rogers contended that transference attitudes of the client toward the counselor occur only in a small percentage of cases. In most cases, attitudes toward the counselor reflect reality rather than the unconscious.

Virginia Axline

Virginia Axline (1947b) studied with Carl Rogers and worked with him in exploring the possibilities of nondirective therapy. She based her nondirective counseling technique on Rogers's work, proposing, as he had, that therapy principles for adults (e.g., the individual's striving for growth and self-realization) could be applied to play therapy for children (p. 27). She believed that "[a] play experience is therapeutic because it provides a secure relationship between the child and the adult, so that the child has the freedom and room to state himself in his own terms, exactly as he is at that moment in his own way and in his own time" (p. 68). The child expresses herself naturally through play, and a child "playing out" during therapy is equivalent to the adult's "talking out" (p. 9). The relatively immature child may not have the words, as do adults, for expressing her deeper conscious or unconscious conflicts. Such expression is possible, however, through play.

Axline's nondirective therapy is based on the assumption that the individual has within herself the ability to solve her own problems and the drive to mature behavior. The therapist must accept the child completely, without pressure to change, to be herself and to chart her own course. Play allows the child to play out accumulated feelings of anxiety, aggression, frustration, and fear. By so doing, she learns to abandon or control such impulses, to make her own decisions, and to become more mature.

The therapist must see the child as the most important person in the therapeutic process. There are no diagnostic interviews and few interpretations. There is no criticism, nagging, directing, or prying into the child's private world. The past is history. The child is allowed to express herself fully. The therapist is sensitive to the child's feelings and reflects them back to her in a way that aids understanding. The therapist conveys the attitude that she is understanding and accepting of her at all times. Consequently, the child digs deeper into her inner world to bring out her real self and begins to direct her own growth. She is psychologically free.

Relationship and Child-Centered Play Therapy

The field of play therapy grew dramatically over the 20th century, and the sheer number of contributors and approaches defies discussing each within the scope of this work (see Table 10–1). Presently, every approach previously discussed—psychoanalysis, structured, nondirective, client centered—and more are alive at the beginning of the 21st century and practiced in a wide range of contexts. The approach chosen for elaboration here is nondirective, or child-centered, play therapy as developed by Rogers (1942, 1951), Axline (1950), Moustakas (1953), Ginott (1961), and Landreth (1991).

Among these authorities on nondirective therapy, all devoted to child-centeredness in the

TABLE 10–1 Approaches to Play Therapy

Approaches	Techniques	Contexts
Psychoanalytic	Puppets	Playrooms
Release	Sand play	Hospitals
Relationship	Costume play	Schools
Nondirective	Board games	Psychiatric settings
Filial	Storytelling	University laboratories
Group	Water play	Homes
Structured	Block play	
Child centered	Role play	
Ecosystem	Telephone play	
Existential	Mud and clay	
Gestalt	Drawing	
Developmental	Painting	
Jungian	Squiggle drawing	
Adlerian	Computer play	
Cognitive-behavioral		
Cognitive-developmental		
Theraplay		
Eclectic		

therapeutic process, certain commonalities and differences in theoretical premises and therapy practices are evident. Each theorist borrowed heavily from other prominent theorists and modified his or her views through extensive practice. The theoretical constructs of Rogers were decidedly influential in subsequent child-centered approaches. He, more than any therapist in the group, is responsible for shifting the focus of therapy from the therapist to the client and highlighting the self-worth of the individual. His nondirective counseling is more a philosophy of human capacities than a set of techniques. The power for growth lies within the client.

Axline offered perhaps the clearest, simplest, yet most profound approach to play therapy with children. Her techniques of play therapy were built from Rogers's principles of self-realization and self-direction. Collectively, Rogers and Axline are preeminent in shifting focus from the therapist to the child.

Haim Ginott (1961), Clark Moustakas (1953), and Garry Landreth (1991) were influenced by Rogers and Axline and were also principal figures in establishing contemporary nondirective or child-centered play therapy.

Ginott gave credit to his "great teacher" Virginia Axline in combining relationship principles with psychotherapy to show that group therapy as well as individual therapy can benefit children and that no one method is effective with all persons. Moustakas (1953, 1998) became interested in play therapy from reading the works of Rogers and Axline. He is credited with framing major portions of the theory and technique used in modern play therapy (James, 1997, p. 140). Landreth was influenced by the work of Axline, Ginott, and Moustakas as well as that of Rogers. Yet he gradually strengthened the theoretical and research bases for his approach and made it uniquely his own. By the turn of the 21st century, the Center for Play Therapy Landreth developed at the University of North Texas was the largest such center in the world, including programs for training master's and doctoral students and housing classroom facilities for workshops and seminars, an extensive collection of play therapy materials (Landreth, Homeyer, Bratton, & Kale, 1995), and playrooms for therapy sessions with children.

CONDUCTING PLAY THERAPY

Setting Up the Playroom

The child-centered play therapist works from the position that play is the language of the child and toys are the child's words. The **playroom** is a special place used for one specific purpose—play therapy—and it is carefully arranged with toys or play materials to accommodate a range of children's play. Different therapists have different views about which play materials to provide and why they are important. Consequently, playrooms differ according to the theoretical views of the therapist and the nature of the child's needs. Special arrangements may be needed for children who are abused, hospitalized, or blind or who have other types of disabilities. The play materials need not be manufactured or expensive, for children can use simple raw materials to represent almost anything. Children's symbolic powers are usually quite remarkable.

Generally, for a given child, the playroom should always be the same when she enters. It should be carefully planned, prepared, cleaned, organized, restocked with disposable materials, and predictable after the first visit. The size of the room will vary with availability in different settings, but typically the desired size is about 12 to 14 feet by 14 to 16 feet, or about 150 to 250 square feet. While specially designed playrooms are desirable, effective therapy can be conducted in a child's hospital room, using play materials carried in by the therapist, or in an equipped section of an unused room (e.g., office, classroom, workroom).

Materials, too, differ with the views of the therapist. Typical materials and arrangement include a sink with cold water; a child-sized bathroom opening to the therapy room; cabinets, counter (child-sized), and shelves for storing materials; clear plastic containers for toys; a child-sized table and chairs; dress-up clothes;

multiethnic dolls; a doctor's bag; one or more doll- or playhouses; playhouse materials; building blocks; clay; toy animals; toy soldiers and army equipment; a dart gun that shoots (safe) rubber darts and a target; rubber knife; small cars, trucks, and airplanes; a sandbox with sand tools; finger paints and other art materials; puppets and a stage; a broom and mop; and a table and easel with drawing and painting supplies. For conducting research and observation, parent viewing, or videotaping for training programs, an observation room with one-way mirror and remote speakers are needed. The room should be well lit, safe, and easily cleaned.

Ginott (1961) groups the desired materials for a playroom, with each category containing multiple play materials: climbing equipment, dollhouse, toy animals, transportation toys, water play, easel painting and water coloring, finger painting, clay play, block play, puppets, aggressive toys, housekeeping equipment, and sand. Landreth (1991) includes toys not mentioned earlier: a pacifier and plastic nursing bottle; pots, pans, and dishes; an all-terrain vehicle for riding; a pounding bench and hammer; musical instruments; a "Bobo bag" (stuffed bag) for hitting; handcuffs; a toy machine gun; blunt scissors; construction paper; and tinker toys.

Play materials should be age- or developmentally appropriate and usable in independent or solitary play. Landreth (1991, p. 116) suggests several criteria for selection. Toys and play materials should engage the child's interest; facilitate creative expression, emotional expression, and exploratory play; allow success without prescribed structure and verbalization; allow for noncommittal play; and be sturdily constructed. In addition, the materials and the child-therapist relationship should remain stable (Moustakas, 1953). That is, the playthings should always be arranged the same way when the child enters the room, and the therapist's attitudes must remain consistent. In the playroom, the child is the guide. She makes the changes.

Beginning Play Therapy

Axline's eight basic play principles (1947b) underlie modern child-centered play therapy and are perhaps the best known and most frequently referenced. They follow in revised form:

- The therapist quickly establishes a warm, friendly relationship.
- The therapist accepts the child exactly as she is.
- The therapist creates a permissive relationship in which the child is free to express her feelings completely.
- The therapist recognizes and reflects back the child's feelings to help her understand her behavior.
- The therapist respects the child's ability to solve her own problems. Responsibility for decisions and change is left to the child.
- The therapist does not attempt to direct the child's actions or conversation. The child leads the way; the therapist follows.
- The therapist does not attempt to hurry therapy. It is a gradual process.
- The therapist sets only the limitations necessary to help the child accept responsibility in the relationship.

Although individual therapists have unique approaches, Axline's basic principles remain the primary guides for child-centered play therapy. Her 1964 book *Dibs in Search of Self* is a detailed account of her methods.

The initial contact with the child is of great importance to the success of therapy. Rapport and structure must be established. This is done through words and through building relationships between the child and the therapist.

Establishing Rapport

The playroom is established, the therapist is on hand, and the child arrives. The initial contact is a time for communicating warmth and friendliness. The therapist greets the child, showing a genuine interest in him. He is the most important person in the room. After the warmup, the therapist invites the child to go to the playroom with her and see all the toys. During this time, the therapist must accept the child exactly as he is, and her language should reflect the child's feelings (Axline, 1947b, pp. 77–78). This is not a time to be dominated by the parent relating the child's history and the therapist directing her attention to the mother. This is the child's time.

Following a brief introduction, the therapist says to the child, "We can go to the playroom now. Your mother will wait here so she will be here when we come back from the playroom" (Landreth, 1991, p. 159). "It is especially important at this time that the child himself decides whether or not he wishes to come to the playroom. Whatever decision the child makes is accepted by the therapist" (Moustakas, 1953, p. 13). Although most children readily go to the playroom, if the child is reluctant, the mother may be invited to walk to the playroom with them and separate at the door or as soon into the session as the therapist judges appropriate.

Structuring the Playroom Experience

Structuring is the process therapists use to convey to the child the special nature of the therapeutic relationship. The child and the therapist enter the playroom, and the therapist structures the situation verbally:

> "You may play with any of the toys in here any way that you want to, Jean. There are paints, clay, finger paints, puppets" (Axline, 1947b, p. 88).

Moustakas (1953) structures the experience this way:

> "You may use these [toys] in any way that you want," "It can be anything you want it to be," "I can't decide that for you; the important thing is that you decide for yourself what you want to do," "You want me to do that for you Janey, but here you do things for yourself" (p. 14).

Landreth (1991, p.162) points out that there are boundaries on freedom in the playroom and the therapist should not communicate that the child can play "any way you want." This could result in withdrawal of approval for play (e.g., being hit with a toy or shot with a dart gun) that threatens the safety of the child or the therapist. He suggests instead saying, for example, "Melissa, this is our playroom, and this is a place where you can play with the toys in a lot of the ways you would like to."

As soon as the child is introduced to the playroom, the therapist sits in a chair (with rollers to facilitate movement) and directs her full attention to the child. The whole body is oriented toward the child as the therapist conveys interest, involvement, and total absorption in the child (see the videotape by Landreth, 1998).

The Playroom Relationship

Following the initial steps of establishing rapport, introducing the child to the playroom, and structuring the relationship, several additional factors influence success in the playroom relationship: (a) accepting the child as she is; (b) making the child safe and comfortable; (c) establishing permissiveness within limits; (d) recognizing and reflecting the child's feelings; (e) maintaining a listening/supportive attitude; (f) facilitating emotional expression; (g) facilitating decision making, responsibility, and control. The overall behaviors and language of the therapist convey these principles of freedom, respect, and responsibility.

The **therapy hour** (often 45 minutes) is a time for children to use the materials in the playroom as they wish, within limits. As the child initially explores the materials in the playroom, the therapist conveys permissiveness and support through her whole being—tone of voice, facial expressions, and actions. The child is given the freedom to play or not to play, to select play materials and to choose how she will play. Even silence is respected. For the reluctant child, the therapist might say, "It's sort of hard to get started. You don't know just what you would like to do. Or maybe you would rather just sit here and not do anything?" (Axline, 1947b, p. 93).

Pressuring the child to talk or play ignores his feelings, removes a degree of freedom, and obviates his role in making decisions. Every behavior, even reluctance to talk or to play, says something about the child.

Therapy cannot be hurried. Taking time for the child to feel comfortable with the playroom and the therapist helps reduce anxiety and allows the child to feel comfortable and supported.

Angela:	(stands right in front of therapist, twisting hands, looking at therapist, and then looks at toys on shelf)
Therapist:	I see you're looking at the toys over there. (pause)
Angela:	(looks at observation mirror, sees herself and grins)
Therapist:	And you saw yourself in the mirror there. (pause) I guess sometimes, maybe . . . it's just hard to decide what to do first (pause) (Landreth, 1991, p. 166).

In a similar manner, the therapist continues to respond to the child's actions in a friendly, accepting, and supporting way. Eventually, emotional barriers come down, and the child begins to communicate verbally with the therapist, explore the playroom, and play. The therapist must remember that the child's behavior at any given time is symbolic of the child's feelings. When the child feels safe and secure with the therapist and the playroom, she may begin to express and explore, through play, emotionally or physically traumatic experiences. Play itself, not the therapist, is the primary therapeutic vehicle. The therapist is a facilitator.

Establishing Limits

Important as freedom is, limits are necessary for learning decision making, self control, and responsibility. Most prominent play therapists (Axline, 1947b; Bixler, 1949; Ginott, 1961; Glasser, 1975; James, 1997; Klein, 1955; Kottman, 2001, 2003; Landreth, 1991; Moustakas, 1953; O'Connor, 1991, 2000) advocate **establishing limits.** Some advocate more clearly defined restrictions than others, but all see limits as essential to the therapeutic process and to learning to act responsibly.

No one is truly free without certain limitations. However, limits should be accompanied by trust and confidence. James (1997, p. 22) explains: Her 7-year-old son, Hunt, was at a friend's house for a sleepover. A tree branch scratching against a window frightened his young friend, and Hunt explained, "in our house, you don't ever have to be afraid. Even if a lion comes to the door, my mom would stop it." Such trust helps the child cope with scary situations.

Confidence in the therapist and the safety of the playroom is established by the limits that protect the sanctity of the playroom and make it safe. Limits are established as the need arises and are designed to:

1. Enhance the child's feeling of security;
2. Prevent the destruction or loss of property;
3. Protect the physical safety of the child and the therapist;
4. Promote consistent behavior;
5. Facilitate the development of self-control, responsibility, and decision making;
6. Prevent harm to the child;
7. Establish time parameters for the therapy session;
8. Define the boundaries of the therapy relationship; and
9. Establish both psychological and physical limits.

Limits help form secure relationships and link them to reality. The therapist must attend to certain basic principles (limitations) in therapeutic practice to establish rapport and support the child's development. Similarly, the child needs limits to guide her emotional growth and to ensure her physical safety. Reasonable limits are essential for healthy growth. Possible alternatives are guilt, anxiety, irresponsibility, barriers in relationships, and threatened health and safety.

Progress in Play Therapy

The therapist has prepared the playroom and materials; the relationship between the child and the therapist has been initiated; the child has been introduced to the playroom; the relationship in the playroom has been structured; limitations are being established. The therapist and child settle in for a series of playroom interactions that gradually free the child to sort out negative feelings, to feel safe, to accept herself as a person of worth, to learn to trust the therapist, and to establish a caring, respectful, and responsible relationship. The successful therapeutic process results in growth in the child, the therapist, and the relationship.

The stages in child-centered (nondirective) play therapy differ from those in psychoanalytic and directive therapy. In these more structured approaches, greater emphasis is given to history and diagnosis, observation and analysis of children's conflicts, and various stages of interpretation from indirect to direct (James, 1997). Toys and stories may be used initially to help the child interpret meanings and incorporate them into her consciousness. Later stages involve interpretive comments made directly to the child.

In nondirective therapy, toys are used to develop the relationship between child and therapist and to allow the child to "play out" her fears and conflicts. There is no pattern of diagnosis or tracing the origins of the child's phobias or conflicts. The successful conclusion of therapy is the child gaining confidence to "go ahead on [her] own" and to be comfortable in expressing her feelings openly and honestly (Axline, 1947b).

The success of play therapy is directly related to the degree to which the therapist is able to establish an atmosphere of safety and acceptance in the child's mind. The learning is not so much cognitive as it is a "developing experiential, intuitive learning about self that occurs over the course of the therapeutic experience" (Landreth, 1991, p. 82). Landreth identifies expected outcomes of the therapeutic experience: Children learn self-control, responsible freedom of expression, respect for self, ability to control their feelings, responsibility for self, creativity and resourcefulness in confronting problems, self-direction, acceptance of self, and responsibility for their choices.

The climate created by the therapist and the unconditional acceptance and support provided by the therapist make these changes possible. They are primarily accomplished within the child, by the child, and are not dependent on analysis or instruction. Child-centered play therapy is an experience to be lived, not a set of principles to be taught and learned.

SETTINGS AND APPLICATIONS

Our focus has been on play therapy in a prepared playroom with one therapist and one child. However, play therapy can be used effectively in many other settings and applications. Only a selected few are discussed here.

Group Play Therapy

Group play therapy is growing in popularity. Ginott's (1961) book, *Group Psychotherapy with Children: The Theory and Practice of Play Therapy,* is the most extensive reference on the topic and remains an important guide for therapists. The basic concepts in Ginott's group approach were derived from psychoanalytical theory. He believed that group therapy applied equally well to individual therapy, and his procedures were applicable to the needs of individual children.

Initially, the presence of two or three other children of her age group may help allay a child's anxiety about going to the play therapy room with an adult therapist. In the group playroom, the individual child may gain comfort in identifying with other children. There are no group goals. Each child has the freedom to engage in individual or group play experiences, and there are two media for catharsis: play and verbalization. Each child

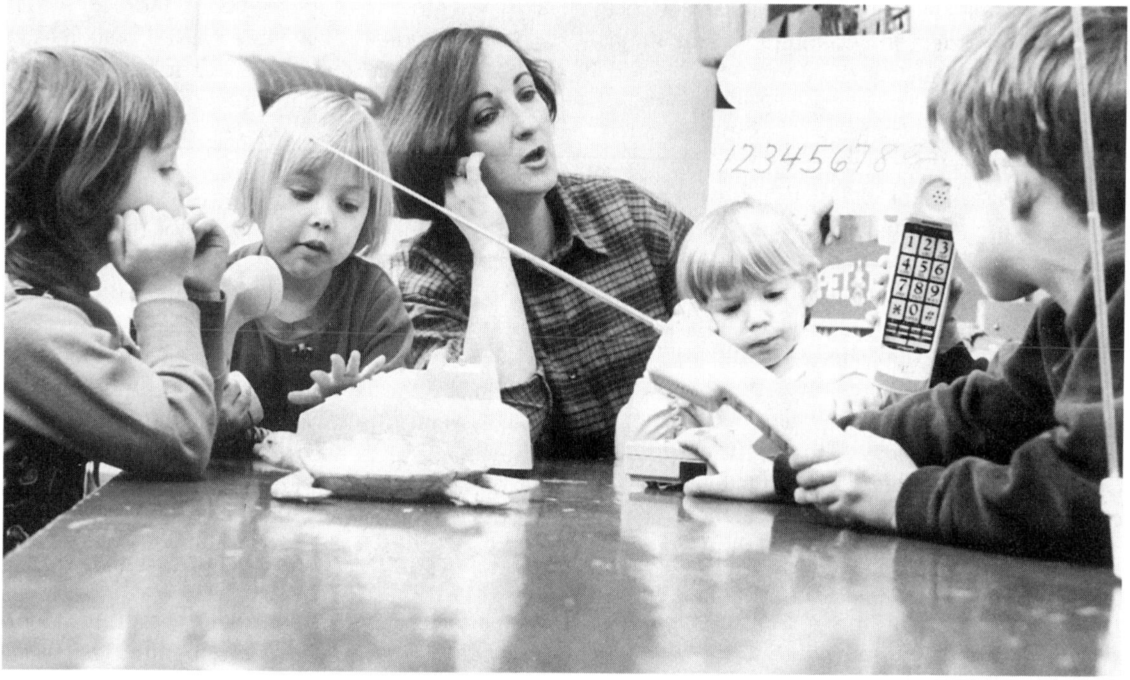

Play therapy may be conducted with individuals or with groups.

learns from the other children and from both giving and receiving. Ginott (1961) illustrates:

> Barbara, age eight, had not seen her father in two years. She missed him keenly. During one of the therapy sessions, while handling a gun, she hurt her finger. It was a minor injury, but she reacted with much emotion. She cried bitterly and pleaded with the therapist.
>
> *Barbara:* Please let me go. My finger hurts, and I need my mother.
>
> *Therapist:* It's not only your finger that hurts. Something hurts inside.
>
> *Barbara:* Yes.
>
> *Therapist:* You miss your Daddy.
>
> *Barbara:* My Daddy went away and I don't have a Daddy. He never comes home, and I need my Daddy.
>
> Barbara stood close to the therapist and cried.
>
> Shirley, age 9, came over, put her arm around Barbara and said: "I don't have a Daddy either. My parents are divorced, and my father is far away in California."
>
> The two girls stood close to each other, sharing their common sorrow. (p. 6)

A number of specialists have raised concerns about the appropriate focus in group play therapy. Ginott (1961) believed, "The focus of treatment in group play therapy is always the individual child. No group goals are set and no group cohesion is looked for" (p. 5). Later writers had different views, maintaining that to fully comprehend the nature of child group therapy, is necessary to clarify the constructs of **group dynamics** (Hansen & Cramer, 1971). Dies and Riester (1986) conducted a comprehensive review of research and concluded that researchers had yet to identify specific mechanisms of group dynamics or mechanisms of change explaining the contributions of group therapy to children's progress.

Researchers and practitioners continue to seek answers to concerns about criteria for selecting or rejecting children for group therapy (Brady, 1991; Celano, 1990; Schaefer, Johnson, & Wherry, 1982). Some favor homogeneous grouping (similar areas of dysfunctionality); others favor heterogeneous grouping (different personalities, different symptoms).

Interdisciplinary Teams

Interdisciplinary teams work together in school and hospital settings to assist with behavior problems and learning disabilities. In schools, the team may consist of a parent, teacher, play therapist, nurse, and remedial personnel. In hospitals, nurses, doctors, play therapists, and diagnosticians are team members. Collectively, such teams make plans for the child's total learning environment and experiences. In schools, the play therapist receives and contributes information about the child's total developmental needs and makes recommendations for enhancing emotional, social, and academic progress. Learning disabilities affect the **whole child.**

In hospitals, the team members work to make the initial hospital experience positive and as comfortable as possible. They understand that play assists recovery from illness or injury, not only emotionally but also physically. The return to normal play following a traumatic experience is a primary marker for such progress.

Filial Therapy

As focus in the therapeutic profession shifted from intrapsychic concerns (e.g., psychoanalysis) to sociocultural concerns, a number of approaches emerged that involved parents in their children's play therapy. Including children in family therapy allows the clinicians to work from observed patterns of communication, roles, and coalitions rather than working from assumptions based on self-reports of a few individuals (Sweeney & Rocha, 1999).

Louise Guerney (1964) developed a model of **filial therapy** for training parents to conduct weekly home play therapy sessions with their children (Andronico, Fidler, Guerney, & Guerney, 1967). This model substitutes a trained parent for the traditional therapist. During parent training sessions, the parents may observe or join the sessions. Observing, sometimes with interpretations by the therapist, helps the parent understand what their children are doing. Parent participation may be highly structured, with the therapist assigning parents tasks to accomplish with the child. Common outcomes of this approach are both changed behavior of the child and changed parental perceptions of the child.

Filial therapy sessions may be supplemented with a "special time" (O'Connor, 1991) that gives the child 15 to 20 minutes of daily contact with parents. During this time, the parent focuses exclusively on the child's needs without waiting for the child to display symptoms. Getting the parent's attention and gaining a sense of control make these sessions valuable for the structured therapy sessions and help develop understanding and rapport between parent and child.

Yet another approach, **theraplay** (Jernberg, 1979), uses structured play for problem families. The delicate interplay of the early bonding ritual between mother and child form the basis for theraplay. The therapy is purposefully physical, sensorimotor play intended to engage the senses and to replicate earlier child-parent bonding rituals. With roots in psychoanalysis, developmental psychology, and nursery school practice, the theraplay process is a mix of empathy and adult authority with the goal of treating troubled children and reducing mental illness.

The principles underlying theraplay rely on the basics of bonding between mother and infant. What does a normal mother do for her baby, and how does the baby respond? The normal actions of the mother—singing, whispering, playing, rocking, washing, rubbing, nuzzling, and protecting—and those of the infant—cooing, imitating, gurgling, staring, and smiling—are essential to the bonding process. Jernberg (1979) groups these reciprocal nurturing and responding behaviors into **structuring, challenging, intruding,** and **nurturing** interactions—all in the context of empathy, authority, and fun. Those deprived of such behaviors may well grow up incapable of bonding with their own babies or forming healthy love relations (Stringer, 1971). Prescott (cited in Hoover, 1976) links such childhood deficits to later violence and drug abuse, and Jernberg (1979) stresses, "Since abusing parents generally are under stress, were never properly parented, are friendless and isolated, and are depressed, dependent, deprived, and need care as much as their children do, Theraplay is often indicated" (p. 32).

Different theraplay techniques are needed because children differ in developmental levels, temperament, and pathology or disturbances. The overactive, aggressive tough guy who disregards boundaries may need limits and firm organization (structure). The little boy with a macho swagger may need soft cuddling and gentle play (nurture). The shy, withdrawn child who has sealed out the world may need invigorating, exciting play (intrusion). He needs to know that he can do better (challenge) (1979, pp. 22–23). Theraplay may need to be modified or another form of therapy chosen for certain cases among sociopathic children, traumatized children, fragile children, and abused children.

Theraplay is used in individual, group, and family therapy. In individual therapy, the child enters a virtually bare room, and play materials are brought in to bolster planned activities. Sessions are designed to be fun, action oriented, and therapist directed. Group theraplay is based on the same principles and assumptions as individual theraplay but is structured for children having difficulty relating to peers. Jernberg believes that the most effective theraplay is that which simultaneously treats the child and her parents. The treatment is enhanced by training all adults who interact with the child on a regular basis—mother, father, grandparents, teacher, principal, and classroom aides.

Hospital Play Therapy

Children often react to medical visits or hospitalization with fear and stress because they are in a strange place where invasive procedures are

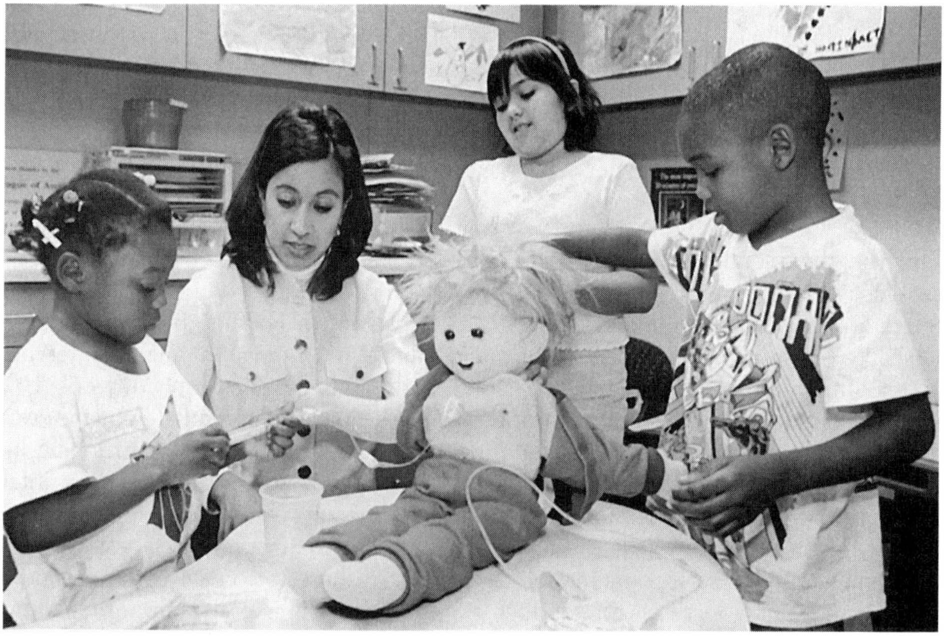

Medical play is used in the outpatient Cancer and Blood Disorder Center.

Source: Photo courtesy of Children's Hospital, Austin, Texas.

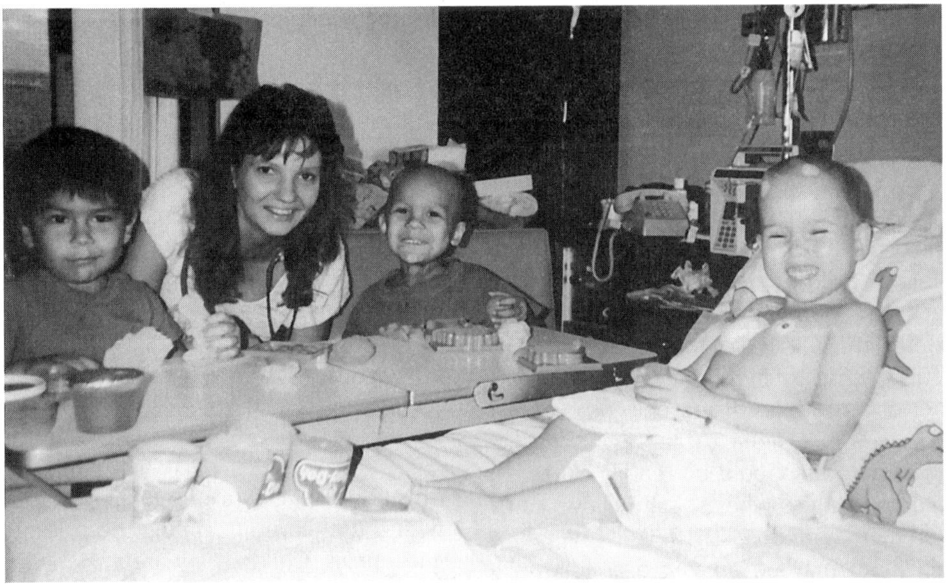

Child life professionals sometimes take play materials directly into children's hospital rooms.
Source: Photo courtesy of Children's Hospital, Austin, Texas.

common. Their perceptions are distorted due to their immature reasoning and active imaginations. Confused by their fantasies, perhaps linked to viewing medical and horror programs on TV and lacking accurate information, they may view medical procedures as punitive and threatening. For example, 5-year-old Kent has been told by his doctor that he will have to have an operation on his stomach to make him well. No one has told Kent that he will be asleep during the operation or that the hole in his stomach will be sewn up after the surgery. Kent believes that he will feel pain during the operation and that all the "things" inside him will fall out (Jessee, 1991, p. 23).

Professionals need not wait until the child is hospitalized to help them cope with impending stays. Teachers can employ simple therapy practices with children during classroom play (Jessee, et al., 2000) by talking with the child about her fears, providing medical play props, reinforcing the child's accurate perceptions, and gently guiding the child to explore medical events through play.

Following World War II, the medical profession's focus shifted from disease-oriented to patient-oriented pediatric care, and the Association for the Care of Children's Health (ACCH) developed the Child Life Program. The intent of ACCH was to minimize stress and anxiety and promote self-esteem and independence for children and adolescents facing medical care. The American Academy of Pediatrics and the Accreditation Council for Graduate Medical Education acknowledge the importance of child life programs and promote the thorough preparation of medical professionals, including child life specialists (Thompson, 1990).

Child life specialists are trained in child development, counseling, education, and family studies. They help children cope with the stress and anxiety of hospital experiences both in the hospital and after returning home (Jessee, 1991). Their work includes the following:

- Preparing children for hospitalization and medical procedures.
- Providing guidance and materials for play.

- Advocating the child's point of view with medical personnel.
- Providing emotional support to parents and siblings.
- Maintaining a positive, receptive environment for children and their families. (Thompson & Stanford, 1981)

Hospitalized children need space to play in a natural, active way and appropriate materials for their play. This may be in a playroom exclusively for that purpose, or it may be a designated area in a corner of a room, end of a hall, or even a covered outdoor play area (Azarnoff & Flegal, 1975). The playroom should be readily accessible to children so those whose health allows can go there on their own (Brooks, 1970).

The playroom may be organized as follows:

- A large central activity table, offering structured play such as handcrafts.
- A sink and work counter for painting and clay play.
- Interest centers such as block corner and housekeeping center for construction and make-believe.
- A medical center with real instruments, doctor bags, and expendable supplies such as tape, bandages, face masks, tongue blades, and stethoscope.
- A convenient storage area with puppets, cloth dolls and animals, medical supplies, and other materials. (Azarnoff & Flegal, 1975)

Therapists sometimes take materials for play therapy directly to children confined in hospital rooms. When choosing materials, the therapist must consider the physical limitations of the child, possible physical harm to the child, and possible damage to medical equipment in the room. A nondirective or child-centered relationship is appropriate, allowing the child to take the lead. The therapist must avoid overwhelming the child with too many play materials and must be alert to avoid overtiring the child. James (1997, p. 95) includes the following materials when planning a hospital room session:

- Small paint pots, brushes, and bed easel
- Puppets and dolls, including nurses, parents, children, and doctors
- Doctor bag stocked with medical toys
- Clay when appropriate
- Small animals
- Folding dollhouse
- Bed tray for small toy play
- Sand tray with lid and small objects
- Books

Medical play is a frequent playroom activity, with the children assuming the roles of doctors and nurses. Children release anxieties and emotions by "treating" one another, sometimes evidenced by violent, relentless shot giving. This play communicates their perceptions, often inaccurate, of examinations and treatments and gives the therapist opportunities to offer accurate, age-appropriate information. The therapist may use doctor play with dolls to model step-by-step procedures for the child to imitate.

Radically differing needs of hospitalized children require different approaches. Short-term stays may require structured or guided play to prepare children for medical treatment, while nonstructured approaches may require extended time for working through feelings and conflicts. A panel of child life experts (Kingson, 1996) concluded that changing health care patterns keep only severely ill or injured children hospitalized for long periods, while less severely ill children are not admitted or dismissed early. This pattern results in the need for highly trained specialists to help children master health care encounters through focused interactions with children and their families. Playroom management, the expert panel maintained, should be delegated to less-trained child life staff and volunteers.

Definitive research on these conclusions is lacking. Jernberg (1979) maintains that highly structured activities with medical objects and concepts may have negative consequences, especially with younger children. This risk may be accentuated when poorly trained or unfamiliar adults engage children in **medical play.** The impact of the total combination of structured and nonstructured episodes may be more critical than any single episode. If medical play is only one of many forms of play, and if there is a variety of structured and unstructured activities, the impact is likely to be different than for exclusively structured or nonexpressive activities (Bolig, Yolton, & Nissen, 1991).

Preschools and Elementary Schools

Among professional groups, play therapy typically refers to play intended to accomplish specific therapeutic outcomes. However, play at any level may be therapeutic in many ways, including improvement in play skills, interpersonal skills, self-confidence, and reduction of stress. The basic principles of play therapy can be adapted by parents, child caretakers, and teachers. Adults who deal with children see a growing array of conflict and stress factors (violence, abuse, physical and emotional disabilities) that far exceed those seen as recently as the 1960s. Children can be assisted in playing out their feelings and phobias in drama, music, storytelling, water play, drawing, painting, clay, puppets, and spontaneous play, both indoors and outdoors. Researchers are even exploring the possible applications of computer play in therapy (Johnson, 1993). Play therapy and its emulation by semiskilled parents, caretakers, and teachers are more than just messing around.

Just as the mental health of teachers is linked to the relationship established with administrators and coworkers, the relationship between the child and the teacher is essential for the child's mental health. Furthermore, good mental health is essential for learning. The teacher should establish rich environments for play, model skills, and help children clarify and deal with fears and disturbing feelings. The teacher should create conditions for enhancing self-reliance, decision making, and initiative, with a focus on preventing problems.

Techniques used in play therapy are effective in helping children settle disputes and improve social behavior and, consequently, reduce discipline problems. Rather than assume a strict authority role, the teacher can use reflective listening, feedback children's feelings and ideas, and reflect a consistent code of values. He can treat the child with respect and honesty and create a warm, friendly climate for living and learning. In so doing, the mental health of the teacher himself can be improved.

East Carolina University developed a model based on Landreth's work for training preschool teachers to use play therapy techniques in their classrooms (Clark, 1995). The model, based on Landreth's (1991) principles, includes the following elements:

- Emotional sharing of feelings
- Being attentive but letting children make decisions
- Basing responses on careful observation
- Allowing children to take the lead
- Making therapeutic responses brief and interactive
- Returning responsibility to the child
- Avoiding interrupting the natural flow of play
- Focusing on the child's efforts rather than the product

Links to Creativity

Even among practicing play therapists, the positive effects of play therapy on creativity are largely unexplored. Yet the linkages are everywhere. Consider the settings in which play therapy is conducted. They include specially prepared rooms stocked with a wide variety of creative materials: dolls, puppets, paints, water, sand, musical instruments, building materials, blocks, tinker toys, and clay. The play bags carried into hospital rooms by therapists contain an assortment of creative materials. Even the techniques or applications of therapy reflect engagement in creative activity—puppet therapy, sand play therapy, storytelling therapy, role play therapy, art therapy, squiggle-drawing therapy, and telephone play therapy.

Indeed, the child's creative impulse may be at the roots of successful play therapy. It is essentially influences from adults and the outside world that stifle the child's natural expression, creating phobias and disturbances that result in the need for play therapy. Lowenfeld (1947) seemed to understand that children's creative impulses can be defeated but can be rekindled.

> [T]he child's creative expression during specific stages of his mental and emotional growth can only be understood and appreciated if the general causal interdependence between creation and growth is understood. . .what civilization has buried we must try to regain by recreating the natural base necessary for such free creation (Lowenfeld, 1947, pp. vi, l).

Play therapy may be considered as a necessary antidote for outside interference with the child's natural growth. We still find creative confidence in remote areas or developing countries where children are not yet deeply affected by technology and unwitting efforts to impose guidelines and restrictions on the child's creative experience. We also see extraordinary levels of creative confidence and expression among children in industrialized countries who live and play with adults who value play and creativity and provide the necessary conditions for their expression. Child-centered play therapy is consistent with Lowenfeld's contention that play and creative activity are therapeutic but growth is linked to freedom of expression.

Creative activity can become a means of overcoming this isolation (physical and mental disabilities) through improving those sensory experiences which deal with the establishment of communications by relieving tensions and inhibitions that stand in the way of sound development (Lowenfeld, 1947, p. 282).

[In creative activity,] don't impose your own images on a child! We should neither influence nor stimulate the child's imagination in any direction which is not appropriate to his thinking and perception. The child has his own world of experiences and expression (Lowenfeld, 1947, p. 3).

RESULTS OF PLAY THERAPY

The research on both process and outcomes of play therapy is limited. The existing studies are marked by methodological inadequacies, lack of conceptual models of how play therapy benefits children, the wide range of techniques used, the wide range of problem areas treated, and failure of the academic community to take play therapy seriously (Phillips, 1985). The available studies cover a wide range of hypotheses and outcome measures. The results, overall, are positive, supporting the efficacy of play therapy for disturbed children and children with problems.

Research has concluded that play therapy is effective for the following:

- Overall functioning (Holloway, Myles-Nixon, & Johnson, 1998; Kaduson, Cangelosi, & Shaefer, 1997; Paul, 1993; Webb, 1999)
- Personality outcomes (Dorfman, 1958)
- Social and emotional adjustment (Andriola, 1944; Burroughs, Wagner, & Johnson, 1997; Conn, 1952; Cox, 1953; Jackson, Rump, Ferguson, & Brown, 1999; Johnson, McLeod, & Fall, 1997; King & Ekstein, 1967; Moustakas, 1951; Smith, 1984; Ude-Pestel, 1977)
- Self-concept (Bleck & Bleck, 1982; Cowden, 1992; Crow, 1989; Pelham, 1971; Quattlebaum, 1970; Wick, Wick, & Peterson, 1997)
- Healing through storytelling (Henderson-Dickson, 1991)
- Temper tantrums, self-control, and aggression (Barlow, Strother, & Landreth, 1985; Stiber, 1991; Trostle, 1984; Willock, 1983)
- Phobias (Mendez & Garcia, 1996)
- Coping with grief (death) (Le Vieux, 1999)

- Progress in reading (Axline, 1947a, 1964; Bills, 1950; Bixler, 1945; Carmichael, 1991; Pumfrey & Elliott, 1970; Winn, 1959)
- Intelligence (Heinecke, 1969; Mundy, 1957)
- Academic performance (Bills, 1950; Guerney, 1983; Moustakas, 1951; Seeman & Edwards, 1954)
- Child abuse (Beezley, Martin, & Kempe, 1976; Berkeley Planning Associates, 1978; Davoren, 1979; Frazier & Levine, 1983; Friedrich & Reams, 1987; Green, 1978; Mann & McDermott, 1983)
- Creativity, emotional adjustment (Lowenfeld, 1939, 1947; Van Fleet, Lilly, & Kaduson, 1999)
- Recovery from sexual abuse (Costas & Landreth, 1999; Johnston, 1997)
- See also *www.a4pt.org/research/#research compilation* for periodically updated synopsis of 100 play therapy studies (2004).

The large majority of studies on the effects of play therapy show positive results. However, there are exceptions. West's (1969) study of short-term play therapy sessions did not yield significant results for experimental subjects over control subjects on measures of self-concept, social adjustment, and intelligence. Levitt (1957) concluded from an examination of child therapy outcome reports that the data failed to support the effectiveness of psychotherapy with neurotic children. Barbour and Beedell (1955) found no differences in results between treated and untreated children. In a long-range follow-up study, Witmer and Keller (1942) noted little difference in the later adjustment of treated children and untreated children. In a study of the efficacy of time-limited (15 weeks) play therapy with maltreated (abused) preschoolers, Reams and Friedrich (1994) found that among 13 outcome measures, their treatment children were superior to the control children on only one measure: amount of isolated play. There were no significant differences at a 10-week follow-up.

Overall, though, the results of play therapy research are positive, demonstrating the efficacy and power of play for therapy and healing. Consequently, interest in play therapy is growing at a rapid rate, and novel applications continue to emerge. The growing patterns of child-against-child violence and adults abusing children pose ever-greater challenges to develop therapeutic as well as preventive measures. There is a pressing need for in-depth process studies and controlled outcome studies, especially for preschool children. None of the experimental studies so far have been as meaningful or valuable for therapists as the detailed analyses of single cases.

Consider Axline's (1964) classic book, *Dibs in Search of Self,* an account of the clinical, play therapy treatment of a 6-year-old boy enrolled in an exclusive private school. The therapy for child and mother resulted in profound changes in the feelings, attitudes, and behaviors of both child and family.

> BEFORE (CHAPTER ONE)
>
> Dibs seemed determined to keep all people at bay. . . . When he started to school, he did not talk and he never ventured off his chair. He sat there mute and unmoving all morning. After many weeks he began to leave his chair and to crawl around the room, seeming to look at some of the things about him. When anyone approached him he would huddle up in a ball on the floor and not move. He never looked directly into anyone's eyes. He never answered when anyone spoke to him. . . . He was a lone child in what must have seemed to him to be a cold, unfriendly world. . . . "He's a strange one," the pediatrician had said. "Who knows? Mentally retarded? Psychotic? Brain-damaged? Who can get close enough to find out what makes him tick?" (pp. 2–4)
>
> AFTER (CHAPTER TWENTY)
>
> Yep, I [Dibs] was afraid, but I'm not afraid any more. . . . I guess I am growing up. . . . As Dibs stood before me now his head was up. He had a feeling of security deep inside himself. He was building a sense of responsibility for his feelings. His feelings of hate and revenge had been tempered with mercy. . . . He could hate and he could love. He

could condemn and he could pardon. . . . Yes, Dibs had changed. He had learned how to be himself, to believe in himself, to free himself. Now he was relaxed and happy. He was able to be a child. . . . They left together—a little boy who had had the opportunity to state himself through his play and who had emerged a happy, capable child, and a mother who had grown in understanding and appreciation for her very gifted child. (A week after play therapy ended, Dib's tested IQ was 168.) (pp. 156, 161, 176, 181, 185)

DIBS AT AGE 15

He is a brilliant boy. Full of ideas. Concerned about everybody and everything. Very sensitive. A real leader. (p. 184)

SUMMARY

Play therapy, the supportive relationship between a child and a therapist in a play context, allows a child to play out feelings and emotions and, hopefully, to heal. This is possible because play by its very nature is therapeutic and healing. The consequences of playing and not playing or playing in bizarre ways, as in excessive violence themes, are profound and lasting. Just as adults talk out their feelings and phobias with a therapist, children play out theirs. Play is the language of children, and healthy play is essential for healthy development.

Play therapy had its roots in the psychoanalytic tradition of Sigmund Freud and his associates and peers. Over the years, it has evolved from the psychoanalytic tradition into a multifaceted treatment option for a wide range of problems, phobias, and disabilities. Currently, play therapy approaches developed by therapists are being integrated into the repertoires of classroom teachers.

Overall, the reports of success for play therapy include improvement in physical, mental, and emotional disabilities; problems in speech; reading and general academics; abused children; phobias; children with attachment problems; hospitalized children; and children who have experienced trauma. Play therapy is carried out successfully in elementary schools, homes, hospitals, child care centers, university laboratories, and psychiatric settings. It also is successfully conducted in individual, group, and family contexts and includes the age ranges from preschool through adolescence.

KEY TERMS

Axline's eight basic play principles
Bonding
Catharsis
Challenging
Child-centered play therapy
Client-centered therapy
Ego
Establishing limits
Filial therapy
Free association
Group dynamics
Group play therapy
Id
Interdisciplinary teams
Intruding
Medical play
Nondirective therapy
Nurturing
Oedipus complex
Playroom
Psychoanalytical method
Psychotherapy
Relationship therapists
Release therapy
Resistance
Self-actualization
Structured play therapy
Structuring
Superego
Theraplay
Therapy hour
Transference
Whole child

STUDY QUESTIONS

1. What is play therapy? Why is play therapy needed?
2. What is the evidence indicating that play is therapeutic?
3. How did play therapy originate and expand over the 20th century? Who were the major players, and what were the major approaches? What were the philosophical likenesses and differences?
4. What were the major principles of Freudian psychoanalysis?
5. What individuals are most responsible for modifying psychoanalysis into play therapy? What modifications did they make to psychoanalysis?
6. What are the fundamental reasons for the emergence of client-centered or child-centered play therapy?
7. How should the playroom be set up? What materials are needed? Why are these materials appropriate? Are there toys that you would not place in the playroom? Why?
8. What are the major roles of the therapist in child-centered play therapy? How would you introduce the child to the playroom? How would you establish rapport with the child? How would you conduct the therapy session?

9. Should limitations be placed on children in therapy? If so, describe the limitations and defend your answer. If not, explain why.
10. Select the individual whom you believe has been the leading play therapist. Why did you select this individual? Compare his or her contributions to other leading therapists.
11. How have Axline's eight basic principles of play therapy influenced the field of play therapy?
12. For which disabilities or problems is play therapy effective?
13. What does research say about the effectiveness of play therapy? What are the present limitations of play therapy research?
14. Can and should play therapy be successfully conducted in elementary school classrooms? By classroom teachers? By play therapists? In hospitals? In playgrounds? By playground supervisors, play leaders, or play workers? Why or why not?
15. In your opinion, what is the future of play therapy? Defend your answer.

Chapter 11 Creating Play Environments

THE SCHOOL grounds had been biologically sealed for years by on unsightly layer of asphalt. The site was almost devoid of plant and animal life and children were so bored that they constantly bickered. Serious fights and bullying occurred frequently among the boys. The girls hated the antisocial conditions, as did the teachers. How could children be expected to live and learn in such a degraded and oppressive place.

(Moore & Wong, 1997, p. xvi)

THAT WAS the main thing about kids then: we spent an awful lot of time-doing nothing. . . . All of us, for a long time, spent a long time picking wild flowers. Catching tadpoles. Looking for arrowheads. Getting our feet wet. Playing with mud. And sand. And water. You understand not doing anything. What there was to do with sand was let it run through your fingers. What there was to do with mud was pat it, and thrust in it, lift it up and throw it down. . . . My world, as a kid was full of things that grownups didn't care about.

(Smith, 1957, pp. 92. 123)

IN PLAY, rules and boundaries are defined by the players themselves. This step is first base—and so it is. This sidewalk square is jail, this broken antenna is a gun—and through the magic of play they are.

(Dargan & Zeitlin, 2000, p. 74)

Although some aspects of indoor play environments will be discussed in this chapter, the major focus is on the creation of outdoor play environments for children of all ages. Chapter 8, Play and the Curriculum, focuses on classroom play viroments. The initial impulse was to title the chapter "*Designing* Play Environments." "Designing" was discarded in favor of "creating," for the former lacks the imagination and energy that children's play environments deserve and need. The current emphasis on "designing" for children is eroding the creativity and imagination that is characteristic of free, spontaneous play in natural environments, and, all too frequently, designers do not involve children in their work. Throughout the industrialized world, designers and engineers are increasingly standardizing children's play equipment and playgrounds and organizing them into tidy, uniform packages that differ little from place to place. As a result, the natural wonders of earlier childhoods are all but lost to a growing number of children, especially those living in the concrete and steel jungles of mega-cities such as New York, Seoul, London, and Hong Kong. We cannot take children to the countryside every day, but we can bring the countryside to them and we can involve children in the ongoing development of their play environments.

THEN AND NOW

A delightful and informative study by Beach (2003) examines children's habitats for play in the rural America of a generation ago. She found that children are still roaming rural America in a free-ranging manner, mostly unaccompanied by adults. When out of school they are not to be found in the school playgrounds but digging in sand, building forts, playing traditional games, climbing, fishing, and playing ball games—overall 60 categories of activities. They are still playing in the natural terrain and employing natural objects in their play.

However, natural play areas are gradually disappearing due to building in common areas, shifting housing patterns, and loss of adult support for natural, creative play. The natural spaces—woods, streams, etc.—are fenced off from school play yards as farms are lost and urban development gains force. Adults are still involved in children's play lives but increasingly in organized play and sports rather than in creative forms of play.

Paul Hogan (1995), a pioneer of children's play and play environments, wrote a delightful book, *Philadelphia Boyhood: Growing Up in the 1930's,* that reveals the joys of growing up in an extended family and a supporting neighborhood before our preoccupation with TV, computers, video games, theme parks, and designer playthings (see Chapter 3). Two of the present authors were growing up in rural areas at that same time, but despite the geographical distinctions, there were more common factors than differences in country and city work and play.

Paul spoke lovingly of the close family ties and his many neighborhood friends, both children and adults—about street peddlers and shopkeepers, the iceman, the butter and egg man, the horseradish man, the snowball man, the organ grinder and monkey, the knife sharpener, and his personal experiences with them. Country children, living in remote hills and on family farms, also enjoyed the occasional peddler who rode a horse or drove a battered, old car along the dirt roads, stopping at houses to spend and hour or two swapping stories with the adults, teasing the children, offering to trade his wares (medicine, spices, etc.) for fresh garden produce, chickens, or anything of value.

Like city kids, country kids worked from an early age. Paul earned his own money from age 7 or 8 and was taught to be very frugal to the point of embarrassment if caught spending too freely. Country kids helped with farm chores before they started to school and were frequently working alongside adults in the fields before completing elementary school. Work was to be done well; it was satisfying and contributed to the welfare of the entire family. When Paul was 10, he sold and delivered the *Saturday Evening Post.* At that age, country kids were selling and delivering a few copies of a weekly newspaper, *Grit,* by horseback to neighbors scattered over several miles.

City kids were inventive, creating such items as diving helmets from cans, surf boards from old ironing boards, bicycles with wings, and what Paul called "skateos"—variations on modern-day scooters, made from old roller skates and scrap lumber. Having no paved surfaces to accommodate rolling devices, country kids carved stick horses from scrap cuttings from sawmills; made rubber guns from pieces of wood, clothes pins, and strips of old inner tubes; and rounded up calves on weekends for rodeos in the barnyard.

No matter where you lived, there always seemed to be a tree house nearby. Paul called his "the greatest tree house in the whole wide world." They could be in a shade tree in a backyard or in a huge oak tree on a hillside. Tree houses were places of great pride, to be shown to friends who came to play, to be club houses, or simply to serve as hideouts for getting away and reflection. They were also places to sharpen tool-using and building skills and for enjoying all sorts of make-believe play. Now, tree houses are prohibited by zoning laws in many urban areas.

Then as now, heroes came from comic books and movies. The movies of the early 1900s were tame and sanitary compared to today's fare of sex and violence. When Clark Gable said, "Frankly, my dear, I don't give a damn," in *Gone with the Wind,* many parents refused to let their children be exposed to such language. Country kids walked, hitched rides, or rode dilapidated buses to county seats to see weekend movies. Paul and his brothers rented movies and showed them in their basement to neighborhood kids for 10 cents. Twenty-five cents paid for a movie, a box of popcorn, and a hot dog after the movie.

City playgrounds were vacant lots, often with hills and valleys for digging, sledding in the winter, and sliding on cardboard boxes year-round. Flat areas were used for the popular sport of the season. No one dumped trash on Paul's neighborhood playground. Early city playground developers bulldozed the trees, leveled the hills, installed playground equipment, paved the area with cinders or asphalt, and designated the site an official playground. Country playgrounds were the hills, streams, rivers, and barn lots. Kids swam and fished during the summer and played traditional games throughout the year. Pets were common companions in their play.

Organized games in neighborhoods and at schools were taught by older peers and adults. These included games of chance using marbles and spinning tops. A wide range of running and chasing games were taught or invented and seemed to follow a season of high interest that could last for several days or weeks before attention was redirected. Groups of kids of all ages would choose up sides for war games and ball games, sometimes playing baseball with homemade balls and no gloves or a hockey-type game called "shinny" using tree limbs and tin cans.

Early 20th-century childhoods were filled with happy memories about work, play, friends, places, family, and community cohesiveness. "Lonely" was not a familiar concept. The downsides included lack of modern prescription drugs and medical expertise. Childhood illnesses were usually long and fraught with risk. Dental care and hospital treatment were relatively primitive and painful.

Among the most compelling differences between childhoods then and now are the early work ethic; the close family ties; the warm, friendly, supportive, personal interactions with family, friends, and community residents; the freedom to roam at will and engage in creative, constructive play; the need to improvise; the pride in good work and the joy of creating with simple, natural, or scrap materials; the favorite places; the time for reflection; the competitive games and socialization with live people and animals rather than machines. Obviously, we cannot go back in time, but adults can help children recapture compelling opportunities to play traditional street games, create from raw materials, and commune with nature (Chapters 3 and 13).

HISTORY OF PLAYGROUNDS IN AMERICA

The first formal playgrounds in the United States were called **outdoor gymnasia.** They were patterned after German playgrounds and introduced to America in 1821 at the Salem, Massachusetts, Latin School (Mero, 1908). They were essentially sets of indoor-type gymnastic equipment adapted for outdoor use. The outdoor gymnasia had succumbed to lack of interest before the end of the 19th century. They were developed for older boys, but later, in 1886, Dr. Marie Zakerzewska, an American visitor to Berlin, wrote to the chairman of the Massachusetts Emergency and Hygiene Association about heaps of sand in Berlin parks where young children played and influenced the establishment of the first **sandgartens** in Boston in 1886 (Sapora & Mitchell, 1948). These rapidly became popular with children of all ages and were gradually integrated into playgrounds for older children.

Friedrich Froebel originated the first kindergarten in Germany in 1837. Despite this early date, he was a proponent of play and considered it very important in the educative process. Indeed, his first playgrounds were nature itself (Froebel, 1887, p. 111). His kindergarten children played much as early 20th-century American children played: channeling streams and building dams, bridges, and mills. They prepared and cared for gardens, observed small insects and animals, explored old walls and vaults, and cared for pets. They used open areas for traditional games such as wrestling, war games, ball games, and chase games. Froebel understood not only the educational benefits of play but also its therapeutic qualities:

> Play is the purest, most spiritual activity of man at this stage, and at the same time, typical of human life as a whole—of the inner hidden natural life in man and all things. It gives, therefore, joy, freedom, contentment, inner and outer rest, peace with the world. (Froebel, cited in Harris, 1906, p. 55)

The first organized playgrounds in the United States were called outdoor gymnasia.

Source: Mero (1908).

He proposed that every town have its own playground to help ensure that children in urban areas were not deprived of the rich physical, mental, and moral advantages available in country children's play.

The early American kindergartens responded to Froebel's call for play and "self-activity" by adding swings, seesaws, various toys, and climbing apparatus to their playgrounds. Over time, such devices supplanted many of the rich natural environments that Froebel favored. Early American child development leaders such as Susan Blow (1909, p. 158) not only supported the creative, natural environments and the gifts and occupations (manipulative materials) proposed by Froebel, but proposed that early childhood programs be focused around children's free, creative play in rich environments, both indoors and outdoors. Both the nursery school movement and the kindergarten movement of the early 1900s were focused much more heavily on play than were public schools and public parks. This was due largely to the influence of Froebel and John Dewey, the creation of child study centers at universities around the country, and the formation of the Association for Childhood Education International and the National Association for the Education of Young Children. As early as the 1920s, playgrounds at the leading nursery schools were superior to practically all contemporary public schools (Frost, 1992, p. 118). Unfortunately, making kindergartens a part of public schools has diminished the role of play and playgrounds in favor of "academic activities."

Early 20th century playgrounds featured manufactured equipment and stressed physical development. Early manufactured playgrounds were established in Charlesbank, Massachusetts, in 1889 and in Boston in 1900. About this time, Massachusetts passed a law requiring all towns with 10,000 or more people to establish public playgrounds (Mero, 1908, p. 242; Playground and Recreation Association of America, 1909, p. 19). By 1913, leaders in the playground and recreation movement saw that the dismal state of public school playgrounds had begun to promote change. Curtis (1913) proposed that schools increase the size of their playgrounds, provide play equipment, keep the equipment and grounds in good condition, and put someone in charge of the playground.

Early 1900s school and park playgrounds featured primarily exercise equipment with heights well over 15 feet, with hard earth surfaces underneath (gradually replaced by asphalt and concrete), and were replete with hazardous elements—giant strides, poorly manufactured equipment, and rotating devices that could inflict serious injury to users. Curtis (1913) lamented these conditions, stating that he "knew of half a dozen broken arms resulting in a week from a new set of poorly made seesaws" (p. 26).

As early as 1905, supervised public park playgrounds had been established in 35 American cities. This number grew to 90 in 1907 and to 336 in 1909 (Knapp & Hartsoe, 1979, p. 28). Rapidly growing interest led to the establishment of the Playground Association of America (PAA) in 1907 and to the creation of its journal, *The Playground.* This journal is a rich source for early history of American playgrounds. By 1910, support had arisen for a broader conception of play and playgrounds, and the PAA was renamed the Playground and Recreation Association of America (PRAA) and the journal retitled *Recreation.* Consequently, the early focus on children's play and playgrounds was modified to include a wide array of social work, civic affairs, and recreation. In 1930, the focus on play and playgrounds was further diluted by changing the PRAA's name to the National Recreation Association (NRA) (Knapp & Hartsoe, 1979, p. 104). Play and playgrounds were by this time a relatively minor consideration in the association. In 1966, the NRA merged with several other associations to form the National Recreation and Park Association (NRPA). In recent years, the NRPA has expanded its interest and activities in play and playgrounds, and, once again, these critical topics are receiving attention and support.

The evolution of public school and public park playgrounds followed a parallel path that can roughly be divided into three eras: (a) **manufactured appliance era,** (b) **novelty era,** and (c) **modern era** (Frost & Wortham, 1988). Because of recent developments, we will redesignate the modern era (1970s–1980s) as the **modular design era** and add a new designation—**standardized era**—for the far-reaching events shaping playgrounds in the late 1980s and 1990s.

Manufactured swings, slides, jungle gyms, merry-go-rounds, giant strides, see-saws, and trapeze devices dominated the playground market throughout most of the 1900s. Following the diversion of steel to war equipment during World War II and its lack of availability for manufacturing play equipment, many manufacturers, designers, architects, engineers, and handymen created novel playground devices to stimulate the imagination and lend aesthetic qualities to playgrounds. This "novelty era," roughly the 1950s and 1960s, emphasized fixed, lifeless, molded concrete forms with bizarre color schemes, theme villages, replicas of amusement park devices, and theme equipment patterned after animal figures and stagecoaches. After Sputnik, rockets and space devices gained popularity, and manufacturers continued to expand their offerings.

During the 1970s and 1980s, a few manufacturers began to seek expert assistance in designing playground equipment. The most influential result was the growing emphasis on modular wood equipment—that is, decks and play devices (play events) attached together to promote challenge, continuity, and linkage. Jay Beckwith (1985), a California designer who continues to influence play equipment design, appears to have been one of the most innovative and influential professionals in this movement.

Beginning in the late 1980s after the publication of the United States Consumer Product Safety Commission's (USCPSC) *Handbook for Public Playground Safety: Volumes I and II* in 1981, followed in 1993 by the publication of the American Society for Testing and Materials' (ASTM) *Standard Consumer Safety Performance Specification for Playground Equipment for Public Use,* a new playground era emerged that we designate as the standardized era. Concerns for safety led to the establishment of specific guidelines/standards for public playground equipment that limited the creativity of designers. Due in part to threat of litigation resulting from injuries, playground sponsors applied safety guidelines/standards intended for manufactured equipment to other features of playgrounds. These included **natural features,** such as terrain and plants, and portable materials, such as construction materials and tools. Consequently, playground equipment gained a degree of standardization never before seen on playgrounds and contributed to limitations on creativity, flexibility, challenge, and natural features of playgrounds. Fortunately, a growing number of public schools and public parks professionals are learning to make playgrounds safer yet more child-friendly and more attuned to nature and basic developmental needs.

INDOORS VERSUS OUTDOORS

Both indoor and outdoor play environments are essential for children's development. The key is to prepare both spaces, complimentary and integrated, to ensure the most significant influence on children's play and development.

Child development centers in industrialized countries typically direct more time and resources to creating indoor play environments than to outdoor environments. This may result from limited space, slim resources, or merely misunderstanding the important roles of the outdoors for children's development. There are indeed advantages of the outdoors that cannot readily be provided indoors. Consequently, the best play and learning places for children flow between the two spaces. A partially or completely covered transition area—deck or porch—provides shaded space for sunny days and shelter from inclement weather. This covered space also allows extension of the classroom that is especially useful for messy play such as sand, water, and art activities.

The unique benefits of outdoor play are extensive. Since large equipment can be available and a greater range of movement is possible, playgrounds enhance motor development (Myers, 1985), promote motor skills (Poest, Williams, Witt, & Atwood, 1990), manipulative skills (Pepler & Ross, 1981), and social skills (Eisenberg & Harris, 1984) in ways that are not feasible in the confined space of indoor classrooms. Playgrounds are superior to indoor settings for activities that are messy or loud (Greenman, 1985). Logistic problems of containing, transporting, and using sand, water, and other fluid materials are reduced. A wider variety of opportunities for sensory stimulation—sounds, smells, textures (Olds, 1987)—are available. Furthermore, friendly, nonviolent, rough-and-tumble play and limited superhero or war play that cannot be allowed indoors can be accommodated outdoors. The loud voices and high activity levels on the playground complement the "inside voices" and controlled movement that must be moderated indoors (Dempsey & Frost, 1991).

The playground appears to be more influential than the classroom in developing the **peer culture** (Ladd & Price, 1993). This results from greater luxury of space and a more flexible environment (Hartup & Larsen, 1993; Olweus, 1993). The relatively unconstrained context of the playground permits greater freedom of selectivity in interacting with peers (Boulton & Smith, 1993), which may lead to learning positive social behaviors if teachers are supportive (Pettit & Harrist, 1993). Consequently, **play leaders** may expect that a greater range of social behavior may result from the freedom and flexibility available in the outdoor environment.

An extensive observational study of preschool children (Shin & Frost, 1995), conducted in well-equipped indoor and outdoor play environments at the University of Texas, concluded that the outdoor environment was more influential on symbolic play than the indoor environment for both boys and girls. This outcome resulted from the relatively greater availability of low-realistic, low-structured, natural materials, spaciousness, and teacher involvement in this particular outdoor environment. The nature and intensity of play on playgrounds is influenced by the availability of materials.

The playground can and should offer a much wider variety of natural materials than the indoors can readily accommodate—many textures, including grass, dirt, stone, brick, plastic, metal, bark, leaves, sand, and water; and a larger variety of plants, gardens, nature areas, and living things. Well-planned storage areas on the playground make a wide range of equipment available that cannot be used as efficiently in the classroom—tricycles, wagons, wheelbarrows, tools, construction materials, and organized game equipment. Together, the indoors and outdoors extend opportunities for complexity, challenge, variety, and novelty—all ingredients for supporting creativity, learning, and development (Frost & Strickland, 1985).

Children play differently outdoors than they play indoors. Language on the playground is more complex than indoor language (Tizard, Philps, & Plewis, 1976). Boys engage in more dramatic play outdoors than indoors (Henniger, 1985). Girls play more assertively outdoors (Yerkes, 1982). Both boys and girls engage in more gross-motor play outdoors (Campbell & Frost, 1985). Active, outdoor play enhances fitness (Poest et al., 1990) and general health. Many extol the virtues of fresh air and the outdoors in reducing respiratory infections, inhibiting the spread of germs, and maintaining healthy immune systems. Some exposure to sunlight is beneficial to children, but too much can be damaging.

PLAYGROUNDS AND CHILD DEVELOPMENT

Perhaps the most common error by adults who design playgrounds is their failure to consider the natural play and development of children. Few child development professionals are skillful in design, and few designers are skillful in child development. The aspiring designer must be an avid student—an observer—of children, one who knows the nature of play across developmental stages. Chronological age, though an approximate indicator of children's cognitive, language, social, and motor abilities, does not reveal precise information about an individual child's play needs.

Children should not always be segregated by age on the playground for there is a **playground culture** (Sutton-Smith, 1990) that must be respected. Children learn from each other, and the culture of the playground, passed on from older to younger children, helps preserve traditional games, promote society's prevailing values and mores, and teach negotiation and cooperation. Younger children play differently than older children, but many possibilities still exist for cooperative play and interrelationships between children of various ages.

One of the most destructive decisions with which we must now contend is that of school boards and administrators who foolishly deprive children of time for free, creative play by abolishing recess. This growing trend, aimed at "more time for academics," robs children of time for play and, consequently, of the many cognitive, social, linguistic, motor, and therapeutic benefits of traditional recess play.

Traditional recess should not be reduced, set aside, or replaced by organized physical education or sports. Recess play, which is essentially free play, is different from organized games or sports in many respects. First, it is free, allowing children to play most any way they choose. Second, it is supported by a wide range of materials—manufactured and natural. Third, it allows children to explore and learn according to their natural tendencies and needs. Finally, it allows children to learn from one another. Consequently, different age groups should have many opportunities to play together, and time-honored recess and free play must be preserved.

Infant and Toddler Indoor and Outdoor Play Environments

Infant and toddler outdoor play spaces are separated from play spaces of older children to prevent accidental contact that could injure the very young child, but skillful play leaders will plan for mutual play times where older children are playing with and assisting younger children in their play under the guidance of adults. Toddlers are beginning to engage in make-believe play, an activity initiated earlier in such games as peek-a-boo with parents, but their major play-related activities are exploration and motor or exercise play (Berk, 1994; Vygotsky, 1966). The key to creating or designing play spaces for this and other age groups is to include materials and opportunities to engage in all the natural play activities that are characteristic of that age group (Frost, 1992, 1997; see also Figure 11–1).

The play of infants is relatively simple in appearance but powerful in developmental consequences. Their sensorimotor play is well named, for they are tasting, feeling, and hearing in a seemingly endless pattern of movement. Their indoor and outdoor play areas are relatively small but clean, with playthings selected for safety and sensory stimulation. As infants grow into toddlerhood, they become avid explorers, testing everything in their immediate surroundings. Their playground contains a wide array of grasping toys, blocks, push-pull toys, textures, and sounds. With adult assistance, they begin to use miniature swings, slides, and small, wheeled vehicles.

Preschool Play Environments

As children grow into the preschool years (2–5 years), they engage in make-believe play in earnest and are learning to use wheeled vehicles and large playground apparatus independently. They are also engaging extensively in gross-motor or exercise play and construction play. Their playgrounds are larger and more complex, providing for a more extensive array of play than needed for toddlers. The materials and equipment needed for make-believe play include playhouses, wheeled vehicles, vehicle tracks, sand, water, and a wide range of **loose parts** or portable materials. For construction play, toddlers need tools, lumber, blocks, sand, and water. As they develop a

FIGURE 11–1 Ages, Dominant Types of Play, and Materials for Play

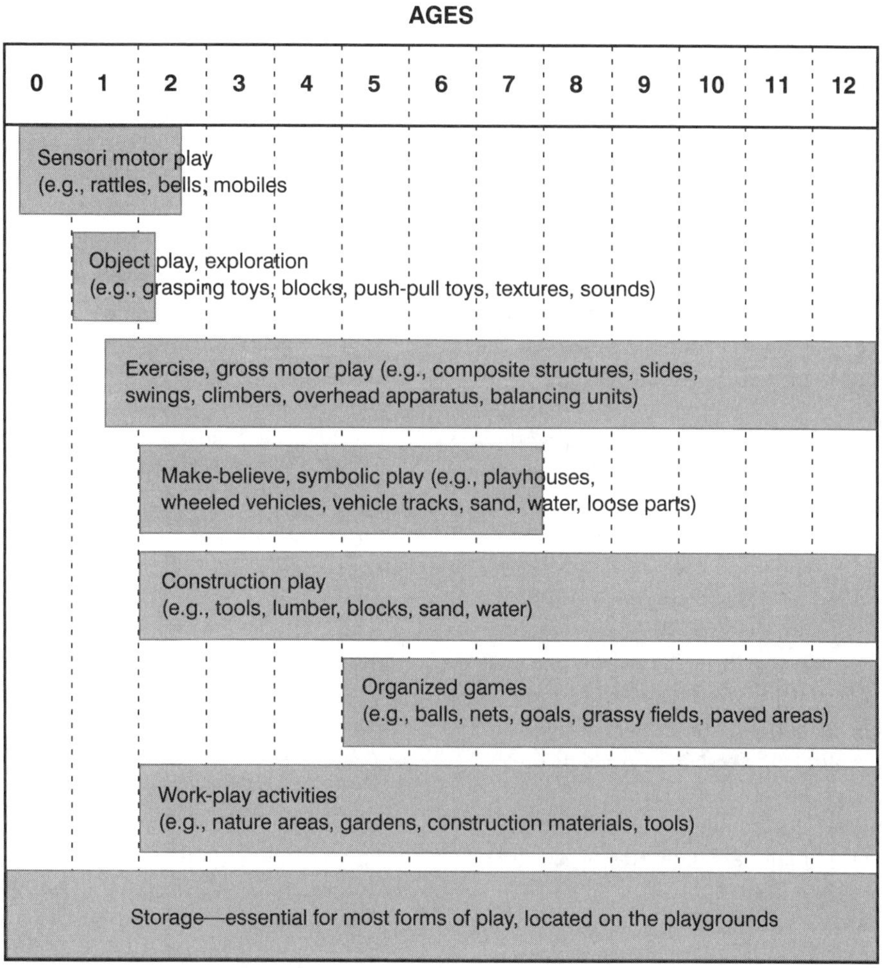

serious interest in organized games, beginning at about age 4 to 5, the playground must be expanded to include flat grassy areas for ball games and chase games, and small paved areas with nets and other equipment for organized games.

The more formal playgrounds, typically seen at child care centers and schools, are organized to accommodate gross-motor (exercise) play, make-believe (symbolic) play, and construction play. There should be storage for portable materials (loose parts), sand and water play equipment, large equipment for gross-motor play (sliding, swinging, climbing, balancing, etc.), materials and areas for make-believe play (cars, boats, sand, wheeled vehicles, playhouses, etc.), and materials for construction (sand, water, tools, building blocks and lumber, etc.). Preschooler's play is further enhanced by including nature areas, gardens, and pets in the playground. The social behavior of children closely parallels the quality and richness of their play environments. Barren, boring playgrounds and lack of supportive adults result in children abusing the environment and one another.

School-Age Play Environments

The play of school-age children (5–12) gradually shifts from an emphasis on make-believe play to organized games (e.g., football, hopscotch, chase games, rough-and-tumble play) and exercise equipment, including overhead equipment such as horizontal ladders and ring treks. Some organized games, such as basketball, require paved surfaces, while others, such as baseball, require flat grassy areas. The shift in focus from make-believe play of the preschooler to the growing frequency of playing organized games of the school-age child should transition gradually, with continual attention to providing play materials and equipment for cognitive, social, and language development through the primary grades. The overall space requirements for playgrounds increase as older children are accommodated.

The school-age child's growing need for order, structure, and industry (Erikson, 1950) can be accommodated on the playground through **work/play** activities such as construction with tools, art, and gardens as well as varied types of games such as soccer, skateboarding, and ice and roller-blade skating. Interest in construction play and work/play activities depends largely on whether storage is available to house the wide array of portable materials needed for such play and whether play leaders are available to encourage such activities. In sum, the playground should meet the developmental play needs of the children who will be playing there (see Figure 11–1).

Children are increasingly influenced by their peers as they approach adolescence; they are changing physically; logical thinking is developing; and they are becoming increasingly interested in the opposite sex. Spaces and equipment for make-believe play are replaced by spaces and equipment for socializing, **hanging out,** and practicing athletic skills. Adolescents need strong, supportive adults who help them sort out changing feelings and conceptions, engage in positive social interactions, and find their way into organized activities (e.g., sports, clubs) that allow them to engage in positive, constructive roles. Of course, contemporary adolescents, even younger children, are increasingly looking to video games, movies, and telephone and computer interaction with both friends and strangers for socialization and information gathering. Such activity should be monitored by adults and should not be allowed to replace traditional creative play.

CREATING PLAY ENVIRONMENTS

The traditional method of preparing a playground is to install fixed equipment in a row, utilizing whatever space is available. Such play places are neither developmentally sound nor economically astute. Contemporary playgrounds are frequently limited in space and must be carefully planned to accommodate large numbers of children and simultaneously provide for a range of play. The first step is to develop a **master plan**—an ultimate, ideal representation of the desired playground (Figure 11–2). The master plan is a sketch or overhead view of the site showing the initial location of fences, adjacent buildings, sidewalks, fixed equipment, storage, water fountains, water sources, shelters, vegetation, gardens, natural features, and any other structures that occupy space.

The master plan should be the joint effort of representative groups: parents, teachers or caretakers, board officials, potential contributors, and people with special skills such as architects, child development specialists, and playground specialists. Children should take active roles in playground planning and in the actual ongoing creation. Good playgrounds are never finished but should be constantly evolving to accommodate users' changing interests and abilities. Many sponsoring groups have limited resources and must prioritize or establish stages for purchasing materials and equipment.

The master plan helps ensure that the steps taken are contributing to a high-quality product. The master plan is merely a first step. The

FIGURE 11–2 Master Plan for a Preschool Playground

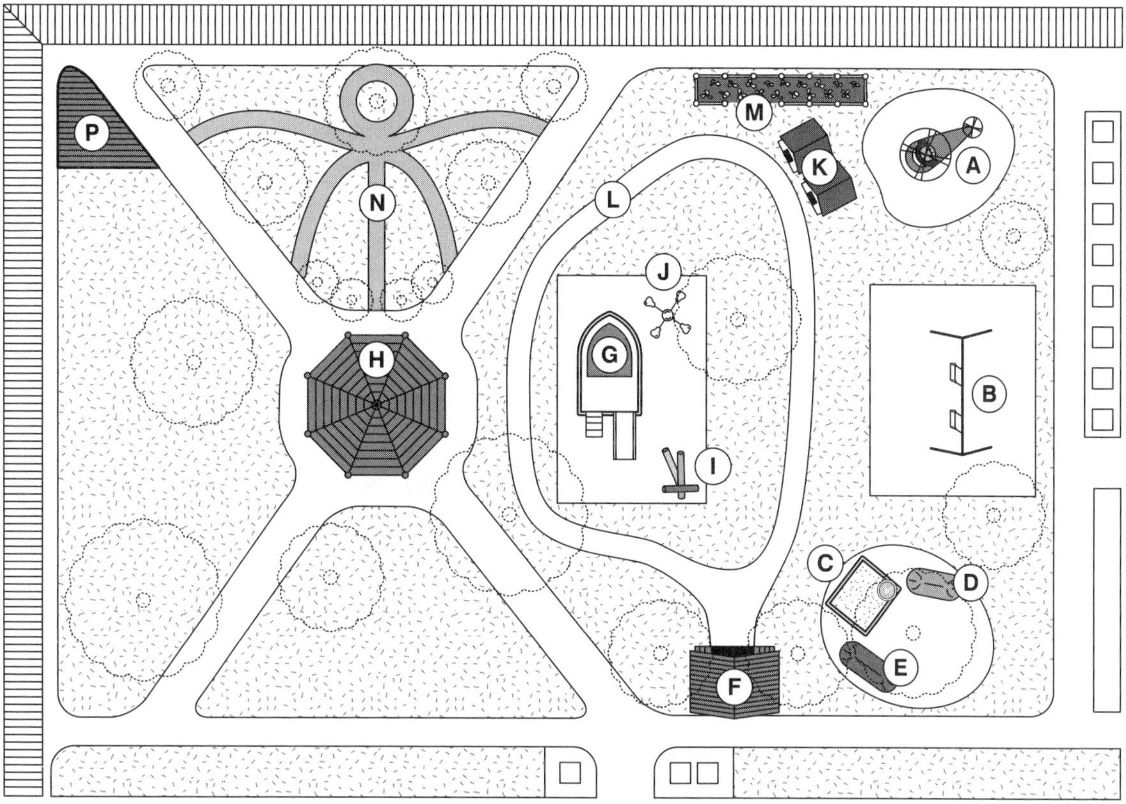

A. HELICOPTER
B. SWINGS
C. SAND / WATER STRUCTURE
D. DIGGER
E. EXPLORATION CENTER
F. TOY GARAGE. SITE BUILT
G. SHIP
H. GAZEBO
I. TALK TUBES
J. FOUR-SEAT TEETER
K. PLAY HOUSES
L. VEHICLE TRACK
M. GARDENS
N. NATURE AREA
O. ORGANIZED GAMES (not shown)
P. DECK

Source: Courtesy of Redeemer Lutheran School, Austin, Texas.

best playgrounds, like the best classrooms, are continually evolving and should be modified day to day and week to week to provide the challenge, novelty, and diversity that developing children need. They should reflect the creative contributions of children at all stages.

Basic factors need to be considered in initial planning of playgrounds (see the appendix, Playground Checklist). These include the **contents of playgrounds**—space, play materials and equipment, natural features, storage, location of utilities, fences, numbers and ages of children, and types of disabilities among children. A second consideration is **safety of playgrounds,** which means compliance with national safety guidelines and standards. A third major factor is **functions of playgrounds**—to nurture, support, encourage, and integrate forms of play, interaction between children, interaction between children and nature, and between children and materials.

Space

Density affects children's play and social behavior, but the results of research are mixed, suggesting that factors other than space affect children's play behavior in environments of varying densities (Frost, Shin, & Jacobs, 1998). Most of the studies of play space are conducted in indoor contexts. Children in crowded physical contexts engage in passive behaviors such as standing around and onlooking and random and deviant behaviors (Preiser, 1972; Shapiro, 1975). Children engage in more fights, involving more children, on high-density playgrounds than on low-density playgrounds (Ginsburg, 1975). A cross-cultural study (Fagot, 1975) of five preschools in the United States and the Netherlands with varying degrees of density concluded that Dutch children in high-density schools spent twice as much time in positive social interaction as American children in low-density schools. Cultural factors appear to play a role in the effects of crowding.

Campbell and Dil (1985) found no significant effect of crowding in space reduced from 46 square feet per child to 29 square feet. However, there was a notable exception. One child was profoundly and negatively affected by the crowded condition, suggesting that effects on individual children should be considered when assessing the impact of crowding. To further complicate the issue of density or crowding, Loo and Kennelly (1972) observed greater passivity (less aggression, less social contact, but more interruption of activities) among 4- and 5-year-old children in small rooms than among those in larger rooms. Social factors appear to play a role in effects of crowding.

Peck and Goldman (1978) found positive effects of increased **social density** on children's play behavior. Greater social density was related to increases in imaginative play and sharing play themes. There was no significant relationship between density and aggression. Exposure to many peers may contribute to sharing play themes.

Collectively, the research shows that a range of factors—including space, numbers of children, individual differences in children, and social and cultural factors—influence play behavior. The ingenuity of adults in planning the play environment and their skills in interacting with children can allow positive play opportunities in limited spaces.

There are clearly thresholds of reasonable density levels beyond which conditions would become intolerable for adults and children. The ideal space for preschool/primary playgrounds is more than 100 square feet per child playing there at a given time and a total area of about 10,000 square feet (100 × 100 feet). Given good design of the playground, this allows for the simultaneous play of about 100 children, including a limited open space for organized games, a feature that may not be available in many urban sites. This amount of space also allows for the inclusion of the various features described in Figure 11–2.

Reducing space significantly means that availability and size of materials and equipment must be reduced, wheeled vehicle tracks and organized games areas must be reduced or downsized, storage must be very carefully designed, special features such as gardens and nature areas must be reduced in size, and greater supervision must be provided. In addition, play schedules must be reworked to prevent overcrowding.

Use of Space

Once the location of the proposed playground is determined, the use of that space must be planned. The first step is to secure utility plans of the site to determine where underground or aboveground utilities (septic systems, sewer lines, telephone cables, etc.) are located. Care must be taken to avoid damaging or conflicting with these, particularly when considering digging holes for supporting superstructures or large, fixed equipment. The second step is to determine **usage patterns** of the site. How many children and what age groups will be involved? How will children be scheduled (schools or child care centers) or anticipated (public parks)?

The third step is to lay out in general fashion a preliminary pattern of arrangement for large, permanent, fixed equipment. Safety guidelines or standards applicable to the geographic region or country must be consulted. A number of countries have adopted playground safety standards, and others are developing standards (see Christiansen, 1997). The most active regions are North America (United States and Canada), northern Europe (Scandinavia, Germany, the Netherlands, and the United Kingdom), and the southeastern Pacific Rim (Australia and New Zealand), with some activity in Singapore, Hong Kong, and Malaysia. Discussions are being held regarding the development of an international playground safety standard. These safety standards will affect manufactured equipment (e.g., swings, superstructures, slides, gross-motor equipment) and will have limited influence on the wide range of creative and natural materials that should be available on playgrounds.

Manufacturer's representatives offer free planning service for laying out space arrangements for the manufactured equipment that they sell. Several are willing to collaborate with environmental professionals in projects that integrate natural features. Unfortunately, not many include children in their planning. They commonly provide computer drawings and specifications for equipment and layout on the site and assist with a range of factors: selecting equipment for various age groups, explaining the differences between materials used in manufacturing equipment (plastic, metal, wood), describing the play value of various equipment components, choosing safety surfaces, evaluating old equipment, and selecting installers. One should bear firmly in mind that manufactured equipment is a minor dimension of highly creative and imaginative playgrounds and turn to other resources for help in integrating manufactured and natural, creative elements into a playground.

The fourth step is to secure materials and equipment and install or develop **permanent features** such as storage, nature areas, organized games areas, and fences. Many communities, child care centers, and schools plan with specialists and build their own playground equipment. The steps involved in one such community built project are detailed in Altmyer and Zeiger (1997). The American Community Built Playground Association (*www.communitybuilt.com*) offers help to those planning to organize the community and build their own playgrounds. Research and experience of long-term designers is useful in selecting manufactured materials and equipment.

Selecting Play Equipment

Research at the University of Texas between 1975 and 2004 included several studies of children's playground equipment choices during free play. These studies were conducted with toddlers through sixth grade children in a number of playgrounds featuring many different types of play equipment. The manufactured equipment used in these studies was graciously provided by several manufacturers including BigToys, Kompan, Grounds for Play, LittleTykes, and GameTime. Since no two playgrounds are identical, caution should be taken in generalizing from one play environment to another. However, over time and in several studies, useful generalizations for selecting and using play equipment have resulted from the research.

The reader should select carefully among the many playground equipment manufacturers. Study the equipment specifications, usually found in catalogs, and compare carefully because quality of equipment is not easily assessed by appearance. Play value of equipment, durability of equipment, customer service, and attention to safety vary greatly among manufacturers. The free-play choices of children, particularly in contexts of multiple equipment options, offer meaningful insight into the play value of equipment and, consequently, help in making wise purchasing decisions.

Special, exciting playgrounds can be created in limited spaces using many natural and inexpensive materials.

In general, the studies reported here indicate that gender differences in play and equipment choices are present from infancy through grade three—the range studied. There are also indications that certain forms of play (e.g., symbolic and organized games) emerge earlier than generally believed, resulting in the need for more complex and challenging equipment than typically provided and more complex than would be recommended by national safety guidelines (CPSC) and standards (ASTM). Safety standards are dumbing down play equipment to the point where many manufacturers are reluctant to market overhead apparatus, sliding poles, or climbers for the age range of 2 to 5 years. Consequently, many children become bored and turn to non-equipment forms of play or use equipment in unintended ways. Just as curriculum materials used in classrooms are individualized to meet the range of cognitive differences among children, playground equipment should be individualized (not restricted by chronological age) to match children's rapidly growing and varied needs for physical challenge.

The typical methods used in the studies that follow included both quantitative and qualitative methods employing collection of anecdotal data, interviews of children and teachers, time sampling observations, and use of wireless transmission systems. Equipment choices were only one of several variables included in the studies. Choices are clustered here to conserve space. For example, climbers may refer to tire climbers, bar climbers, arch climbers, and traditional monkey

bars. Overhead equipment refers to chinning bars, horizontal ladders, ring treks, and track rides. The reader should bear in mind that equipment not present on a playground could well be listed as "most chosen" if available. Percentages are rounded to whole numbers.

Toddler Equipment Choices

Winters's (1983) study of toddlers (24–35 months) focused on both stationary equipment and loose parts (portable materials). The most frequently chosen or most popular fixed equipment in order of preference was the car, fort enclosure, slides, swings, climbers, playhouse, parallel bars and assorted bars, and clatter bridge. Least frequently chosen were picnic table, steering wheel, barrel, and bench.

Most popular loose parts were sand (22% of all play or play choices including fixed equipment choices), tricycles (8%), assorted containers, cooking pots, funnels, and scoops. Least popular were cable spools, tire barrel, potato masher, and sifter. Fixed equipment choices were 25% of total, and loose parts choices were 75% of total.

Keesee's (1990) study of toddlers (ages 18–36 months) began with an analysis of children's play and equipment choices on a very sterile playground and followed with a study after refinement of the playground to make it "developmentally appropriate." The most popular fixed equipment on the redesigned playground was the play cube with climbing elements and symbolic play components (14% of all choices), followed in order of preference by the dirt hill, platform swing, slide, play deck, sound board, and steering wheel.

Most frequently chosen loose parts in order of preference (most to least) were riding vehicles (21% of all choices), sandbox and sand toys (9%), dress-up items, broom, and gardening tools. Least chosen loose parts included steering wheels, ball, wheelbarrow, pea gravel, and bugs. Fixed equipment accounted for 29% of all choices and loose parts for 71%.

In sum, loose parts are much more popular on toddler playgrounds than is fixed equipment. However, superstructures featuring places to engage in symbolic play and well as exercise or motor play are very popular and valuable play elements as are sand, sand play materials, playhouses, dress-up materials, and wheeled vehicles and tracks. Water play, which is also very popular with toddlers, was not provided during the studies reported here. This is a very common fault that should be corrected.

Preschool Equipment Choices

A study of 4- and 5-year-olds at a university child care center (Shin, 1994) examined play choices in both indoor and outdoor play environments. Children engaged in symbolic play at every play area on the playground. However, the frequencies of using equipment varied from area to area. Children's most frequent choice of play area was sand play areas (22% of all choices), followed in descending order by open space (19%), model car (16%), superstructure area (12%), swings (8%), and bushes (8%). Water play and wheeled vehicle play were not available during the study. Boys most often chose open space and car for symbolic play; girls most often chose the sand play areas and the car.

A study of 4- and 5-year-old children's play compared equipment choices on a preschool playground (playground A) featuring well-equipped, expensive, "state-of-the-art" equipment versus a well-equipped playground (playground B) featuring inexpensive equipment built on site by volunteers (Park, 1998). Playground A contained 23 pieces of equipment, and playground B contained 28. Most frequent choices on playground A in order of preference, most to least, were open space (16%), used primarily for rough-and-tumble and chase games, sand areas (14%), swings (11%), superstructure (9%), tricycle play (8%), and garden (4%). Least popular were six instructive panels such as tic-tac-toe (2%), fixed animal figures (3%), and fixed world globe (0%). Water play was very popular during the weekly scheduled activity.

Playground B, featuring equipment made on site by volunteers, did not have a superstructure. Art table and art activity was the top choice (15% of all play), in part due to the interest of a teacher and the availability of many art materials on a deck adjacent to the classroom. Following in descending order were open space (15%), five types of swings (14%), horizontal ladder and climbers (11%), play decks (6%), slide (5%), trampoline (4%), ropes (4%), playhouse (3%), and sandbox (3%). Playhouses are best used in conjunction with wheeled vehicle tracks and sand areas. This playground had no wheeled vehicle equipment, and the extensively stocked art area attracted much of the play away from the sandbox.

A study of 4-year-olds was conducted by Ihn (1998) at the playground designated by Park as playground A (described earlier). The top choice of boys was loose parts (31%), followed in descending order by open space (15%), swing (12%), sand (10%), wheeled vehicles (8%), playhouse (6%), and teeter-totter (6%). Least chosen were the superstructure (containing only one major play event—a slide), fixed animal figures, instructive panels, and world globe. Choices for girls were loose parts (30%), open space (16%), swing (12%), sand (11%), wheeled vehicles (8%), and teeter-totter (4%). Least used were the instructive panels, fixed animals, and world globe.

In both Park's and Ihn's studies, gardening accounted for only 4% of play because gardening was supervised by an interested teacher on a periodic, planned basis. In other words, gardening is not usually considered as free play to be chosen at will by children but is planned and supervised to ensure skills in using tools and good planting and cultivation procedures. Similarly, art activity is rarely seen on playgrounds unless adults take a leadership role in planning, providing space and materials, and scheduling and assisting children. When adults take leadership roles, both gardening and art are rich, developmentally beneficial activities for children.

Both fixed and portable equipment (loose parts) are important for children's play. Each type of equipment stimulates children to engage in different forms of play. Each complements the other in providing broader, richer play. In Chiang's (1985) study of 3-, 5-, and 7-year-old children, both age and gender were identified as important variables in selecting equipment. For example, as symbolic play gradually gives way to organized games and symbolic and constructive play become more elaborate, materials and space to support such play are needed.

Many playgrounds do not contain loose parts or storage facilities to house them. Riddell (1992) studied kindergarten children's play behaviors and equipment choices on two playgrounds. One, playground A, contained a wide range of fixed equipment and loose parts; the other, playground B, featured fixed pieces of equipment that were several decades old and designed for elementary school children. No loose parts were allowed because there was no place to store them.

Playground A choices (most to least) were playhouse, superstructure, swings, loose parts, open space, tire car, sand area (sand was depleted), and plastic train tunnels. Wheeled vehicles were not in service. Playground B choices in order (most to least) were superstructure, open space, swings, slides, horizontal bars, arch climber, S climber, seesaws, and chinning bars. The play on playground A included a range of symbolic, constructive, exercise, and open-space play (organized games, chase games, and rough-and-tumble play). Play on playground B was almost exclusively exercise (climbers, overhead apparatus, swings, and slides) and open-space play.

Clearly, children's play during the preschool years is heavily influenced by the materials and equipment provided for them. Collectively, the studies show that adults can ensure the type of play desired by the choices they provide. From developmental perspectives, playgrounds should be stocked with a rich array of portable and fixed materials for free play and gardens, art areas, nature areas, and animal areas for directed play/work activities.

Superstructures featuring a mix of play events—slides, tunnels, clatter bridges, climbers, sliding poles, parallel bars, and overhead apparatus for exercise play, and contained space for symbolic play—should be available for typical children age 3 and older. Swings and spring-mounted teeter-totters stimulate motor development and a sense of balance and are just plain fun. Instructive panels attached to superstructures appear to be a waste of resources. Children use playground equipment for playing, not for engaging in classroom-type instructional activity. The environment should change as children develop to ensure challenge and novelty. Superstructures that feature limited play events—for example, a superstructure with several slides and no climbers or overhead apparatus—are clearly not wise choices for children's motor development. A wide mix of loose parts, including wheeled vehicles and tracks, with convenient storage on the playground, are needed to enrich children's symbolic and motor play and to support organized games.

School-Age Equipment Choices

Most first grade children engage in every major form of play and need very extensively equipped playgrounds. Their most common choices of play equipment and areas include open spaces, superstructures, loose parts, swings, slides, climbers, overhead equipment, playhouses, sand and water (when provided), and cars or boats for dramatic play (Moore, 1992). Storage continues to be essential. Wheeled vehicles, tracks, and supporting parts such as playhouses, gas pumps, street signs, sand diggers for loading wagons, and talk tubes for conversation continue to be very popular and have high play value.

As children grow into the middle elementary grades, their play equipment needs change. A simple dirt mound continues to attract second graders, especially boys, playing Star Wars games, rough-and-tumble, and King of the Mountain. Girls and boys continue to use loose parts in constructive and make-believe play (Myers, 1981). Linked overhead apparatus such as horizontal ladders, ring treks, and track rides are very popular with second and third grade children (Deacon, 1994; Myers, 1981). By third grade, children are engaging extensively in organized games on open fields and courts; constructing with loose parts; playing in sand, dirt, and water; using overhead apparatus and climbers extensively; and seeking out special places for socialization (especially girls). These special places may be large open decks on superstructures, wheelchair decks, or bounded areas under trees. Interestingly, they still use tricycles when allowed (even though they are quite small for their size) and may use the tricycle paths for "jogging."

Recent and Continuing Research

The most recent studies in the University of Texas playground research project examined 4- to 12-year-olds' choices, developmental use patterns, and motivations in using overhead apparatus (Frost, et al., 2001), climbing apparatus (Frost, et al., 2002), and swings (2004). Yet another study examined the relevance of height for child development (Frost, et al., 2001). These studies include comprehensive reviews of research on each major subject and original studies of children at play. They are valuable for making decisions about creating playgrounds, play leadership, and revising national playground safety guidelines and standards. Space will allow only a brief overview but these studies are being compiled into a book to be published by the Association for Childhood Education International (Frost, Brown, Thornton, & Sutterby, 2005, in press).

In sum, playground equipment designed for climbing, upper body activity, and swinging is extremely valuable for the total development of boys and girls, preschool through elementary school, and such equipment should be carefully selected to provide a wide range of challenging motor and social activities. Chronological age is a weak predictor of individual differences because with increased practice using challenging equipment, children develop perceptual motor skills at a rapid, sometimes remarkable rate. Most children at age three can successfully navigate properly designed overhead apparatus after only a few opportunities to freely use the equipment. The most notable exceptions are obese children who frequently do not have the requisite strength and quickly lose motivation.

Motor development on overhead apparatus, climbing equipment, and swings follows a predictable and observable developmental sequence from awkward, crude, primitive movements to rapidly refined, elaborate movements requiring considerable strength, coordination, and flexibility.

Extensive observations, and interviews with children and teachers indicate that children's motivations for such motor activity are to some degree inborn or genetic (e.g., they climb because it's there). Yet modeling and encouragement (cheering on) by other children and adults, and apparent feelings of power and success lead children to continue the activity and to expand and elaborate the motor patterns employed.

Height is a key variable in provision of challenge and attraction and simultaneously a major variable in weighing hazards. The higher the child climbs, the faster she falls, and the more serious the consequences. Consequently, playground equipment must be limited in height while presenting challenge and an acceptable level of risk. Resilient surfacing under and around equipment, selected to match the potential fall height from equipment, are key variables in playground safety.

Having considered the steps essential in creating conventional playgrounds featuring manufactured equipment, we now consider the natural, magical qualities that transform play environments from merely good to very special.

CREATING SPECIAL PLAY PLACES: NATURE AND MAGICAL QUALITIES*

The typical playground is far too tame (Shell, 1994). Children need wild places (Nabhan & Trimble, 1994). Current play practice mitigates against children making mudholes, cooking over open fires, building their own houses, resolving their own disputes, creating their own special play places. The best natural play places may lack the glitz of arcades and theme parks, but they still catch and hold the attention of "technosavvy" youth. No piece of equipment designed by an adult can substitute for the child's own creation.

Unfortunately, few countries have extended thought and action about children's playgrounds beyond the traditional concept of swings, slides, monkey bars, and merry-go-rounds, all in a row around an open field. The best of the adventure playgrounds (Frost, 1992) of Scandinavian countries and Western Europe come closest among large-scale organized playgrounds to meeting criteria for "**magical playscapes**" (Talbot & Frost, 1989). Only a few adventure playgrounds exist in the United States, but many playgrounds developed in recent years do contain some adventure components, and gardens for children are gaining popularity.

How do we transform playgrounds from the conventional to natural, magical, special places, which preserve and enhance children's sense of wonder? We first extend the concept of playground from structured, high-tech, manufactured, designed, standard, developmentally appropriate, and age appropriate, to natural, creative, enchanted, vibrant, unique, mystical, rich, and abundant.

Children of all ages need wild places.

*We express appreciation to Jimi Jolley, James Talbot, Suzanne Winter, Robin Moore, Roger Hart, and Paul Hogan for influencing our perspectives about natural, special, magical play places.

Children and sensitive, skillful adults working together can provide natural elements and magical qualities in a continuing process. The needs are extensive—sand, water, storage, portable materials, tools, gardens, nature areas, hills, streams, trails, animal habitats, construction materials, spaces for group and solitary play, and transition areas (porches and decks) between classrooms and playgrounds.

Children's Gardens

Children's gardens are springing up around the country in a variety of contexts: child care centers, schools, children's museums, community gardens, botanical gardens, and, of course, home gardens.

The Michigan State University (MSU) 4-H Children's Gardens

The MSU children's gardens are part of the 7-acre Horticultural Demonstration Gardens. MSU's mission for the gardens is to promote understanding of plants and the role they play in everyday life, to nurture children's imagination and curiosity, and to provide places for delighting children and enriching their lives (Taylor, 1998). Children participate in planning the ever-changing gardens, which draw about 200,000 visitors annually. The 60 theme areas include the Pizza Garden, the Dinosaur Garden, the Crayon Garden, the Jack and the Giant's Garden, the Cloth and Color Garden, the ABC-Kinder-Garten, the Storybook Garden, the Science Discovery Garden, the Secret Garden, the Peter Rabbit Garden, and the Cereal Bowl Garden.

The founder and curator of the MSU gardens offers tips (adapted by permission) for designing special gardens (Taylor, 1998, pp. 56–57):

1. Observe who's coming in the garden gate, and modify the gardens to meet emerging needs.
2. Dazzle children with a rainbow of colors—structures as well as plants.
3. Keep theme areas to children's scale. Bigger is not better.
4. Attend to details. Embed prints and shapes in walks. Cut peek holes in fences.
5. Attract children to interactive displays.
6. Use common names for plants instead of Latin names.
7. Create mini–green worlds of enchantment and magic—plant mazes, arbors, houses.
8. Reach kids through their stomachs. Help them learn about the foods they eat.
9. Make gardens accessible for all abilities.
10. Fence the gardens for security.
11. Make the gardens ageless, for the young and the young at heart.
12. Listen, look, see what is not working; change it.

The Berkeley, California, Elementary School Project

Over a 10-year period, Moore and Wong (1997) worked with teachers, parents, and children to reinvent a barren elementary school landscape into a school-based ecosystem, populated with hundreds of species of plants and animals enriched with gardens, ponds, private places, cageless zoos, ant cities, meadowlands, logs, spools and tires, fruit trees, weather stations, dirt theaters, running water, indoor–outdoor connections, storage, gathering places, play structures, barnyards, compost piles, and fishing holes. The entire process was integrated into the school curriculum and focused on the development of a natural educational environment to be used as a vehicle for teaching all subjects and for motivating children to learn through play and instinctive curiosity.

Despite the protests of neighborhood residents, the Environmental Yard has been replaced with grass and basketball courts, but valuable lessons were learned: children can peacefully coexist with nature; nature reclaims itself through remarkable powers; nature is an economic, social, scientific, and cultural resource. Furthermore, the community nature of the process fostered peaceful coexistence and the absence of boredom and antisocial behavior. The space was truly the children's space. They participated in the planning, design, construction, and management of the yard.

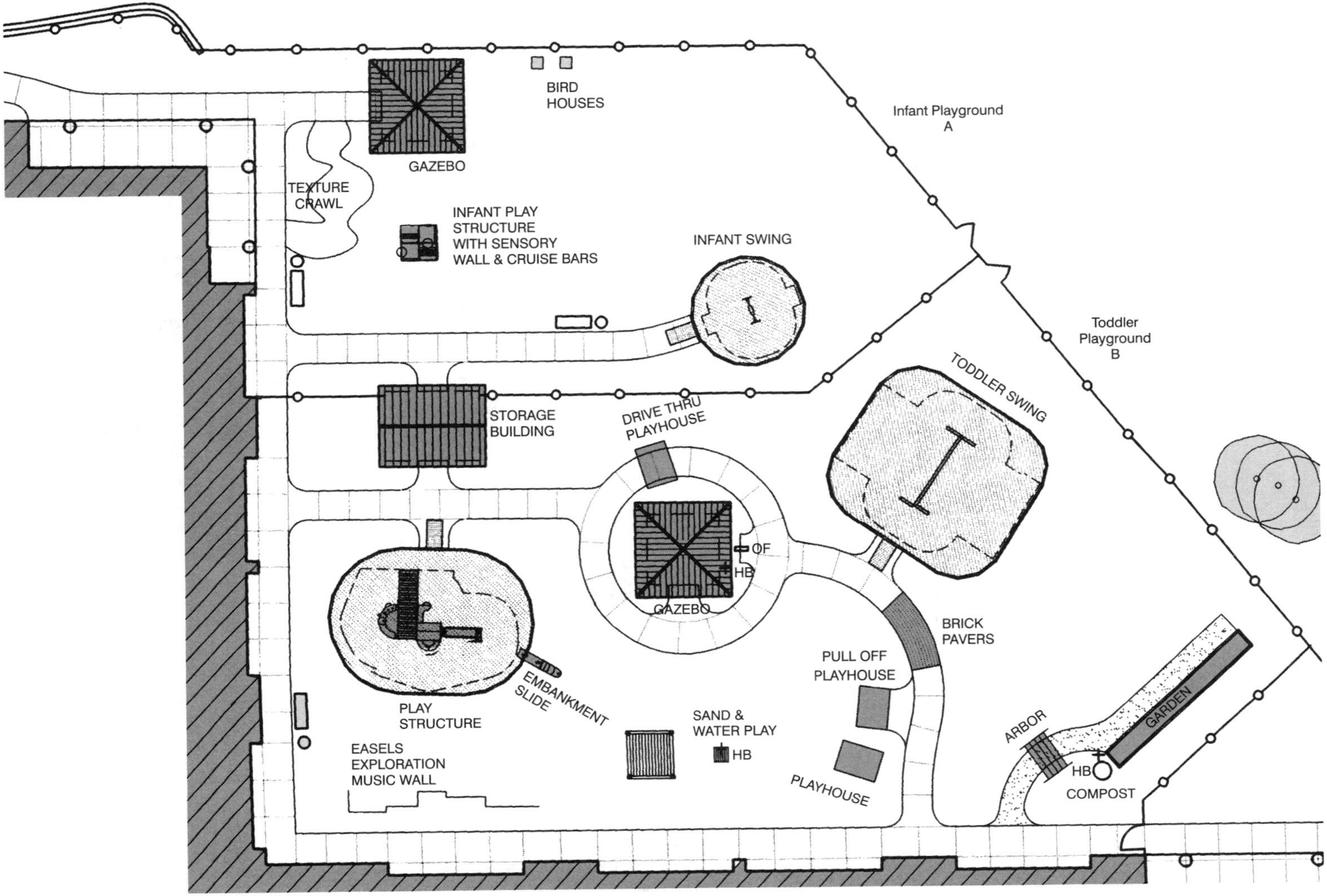

FIGURE 11–3

Source: Printed by permission of the United States Services Automobile Association (USAA), Bright Horizons, and HKS Incorporated (Joe Frost, design consultant). Draft plan current as of February 15, 2000.

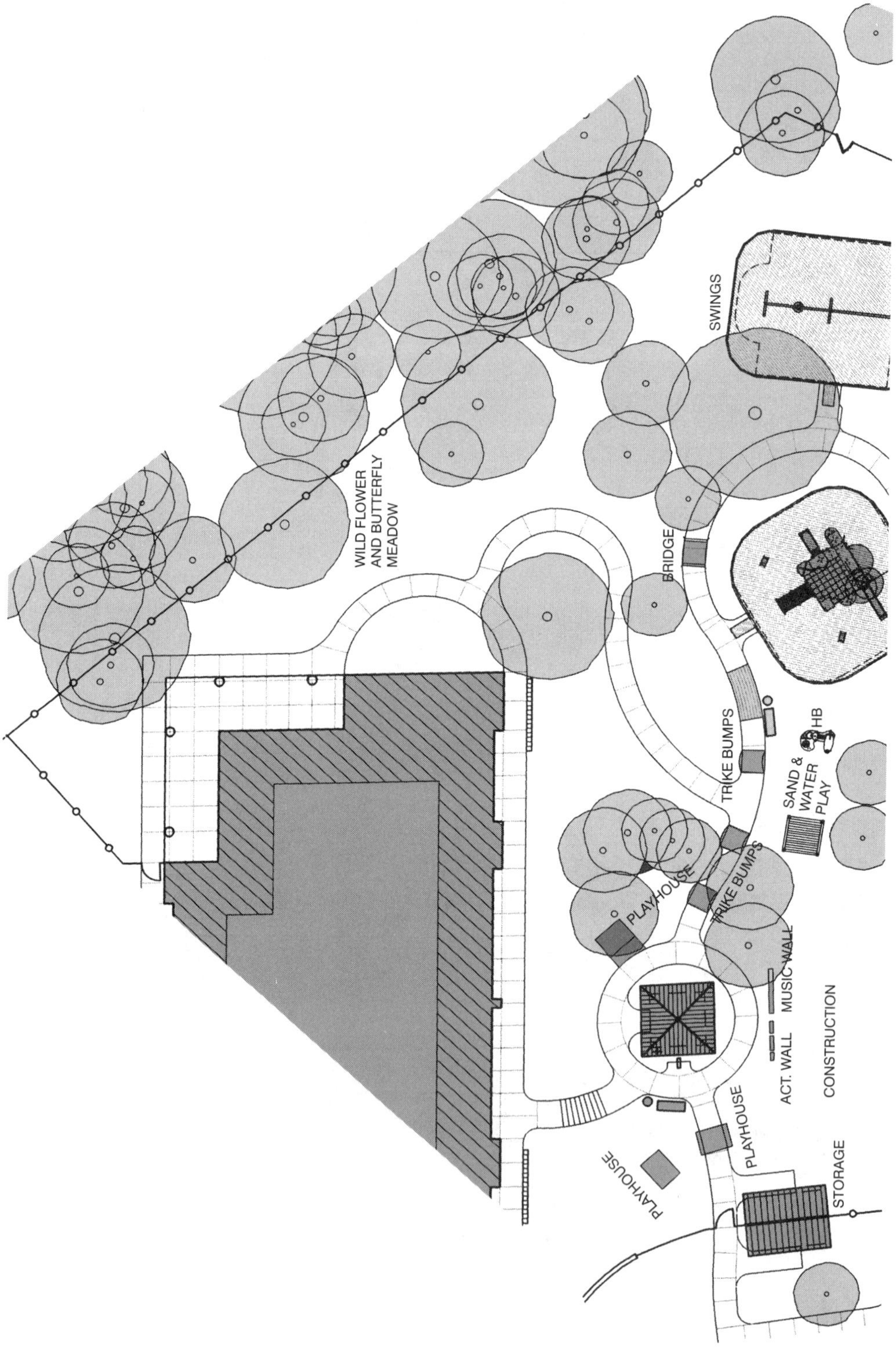
SWINGS
WILD FLOWER
AND BUTTERFLY
MEADOW
BRIDGE
TRIKE BUMPS
HB
SAND &
WATER
PLAY
PLAYHOUSE
TRIKE BUMPS
MUSIC WALL
ACT. WALL
CONSTRUCTION
PLAYHOUSE
STORAGE
PLAYHOUSE

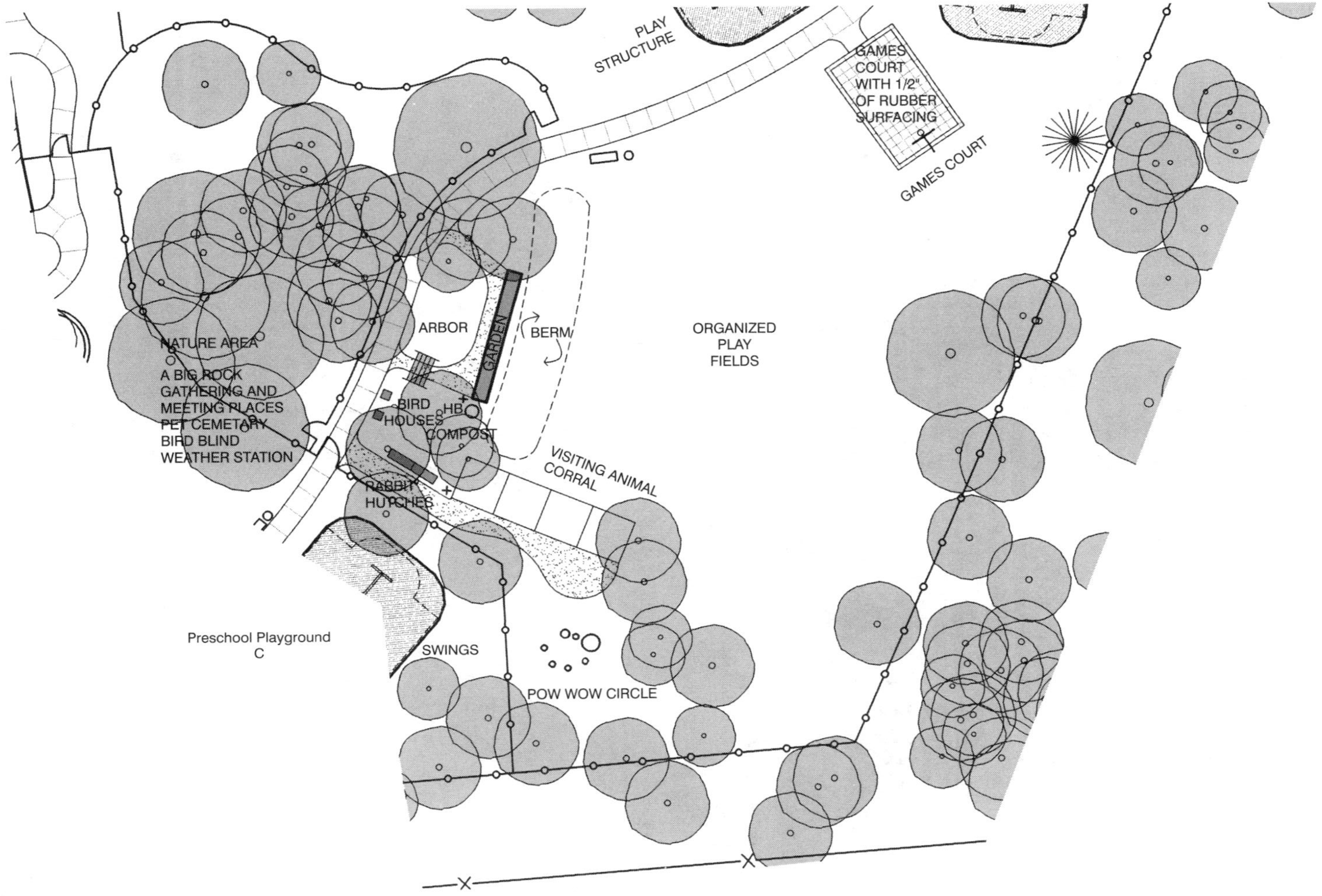
PLAY
STRUCTURE
GAMES
COURT
WITH 1/2"
OF RUBBER
SURFACING
GAMES COURT
NATURE AREA
A BIG ROCK
GATHERING AND
MEETING PLACES
PET CEMETARY
BIRD BLIND
WEATHER STATION
ARBOR
GARDEN
BERM
BIRD
HOUSES
HB
COMPOST
RABBIT
HUTCHES
VISITING ANIMAL
CORRAL
ORGANIZED
PLAY
FIELDS
Preschool Playground
C
SWINGS
POW WOW CIRCLE

FIGURE 11–3 *(continued)*

Gardening motivates children to learn through play and instinctive curiosity.

> The natural diversity of the yard functioned as a tripartite vehicle—stimulating healthy child development through informal play, supporting formal curriculum development in interdisciplinary environmental education, and accommodating a variety of informal in-school and out-of-school educational and recreational programs. (Moore & Wong, 1997, p. 13)

American Horticultural Society

Horticulturists, landscape architects, science educators, and others who know the value of gardens for children are increasingly studying and sponsoring gardening activities for children. The American Horticultural Society and the W. Atlee Burpee Company sponsored a national children's gardening symposium to help kindergarten through eighth grade educators initiate or improve gardening programs for children (Heffernan, 1994). Over 550 educators, horticulturists, and others attended 60 workshops designed to be a call to arms to help ensure the next generation of gardeners. Twelve children's gardens, designed by children and landscape designers, were built overlooking the Potomac River in Alexandria, Virginia, as models for parents, teachers, and youth leaders.

Healing Gardens

Gardens for healing are rapidly finding their way into outdoor spaces at children's hospitals (Coates & Siepl-Coates, 1998; Olds & Daniel, 1987). The natural wonders of artistic creations (sculpture, fountains, color, ceramics), music, sunshine, fragrance of flowers, trickling waters, fish, birds and other small animals, and play places may have healing effects for ill and injured children and provide solace for their families. Covered areas, natural shade, playscapes, gardens, herbs, and plants, all connected with user-friendly paths, are linked to natural wonders for the enjoyment, self-esteem, and spiritual benefit those of hospitalized children and their entire families. Examples are the Children's Hospital of Austin, Texas (under development); the Children's Hospital of

San Diego (*www.chsd.org*); Duke University Children's Hospital (*www.dukenews.duke.edu*); the University of Virginia's Children's Medical Center (*www.people.virginia.edu*); and the West Seattle Natural Health Clinic (*www.wln.com*).

Favorite Places

Francis (1995) interviewed gardeners in California and Norway to identify the different meanings that people attach to childhood gardens. Using childhood memories of gardens, he identified common qualities to illustrate design, planning, and management issues for children's gardens. The order of most to least frequently mentioned, remembered element were vegetation and natural elements such as trees bushes and flowers; structures such as cabins, barns, tool sheds, and fire pits; specific gardens areas such as flower beds, paths, sandboxes, tree swings, and sports areas; shelter and privacy areas such as those among the big trees and in naturally sheltered areas. In describing favorite places, most mentioned protected, sheltered, or hidden areas, mostly under trees or bushes. Other researchers (Bartlett, 1990; Hart, 1979; Hester, 1985) confirm Francis's conclusions that rough, natural places are remembered and sought out more frequently than manicured places.

Children's gardens should contain certain essential elements including good soil, water, trees (some large), places for tending growing vegetables, fruit trees, habitats for birds and insects, pets, a playhouse, hiding places, places to dig in the earth, a compost area, an area for native plants, and a storage shed with tools and supplies. For help on getting started with a schoolyard habitat see the National Wildlife Federation Web site at *www.nwf.org/schoolyardhabitats/creatinghabitatsites.cfm* (2004).

Making Play Environments Magical

We seek to help children recapture the enchanted moments of early childhood, the special memories of dewy mornings in the countryside, the special hiding places in the forest, the captivating moments with sand castles on a beach, the special comfort and aromas of grandmother in her kitchen, the sense of accomplishment from creating with found and natural materials. What are these magical qualities that can be included in any playground?

Big and Little

The miniature worlds of storybooks capture most effectively the fairy-tale imaginations of young children. Children of all ages delight in the tiny, miniature, charming, or diminutive, which offer a sense of power and allow them to play out their deepest conflicts or desires. As they grow, their fascination with the miniature is extended to model building, dolls, figurines, toy trains, small trains in parks, and the miniature in nature—insects, tiny animals, snowflakes, cocoons, pebbles, veins in a leaf.

The giant, heroic, colossal scale reduces children and adults to equals and creates a new sense of grandeur. Children are in awe of dinosaurs, full-size trains, 18-wheelers, and airplanes. Where space allows, replicas or antiques enhance the wonder of the playground. In small playgrounds, elevated platforms can capture views of distant places, opening up a world of huge buildings and expansive, changing skies and clouds, and enabling children to gain a sense of distance and vastness of scale.

Story Time

The fairy-tale world of children's literature is peopled with brownies, pixies, elves and leprechauns, and animals that live and talk like people. Children love hearing stories of these creatures and delight in reliving their fantasies in make-believe play. The outdoor setting for story time and reliving time-honored fairy tales and favorite stories can be one and the same—a cozy enclosure, framed by trees and flowering shrubs.

Real versus Sham

Children often prefer the real thing over the sham. The real may be more durable, more valuable, more functional, or associated with past experience. The hammer Mom or Dad uses is more valuable than a plastic imitation. The real truck or fire engine, complete with horn, whistle, steering wheel, levers, and gauges, imparts attributes that a mere copy cannot have.

Sensuality

Infants and toddlers are essentially sensory beings, trying out and sharpening their senses with everything within visual, auditory, or tactile reach. Create with children a sensory path with textures, sounds of animals and mobiles, smells and colors of blooming plants, trickling water and shifting sand—all combining to engage children's senses and remain in their memories. People never outgrow their need for sensory stimulation and beauty. Play spaces should be beautiful as well as functional (Olds, 1989).

Connection with the Past

A centuries-old oak tree in Austin, Texas, drew worldwide attention when it was deliberately poisoned by a vandal. Money and letters of advice for saving the tree poured in from many places. The media covered the story for months. Similar scenarios are played out around the world as, historical artifacts or elements of nature are threatened.

Age and history bestow a magical aura. Natural forests are more compelling than pine plantations; hoary old oaks are more magical than young saplings; old coal-fired locomotives are more awe-inspiring than modern electrical engines.

The prevailing mentality is to bulldoze everything of value from a site before creating a playground. Thus, everything of historical value—old ivy-covered stone fences, brick and stone walks, old buildings, rare plants, hills, streams—is damaged or destroyed. Somehow, the contrived replacements are never quite so imaginative, never have the tales to tell, never conjure up the images, and never quite have the lasting effects of the real thing.

The Unique and Exotic

Children are intrigued by novelty, incongruity, unpredictability, out-of-placeness—something not provided by the playground catalog and not seen except in special places. Giant musical instruments made durable for outdoor use and requiring whole bodies to manipulate, tire dinosaurs that stretch the scale of the usual, enclosures of winding vines—all lend uniqueness and a special state of pride, awe, and consciousness to surroundings.

Objects need not have obvious purpose. If they are foreign, strange, or rare, they lend a special quality that transcends utility beyond their static nature. "Within sameness there is difference" (Huxley, 1954, p. 61). A flower garden and an old fountain may yield nothing of concrete worth, yet they lend beauty and elicit reflection and awareness of a larger or higher order of things.

Loose Parts (Portable Materials) and Simple Tools

Children of industrialized countries are losing their ability to use tools (Ikeda, 1979), for fearful parents restrict their use and plastic imitations supplant the real things. The freedom to roam, explore, and create from scratch that children of previous generations enjoyed has all but disappeared for millions of children. Places children build for themselves are far more valuable than those built for them. Children in playgrounds and gardens need tools, a wide selection of building materials, and a play leader who knows when to help and when to step out. Tools and loose parts allow children to be their own designers. The best playgrounds and gardens are changed and transformed by children and are never finished.

Special or Sacred Places

For a place to be special and enchanting, it needs to have a certain atmosphere, a sense of enclosure about it, a feeling of serenity, an atmosphere of natural beauty. An amphitheater built for children, surrounded by plants, and made special with a pool for fish, a bird bath, or wind chimes creates a mood-setting focus. Light and shadowy features created by the sun filtering through an overhead trellis covered with flowering vines create a pattern of beauty and mystique.

In his study of children's special places in England and on the island of Carriacou in the West Indies, Sobel (1993) learned from children about their special places—forts, bases, houses, tree houses, tree forts, dens, playhouses, and bush houses—all referring to places that were special or important to the children. He found that shared places were important throughout middle childhood (ages 8–11), for both boys and girls, but that private places became more important around ages 10 and 11. Children 5 to 7 years old and 12 to 15 claimed that they did not build or use such places; the older children implied that this was "kid's stuff."

These places ranged from those constructed from found or scavenged materials to those merely found and claimed. At first, they were found close to home but tended to be located farther away as children grew older. Sobel surmised that basic to children's attraction to such special places is their need for privacy and self-sufficiency, and creating them is one of the ways that they physically and psychologically prepare themselves for puberty in adolescence.

Special places are places to retreat, places to look at the world from a place of one's own, places to transform the environment, to make a place for oneself and develop a sense of personal order, a **sense of place** (Hart, 1979). Sobel (1993) adds that forts are special places, that these often secret places are sacrosanct and defended, and outsiders are not welcome.

Small, manageable places in the world should be safe, calm, and reassuring. They are our own, whether for having doll parties or for a clubhouse. "To experience a place deeply is to bond with a place" (Sobel, 1993, p. 159). Taking one's place in the larger community depends on children's bonding with natural places during childhood. "Sense of place describes the feeling that exists between people and the environments in which they live" (Moore & Wong, 1997, p. 65).

The responsibility of adults is to ensure that children have opportunities and access to special or "sacred" places (Singer & Singer, 1990), with unstructured time and a few props for cultivating games of pretend and developing their imagination—where they can find and create their own natural, private, special places and, in so doing, develop a sense of place and bond with nature.

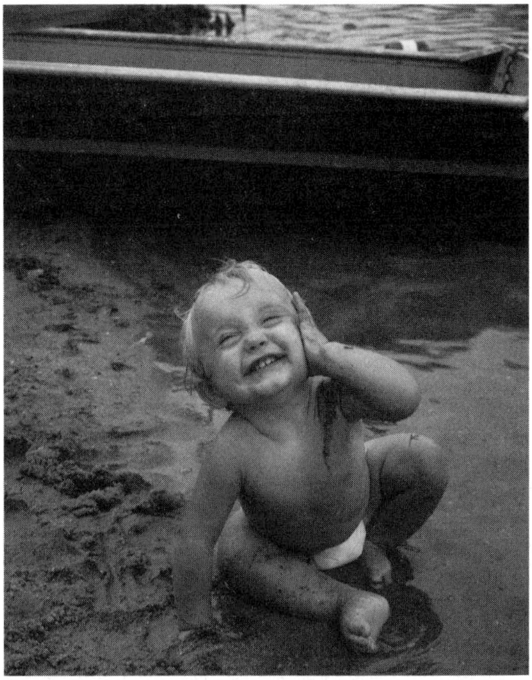

Good play environments have magical qualities. They are permeated with awe and wonder.

Doing Nothing

Smith (1957, p. 92), reflecting on his childhood play, says, "[W]e spent an awful lot of time doing nothing. There was an occupation called 'just running around.' It was no game. It had no rules. It didn't start and it didn't stop." When Christopher Robin told Pooh, "What I like doing best is nothing" (Milne, 1928), he was living in a world that allowed reflecting, daydreaming, messing around, playing or not playing, working or not working. Today's children of industrialized nations live in a world of schedules, lessons, and practices that no longer values daydreaming, reflecting, relaxing, enjoying free play, or doing nothing. Adults unwittingly assume that television compensates for privacy, reflection, and reading, but in reality television structures time, distorts reality, and robs children of reading, playing, and reflecting. Children need time to mess around in enchanted places and time to just be kids. The favorite fishing or swimming hole or the fish pond, wild places, tree-shaded picnic grounds, vine-covered enclosures, fire pits for warming or cooking, and shaded nooks for reading books all invite children to stop and reflect, to slow down and experience the magical.

SUMMARY

Where do we look for models that will support the creation of imaginative play environments? The countryside, of course, is nature's own, unexcelled outdoor play environment. Here, children experience an infinite range of qualities that are both the concrete and the symbolic stuff of play—rarity, incongruity, unpredictability, mystery, abundance, color, texture, ambiance, scale, imagery, creation, shape, risk, and motion. Compact gardens are yet another example of the wisest adaptations of the countryside to confined spaces and limited resources. For adults, a small garden, even a square foot, offers food and aesthetic beauty. For children, the potential benefits extend well beyond these basic needs to support expanding knowledge of nature and incorporate an infinite range of creative activities.

Creating play places in restricted spaces is not merely a matter of cost or of space, but of imagination and ingenuity. Just as there is good play (healthy play) or play with positive effects and bad play (unhealthy play) (e.g., bullying, cruelty, sadism, extreme violence), with deleterious effects, there are also good play environments and bad play environments.

Good play environments have magical qualities that transcend the here and now, the humdrum, and the typical. They have "flow" qualities that take the child to other places and other times. They are permeated with awe and wonder, both in reality and in imaginative qualities. Bad play environments are stark and immutable, controlled by adults, lacking resiliency and enchantment. Few dreams can be spun there, and few instincts can be played out. The wonders of nature, the joys of imagery, the delights of creating are all but lost for children restricted to such play places. Those who create play environments for children have a choice, no matter what the context—small town, city, or megalopolis. The difference lies in how we value children's play, what we are willing to do, and how much energy we are willing to expend.

KEY TERMS

Contents of playgrounds
Functions of playgrounds
Hanging out
Loose parts
Magical playscapes
Manufactured appliance era
Master plan
Modern era
Modular design era
Natural features
Novelty era
Outdoor gymnasia
Peer culture
Permanent features
Play leaders
Playground culture
Safety of playgrounds
Sandgartens
Sense of place
Social density
Standardized era
Traditional recess
Usage patterns
Work/play

STUDY QUESTIONS

1. How did city and country play environments of the Depression era differ from today's play environments? How do these differences affect children's development?
2. Trace the development of formal playgrounds from their beginnings in the United States to the present time. Which era best represented developmentally appropriate play environments? Why?
3. Why is it necessary to provide different play opportunities indoors versus outdoors? Describe how indoor and outdoor play environments can be complementary.
4. Why is it important for creators/designers of play environments to have a working knowledge of child development?
5. Identify key differences in "good" playgrounds for different age groups—infants/toddlers, preschoolers, and school-age children. Locate playgrounds in your neighborhood or city that were prepared for these age groups. Using the Playground Rating System, assess their relative merits.
6. Why is a master plan needed when designing or creating playgrounds? What are the appropriate steps in creating a master plan? How can children be involved? Should there be deviations from the plan? Why?

7. How does social density on playgrounds affect play behaviors?
8. What are the major factors to consider in determining equipment layout and use patterns on playgrounds?
9. How does one transform conventional playgrounds into magical playgrounds? Why is this important?
10. Explain "sense of place." Observe at neighborhood homes, parks, schools, and woodlands for "special places." Describe them. How do they contribute to healthy development?
11. Why is recess important for children? How is recess time used by teachers and children in your area schools? What changes would you propose? Why?

Chapter 12 Child Safety in Public Places

EVERY TIME someone gets accidentally injured, someone, somewhere made a mistake. God ain't doing this stuff—we are.

(Dr. Red Duke, director of Trauma and Emergency Medical Services at Hermann Hospital in Houston, TX, quoted in *Modern Maturity,* July–August 1995)

IT IS clear that we need to find ways to let children roam beyond the pavement, to gain access to vegetation and earth that allows them to tunnel, climb, or even fall. . . . Better to let kids be a hazard to nature than let nature be a hazard to them. . . . Learning what to fear, and what not to fear, is a large part of growing up.

(Nabhan & Trimble, 1994, pp. 9, 152)

SOME PEOPLE think that accidents just happen—that they are due to fate or bad luck and are unavoidable. . . . [I]njuries result from hazardous conditions, which can be corrected, and unsafe behaviors, which can be changed.

(National Safety Council, 1999, p. iv)

The literature on children's indoor safety, particularly for schools and child care centers, is extensive, and safety guidelines and standards are detailed and generally enforced through inspections by various agencies. However, children's safety in public outdoor places for play, amusement, and entertainment receives only marginal attention, and children are frequently exposed to unacceptable levels of **risk** for injury. This chapter will illuminate types of hazards and the nature of physical risks that children and their caretakers may encounter in public places, and will make recommendations for improving child safety while preserving acceptable levels of risk and ensuring **play value**, challenge, diversity, and learning. It is not reasonable to anticipate that attention to safety will result in prevention of all injuries, particularly minor ones such as scrapes, abrasions, bruises, and small splinters. However, it is reasonable to expect that careful, organized safety programs will dramatically reduce the probability of serious injuries.

In a safety context, physical risk refers to an action chosen by an individual that poses a chance of injury. The level of risk may vary widely, depending on the nature of the hazard, the abilities of the individual, and related factors such as weather, adult supervision, and maintenance. **Hazard** refers to a condition, seen or unseen, that is likely to cause injury, ranging from minor to serious, debilitating, or life-threatening. Hazards are encountered during normal, anticipated activity or as a result of reasonably foreseeable abuse or misuse of materials and equipment in the play environment.

Risk management is the systematic, planned prevention and reduction of accidents through selecting safe equipment, reducing hazardous conditions, and providing information and supervision that identifies potential hazards and how to avoid them. Safety specialists are concerned with levels of hazards. Level I, or **limited hazards**, are conditions likely to cause minor or nondisabling injuries. Level II, or **moderate hazards**, are conditions that are likely to cause serious injury resulting in temporary disability. Level III, or **extreme hazards**, are conditions that are likely to cause permanent disability or loss of life or body parts. When examining playgrounds, certified inspectors may identify levels of hazards and make recommendations for immediate and protracted corrections based on the level of hazard. For example, playground equipment posing extreme hazards is immediately removed from the playground or secured from use until the hazards are corrected. Limited hazards may be subject to correction on a more extended schedule of regular maintenance. See Christiansen and Vogelsong (1996) and Kutska and Hoffman (1992) for detailed information on developing playground safety and maintenance programs.

A reasonable level of risk is necessary in play, but as in other life activities, there must be limitations on the degree of physical risk taken. Yet, we must ensure that children have access to play environments that challenge, provide acceptable risks, and even pose degrees of danger. By its very nature, spontaneous play is purposeless and pleasure giving and exposes children to risk. All healthy, well-fed mammals play, and their fundamental play moves include leaping, defying gravity, climbing, jumping, horsing around—all activities that place the player at risk (Brown, 1997, 1998). Through experience with risk taking, adult and older peer **scaffolding** (presenting gradually increasing levels of risk and assisting children in developing skills), and exposure to increasingly complex materials and problems, levels of challenge and complexity are constantly expanded. Risk is essential for play and for healthy development.

Risks are inherent in children's play activities. They may be **physical risks**, as when exposed to challenges and hazards; **emotional risks**, as when expressing anger, trusting others, and admitting fear; or **intellectual risks**, as when admitting error or trying to outwit a peer. These types of risks are often interconnected (Smith, 1998). Adults frequently engage in yet other types of risk—**financial risks** (investing in the stock market, gambling, overextending credit card debt) and **supervisory risks** (standing back and observing children taking manageable risks, responding to them, considering what is good for them, and letting them grow and mature).

Neither parents nor teachers can be aware of all the hazards that children face, nor can they be watching every child at every moment. Providing safe places for children to play means that caretakers need the help of many others whose decisions can reduce the risk of injury to children—legislators, police, firefighters, social workers, designers, architects, reporters, manufacturers, service groups, the business community, and safety organizations (Wilson, Baker, Teret, Shock, & Garbarino, 1991). When all responsible adults attend to their respective responsibilities for child safety, children escape serious injury. Caretakers (parents and teachers) cannot be expected to have unlimited knowledge of safety, infallible powers of perception, or total control of children.

The **U.S. Consumer Product Safety Commission (CPSC)** (*www.cpsc.gov*) makes available a huge range of safety resources to assist the public in evaluating and regulating the safety of approximately 15,000 types of consumer products (manufactured products), from coffeemakers, to toys, to lawn mowers, to playground equipment. This independent regulatory agency of the U.S. government protects the public against unreasonable risks of injuries and deaths resulting from consumer products. Information on consumer product–related injuries and deaths, product recalls, and other CPSC activities are available by telephone, Internet, letter, or messenger service. Contact numbers are included in the "General Information" section at the end of this chapter, and the news releases referenced herein are available from these same sources.

The home, the shopping mall, and the classroom are places where children encounter hazards and take risks, but these places are not designed for taking physical risks during play, as are playgrounds. Failure to foresee that children tend to play in almost all contexts using anything that remotely resembles a play device, and failure to take preventive safety measures, is a frequent cause of child injury. Children are naturally attracted to water, equipment, or devices, including furniture and railings, that can be climbed or manipulated, and, even in public places not designed for play, children commonly engage in risk taking in hazardous settings.

For example, one of the most common unacceptable, yet easily preventable, physical risks for young children is seen in grocery stores and shopping malls where young children are allowed to stand up, jiggle, jump, reach for merchandise, and play in shopping carts rolling over concrete floors. Injuries resulting from shopping cart falls increased from 7,800 in 1985 to more than 16,000 in 1996. Two-thirds of the victims were treated in emergency rooms for head injuries, with more than half suffering severe injuries such as concussions and fractures (CPSC Press Release #97-116). Parents should require children to use safety belts when in shopping carts. Following an analysis of shopping cart injuries, Smith, Dietrich, Garcia, and Shields (1997) concluded that shopping carts should be redesigned to decrease the risk of injury, and children should be prohibited from riding in carts of current design.

Regardless of the setting, careful planning can reduce or eliminate hazards while preserving challenge and acceptable levels of risk. On outdoor playgrounds, fast slides, challenging climbing equipment, supervised outdoor cooking over open fires, and building and gardening with tools can all be available with reasonable levels of safety. Growth demands taking reasonable risks and learning from one's mistakes. Those deprived of such opportunities grow up fearful, timid, and brittle. Children of an earlier, more rural era learned to identify hazards and handle risks through extensive play and work activities. From an early age they interacted with animals, nature, tools, and farm equipment under the careful tutelage of adults. They learned to use tools, to appreciate heights, to plant and nurture gardens, and to sort out dangerous and wild animals from docile, domesticated ones; in so doing, they developed highly refined perceptual and motor skills.

Contemporary kids, because of fragmented parenting, latch-key living, television addiction, junk food, gangs, perceived and real neighborhood dangers, absence of places to play, elimination of recess, reduction of physical education, and a host of other modern pressures, have fewer opportunities to develop the motor and cognitive skills needed for safe play (Sutterby & Frost, 2002). American children rank lowest among developed countries on measures of physical fitness (Dennison et al., 1988; Javernick, 1988; Ross & Gilbert, 1985), and their sedentary lifestyles and consumption of junk food are now seen by pediatricians as contributing to obesity (Deitz & Gortmaker, 1985), diabetes (Thompson, 1998), and early symptoms of later heart disease (Winston, 1984).

The solution to this fitness dilemma is to ensure that children at home and at school receive a balanced diet of nutritious food and that they engage in regular, sustained physical activity. The National Association for Sport and Physical Education recommends (Fukushima, 1998) that elementary-school-age children have at least 1 hour of vigorous physical activity each day. Vigorous activities should last 10 to 15 minutes or more with brief rest periods and children should engage in a variety of activities of various intensities.

A national online survey of more than 800 mothers in the United States (Clements, 2003) found that children play outdoors on a daily basis less often than did children a decade ago—declining from 70% then to 31% today. Children's current engagement in television viewing, playing computer and video games, reading, and playing board games helps account for this decrease. Concerns about crime and safety coupled with lack of adult supervision also contributed to the decline in outdoor play. The results indicated that 71% of parents do not have adequate time to spend outdoors with their children.

Children are naturally drawn to challenging environments rich with play materials—free or expensive, natural or manufactured. Construction sites, adventure playgrounds, swimming pools, ice skating areas, zoos, and wilderness areas invite and challenge children, but all pose unseen hazards, particularly for very young children who have not developed logical thought (reflective, evaluative, cause–effect thinking) and those with poorly developed motor skills (clumsy, uncoordinated). Children must be exposed to managed levels of hazards, learn to see hazards, evaluate hazards, and cope with or master hazards. This is best done through experiencing challenges regularly, from an early age, under the watchful eyes and helpful hands of adults. Many children are unsafe in any play environment because they spend too little time in challenging, complex settings to develop perceptual-motor and safety skills (Frost & Henniger, 1979), or they receive little or no guidance on safety from adults.

HAZARDS IN PUBLIC PLACES

Throughout this chapter, we use injury data from the National Electronic Injury Surveillance System (NEISS) to illustrate the scope of injuries, type of injuries, and consumer products implicated in injuries. NEISS is a federal agency that collects injury data associated with 15,000 consumer products from hospital emergency departments across the United States. The examples of very serious hazards in Figure 12–1 were selected from personal litigation documents, CPSC data which includes NEISS data, Safe Kids 2000 data, personal communication with specialists in child safety, inspection of injury/fatality sites, and safety conferences. These examples represent very serious **play-related hazards** that are likely to result in permanent disability, loss of body parts, or loss of life.

CHILD DEVELOPMENT AND SAFETY

The ages and **developmental abilities** of children must be taken into account in formulating a safety program. The following sections consider the unique characteristics of toddlers, preschoolers, and early-school-age children, and how those characteristics affect safety concerns.

FIGURE 12–1 Examples of Very Serious Hazards

- Cords on children's clothing, jewelry around necks, and jump ropes can catch on playground apparatus, in car or bus doors, and choke children. Heavy handles and protrusions on jump ropes injure eyes and other body parts.
- Openings on playground apparatus between $3\frac{1}{2}$ inches and 9 inches can entrap children's heads and lead to strangulation.
- Falls onto concrete, asphalt, and hard-packed earth under and around playground equipment can result in fractures, paraplegia, quadriplegia, brain damage, damaged internal organs, and death. Wherever children climb, hard surfaces, indoors or outdoors—including homes, child care centers, and commercial establishments—are extremely hazardous.
- Heavy wood, plastic, or metal swings, especially those with protruding bolts, can cause serious or fatal injury to children upon impact.
- Excessive heights on playground equipment or other climbing equipment (generally, equipment above the standing reaching height of tallest child users) can result in serious injury or death from falls.
- Wearing jewelry (rings, earrings, necklaces) on playgrounds can result in hang-ups on protruding equipment parts, causing finger amputation or injury to neck or ear.
- Open S-hooks and protruding elements on playground and sports equipment can entangle children's clothing or jewelry and lead to suffocation.
- Exposed electrical apparatus (e.g., playground slides and decks, sewer covers, black or heat-absorbing padded surfaces) can result in severe burns, especially to toddlers who tend to "freeze" or "stick" to hot surfaces.
- Swimming pools, improperly protected by fences, secure gates, and alarms, are the sites of many drownings each year, especially of toddlers.
- Improperly designed or improperly anchored soccer goals can collapse on children, resulting in serious injuries or death.
- Beginning ice skaters, in-line skaters, roller skaters, and skiers are at high risk of head injury in falls. Helmets would prevent most of these injuries.
- Riding bicycles without a helmet can result in serious injury and fatalities in collisions and falls.
- Unsupervised children can gain access to dangerous animals in zoos by crossing barriers, inserting fingers and hands into animal containment areas, and falling into animal containment pits and moats. Most existing barriers at zoos do not prevent such access.
- Trampolines are frequently poorly designed and maintained, leading to the risk of serious injuries in falls onto unpadded frames of trampolines or onto unprotected surrounding floor or ground.
- In many states, carnival and theme park rides are poorly regulated or unregulated and many are involved in serious injuries and deaths. This is especially true of traveling carnivals.
- Many car trunks, abandoned refrigerators, storage boxes, and toy chests have doors or lids that can be opened and closed by children, allowing them to become entrapped and suffocate.
- Window guards should be installed in multifloor apartments and homes to prevent young children from falling out. Window screens do not protect from falling.
- Loose cords such as those used for window blinds should be secured so that they cannot form a loop around a child's head and lead to strangulation.
- Standing up in shopping carts is very hazardous because children can easily lose their balance and the carts are unstable and tilt over easily. Falls from the height of a shopping cart onto a concrete floor covered with vinyl can be fatal.
- Young children can pull out heavy furniture drawers, and cause furniture to topple or appliances and television sets to topple from tables or chests onto them. This can result in serious injury or death.

(continued)

FIGURE 12–1 *(continued)*

- Fireworks cause many serious burns to children each year. Many fireworks entering the United States do not meet U.S. federal standards. Young children should not be allowed to use fireworks in any manner.
- Toddlers must be given extra protection from water in buckets, toilets, pools, and streams because they are attracted to water, do not realize the dangers of water, and cannot easily extricate themselves from falls into water. Drowning is the number two cause of death for young children.
- Children should be properly secured in car seats taking into account type of air bags, quality of car seats, and age of child. Auto accidents are the number one cause of accidental death for young children.
- Extreme caution should be used to protect children against exposure to pesticides, prescription drugs, housekeeping products, and other toxic materials.
- Firearms should be kept locked away and unloaded.
- Adults and children should get up-to-date recall and product safety information from the Consumer Product Safety Commissions Web site *(www.cpsc.gov)* so they will know which products are causing injuries and deaths.
- Adults who care for children—parents, grandparents, teachers, caretakers, and others—should secure federal and state safety guidelines for toys, playground equipment, swimming pools, and other consumer products used by children and use them in their injury prevention programs.

Toddlers

As children grow into the toddler stage ages (1–3 years), beginning with the onset of walking, they become increasingly mobile. During the toddler period, cognitive, social, motor, and emotional development is rapid and leads to a growing sense of independence. Toddlers are avid explorers, trying out everything in the immediate environment, but their curiosity frequently threatens their safety. They will walk into pools of water, touch hot surfaces, step off high places, or run into the paths of cars. They may be unaware of the consequences of their actions and must be carefully protected by adults.

As toddlers learn to understand and accept common rules of behavior, adults must supervise them closely and take steps to reduce hazards they may encounter, indoors and outdoors. This is frequently called "childproofing," but "proofing" is not really possible under normal conditions. Toddlers must take acceptable risks to learn how to protect themselves. Adults attempt to reduce hazards to a reasonably acceptable level, focusing on avoiding or removing those hazards that could result in loss of life or debilitating injury. Even animals take care to protect their young from extreme hazards. Such care by human adults need not extend to overprotection, paranoia, or interference with creativity. As toddlers experience challenges and think about steps for solving problems, they gradually learn to anticipate the consequences of their actions and are better able to protect themselves from previously unrecognized hazards. Adults should encourage experimentation in reasonably safe environments, for "trying on for size" is essential to toddler's learning and safety.

Toddlers are sometimes referred to as the "terrible twos." Their curiosity and extreme activity can cause considerable anxiety for caretakers, especially in public play and entertainment environments such as playgrounds, pools, zoos, and amusement parks. In such places, the caretaker must stay in visual and auditory range at all times and attempt to stay in range for physical restraint when necessary. With toddlers, there will be breakdowns or lapses in supervision, including times when they run out of auditory or visual range. This is especially true when a single adult is responsible for supervising more than one child. Consequently, both child supervisors and sponsors of play sites should carefully evaluate the environments they allow toddlers to enter. In extremely hazardous places, such as along busy streets or adjacent to steep drop-offs, adults must hold toddlers by the hand because they can move quickly and unexpectedly. Those responsible for operating public play and entertainment places must meet or exceed common regulations and standards for child safety.

Children are most active at ages 2 and 3, and their activity levels decrease during the preschool years. Because of their high activity levels and their relatively immature motor and cognitive skills, toddlers are at greater risk of accidental injuries than preschoolers and must be supervised more closely. This is graphically and poignantly illustrated by a wide range of data: toddlers walking or running into the path of cars, climbing through gates and fences and drowning in pools, standing up in shopping carts or other wheeled devices and falling onto concrete floors, locking themselves in refrigerators and car trunks, sitting down or placing hands on hot metal and "sticking" to the surface, and walking into the path of swings on the playground. More boys are injured accidentally than girls, resulting from higher activity levels, high-risk behavior, and reluctance to submit to authority.

Preschoolers and Early-School-Age Children

Preschoolers (ages 3–5) and early-school-age children (ages 5–7) have generally developed beyond toddlers in physical appearance, height and weight, levels of activity, refinement of motor skills, thinking processes, knowledge of events, language and communication, social skills, and emotional maturity. Their motor skills allow them to gain access to previously forbidden or inaccessible places such as pools, high places, trees, walls, deck railings, and fences, and they are motivated to play on such challenging devices. The conceptual development of these age groups is progressing rapidly, but most are still engaging in prelogical thought and lack high levels of skill in recognizing and evaluating potentially hazardous conditions. Furthermore, they are increasingly influenced by peers and may participate in motor challenges beyond their abilities in order to impress or compete with them. Such risks often lead to injury, particularly on playgrounds but also in other public places.

Preschoolers experience an increase in fears and anxieties. They have vivid imaginations, engage frequently in symbolic (make-believe) play, and may have difficulty distinguishing reality from fantasy. The fears of some children are specific to certain events. The child who has been mauled by a dog or burned on a hot surface may generalize her fears to other animals or to other surfaces. Some children may show little fear in most contexts, even in very hazardous situations. They may approach vicious animals as though they were docile pets; they may display little fear of heights, water, or automobiles in streets. They may play hangman in realistic fashion ("like on television"), actually forming a noose, placing it around one's head, and jumping off a deck or chair. Learning such concepts as "injuries can cause severe pain" and "death is permanent" is one of the many tasks of young children that takes time, experience, and adult guidance.

Adult (parent, teacher, caretaker), peer, and television models heavily influence the social skills, moral values, and hazard avoidance behaviors of young children. Many adults do not recognize many of the serious hazards that children regularly face, yet young children look to them as models. Some children learn cruelty, aggression, and disruptive behavior from their adult models and play out these influences by teasing and fighting peers, throwing things at zoo animals and feeding them food dangerous to their health, abusing the property of others, ignoring safety rules, and generally disrupting group activities in public places. Such behavior is reinforced by parents, teachers, and caretakers who fail to plan with children, do not teach self-control, employ poor child management skills, or lack basic knowledge of common safety guidelines/standards.

GUIDELINES/STANDARDS FOR SAFETY

Because of young children's vulnerability to hazards, growing numbers of child injuries, and mushrooming litigation, concerned professionals are rapidly developing safety guidelines, standards and regulations, or laws to help ensure that play equipment and environments are reasonably safe. These range from guidelines prepared by schools and child care centers relevant to their own contexts; to mandatory regulations of state departments of health, human services, and education; to voluntary standards prepared and distributed by national standards organizations and U.S. government agencies such as the CPSC.

The safety standards established by organizations such as the **American Society for Testing and Materials (ASTM)** and by agencies of the U.S. government usually become recognized as national standards of care, meaning that they prevail in litigation. In other words, if a child is injured or killed in an accident on a playground or other public place where national standards apply and a lawsuit is filed, the winner is often determined by compliance or noncompliance with the national standard. Compared to national playground and play equipment standards, state playground standards or regulations are typically sterile and extremely limited in scope and clarity. Consequently, many child care providers, unwittingly relying on compliance with state regulations to protect themselves in litigation, find themselves facing huge liability settlements because they failed to meet national standards of care (e.g., ASTM, CPSC). Every sponsor of facilities where children gather should check all levels of safety standards and laws, local to national, to ensure that their facilities are in compliance with those that best represent reasonable levels of safety for children and those that will best protect against legal claims.

History of Playground Equipment Standards

This section will trace the development of national playground and play equipment standards because most serious injuries at child care centers and schools occur on outdoor playgrounds and because the process of safety standards development is similar across products intended for children.

The ASTM, organized in 1898, is the leading national voluntary standards development system in the world for publishing safety standards for consumer materials, products, systems, and services. More than 34,000 technically qualified volunteers, working in more than 132 committees, write about 1,000 standards each year. These are sold throughout the world. A number of the ASTM standards were prepared for materials and equipment that children use in their play. Separate standards are available for public playground equipment, home playground equipment, sports equipment and facilities, playing surfaces, nonpowder guns, amusement rides and devices, baseball face guards, toys, baby cribs, infant walkers, helmets, pool covers, bunk beds, bicycle carriers, and toddler beds.

The section to follow traces the development of safety guidelines and standards for public playground equipment—that is, equipment designed for parks, schools, child care facilities, multiple-family dwellings, restaurants, resorts and recreational developments, and other areas of public use. These guidelines and standards cover children ages 2 to 12. Standards for toddlers are under development as of November, 2003.

In the early 20th century, manufactured playground equipment was constructed primarily of heavy-duty steel and wood. The most common devices were swings, slides, jungle gyms, teeter-totters, and giant strides. They featured fast rotation and extreme heights, accommodated large numbers of children, and the surface underneath equipment was commonly hard-packed earth, packed cinders, or asphalt. As early as 1917, concern about injuries was evident, and a lawsuit, resulting from an injury to a child who fell from a swing, was successfully litigated against a school board in Tacoma, Washington. During the 1920s, the design, selection, installation, and use of playground equipment was debated in professional publications (Playground and Recreation Association of America, 1928). Concerns about playground injuries led the National Recreation

Association (NRA) to form the Committee on Standards in Playground Apparatus for the purpose of developing a guide for communities in selecting playground equipment (NRA, 1931). The resulting document included essential elements for playground success: location, arrangement, and erection of equipment; supervision; apparatus zones; care of ground under equipment; instructions for use of equipment; age designations; and types of equipment.

Even during this early period, park professionals recognized the hazards of hard surfacing under equipment, and in 1932 the NRA published a two-part report on problems in surfacing children's playgrounds in its periodical *Recreation*. Based on his knowledge of law and of lawsuits, Jacobson (1940) made specific recommendations for playground safety. He emphasized purchasing the best equipment, observing equipment in use, setting up inspection systems, creating printed inspection and repair forms, recording all inspections and work, employing careful supervision by trained professionals, and posting warning signs for unsafe conditions. Ironically, over a half century later, professionals are still debating and encouraging the same or similar recommendations.

By the 1950s, injuries and fatalities on the school playgrounds of Los Angeles (Brashear, 1952; Zaun, 1952, 1955) resulted in public protest about asphalt surfaces under and around play equipment. With 190 school playgrounds surfaced with asphalt, several children suffered fatal injuries in falls onto the hard surfaces. Following citizen action and a lawsuit, Los Angeles installed rubber surfacing under playground equipment and had no additional fatalities over the following decade.

In 1972, NEISS was established to gather information from a sample of hospital emergency departments about consumer product–related injuries in the United States and its territories. The data collected on some consumer products, including those associated with playground injuries, were influential in later decisions to develop national safety guidelines and standards for playground equipment.

Systematic efforts to collect scientific data on playground injuries were initiated in 1972, resulting in a report by the Bureau of Product Safety, U.S. Food and Drug Administration (1972), which drew from NEISS data to reveal a dismal picture of playground injuries and hazards, and ranked playground equipment, eighth in number of injuries on the Consumer Product Safety List. A University of Iowa report (McConnell, Parks, & Knapp, 1973) utilized data from NEISS, the National Safety Council, in-depth studies by the CPSC, and anthropometric data. Yet another study (CPSC, 1975) explored playground injuries in depth and estimated from NEISS data that 117,951 playground injuries were treated in emergency rooms in 1974. During this same period, the Playground Equipment Manufacturer's Association and the National Recreation and Park Association (NRPA) were working with the CPSC to develop preliminary safety standards for playground equipment.

Spurred by this activity and petitions by Butwinick (1974), endorsed by the Americans for Democratic Action and the Consumers Union, and a second petition by Sweeney (1974), the stage was set for the CPSC to contract with the NRPA to develop a standard for public playground equipment (NRPA, 1976). The National Bureau of Standards revised the standards and published them as two handbooks in 1978. On October 4, 1979, commentaries on the handbooks were requested by the CPSC in the *Federal Register,* and, following revisions, the reports were published and made available to the public by the CPSC in two handbooks (CPSC, 1981a, 1981b). These handbooks, with periodic revisions (revised in 1991, 1993, and 1997) and combined with the ASTM standards published in 1993 (revised in 1995), would become the national standard of care in play equipment safety (Frost, 1985, 1989).

By the year 2000, six states—California, Connecticut, Michigan, New Jersey, North Carolina, and Texas—had passed legislation addressing playground safety with a common requirement to meet CPSC guidelines (voluntary in Connecticut) and, in some states, ASTM standards.

Accessibility Standards and Regulations for Children with Disabilities

In 1993, the ASTM included accessibility standards in its *Standard Consumer Safety Performance Specification for Playground Equipment for Public Use*. These standards included such factors as accessible routes, access to equipment, ramps, equipment landings, dimensions of routes and equipment, structural integrity of equipment, and transfer stations.

In July 1997, following several years of study and negotiations, the Architectural and Transportation Barriers Compliance Board (1997) issued a preliminary draft of minimum accessibility guidelines for play areas (Americans with Disabilities Act Accessibility Guidelines or ADAAG). These guidelines, now enforced, address age ranges; safety factors; access to ground-level play components; access to elevated play components; accessible routes within play areas; width, height, and slope guidelines; transfer (from wheelchair) systems; equipment platforms; and **soft contained play structures**. The accessibility guidelines are published in Section 15.6 of ADAAG and are a national building code for accessible play areas. The guidelines help to ensure that play areas are accessible, but do not require that they facilitate imaginative, interactive, dramatic, or social play (Malkusak, et al., 2002).

Playground Safety Surveys

During the period when the early CPSC guidelines were being developed, three national surveys of playground safety were conducted by teams of professionals (child development, architecture, physical education, recreation, and playground design) and published by the American Alliance for Health, Physical Education, Recreation, and Dance (AAHPERD). These surveys were conducted in most of the United States following training sessions for the surveyors at international conferences. First was the survey of elementary school playgrounds (Bruya & Langendorfer, 1988), followed by the survey of public park playgrounds (Thompson & Bowers, 1999) and the survey of preschool playgrounds (Wortham & Frost, 1990). Collectively, these surveys revealed an overall pattern of antiquated design, hazardous conditions, and poor or absent maintenance. The worst of the lot are accidents waiting to happen, sterile in play value, and essentially unfit for children's play (Frost, Bowers, & Wortham, 1990, p. 21).

Overall, the surveys concluded that the safety of American public playgrounds was unconscionably bad. Common hazards included head entrapment areas, open-base merry-go-rounds, crushing rotating mechanisms, open S-hooks, protruding bolts, excessive heights, poor or absent resilient surfacing, rigid and heavy swing seats, and very little evidence of maintenance. Statistical analyses are available in each of the reports. These surveys were influential in the work of standards committee groups in developing and revising national playground standards. National surveys later conducted by the U.S. Public Interest Research Group and the Consumer Federation of America (Mierzwinski, Fise, & Morrison, 1996; Sikes, Fise, & Morrison, 1992; Wood, Fise, & Morrison, 1994) reinforced the earlier national surveys' findings of neglect in playground safety. Later, national surveys of playgrounds were conducted by the National Program for Playground Safety (1999) (see General Information, on pp. 505–506) and the Consumer Federation of America (2000).

PROMOTING SAFETY WHERE CHILDREN PLAY

Annually, 20–25% of all children sustain an injury sufficiently severe to require medical attention, missed school, or bed rest. Unintentional injury is the leading cause of death for children under age 21. The leading causes of fatal injuries are motor vehicles, fires/burns, drowning, falling, and poisoning (National Center for Injury Prevention and Control, 2003).

Children encounter hazards wherever they play, and they play wherever they happen to be—from their bedrooms to classrooms, theme parks, and shopping centers. The large numbers of children's accidents are not merely a natural consequence of growing up and are not simply to be tolerated. This is a particularly pernicious view, for virtually all fatal and permanent accidental injuries are preventable. Numerous safety measures have demonstrated success in reducing injuries and fatalities—for example, seat belts in cars, bicycle helmets, proper barriers around pools, resilient surfacing around play equipment, even removing cords from children's clothing and small parts from infant–toddler toys (no child has ever been choked by the absence of a cord or strangled by the absence of an object).

A second common misconception is the view that requiring playground equipment to conform to national safety standards must result in sterile, unimaginative, unchallenging playgrounds. Interpretations of CPSC and ASTM guidelines/standards can and often do result in such playgrounds, but that may be the choice or fault of the designer or sponsor. CPSC guidelines and ASTM standards deal essentially with consumer products—that is, manufactured equipment. They barely touch natural features—gardens, woodlands, tools, building or construction materials, living things, shelters, cooking facilities, wheeled-vehicle paths, sand and water play areas, streams, hills, and vegetation. These are the stuff of creative, imaginative, magical playgrounds and should be integrated into playgrounds generally. Manufactured playground equipment and the surfaces around the equipment are implicated in an overwhelming majority of serious playground injuries. Those who create play environments are responsible for ensuring that safety standards are used to protect children from serious injury, not to dumb down their play environments.

One of the most visible success stories in America for safety while delivering high-quality service is that of Southwest Airlines. Over the 30-plus years the company has been in business, hundreds of Southwest Airlines planes have flown millions of miles and carried millions of passengers. They have never lost a passenger in an accident, and year after year they have won

The Houston Parks and Recreation Department trains workers and equips vans for playground maintenance.

FIGURE 12–2 Overview: CPSC *Handbook for Public Playground Safety*

Scope of *Handbook*

- *Handbook* specifies separate play areas for 2- to 5-year-olds and 5- to 12-year-olds.

Source of Guidelines

- Guidelines are based on injury data from NEISS, expert opinion, public commentaries, and research data.

Supervision

- Supervisors should understand the basics of play safety.
- Preschool children require more attentive supervision than older children.
- Supervisors should be aware of age appropriateness of equipment (look for posted signs).

Selecting, Purchasing, and Installing Equipment

- Confirm that equipment meets CPSC guidelines (e.g., select equipment approved by the International Play Equipment Manufacturers Association, IPEMA).
- Select experienced installers. Require CPSC compliance and insurance.
- Check equipment for durability and finish.
- Follow manufacturer's assembly and installation instructions.
- Have equipment and play area inspected by a qualified playground inspector during and after installation.

Surfacing

- Concrete, asphalt, soil, hard-packed earth, and grass are not acceptable.
- Properly tested rubber materials—unitary and loose-fill—are acceptable.
- Properly selected loose-fill materials—wood chips, engineered wood chips, sand, pea gravel, and shredded tires—are acceptable.
- Depth of material is dependent on potential fall height, type of material, and scientific tests (see CPSC critical height tables).
- Extreme cold and hot climates require special attention to type of surface. Sand freezes solid, but pea gravel and some manufactured surfaces are less prone to freezing (not in CPSC Handbook for Public Playground Safety).
- Loose-fill surfacing should not be installed over concrete or asphalt.
- Surfacing should be kept in place under and around equipment according to specified dimensions and maintained regularly.
- The use zone of stationary equipment (area to receive resilient surfacing) should extend a minimum of 6 feet in all directions. Check *Handbook* regarding use zones for swings, slides, moving equipment, and overlap zones.
- The guidelines do not address indoor equipment, but a CPSC Safety Alert dated May 1995 (available at *www.cpsc.gov*) warns consumers never to put children's climbing gyms on hard surfaces, including wood or carpeted floors, indoors or outdoors.

Safety and Maintenance

- Develop a comprehensive maintenance program.
- Inspect all equipment and play areas frequently.
- Follow the CPSC *Handbook* and manufacturer's recommendations for maintenance.
- Use inspection checklists, repair promptly, and keep records.

- Check protective surfacing for reduced depth, compacted areas, and foreign material.
- Check for head entrapment (most components should not form openings between 3.5 and 9 inches; check the *Handbook* for details. CPSC Guidelines do not address extreme climate conditions, but ice may form in a manner that could create head entrapments. Ice may also fall from play structure roofs when thawing.
- Check for suspended hazards.
- Check for ropes or cables that can form loops around neck.
- Check all equipment for CPSC-prescribed dimensions (height, width, diameter, elevation, transition, guardrails, protective barriers, etc.).
- Check for sheet metal (e.g., slides and decks) in direct sunlight.
- Check for sharp points, missing or damaged parts, protrusions, potential clothing entanglement hazards (open S-hooks and bolts), shearing points, trip hazards.
- Check for rust, rot, cracks and splinters, and termites (probe underground).
- Check for broken or missing play components, fences, benches, and signs.
- Check that all equipment is securely anchored.
- Check for loose fasteners and worn connections.
- Check for worn swing hangers and bearings of moving devices.
- Check area for drainage, especially in heavy-use areas (e.g., under swings).
- Check for lead paint and cracked, chipped, and peeling paint.
- Check for toxic materials (wood preservatives, insecticides, pesticides, and herbicides).
- Check entire area for litter.
- Check entire area for damaged or missing parts, signs, and fence components.
- Check all equipment for structural stability, excessive wear, and damage.

major awards for excellence of service. The distinction that sets Southwest apart is that the airline balances its safety program with concern for passengers. We can strike the same balance with children's play environments. We must insist on having it both ways: play environments that are safer but also more creative and more challenging than traditional hazardous, sterile ones.

Playground Safety

Data from NEISS show a rising incidence of playground injuries from a level of about 118,000 annually from 1974 through 1984; to about 200,000 annually from 1984 through 1988; and another jump to almost a quarter million annually from 1991 through the remainder of the decade. About 45% of playground injuries are severe; 75% occur on public playgrounds; girls sustain slightly more injuries than boys; children ages 5 to 9 are the most frequently injured; climbers are the site of most injuries (National Center for Injury Prevention and Control, 2003b). Reasons for the growing number of injuries are somewhat speculative, but improved reporting, the growing numbers of formal playgrounds at schools, child care centers, and public parks, the aging of playgrounds, neglected maintenance, the absence of adult supervision, and declining fitness levels of children are all probable factors.

Sponsors of playgrounds, whether at schools, child care centers, public parks, pay-for-play facilities, or backyards, should rely on the current and appropriate ASTM standards and CPSC guidelines in designing sites, selecting equipment, and inspecting and maintaining playground equipment. Figure 12–2 provides an overview of recommendations from the **CPSC *Handbook for Public Playground Safety***; consult that source for details.

Limitations of CPSC Guidelines and ASTM Standards

Some play and play environment professionals believe that the CPSC guidelines and the ASTM standards are unduly restrictive and tend to influence "cookie-cutter" or standardized playgrounds. This approach is indeed taking place, particularly in schools and parks where sponsors tend to limit their playgrounds to an array of commercial equipment, fixed in concrete, and devoid of loose materials, natural features, and children's creations. The safety specifications of the guidelines/standards are heavily influenced by play equipment manufacturers who initially resisted regulations but later came to embrace them, as old, outmoded, out-of-compliance equipment was destroyed and sales of new equipment skyrocketed.

Unfortunately, architects, child development professionals, recreation professionals, and other ASTM members expert in children's play have relatively limited roles in establishing playground safety standards. They can vote but may not be sufficiently motivated to expend the time and money required to attend standards-setting meetings in areas of the country remote from their work places. Consequently, much of the existing research may not be available in setting standards.

Consider, for example, that a range of equipment is "not recommended" for preschool-age children, including vertical sliding poles and overhead apparatus. Extensive research shows that preschool children can and do use such equipment when it is available (Frost et al., 2001). The decision to not recommend is based on injury data arising from preschoolers using equipment designed for elementary schools—excessively tall, lacking protective resilient surfacing, and often having exposed concrete footings. The issue of height of equipment is of particular importance in determining safety parameters of equipment (Frost et al., 2002). Safety specifications prescribe narrow diameters (less than 1.9 inches) for sliding poles. Very young children like to hug broad sliding poles (3–4 inches in diameter) for their short descent. Much of the prohibited equipment can be used with reasonable safety if scaled to the ability of users. The playground manufacturing industry is beginning to sponsor limited research on children's play and play environments.

All too frequently, playgrounds are merely selections of purchased equipment arranged in standardized form. Such playgrounds may be neat and tidy but may lack child appeal, creative function, challenge, and diversity. In addition to using safety guidelines and standards, designers and consumers should seek information on integrating manufactured equipment with more creative play materials and opportunities. These include most portable materials, trike paths, wheeled vehicles, sand, water and dirt, construction materials and tools, gardening and gardening materials, nature areas and materials, provision for pets, art materials, storage, and special places. Many purchasers assume that such materials and activities are hazardous, unimportant, and frivilous.

The national playground safety standards and guidelines (CPSC and ASTM) have been very influential in promoting the safety of manufactured equipment (consumer products). We should now direct attention to identifying safety restrictions of documented importance, making them simple and understandable to consumers, and orienting them to developmental needs of children.

Amusement Parks

In 2003, the National Safety Council reported that about 6,700 people are injured on amusement park rides annually. This is considered low by the industry since about 300 million people visit amusement parks with rides every year. Between 1973 and 1997, 133 deaths were reported to the CPSC; 57 were at permanent sites, 40 at carnivals, and 36 at unspecified sites. This number is relatively low, considering that 270 million people visit carnivals and amusement parks each year (Wear, 1998). According to CPSC data, the types of rides implicated in deaths between 1973 and 1997 ranged from roller coasters (34), whirling rides (40), and Ferris wheels (15) to sky rides (15), trains (5), and bumper cars and boats (3). However, these data are misleading. "The actual reporting of an accident is made by the park

Both installation and design are important for play equipment safety.

itself," and there are incentives to underreport accidents (Kaplan, 1998, p. 140).

On opening day of the terrifying Timber Wolf roller coaster in Kansas City, a computer allegedly went haywire and two coaster trains collided. Forty-eight people suffered broken bones, broken teeth, punctured tongues, twisted necks, and split heads (Fritz, 1996). In March 1998, a child was killed and two others injured when a restraining bar latch allegedly failed on a Himalaya carnival ride at a livestock show and rodeo in Austin, Texas, allowing two children to be thrown out of the car. An intensive investigation by law enforcement officials and experts revealed an alleged pattern of injuries on Himalaya rides operated by the same company in several states, and alleged defective restraining devices on the implicated ride. Consequently, a grand jury indicted nine people, including the owners of the ride, ride operators, and inspectors, for murder (Fritz, 1996).

Perkes (1998) collected accident data for the carnival company that owned the Himalaya ride implicated in the Austin death and found an alleged pattern of accidents (from news reports) on their rides in other states. In 1991, a cyclone roller coaster injured 14 people at the Arizona State Fair; in 1992, seven people suffered ride injuries at the same fair. In 1992, there were 28 ride-related injuries in 17 days in Orange County, California. In 1993, eight people were injured in a Cyclone roller coaster crash at the Orange County Fair. In 1994, an employee of the company was electrocuted while working on a ride at the Orange County Fair. Numerous other accidents were noted for the 1980s. This same company "was sued at least 15 times in California between 1983 and 1993 after patrons were injured on rides it owned" (Banta, 1998, p. A-7).

Federal regulations are badly needed, for rides judged unsafe in one state would be considered safe in other states. Some states, including Missouri, Montana, North and South Dakota, Alabama, and Kansas, do not regulate rides at all, and several others—California, Rhode Island, and Mississippi—and Washington, D.C., regulate traveling carnivals but do not regulate permanent ones (Kaplan, 1998). Florida and Pennsylvania employ full-time inspectors.

Despite the amusement industry's insistence that today's technology has made thrill rides scarier yet safer, an extensive study by the Associated Press has found an industry in which blunders and bad judgment are commonplace, government oversight is lax or nonexistent, and injury reporting is incomplete and inaccurate (Fritz, 1996, p. A-25).

As amusement rides become ever more extreme, accidents are increasing. In one week alone in August 1999, four people were killed in accidents at three different amusement parks. In 1998, there were an estimated 9,200 injuries, a jump of 24% from 1994 despite an increase of visitorship of only 12%. The incomplete data do not account for scores of injuries to backs, necks, legs, and heads resulting from "violent shaking, jolting, and jouncing." Older people may be at greater risk than children (Silver, 1999). There is evidence that extreme rides can cause brain injury, but a number of studies conclude that there is no such risk (National Safety Council, 2003).

Fritz (1996) describes the state of thrill rides: the successful, lucrative, thrill ride is the ride that is faster, bigger, and better. Amusement parks are under pressure to open rides on schedule and tend to fix their flaws after they open for business, making the customers their guinea pigs. For example, Six Flags said at least 70 were injured at three of their roller coasters in three states, costing almost $2 million for revamping; scores of people were hurt on the Fiesta Texas theme park Rattler roller coaster before it was "toned down." Regulation of theme parks can even be tied to politics. Florida inspectors do not inspect the high-tech rides at Disney World, Busch Gardens, and Universal Studios because they were granted exemptions by state laws (Fritz, 1996). The lack of stiff state and national regulations encourages many amusement parks, particularly traveling carnivals, to do business in those states with the least inspections. Consequently, some businesses have five to seven times more safety violations than others. Fortunately, in 2003 the World Standards Task Force of ASTM was creating international guidelines for theme park equipment.

Overall, rides at permanent theme parks appear to be in safer condition that those at traveling carnivals. A growing problem at parks and carnivals is unsupervised adolescents who engage in mischief, shoplifting, boisterous behavior, and, at times, gang-related violence. Adults should ensure that their children are properly supervised (observe the supervisors) and not allow them to ride carnival equipment unless strict inspections have been conducted and the equipment is in safe condition (contact the sponsoring agency) and properly supervised. Figure 12–3 summarizes points for theme park and carnival ride safety.

Water Safety

In some states, including California, Texas, and Arizona, drowning is the top killer of young children (CPSC, 1992). The National Center for Injury Prevention and Control (NCIPC, 2003b) reports that in 2000, 943 children ages 0 to 14 years died from drowning. For every child who drowns, six receive emergency room care for near-drowning which may result in brain damage. Children under age 1 most frequently drown in buckets, bathtubs, and toilets. Children ages 1 to 4 most frequently drown in residential swimming pools. As children get older they are more likely to drown in lakes, ponds, and rivers (NPIPC, 2003b). In Florida, there were 365 drownings in 1996, including 75 toddlers (Sharp, 1997). Toddlers are at great risk around water for they are attracted to water, have limited cause–effect thinking ability, usually cannot swim, are poorly coordinated, and may walk or jump into pools or streams and drown without a sound. Even momentary lapses in supervision such as answering a phone or stepping inside can result in disaster.

Consumer Product Safety Commission studies (1996a) of children under 5 years old in Arizona, California, and Florida show that 75% were between 1 and 3 years old; 65% were boys; most were being supervised by one or both parents;

FIGURE 12–3 Theme Park and Carnival Thrill Ride Safety

- Do not assume that rides at theme parks and carnivals are reasonably safe.
- Never allow young children to visit parks or use rides without close adult supervision.
- Avoid allowing children to ride equipment designed for older children. Age information should be posted.
- Observe rides in operation. Look for unsafe features: broken or worn parts, worn-out condition, excessive speed, inadequate security devices for riders.
- Observe quality of supervision. Are supervisors alert, skillful, helpful? Do they give clear instructions? Do they focus on their work?
- Are warnings and instructions prominently posted?
- Instruct children to follow all safety rules.
- Avoid newly designed rides that have recently opened.
- Check with park administration to determine the nature and extent of safety regulations for equipment. Are safety inspections, maintenance records and injury records available to the public?
- Insist that local sponsors check safety and injury records and require strict inspections and regulations for carnivals brought to the city.
- If there are unresolved safety problems, discuss concerns with children and select other forms of entertainment.

69% were not expected to be at or near the water; 65% happened at a pool owned by the family.

Growing awareness of the scope of drownings is leading communities, cities, and states to implement laws and regulations for child protection. Existing national regulations/guidelines include those by the National Spa and Pool Institute (1991, 1992), the Southern Building Code Congress (1992), the American Public Health Association (1981), and the CPSC (1996b). These regulations and guidelines typically specify barriers (fences, walls) around pools at least 4 feet high with self-closing, self-latching gates. The authors and some municipalities recommend that barriers be 6 feet tall because many preschool-age children can scale 4-foot fences, particularly those of chain-link construction. Barriers should have openings no greater than 4 inches wide; they should be difficult to climb; and gate latches should be out of reach of young children. If the home or adjacent house forms one side of the pool barrier, doors leading to the pool should be equipped with alarms as well as locking devices than cannot be operated by young children. During the off-season, pools should be covered with durable covers that support a child's weight and that cannot collapse under a child's weight into the water.

The water safety program must extend beyond mere provision of physical barriers and alarms. Supervision and emergency preparation are essential. Alert, trained supervisors know that they cannot depend on flotation devices to provide protection for nonswimmers. Children can slip off or out of such devices and drown in a matter of seconds. Nor should they assume that the pool or spa itself is safe. The CPSC reported that long hair entanglement in drain grates of spas and hot tubs resulted in at least 10 deaths between 1990 and 1997. In addition, at least seven children died when their bodies were held against drains by the circulation system. Several children suffered permanent injuries when disemboweled from sitting on circulation pump drain grates. Such accidents are easily prevented by proper design and maintenance.

Supervisors should ensure that the pools they use meet local, state, and national safety codes and regulations since many children drown each year because of faulty pool design, maintenance, and operation. Caretakers of young children should not assume that lifeguards are well trained or that emergency equipment (e.g., phone, ring buoy, rope, Shepherd's hook) is available at poolside, and they should ensure that baby-sitters, nannies, friends, or relatives supervising their children around water hazards are careful and competent. Parents, teachers, and other child caretakers should know cardiopulmonary resuscitation (CPR) and read pool safety literature so they can judge for themselves the level of safety at public or private pools. The CPSC (1992) offers free publications available by calling its hotline (800-638-2772) or visiting its Web site (*www.cpsc.gov*). ASTM provides an update at *www.astm.org/SNEWS/MARCH_2003/stoner_mar03.html*.

Young children can drown in a few inches of water in bathtubs, spas, hot tubs, creeks, wading pools, ponds, toilets, and buckets. With a toddler in the house or child care center, bathrooms must be secured, buckets stored empty, and multiple levels of protection installed between indoor places and pools. In addition, water hazards must be secured against entry by neighborhood children when home owners are absent or child care centers or schools are closed. This requires tall, difficult-to-climb fences (6-foot minimum height) and secure locks on all entrances.

With the growing number and popularity of water parks, special safety precautions are needed. Risk management surveys provide insight into the risks for children and for operators. Over 2,400 risk management surveys demonstrated a consistent pattern of risk. Sixty-six percent of risk exposures were attributed to operational oversights, mistakes, and/or staff ignorance, and 33% to physical plant malfunctions. Heath (1995) provides detailed information about the top 20 water park risk exposures, and a special issue of *Parks and Recreation* (1998) examines aquatic facility safety.

Homeowners, child care center operators, parks, and school systems are usually held accountable for meeting existing local, state, and national codes and regulations in the event of injury or near-drowning (e.g., brain damage) or drowning of children attracted to their pools at any time—during or after hours of operation. Pools of water are typically seen in litigation as "attractive nuisances," and reasonable adults are expected to know that young children are attracted to water, that they may enter pools uninvited, and that they are at high risk of drowning because of their age. Unfortunately, child care center regulations of state regulatory agencies typically fail to give detailed safety information or provide appropriate training for center operators about pool risks and hazards. Such practices place centers at risk for child injury, drowning, and large legal judgments in lawsuits.

Noise

Noise is commonly described as unwanted sound and has adverse effects on people of all ages. The effects are cumulative and more severe for children than for adults. The extent of damage resulting from high levels of noise depends on the duration of the noise, its intensity or volume, and the individual's relative susceptibility. The damage includes stress, hearing loss, psychiatric disorders, cardiovascular disease, and decline in school performance (Kryter, 1994). The effects of noise are cumulative; long-term exposure can result in permanent damage to the inner ear and central nervous system.

The opportunities for damage from noise are perhaps greatest in large urban areas of congregated living where airports (Kryter, 1994), trains (Bronzaft & McCarthy, 1975), expressways (Glass & Singer, 1972), rock music (Danenberg, Loos-Cosgrove, & LoVerde (1987), and other noise-producing sources, such as factory and construction activity, are concentrated. Concentrations of children at schools and apartment buildings with unprotected noise sources result in large numbers being exposed on a regular basis. Many such concentrations are present throughout the world, particularly in flight paths of airports and adjacent to expressways. Damaging levels of noise may be present both indoors and outdoors, so steps should be taken to reduce or eliminate exposure.

Noise levels above 60 decibels (dBA) interfere with classroom work, and 75 to 80 dBA destroy the communication process (Kryter, 1970; Miller, 1974). Many educators have observed or worked in classrooms where lessons are stopped or delayed while trains pass by or planes fly overhead, and the noise levels on playgrounds outside these same schools are much more intense.

Solutions and partial solutions to noise include (a) avoidance of noise, (b) reduction or elimination of noise at its source, and (c) reduction or elimination of noise by installing sound-reducing materials (Frost, 1996a). The solution begins at home and is carried over to child care centers and schools. Adults should review noise conditions when selecting homes and schools, spending time indoors and outdoors, observing and listening to types and levels of noise. They should also restrict children from participating in excessive noise-producing activities, such as most rock concerts, and instruct them in using earphones and acoustical equipment.

The most effective method of controlling noise is identifying its source and taking steps to reduce or eliminate it. Airport runways are sometimes designed to avoid heavily populated areas. Flight schedules are modified to reduce landings and takeoffs during late-night periods when people are asleep. Train and subway noises can be buffered in a variety of ways, including use of shock-absorbing rubber pads between rails and supporting structures. Factories are frequently located away from populated areas in industrial zones. Loud music can be controlled by checking decibels and modifying the volume at its source. Offensive as it may be to teens, adults should take the initiative to plan with children and youth and regulate noise in homes, schools, automobiles, video arcades, and entertainment venues, particularly noise produced by high-tech entertainment equipment.

Noise can be reduced indoors by replacing sound-reflecting materials (e.g., highly reflective tiles, walls, ceilings) with sound-absorbing materials (e.g., carpets, draperies, acoustic materials), installing sound barriers, and sealing cracks or openings. Excessive noise at musical events should be limited to Occupational Safety and Health Act regulations (Beranek, 1996; Hodge & Price, 1978). Outdoor noise may be a more serious problem than indoor noise because the protection of walls and insulation is not present there. The first step in outdoor noise control is locating playgrounds away from noise sources or locating them on the opposite side of the school building from the source. That failing, landscape architects can assist in buffering and redirecting noise with hills, fences, and dense vegetation. It is cheaper and more effective to design and construct quiet facilities and equipment than to attempt remedies later. Noise avoidance can be expensive and very difficult to achieve in poverty areas where resources are limited.

Toy Safety

At least 25 children under age 12 died and about 202,500 were treated in hospital emergency rooms from toy-related injuries in 2000 (National Safe Kids Campaign, 2003). The CPSC reported that toy-related injuries are preventable. Slipshod manufacture and importation of toys from foreign countries represent a major risk to children because the large volume reaching American entry points cannot be thoroughly evaluated by customs inspectors. Consequently, the CPSC and other government agencies are constantly recalling dangerous products after they have been placed in the hands of children and resulted in injuries. Wise caretakers of children will inspect all toys intended for children upon purchase and periodically thereafter. The CPSC report *Age Determination Guidelines* (Therrell et al., 2002) is an extensive analysis of toy characteristics and developmental guidelines and Figure 12–4 summarizes some safety points for toys for various ages.

FIGURE 12–4 Safety in Toy Play

Ages 0–3

- Select toys appropriate to the child's age. Toddlers put objects in their mouth, creating choking hazards.
- Avoid objects including balls, marbles, buttons, pea gravel on playgrounds, pellets from bean bag chairs, and removable toy parts that are less than 1.75 inches in diameter. Check all toys carefully to ensure that parts cannot be torn off.
- Never allow children to play with uninflated balloons because they pose a choking hazard.
- Never allow children to play with plastic bags, including dry cleaning bags and bags that package merchandise, because of the suffocation hazard. Any material that covers the entire head can be hazardous.
- Check toys for parts that active children can pull off and put in their mouths.
- Check toys for sharp edges and points.

Ages 3–5

- Instruct older children to keep toys that are hazardous for younger children away from them.
- Select art materials marked "ASTM D-4236," which means they have been reviewed for toxic content.
- Avoid toys constructed of brittle material that might break into small pieces with jagged edges.

All Ages

- Review age designations and safety warnings on toys before purchasing or giving them to children.
- Check toys regularly for breakage, excessive wear, and potential hazards.
- Require children to wear helmets when riding bicycles and when learning to roller skate, ice skate, or ski in snow.
- Teach children to put toys away when not in use and not leave them where others can fall over them.
- Be sure that toy guns are brightly colored and cannot be mistaken for a real gun.
- Never allow young children to play with fireworks. Fireworks displays are best conducted by experts for the entertainment of all ages.
- Avoid purchasing toys, such as dart guns, that fire projectiles.
- Check areas where children play for chests and trunks that can close on them, leading to suffocation. Some automobile trunks can be opened without a key. Presently, automobile trunks cannot be opened from the inside.
- Never allow children to play with automatic garage door openers. Ensure that safety reversal systems are installed and operational.
- Secure a copy of American Society for Testing and Materials (ASTM, 1996), *Standard Consumer Safety Specification on Toy Safety* (phone [610] 832-9585; Web site: *www.astm.org*).
- Check Web pages of the CPSC (*www.cpsc.gov*) to secure safety alerts and related data on hazardous toys and devices.
- Get involved with the National Safe Kids Campaign (*www.safekids.org*), a nonprofit organization that conducts efforts to prevent unintentional deaths and injuries to children. Read its literature.

Other Hazards

Fireworks

In 2000, 10 people were killed and 11,000 were treated in hospital emergency rooms from fireworks-related injuries (National Safety Council, 2002). Because of the extreme hazards associated with igniting fireworks, they are best left to professionals. Every year fireworks, frequently illegal ones imported from Asia, and their improper use result in deaths, blindings, amputations, and severe burns. Most of these occur around the Fourth of July. From 1988 to 1998, the CPSC enforcement program prevented over 400 million hazardous fireworks from reaching consumers by stopping them at import docks.

Even improperly made caps for children's cap pistols are sometimes hazardous. For example, in one lawsuit against a fireworks importer, this writer inspected caps implicated in spontaneous ignition and severe burning of a young boy. The caps ignited while in the child's pocket merely by rubbing together. These individual caps were filled (illegally) to overflowing with powder, overriding the protective capsule designed to prevent contact. In another case, a child examined a rocket that had failed to fire after a city display and was left undiscovered on the grounds. The rocket exploded, severely burning much of his body. Common fireworks regulations require careful cleanup of display areas immediately after shows.

Whatever the motive, young children should never be allowed to play with fireworks. Adults who decide to use them should read the warnings and instructions and follow them carefully. They should never attempt to relight misfired fireworks, and all fireworks activities should take place well away from flammable materials. The American Academy of Pediatrics (AAP) and the National Fire Protection Association urge that private use of fireworks be banned (AAP, 2003).

Head Injuries and Helmets

Proper helmets, approved by CPSC, ASTM, and/or the American National Standards Institute (ANSI) should be worn by children in a number of play and recreational activities. In 1998, 275 deaths and 430,000 visits to emergency rooms resulted from bicycle-related injuries to children under age 21. About 23,000 children sustained a traumatic brain injury while bicycling (AAP, 2001). Helmet's if used, can reduce head injuries by up to 85%. Evidence is accumulating that young children, especially beginners, should wear helmets for all types of skating, including in-line, roller, and ice, as well as skateboarding and snow skiing.

Fortunately, a growing number of child care centers are using helmets for tricycle riders. Powell, Tanz, and DiScala (1997) determined from the National Pediatric Trauma Registry (NPTR) and CPSC data that injuries related to bicycle use are far more common than injuries associated with the use of tricycles or wheeled toys. However, more than half the children in their data pool had head injuries regardless of cycle type. Although the available data do not specify how tricycle riders sustain head injuries, falling onto asphalt and concrete tracks appears to be a reasonable conclusion. Replacing such tracks with discarded (or new, if affordable) rubber/fiber conveyor belts would provide a much more resilient surface for tricycles and should drastically reduce serious head injuries. Discarded conveyor belts can usually be obtained free of charge from sand and gravel companies, airports, factories, and other places that use them. Poured rubber surfacing is an expensive but probably effective alternative.

Cords, Clothing, Strangulation, and Sudden Infant Death Syndrome

Loops on window blind cords at homes, schools, and child care centers should be cut and separate tassels attached to prevent entanglement and strangulation. The CPSC (1998, News Release #98-157) reported that about one child a month dies from strangulation with window cord blinds, but a study by the American Medical Association and CPSC found that about half of the deaths were not reported to CPSC. Children's clothing should not have cords attached. Between 1985 and 1998, 21 children died when drawstrings caught on school buses, playground equipment, and other products. The entry to playground slides is particularly vulnerable to entanglement and should be examined for protruding parts or cracks that could entrap cords and clothing.

Adults should also examine play equipment for protruding parts that can entangle clothing. In November 1998, the CPSC recalled 9.6 million play yards/playpens with protruding rivets that could strangle children if pacifier strings or loose clothing caught on them. The mesh on some playpens may unravel, creating choking hazards, and some playpens have top rails that can collapse, trapping children at the neck. Cribs and bunk beds should also be examined for head entrapment hazards. Twelve children died between 1985 and 1996 because crib slats came loose, trapping children's heads. Infant swings and carriers should be examined for straps that can entangle the head and leg openings through which infants can slip, trapping the head.

Sudden infant death syndrome (SIDS) is the leading cause of infant death beyond the neonatal period (AAP, 2000). SIDS is described as the sudden death of an infant under 1 year of age. The risk factors include prone sleeping position, soft or loose sleeping surfaces, overheating, and bed sharing. Comprehensive guidelines for preventing SIDS are available from CPSC and AAP (2000).

Toxic Materials

Some children's toys and play equipment may contain toxic materials. The amount of a particular substance required to cause harm to young children is disputed and debated, even by professionals. Some children are at greater risk than others, for individual factors—health, previous exposure to toxic materials, and type and length of exposure—appear to be implicated. The ACTS Testing Laboratories (1998, Release #8N-123, 124) reported that soft polyvinyl chloride (PVC) toys and other products for children under age 3 may contain alleged toxic phthalate ester plasticizers. The United States, Canada, and the European Union issued health warnings or banned the use of this material in vinyl teethers, pacifiers, and rattles. The CPSC reported that "few if any children are at risk" but continues to conduct scientific research.

Each year, approximately 50 children under age 5 die from poisoning, and more than a million consumers call poison control centers about child poisonings from medicines, pesticides, or household chemicals (CPSC, 1997, News Release #97-077). More than 700 children were saved between 1970 and 1997 due to child-resistant packaging for aspirin and oral prescription medicines. Many school districts and park systems use toxic pesticides and herbicides to control insects and weeds on and around children's playgrounds. This is a hidden hazard that can threaten the health of young children.

Ingestion of lead from deteriorating paint is a major source of lead poisoning for children 6 years and younger. Lead poisoning is associated with behavioral problems, learning disabilities, hearing problems, and stunted growth. In 1978, the CPSC banned the sale of toys and playground equipment using paint containing more than 0.06% lead, but many older school, park, and community playgrounds have painted wood and metal playground equipment that presents lead hazards. Over time, the lead-laced paint deteriorates into chips and dust, allowing children to ingest lead by putting their hands on the equipment and then in their mouths. The CPSC (1996a) recommends a series of steps to eliminate lead on playground equipment, including visual inspection, laboratory tests, and control or eradication steps. This is best done by professionals.

Preservatives in wood playground equipment are a subject of ongoing controversy. The CPSC tests and approves certain types of preservatives for playground equipment use, but consumer groups increasingly push for toxic-free, totally inert products. If contemplating the purchase of wood equipment, the purchaser should determine the type of preservative used and ensure that it has been judged acceptable for children's play by a federal agency such as the CPSC. See (*www.CPSC.gov*) for action taken in 2003 by the Environmental Protection Agency to ban common preservative Chromated Copper Arsenate (CCA) from all residential uses.

Baby Walkers

More children are injured with baby walkers than with any other nursery product. In 1997 about 14,300 children less than 15 months of age were treated at emergency rooms for baby walker injuries, most from falling down stairs. Walkers were involved in 34 deaths between 1973 and 1998 (CPSC News Release #98-142). A baby walker certified by the Juvenile Products Manufacturers Association must meet one of two requirements: (a) it must be too wide to fit through a standard doorway, or (b) it must have a feature, such as a gripping mechanism, to stop the walker at the edge of a step. Some child development specialists recommend against use of baby walkers for their possible interference with normal motor development.

Field Trips and Safety: Zoos

Every year hundreds of thousands of schoolchildren take field trips to special places of educational and recreational value. These trips are often under the care of teachers, child care center caretakers, or parents. The scope of this chapter will not allow discussion of all the popular field trip destinations. A trip to a zoo is used as an example of the nature and extent of planning for safety that should be a part of every field trip. Zoos are among the popular choices and appear to be among the safer public entertainment/educational places for children, but, as in all field trip destinations, hazards exist and precautions should be taken. Perhaps the most common errors by child supervisors on trips to zoos involve failing to prevent children from climbing on objects in the zoo or failing to appreciate the danger posed by wild animals. Children must be taught that wild animals are not pets and, with certain exceptions, can cause great bodily harm if approached or touched.

Zoos generally do a good job of containing animals but face a very difficult task of keeping children from accidental, deliberate, or mischievous intrusion into animal containment spaces. The behavior of wild animals is not predictable, especially by children. For certain animals (e.g., wolves), merely inserting fingers through a mesh fence may result in the loss of one or more fingers. Some barriers are so poorly constructed that very young children can easily gain access or fall into dangerous animal containments

Play leaders (parents, teachers) should plan with children for field trips.

FIGURE 12–5 Kronkosky's Tiny Tot Nature spot, San Antonio Zoo.

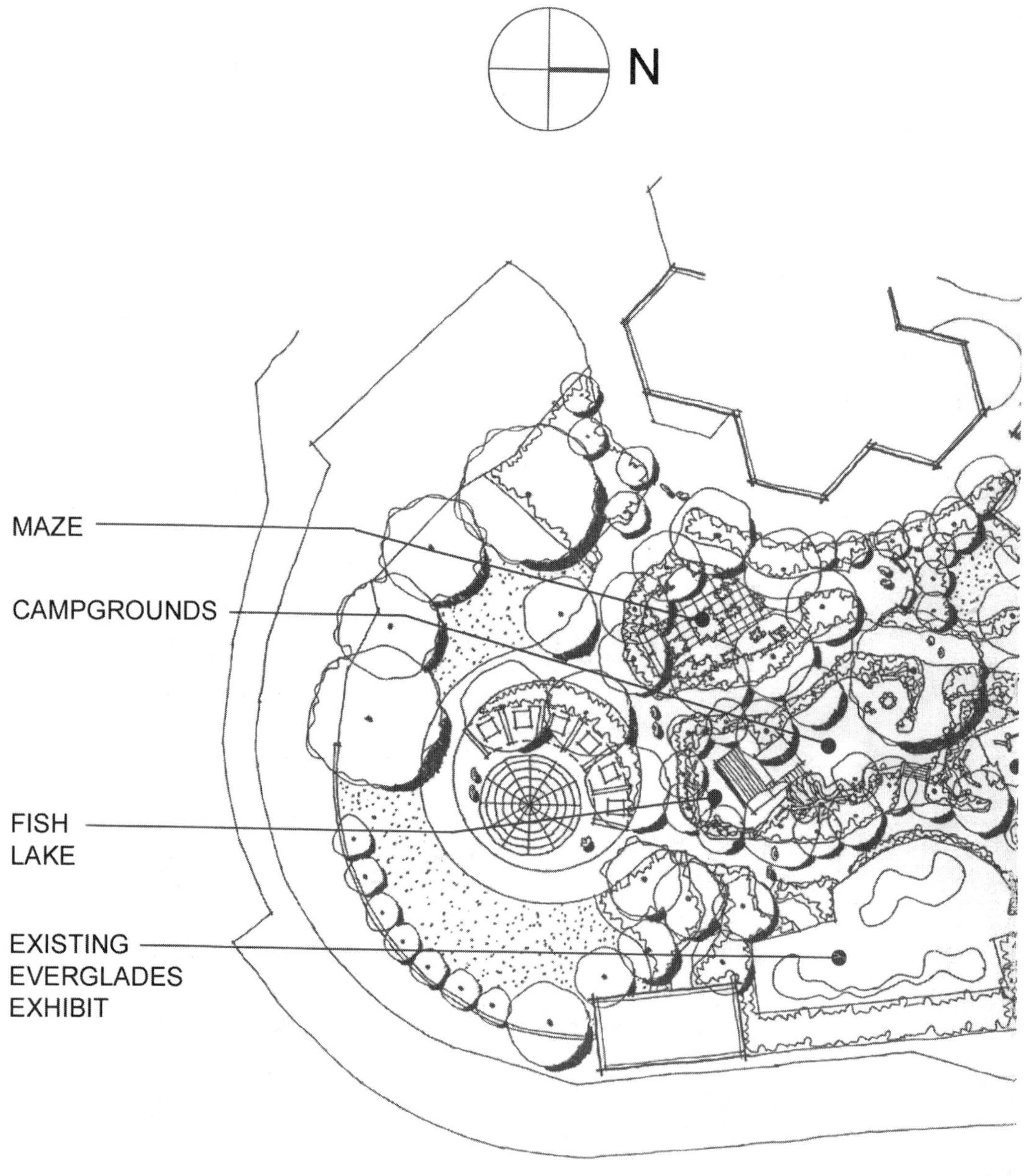

Source: Jones & Jones, Riatto Studio, MIG (Joe Frost, Consultant). By permission of Jones and Jones, Architects, Seattle, Washington.

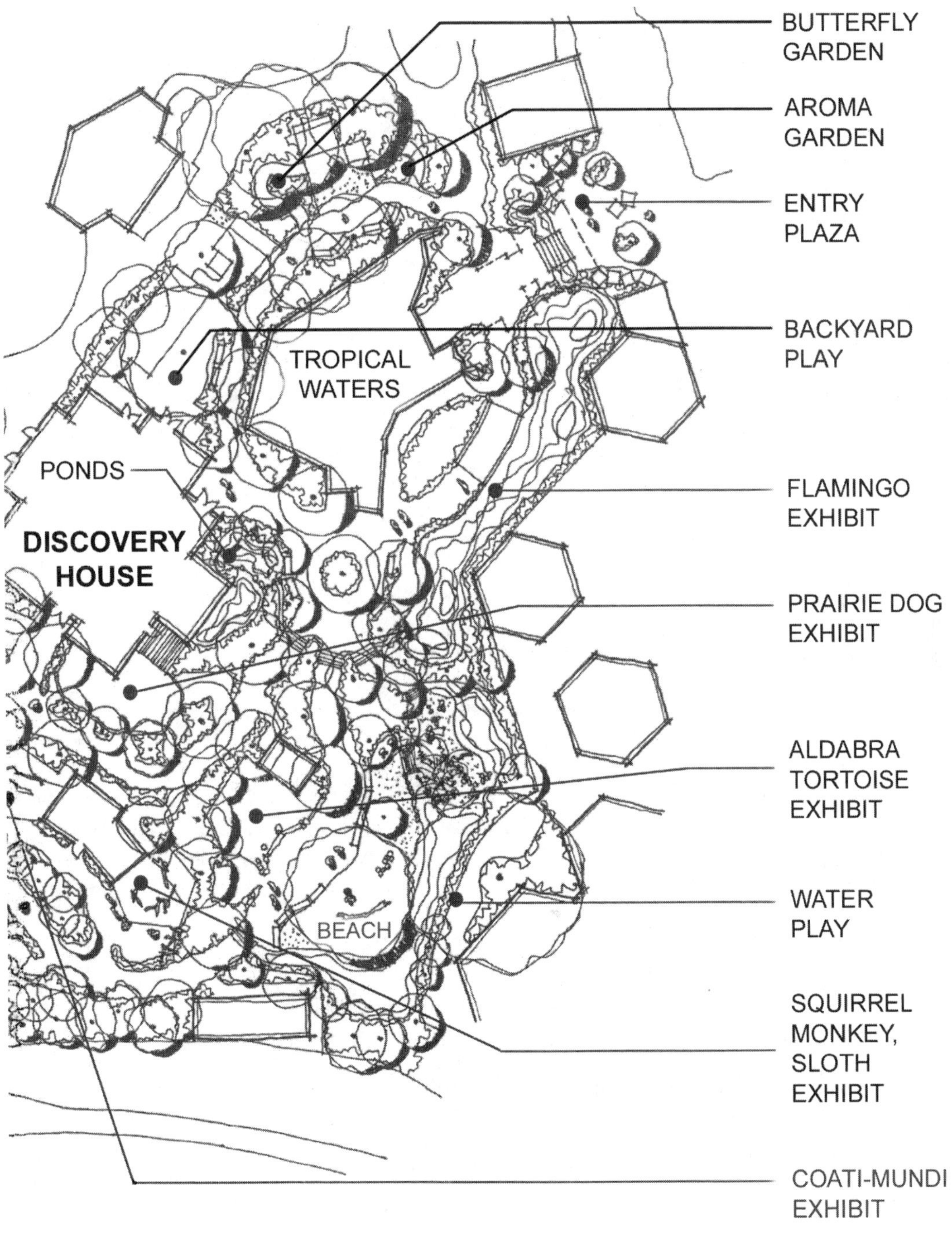
BUTTERFLY GARDEN
AROMA GARDEN
ENTRY PLAZA
BACKYARD PLAY
TROPICAL WATERS
PONDS
FLAMINGO EXHIBIT
DISCOVERY HOUSE
PRAIRIE DOG EXHIBIT
ALDABRA TORTOISE EXHIBIT
WATER PLAY
BEACH
SQUIRREL MONKEY, SLOTH EXHIBIT
COATI-MUNDI EXHIBIT

(e.g., gorilla habitats). Alligators in their native habitats (swamps) may be separated from visitors merely by bridge railings spanning the habitats. Some zoos install nets to catch children who fall from bridges before they enter the water.

There are levels of hazards and risks with zoo animals (Frost & Griffith, 1997). Those posing minimal danger to humans if humanely treated include animals commonly found in petting zoos (e.g., guinea pigs, rabbits). Those posing moderate danger, especially to young children who contact them directly, include small-hoof stock (goats, sheep, calves) under 100 pounds; and those posing greater danger include large-hoof stock (cows, horses, deer) and large wild animals in general (lions, tigers, elephants).

Zoos routinely construct barriers of various types, depending on the type of animal, to keep animals contained and to keep visitors from contacting animals. This must be done without compromising views of the habitat and the animals' natural behavior. The total zoo experience includes interaction with some animals, observation of animals, visitor education, animal preservation, and research. These experiences must be preserved while ensuring reasonable degrees of safety.

Visitors and animals are separated by barriers according to the type of animal. Types of barriers include **primary barriers** (solid impenetrable barriers, deep pits, moats, and partially solid barriers such as fences), **setback zones** (several feet of vegetation between primary and public barriers to hamper access), and **public barriers** (low fences adjacent to visitor trails) to reduce accessibility, particularly by young children. Adult supervisors should never allow children to violate any of these barriers.

The primary safety goal of zoo staff appears to be animal containment. An equally important goal should be to ensure that visitors, especially young children, do not gain access to animals except in petting zoos supervised by zoo professionals. The *American Zoo and Aquarium Accreditation Handbook* safety criteria are limited and general in nature, providing no specific guidelines for barrier design or for protecting children from gaining access to dangerous animals.

Zoos vary widely from city to city in the degree of safety they provide for visitors. Adults who take children to zoos should plan with children in advance and maintain contact with them throughout the zoo visit. Figure 12–6 lists safety precautions for field trips to zoos and other general destinations with children.

CHILD INJURIES AND LITIGATION

CPSC and NEISS data describe thousands of injuries, but depth of analysis is limited. Frost and Sweeney (1996) report data from 190 lawsuits on child injury and fatalities in public places, including swimming pools, carnivals, ice skating rinks, amusement parks, wilderness camps, fast-food restaurants, indoor entertainment complexes, and playgrounds at city parks, public and private schools, and child care centers. These lawsuits were spread over 38 states, from Alaska to Florida and from Hawaii to Washington, D.C. The sources of data were personal inspection of injury sites, depositions, police reports, private investigator reports, safety standards, regulations and laws, photographs of injury sites, medical records, interviews with children and caretakers, and autopsies. These data were supplemented by personal safety inspections of playgrounds, zoos, theme parks, and entertainment centers for children, personal interaction with safety specialists, and the vast array of data available from safety organizations. Most litigation data are not available to the public because about 90% of child injury/fatality cases settle out of court and records remain private.

Injuries to children in this study were serious, ranging from serious limb fractures to brain trauma, quadriplegia, and death. The leading cause of injuries, 113 of 190 cases, was falling onto hard ground surfaces—concrete, asphalt, or hard-packed earth. Falling onto equipment accounted for 21 additional cases, with 71% of all cases resulting from falling onto hard surfaces. Entrapments, shearing mechanisms, heavy, battering

FIGURE 12–6 Zoos and Field Trips

- Visit field trip site in advance. Check access for children with disabilities.
- Get permission forms from parents.
- Send information to parents regarding schedule, clothing, food, and transportation.
- Increase the normal adult/child ratio for field trips.
- Check liability insurance for drivers and vehicles. Check maintenance and fuel for vehicles.
- Plan all steps, including safety procedures, with children and supervisors before reaching the site.
- Plan with supervisors where and when entire group will meet in the event they become separated.
- Check carefully the location of transportation vehicles before leaving parking lots. Inform driver(s) of plans for departure.
- Take advantage of orientations provided by zoo personnel.
- Read and heed all warning signs throughout the zoo.
- Check locations of water fountains, toilets, first aid stations, and food concessions upon entry to zoo.
- Do not assume that all zoos have high-quality safety programs. Look for obvious and hidden hazards.
- Young children should never be left unsupervised. Toddlers are generally unaware of hazards and must be supervised closely. Many zoos do not have sufficient protective devices to prevent toddlers and very young children from gaining access to animals or pools of water during momentary lapses of supervision.
- Children should not be allowed to run or engage in horseplay in zoos.
- Never touch animals unless allowed by zoo personnel.
- Avoid climbing over or through barriers.
- Never place small children on top of fences or barriers for better views of animals.
- Be alert to changing circumstances (weather, obstacles, etc.).
- Avoid teasing animals or throwing objects at animals.
- Avoid feeding animals. Certain foods are not good for animals.
- Carry a portable phone and emergency phone numbers.
- Notify zoo personnel if you see safety conditions that need attention.
- Falls onto hard surfaces appear to be the chief cause of injuries at field trip destinations. Do not allow children to climb or play on structures not intended for climbing—railings, tables, strollers or rolling devices, fences, safety barriers, water fountains, or statues.

ram-type swings, protrusions, and open S-hooks accounted for an additional 41 injuries (22%), and a range of factors accounted for the remaining 15 injuries (7%) (Figure 12–7). The injuries to 13 children were fatal—6 asphyxiated by entrapment, entangled clothing, and a jump rope; 2 from being struck by heavy swings; and 1 each from hitting a concrete culvert, falling onto concrete, falling onto rocks, being hit by a car (unfenced playground), and being hit by a motorcycle (on the playground).

The equipment most frequently implicated in serious injuries was slides (38 cases) and swings (38 cases), followed by climbers (24 cases), merry-go-rounds (16), horizontal ladders (14), fire poles (sliding poles) (8), superstructures (7), chinning bars (6), and jungle gyms (6). The three types of equipment most often implicated in injuries—slides, swings, and climbers—are the types most frequently found on playgrounds (see Figure 12–7). Although the height of equipment and design of safety features are frequently implicated in injuries, including falls, the most common direct cause of injuries is falling onto hard surfaces under and around the equipment.

FIGURE 12–7 Avoiding Serious Playground Injuries and Lawsuits

- Develop a carefully documented safety inspection and maintenance program.
- Adopt the CPSC and ASTM playground safety guidelines and standards as minimum requirements for playgrounds. Do not depend on limited state safety regulations for protection from liability.
- Replace hard surfaces with approved resilient surfacing.
- Destroy all outmoded equipment such as battering ram type swings and vintage open-base merry-go-rounds.
- Ensure that very young children do not use overhead apparatus designed for school-age children.
- Replace bare metal slides and decks that can cause serious burns.
- Ensure that concrete footings, especially at the base of fire or sliding poles, are recessed well under base ground and then covered with recommended resilient surfacing.
- Do not allow children to wear jewelry (rings, necklaces, earrings) or loose cords on playgrounds.
- Replace all S-hooks with permanently closed hooks.
- Fence playgrounds for young children from streets, cliffs, and water hazards.
- Require manufacturers and installers to certify in writing that their equipment and installation conform to CPSC guidelines, ASTM standards, IPEMA regulations, and ADA regulations.
- Require manufacturers and installers to provide evidence of liability insurance ($5 million minimum).
- Provide NPSI training and certification for one or more maintenance personnel.
- Provide annual safety training for all adults who supervise playgrounds.
- Document and keep records for all the above.

Public school playgrounds, which were identified by national surveys of playgrounds (AAHPERD) as the most hazardous among three groups—public schools, public parks, and preschools—were also the most common sites for injuries leading to lawsuits. Seventy of the 190 cases (37%) were at public schools, 48 involved public parks, 25 were at child care centers, 15 at fast-food restaurants, 13 at backyards, 7 at apartment complexes, and the others at camps, drive-in theaters, state schools, zoos, swim clubs, retail stores, private schools, and theme parks.

Children in the early childhood range were the most often injured, with 2- to 8-year-olds accounting for 137 of the 190 injuries and fatalities, or 72%. This statistic appears to be due to immature physical skills, extensive time on playgrounds, hazardous playgrounds, and poor supervision (Frost, 1997). Boys were more frequently injured than girls (57% to 43%). As children enter the primary grades, their playground time is supplanted by organized sports activities and physical education.

One of the most compelling findings was that 179 of the 190 injuries and fatalities (94%) involved violations of CPSC playground safety guidelines and ASTM safety standards. Falls and failure to install and maintain resilient surfacing under and around equipment dominated these findings, involving 101 of the 190 cases. Concrete, asphalt, and hard-packed earth accounted for almost all of these data. Does this mean that the injuries would not have happened if recommended surfacing practices had been followed? The answer is somewhat speculative, for children do sustain injuries from falling onto approved surfaces, but the injuries are less serious and less frequent. For example, children sometimes suffer broken arms when falling onto resilient surfacing but are unlikely to suffer brain damage or death. These differences are worth the effort and expense of installing and maintaining resilient surfacing. For detailed information on selecting, installing, and maintaining resilient surfacing on playgrounds, see CPSC (1997), ASTM (1995, 1996b) and Frost (1996b).

The most common case profile resulting from the data in the Frost and Sweeney (1996) study is a seriously injured male child between the ages of 2 and 8 years, who fell from a slide, swing, or climber onto concrete, asphalt, or hard-packed earth while playing at a public school, public park, or child care center playground. The child suffered a broken limb or head injury resulting in litigation that endured for 2 to 4 years before being settled out of court in an agreement negotiated by attorneys and favoring the plaintiffs (p. 14).

The pattern of spiraling actual and punitive damages in American courts is influencing the design and use of playground equipment, resulting in what we earlier designated the "standardized era" in playgrounds. In the United States, those who depend on manufactured equipment as a central feature in playgrounds have little choice but to comply with safety guidelines and standards that prevail in litigation. Case studies from litigation are instructive for preventing some of the most serious playground injuries that are likely to result in lawsuits (see Figure 12–7).

Standards and Lawsuits: The United States Versus Europe

"The notion of a **riskless society** is a peculiarly American one" (Andrews, 1998, p. D-1). Playgrounds in much of Europe are more challenging, more hazardous, and more fun than typical American playgrounds. These conditions may change because the European safety standards (European Committee for Standardization, 1998), prepared by representatives of 18 European countries, are stringent and similar in most respects to American standards. The Europeans wisely exclude adventure playgrounds—"fenced, secured playgrounds, run and staffed according to pedagogical principles, that encourage children's development and often use self-build equipment" (p. 4)—in their draft standard. In Europe, staffing "according to pedagogical principles" frequently means that a trained **play leader** or **play worker** is available to play and work with children on playgrounds (see Chapter 13). American standards contain no such exclusion, and self-build adventure playgrounds are rare.

European children typically swing from greater heights, play on more challenging equipment, depend less on adult directives than American children, and, if injured, are unlikely to collect huge damage awards in lawsuits. European courts offer little financial compensation for injuries and virtually no punitive damages for negligence. Even for very serious injuries, plaintiffs may not recover damages from careless manufacturers, operators, and doctors. This is balanced by generous European systems of government health care.

One factor accounting for these differences between the American and European systems is their views of responsibility and risk. The Europeans place greater responsibility on children and allow greater freedom to take risks because risk taking is essential to development. Too much supervision or inappropriate supervision can hinder opportunities for development. The adventure playgrounds of Scandinavian countries, Germany, the United Kingdom, and the Netherlands are concrete testimony to the efficacy of such beliefs, practices, and results (see Chapter 13).

SUMMARY

Striking a reasonable balance between allowing healthy development through play and managing risk of physical harm is a prevailing dilemma in promoting the play of children. Risk is inherent in all human behavior and, indeed, is essential to survival in mammals, especially the smarter ones (Brown, 1997). Play enhances risk and the more adventuresome the child, the greater the risk may be. The roles of adults are to be smart (get educated) about what constitutes excessive risk, that is, risk likely to result in serious injury or death; to see that children have extensive daily opportunities to play in challenging, stimulating places that promote creativity, learning, fitness, and motor development; to carefully check all consumer products that children play with and help children examine them for safety, without encouraging paranoia; to spend time with children ensuring that they develop both motor and cognitive skills that make them smarter, safer players; and to intervene on behalf of children against distribution and use of slipshod manufactured products and hazardous play places. Take reasonable precautions, then stand back and *let children play*.

KEY TERMS

American Society for Testing and Materials (ASTM)
CPSC *Handbook for Public Playground Safety*
Developmental abilities
Emotional risks
Extreme hazards
Financial risks
Hazard
Intellectual risks
Limited hazards
Moderate hazards
Noise
Physical risks
Play leader
Play value
Play worker
Play-related hazards
Primary barriers
Public barriers
Risk
Risk management
Riskless society
Scaffolding
Setback zones
Soft contained play structures
Supervisory risks
U.S. Consumer Product Safety Commission (CPSC)

STUDY QUESTIONS

1. What is the meaning of the following terms: *risk, risk management, hazard, limited hazards, moderate hazards,* and *extreme hazards*? What is the importance of risk for child development? How should risk at play be balanced with children's need to play?
2. How can the Consumer Product Safety Commission be helpful to children's teachers and caretakers in reducing play hazards?
3. Identify key elements in managing risk (risk management). That is, how can play hazards be managed to reduce physical risk to reasonable levels?
4. In what ways does a contemporary lifestyle (e.g., TV, fast food, busy schedules, pay-for-play) contribute to making kids unsafe?
5. What steps would you take to help ensure safety for young children you are taking to a mall? On a field trip? To a playground?
6. How do safety needs of infants and toddlers differ from those of preschoolers? Of school-age children?
7. Why are standards, regulations, and codes important for play safety? What are their limitations and problems? How do consumer products threaten children's safety? Should standards, regulations, and codes be applied to natural features of playgrounds? Why?
8. How safe are American playgrounds? Are they developmentally appropriate? Why or why not?
9. Identify the 10 to 12 major safety hazards on playgrounds. How can these be corrected? Must correction of these hazards reduce the play value of the playground? Why or why not?
10. What is the general state of safety at pay-for-play places such as amusement parks, video arcades, carnivals, museums, swimming pools, and water parks?
11. What steps would you take to protect infants and toddlers against hazardous toys?
12. When should safety helmets be used? Cite evidence. Should tricycle riders wear helmets? Why or why not?
13. How is litigation affecting the safety of American playground equipment and toys? How is it influencing their design and distribution? How is it affecting challenge, creativity, and diversity in play? How does this situation differ from European conditions? Which do you prefer, the American or the European system? Why?

Chapter 13

Play Leadership in American and European Playgrounds

FIRST AND FOREMOST . . . play is a voluntary activity. . . . It is never a task. . . . Second, play is not "ordinary" or "real" life. It is rather a stepping out of "real" life into a temporary sphere of activity . . . . Third, play is distinct from "ordinary" life both as to location and duration. It is "played out" within certain limits of time and space . . . . It plays itself to an end.

(Huizinga, 1950, pp. 7–9)

A CERTAIN supervision and guidance will, of course, be necessary but I am firmly convinced that one ought to be exceedingly careful when interfering in the lives and activities of children. The object must be to give the children of the city a substitute for the rich possibilities for play which children in the country possess.

(Allen, 1968, p. 55)

The influences of history and theories of play permeate this text. Initially, we explained that over the centuries, philosophers and scholars held different views about the nature of play and its importance in social, cognitive, motor, and cultural aspects of development. In this chapter, we draw from various leading theories, research, and accounts of experience to focus on the role of adults in children's outdoor play environments or playgrounds. The reader should bear in mind that the concept and reality of "playground" is rapidly broadening to reflect (a) the need to reintroduce natural features, (b) the rapid introduction of technology into children's lives, (c) a growing emphasis on safety, (d) the introduction of new equipment designs and materials, and (e) the appearance of playgrounds in a broadening context (e.g., backyards, neighborhood spaces, public parks, schools, child development centers, shopping malls, children's museums, gambling casinos, theme parks, and vacation destinations).

The roles of adults in most dimensions of teaching and caring for children are carefully prescribed and protected by bodies of theory. Teachers do not all teach the same way, but they can point to theory that supports their behavior. Play therapists identify several alternate, sometimes conflicting, theories to support their practice. Theory is available for behavior management, language teaching, reading, and a host of other child development tasks faced daily by adults, but the foundations for playground supervision have yet to rise beyond the level of fragmented research and theory. Despite such shortcomings, common practice is to apply these classroom theories and resulting methods to children's outdoor play and play environments. We will visit indoor play intervention views and theories in this chapter, but the major emphasis will be on play leadership and play work principles emerging in Europe, which are rooted in a century of extensive attention to children's play and play environments, and to the appropriate roles of play leaders or playworkers.

Some of the most thoughtfully developed and highly respected early childhood programs (e.g., High Scope, Head Start, Reggio Emilio, Bank Street; see Chapter 8) integrate play into virtually all aspects of classroom environment, materials and equipment, teaching techniques, and curricula. These programs draw from the work of such noted persons as Jean Piaget, John Dewey, Jerome Bruner, and Lev Vygotsky. All of these prominent figures valued and described the processes and benefits of play, but none attempted extensive application of their views to outdoor play in public settings. Consequently, leaps of faith are taken when adults apply their theories to practical applications.

The role of adults in young children's classroom play has been extensively studied, carefully explained, and applied in programs throughout the United States (discussed in Chapter 8). However, with limited exceptions, only minimal attention has been directed to the role of adults in American children's out-of-classroom or outdoor play environments during recent decades. Consequently, a common pattern on school and child care center playgrounds across America is adult supervisors sitting in the shade gossiping with their peers—taking a break—while their young charges play, or applying academic-related strategies proven during indoor play to outdoor play contexts. The pattern of supervision in American city park playgrounds is even less planned. Many cities employ out-of-school teenagers to oversee park play during the summer months and provide no adult supervision for the remainder of the year.

In the following sections, we will review the history of adult roles in outdoor play, summarize theories and research on adult roles, and describe the practices of select programs in the United States and Europe. Finally, we will make recommendations for application in child care center, school, and other organized public playgrounds. The emphasis is on outdoor play environments, but many of the principles are applicable to all contexts where children play. We will draw from personal views and experiences, from American research and practice in play leadership in playgrounds, and from extensive on-the-job experiences of play leaders in European playgrounds. We believe that these sources are all relevant in building and conducting play leadership programs in playgrounds.

Play professionals in the United States and other countries, notably the Scandinavian countries, the United Kingdom, and the Netherlands, struggle in vain to find language that clearly describes the preferred roles of adults on playgrounds. The concept of supervisors is seen as inconsistent with the desired freedom, independence, and creativity of children at play. **Play leaders** was a popular approach for many years but has recently been replaced with **playworkers** in some European countries, notably the United Kingdom. We have chosen the term play leaders for this discussion of the roles of adults (including teachers) in children's play.

HISTORY OF PLAY LEADERSHIP IN AMERICA

The history of American **play leadership** is erratic and spread across various play contexts. Major contexts for play include urban parks, public and private schools, child development centers, and both rural and urban neighborhoods. The adults responsible for play leadership across these contexts hold differing views about the nature and importance of children's play, play environments, and the appropriate roles and training of play leaders. These views also differ across countries, particularly the United States versus the United Kingdom, the Netherlands, and Scandinavia.

Play Leadership in Public Parks

During the early 1900s, organized city park playgrounds in the United States were developed in unprecedented numbers (Frost, 1992). Soon, the public came to believe that without trained leadership playgrounds fostered idleness, immorality, and vandalism (Lee, 1927). Consequently, the **Playground Association of American (PAA)** developed guidelines for training play leaders, often called *play directors,* and courses were established in normal schools (Cavallo, 1976; Curtis, 1917). The initial goals established for these training programs focused on physical education and recreation but included courses in sociology, social psychology, biology, industrial arts, and civic relationships. By 1915, there were 774 full-time and 5,000 part-time directors in the United States. The recreation emphasis was reinforced during the 1930s when the name of the Playground Association of America was changed to the National Recreation Association. The important role of play leader during the 1920s and 1930s was gradually deemphasized to become a subcategory of workers under the recreation supervisor, and the emphasis on trained play leaders shifted from playground play to organized recreation and sports (Butler, 1950). The early ideals of training play leaders have not regained their importance in the structure of American public park playgrounds.

Play Leadership in Preschools

Early 20th-century views held by preschool professionals—child care, nursery school, and kindergarten—about the roles of adults in children's play were founded on radically different premises than were those of public park and public school personnel. Rather than focusing on the limited views of physical development and recreation, preschool professionals adopted the views of Friedrich Froebel and the early child development research centers. Froebel (1887) viewed play as important for developing the mind, body, and character. College and university training programs and the best preschool programs promoted context (providing space and a wide range of materials) and a general policy of "hands off," but specific steps for adult intervention were taken (Iowa Child Welfare Research Station, 1934):

- Expose the child to materials.
- Explain correct uses when materials are misused.
- Support the child in using new materials.
- Praise the child for accomplishing difficult tasks.

- Give slow, timid children time, then encourage use of materials.
- Encourage reluctant but capable children to "Try it yourself."
- Support the child's inclinations to try new or difficult materials or equipment.
- Redirect the child when he overused materials or equipment.
- If the child throws materials, ask her to pick them up before playing with anything else.
- If the child continues to abuse materials or use a toy unsafely, remove it until she is willing to comply.
- The child should use large equipment properly and safely.

Early leaders in the nursery-kindergarten movement promoted adults' role in shaping the development of children during play (Palmer, 1916). They were aided in this effort by the training of preschool teachers in college and university programs that emphasized child development. This contrasted sharply with the typical didactic training of elementary school teachers with virtually no attention to supervising playground play—a difference that prevails today and continues to shape play leadership across the two contexts.

Play Leadership in Public and Private Elementary Schools

Unfortunately, the views and practices of elementary school professionals concerning the roles of adults in children's play roughly parallel those of public park professionals. Throughout most of the 20th century, public and private elementary school playgrounds were equipped to promote exercise, organized games, and sports. Play rested on old "excess energy" theory rather than developmental foundations; equipment for play was antiquated, hazardous, and limited in function; and loose or portable materials were virtually nonexistent. Teacher education institutions rarely devoted attention to play or play leadership and play time was widely viewed as trivial and inconsequential. These patterns are slowly improving.

The role of adults in elementary school playgrounds has been subjected to limited study. Available studies include those by Block and King (1987), Evans (1989, 1990), Finnan (1982), Frost (1992), Moore (1974), and Sluckin (1981). Since playground play in elementary schools typically takes place during recess, the reader should also see Pellegrini's (1995) book on school recess and playground behavior.

Evans' (1990) studies in American and Australian schools are among the most insightful for understanding the roles assumed by teachers on playgrounds during recess. Teachers generally view recess as an activity break or a time for children to let off steam, but many children, especially those in upper elementary grades, use recess to talk with peers, sit on equipment, wait in line for equipment, or wander around. Children do not always return to the classroom relaxed and attentive but may be agitated or excited about events that transpired.

Teachers may use recess as a time to take a break, have coffee, or converse among themselves. Many school systems hire parents or unskilled workers to supervise recess while teachers have lunch, prepare lessons, or simply be alone. Recess is commonly seen as an unpleasant duty, especially by teachers of older children who may engage in confrontations with the teacher and require policing.

Evans (1987, 1990) found that teachers' assumed roles on playground duty varied widely. Some stood or sat near the school building; some wandered around the playground; others joined in games or talked with children. Some teachers avoided contact with the children, remained aloof, and discouraged children from bringing grievances to them. Younger children sought out the teachers more frequently than did older ones. Teachers basically saw their roles as supervisory, ensuring a safe environment and alternately acting as police officer, referee, counselor, or coplayer.

Despite teachers assuming multiple roles on playgrounds, they are generally given little or no advice by school administration for performing their roles and are unclear as to the value of recess. Little wonder that some abhor the role, many try to avoid it, and few feel competent doing it. Teachers do believe that supervision is necessary, and that children, even older children, should not be left unsupervised, in part due to legal concerns. Those who understand play's value for child development believe that children should be supervised and this should be done by adults who know the children and have been trained for the role.

Our research and personal experiences reveal that appropriate adult roles on children's playgrounds are varied and complex, extending well beyond enforcement of rules. Roles should also include ensuring that children have rich, challenging, and ever changing environments for play. As playgrounds are improved, behavior problems decline. Good playgrounds breed good behavior. Rules are needed—but only necessary ones established *with* the children.

One of the most pressing issues in recess supervision remains: how much intervention by adults? Evans (1990) concludes that "there are sound moral and legal reasons why adult presence is required when children are at recess, but . . . the more we can leave them to their own devices in the playground the better" (p. 233). During recess, children have unique opportunities not available in the classroom to learn organization, negotiation, and physical and social skills. Qualified, well-trained teachers can assist without excessive intervention. See *www.ericfacility.net/ericdigests/ed466331/html* (2002) for research on benefits of recess.

THEORETICAL BASES FOR ADULT INTERVENTION IN CHILDREN'S PLAY

Play leadership takes place in many physical contexts, and play takes many forms, so no one theory or philosophy taps the conceptual depth and range necessary to establish a scientific basis for play leadership for all children in all settings. For example, both Piaget and Vygotsky seemed to realize that play had emotional and therapeutic components, but neither gave this critical factor much attention. One could hardly rely on either of these theorists to explain the appropriate roles of adults in play therapy. The work of Anna Freud, Carl Rogers, and Virginia Axline (see Chapter 10) are far more significant for assisting children in dealing with serious problems of neglect, abuse, conflict, and trauma. This examination of theory and practice identifies appropriate roles for adults in children's play in typical home, child care center, and school contexts.

In *The Republic,* Plato wrote that children from the earliest ages must take part in the more lawful forms of play if they are to grow up to be well-conducted and virtuous citizens. He stressed that adults should learn about children by observing their play. In the 1st century, Quintilian thought that play could be arranged by adults to develop children's intellects. In the 16th century, John Amos Comenius considered playgrounds to be essential to a well-ordered school and encouraged adults to provide objects, pictures, and puzzles in lower schools to encourage the play interests of children (Caplan & Caplan, 1973; Frost & Kissinger, 1976). Jean-Jacques Rousseau, in the 18th century, emphasized the value of play and the vast differences in the interests and values of adults and children. Rousseau believed the child should receive no kind of verbal instructions, and his learning was to come from direct experience. Growth was to be natural and unfettered by society.

Johann Pestallozi, in the late 1700s, also attacked the harsh, rote instruction of his era, emphasizing instead learning through direct experiences. The adult or teacher was not to adopt the tone of an instructor, Pestallozi thought, but should gently help children engage in real-life activities such as setting up a business and utilizing nature. The older children should teach the younger children. However, no system of educational play was to be followed until Froebel's time.

Froebel, a student of Pestallozi's, established the first kindergarten (literally **garden of children**) in Blankenburg, Germany, in 1837. These were seen as enclosures in which human plants were nurtured. Schools for very young children existed before Froebel's kindergarten, but they focused on the mothers more than on the children (Quick, 1896). To Froebel, the children's employment (activity) was play, and any occupation in which children gained delight was play to them. In Froebel's kindergarten, work or learning activities were infused with the pleasure of play and became **play/work**, with the intent that pleasurable activities would have an educational object. Learning from simple playthings (gifts and occupations) in the classroom was further strengthened by extensive creative self-activity with games and nature in the outdoors.

Froebel's outdoor gardens combined practical work with the literary school and served to assist physical health. Children tended a patchwork of plants, vegetables, shrubs, and meadows and modeled mountain chains, river valleys, canals, and ponds complete with fishes and frogs (Von Marenholz-Bulow, 1897). Nothing lay closer to Froebel's heart than the study of animals and plants, and the outdoors in general (Kilpatrick, 1916, p. 187). Consider his views of the garden:

> The kindergarten . . . necessarily requires a garden. . . . Personal responsibility is fixed by the provision that in their own little beds the children can plant what and how they will, also deal with the plants as they will, that they may learn from their own judicious treatment. . . . This will be shown to them by the plants in the common bed [a separate garden planned by the group], which they must observe carefully. The seeds and plants should be so compared and discussed that the children may learn to recognize them readily. Seeds preserved for the next planting should be kept in little paper boxes previously made by the children themselves. The beds should be so labeled as to name plant and child. Through this the child is not only carried along the road towards reading, but receives the merited silent praise or blame, according as his work has been. (Kilpatrick, 1916, pp. 193–194)

Froebel believed that not only kindergartens but every town should have its common playground where the games of children could be carried out. The adult (teacher) was to watch the children at play and recast their games to form the habit of "association with comrades" (Kilpatrick, 1916, p. 153). The true kindergarten teacher "will listen to the suggestion of children and will be guided by circumstances" (p. 154). Froebel did not propose to do away with free play. He understood that there was much time for free play outside the 3 hours of the kindergarten. (In the 21st century, however, kindergarten and child care may occupy most of a child's waking hours.) In Froebel's school, traditional and instinctive games furnish the material that may be transfigured into truly educative play. Through insight into the ideal, the adult (teacher) can help children select games that form a logically related sequence and develop the child into the chosen game's image. As each new generation gains experience, fresh images are added to the children's dramatic reproductions of the vital and formative facts of their own lives (Blow, 1909). (Consider the images that are introduced into contemporary children's play via television and the Internet.) As the reader will see, the views and practices of contemporary play leaders on Europe's adventure playgrounds have much in common with Froebel's outdoor kindergarten activities.

John Dewey acknowledged that Froebel was perhaps the first to consciously set forth that children's play was not only essential to their growth but that their games and activities "are the foundational stones of educational method" (Tanner, 1997, p. 30). However, Dewey believed that elaborate **symbolism** (sweeping a make-believe room with a make-believe broom, for example), perhaps essential in the Germany of Froebel's time, was not essential in early 20th-century America. Societal change justified making kindergarten activities more natural and representative of current life. Dewey's children, like Froebel's, worked in gardens in their school yard, applied principles learned in classrooms in cooperatively building club houses outdoors, learned to use tools in shops, planned and prepared meals using natural grains, studied elementary biology in natural outdoor settings, and built models of their community while studying community life. The classroom was extended, through both play and work, into the community.

Dewey's teachers used a range of approaches including **cooperative planning** with children, group discussion, writing about experiences, laboratory experiments, practical and fine arts experiences, and reproduction of home and family life. The school must be a community in which children work and play in a social context and in which the subject matter of formal instruction is integrated with the subject matter of life experiences. Formal instruction easily becomes "remote and dead." The danger of improper balance increases as societies become more complex in structure and resources. Learners must test their ideas through applications. "Only by wrestling with the conditions of the problem at first hand, seeking and finding his own way out, does he [the child] think" (Dewey, 1916, p. 160).

What, then, are the conditions for balancing formal instruction with life experiences? For balancing play and work? What is the role of the teacher? First, he provides the context—a rich blend of classrooms, playgrounds, laboratories (indoor and outdoor), and workrooms. Second, he ensures opportunity for interaction—the social context. Playgrounds, for example, involve intercourse, communication, and connection (Dewey, 1916, p. 358). Third, cooperative planning and acting occur to develop a spirit of companionship and shared activity. Fourth, there is carry-over of social concern and understanding into the broader community outside the school, lest the "social life of the school . . . no more represent or typify that of the world beyond the school walls than that of a monastery" (p. 359). Fifth, the teachers strive to keep a proper balance between the informal and the formal, the abstract and the practical. Gardening, for example, is more than the preparation of future gardeners or an agreeable way of passing time. It allows for the study of growth, soil chemistry, animal life, and human relations. Playing in sand and water or engaging in chase games or symbolic housekeeping play carries similar advantages beyond the sheer joy and delight experienced by the player. Finally, the teacher ensures that the joy and delight of play permeates the work experience.

"From a very early age . . . there is no distinction of exclusive periods of play activity and work activity, but only one of emphasis . . . both involve ends consciously entertained and the selection and adaptations of materials and processes designed to effect the desired ends" (Dewey, 1916, pp. 202–203). "The defining characteristic of play is not amusement nor aimlessness. . . . Work which remains permeated with the play attitude is **art-in-quality** if not in conventional designation" (pp. 205–206).

During the early 1900s, psychoanalysis was integrated into play therapy for children and two schools of thought developed (see Chapter 10), each advocating a particular form and frequency of intervention. The **directive school** emphasized directed play and prescribed materials, and interpreted play to determine the source and nature of phobias and conflicts. The **nondirective school** confirmed, repeated, and clarified the child's play acts, emphasizing the importance of nonintervention by adults in children's play. Play itself, aside from the adult's direction or interpretation, was seen as the critical factor in fostering the child's social and intellectual development. Today scholars continue to debate the relative importance of these approaches to adult intervention in children's play (see Chapter 8).

Piaget and Constructivism

Piaget's cognitive theories of play and implications for the roles of adults in children's play were dominant among early childhood educators from the 1960s until the late 1980s. Now, growing numbers of scholars recommend specific roles for adults in children's play and visionary programs are shifting from a **constructivist** to a **social-constructivist** approach. The Piagetian "watching and waiting" approach is tempered by the Vygotskian view that children do not merely construct their knowledge but that their performance can be assisted by others. Following the translation of Vygotsky's work and its dissemination and interpretation throughout the English-speaking world, growing numbers of early childhood educators modified their views to place greater emphasis on the social context of children's play, especially with respect to the role of adults (teachers and parents).

Vygotsky and Social Constructivism

Vygotsky (1933/1966) broke with the views of Piaget (1962) about play in several ways that have implications for adults' role in play. For example, Vygotsky maintained that there is no such thing as play without rules laid down in advance by real-life behavior. If the child is "nurturing" a baby, she is obeying rules of maternal behavior. Unlike Piaget, who held that rules emerge after the preschool period, primarily in organized games, Vygotsky believed that children under age three engaged in imaginary play and that all imaginary play contains rules. Piaget focused only marginally on sociocultural dimensions of development and the roles of adults in development, maintaining that education was the "American question," yet he included **social transmission** as one of four fundamental factors influencing children's development.

For Piaget, make-believe play emerges spontaneously with the onset of representational thought, and cognitive construction takes place largely through interaction with physical objects. Vygotsky and his followers contend that from its beginnings, make-believe play is a social activity—a product of **social collaboration** (Haight & Miller, 1993; Smolucha, 1992).

Vygotsky identified a **zone of proximal development (ZPD)**, a range of tasks between those the child can handle independently and those at the highest level he can handle with the help of adults or more competent peers), which placed adults in a prominent role in the child's play and educational life. He identified play as the "highest level of preschool development" (Vygotsky, 1933/1966, p. 16). His followers maintained that adults and more competent peers could effectively **scaffold** intervention to match the child's learning ability (introduce tasks more complex than the child's independent level but not beyond his potential level), helping him achieve higher levels of development than possible by working independently. Thus, the constructivism of Piaget's followers was tempered by the **co-constructivism** of Vygotsky's followers.

Following the Vygotskian approach, the child engages in joint problem solving with a more skilled partner (teacher or parent) who introduces the intellectual tools of the society to the child within the manageable ZPD (Rogoff et al., 1993). This reciprocal relationship between child, teacher, and social environment promotes movement through the ZPD as knowledge is continuously reconstructed (Wertsch & Hickman, 1987) or coconstructed (Rogoff, 1990; Winegar, 1989). Teaching is assisted performance (Tharp & Gallimore, 1988), and a social environment is essential for cognitive development (Newman, Griffin, & Cole, 1989).

Chaos Theory

The rationale for **chaos theory** draws from the growing national, and to some degree international, paradox that postmodern families and institutions—indeed, societies—are experiencing a transformation from traditional predictable structures to ever more complex and interdependent ones. Chaos theory holds that social systems are nonlinear, interdependent, and unpredictable. Workers must now have portable skills allowing them to move from job to job. The traditional intact nuclear family is declining. Global interests and concerns touch everyone's community (Naisitt, 1994; Vander Ven, 1998). The reality of the world is essentially chaotic (Goerner, 1994). Consequently, an essential question arises: What kind of persons will be needed to survive in such a world, and how can parents and educators help children cope in a chaotic world?

Despite growing knowledge of the prevailing, creeping chaos in society, those parents and teachers most directly responsible for helping children adapt to chaos cling to outmoded, antiquated views about teaching, parenting, and the role of play as a legitimate educational enterprise. In resolution, Vander Ven (1998) proposes a chaotically oriented approach to education that incorporates play at every developmental level—an approach that unifies play and school curriculum. Her views are based on two basic principles: (a) play is a complex adaptive system that embraces and generates other complex adaptive systems, and (b) play is essential for young children to experience pervasive chaos and to identify themselves as complex adaptive beings. When children play, they seek chaotic experiences—novelty, surprise, loss of control, and disequilibrium—the very experiences that adults avoid (Wheatley, 1992). Many of the underlying principles of chaos theory were discovered through free play with computers and computer games (Peitgen, Jurgens, & Saupe, 1992, p. 35; Whitton, 1998, p. 480).

Many parents, child caretakers, and educators resist the ideas that play is an essential component of parenting, child care programs, and school curricula and that adults should have an active role in supporting play. Vander Ven (1998), following the leads of Smilansky and Shefatya's (1990) research and Berk and Winsler's (1995) interpretations of Vygotsky, contends that adult facilitation of play is essential for children's development and for adaptation to a chaotic world. She proposes a number of chaos theory concepts of play facilitation:

- *Determinism.* A system or process can be predetermined *and* have unpredictable outcomes. Adults need not resist play facilitation strategies (e.g., suggesting a theme) simply because the outcomes may be unpredictable.
- *Weak chaos.* Any play facilitation strategy by an adult injects weak chaos (a change in the dynamic) and keeps it changing, evolving, and dynamic.
- *Bifurcation.* The adult facilitator may introduce a bifurcation or transition into a new form or state by scaffolding, as suggested by Vygotsky's followers.
- *Attractor.* As play runs down, adult facilitators may introduce novel "attractors" to reengage the child's attention and energy by, for example, introducing a new toy or material.

Following chaos theory, the early childhood or elementary teacher would abandon prescriptive curricula focusing on memorization, prescriptive thinking, and linear instruction and implement a play–based curriculum focusing on flexibility, extended options, divergent thinking, risk taking, learning through error, and flexible planning. Vander Ven playfully proposes that **supersymmetry** (Freedman, 1991; Weinberg, 1992), a concept embracing both symmetry and chaos, will be the new worldview beyond chaos. Games, play, and highly skilled adults can help children to adapt to change and meet the complex challenges of a chaotic world.

RESEARCH BASES FOR ADULT INTERVENTION IN CHILDREN'S PLAY

Since 1960, a number of researchers have studied the effects of intervention, commonly referred to as **play tutoring** or training, on children's play. In these studies, adults participated in children's play through such activities as discussing topics that might be used in play, encouraging use of nonstructured materials, encouraging children to invite others to join their play, helping elaborate themes, making imaginative uses of play materials, encouraging invention, helping create pretend episodes, and taking children on trips to community centers (fire stations, doctor's office, grocery store, etc.) and encouraging reenactment in dramatic play. The terms *training* and *tutoring* are misleading because the adult interventions were generally informal and consisted of adults unobtrusively suggesting, questioning, supporting, and encouraging rather than teaching, telling, directing, or requiring.

Correlations were found between parent's verbal behavior (e.g., discussing topics that could be used in the child's dramatic play) and the amount of nursery school children's dramatic play (Marshall, 1961). Doll play training increased the frequency of dramatic play for nursery school children (Marshall & Hahn, 1967). Imaginative training sessions for "ghetto school" kindergarten children resulted in significant improvement in imaginativeness and concentration (Freyberg, 1973). Kindergarten children from working-class families exposed to play tutoring made significant gains in combinatory play and creativity. There were no significant gains for nontutored children in the same play environment (Feitelson & Ross, 1973). Kindergartners from low socioeconomic groups who received sociodramatic play tutoring showed significantly higher gains than a control group on measures including manipulation of objects, interaction with coplayers, use of verbal descriptions, problem-solving tasks, and perceptual role taking (Rosen, 1974).

Additional positive results of play intervention for young children include enhanced imaginative play (Feitelson & Ross, 1973; Smilansky, 1968; Smilansky & Shefatya, 1990); improvement in cognitive tasks, impulse control, verbal intelligence, story interpretation, and spontaneous engagement in sociodramatic play (Saltz, Dixon, & Johnson, 1977); creativity, group activity, attention span, cognitive ability, and amount of group activity (Smith & Sydall, 1978); perspective taking (Burns & Brainerd, 1979); verbal comprehension, cognitive tasks, and verbal comprehension (Dansky, 1980); cognitive complexity (Sylva, Roy, & Painter, 1980); conservation tasks (Golomb & Bonen, 1981); verbal fluency, amount of imaginative play, social interaction, reduced aggression, social adjustment (Udwin, 1983); associative fluency (Dempsey, 1985); attention span (Hutt, Tyler, Hutt, & Christopherson, 1989); language development (Levy, Wolfgang, & Koorland, 1992); attachment to adults and peer interaction (Howes & Smith, 1995); and play enrichment (Bennett, Wood, & Rogers, 1997).

Smilansky (1966) conducted studies of low-income immigrant children in Israel and concluded that they engaged in less sociodramatic play than did middle-income Israeli children. The preschool and kindergarten children were assigned to four treatments: (a) direct or preparatory experiences (guided visits and discussions), (b) teaching how to play, (c) a combination of direct experiences and teaching, and (d) control. She concluded that direct teaching and a combination of teaching and provision of direct experiences were effective in increasing the extent and quality of sociodramatic play.

Although the most compelling conclusion from play intervention studies is that play tutoring or training results in academic and developmental outcomes, a central concern remains: what form of intervention for which children? Gains in developmental indices among earlier studies were questioned by Smith and Sydall (1978), who concluded that advantages in language and cognitive skills ascribed to play tutoring may have been due to lack of adult contact with children in the non-play tutored or control groups. Christie and Johnsen (1985) questioned whether the cognitive and social benefits of play training are caused by children's social interaction during play or by the adult play component. Failure to control experiments for effects of peer interaction and adult tutoring are seen as methodological weaknesses in the research. Which is the major factor in determining effectiveness of adult intervention, play per se or adult contact? However, "If the tutors playing with children produce important scholarly results, this is an important finding regardless of the exact nature of the antecedents" (Sutton-Smith, 1993, p. 23). Researchers are still divided as to *how* adults should play with children.

The approaches used in experimental studies ranged from informal to directive, and the subjects included a range of ages, developmental abilities, and ethnic groups. Those children who do not engage in play have different intervention needs than those who are skilled and secure in their play. Unwitting or unskilled adults can interrupt the flow of children's play, discourage certain types of play (e.g., rough-and-tumble), inhibit play activities, reduce problem solving and peer interaction, interfere with learning during play, stifle imagination, or even prohibit play (Frost, 1992; Johnson, Christie, & Yawkey, 1998; Jones & Reynolds, 1992; Miller, Fernie, & Kantor, 1992; Pellegrini & Galda,

1993; Sutton-Smith, 1992; Wood, McMahon & Cranstoun, 1980). Overall, research indicates that more, not less, adult-child play would benefit children's play and development.

PRACTICING PLAY LEADERSHIP

We conclude that decisions about the nature, type, and timing of intervention into children's play involves a complex mix of approaches:

1. Providing natural and designed spaces for play
2. Scheduling extensive time for play
3. Providing a challenging mix of natural and manufactured play materials and equipment
4. Individualizing play intervention through observation and study of children
5. Deciding what strategies to use during personal interactions with children

These approaches are more fully explained in Chapter 11, "Creating Play Environments" (outdoors), and Chapter 8, "Play and Curricula" (indoors).

Pacific Oaks College Perspectives on Practice

For many years, the faculty of Pacific Oaks College in Pasadena, California, has operated one of the most visionary and creative sets of play yards in the United States. There children spend many hours playing and learning in well-designed and skillfully managed outdoor play yards. These play yards contain many imaginative do-it-yourself play structures; exciting linkages between indoor curricula and outdoor play; storage and loose parts; an abundance of natural materials including sand, dirt, vegetation, and even fire for cookouts; and adults trained in enhancing children's spontaneous play. The success of the Pacific Oaks faculty and its long-term studies of children at play deserves special recognition and offers a model to emulate.

The Pacific Oaks program was developed over many years at Pacific Oaks College, but was influenced by the developmental approaches of Bank Street College and the High/Scope curriculum and refined in collaboration with the Pasadena Unified School District. Its theoretical bases reside in both cognitive and interactionist theory, especially Piaget's constructivism (Jones & Reynolds, 1992). "Young children learn the most important things not by being told but by constructing knowledge for themselves in interaction with the physical world and with other children—and the way they do this is by playing" (Johnson & Reynolds, 1992, p. 1). The Pacific Oaks program emphasizes the importance of language, construction with materials, and bodies in action during both fantasy and reality play themes (scripts) (p. 9). They break with scholars who believe that Piaget ignores or deemphasizes the socioemotional benefits of play and with educators who see the role of adults as teller or "interrupter" of children's play—as one who merely teaches (p. 1). They acknowledge the work of Vygotsky stressing the cognitive challenge that play offers children (p. 5) and identify intervention strategies for teachers to assume during children's play.

Since becoming a master player represents a high level of development for preschool children and has high educational significance (Jones & Reynolds, 1992; Reynolds & Jones, 1997), the teacher pays attention to play; that is, she carefully observes children at play to take their perspectives and to answer such questions as, What is happening for this child in his play? What is the child's agenda? Does he have the skills and materials he needs to accomplish his intent? How can I support the child's play? Using observation as a guide, the teacher takes steps to make play possible. These steps include assuming the roles of stage manager, mediator, player, scribe, assessor and communicator, and planner.

Vygotskian Perspectives on Practice

Bodrova and Leong (1996, 1998), and Berk and Winsler (1995) conducted extensive analyses of Vygotsky's work, resulting in recommendations for the roles of adults in children's play. Just as many other play scholars have done, Bodrova and Leong (1998, p. 279) recognize that adults have indirect influences on children's play, including preparing the environment, choosing toys and materials, and encouraging children to play together. Vygotskians reach beyond indirect influences to exert direct influences on play, especially for infants, toddlers, and preschoolers. These include providing experiences that can become play themes, modeling how to play with a toy, taking turns, settling disputes, and describing sequences.

As children mature in their play, adult intervention should change and decline. Adults help infants establish attachment with adults and provide for interaction with other people, toys, books, and objects. Toddlers are helped to use language to describe actions and interact socially with peers, and to see roles, implicit rules, and imaginary situations. Preschoolers are assisted by offering props for play, organizing activities, planning with children before and after play, expanding pretending and role taking, and providing for scaffolding by older children and adults. Fantasy play is encouraged well into elementary school, but adults assume a minor role in play, and adult domination is avoided. Interaction with slightly older peers is encouraged, and self-regulation is promoted (Bodrova & Leong, 1998).

Working independently, numerous individuals and groups have identified strategies for adult intervention in children's play (Figure 13–1). These strategies resulted from study of children on playgrounds, analysis of research literature, and practical experience. The contexts were primarily indoor classrooms, but the findings are adaptable to some degree in outdoor playgrounds, bearing in mind that most outdoor play should basically be free of academic motives. Such outdoor skills as basic gardening, animal care, and other work-play activities do require sensitive, skillful adult involvement.

Adventure Play and Play Leadership in Europe

Play professionals everywhere have noticed the excitement and energy of children playing in

FIGURE 13–1 Adult Intervention

Smilansky (1966)	*Bennett, Wood, & Rogers (1997)*
Observer	Observer
Outside intervention	Provider
Inside intervention	Participant
Coplayer	Model
Jones & Reynolds, (1992)	Review and feedback
Observer	*Van Hoorn, Nourot, Scales, & Alward (1999)*
Stage manager	Observer
Mediator	Stage manager
Player	Scaffolder
Scribe	Peacemaker
Assessor and communicator	Gate guardian
Planner	Parallel player
Johnson, Christie, & Yawkey (1999)	Spectator
Observer	Participant
Stage manager	Matchmaker
Coplayer	Storyplayer
Play leader	Play tutor
Provider	Assessor

construction sites, vacant lots, and natural areas. In 1943, the first of many junk playgrounds, later named building playgrounds or **adventure playgrounds**, was developed by C. T. Sorensen, a Danish landscape architect, in Emdrup, Denmark. John Bertelson, a nursery school teacher and former seaman, was named as the first play leader. Adventure playgrounds start with basically nothing. A fenced space is provided within walking distance of many children's homes, and one or more play leaders are assigned to the space and the children. Within this space, children are free to play almost any way they choose (Lambert, 1992). The playground is essentially a place for building with scrap materials. Children build dens, huts, and secret places. They play with water and mud. They care for animals, tend gardens, construct play equipment, and build fires for warming and cooking.

The American Adventure Playground Association was formed in California in 1976, and 16 adventure playgrounds were identified in the United States by 1997. The association later succumbed to lack of support. Americans object to adventure-type playgrounds because of their untidy appearance, ignorance concerning the nature of children's play, and misplaced fear of injury and liability (Frost & Klein, 1979). The only organized adventure playgrounds known to exist in the United States at the turn of the 21st century were those organized by the Houston Adventure Playground Association in Houston, Texas.

Unlike in the United States, where most playgrounds are basically standardized, limited in play function, and either unstaffed or staffed by "supervisors" or "baby-sitters," playgrounds in Denmark and some other countries "are recognized as so important they are provided by law" (Lambert, 1992, p. 14). **Playwork** or play leadership is a nationally recognized profession in some countries, and training programs range from on-the-job to university programs. Playwork as a profession is active in the United Kingdom, Scotland, Scandinavian countries, the Netherlands, and Australia, and is gaining momentum in Japan and Hong Kong (Jacobs, 1998).

Children in European adventure playgrounds enjoy a wide range of challenging play under the direction of trained play leaders.

Bonel and Lindon's (1996) strategies (Figure 13–2) were prepared as a text for playwork students in four National Centres for Playwork Education in England, underpinning the system of National Vocational Qualifications for play workers. The contexts for implementation are adventure playgrounds, play centers, school play centers, and after-school clubs. Playwork strategies are based on the experiences of play workers or play leaders since the early 1940s and do not appear to be tied to a particular scientific theory.

Jack Lambert (1974), a former adventure playground leader, quotes John Bertelsen (the first adventure playground play leader) regarding the appropriate roles of the play leader:

> The children are sovereign and the initiative must come from them. The leader can make suggestions but must never demand. He must obtain the tools and material needed or requested by the children but must at any time be prepared to give way to new activities. To organize and arrange programmes is to stifle imagination and initiative and preclude children whose lively curiosity and interests constantly demand new outlets. (p. 18)

This basic philosophical intent, adopted informally but widely throughout European adventure playgrounds, is rejected in American playground contexts, where the practices of adults are basically laissez-faire or didactic. Lady Allen of Hurtwood (1968, p. 56), who introduced adventure playgrounds to the United Kingdom and established the London Handicapped Adventure Playground Association, helped explain this: "Only rarely do the . . . school teachers feel at home in so unorthodox a situation. Perhaps they have too much to unlearn before they can begin." She quotes a personal letter from Sorensen, the famous Danish landscape architect mentioned earlier:

> A certain supervision and guidance will, of course, be necessary but I am firmly convinced that one ought to be exceedingly careful when interfering in the lives and activities of children. The object must be to give the children of the city a substitute for the rich possibilities for play which children in the country possess. (Allen, 1968, p. 55)

Functionally, adventure play leaders perform many roles:

- They nurture play in an unrestrictive setting (Bengtsson, 1972).
- They act as referees when a situation is getting out of hand (Allen, 1968).
- They maintain order but are friends to the children (Benjamin, 1974; Nicholson, 1971).
- They ensure that the playground is well staffed, equipped, and safe (Jacobs, 1998).
- They attract voluntary workers to the playground and involve families (Allen, 1968).
- They scrounge for tools and materials needed by the children (Lambert, 1992).
- They make suggestions but do not demand. They are never too busy to talk (Lambert, 1992).
- They don't interfere in play but teach an interesting skill if asked (Lambert, 1992).
- They accept a wide range of ages and individual differences (Frost & Klein, 1979).

FIGURE 13–2 Playwork Strategies: Adventure Playgrounds

Friendly companion	Impartial referee
Source of ideas and suggestion	Gatekeeper of boundaries
Model of behavior	Assessor of risks
Balancer—joining play and standing back	Balancer—initiating play or follower
Resource to children	Encourager of older to coach younger
Reviewer and planner with children	Confidence builder

Source: Adapted from Bonel and Lindon (1996).

- They support the work and play of children with minimum interference (Frost & Klein, 1979).
- They create opportunities that allow children to pursue their own play agendas (Brown, 2003).
- They help children create environments that address the negative effects of play deprivation and play bias (Brown, 2003).
- They introduce flexibility and adaptability into play environments (Brown, 2003).

The secret is to learn from children, to listen to them, and to understand what they are saying. Play leadership is being among children with a mind free of preconceptions (Lambert, 1992).

Personal observations of play leaders at work in several European countries and Japan confirm that the best of the group meet these criteria and support children's play at a level rarely seen in the United States. Some of the most memorable observations were children in Stockholm consoling a sow giving birth; children in Denmark feeding and cleaning burros in preparation for a ride; children in Birmingham, England, cultivating vegetable and flower gardens; children in Tokyo creating beautiful pieces of pottery; children in London bringing scraps of food from home to cook over open fires; children in Copenhagen organizing volunteers to help them build their own wading pool; children near Ringe, Denmark, planning, creating, and running their own operational village, built to child scale—all under the watchful yet unobtrusive tutelage and support of trained play leaders.

For additional information and photos of adventure playgrounds in London and Tokyo, see *www.arunet.co.uk/fairplay/facts/adplay.htm* (2004).

CONCLUSIONS AND RECOMMENDATIONS

The initial tendency is to assign the same play leadership roles to adults regardless of whether the context is classroom play or playground play. However, even in the better play-oriented classrooms for young children, there is a mix of academic pursuits integrated with play activities; the degree of integration depends on the ages and developmental levels of the children and the nature of the topic or problem under consideration. Space in the classroom is limited and unsuitable for the free, active, unfettered play of the playground. Applying the same intervention strategies in the playground that are used in the classroom may restrict play opportunities, flow and enthusiasm of play, and the spontaneity, creativity, and independence of playing children. Much playground play should be essentially free—free to make choices for self, free to choose play materials, free to create topics and themes, free to choose play partners, free to play themes to an end without undue interference from adults.

In the outdoors, compared to indoors, children have more space, larger equipment, greater variety of natural materials and features, real tools, more challenge and flexibility, higher activity levels, less structure and constraint, fuller expression, messier and louder activities, a wider range of sensory experiences, a greater range of social behaviors, uncontrolled movement, greater range of gross motor activities, more assertive play—all conducive to free, unfettered, spontaneous play. Although some adult roles are appropriate wherever children play, it does not follow that the same adult-imposed constraints, directives, rules, admonitions, requirements, and expectations extant indoors should be operable in the outdoor play environment. What, then, are the appropriate roles of adults on playgrounds?

First, the play leader studies children to understand whether intervention into their play is needed. In simplest terms, this means getting to know children. One does not get to know merely through observing or applying a checklist of behaviors. Knowing a child requires a degree of intimacy resulting from a two-way process of sensitive relating—talking, listening, planning, sharing, negotiating, helping, and trusting.

Children whose play is consistently outside a broad normal range may indeed benefit from direct prompting, modeling, scaffolding, refereeing, or even tutoring (direct support or instruction) by adults (e.g., children who are abnormally shy, withdrawn, or overly aggressive). A few children are too damaged (traumatized, abused, disabled) to play in a healthy manner, and an occasional child does not know how to play. Damaged or unhealthy children or children who engage in unhealthy play (cruel teasing, demeaning others, behaving violently) need direct help from adults. "There is sufficient data correlating the lack of play competence with various forms of pathology to support the value of amplifying play opportunities just for their own sake" (Sutton-Smith, 1993, p. 23). Times have changed since children settled disagreements with brief fisticuffs. Some disabled or frightened children now take real guns to school, and adults must constantly be alert to bizarre patterns of behavior that might signal impending violence. Most children, given rich natural or prepared play environments, need only minimal intervention by adults to engage in a wide range of healthy play—play that is fun, intense, creative, but not likely to inflict serious damage to others.

Second, the play leader ensures that children have access to challenging playscapes that integrate multiple levels of complexity, using both natural and built materials (see Chapter 11). The provision of exciting, magical, natural playscapes is perhaps the most formidable task facing teachers and play leaders at public playgrounds, and perhaps the most important. Over the past half century, many American children have lost contact with wilderness areas and wild places. They have lost contact with the land—the rivers, forests, and native animals—and, consequently, their ability to cope in the wild and to understand and value nature. They have, in sum, lost important parts of their souls and senses.

> In the child's best playground, the country, he can climb trees and fences, hang from a branch, swing from the apple tree, make a wreath of leaves or flowers or a basket of burrs, seesaw across the watering trough or a fallen log, wade in the brook, dig in the earth, slide down the haymow, skip stones on the water, or skate on the pond. (Palmer, 1916, p. 252)

How can adults compensate for such loss in inner cities and in crowded schools with limited space? The selection of teachers should include searching for individuals who not only teach the typical subject matter but who also have special skills in motor development, gardening, conservation, animal care, horticulture—people who know about tools, rocks, dirt, pollution, clearcutting, minerals, hills, hollows, cliffs, reefs, volcanoes, hurricanes, tides, salamanders, snakes, rabbits, and pigs; people who have childhood memories about special places and games like dens, tree houses, spinning tops and shooting marbles, kick-the-can, stick hockey, working in fields and shops; adults who remember how children express their fantasies in creative and wonderful ways. Such people are needed to help children shape small sterile spaces into growing, blooming, mysterious, challenging places. They are needed to move children beyond the classroom, to take children back to the land, to build with scrap and inexpensive materials, and to introduce traditional games that many, even adults, have forgotten or never known.

Third, the play leader prepares the child for risks, challenges, and hazards. Children must take risks to grow. During the early years, the child can be prepared by gradually introducing more complex challenges. Small climbing equipment makes way for larger, more complex, equipment. Ever more complex tools and tasks are introduced. Young children must learn to negotiate and to respect and yield to the rights of others. Even during the early 20th century, leading early educators recognized the need to let go and to limit their interference in children's play.

> In these [playgrounds] he should learn two things—to take care of himself while playing, and to respect the rights of others. . . . Even with little children the frequent "Don't, you will hurt yourself," should be changed to "Do, but be careful." A few falls and bruises will teach a child more than much caution and advice, but the adult must use judgment in allowing the child to endanger himself—always guarded but seldom interfered with. (Palmer, 1916, p. 253)

If adults are to help children counter the loss of nature and wildness, they must pay more attention to preserving and planting and less to building monolithic-like plastic and steel jungle gyms. They must be prepared to create a *compact countryside* in the playground or to take the children to the countryside.

> [I]t is clear that we need to find ways to let children roam beyond the pavement, to gain access to vegetation and earth that allows them to tunnel, climb, or even fall. . . . Better to let kids be a hazard to nature than let nature be a hazard to them. . . . Learning what to fear, and what not to fear, is a large part of growing up. (Nabhan & Trimble, 1994, pp. 9, 152)
>
> [E]xtremely safe tends to equate with extremely boring. . . . Learning anything new will also bring some level of risk—social, psychological or physical—and children can cope with adult support along with their own personal resources. (Bonel & Lindon, 1995, p. 96)

None of this should mean that the play leader is a push-over or overly permissive, nor is he overly authoritarian. Play leaders explain their perspectives and listen to those of the children. They establish friendly relationships but are not "just one of the kids." They can be both firm and kind, strict and fun, capable of stepping in and taking charge when situations get out of hand. They sometimes mediate disputes or impose consequences for ignoring ground rules. They help children understand the importance of maintaining their own play areas and raise their awareness of health and safety hazards.

Fourth, play leaders prepare children for play. The wise play leader engages children in planning before play and after play as needed. Planning for play is not to restrict places, opportunities, and materials for play but to allow children opportunities to learn to plan, to consider safe and unsafe play, to examine the play needs of all the players, and to determine how to secure and use materials for play projects. Learning to plan results from planning. As children's planning skills develop, they can assume the role of planning leader from the play leader who gradually becomes an adviser and consultant. The perspectives of children must be seriously considered in planning for play.

Initially, the play leader conducts a tour of the playground, discussing safety issues, asking open-ended questions of children, and establishing written ground rules necessary to avoid serious injury and to protect rights of others. These are best established as positive (do's) rather than negative (don'ts). Before outdoor play time, the group comes together to jointly lay plans. For example, one subgroup is building an aboveground wading pool with materials donated by a local contractor, another subgroup has chosen today to plant and tend the garden, and yet another will continue the organized game begun the day before. Many play times are simply free choice—doing whatever one chooses to do.

After-play planning takes place whenever unresolved conflicts remain, either conflicts between players or conflicts resulting from frustration in the projects undertaken. Group A will not share building materials and tools with group B. Ryan and Lisa are throwing gravel at one another. The water continues to leak from the new wading pool despite best efforts. Clearly, there are times when the play leader needs to step in to resolve disputes on the spot or to stop activities that threaten children's safety. Negotiating and arguing may be constructive and are necessary for growth; bitter conflicts and physical violence are destructive.

Fifth, the play leader focuses on creative aspects of play. Creativity refers to "mental processes that lead to solutions, ideas, conceptualization, artistic forms, theories or products that are unique and novel" (Reber, 1995, p. 172). The spontaneous play of children is freely chosen, takes place within a given space and time span, is linked to materials, carries opportunities for divergent thinking and problem solving, and supports the creation of new images, ideas, products and artistic forms. In sum, spontaneous play *is* a creative process. Play loses these qualities when there is a paucity of resources, when there is not enough time for play to take form and gain power and intensity, or when play is directed or oversupervised. Many forms of play, including organized sports and video games, and entertainment, including television, have limited creative benefits. Such

Sometimes the play leader needs to step in to resolve disputes. Resolution may merely require providing more equipment choices.

activities should be carefully selected and supervised and should not be allowed to substitute for opportunities for spontaneous, creative play. Playful learning and teaching foster creative expression through music, movement, and the visual arts, whether indoors or outdoors (Kieff & Casbergue, 2000).

> Whereas, children may play without encouragement or help, adults can, through the provision of an appropriate human and physical environment, significantly enhance opportunities for the child to play creatively and thus develop through play. (Bonel & Lindon, 1996, p. 15)

Sixth, the play leader extends the child's world. Children need extensive experiences to produce mental images for imaginative play and to support their growth in problem solving. These experiences should take them outside the playground to visit points of interest in the community: museums, factories, botanical gardens, and farms. They also include reading great children's books, storytelling, and interacting with grandparents, community artists, and leaders. Now children can take virtual tours of far away places—Indian reservations, theme parks, even other countries—via the medium of computerized virtual reality equipment. Such equipment promises to offer positive, growth-enhancing opportunities to balance the negative influences of much television and Internet play.

Extending the child's world also refers to providing opportunities for children from different cultures to interact with one another and for children with disabilities to have equal access to all the activity areas on the playground. Children learn from one another. When children are allowed to play in mixed-age groups, older children can assume some of the roles often left to adults—teach traditional games to younger children, support them in learning play skills, and show them how to deal with safety hazards. Generally, children should be free to choose their own friends, but the play leader makes exceptions for children who are ignored or excluded from play and helps them develop positive relationships.

Seventh, play leaders help children cope in an increasingly chaotic world. In a culture of fragmented and absent families, play leaders carry responsibilities once assumed by parents. They interact with growing numbers of children who are alienated, abused, traumatized, and disabled—kids who are dependent on drugs to help them cope, who are shifted from caretaker to caretaker, who have little security and support, or who move from place to place. Helping these kids within a mix of kids with no such problems is a constant and growing challenge to contemporary teachers and play leaders. Many simply need an understanding adult who recognizes and expresses appreciation for work well done and trusts them to assume growing responsibility. Others need help in securing special, professional assistance to cope with their problems and disabilities. Some need adults who recognize the signs of child abuse, communicate with other professionals, and promptly report their findings to the proper authorities.

Providing for extensive time in healthy play, under the guidance of skilled adults who integrate flexible indoor and outdoor curricula (work and play), is a profound challenge for 21st-century teachers and play leaders. Schools must come to understand that recess is a critical component of the educative process.

Eighth, play leaders step aside and let children play. Adults step aside and let children play when their joint consciousness is riveted to a powerfully satisfying theme, enveloped with intensity and ecstasy, and functioning freely and creatively. Consider Ackerman's **deep play** (1999), Csikszentmihalyi's **flow** (1975, 1990), Maslow's **self-actualization** (1962), and Rogers's **fully functioning** person (1962). Deep play, a concept Ackerman borrowed from Jeremy Bentham (1748–1832), is characterized by rapture, ecstasy, risk, obsession, pleasure, distractedness, timelessness, and a sense of the holy or sacred.

> In those rare moments of deep play, we can lay aside our sense of self, shed time's continuum, ignore pain. . . . No mind or heart bobbles. No analyzing or explaining. No questing for logic. No promises. No goals. No worry. . . . What is the difference between simple play and deep play? Simple play can take many forms and have many purposes, but it goes only so far. When it starts focusing one's life and offering ecstatic moments, it becomes deep play. . . . [I]n deep play's altered mental state one most often finds clarity, revelation, acceptance of self, and other life affirming feelings. (Ackerman, 1999, pp. 23, 24)

For many years, Csikszentmihalyi (1975, 1990; Csikszentmihalyi & Csikszentmihalyi, 1995) studied states of **optimal experience**—those times when people report heightened, more intense states of enjoyment, concentration, and absolute absorption in an activity. He calls those times "flow experiences." Flow is most consistently experienced in sports, games, art, hobbies, and play. The characteristics of flow that are recognizable in play include the merging of action and awareness, a centering of attention, a narrowing of consciousness to an immediate activity as in a play theme, a loss of ego and self-consciousness, a sense of being in control, an integration of one's activities with those of another, motivated by the activity itself, and the existence of a **spirit of play.**

Self-actualizing people (Maslow, 1962) are those who accept and express the inner self and who have minimal presence of ill health or loss of capacities. There are requirements for controls as capacities are organized and higher forms of expression are sought, but there must be a balance between controls and spontaneity. Education and healthy development are directed by both the cultivation of inner controls by the child and the cultivation of spontaneity, expression, and creativity. In the playground culture, spontaneity should rule over controls. To be strong, a child must develop frustration tolerance—that is, experience frustration in a helping context, grapple with it, win or cope, and survive to play again. For self-actualizing people, work can be playful, having its qualities of spontaneity, expression, and creativity. The highest levels of self-actualization have childlike qualities of fun, humor, silliness, whimsicalness, and craziness. The ultimate experience during play is those peak experiences in which time disappears.

The fully functioning person (Rogers, 1962) is a person in flow, in process, rather than one who has achieved some state. He is a creative being who permits himself to experience freely, to delve into the unique, to explore the mysterious, to stretch and grow, to express himself in his own unique way. Is it any wonder that children's playgrounds must possess matching qualities of mystery, uniqueness, wildness, and magic?

Frost (2003) sums the transcendental experiences described by these scholars as **transcendental play**—play that *transcends* the real and the make-believe—a state of being in which the child loses contact with the outside world, places herself into mental oneness with the activity, loses inhibitions, revels in physical risk and mental challenge, and creates a profound play world of magic and intrigue.

Transcendental play, deep play, or flow, are perhaps understandable only to those who have experienced such phenomena as children. When school recess was long, adult supervision was casual, and natural materials were abundant, such experiences were regular and profound. One of us recalls one such experience that permeated school recess for a week following a rain that gorged a small stream running through the school grounds. Void of any adult supervision except for curious observation near the end of the intense activity, a group of children built a mud dam across the stream and backed up the water, forming an increasingly deep pond. This eventually captured the attention of a second group, who went upstream to build their own dam and later released the water to "wash out" the downstream dam. This led to several days of intense experimentation with various materials—mud, clay, sticks, limbs, boards, rocks, scrap iron—to strengthen new dams in efforts to entrap more water or to prevent wash-out by the opposing group's dam. The sight of 20-plus children sloshing through classrooms in dripping clothing could easily have drawn reprimands and closure on dam building. Fortunately, the teachers allowed the activity to continue until it ran its course (the water dried up), and the children experienced those rare levels of intensity, creativity, loss of self, pushing limits, and ecstasy described as deep play or flow. Such is the stuff from which joy, creativity, learning, and development are formed.

For even keener insight into the nature or meaning of transcendental play, deep play, and flow as they relate to children's play, absorb the wonderful book for children *Roxaboxen* (McLerran & Cooney, 1991), powerfully but simply written by Alice McLerran and sensitively illustrated by Barbara Cooney. *Roxaboxen* is a celebration of children's play and special play places enjoyed by the author's mother during her childhood. On a hill in Arizona exists the remains of the magical town of Roxaboxen—a simple scattering of rocks, plants, broken glass, and an old car chassis; a place never forgotten by the children who played there.

KEY TERMS

Adventure playgrounds
Art-in-quality
Attractor
Bifurcation
Chaos theory
Co-constructivism
Constructivist
Cooperative planning
Deep play
Determinism
Directive school
Flow
Fully functioning
Garden of children
Nondirective school
Optimal experience
Play leaders
Play leadership
Play tutoring
Play/work
Playworkers
Playground Association of America (PAA)
Playwork
Scaffold
Self-actualization
Social collaboration
Social transmission
Social-constructivist
Spirit of play
Supersymmetry
Symbolism
Transcendental play
Weak chaos
Zone of proximal development (ZPD)

STUDY QUESTIONS

1. How is the concept of "playground" changing? What are the implications for changing the nature of playground supervision or "play leadership"?
2. How did play leadership in the United States change during the 20th century? Compare play leadership in city park and school playgrounds.
3. What do major theorists believe are adults' primary roles in playgrounds for children? How do these beliefs compare to your personal beliefs?
4. What challenges does Vygotsky's work pose for proponents of Piaget's theories, particularly in regard to adult roles in children's play?
5. What general conclusions do you draw from research regarding adult roles in children's play? How do conclusions from research compare with views of early theorists?
6. What are the qualities of adventure playgrounds? How do they differ from typical American playgrounds? What are the advantages and disadvantages of each? Would you propose establishing adventure playgrounds at American parks and schools? Why or why not?
7. How does the content of the "Conclusions and Recommendations" section of this chapter differ from theoretical and research perspectives discussed earlier in the chapter? How are they consistent?
8. Reflecting on your own childhood play, describe one or more play experiences that you would characterize as "flow," "deep play," or "transcendental play." How do you believe that these experiences would contribute to "self-actualization" or becoming "fully functioning"?

Playground Checklist

Appendix

Note: This checklist is not intended as a research tool but as an aid to planning and evaluating playgrounds.

CHECK	SECTION I. What does the playground contain?
	1. A hard-surfaced area with space for games and a network of paths for wheeled toys. Strategically placed goals for such activities as basketball and soccer.
	2. Sand and sand play equipment including a variety of toys, blocks, scoops, and containers.
	3. Water play areas with fountains, pools and sprinklers, and water play equipment.
	4. Dramatic play structures (playhouses, cars or boats with complementary equipment such as adjacent sand and water, and housekeeping equipment).
	5. A superstructure with room for many children at a time and with a variety of challenges and exercise options (entries, exits, and levels).
	6. Mound(s) of earth for climbing and digging.
	7. Trees and natural areas for shade, nature study, and play.
	8. Continuous challenge, linkage of areas, functional physical boundaries, vertical and horizontal treatment (hills and valleys).
	9. Construction area with junk materials such as tires, crates, planks, boards, bricks, and nails; tools should be provided and demolition and construction allowed.
	10. A purchased or built vehicle, airplane, boat, or car that has been made safe, but not stripped of its play value (should be changed or relocated after a period of time to renew interest).
	11. Equipment for active play: a variety of overhead apparatus, climbers, slides, balancing devices, swings, etc.
	12. A large soft area (grass, bark mulch, etc.) for organized games. A concrete or asphalt area for organized games.
	13. Small semi-private spaces at the child's own scale: tunnels, niches, playhouses, private or special places partially enclosed by trellises, plants, beams.
	14. Fences, gates, walls, and windows that provide security for young children and are adaptable for learning/play.
	15. A garden for flowers located so that they are protected from play, but with easy access for children to tend them. Special nature areas such as butterfly gardens. Gardening tools are available. A greenhouse for plants greatly enhances nature study.
	16. Provisions for housing of pets. Pets and supplies available. Special areas to attract birds and insects. Storage for supplies.
	17. A transitional space from outdoors to indoors. This can be a covered play area immediately adjoining the playroom, which will protect the children from the sun and rain and extend indoor activities to the outdoors.
	18. Storage for outdoor play equipment, tools for construction and garden areas, and maintenance tools. Storage can be separate: wheeled toys stored near the wheeled vehicle track, sand play equipment near the sand enclosure, tools near the construction area. Storage can be next to the building or fence. Storage should aid in children's picking up and putting away equipment at the end of each play period.
	19. Easy access from outdoor play areas to coats, toilets, and drinking fountains. Shaded areas, benches, tables, and support materials for group activities (art, reading, etc.).
	20. Accessibility, materials, and equipment for children of all abilities/disabilities.

CHECK	SECTION II. Is the playground in good repair and relatively safe?*
	1. A protective fence (with lockable gates) next to hazardous areas (streets, deep ditches, water, etc.).
	2. Ten to twelve inches of non-compacted sand, wood mulch, or equivalent manufactured surfacing under all climbing and moving equipment, extending through fall zones and secured by retaining walls, as needed.
	3. Size of equipment appropriate to age and skill levels served. Climbing heights limited to six to seven feet, or just above standing/reaching height of children. Special attention to reduced heights for preschool children.
	4. Area free of litter (e.g., broken glass), electrical hazards, high voltage power lines, toxic hazards. See CPSC for toxic hazards in wood products.
	5. Moving parts free of defects (e.g., no pinch and crush points, bearings not excessively worn).
	6. Equipment free of sharp edges and broken, loose, and missing parts.
	7. Swing seats constructed of soft or lightweight material (e.g., rubber, plastic). Basketball goal posts padded. Soccer goals secure in ground.
	8. All safety equipment in good repair (e.g., guard rails, padded areas, protective covers).
	9. No openings that can entrap a child's head (approximately 3.5" x 9"). See CPSC/ASTM for measurements and tests.
	10. Equipment structurally sound. No bending, warping, breaking, sinking, etc. Heavy fixed and moving equipment secured in ground and concrete footings recessed under ground at least four inches.
	11. Adequate space between equipment—typically six feet, depending upon type and location of equipment (see CPSC/ASTM).
	12. No signs of underground rotting, rusting, or termites in support members (probe underground).
	13. No metal slides or decks exposed to sun. Use plastic components or place in permanent shade.
	14. Guardrails and protective barriers in place that meet CPSC/ASTM height and other requirements.
	15. No loose ropes, suspended ropes, or cables in movement area.
	16. All balance beams, cables, and chains at low heights—prescribed by CPSC/ASTM.
	17. Signs at entry alerting to appropriate ages of users, need for adult supervision, and any hazards.
	18. No protrusion or entanglement hazards.
	19. No tripping or fall hazards in equipment use areas. For example, exposed concrete footings.
	20. No water hazards—access to pools, creeks. No traffic hazards—streets, parking lots, delivery areas.

*This is an overview of relevant safety items. For details, refer to current issues of the United States Consumer Product Safety Commission's (CPSC's) *Handbook for Public Playground Safety* and the American Society for Testing Materials' (ASTM's) *Standard Consumer Safety Performance Specification for Playground Equipment for Public Use.*

CHECK	SECTION III. How should the playground and/or the playleader function?
	1. Encourages play: • Inviting, easy access • Open, flowing, and relaxed space • Clear movement from indoors to outdoors • Appropriate equipment for the age group(s)
	2. Stimulates the child's senses: • Changes and contrasts in scale, light, texture, and color • Flexible equipment • Diverse experiences
	3. Nurtures the child's curiosity: • Equipment that the child can change • Materials for experiments and construction • Plants and animals
	4. Supports the child's social and physical needs: • Comfortable to the child • Scaled to the child • Physically challenging
	5. Allows interaction between the child and the resources: • Systematic storage that defines routines • Semi-enclosed spaces to read, work a puzzle, or be alone
	6. Allows interaction between children: • Variety of spaces • Adequate space to avoid conflicts • Equipment that invites socialization
	7. Allows interaction between the child and adults: • Organization of spaces to allow general supervision • Rest areas for adults and children
	8. Supports functional, exercise, gross motor, active play. Children are not denied a range of challenging swings, overhead equipment, and climbing equipment scaled to age and skill levels of children.
	9. Supports constructive, building, creating play. Children are taught safe ways of using tools and materials for construction.
	10. Supports dramatic, pretend, make-believe play. Sufficient time is given during recess or playtime for children to generate and engage fully in pretend play.
	11. Supports organized games and games with rules. Adults and older children teach traditional games then step out of the way, and provide equipment for sports activities.
	12. Supports special play forms (e.g., chase games, rough-and-tumble, sand and water play). Chase and rough-and-tumble are carefully but unobtrusively supervised.

CHECK	SECTION III. How should the playground and/or the playleader function?
	13. Promotes solitary, private, meditative play. Children assist in preparing nature areas and small built spaces (e.g., gazebos) for semi-privacy.
	14. Promotes group, cooperative, sharing play. Children are encouraged to include new and reticent peers in their play groups.
	15. Involves children in care and maintenance of playground. Adults model and teach maintenance skills—tool use, hazard identification, etc.
	16. Involves adults in children's play—regular adult/child planning and evaluation. Adults help children learn to solve playground problems through cooperative planning and analysis of problems.
	17. Integrates indoor/outdoor play and work/play activities—art, music, science, etc.
	18. Promotes interaction between children and nature—plants, animals, etc. Knowledgeable adults are identified to lead field trips, provide direct instruction, and interact with children.
	19. Adults are trained in play values, playground maintenance and safety, emergency procedures. Playleaders receive annual workshops to maintain skills.
	20. The play environment is constantly changing—growing in appeal, challenge, and complexity. Good playgrounds are never finished.

References

ABC News. (1996). Romania: What happened to the children? In *Turning point*. New York: American Broadcasting Company.

Abrahams, R. D. (1962). Playing the dozens. *Journal of American Folklore, 75,* 209–220.

Ackerman, D. (1999). *Deep play*. New York: Random House.

Acredelo, C., Adams, A., & Schmid, J. (1984). On the understanding of the relationships between speed, duration, and distance. *Child Development, 55,* 2151–2159.

Adler, A. (1927). *Understanding human nature* (W. B. Wolfe, Trans.). Garden City, NY: Garden City.

Alessandri, S. M. (1994). Play and social behavior in maltreated preschoolers. *Development and Psychopathology, 3,* 191–205.

Allen, F. H. (1942). *Psychotherapy with children*. New York: Norton.

Allen, Lady of Hurtwood. (1968). *Planning for play*. Cambridge, MA: MIT Press.

Alliance for Childhood (2000). Fool's gold: A critical look at computers and childhood. Retrieved March 29, 2004 from http://www.allianceforchildhood.net/projects/computers/

Al-Shatti, A., & Johnson, J. (1984). *Free play behaviors of middle class Kuwaitis and American children*. Paper presented at the annual meeting of the American Educational Research Association, New Orleans.

Altmyer, D. J., & Zeiger, J. B. (1997). Project playgrounds: "We can do this together." *Parks and Recreation, 32*(4), 74–82.

American Academy of Child and Adolescent Psychiatry. (1999). Children and TV violence. Re trieved March 29, 2004 from http://www.aacap.org/publications/factsfam/

American Academy of Pediatrics. (2000). *Changing concepts of sudden infant death syndrome*. Policy statement RE9946. Elk Grove Village, IL: The Academy. Retrieved March 29, 2004 from http://www.aap.org

American Academy of Pediatrics and National Fire Protection Association (2003). AAP and NFPA urge ban on private use of fireworks. News release. Elk Grove Village, IL: The Academy. Retrieved March 29, 2004 from http://www.aap.org

American Public Health Association. *Public swimming pools: Recommended regulations for design and construction, operation and maintenance*. Washington, DC: Author.

American Society for Testing and Materials. (1995). *Standard consumer safety performance specification for playground equipment for public use*. West Conshohocken, PA: Author.

American Society for Testing and Materials. (1996a). *Standard consumer safety specification on toy safety*. West Conshohocken, PA: Author.

American Society for Testing and Materials. (1996b). *Standard specification for impact attenuation of surface systems under and around playground equipment*. West Conshohocken, PA: Author.

American Society for Testing and Materials. (1998). *Standard consumer safety performance specification for playground equipment for public use*. West Conshohocken, PA: Author.

Amrein, A. L., & Berliner, D. C. (2002). The impact of high-stakes tests on student academic performance. Research Report. Tempe, AZ: Arizona State University Education Policy Studies Laboratory. Retrieved March 29, 2004 from http://www.asu.edu/educ/epsl/EPRU/epru_2002_Research_Writing.htm

Andrews, E. L. (1998, March 15). Where a lawsuit can't get any respect. *New York Times*.

Andriola, J. (1944). Release of aggressions through play therapy for a ten-year-old patient at a child guidance clinic. *Psychoanalytic Review, 31,* 71–80.

Andronico, M., Fidler, J., Guerney, G., & Guerney, L. (1967). *International Journal of Group Psychotherapy, 17,* 10–17.

Angier, N. (1992, October 22). The purpose of playful frolics: Training for adulthood. *New York Times,* pp. B5–B6.

Anonymous. (1997). An organization at play. *The Exceptional Parent, 36,* 36–37.

Architectural and Transportation Barriers Compliance Board. (1997). *Regulatory Negotiation Committee on Accessibility Guidelines for Play Facilities: Final report*. Washington, DC: Author.

Ariel, S., & Sever, I. (1980). Play in the desert and play in the town: On play activities of Bedouin Arab children. In H. Schwartzman (Ed.), *Play and culture* (pp. 164–174). West Point, NY: Leisure Press.

Armbruster, B. B., Lehr, F., & Osborn, J. (2002). *A child becomes a reader. Birth to preschool*. Jessup, MD: National Institute for Literacy.

Arnett, J. (1989). Caregivers in day-care centers: Does training matter? *Journal of Applied Developmental Psychology, 10,* 541–552.

Association for Childhood Education International. Perrone, V. (1991). ACEI position paper on standardized testing. Olney, MD: Author.

Association of Children's Museums (2003) ACM press room [Electronic version]. Retrieved from www.childrensmuseums.org

Athey, I. (1984). Contributions of play to development. In T. D. Yawkey & A. D. Pellegrini (Eds.), *Child's play: Developmental and applied* (pp. 9–28). Hillsdale, NJ: Erlbaum.

Atlas, J. A., & Lapidus, L. B. (1987). Patterns of symbolic expression in subgroups of the childhood psychoses. *Journal of Clinical Psychology, 43*, 177–188.

August, R. L., & Forman, B. D. (1989). A comparison of sexually abused and non-sexually abused children's responses to anatomically correct dolls. *Child Psychiatry and Human Development, 20,* 39–47.

Ausch, L. (1994). Gender comparisons of young children's social interaction in cooperative play activity. *Sex Roles, 31,* 225–239.

Axline, V. (1947a). Nondirective play therapy for poor readers. *Journal of Consulting Psychology, 11,* 61–69

Axline, V. (1947b). *Play therapy: The inner dynamics of childhood*. Boston: Houghton Mifflin.

Axline, V. (1950). Entering the child's world via play experiences. *Progressive Education, 27,* 68–75.

Axline, V. (1964). *Dibs: In search of self*. Boston: Houghton Mifflin.

Axline, V. (1969). *Play therapy*. New York: Ballantine.

Azarnoff, P., & Flegal, S. (1975). *A pediatric play program: Developing a therapeutic play program for children in medical settings*. Springfield, IL: Thomas.

Babcock, B. (Ed.). (1978). *The reversible world: Symbolic inversion in art and society*. Ithaca, NY: Cornell University Press.

Bagley, D. M., & Chaille, C. (1996). Transforming play: An analysis of first-, third-, and fifth-graders' play. *Journal of Research in Childhood Education, 10,* 134–142.

Bailey, D. (1989). Assessment and its importance in early intervention. In D. Bailey & M. Wolery (Eds.), *Assessing infants and preschoolers with handicaps* (pp. 1–21). Upper Saddle River, NJ: Merrill/Prentice Hall.

Baird, W. E., & Silvern, S. B. (1990). Electronic games: Children controlling the cognitive environment. *Early Child Development and Care, 61,* 43–49.

Bakeman, R., & Brownlee, J. (1980). The strategic use of parallel play: A sequential analysis. *Child Development, 51,* 873–878.

Baker, D. (1937). *The kindergarten centennial 1837–1937*. Washington, DC: Association for Childhood Education International.

Ballargeon, R., & DeVos, J. (1991). Object permanence in young infants: Further evidence. *Child Development, 62,* 1227–1246.

Banta, B. (1998, March 24). Report: Ride's lap bar broke. *Austin American-Statesman,* pp. A-1, A-7.

Barbour, R. F., & Beedell, C. J. (1955). The follow-up of a child guidance clinic population. *Journal of Mental Science, 101,* 794–809.

Barker, R., & Wright, H. F. (1966). *One boy's day*. Hamden, CT: Archon.

Barker, S. (1996). Brain science benefits from budget plan. *Nature, 382,* 105.

Barlow, K., Strother, J., & Landreth, G. (1986). Sibling group play therapy: An effective alternative with an elective mute child. *School Counselor, 34,* 44–50.

Barnes, B. J., & Hill, S. (1983). Should young children work with microcomputers—Logo before Lego? *Computing Teacher, 10*(9), 11–14.

Barnes, K. E. (1971). Preschool play norms: A replication. *Developmental Psychology, 5,* 99–103.

Baron-Cohen, S., Leslie, A. M., & Frith, U. (1985). Does the autistic child have a theory of mind? *Cognition, 21,* 37–46.

Barta, J., & Schaelling, D. (1998). Games we play: Connecting mathematics and culture in the classroom. *Teaching children mathematics, 4,* 388–393.

Bartlett, S. (1990). A childhood remembered. *Children's Environments Quarterly, 7*(4), 2–4.

Bateson, G. (2000). *Steps to an ecology of mind.* Chicago: University of Chicago Press.

Bauer, K. L., & Dettore, E. (1997). Superhero play: What's a teacher to do? *Early Childhood Education Journal, 25,* 17–21.

Baumrind, D. (1991). To nurture nature. *Behavioral and Brain Sciences, 14,* 386.

Baumeister, R. (2001). Violent pride: Do people turn violent because of self-hate or self-love? *Scientific American, 284,* 96–101.

Bayley, N. (1993). *Bayley Scales of Infant Development (BSID-II)* (2nd ed.). San Antonio, TX: Psychological Corporation.

Beal, B. (1998). Symbolic inversion in the subculture of skateboarding. In S. Reifel (Ed.), *Play and culture studies: Vol. I. Diversions and divergences in fields of play*. Stamford, CT: Ablex.

Beckman, P. J., & Kohl, F. L. (1987). Interactions of preschoolers with and without handicaps in integrated and segregated settings: A longitudinal study. *Mental Retardation, 25,* 5–11.

Beckwith, J. (1985). Equipment selection criteria for modern playgrounds. In J. L. Frost & S. Sunderlin (Eds.), *When children play* (pp. 209–214). Washington, DC: Association for Childhood Education International.

Beckwith, L. (1986). Parent-infant interaction and infants' social-emotional development. In A. W. Gottfried & C. C. Brown (Eds.), *Play interactions* (pp. 279–292). Lexington, MA: Lexington.

Beezley, P., Martin, H. P., & Kempe, R. (1976). Psychotherapy. In H. P. Marrin & C. H. Kempe (Eds.), *The abused child: A multidisciplinary approach to developmental issues and treatment*. Cambridge, MA: Ballinger.

Begley, S. (1996, February 29). Your child's brain. *Newsweek,* pp. 55–58.

Begley, S. (1997, Spring–Summer). How to build a baby's brain. *Newsweek Special Edition*, pp. 28–32.

Begley, S. (2000, February 22). Getting inside the brain. *Newsweek,* pp. 58–59.

Begley, S. (2001, May 6). Religion and the brain. *Newsweek*, pp. 50–57.

Beigel, A. R. (1996). Developing computer competencies among special needs educators. *Learning and Leading with Technology, 23,* 69–70

Bekoff, M., & Byers, J. A. (Eds.). (1998). *Animal play: Evolutionary, comparative, and ecological perspectives*. Cambridge: Cambridge University Press.

Belka, D. E. (1998). Strategies for teaching tag games. *Journal of Physical Education, 69,* 40–43.

Belsky, J. (1984). Two waves of day care research: Developmental effects and conditions of quality. In R. Ainslie (Ed.), *The child and the day care setting* (pp. 1–34). New York: Praeger.

Belsky, J. (1990). Parental and nonparental child care and children's socioemotional development: A decade in review. *Journal of Marriage and Family, 52,* 885–903.

Belsky, J., & Most, R. (1981). From exploration to play: A cross-sectional study of infant free play behavior. *Developmental Psychology, 17,* 630–639.

Bengtsson, A. (Ed.). (1972). *Adventure playgrounds*. New York: Praeger.

Benjamin, J. (1974). *Grounds for play: In search of adventure*. London: Bedford Square.

Bennett, N., Wood, L., & Rogers, S. (1997). *Teaching through play: Teachers' thinking and classroom practice*. Philadelphia: Open University Press.

Beranek, L. (1996). *Concert and opera halls: How they sound*. Woodbury, NY: Acoustical Society of America.

Bereiter, C., & Engelmann, S. (1966). *Teaching the culturally disadvantaged child in the preschool*. Upper Saddle River, NJ: Prentice Hall.

Beresin, A. R. (1989). Toy war games and the illusion of two-sided rhetoric. *Play & Culture, 2,* 218–224.

Bergen, D. (1991). *Play as the vehicle for early intervention with at-risk infants and toddlers*. Paper presented at the Annual conference of the American Educational Research Association (ED 335 115).

Bergen, D. (1994). Should teachers permit or discourage violent play themes? *Childhood Education, 70,* 300–301.

Bergen, D., & Coscia, J. (2001). *Brain research and childhood education: Implications for Educators*.

Olney, MD: Association for Childhood Education International.

Berger, K. S. (2000). *The developing person through childhood* (3rd ed.). New York: Worth.

Berk, L. (1994). *Child development*. Needham Heights, MA: Allyn & Bacon.

Berk, L. E. (1994). Vygotsky's theory: The importance of make-believe play. *Young Children, 50,* 30–39.

Berk, L. E. (2002). *Infants, children, and adolescents* (3rd ed.). Boston: Allyn & Bacon.

Berk, L. E., & Winsler, A. (1995). *Scaffolding children's learning: Vygotsky and early childhood education*. Washington, DC: National Association for the Education of Young Children.

Berkeley Planning Associates (1978). *Evaluation of child abuse and neglect demonstration projects, 1974–1977* (Vols. 1 and 22). (DHEW Report No. 79-3217-1). Washington, DC: National Center for Health Services Research.

Best, E. (1925). *Games and pastimes of the Maori*. Dominion Museum Bulletin, No. 8.

Betancourt, F., & Zeiler, M. (1971). The choices and preferences of nursery school children. *Journal of Applied Behavior Analysis*, *4*, 299–304.

Beyer, L., & Bloch, M. (1996). Theory: An analysis (Part 1). In J. Chafel & S. Reifel (Eds.), *Advances in early education and day care: Vol. 8. Theory and practice in early childhood teaching* (pp. 1–40). Greenwich, CT: JAI.

Biben, M. (1989). Effects of social environment on play in squirrel monkeys: Resolving Harlequin's dilemma. *Ethology, 81, 72–82.*

Biber, B. (1977). A developmental-interaction approach: Bank Street College of Education. In M. Day & R. Parker (Eds.), *The preschool in action* (pp. 421–460). Boston: Allyn & Bacon.

Biber, B. (1984). *Early education and psychological development.* New Haven, CT: Yale University Press.

Biber, B., Shapiro, E., & Wickens, D. (1971). *Promoting cognitive growth from a developmental interaction point of view.* Washington, DC: National Association for the Education of Young Children.

Bills, R. C. (1950). Nondirective play therapy with retarded readers. *Journal of Consulting Psychology, 14,* 140–149.

Bixler, R. (1945). Treatment of a reading problem through nondirective play therapy. *Journal of Consulting Psychology*, *9,* 105–118.

Bixler, R. (1949). Limits are therapy. *Journal of Consulting Psychology, 13,* 1–11.

Blakeslee, S. (1997, April 17). Studies show talking with infants shapes basis of ability to think. *New York Times,* p. A-14.

Blasco, P. M., Bailey, D. B., & Burchinal, M. A. (1993). Dimensions of mastery in same-age and mixed-age integrated classrooms. *Early Childhood Research Quarterly, 8,* 193–206.

Bleck, R., & Bleck, B. (1982). The disruptive child's play group. *Elementary School Guidance and Counseling, 17,* 137–141.

Blisset, G., & Adkins, M. (1993). Are they learning? A study of the use of interactive video. *Computers and Education, 21,* 31–39.

Bloch, M. N. (1984). Play materials. *Childhood Education, 60,* 345–348.

Bloch, M. N. (1989). Young boys' and girls' play at home and in the community: A cultural-ecological framework. In M. N. Bloch & A. D. Pellegrini (Eds.), *The ecological context of children's play* (pp. 120–154). Norwood, NJ: Ablex.

Bloch, M. N., & Adler, S. (1994). African children's play and the emergence of the sexual division of labor. In J. L. Roopnarine, J. E. Johnson, & F. H. Hooper (Eds.), *Children's play in diverse cultures* (pp. 148–178). Albany: State University of New York Press.

Block, J., & King, N. (1987). *School play: A source book*. New York: Guilford.

Blow, S. E. (1909). *Symbolic education: A commentary on Froebel's "mother play."* New York: Appleton.

Blurton Jones, N. (Ed.). (1972). *Ethological studies of child behaviour*. Cambridge: Cambridge University Press.

Board of Directors, Association for Play Therapy. (1997). Minutes. *Association for Play Therapy Newsletter, 16,* p.14.

Bodrova, E., & Leong, D. J. (1996). *Tools of the mind: The Vygotskian approach to early childhood education*. Upper Saddle River, NJ: Merrill/Prentice Hall.

Bodrova, E., & Leong, D. J. (1998). Adult influences on play. In D. P. Fromberg & D. Bergen (Eds.), *Play from birth to twelve and beyond: Contexts, perspectives, and meanings*. New York: Garland.

Bodrova, E., & Leong, D. J. (1998). Development of dramatic play in young children and its effects on self-regulation: The Vygotskian approach. *Journal of Early Childhood Teacher Education, 20,* 115–124.

Bohren, J. M., & Vlahov, E. (1989, July). *Comparison of motor development in preschool children*. ERIC Document 312053.

Bolig, R., Yolton, K. A., & Nissen, H. L. (1991). Medical play and preparation: Questions and issues. *Children's Health Care, 20,* 225–229.

Bonel, P., & Lindon, J. (1996). *Good practice in playwork*. Cheltenham, England: Thornes.

Bott, H. (1928). Observations of play activities in a nursery school. *Genetic Psychology Monographs, 4,* 44–88.

Boulton, M., & Smith, P. (1993). Ethnic, gender partner, and activity preferences in mixed-race schools in the U.K.: Playground observations. In C. Hart (Ed.), *Children on playgrounds* (pp. 210–238). Albany: State University of New York Press.

Bower, E., Ilgaz-Carden, A., & Noori, K. (1982). Measurement of play structures: Cross-cultural considerations. *Journal of Cross-Cultural Psychology, 13,* 315–329.

Bower, T. G. R. (1989). *The rational infant: Learning in infancy*. New York: Freeman.

Boyd, B. J. (1997). Teacher response to superhero play: To ban or not to ban? *Childhood Education, 74,* 23–28.

Boyer, W. A. R. (1997a). Enhancing playfulness with sensorial stimulation. *Journal of Research in Childhood Education, 12,* 78–87.

Boyer, W. A. R. (1997b). Playfulness enhancement through classroom intervention for the 21st century. *Childhood Education, 74,* 90–96.

Bradley, D. H., & Pottle, P. R. (2001). Supporting emergent writers through on-the-spot conferencing and publishing. *Young Children, 56,* 20–27.

Brady, E., & Hill, S. (1984). Young children and microcomputers. *Young Children, 39*(3), pp.49–61.

Brady, G. L. (1991). A group-work approach for sexually abused preschoolers. *Journal of Group Psychotherapy Psychodrama and Sociometry, 43*(4), 174–183.

Brandon, K. (2002). Pressure, stress and evaluations—all at age 5. *Chicago Tribune*. In *Austin American-Statesman*. Austin, TX: p. A1

Bransford, J. D., Brown, A. L., & Cocking, R. R. (Eds.). (1999). *How people learn: Brain, mind, experience, and school*. Washington, DC: National Academy Press.

Brashear, E. (1952). "But suppose she falls": Safety education. *National Safety Council, 32*(1), 2, 5, 26.

Bredekamp, S., & Copple, C. (1997). *Developmentally appropriate practice in early childhood programs* (rev. ed.). Washington, DC: National Association for the Education of Young Children.

Breig-Allen, C., & Dillon, J. U. (1997). Implementing the process of change in a public school setting. In J. Hendrick (Ed.), *First steps toward teaching the Reggio way* (pp. 126–140). Upper Saddle River, NJ: Merrill/Prentice Hall.

Bretherton, I. (1985). Attachment theory: Retrospect and prospect. In I. Bretherton & E. Waters (Eds.), Growing points of attachment theory and research. *Monographs of the Society for Research in Child Development, 50*(1–2, Serial No. 209).

Bretherton, I. (1989). Pretense: The form and function of make-believe play. *Developmental Review, 9,* 383–401.

Brewster, P. G. (1939). Rope-skipping, counting-out and other rhymes of children. *Southern Folklore Quarterly, 3,* 173–184.

Bronson, M. B. (1995). *The right stuff for children birth to 8*. Washington, DC: National Association for the Education of Young Children.

Bronzaft, A. L., & McCarthy, D. P. (1975). The effects of elevated train noise on reading ability. *Environmental Behavior, 7,* 517–527.

Brooker, L. (2003). Integrating new technologies in U.K. classrooms. *Childhood Education, 79,* 261–267.

Brooks, M. M. (1970). Why play in hospitals? In E. C. Rothrock & E. Wesseling (Eds.), *The nursing clinics of North America*. Philadelphia: Saunders.

Brooks, P. H., & Roberts, M. C. (1990, Spring). Social science and the prevention of children's injuries. *Social Policy Report of the Society for Research in Child Development, 4*(1).

Brooks-Gunn, J., & Lewis, M. (1981). Assessing young handicapped children: Issues and solutions. *Journal of the Division for Early Childhood, 2,* 84–95.

Brophy, K., & Hancock, S. (1985). Adult-child interaction in an integrated preschool programme: Implications for teacher training. *Early Child Development and Care, 22,* 275–294.

Brosterman, N. (1997). *Inventing kindergarten*. New York: Abrams/Times Mirror.

Brown, F. (Ed.) (2003). *Playwork: Theory and practice*. Philadelphia, PA: Open University Press.

Brown, J. E., Serdula, M., Cairns, K., Godes, J. R., Jacobs, D. R., Elmer, P., & Trowbridge, F. L. (1986). Ethnic group difference in nutritional status of young children from low-income areas of an urban county. *American Journal of Clinical Nutrition, 44,* 938–944.

Brown, P., & Frost, J. L. (Puckett, M. B., ed.) (2002). Play and neuroscience. *Room to grow* (pp. 24–31). Austin, Texas: Texas Association for the Education of Young Children.

Brown, S. (1997). *Discovering the intelligence of play: A new model for a new generation of children* [videotape]. (Available from Touch the Future, 4350 Lime Ave., Long Beach, CA, 90807.)

Brown, S. (1998). Play as an organizing principle: Clinical evidence and personal observations. In M. Bekoff & J. Byers (Eds.), *Animal play: Evolutionary, comparative, and ecological perspectives* (pp. 243–259). Cambridge: Cambridge University Press.

Brown, S. L. (1994, December). Animals at play. *National Geographic,* pp. 2–35.

Brownback, S. (2003). Hearing examines impact of entertainment on children's health. Washington, DC: Senate Subcommittee on Science, Technology, and Space. Retrieved March 15, 2004 from http://www.lionlamb.org

Brownlee, S. (1997, February 3). The case for frivolity. *U.S. News and World Report*, pp. 45–49.

Brownlee, S. (1999, Aug. 9). Inside the teen brain. *U. S. News and World Report*, 44–54.

Bruer, J. T. (1997). Education and the brain: A bridge too far. *Educational Researcher*, *26*, 4–16.

Bruer, J. T. (1999, May). In search of brain-based education. *Phi Delta Kappan,* pp. 649–657.

Bruner, J. (1974). The ontogenesis of speech acts. *Journal of Child Language, 2,* 1–19.

Bruner, J. (1975). From communication to language—A psychological perspective. *Cognition, 3,* 255287.

Bruner, J. S. (1972). The nature and uses of immaturity. *American Psychologist, 27,* 686–708.

Bruner, J. S. (1990). *Acts of meaning*. Cambridge, MA: Harvard University Press.

Bruner, J. S., Jolly, A., & Sylva, K. (Eds.). (1976). *Play: Its role in development and evolution*. New York: Penguin.

Bruner, J. S., & Sherwood, V. (1976). Peekaboo and the learning of rule structures. In J. S. Bruner, A. Jolly, & K. Sylva (Eds.), *Play: Its role in development and evolution* (pp. 277–285). New York: Basic Books.

Bruya, L. D., & Langendorfer, S. J. (Eds.). (1988). *Where our children play: Elementary school playground equipment*. Reston, VA: American Alliance for Health, Physical Education, Recreation, and Dance.

Buchanan, A. M., Gentile, D. A., Nelson, D., Walsh, D. A., & Caillois, R. (1961). *Man, play, and games*. New York: Free Press.

Buchman, D. D., & Funk, J. B. (1996). Video and computer games in the 90s: Children's time commitment and games preference. *Children Today, 24,* 12–16.

Buhler, K. (1937). *The mental development of the child*. London: Routledge & Kegan Paul.

Bullock, J. R. (2002). Bullying among children. *Young Children, 78,* 130–133.

Bureau of Product Safety, U.S. Food and Drug Administration. (1972). *Public playground equipment*. Washington, DC: Author.

Burk, F., & Burk, C.F. (1920). *A study of the kindergarten problem in the public kindergartens of Santa Barbara, California, 1898–1899*. New York: Teachers College, Columbia University.

Burkour, C. K. (1998). We want to play too! *The Exceptional Parent, 28,* 72–74.

Burlingham, D. (1961). Some notes on the development of the blind. *Psychoanalytic Study of the Child, 16,* 187–198.

Burlingham, D. (1965). Some problems of the ego development in blind children. *Psychoanalytic Study of the Child, 20,* 194–208.

Burlingham, D. (1967). Developmental considerations in the occupations of the blind. *Psychoanalytic Study of Child, 22,* 187–198.

Burlingham, D. (1972). *Psychoanalytic studies of the sighted and the blind*. New York: International Universities Press.

Burlingham, D. (1975). Special problems of blind infants: Blind baby profile. *Psychoanalytic Study of the Child, 30,* 3–14.

Burns, S., & Brainerd, C. (1979). Effects of constructive and dramatic play on perspective taking in young children. *Developmental Psychology, 15,* 512–521.

Burroughs, M. S., Wagner, W. W., & Johnson, J. T. (1997). Treatment with children of divorce: A comparison of two types of therapy. *Journal of Divorce and Remarriage, 27,* 83–99.

Burts, D., Hart, C., DeWolf, D., Ray, J., Manual, K., & Fleege, P. (1993). Developmental appropriateness of kindergarten programs and academic outcomes in first grade. *Journal of Research in Childhood Education, 8,* 23–31.

Bushell, D. (1970). *The behavior analysis classroom*. Lawrence: University of Kansas Follow Through Project.

Bushell, D., Wrobel, P., & Michaelis, M. (1968). Applying group contingencies to the classroom study behavior of preschool children. *Journal of Applied Behavior Analysis, 1,* 55–62.

Butler, G. D. (1950). *Playgrounds: Their administration and operation*. New York: Barnes.

Butwinick, E. (1974). *Petition requesting the issuance of a consumer product safety standard for public playground equipment*. Washington, DC: Consumer Product Safety Commission.

Cairns, R. B., Cairns, B. D., Neckerman, H. J., Gest, S. D., & Gairepy, J. (1988). Social networks and aggressive behavior: Peer support or peer rejection? *Developmental Psychology, 24,* 815–823.

Campbell, L. (1997). Perceptual-motor programs, movement and young children's needs: Some challenges for teachers. *Australian Journal of Early Childhood, 22,* 37–42.

Campbell, S. D., & Dil, N. (1985). The impact of changes in spatial density on children's behaviors in a day care setting. In J. L. Frost & S. Sunderlin (Eds.), *When children play* (pp. 255–264). Wheaton, MD: Association for Childhood Education International.

Campbell, S. D., & Frost, J. L. (1985). The effects of playground type on the cognitive and social play behaviors of grade two children. In J. L. Frost & S. Sunderlin (Eds.), *When children play* (pp. 81–88). Wheaton, MD: Association for Childhood Education International.

Caplan, F., & Caplan, T. (1973). *The power of play*. New York: Anchor.

Carlsson-Paige, N., & Levin, D. E. (1987). *The war play dilemma*. New York: Teachers College Press.

Carlsson-Paige, N., & Levin, D. E. (1990). *Who's calling the shots?: How to respond effectively to children's fascination with war play and war toys.* Philadelphia, PA: New Society Publishers.

Carlsson-Paige, N., & Levin, D. E. (1991). The subversion of healthy development and play: Teachers' reactions to the Teenage Mutant Ninja Turtles. *Day Care and Early Education, 19,* 14–20.

Carlsson-Paige, N., & Levin, D. E. (1995). Can teachers resolve the war-play dilemma? *Young Children, 50,* 62–63.

Carmichael, K. (1991). Play therapy: Role in reading improvement. *Reading Improvement, 4,* 273–276.

Casby, M. W. (1997). Symbolic play of children with language impairment: A critical review. *Journal of Speech, Language, and Hearing Research, 40,* 468–479.

Caster, T. J. (1984). The young child's play and social and emotional development. In T. D. Yawkey & A. D. Pellegrini (Eds.), *Child's play and play therapy* (pp. 17–30). Lancaster, PA: TECHNOMIC.

Castle, K. (1998). Children's rule knowledge in invented games. *Journal of Research in Childhood Education, 12,* 197–209.

Cataldo, C. Z. (1983). *Infant and toddler programs: A guide to very early childhood education*. Reading, MA: Addison-Wesley.

Cavallo, D. J. (1976). *The child in American reform: A psychohistory of the movement to organize children's play, 1880–1920*. Unpublished doctoral dissertation, State University of New York, Stony Brook. Ann Arbor, MI: University Microfilms International.

Cazden, C. (1974). Play with language and metalinguistic awareness: One dimension of language experience. *Urban Review, 7,* 23–39.

Celano, M. P. (1990). Activities and games for group psychotherapy with sexually abused children. *International Journal of Group Psychotherapy, 40*(4), 419–429.

Center for the Future of Children. (1996). *The future of children.* Los Altos, CA: Author.

Chafel, J., & Reifel, S. (Eds.). (1996). *Advances in early education and day care: Theory and practice in early childhood teaching* (Vol. 8). Greenwich, CT: JAI.

Chaille, C., & Silvern, S. (1996). Understanding through play. *Childhood Education, 72,* 274–279.

Chambers, P. (1997). IV and SEN: Using interactive video with special education pupils. *British Journal of Educational Technology, 28,* 31–39.

Chang, L.-C., & Reifel, S. (2003). Play, racial attitudes, and self-concept in Taiwan. In D. Lytle (Ed.), *Play and Culture Studies: Vol. 5. Play and educational theory and practice* (pp. 257–275). Westport, CT: Praeger.

Chang, P.-Y. (2003). Contextual understanding of children's play in Taiwanese kindergartens. In D. Lytle (Ed.) *Play and Culture Studies: Vol. 5. Play and educational theory and practice* (pp. 277–297). Westport, CT: Praeger.

Chang, P.-Y., & Yawkey, T. D. (1998). Symbolic play and literacy learning: Classroom materials and teacher's roles. *Reading Improvement, 35,* 172–177.

Chedekel, L. (1999, May 1). Can Hartford schools learn their lesson? *Hartford Courant*, p. 1.

Cheney, D. (1978). The play partners of immature baboons. *Animal Behavior, 26,* 1038–1050.

Chiang, L. (1985). *Developmental differences in children's use of play materials*. Unpublished doctoral dissertation, University of Texas, Austin.

Child, E. (1983). Play and culture: A study of English and Asian children. *Leisure Studies, 2,* 169–186.

Children's Defense Fund. (1996). *The state of America's children: Yearbook.* Washington, DC: Author.

Children's Defense Fund. (1998). *The state of America's children: Yearbook.* Washington, DC: Author.

Chomsky, C. (1969). *The acquisition of syntax in children from five to ten*. Cambridge, MA: MIT Press.

Chomsky, N. (1957). *Syntactic structures*. The Hague: Mouton.

Christiansen, M. (1997). International perspectives of playground safety. *Parks and Recreation, 32*(4), 100–101.

Christiansen, M. L., & Vogelsong, H. (Eds.). (1996). *Play it safe: An anthology of playground safety*. Arlington, VA: National Recreation and Park Association.

Christie, J. (1983). The effects of play tutoring on young children's cognitive performance. *Journal of Educational Research, 76,* 326–330.

Christie, J. (1994). Literacy play interventions: A review of empirical research. In S. Reifel (Ed.), *Advances in early education and day care* (Vol. 6, pp. 3–24). Greenwich, CT: JAI.

Christie, J., Enz, B., & Vukelich, C. (1997). *Teaching language and literacy: Preschool through the elementary grades.* New York: Addison-Wesley Educational.

Christie, J., & Johnsen, P. (1985). Questioning the results of play training research. *Educational Psychologist, 20,* 7–11.

Christman, M. (1979). A look at sociodramatic play among Mexican-American children. *Childhood Education, 55,* 106–110.

Chugani, H. T. (1994). Development of regional brain glucose metabolism in relation to behavior and plasticity. In G. Dawson & K. W. Fischer (Eds.), *Human behavior and the developing brain* (pp. 153–175). New York: Guilford.

Chuoke, M., & Eyman, B. (1997). Play fair—And not just at recess. *Educational Leadership, 54,* 53–55.

Clark, R. J. (1995). Research review: Violence, young children and the healing power of play. *Dimensions, 23,* 28–30, 39.

Clarke-Stewart, A. (1978). And daddy makes three: The father's impact on mother and young child. *Child Development, 49,* 466–478.

Clarke-Stewart, K. A. (1987). Predicting child development from child care forms and features: The Chicago Study. In D. Phillips (Ed.), *Quality in child care: What does research tell us?* (pp. 21–41). Washington, DC: National Association for the Education of Young Children.

Clawson, M. A. (2002). Play of language-minority children in early childhood settings. In J. L. Roopnarine (Ed.), *Play and culture studies: Vol. 4. Social-cognitive, and contextual issues in the fields of play* (pp. 93–110). Westport, CT: Ablex.

Clements, D. H. (1986). Effects of Logo and CAI environments on cognition and creativity. *Journal of Educational Psychology, 78,* 309–318.

Clements, D. H., & Nastasi, B. K. (1992). Computers and early childhood education. In M. Gettinger, S. N. Elliott, & T. R. Kratochwill (Eds.), *Advances in school psychology: Preschool and early childhood treatment directions* (pp. 187–246). Hillsdale, NJ: Erlbaum.

Clements, D. H., Nastasi, B. K., & Swaminathan, S. (1993). Young children and computers: Crossroads and directions from research. *Young Children, 48*(2), 56–64.

Clements, R. (2003, June). New research finds a decrease in USA outdoor play. *PlayRights, 25*(1–2), 11–13.

Coakly, J. (1990). *Sport and society: Issues and controversy* (4th ed.). St. Louis: Mosby.

Coates, G. J., & Siepl-Coates, S. (1998). New design technologies: Healing architecture: A case study of the Vidarkliniken. *Journal of Healthcare Design, 8,* 1–12.

Cohen, D., & Stern, V. (1983). *Observing and recording the behavior of young children* (2nd ed.). New York: Teachers College Press.

Cohn, D. (1991). Anatomical doll play of preschoolers referred for sexual abuse and those not referred. *Child Abuse and Neglect, 15,* 455–466.

Comenius, J. A. (1896). *The great didactic*. London: Black.

Conn, J. H. (1952). Treatment of anxiety states in children by play interviews. *Sinai Hospital Journal, 1,* 57–65.

Conner, K. (1989). Aggression: Is it in the eye of the beholder? *Play and Culture, 2,* 213–217.

Consumer Federation of America. (2000). *Fifth nationwide investigation of public playgrounds.*

Consumer Product Safety Commission. (1975). *Hazard analysis of injuries relating to playground equipment*. Washington, DC: Author.

Consumer Product Safety Commission. (1981a). *A handbook for public playground safety: Vol. I. General guidelines for new and existing playgrounds*. Washington, DC: Author.

Consumer Product Safety Commission. (1981b). *A handbook for public playground safety: Vol. II. Technical guidelines for equipment and surfacing*. Washington, DC: Author.

Consumer Product Safety Commission. (1992). *Barriers for residential swimming pools, spas, and hot tubs*. Washington, DC: Author.

Consumer Product Safety Commission. (1996a). *Identifying and controlling lead paint on public playground equipment*. Washington, DC: Author.

Consumer Product Safety Commission. (1996b). *Pool safety guidelines*. Washington, DC: Author.

Coplan, R. J., & Rubin, K. H. (1998). Social play. In D. P. Fromberg & D. Bergen (Eds.), *Play from birth to twelve and beyond: Contexts, perspectives, and meanings* (pp. 368–377). New York: Garland.

Coplan, R. J., Rubin, K. H., Fox, N. A., Calkins, S. D., & Stewart, S. L. (1994). Being alone, playing alone, and acting alone: Distinguishing among reticence, and passive- and active-solitude in young children. *Child Development, 65,* 129–138.

Corsaro, W. (1979). We're friends, right? Children's use of access rituals in a nursery school. *Language in Society, 8,* 315–336.

Corsaro, W., & Rizzo, T. (1988). *Discussione* and friendship: Socialization processes in the peer culture of Italian nursery school children. *American Sociological Review, 53,* 879–894.

Corsaro, W. A. (1985). *Friendship and peer culture in the early years*. Norwood, NJ: Ablex.

Corsaro, W. A., & Schwarz, K. (1991). Peer play and socialization in two cultures: Implications for research and practice. In B. Scales, M. Almy, A. Nicolopoulou, & S. Ervin-Tripp (Eds.), *Play and the social context of development in early care and education* (pp. 234–254). New York: Teachers College Press.

Costas, M., & Landreth, G. (1999). Filial therapy with nonoffending parents of children who have been sexually abused. *International Journal of Play Therapy, 8,* 43–66.

Cowden, S. T. (1992). *The effects of client-centered group play therapy on self concept* (Masters Abstracts International 31/01). Unpublished master's thesis, University of West Florida, Pensacola.

Cowley, G. (1997, Spring–Summer). The language explosion. *Newsweek Special Edition,* pp. 16–21.

Cox, F. E. (1953). Sociometric status and individual adjustment before and after play therapy. *Journal of Abnormal Psychology, 40,* 354–356.

Cox, T. (1996). Teachable moments: Socially constructed bridges. In S. Reifel (Ed.), *Advances in early education and day care: Vol. 8. Theory and practice in early childhood teaching* (pp. 187–200). Greenwich, CT: JAI.

Cratty, B. J. (1986). *Perceptual and motor development in infants and children* (3rd ed.). Upper Saddle River, NJ: Prentice Hall.

Creasey, G. L., Jarvis, P. A., & Berk, L. E. (1998). Play and social competence. In O. N. Saracho & B. Spodek (Eds.), *Multiple perspectives on play in early childhood education* (pp. 116–143). Albany: State University of New York Press.

Crenson, M. (2001, January 6). Research into brain growth explains some of teens' troubles. Associated Press and *Austin American-Statesman*, A20.

Cross, G. (1997). *Kids' stuff: Toys and the changing world of American childhood*. Cambridge, MA: Harvard University Press.

Crow, J. (1989). *Play therapy with low achievers in reading*. Unpublished doctoral dissertation, University of North Texas, Denton.

Csikszentmihalyi, M. (1977). *Beyond boredom and anxiety*. San Francisco: Jossey-Bass.

Csikszentmihalyi, M. (1979). The concept of flow. In B. Sutton-Smith (Ed.), *Play and learning*. New York: Gardner.

Csikszentmihalyi, M. (1990). *Flow: The psychology of optimal experience*. New York: Harper & Row.

Csikszentmihalyi, M., & Csikszentmihalyi, I. S. (Eds.). (1995). *Optimal experience*. New York: Cambridge University Press.

Cuffaro, H. (1995). *Experimenting with the world: John Dewey and the early childhood classroom*. New York: Teachers College Press.

Curtis, H. S. (1913). *The reorganized school playground*. U.S. Bureau of Education, No. 40. Washington, DC: U.S. Government Printing Office.

Curtis, H. S. (1917). *Education through play*. New York: Macmillan.

Cutler, K. M., Gilkerson, D., Parrott, S., & Bowne, M. T. (2002). Developing math games based on children's literature. *Young Children, 58*(1), 22–27.

Damon, W. (1990). Self-concept, adolescent. In R. M. Lerner, A. C. Petersen, & J. Brooks-Gunn (Eds.), *The encyclopedia of adolescence* (Vol. 2. pp. 87–91). New York: Garland.

Danenberg, M. A., Loos-Cosgrove, M., & LoVerde, M. (1987). Temporary hearing loss and rock music. *Language, Speech and Hearing Services in Schools, 18,* 267–274.

Dansky, J. L. (1980). Cognitive consequences of sociodramatic play and exploration training for economically disadvantaged preschoolers. *Journal of Child Psychology and Psychiatry, 21,* 47–58.

Dargan, A., & Zeitlin, S. (1998). City play. In D. P. Fromberg & D. Bergen (Eds.), *Play from birth to twelve and beyond: Contexts, perspectives, and meanings* (pp. 219–224). New York: Garland.

Darwin, C. (1859). *On the origin of species by means of natural selection, or the preservation of favoured races in the struggle for life*. London: Murray.

David and Lucile Packard Foundation. (2001). The future of children [Electronic version]. Retrieved from www.futureofchildren.org/cct/index/htm

Davidson, J. I. F. (1998). Language and play: Natural partners. In D. P. Fromberg & D. Bergen (Eds.), *Play from birth to twelve and beyond: Contexts, perspectives, and meanings* (pp. 175–184). New York: Garland.

Davoren, E. (1979). Low budget play therapy for very young children. *Child Abuse and Neglect, 3,* 199–204.

DeAngelis, T. (1997, June). Trauma at an early age inhibits ability to bond. *Monitor: American Psychological Association,* pp. 11–13.

Deacon, S. R. (1994). *Analysis of children's equipment choices and play behaviors across three play environments.* Unpublished doctoral dissertation, University of Texas, Austin.

Deiner, P. L. (1997). *Infants and toddlers: Development and program planning*. Fort Worth, TX: Harcourt Brace.

Deitz, W. H., & Gortmaker, S. L. (1985). Do we fatten our children at the television set? Obesity and television viewing in children and adolescents. *Pediatrics, 75,* 807–812.

Dell, A. G., & Newton, D. Software for PLAY and ACTIVE Early Learning. *The Exceptional Parent, 28,* 39–43.

deMarrais, K. B., Nelson, P. A., & Baker, J. H. (1994). Meaning in mud: Yup'ik Eskimo girls at play. In J. L. Roopnarine, J. E. Johnson, & F. H. Hooper (Eds.), *Children's play in diverse cultures* (pp. 179–209). Albany: State University of New York Press.

Dempsey, J. D. (1985). *The effects of training in play on cognitive development in preschool children*. Unpublished doctoral dissertation, University of Texas, Austin.

Dennis, W. (1960). Causes of retardation among institutionalized children. *Journal of Genetic Psychology, 99,* 47–59.

Dennison, B., et al. (1988) Childhood physical fitness tests: Predictor of adult physical activity levels? *Pediatrics, 82,* 3.

Devereux, E. (1976). Backyard versus Little League baseball: The impoverishment of children's games. In D. Landers (Ed.), *Social problems in athletics*. Urbana: University of Illinois Press.

DeVries, R. (1998). Games with rules. In D. P. Fromberg & D. Bergen (Eds.), *Play from birth to twelve and beyond: Contexts, perspectives, and meanings* (pp. 409–415). New York: Garland.

DeVries, R., & Fernie, D. (1990). Stages in children's play of tic tac toe. *Journal of Research in Childhood Education, 4,* 98–111.

DeVries, R., Hildebrandt, C., & Zan, B. (2002). *Developing a constructivist early childhood curriculum*. New York: Teachers College Press.

DeVries, R., & Kohlberg, L. (1990). *Constructivist early education: Overview and comparison with other programs* (2nd ed.). Washington, DC: National Association for the Education of Young Children.

DeVries, R., & Zan, B. (1994). *Moral classrooms, moral children*. New York: Teachers College Press.

Dewey, J. (1896). Imagination and expression. In *John Dewey: The Early Works, 1882–1898: Vol. 5. 1895–1898* (pp. 192–201). Carbondale: Southern Illinois University Press. (Originally published 1972, Feffer & Simons.)

Dewey, J. (1913). *Interest and effort in education*. Edwardsville: Southern Illinois Press.

Dewey, J. (1916). *Democracy and education*. New York: Free Press.

Dewey, J. (1938). *Experience and education*. New York: Collier.

Diaz, R. M. (1985). Bilingual cognitive development: Addressing three gaps in current research. *Child Development, 56,* 1376–1388.

Dies, R. R., & Riester, A. E. (1986). Research on child group therapy: Present status and future directions. In A. Riester & I. Kraft (Eds.), *Group child psychotherapy: Future tense* (pp. 173–220). Madison, CT: International Universities Press.

Dillard, A. (1987). *An American childhood*. New York: Harper & Row.

Dix, T. (1991). The affective organization of parenting: Adaptive and maladaptive processes. *Psychological Bulletin, 110,* 3–25.

Dockett, S., & Fleer, M. (1999). *Play and pedagogy in early childhood: Bending the rules*. Orlando, FL: Harcourt, Brace.

Dodge, D. T., Colker, L. J., & Heroman, C. *The creative curriculum for preschool.* Washington, DC: Teaching Strategies, Inc.

Dodge, K., & Frame, C. (1982). Social cognitive deficits and biases in aggressive boys. *Child Development, 53,* 620–635.

Dodge, K. A., Coie, J. D., Pettit, G. S., & Price, J. M. (1990). Peer status and aggression in boys' groups: Developmental and contextual analyses. *Child Development, 61,* 1289–1309.

Dolgin, K. G., & Behrend, D. A. (1984). Children's knowledge about animates and inanimates. *Child Development, 55,* 1646–1650.

Donovan, M. S., Bransford, J. D., & Pellegrino, J. W. (Eds.). (1999). *How people learn: Bridging research and practice*. Washington, DC: National Academy Press.

Dorfman, E. (1958). Personality outcomes of client-centered play therapy. *Psychological Monographs, 72,* 1–22.

Duncan, M. C. (1988). Play discourse and the rhetorical turn: A semiological analysis of *Homo ludens*. *Play & Culture, 1,* 28–42.

Dundes, A., Leach, J. W., & Ozkok, B. (1970). Strategy of Turkish boys' verbal dueling rhymes. *Journal of American Folklore, 83,* 325–349.

Dunn, J. (1983). Sibling relationships in early childhood. *Child Development, 54,* 787–811.

Dunn, J. (1998). "This time I'll be the golden bird": A call for more child-structured dramatic play. *Research in Drama Education, 3,* 55–66.

Dweck, C. S., & Leggett, E. L. (1988). A social-cognitive approach to motivation and personality. *Psychological Review, 95,* 256–273.

Dyson, A. H. (1997). *Writing superheroes: Contemporary childhood, popular culture, and classroom literacy*. New York: Teachers College Press.

Dyson, A. H., & Genishi, C. (1993). Visions of children as language users: Language and language education in early childhood. In B. Spodek (Ed.), *Handbook of research on the education of young children* (pp. 122–136). New York: Macmillan.

Eccles, J. S., & Harold, R. D. (1991). Gender differences in sport involvement: Applying the Eccles' expectancy-value model. *Journal of Applied Sport Psychology, 3,* 7–35.

Edelman, M. W. (1994, Autumn). Cease fire! Stopping the war against children. *Harvard Medical Bulletin, 68,* 18–23.

Education Commission of the States and the Charles A. Dana Foundation. (1996). *Bridging the gap between neuroscience and education.* Denver, CO: Education Commission of the States.

Edwards, C. P., Gandini, L., & Forman, G. (1998). *The hundred languages of children: The Reggio Emilia approach to early childhood education* (rev. ed.). Stamford, CT: Ablex.

Eifermann, R. (1971). Social play in childhood. In R. Herron & B. Sutton-Smith (Eds.), *Child's play* (pp. 270–297). New York: Wiley.

Eisenberg, N., Fabes, R. A., Bernzweig, J., Karbon, M., Poulin, R., & Hanish, L. (1993). The relations of emotionality and regulation to preschoolers' social skills and sociometric status. *Child Development, 64,* 1418–1438.

Eisenberg, N., & Harris, J. D. (1984). Social competence: A developmental perspective. *School Psychology Review, 13,* 267–277.

Eisenberg, N., & Miller, P. A. (1987). The relations of empathy to prosocial and related behaviors. *Psychological Bulletin, 101,* 91–119.

Eisert, D., & Lamorey, S. (1996). Play as a window on child development: The relationship between play and other developmental domains. *Early Education and Development, 7,* 221–235.

Elias, M. (1995, February 27). Teens themselves say TV is a bad influence. *USA Today*.

Elkind, D. (1968). Editor's introduction. In J. Piaget, *Six psychological studies* (pp. v–xviii). New York: Vintage.

Elkind, D. (1981). *The hurried child: Growing up too fast, too soon*. Reading, MA: Addison-Wesley.

Elkind, D. (1985). The child, yesterday, today and tomorrow. *Young Children, 42*(4), 6–11.

Ellis, J. J. (1973). *Why people play*. Upper Saddle River, NJ: Prentice Hall.

Enz, B., & Christie, J. (1997). Teacher play interaction styles: Effects on play behavior and relationships with teacher training and experience. *International Journal of Early Childhood Education, 2,* 55–75.

ERIC Clearinghouse on Elementary and Early Childhood Education. (2000). Computers and young children. Retrieved March 29, 2004, from http://ecap.crc.uiuc.edu/eecearchive/digests/2000/haugland00.html

Erikson, E. H. (1941). Further exploration in play construction: Three spatial variables in their relation to sex and anxiety. *Psychological Bulletin, 38,* 748.

Erikson, E. H. (1950). *Childhood and society*. New York: Norton.

Erikson, E. H. (1963). *Childhood and society* (rev. ed.). New York: Norton.

Erikson, E. H. (1972). Play and actuality. In M. W. Piers (Ed.), *Play and development* (pp. 127–168). New York: Norton.

Erin, J. N. (1990). Language samples from visually impaired 4- and 5-year-olds. *Journal of Childhood Communication Disorders, 13*, 181–191.

Escalona, S. (1968). *The roots of individuality*. Chicago: Aldine.

Escobedo, T. H. (1992). Play in a new medium: Children's talk and graphics at computers. *Play and Culture, 5, 120–140.*

Esposito, B. G., & Koorland, M. A. (1989). Play behavior of hearing impaired children: Integrated and segregated settings. *Exceptional Children, 55,* 412–419.

European Committee for Standardization. (1998). *European Standard for Playground Equipment*. Brussels: Central Secretariat.

Evans, J. (1989). *Children at play: Life in the school playground*. Victoria, Australia: Deakin University Press.

Evans, J. (1990). The teacher role in playground supervision. *Play & Culture, 3,* 219–234.

Evans, J. (1992). Children's leisure patterns: The shift to organized recreation. *Recreation Australia, 3*(4), 19–26.

Factor, J. (1993). Enriching the play environment: Creativity, culture and tradition. In *Proceedings* (Vol. 5), World Play Summit, Melbourne, Australia.

Factor, J. (1998). *Captain Cook chased a crook*. Australia: Penguin.

Fagen, R. (1981). *Animal play*. New York: Oxford University Press.

Fagot, B. I. (1977). Variations in density: Effects on task and social behaviors of preschool children. *Developmental Psychology, 13,* 166–167.

Fagot, B. I. (1994). Peer relations and the development of competence in boys and girls. *New Directions for Child Development, 65,* 53–65.

Fagot, B. I., Hagan, R., Youngblade, L. M., & Potter, L. (1989). A comparison of the play behaviors of sexually abused, physically abused, and non-abused children. *Topics in Early Childhood Special Education, 9,* 88–100.

Fagot, B. I., & Kronsberg, S. J. (1982). Sex differences: Biological and social factors influencing the behavior of young boys and girls. In S. G. Moore & C. R. Cooper (Eds.), *The young child: Reviews of research* (Vol. 3, pp. 193–210). Washington, DC: National Association for the Education of Young Children.

Fagot, B. I., & Leinbach, M. D. (1989). The young child's gender schema: Environmental input, internal organization. *Child Development, 60,* 663–672.

Fagot, B. I., Leinbach, M. D., & Hagan, R. (1986). Gender labeling and the adoption of sex-typed behaviors. *Developmental Psychology, 22,* 440–443.

Fagot, B. I., & Leve, L. (1998). Gender identity and play. In D.P. Fromberg & D. Bergen (Eds.), *Play from birth to twelve and beyond: Contexts, perspectives, and meanings* (pp. 187–192). New York: Garland.

Farver, J. (1993). Cultural differences in scaffolding pretend play: A comparison of American and Mexican American mother-child and sibling-child pairs. In K. MacDonald (Ed.), *Parent-child play: Descriptions and implications* (pp. 349–366). Albany: State University of New York Press.

Farver, J., & Howes, C. (1993). Cultural differences in American and Mexican mother-child pretend play. *Merrill-Palmer Quarterly, 39,* 344–358.

Farver, J., Kim, Y. K, & Lee, Y. (1995). Cultural differences in Korean- and Anglo-American preschoolers' social interaction and play behaviors. *Child Development, 66,* 1088–1099.

Farver, J., & Wimbarti, S. (1995). Indonesian toddlers' social play with their mothers and older siblings. *Child Development, 66,* 1493–1503.

Farwell, L. (1930). Reactions of kindergarten, first, and second grade children to constructive play materials. *Genetic Psychology Monographs, 8,* 431–562.

Fein, G., & Stork, L. (1981). Sociodramatic play in a socially integrated setting. *Journal of Applied Developmental Psychology, 2,* 267–279.

Fein, G., & Wiltz, N. (1998). Play as children see it. In D. Fromberg & D. Bergen (Eds.), *Play from birth to twelve and beyond: Contexts, perspectives, and meanings* (pp. 37–49). New York: Garland.

Fein, G. G. (1975). A transformational analysis of pretending. *Developmental Psychology, 11,* 291–296.

Fein, G. G. (1981). Pretend play in childhood: An integrative review. *Child Development, 52,* 1095–1118.

Fein, G. G. (1987). Technologies for the young. *Early Childhood Research Quarterly, 2,* 227–243.

Fein, G. G. (1989). Mind, meaning, and affect: Proposals for a theory of pretense. *Developmental Review, 9,* 345–363.

Fein, G. G. (1999). Commentary on Rhetorics Redux. In S. Reifel (Ed.), *Advances in early education and day care: Vol. 10. Foundations, adult dynamics, teacher education and play* (pp. 189–200). Greenwich, CT: JAI.

Fein, G. G., & Kinney, P. (1994). He's a nice alligator: Observations on the affective organization of pretense. In A. Slade & D. P. Wolf (Eds.), *Children at play* (pp. 188–204). Boston: Oxford University Press.

Feitelson, D., & Ross, G. S. (1973). The neglected factor—play. *Human Development, 16,* 202–223.

Fenson, L. (1986). The developmental progression of play. In A. Gottfried & C. C. Brown (Eds.), *Play interactions: The contribution of play materials and parental involvement to children's development.* Lexington, MA: Heath.

Fernald, A., & Morikawa, H. (1993). Common themes and cultural variations in Japanese and American mothers' speech to infants. *Child Development, 64,* 637–656.

Fewell, R., & Kaminski, R. (1988). Play skills development and instruction for young children with handicaps. In S. Odom & M. Karnes (Eds.), *Early intervention for infants and children with handicaps* (pp. 145–158). Baltimore, MD: Brookes.

Fewell, R., & Rich, J. (1987). Play assessment as a procedure for examining cognitive, communication and social skills in multihandicapped children. *Journal of Psychoeducational Assessment, 2,* 107–118.

Fewell, R. R., & Wheeden, C. A. (1998). A pilot study of intervention with adolescent mothers and their children: A preliminary examination of child outcomes. *Topics in Early Childhood Special Education, 18,* 18–25.

Feynman, R. P. (1985). *Surely you're joking Mr. Feynman! Adventures of a curious character.* New York: Bantam.

Fields, M. V., & Spangler, K. L. (1995). *Let's begin reading right* (3rd ed.). Upper Saddle River, NJ: Merrill/Prentice Hall.

Figler, S., & Whitaker, G. (1991). *Sport and play in American life.* Dubuque, IA: Brown.

File, N. (1994). Children's play, teacher-child interactions, and teacher beliefs in integrated early childhood programs. *Early Childhood Research Quarterly, 9,* 223–240.

File, N., & Kontos, S. (1993). The relationship of program quality to children's play in integrated early intervention settings. *Topics in Early Childhood Special Education, 13,* 1–18.

Fine, G. A. (1983). *Shared fantasy: Role-playing games as social worlds.* Chicago: University of Chicago Press.

Finnan, C. (1982). The ethnography of children's spontaneous play. In G. Spindler (Ed.), *Doing the ethnography of schooling: Educational anthropology in action* (pp. 356–380). New York: Holt, Rinehart & Winston.

Fisher, E. (1992). The impact of play on development: A meta-analysis. *Play & Culture, 5,* 159–181.

Fischer, M. A., & Gillespie, C. W. (2003). Computers and young children's development. *Young Children.* Washington, DC: National Association for the Education of Young Children. *58*(4), 85–91.

Flavell, J. H., Green, F. L., & Flavell, E. R. (1987). Development of knowledge about the appearance-reality distinction. *Monographs of the Society for Research in Child Development, 51*(1, Serial No. 212).

Flavell, J. H., Miller, P. H., & Miller, S. A. (1993). *Cognitive development* (3rd ed.). Upper Saddle River, NJ: Prentice Hall.

Fogel, A. (1979). Peer vs. mother-directed behavior in 1- to 3-month-old infants. *Infant Behavior and Development, 2,* 215–216.

Forman, F. (1998). Constructive play. In D. Fromberg & D. Bergen, D. (Eds.), *Play from birth to twelve and beyond: Contexts, perspectives, and meanings* (pp. 392–400). New York: Garland.

Fraiberg, S. (1968). Parallel and divergent patterns in blind and sighted infants. *Psychoanalytic Study of the Child, 23,* 264–300.

Fraiberg, S. (1977). *Insights from the blind: Comparative studies of blind and sighted infants.* New York: Basic Books.

Fraiberg, S., & Adelson, E. (1973). Self-representation in language and play: Observations of blind children. *Psychoanalytic Quarterly, 42,* 539–562.

Francis, M. (1995). Childhood's garden: Memory and meaning of gardens. *Children's Environments, 12*(2), 183–191.

Frank, D. A., Klass, P. E., Earls, F., and Eisenberg, L. (1996). Infants and young children in orphanages: One view from pediatrics and child psychiatry. *Pediatrics, 97,* 573–580.

Frankenburg, W. K., Frandel, A., Sciarillo, W., & Burgess, D. (1981). The newly abbreviated and revised Denver Developmental Screening Test. *Journal of Pediatrics, 99,* 995–999.

Frazier, D., & Levine, E. (1983). Reattachment therapy: Intervention with the very young physically abused child. *Psychotherapy: Theory, Research, and Practice, 20,* 90–100.

Freedman, D. (1991). The new theory of everything. *Discover, 12,* 53–61.

Freeman, R. D., Goetz, E., Richards, P., Groenveld, M., Blockberger, S., Jan, J. E., & Skylanda, A. M. (1989). Blind children's early emotional development: Do we know enough to help? *Child: Care, Health and Development, 15,* 3–28.

Freud, A. (1928). *Introduction to the technique of child analysis* (trans. L. P. Clark). New York: Nervous and Mental Disease Publishing.

Freud, A. (1946). *The psychoanalytical treatment of children*. London: Imago.

Freud, A. (1964). *The psychological treatment of children*. New York: Schocken.

Freud, S. (1909). Analysis of a phobia in a five year old boy. In *The standard edition of the complete psychological works of Sigmund Freud*. London: Hogarth.

Freud, S. (1918). *Totem and taboo*. New York: New Republic.

Freud, S. (1935). *A general introduction to psychoanalysis* (Joan Riviare, Trans.). New York: Modern Library.

Freud, S. (1938). *The basic writings of Sigmund Freud*. (A. A. Brill, Trans. & Ed.). New York: Modern Library.

Freud, S. (1959). Beyond the pleasure principle. In J. Strachey (Ed.), *The standard edition of the complete psychological works of Sigmund Freud*. London: Institute of Psychoanalysis. (Originally published 1922.)

Freud, S. (1961). *Beyond the pleasure principle*. New York: Norton.

Freud, S. (1965). *The psycho-analytical treatment of children*. London: Imago.

Freund, L. S. (1989). Maternal regulation of children's problem solving behavior and its impact on children's performance. *Child Development, 61,* 113–126.

Freyberg, J. T. (1973). Increasing the imaginative play of urban disadvantaged kindergarten children through systematic training. In J. L. Singer (Ed.), *The child's world of make-believe* (pp. 129–154). New York: Academic Press.

Friedrich, W. N., & Reams, R. A. (1987). The course of psychological symptoms in sexually abused young children. *Psychotherapy: Research, Theory, and Practice, 24,* 160–170.

Fritz, M. (1996, September 1). Thrill, chill, occasionally kill. *Austin American-Statesman,* pp. A-1, A-25.

Froebel, F. (1887). *The education of man* (W. N. Hailmann, Trans.). New York: Appleton.

Froebel, F. (1897). *Mother's songs, games, and stories* (F. & E. Lord, Trans.). London: Rice. (Originally published 1844.)

Froebel, F. (1902). *Education of man* (W. N. Hailmann, Trans.). New York: Appleton. (Originally published 1826.)

Fromberg, D. P. (1997). Play issues in early childhood education. In C. Seefeldt (Ed.), *Continuing issues in early childhood education* (2nd ed.). (pp. 190–212). Upper Saddle River, NJ: Merrill/ Prentice Hall.

Fromberg, D. P. (1999). A review of research on play. In C. Seefeldt (Ed.), *The early childhood curriculum: Current findings in theory and practice* (3rd ed.). (pp. 190–212). New York: Teachers College Press.

Froschl, M., & Sprung, B. (1999). On purpose: Addressing teasing and bullying in early childhood. *Young Children, 54,* 70–72.

Frost, J. L. (1968). *Early childhood education rediscovered*. New York: Holt, Rinehart & Winston.

Frost, J. L. (1975). *At risk! Childhood Education, 51,* 298–304.

Frost, J. L. (1985). History of playground safety in America. *Children's Environments Quarterly, 2*(4), 13–23.

Frost, J. L. (1986). Children in a changing society. *Childhood Education, 62,* 242–249.

Frost, J. L. (1987). Conference reflections. In P. J. Heseltine (Ed.), *Creativity through play: Report from the IPA 10th World Conference*. Stockholm: International Association for the Child's Right to Play.

Frost, J. L. (1989). Play environments for young children in the USA: 1800–1990. *Children's Environments Quarterly, 6*(4), 17–24.

Frost, J. L. (1992). *Play and playscapes*. Albany, NY: Delmar.

Frost, J. L. (1996a). The effects of noise on children. *International Journal of Early Childhood Education, 1*(1), 21–35.

Frost, J. L. (1996b). *Protective surfacing for playgrounds*. Report prepared for the U.S. Air Force (ERIC PS024092).

Frost, J. L. (1997). Child development and playgrounds. *Parks and Recreation, 32*(4), 54–60.

Frost, J. L. (1998). *Neuroscience, play and child development*. Paper presented at the American Association for the Child's Right to Play Conference, Longmont, CO.

Frost, J. L. (1999). The changing face of play. *Play, Policy, and Practice Connections, 4,* 6–7, 11. (Newsletter of the play, policy, and practice caucus of the National Association for the Education of Young Children.)

Frost, J. L. (2003). Bridging the gaps: Children in a changing society. *Childhood Education, 80,* 29–34. Olney, MD: Association for Childhood Education International.

Frost, J. L. (2004). Introduction. In K. G. Burriss (Ed.) (In press), *Outdoor learning and play for elementary school*. Olney, MD: Association for Childhood Education International.

Frost, J. L., Bowers, L. E., & Wortham, S. C. (1990). The state of American preschool playgrounds. *Journal of Physical Education, Recreation and Dance, 61*(8), 18–23.

Frost, J. L., Brown, P., Sutterby, J. A., & Wisneski, D. (2004). *Young children's development of swinging behaviors.* Austin, TX: University of Texas. Unpublished research report.

Frost, J. L., Brown, P., Thornton, C. D., Sutterby, J. A., & Therrell, J. A. (2001). *The developmental benefits and use patterns of overhead equipment on playgrounds.* Austin, TX: University of Texas. Unpublished research report.

Frost, J. L., Brown, P., Thornton, C. D., & Sutterby, J. A. (2002). *The nature and benefits of children's climbing behaviors*. Austin, TX: University of Texas. Unpublished research report.

Frost, J. L., Brown, P., Thornton, C. D., & Sutterby, J. A. (2005, in press). *The developmental benefits of playground equipment.* Olney, MD: Association for Childhood Education International.

Frost, J. L., & Griffith, L. (1997). *Visibility, accessibility and safety assessment.* Houston, TX: Houston Zoological Gardens.

Frost, J. L., & Henniger, M. L. (1979). Making playgrounds safe for children and children safe for playgrounds. *Young Children, 34*(5), 23–30.

Frost, J. L., & Jacobs, P. (1995, Spring). Play deprivation and juvenile violence. *Dimensions, 23,* 14–20, 39.

Frost, J. L., & Kissinger, J. B. (1976). *The young child and the educative process*. New York: Holt, Rinehart & Winston.

Frost, J. L., & Klein, B. L. (1979). *Children's play and playgrounds*. Boston: Allyn & Bacon.

Frost, J. L., Shin, D., & Jacobs, P. J. (1998). Physical environments and children's play. In O. N. Saracho & B. Spodek (Eds.), *Multiple perspectives on play in early childhood education*. Albany: State University of New York Press.

Frost, J. L., & Strickland, E. (1985). Equipment choices of young children during free play. In J. L. Frost & S. Sunderlin (Eds.), *When children play* (pp. 93–101). Wheaton, MD: Association for Childhood Education International.

Frost, J. L., Sutterby, J. A., Therrell, J. A., Brown, P., & Thornton, C. D. (2001). *The relevance of height for child development and playground safety*. Austin, TX: University of Texas. Unpublished research report.

Frost, J. L., Sutterby, J. A., Therrell, J. A., Brown, P., & Thornton, C. D. (2002). Does height matter? *Parks and Recreation, 37*(4), 74–83.

Frost, J. L., & Sweeney T. B. (1996). *Cause and prevention of playground injuries and litigation: Case studies*. Olney, MD: Association for Childhood Education International.

Frost, J. L., & Wortham, S. C. (1988). The evolution of American playgrounds. *Young Children, 43*(5), 19–28.

Fukushima, R. (1998, December 29). Study: Kids need an hour of exercise. *Austin American-Statesman*, p. E-3.

Funk, J. B., & Buchman, D. D. (1996). Children's perceptions of gender differences in social approval for playing electronic games. *Sex Roles, 35,* 219–231.

Gabbard, C. (1979). Playground apparatus experience and muscular endurance among children 4–6. (ERIC Document Reproduction Service, SP 022 020; ED 228 190.)

Gabbard, C. (1995). P. E. For preschoolers: The right way. *Principal, 74,* 21–24.

Galda, L. (1982). Playing about a story: Its impact on comprehension. *The Reading Teacher, 55,* 52–55.

Galda, L. (2000). *Looking through the far away end: Creating a literature-based reading curriculum with second graders*. Newark, DE: International Reading Association.

Gallahue, D. L. (1989). *Understanding motor development: Infants, children, adolescents*. Dubuque, IA: Brown & Benchmark.

Gallahue, D. L. (1993). Motor development and movement skill acquisition in early childhood education. In B. Spodek (Ed.), *Handbook of research on the education of young children* (pp. 24–41). New York: Macmillan.

Gandini, L. (1997). Foundations of the Reggio Emilia approach. In J. Hendrick (Ed.), *First steps toward teaching the Reggio way* (pp. 14–25). Upper Saddle River, NJ: Merrill/Prentice Hall.

Gardner, H. (1983). *Frames of mind: The theory of multiple intelligences*. New York: Basic Books.

Gardner, H. (1993). *Multiple intelligences: The theory in practice*. New York: Basic Books.

Gardner, H., & Hatch, T. (1989). Multiple intelligences go to school. *Educational Researcher, 18,* 4–10.

Garner, B. P. (1998). Play development from birth to age four. In D. P. Fromberg & D. Bergen (Eds.), *Play from birth to twelve and beyond: Contexts, perspectives, and meanings* (pp. 137–145). New York: Garland.

Garvey, C. (1977). Play with language and speech. In S. Ervin-Tripp & C. Mitchell-Kernan (Eds.), *Child discourses*. New York: Academic Press.

Garvey, C. (1990). *Play*. Cambridge, MA: Oxford University Press.

Garvey, C. (1993). *Play* (enlarged ed.). Cambridge, MA: Harvard University Press.

Garza, M., Briley, S., & Reifel, S. (1985). Children's view of play. In J. L. Frost & S. Sunderlin (Eds.), *When children play* (pp. 31–37). Wheaton, MD: Association for Childhood Education International.

Geist, E. (2003). Infants and toddlers exploring mathematics. *Young Children, 58,* 10–13.

Gelman, R. (1972). Logical capacity of very young children: Number invariance rules. *Child Development, 43,* 75–90.

Gelman, R., & Shatz, M. (1978). Appropriate speech adjustments: The operation of conversational constraints on talk to two-year-olds. In M. Lewis & L. A. Rosenblum (Eds.), *Interaction, conversation, and the development of language* (pp. 27–61). New York: Wiley.

Genishi, C., & Dyson, A. H. (1984). *Language assessment in the early years*. Norwood, NJ: Ablex.

Gentile, D. A., Lynch, P. J., Linder, J. R., & Walsh, D. A. (2002 under review). The effects of violent video game habits on adolescent hostility, aggressive behaviors, and school performance.

Gesell, A. (1934). *An atlas of infant behavior*. New Haven, CT: Yale University Press.

Gesell, A. (1939). *Biographies of child development*. New York: P. B. Hoeber.

Ginott, H. G. (1961). *Group psychotherapy with children*. New York: McGraw-Hill.

Ginsburg, H. J. (1975). *Variations of aggressive interaction among male elementary school children as a function of spatial density*. Paper presented at the meeting of the Society for Research in Child Development, Denver, CO.

Ginsburg. M. (2001). Early years are learning years: Computers and young children. Washington, DC: National Association for the Education of Young Children. Retrieved March 29, 2004, from http://www.naeyc.org/resources/eyly/2001

Gitlin-Weiner, K. (1998). Clinical perspectives on play. In D. P. Fromberg & D. Bergen (Eds.), *Play from birth to twelve and beyond: Contexts, perspectives, and meanings* (pp. 77–92). New York: Garland.

Glass, D. C., & Singer, J. E. (1972). *Urban stress: Experiments on noise and social stressors*. New York: Academic Press.

Glasser, W. (1975). *Reality therapy*. New York: Harper & Row.

Gleason, J. J. (1990). Meaning of play: Interpreting patterns in behavior of persons with severe developmental disabilities. *Anthropology & Education Quarterly, 21,* 59–77.

Glickman, C. D. (1984). Play in public school settings: A philosophical question. In T. D. Yawkey & A. D. Pellegrini (Eds.), *Child's play: Developmental and applied* (pp. 255–271). Hillsdale, NJ: Erlbaum.

Gmitrova V., & Gmitrov, J. (2002).The impact of teacher-directed and child-directed pretend play on cognitive competence in kindergarten. *Early Childhood Education Journal, 30,* 241–246.

Goerner, S. (1994). *Chaos and the evolving ecological universe*. Langhorne, PA: Gordon & Breach.

Goffman, I. (1974). *Frame analysis: An essay on the organization of experience*. Cambridge, MA: Harvard University Press.

Golbeck, S., Rand, M., & Soundy, C. (1986). Constructing a model of large-scale space with the space in view: Effects of guidance and cognitive restructuring in preschoolers. *Merrill-Palmer Quarterly, 32,* 187–203.

Golbeck, S. L. (1995). The social context and children's spatial representations: Recreating the world with blocks, drawings, and models. In S. Reifel (Ed.), *Advances in early education and day care* (Vol. 7, pp. 213–250). Greenwich, CT: JAI.

Goldfarb, W. (1953). The effects of early institutional care on adolescent personality. *Journal of Experimental Education, 12,* 106–129.

Goldstein, J. (1995). Aggressive toy play. In A. D. Pellegrini (Ed.), *The future of play theory* (pp. 127–147). Albany: State University of New York Press.

Goldstein, K. S. (1971). Strategy in counting out: An ethnographic folklore field study. In E. Avedon & B. Sutton-Smith (Eds.), *The study of games* (pp. 167–178). New York: Wiley.

Goleman, D. (1995). *Emotional intelligence*. New York: Bantam.

Golomb, C., & Bonen, S. (1981). Playing games of make-believe: The effectiveness of symbolic play training with children who failed to benefit from early conservation training. *Genetic Psychology Monographs, 104,* 137–159.

Goncu, A. (1993). Development of intersubjectivity in the dyadic play of preschoolers. *Early Childhood Research Quarterly, 8,* 99–116.

Goncu, A., & Mosier, C. (1991). *Cultural variations in the play of toddlers*. Paper presented at the biannual meeting of the Society for Research in Child Development, Seattle, WA.

Goodman, F. (1981). *Computers and the future of literacy*. Proceedings of the National Computer Conference.

Gossen, G. H. (1976). Verbal dueling in Chamula. In B. Kirshenblatt-Gimblett (Ed.), *Speech play* (pp. 121–146). Philadelphia: University of Pennsylvania Press.

Gottlieb, G. (1983). The psychobiological approach to developmental issues. In M. M. Haith & J. J. Campos (Eds.), P. H. Mussen (Series Ed.), *Handbook of child psychology: Vol. 2. Infancy and developmental psychobiology* (pp. 1–26). New York: Wiley.

Gottman, J. M., & Katz, L. F. (1989). Effects of marital discord on young children's peer interaction and health. *Developmental Psychology, 25,* 373–381.

Gove & the Merriam-Webster Editorial Staff. (1986). *Webster's third new international dictionary of the English language unabridged*. Springfield, MA: Merriam.

Green, A. H. (1978). Psychiatric treatment of abused children. *Journal of the American Academy of Child Psychiatry, 17,* 356–371.

Greenman, J. (1985). Babies get out: Outdoor settings for infant-toddler play. *Beginnings, 2,* 7–10.

Gregory, K. M., Kim, A. S., & Whiren, A. (2003) The effect of verbal scaffolding on the complexity of preschool children's blockconstructions. In D. Lytle (Ed.), *Play and Culture Studies: Vol. 5. Play and educational theory and practice* (pp. 117–133). Westport, CT: Praeger.

Griffiths, M. (2003). Column: Playground games reply. *Edge Online*. Retrieved March 29, 2004, from http://www.edge-online.com/news_main.asp?news_id=3468

Groos, K. (1898). *The play of animals*. New York: Appleton.

Groos, K. (1901). *The play of man*. New York: Appleton.

Gross, D. L. (2003). An introduction to research in psychology: Learning to observe children play. In D. Lytle (Ed.), *Play and Culture Studies: Vol. 5. Play and educational theory and practice* (pp. 33–41). Westport, CT: Praeger.

Guerney, L. (1964). Filial therapy: Description and rationale. *Journal of Consulting Psychology, 28,* 304–310.

Guerney, L. (1983). Play therapy with learning disabled children. In C. E. Schaefer & K. L. O'Connor (Eds.), *Handbook of play therapy* (pp. 419–435). New York: Wiley.

Guilford, J. P. (1957). Creative abilities in the arts. *Psychological Review, 64,* 110–118.

Guralnick, J., & Groom, J. (1987). The peer relations of mildly delayed and nonhandicapped children in mainstreamed playgroups. *Child Development, 58,* 1556–1572.

Guralnick, M. J. (1990). Social competence and early intervention. *Journal of Early Intervention, 14,* 3–14.

Guralnick, M. J., Conner, R. T., Hammond, M. A., Gottman, J. M., & Kinnish, K. (1996). The peer relations of preschool children with communication disorders. *Child Development, 67,* 472–489.

Guralnick, M. J., & Groom, J. M. (1988). Friendships of preschool children in mainstreamed playgroups. *Developmental Psychology, 24,* 595–604.

Guralnick, M. J., Weinhouse, E. M. (1984). Peer-related social interactions of developmentally delayed young children: Development and characteristics. *Developmental Psychology, 20,* 815–827.

Hadley, P. A., & Rice, M. L. (1991). Conversational responsiveness of speech- and language-impaired preschoolers. *Journal of Speech and Hearing Research, 34,* 1308–1317.

Haigh, K. (1997). How the Reggio approach has influenced an inner city program: Exploring Reggio in Head Start and subsidized child care. In J. Hendrick (Ed.), *First steps toward teaching the Reggio way* (pp. 152–166). Upper Saddle River, NJ: Merrill/Prentice Hall.

Haight, W. (1998). Adult direct and indirect influences on play. In D. P. Fromberg & D. Bergen (Eds.), *Play from birth to twelve and beyond: Contexts, perspective, and meanings* (pp. 259–265). New York: Garland.

Haight, W., Masiello, T., Dickson, L., Huckeby E., & Black, J. (1994). The everyday contexts and social functions of spontaneous mother-child play in the home. *Merrill-Palmer Quarterly, 40,* 509–533.

Haight, W., Parke, R., & Black, J. (1997). Mothers' and fathers' beliefs about and spontaneous participation in their toddler's pretend play. *Merrill-Palmer Quarterly, 43,* 271–290.

Haight, W., & Sachs, K. (1995). A longitudinal study of the enactment of negative emotion during mother-child pretend play from 1–4 years. In L. Sperry & P. Smiley (Eds.), *New directions in child development: Developmental dimensions of self and other* (pp. 33–46). San Francisco: Jossey-Bass.

Haight, W., Wang, X., Fung, H., Williams, K., & Mintz, J. (1995). *The ecology of everyday pretending in three cultural communities*. Paper presented at the biannual meeting of the Society for Research in Child Development, Indianapolis, IN.

Haight, W. L., & Miller, P. J. (1992). The development of everyday pretend play: a longitudinal study of mothers' participation. *Merrill-Palmer Quarterly, 38,* 331–349.

Haight, W. L., & Miller, P. J. (1993). *Pretending at home: Early development in a sociocultural context*. Albany: State University of New York Press.

Haight, W. L., Parke, R. D., & Black, J. E. (1997). Mothers' and fathers' beliefs about and spontaneous participation in their toddlers' pretend play. *Merrill-Palmer Quarterly, 43,* 271–290.

Hale-Benson, J. E. (1986). *Black children: Their roots, culture, and learning styles*. Baltimore: Johns Hopkins University Press.

Hall, G. S. (1911). *Educational problems* (vol.1). New York: Appleton and Company.

Hambridge, G. (1955). Release therapy. *American Journal of Orthopsychiatry, 9,* 601–617.

Handen, B. L., McAuliffe, S., Janosky, J., Feldman, H., & Breaux, A. M. (1998). A playroom observation procedure to assess children with mental retardation and ADHD. *Journal of Abnormal Child Psychology, 4,* 269–277.

Hansen, J. C., & Cramer, S. H. (1971). *Group guidance and counseling in the schools*. New York: Meredith.

Harper, J. (1991). Children's play: The differential effects of intrafamilial physical and sexual abuse. *Child Abuse and Neglect, 15,* 89–98.

Harris, J. R. (1998). *The nurture assumption: Why children turn out the way they do*. New York: Free Press.

Harris, W. T. (Ed.). (1906). *The mottoes and commentaries of Friedrich Froebel's mother play*. New York: Appleton.

Hart, C., Burts, D., Durland, M. A., Charlesworth, R., DeWolf, M., & Fleege, P. (1998). Stress behaviors and activity type participation of preschoolers in more or less developmentally appropriate classrooms: SES and sex differences. *Journal of Research in Childhood Education, 12,* 98–116.

Hart, R. A. (1979). *Children's experience of place*. New York: Irvington.

Harter, S. (1990). Issues in the assessment of the self-concept of children and adolescents. In A. LaCreca (Ed.), *Through the eyes of a child* (pp. 292–325). Boston: Allyn & Bacon.

Hartup, W. & Larsen. (1993). Conflict and context in peer relations. In C. Hart (Ed.), *Children on playgrounds* (pp. 44–84). Albany: State University of New York Press.

Haugland, S. W. (1992) The effect of computer software on preschool children's developmental gains. *Journal of Computing in Childhood Education, 3*(1), 15–30.

Haugland, S. W., & Shade, D. D. (1988). Developmental evaluations of software for young children. *Young Children, 43*(4), 37–43.

Hartup, W. W. (1992). *Having friends, making friends, and keeping friends: Relationships as educational contexts. ED 345 854*. Urbana, IL: ERIC Clearinghouse on Elementary and Early Childhood Education.

Hayes, C. D., Palmer, J. L., & Zaslow, M. J. (Eds.). (1990). *Child care choices*. Washington, DC: National Academy Press.

Healy, J. H. (1997, August–September). Current brain research. *Scholastic Early Childhood Today* (pp. 42–43).

Healy, J. H. (1998) Failure to connect: *How computers affect our children's minds*. NY: Simon and Schuster.

Heath, P. J. (1995). The top 20 waterpark risk exposures. *Parks and Recreation, 30*(7), 66–70.

Heffernan, M. (1994). The children's garden project at River Farm. *Children's Environments, 11*(3), 221–231.

Heinecke, C. M. (1969). Frequency of psychotherapeutic sessions as a factor affecting outcome: Analysis of clinical rating and test results. *Journal of Abnormal Psychology, 74,* 553–560.

Hellerdorn, J., Van Der Kooij, R., & Sutton-Smith, B. (1994). *Play and intervention*. Albany: State University of New York Press.

Helm, J. H., & Boos, S. (1996). Increasing the physical educator's impact: Consulting, collaborating, and teacher training in early childhood programs. *Journal of Physical Education, Recreation & Dance, 67,* 26–31.

Helm, J. M., Comfort, M., Bailey, D. B., & Simeonsson, R. J. (1990). Adolescent and adult mothers of handicapped children: Maternal involvement in play. *Family Relations, 39,* 432–437.

Henderson-Dixon, A. S. (1991). *The child's own story: A study of the creative process of healing in children in play therapy* (Dissertation Abstracts International 52/09A). Unpublished doctoral dissertation, Union Institute, Cincinnati.

Henniger, M. L. (1985). Preschool children's play behaviors in an indoor and outdoor environment. In J. L. Frost & S. Sunderlin (Eds.), *When children play* (pp. 145–149). Wheaton, MD: Association for Childhood Education International.

Henniger, M. L. (1994). Computers and preschool children's play: Are they compatible? *Journal of Computing in Childhood Education, 5,* 231–239.

Henricks, T. S. (1999). *Huizinga's legacy.* Paper presented at the 25th annual meeting of the Association for the Study of Play, Santa Fe, NM.

Hensel, J. (2002). What goes in must come out: Children's media violence consumption at home and aggressive behaviors at school. Paper presented at the *International Society for the Study of Behavioural Development Conference,* Ottawa, Ontario.

Hess, R. D., & Bear, R. M. (Eds.). (1968). *Early education.* Chicago: Aldine.

Hester, R. T. (1985) Subconscious landscapes in the heart. *Places, 2,* 10–22.

Hewitt, P. (1997). Games in instruction leading to environmentally responsible behavior. *Journal of Environmental Education, 28,* 35–37.

Hill, P., & McCune-Nicolich, L. M. (1981). Pretend play and patterns of cognition in Down's syndrome children. *Child Development, 52,* 611–617.

Hill, P. S., & Langdon, G. (1930). Nursery school procedures at Teachers College. *Revue internationale de l'enfant, 9*(53), 398–407.

Hilliard, D. C. (1998). Sport as play (and work). In D. P. Fromberg & D. Bergen (Eds.), *Play from birth to twelve and beyond: Contexts, perspectives, and meanings* (pp. 416–423). New York: Garland.

Hirsh-Pasek, K., & Golinkoff, R. M. (2003). Einstein never used flash cards. Retrieved March 12, 2004, from http://www.rodale.com

Hodge, D. C., & Price, G. R. (1978). Hearing damage risk criteria. In D. M. Lipscome (Ed.), *Noise and audiology* (pp. 167–191). Baltimore: University Park Press.

Hogan, P. (1995). *Philadelphia boyhood.* Vienna, VA: Holbrook & Kellogg.

Hohmann, C., & Weikart, D. P. (1995). *Educating young children: Active learning practices for preschool and child care programs.* Ypsilanti, MI: High/Scope Press.

Holloway, P. J., Myles-Nixon, C. & Johnson, W. M. (1998). *Identification, differentiation and intervention of the demographically diverse four year old: Strategies for rural special education* (EDRS, ED417917).

Holmberg, M. C. (1980). The development of social exchange patterns from 12 to 42 months. *Child Development, 51,* 618–626.

Holmes, R. (1999). Kindergarten and college students' view of play and work at home and at school. In S. Reifel (Ed.), *Play and Culture Studies: Vol. 2. Play contexts revisited* (pp. 59–72). Stamford, CT: Ablex.

Hoorn, J. V., Noorot, P. M., Scales, B., & Alward, K. R. (1999). *Play at the center of the curriculum.* Upper Saddle River, NJ: Merrill/Prentice Hall.

Hoover, E. (1976, January). Affection as an inoculation against aggression. *Human Behavior,* pp. 10–11.

Hopkins, B., & Westra, T. (1988). Maternal handling and motor development: An intracultural study. *Genetic, Social, and General Psychology Monographs, 14,* 377–420.

Hopper, T. F. (1996, October). *Play is what we desire in physical education. A phenomenological analysis.* (EDRS ED 398 805)

Howard, J., Greyrose, E., Kehr, K., Espinosa, M., & Beckwith, L. (1996). Teacher-facilitated microcomputer activities: Enhancing social play and affect in young children with disabilities. *Journal of Special Education Technology, 13,* 36–47.

Howes, C. (1983). Patterns of friendship. *Child Development, 54,* 1041–1053.

Howes, C. (1987). Social competence with peers in young children: Developmental sequences. *Developmental Review, 7,* 252–272.

Howes, C. (1987). Peer interaction of young children. *Monographs of the Society for Research in Child Development, 53*(1, Serial No. 217).

Howes, C. (1992). *The collaborative construction of pretend: Social pretend play functions.* Albany: State University of New York Press.

Howes, C., & Matheson, C. C. (1992). Sequences in the development of competent play with peers:

Social and social pretend play. *Developmental Psychology, 28,* 961–974.

Howes, C., & Smith, E. (1995). Relations among child care quality, teacher behavior, children's play activities, emotional security, and cognitive activity in child care. *Early Childhood Research Quarterly, 10,* 381–404.

Howes, C., Phillips, D., & Whitebrook, M. (1992). Thresholds of quality in child care centers and children's social and emotional development. *Child Development, 63,* 449–460.

Howes, C., Ritchie, S., & Bowman, B. (2002). *A matter of trust: Connecting teachers and learners in the early childhood classroom.* New York: Teachers College Press.

Howes, C., & Smith, E. W. (1995). Relations among child care quality, teacher behavior, children's play activities, emotional security, and cognitive activity in child care. *Early Childhood Research Quarterly, 10,* 381–404.

Howes, C., & Stewart, P. (1987). Child's play with adults, toys, and peers: An examination of family and child-care influences. *Developmental Psychology, 23,* 77–84.

Howes, C., Unger, O., & Seidner, L. B. (1989). Social pretend play in toddlers: Parallels with social play and with solitary pretend. *Child Development, 60,* 77–84.

Howes, C., & Wu, F. (1990). Peer interactions and friendships in an ethnically diverse school setting. *Child Development, 61,* 537–541.

Hrncir, E., Speller, G., & West, M. (1983). *What are we testing? A cross-cultural comparison of infant competence.* (ERIC Document Reproduction Service No. ED 230 309)

Hug-Hellmuth, H. (1921). On the technique of child analysis. *International Journal of Psychoanalysis, 2,* 287.

Hughes, B. (1998). Playwork in extremis: One of many applications of playwork's values, methods, and worth. In *Proceedings,* International World of Play Conference. San Antonio, TX: University of the Incarnate Word.

Hughes, F. P. (1995). *Children, play, and development.* Boston: Allyn & Bacon.

Hughes, F. P. (1998). Play in special populations. In O. N. Saracho & B. Spodek (Eds.), *Multiple perspectives on play in early childhood education.* Albany: State University of New York Press.

Hughes, M., Dote-Kwan, J., & Dolendo, J. (1998). A close look at the cognitive play of preschoolers with visual impairments in the home. *Exceptional Children, 64,* 451–462.

Hughes, P., & MacNaughton, G. (2001). Fractured or manufactured: Gendered identities and culture in the early years. In S. Grieshaber & G. Cannella (Eds.), *Embracing identities in early childhood education: Diversity and possibilities* (pp. 114–130). New York: Teachers College Press.

Huizinga, J. (1938). *Homo ludens: A study of the play-element in culture.* Boston: Beacon.

Huizinga, J. (1950). *Homo ludens.* Boston: Beacon. (Originally published 1938.)

Humphreys, A. P., & Smith, P. K. (1984). Rough-and-tumble in preschool and playground. In P. K. Smith (Ed.), *Play in animals and humans* (pp. 241–270). Oxford: Blackwell.

Hunt, J. M. (1961). *Intelligence and experience.* New York: Ronald.

Hupp, S. C., Boat, M. B., & Alpert, A. S. (1992). The impact of adult interaction on play behaviors and emotional responses of preschoolers with developmental delays. *Education and Training in Mental Retardation, 27,* 145–152.

Hutt, C. (1970). Specific and diverse exploration. In H. W. Reese & L. P. Lipsett (Eds.), *Advances in child development and behavior* (Vol. 5). New York: Academic Press.

Hutt, C. (1976). Exploration and play in children. In J. S. Bruner, A. Jolly, & K. Sylva (Eds.), *Play: Its role in development and evolution* (pp. 202–213). New York: Basic Books.

Hutt, S., Tyler, S., Hutt, C., & Christopherson, H. (1989). *Play, exploration, and learning: A natural history of the pre-school.* London: Routledge.

Huxley, A. (1954). *The doors of perception: Heaven and hell.* New York: Harper & Row.

Ihn, H. J. (1998). *Preschool children's play behaviors and equipment choices in an outdoor environment.* Unpublished research report, University of Texas, Austin.

Ikeda, D. (1979). *Glass children and other essays* (B. Watson, Trans.). Tokyo: Kodanska International.

International Association of Amusement Parks and Attractions (2003). Web site, http://www.saferparks.org

Iowa Child Welfare Research Station. (1934). *Manual of nursery school practice.* Iowa City: State University of Iowa.

Isaacson, R. L. (1954). *Recovery "?" from early brain damage*. Paper presented at the National Conference on Early Intervention with High Risk Infants and Young Children, University of North Carolina at Chapel Hill.

Isenberg, J. P., & Jalongo, M. R. (1997). *Creative expression and play in early childhood* (2nd ed.). Upper Saddle River, NJ: Merrill/Prentice Hall.

Izard, C. E. (1991). *The psychology of emotions*. New York: Plenum.

Jacobs, P. J. (1998). *A constructivist inquiry into the issues in the contemporary practice of playwork in England*. Unpublished doctoral dissertation, University of Texas, Austin.

Jacobson, W. (1940). Safety versus lawsuits. *Recreation, 34*(2).

Jambor, T. (1990). Promoting perceptual-motor development in young children's play. In S. C. Wortham & J. L. Frost (Eds.), *Playgrounds for young children: National survey and perspectives* (pp. 147–166). Reston, VA: American Alliance for Health, Physical Education, Recreation, and Dance.

Jambor, T. (1998). Challenge and risk-taking in play: In D. P. Fromberg & D. Bergen (Eds.), *Play from birth to twelve and beyond: Contexts, perspectives, and meanings* (pp. 319–323). New York: Garland.

James, O. O., (1997). *Play therapy: A comprehensive guide*. Northvale, NJ: Aronson.

Jampole, L., & Weber, M. K. (1987). An assessment of the behavior of sexually abused victims in anatomically correct dolls. *Child Abuse and Neglect, 11,* 187–192.

Janney, R. E., Snell, M. E., Beers, M. K., & Raynes, M. (1995). Integrating students with moderate and severe disabilities into general education classes. *Exceptional Children, 61,* 425–439.

Jarrett, O. S, (1997). Science and math through role-play centers in the elementary school classroom. *Science Activities, 34,* 13–19.

Jarrett, O. S., Farokhi, B., Young, C., & Davies, G. (2001). Boys and girls at play: Recess at a southern urban elementary school. In S. Reifel (Ed.), *Play and culture studies: Vol. 3. Play in and out of context* (pp. 147–170). Stamford, CT: Ablex.

Javernick, E. (1988). Johnny's not jumping: Can we help obese children? *Young Children, 43,* 18–23.

Jernberg, A. (1979). *Theraplay*. San Francisco: Jossey-Bass.

Jersild, A. T. (1933). *Child psychology*. New York: Prentice Hall.

Jersild, A. T. (1942). *Child psychology* (rev. ed.). New York: Prentice Hall.

Jersild, A. T. (1946). *Child psychology* (3rd ed.). New York: Prentice Hall.

Jersild, A. T., & Fite, M. D. (1939). *The influence of nursery school experience on children's social adjustments*. New York: Teachers College, Columbia University.

Jersild, A. T., Telford, C. W., & Sawrey, J. M. (1975). *Child psychology* (7th ed.). New York: Prentice Hall.

Jessee, P. O. (1991, Fall). Making hospitals less traumatic: Child life specialists. *Dimensions,* 23–24, 37.

Jessee, P. O., Wilson, H., & Morgan, D. (2000, Summer). Medical play for young children. *Childhood Education, 76,* 215–218.

Johnson, A. P. (1998). How to use creative dramatics in the classroom. *Childhood Education, 75,* 2–6.

Johnson, H. (1928). *Children in the nursery school*. New York: Agathon.

Johnson, J., & Roopnarine, J. (1983). The preschool classroom and sex differences in children's play. In M. Liss (Ed.), *Social and cognitive skills* (pp. 193–218). New York: Academic.

Johnson, J. E. (1976). Relations of divergent thinking and intelligence test scores with social and nonsocial make-believe play of preschool children. *Child Development, 47,* 1200–1203.

Johnson, J. E. (1998). Play development from ages four to eight. In D. Fromberg & D. Bergen (Eds.), *Play from birth to twelve and beyond: Contexts, perspectives, and meanings* (pp. 146–153). New York: Garland.

Johnson, J. E., Christie, J. F., & Yawkey, T. D. (1999). *Play and early childhood development* (2nd ed.). New York: Longman.

Johnson, L., McLeod, E. H., & Fall, M. (1997). Play therapy with labeled children in the schools. *Professional School Counseling, 1,* 31–34.

Johnson, R. G. (1993). High tech play therapy. In C. E. Schaefer & D. M. Cangelosi (Eds.), *Play therapy techniques* (pp. 281–286). Northvale, NJ: Aronson.

Johnston, S. M. (1997). The use of art and play therapy with victims of sexual abuse: A review of the literature. *Family Therapy, 24,* 101–113.

Jones, E. & Reynolds, G. (1992). *The play's the thing: Teacher's role in children's play*. New York: Teacher's College Press.

Jones, N. B. (1972). Categories of child-child interaction. In N. Blurton Jones (Ed.), *Ethological studies of child behaviour* (pp. 97–127). Cambridge: Cambridge University Press.

Jones, N. B. (1976). Rough-and-tumble-play among nursery school children. In J. S. Bruner, A. Jolly, & K. Sylva (Eds.), *Play: Its role in development and evolution* (pp. 352–363). New York: Basic Books.

Joyce, A. (1998, October 8). Fun and games becoming part of company cultures. *Austin American-Statesman*, pp. D-1–D-2.

Jung, C. G. (1954). *The practice of psychotherapy* (R. F. C. Hull, Trans.). New York: Pantheon.

Jwa, S., & Frost, J. L. (2003). Contextual differences in Korean mother-child interactions: A study of scaffolding behaviors. In D. Lytle (Ed.), *Play and culture studies: Vol. 5. Play and educational theory and practice* (pp. 299–322). Westport, CT: Praeger.

Kaduson, H. G., Cangelosi, D. M., & Schaefer, C. E. (Eds.). (1997). *The playing cure: Individualized play therapy for specific childhood problems*. Northvale, NJ: Aronson.

Kafai, Y. B. (1998). Play and technology. In D. P. Fromberg & D. Bergen (Eds.), *Play from birth to twelve and beyond: Contexts, perspectives, and meanings* (pp. 93–99). New York: Garland.

Kagan, J. (1977). The uses of cross-cultural research in early development. In P. H. Leiderman, S. R. Tulkin, & A. Rosenfeld (Eds.), *Culture and infancy: Variations in the human experience* (pp. 271–286). New York: Academic Press.

Kagan, J. (1994, October 5). The realistic view of biology and behavior. *Chronicle of Higher Education*, p. A64.

Kagan, J., Kearsley, R. B., & Zelazo, P. R. (1998). *Infancy: Its place in human development*. Cambridge, MA: Harvard University Press.

Kagan, J., Reznick, J. S., & Snidman, N. (1988). Biological basis of childhood shyness. *Science, 240,* 167–171.

Kalb, C., & Namuth, T. (1997, Spring–Summer). When a child's silence isn't golden. *Newsweek Special Edition,* p. 23.

Kamii, C., & DeClark, G. (1985). *Young children reinvent arithmetic: Implications of Piaget's theory*. New York: Teacher's College Press.

Kamii, C., & DeVries, R. (1980). *Group games in early education: Implications of Piaget's theory*. Washington, DC: National Association for the Education of Young Children.

Kamps, D. M., Kravits, T., Lopez, A., Kemmerer, K., Potucek, J., & Harrell, L. G. (1998). What do the peers think? Social validity of peer-mediated programs. *Education and Treatment of Children, 21,* 107–134.

Kaplan, M. (1998, June). Ten things theme parks won't tell you. *Smart Money,* pp. 137–145.

Katz, L. G. (1970). Teaching in preschools: Roles and goals. *Children, 17,* 43–48.

Katz, L. G. (1994). What can we learn from Reggio Emilia? In C. Edwards, L. Gandini, & G. Forman (Eds.), *The hundred languages of children: The Reggio Emilia approach to early childhood education* (pp. 19–37). Norwood, NJ: Ablex.

Katz, L. G. (1997). The challenges of the Reggio Emilia approach. In J. Hendrick (Ed.), *First steps toward teaching the Reggio way* (pp. 103–111). Upper Saddle River, NJ: Merrill/Prentice Hall.

Keesee, I. H. (1990). *A comparison of outdoor play environments for toddlers*. Unpublished doctoral dissertation, University of Texas, Austin.

Kelly, J. (1976). Work and leisure: A simplified paradigm. *Journal of Leisure Research, 4,* 50–62.

Kelly-Byrne, D. (1989). *A child's play life: An ethnographic study*. New York: Teachers College Press.

Kemple, K. M. (1991). Preschool children's peer acceptance and social interaction. *Young Children, 40*(5), 47–54.

Kendrick, A., Kaufman, R., & Messenger, K. (1991). *Healthy young children*. Washington, DC: NAEYC.

Kieff, J. E., & Casbergue, R. M. (2000). *Playful learning and teaching*. Boston: Allyn & Bacon.

Kilpatrick, W. H. (1916). *Froebel's kindergarten principles: Critically examined*. New York: Macmillan.

Kimmerle, M., Mick, L. A., & Michel, G. E. (1995). Bimanual role-differentiated toy play during infancy. *Infant Behavior and Development, 18,* 299–307.

Kinder, M. (1991). *Playing with power.* Berkeley: University of California Press.

King, N. R. (1982). Work and play in the classroomn. *Social Organization, 46,* 110–113.

King, P., & Ekstein, R. (1967). The search for ego controls: Progression of play activity in psychotherapy with a schizophrenic child. *Psychoanalytic Review, 54,* 25–37.

Kingson, J. F. (1996). Playing for keeps: Supporting children's play. *Topics in Early Childhood Education, 2,* 25–50.

Kleiber, D., & Barnett, L. A. (1980). Leisure in childhood. *Young Children, 35*(5), 47–53.

Klein, M. (1932). *The psychoanalysis of children*. London: Hogarth.

Klein, M. (1955). The psychoanalytic play technique. *American Journal of Orthopsychiatry, 25,* 223–237.

Klenk, L. (2001). Playing with literacy in preschool classrooms. *Childhood Education, 77,* 150–157.

Knapp, R. F., & Hartsoe, C. E. (1979). *Play for America: the National Recreation Association 1906–1965.* Arlington, VA: National Recreation and Park Association.

Kochanska, G. (1993). Toward a synthesis of parental socializations and child temperament in early development of conscience. *Child Development, 64,* 325–347.

Kohlberg, L. (1966). A cognitive-developmental analysis of children's sex role concepts and attitudes. In E. E. Maccoby (Ed.), *The development of sex differences* (pp. 82–172). Stanford, CA: Stanford University Press.

Kontos, S., & Dunn, L. (1993). Caregiver practices and beliefs in child care varying in developmental appropriateness and quality. In S. Reifel (Ed.), *Advances in early education and day care: Vol. 5. Perspectives on developmentally appropriate practice* (pp. 53–74). Greenwich, CT: JAI.

Kontos, S., & Fiene, R. (1987). Child care quality compliance with regulations, and children's development: The Pennsylvania Study. In D. A. Phillips (Ed.), *Quality and childcare: What does research tell us?* (pp. 57–79). Washington, DC: National Association for the Education of Young Children.

Kontos, S., Moore, S., & Giorgetti, K. The ecology of inclusion. *Topics in Early Childhood Special Education, 18,* 38–48.

Kottman, T. (2001). *Play therapy: Basics and beyond.* Alexandria, VA American Counseling Association.

Kottman, T. (2003). Partners I play: *An Adlerian approach to play therapy.* Alexandria, VA: American Counseling Assocition.

Kozub, F. M., & Porretta, D. (1996). Including athletes with disabilities: Interscholastic athletic benefits for all. *Journal of Physical Education, Recreation & Dance, 67,* 19–24.

Kryter, K. D. (1970) *The effects of noise on man.* New York: Academic Press.

Kryter, K. D. (1994). *The handbook of hearing and the effects of noise: Physiology, psychology, and public health.* New York: Academic Press.

Kuschner, D. (2001). The dangerously radical concept of free play. In S. Reifel & M. Brown (Eds.), *Advances in early education and day care: Vol. 11. Early education and care, and reconceptualizing play* (pp. 275–293). Oxford, UK: JAI/Elsevier Science.

Kutska, K. S., & Hoffman, K. J. (1992). *Playground safety is no accident.* Arlington, VA: National Recreation and Park Association.

Kuykendall, J. (1996, January). Is gun play OK for kids? *Education Digest,* pp. 12–15.

Ladd, G., & Price, J. (1993). Play styles of peer-accepted and peer-rejected children on the playground. In C. Hart (Ed.), *Children on playgrounds* (pp. 130–161). Albany: State University of New York Press.

Ladd, G. W., & Hart, C. H. (1992). Creating informal play opportunities: Are parents' and preschoolers' initiation related to children's competence with peers? *Developmental Psychology, 28,* 1179–1187.

Lambert, J. (1992). *Adventure playgrounds: A book for play leaders.* N.p.: Out of Order Books.

Lancy, D. F. (1996). *Playing on the mother-ground: Cultural routines for children's development.* New York: Guilford.

Lancy, D. F. (2002). Cultural constraints on children's play. In J. L. Roopnarine (Ed.), *Play and culture studies: Vol. 4. Social-cognitive and contextual issues in the fields of play* (pp. 53–60). Westport, CT: Ablex.

Landreth, G. L. (1991). *Play therapy: The art of the relationship.* Bristol, PA: Accelerated Development.

Landreth, G. L. (1998). *Child centered play therapy: A clinical session* [videotape]. Denton: University of North Texas Center for Play Therapy.

Landreth, G. L. (Ed.). (2001). *Innovations in play therapy: Issues, process, and special populations.* Philadelphia: Taylor & Francis.

Landreth, G., & Hohmeyer, L. (1998). Play as the language of children's feelings. In D. P. Fromberg & D. Bergen (Eds.), *Play from birth to twelve and beyond: Contexts, perspectives, and meanings* (pp. 193–198). New York: Garland.

Landreth, G., Hohmeyer, L., Bratton, S., & Kale, A. (Eds.). (1995). *The world of play therapy literature: A definitive guide to authors and subjects in the field* (2nd ed.). Denton: University of North Texas Center for Play Therapy.

Leaper, C. (1994). Exploring the consequence of gender segregation on social relationships. In C. Leaper (Ed.), W. Damon (Series Ed.), *New directions for child development: Vol. 65. Childhood gender segregation: Causes and consequences* (pp. 67–86). San Francisco: Jossey-Bass.

Learning Channel. (1998, October 18). *Adventures for your mind.*

Lee, J. (1927). Play, the architect of man. *The Playground, 21,* 460–463.

Lefever, A., Wolfgang, C., & Koorland, M. (1992). Sociodramatic play as a method for enhancing language performance of kindergarten age students. Early Childhood Research Quarterly, 7, 256–262.

Lefever, H. (1981). "Playing the dozens": A mechanism for social control. *Phylon, 42,* 73–85.

Leslie, A. M. (1987). Pretense and representation: The origins of "theory of mind." *Psychological Review, 94,* 412–426.

Levenstein, P. (1988). *Mother-child home program.* Columbus: Ohio State University Press.

Le Vieux, J. (1999). Group play therapy with grieving children. In L. E. Homeyer (Ed.), *The handbook of group play therapy: How to do it, how it works, whom it's best for.* San Francisco: Jossey-Bass.

Levitt, E. E. (1957). The results of psychotherapy with children, an evaluation. *Journal of Consulting Psychology, 21,* 189–196.

Levy, A., Wolfgang, C., & Koorland, M. (1992). Sociodramatic play as a method for enhancing language performance of kindergarten age students. *Early Childhood Research Quarterly, 7,* 245–262.

Levy, D. M. (1939). Trends in therapy III: Release therapy. *American Journal of Orthopsychiatry, 9,* 713–736.

Lewis, C. C. (1994). The roots of discipline in Japanese preschools: Meeting children's needs for friendship and contribution. In S. Reifel (Ed.), *Advances in early education and day care: Vol. 6. Topics in early literacy, teacher preparation, and international perspectives on early care* (pp. 259–278). Greenwich, CT: JAI.

Lewis, V., & Boucher, J. (1988). Spontaneous, instructed and elicited play in relatively able autistic children. *British Journal of Developmental Psychology, 6,* 325–339.

Lickona, T. (2000). Sticks and stones may break my bones AND names will hurt me. Thirteen ways to prevent peer cruelty. *Our children, 26,* 12–14.

Lieberman, J. N. (1965). Playfulness and divergent thinking: An investigation of their relationship at the kindergarten level. *Journal of Genetic Psychology, 107,* 219–224.

Lillard, A. S. (1993). Pretend play skills and the child's theory of mind. *Child Development, 64,* 348–371.

Lillard, A. S. (1998a). Wanting to be it: Children's understanding of intentions underlying pretense. *Child Development, 69,* 979–991.

Lillard, A. S. (1998b). Playing with a theory of mind. In O. N. Saracho & B. Spodek (Eds.), *Multiple perspectives on play in early childhood* (pp. 11–33). Albany: State University of New York.

Lillard, A. S. (2000). Pretending, understanding pretense, and understanding minds. In S. Reifel (Ed.), *Play and culture studies: Vol. 3. Play in and out of context.* Stamford, CT: Ablex.

Lin, S.-H., & Reifel, S. (1999). Context and meanings in Taiwanese kindergarten play. In S. Reifel (Ed.), *Play and Culture Studies: Vol. 2. Play contexts revisited* (Vol. 2, pp. 151–176). Stamford, CT: Ablex.

Lincoln, B. (1989). *Discourse and the construction of society: Comparative studies of myth, ritual, and classification.* New York: Oxford University Press.

Lindemann, P. (1992, May). The Americans with Disabilities ACT (ADA) is now law. *ASTM Standardization News,* pp. 48–51.

Linder, T. (1990). *Transdisciplinary play-based assessment: A functional approach to working with young children.* Baltimore, MD: Brookes.

Lindsey, E. W., Mize, J. (2001). Contextual differences in parent-child play: Implications for children's gender role development. *Sex Roles: A Journal of Research, 44*(3-4), 55–76.

Lindsey, E. W., Mize, J., & Pettit. G. S. (1997). Differential play patterns of mothers and fathers of sons and daughters: Implications for children's gender role development. *Sex Roles, 37,* 643–661.

Lipton, M. A. (1974). *Early experience and plasticity of the central nervous system.* Paper presented at the National Conference on Early Intervention with High Risk Infants and Young Children, University of North Carolina at Chapel Hill.

Locke, J. (1968). *Some thoughts on education.* Cambridge: Cambridge University Press. (Originally published 1693.)

Locke, P. A., & Levin, J. (1998). Creative play . . . begins with fun objects, your imagination, and simple-to-use technology. *The Exceptional Parent, 28,* 36–40.

Lockman, J. J., & McHale, J. P. (1989). Object manipulation in infancy: Developmental and contextual determinants. In J. J. Lockman & N. L. Hazen (Eds.), *Action in social context: Perspectives on early development* (pp. 129–167). New York: Plenum.

Lombardino, L., Stein, J., Kricos, P., & Wolf, M. (1986). Play diversity and structural relationships in the play and language of language-impaired and language-normal preschoolers: Preliminary data. *Journal of Communication Disorders, 19,* 475–489.

London Handicapped Adventure Playground Association. (1978). *Adventure playgrounds for handicapped children*. Unbridge, England: Bamber.

Long, K. (1997, June 4). Baby's brain begins distinguishing life experiences very early. *Austin American-Statesman*, pp. E-4, E-6.

Lonsdale, S. (1993). *Dance and ritual play in Greek religion*. Baltimore, MD: Johns Hopkins University Press.

Loo, C., & Kennelly, D. (1979). Social density: Its effects on behaviors and perceptions of preschoolers. *Environmental Psychology and Non-Verbal Behavior, 3,* 131–146.

Lott, D. H. (1998). Brain development, attachment, and impact of psychic vulnerability. *Psychiatric Times, xv*. Retrieved June, 1999, from http://babyparenting.about.com

Lovell, K., Hoyle, H., & Siddall, M. (1968). A study of some aspects of the play and language of young children with delayed speech. *Journal of Child Psychology and Psychiatry, 9,* 41–50.

Lowenfeld, V. (1939). *The nature of creative activity*. New York: Harcourt, Brace.

Lowenfeld, V. (1947). *Creative and mental growth*. New York: Macmillan.

Lowenfeld, V. (1947). For an education based on relationships. *Young Children, 49,* 9–12.

Lowenthal, B. (1999). Effects of maltreatment and ways to promote children's resiliency. *Childhood Education, 75,* 204–209.

Luebke, J., Epstein, M. H., & Cullinan, D. (1987). First- and second-order factor analyses of the Behavior Problem Checklist with behaviorally disordered pupils. *Behavioral Disorders, 12,* 193–197.

Lutz, P. (1983). The stepfamily: An adolescent perspective. *Family Relations, 32,* 367–375.

Maccoby, E. E. (1988). Gender as a social category. *Developmental Psychology, 24,* 755–756.

Maccoby, E. E. (1990). Gender and relationships: A developmental account. *American Psychologist, 45,* 513–520.

Maccoby, E. E. (1998). Gender as social category. *Developmental Psychology, 24,* 755–765.

Maccoby, E. E., & Jacklin, C. N. (1974). *The psychology of sex differences*. Stanford, CA: Stanford University Press.

MacDonald, K., & Parke, R. (1984). Bridging the gap: Parent-child play interaction and peer interactive competence. *Child Development, 55,* 1265–1277.

MacNaughton, G. (1997). Who's got the power? Rethinking equity strategies in early childhood. *International Journal of Early Years Education, 5,* 57–66.

MacNaughton, G. (1999). Even pink tents have glass ceilings: Crossing the gender boundaries in pretend play. In E. Dau & E. Jones (Eds.), *Child's play: Revisiting play in early childhood settings*. Australia New South Wales. (ERIC Document Reproduction Services No. ED 433 969).

Mahler, M. S., Pine, F., & Bergman, A. (1976). *The psychological birth of the human infant: Symbiosis and individuation*. New York: Basic Books.

Malkusak, T., Schappet, J., & Bruya, L. (2002, April). Turning accessible playgrounds into fully integrated playgrounds. *Parks and recreation, 37*(4), 66–69.

Malone, D. M., & Stoneman, Z. (1990). Cognitive play of mentally retarded preschoolers: Observations in the home and school. *American Journal on Mental Retardation, 94,* 475–487.

Malone, T. W., & Lepper, M. R. (1987). Making learning fun: A taxonomy of intrinsic motivations for learning. In R. E. Snow & M. J. Farr (Eds.), *Aptitude, learning and instruction* (Vol. 3, pp. 223–253). Hillsdale, NJ: Erlbaum.

Mandler, J. M., Bauer, P. J., & McDonough, L. (1991). Separating the sheep from the goats: Differentiating global categories. *Cognitive Psychology, 23,* 263–298.

Mann, E., & McDermott, J. F. (1983). Play therapy for victims of child abuse and neglect. In C. E. Schaefer & K. L. O'Conner (Eds.), *Handbook of play therapy* (pp. 283–307). New York: Wiley.

Manning, M. L. (1993). *Developmentally appropriate middle level schools*. Wheaton, MD: Association for Childhood Education International.

Manning, M. L. (1998). Play development from ages eight to twelve. In D. P. Fromberg & D. Bergen (Eds.), *Play from birth to twelve and beyond: Contexts, perspectives, and meanings* (pp. 154–162). New York: Garland.

Marriott, M. (1998, March). When love turns to obsession, games are no game. *New York Times*, p. D8.

Marshall, H. R. (1961). Relations between home experiences and children's use of language in play interaction with peers. *Psychological Monographs, 75*(5), no. 509.

Marshall, H. R., & Hahn, S. (1967). Experimental modification of dramatic play. *Journal of Personality and Social Psychology, 5,* 119–122.

Martini, M. (1994). Peer interactions in Polynesia: A view from the Marquesas. In J. L. Roopnarine, J. E. Johnson, & F. H. Hooper (Eds.), *Children's play in diverse cultures* (pp. 73–103). Albany: State University of New York Press.

Maslow, A. H. (1962). Some basic propositions of a growth and self-actualization psychology. In A.S.C.D. *Yearbook: Perceiving, Behaving, Becoming* (pp.34–49). Washington, DC: Association for Supervision and Curriculum Development.

McCall, R. (1979). *Infants*. Cambridge, MA: Harvard University Press.

McCaslin, N. (1990). *Creative drama in the classroom*. White plains, NY: Longman.

McConnell, W. H., Parks, J. T., & Knapp, L. W. (1973). *Public playground equipment (The Iowa Study)*. Washington, DC: Consumer Product Safety Commission.

McCune, L. (1985). Play-language relationships and symbolic development. In C. C. Brown & A. W. Gottfried (Eds.), *Play interactions: The role of toys and parental involvement in children's development* (pp. 28–45). Skillman, NJ: Johnson & Johnson Baby Products.

McCune, L. (1986). Symbolic development in normal and atypical infants. In G. Fein & M. Rivkin (Eds.), *The young child at play. Reviews of research* (Vol. 4, pp. 45–62). Washington, DC: National Association for the Education of Young Children.

McLerran, A., & Cooney, B. (1991). *Roxaboxen*. New York: Penguin.

McLoyd, V. (1980). Verbally expressed modes of transformation in the fantasy play of black preschool children. *Child Development, 51,* 1133–1139.

McLoyd, V. (1983). Class, culture, and pretend play: A reply to Sutton-Smith and Smith. *Developmental Review, 3,* 11–17.

McLoyd, V. (1986a). Scaffolds or shackles? The role of toys in preschool children's pretend play. In G. Fein & M. Rivkin (Eds.), *The young child at play: Reviews of research* (Vol. 4, pp. 63–78). Washington, DC: National Association for the Education of Young Children.

McLoyd, V. C. (1986). Social class and pretend play. In A. W. Gottfried & C. C. Brown (Eds.), *Play interactions: The contributions of play materials and parental involvement to children's development* (pp. 175–193). Lexington, MA: Heath.

Mclure, J. (2003, July 14). Education: Summa cum laude in grand theft auto? *Newsweek,* p. 10.

Mead, G. H. (1934). *Mind, self and society*. Chicago: University of Chicago Press.

Meckley, A. (1995). Studying children's social play through a child cultural approach: Roles, rules, and shared knowledge. In S. Reifel (Ed.), *Advances in early education and day care* (Vol. 7, pp. 179–211). Greenwich, CT: JAI.

Medrich, E., Roizen, J., Rubin, V. & Buckley, S. (1982). *The serious business of growing up*. Los Angeles: University of California Press.

Mellou, E. (1994). Tutored-untutored dramatic play: Similarities and differences. *Early Child Development and Care, 100,* 119–130.

Meltz, B. F. (2003, November 22). Toddlers' hours with T.V. erode their development. *Austin American-Statesman*. From *Boston Globe.*

Melzack, R., & Scott, T. H. (1957). The effects of early experience on the response to pain. *Journal of Comparative and Physiological Psychology, 50,* 155–161.

Melzack, R., & Thompson, W. R. (1956). Effects of early experience on social behavior. *Canadian Journal of Psychology, 10,* 82–90.

Mendez, F. J., & Garcia, M. J. (1996). Emotive performances: A treatment package for children's phobias. *Child & Family Behavior Therapy, 3,* 19–34.

Mergen, B. (1995). Past play: Relics, memory, and history. In A. D. Pellegrini (Ed.), *The future of play theory* (pp. 257–274). Albany: State University of New York Press.

Mero, E. B. (1908). *American playgrounds: Their construction, equipment, maintenance and utility*. Boston: American Gymnasia.

Mervis, C. B., & Crisafi, M. A. (1982). Order of acquisition of subordinate-, basic-, and superordinate-level categories. *Child Development, 53,* 258–266.

Mierzwinski, E., Fise, M. E., & Morrison, M. (1996). *Playing it safe: A third nationwide safety survey of public playgrounds*. Washington, DC: U.S. Public Interest Research Group and Consumer Federation of America.

Miller, J. D. (1974). Effects of noise on people. *Journal of the Acoustical Society of America, 56,* 729–764.

Miller, L. B., & Bizzell, R. P. (1983). Long-term effects of four preschool programs: Sixth, seventh, and eighth grades. In J. Trawick-Smith (Ed.), *Preschool education* (pp. 41–56). Bloomington, IN: Phi Delta Kappa.

Miller, P. H. (1993). *Theories of developmental psychology* (3rd ed.). New York: Freeman.

Miller, S. M., Fernie, D., & Kantor, R. (1992). Distinctive literacies in different preschool contexts. *Play & Culture, 5,* 107–119.

Milne, A. A. (1928). *House at Pooh corner*. New York: Dutton.

Mindes, G. (1982). Social and cognitive aspects of play in young handicapped children. *Topics in Early Childhood Special Education, 2,* 39–52.

Minuchin, P., Biber, B., Shapiro, E., & Zimiles, H. (1969). *The psychological impact of school experience*. New York: Basic Books.

Mitchell, L. S. (1950). *Our children and our schools*. New York: Simon & Schuster.

Moller, L. C., & Serbin, L. A. (1996). Antecedents of toddler gender segregation: Cognitive consonance, gender-typed toy preferences and behavioral compatibility. *Sex Roles, 28,* 136–147.

Moller, L. C., Hymel, S., & Rubin, K. H. Sex typing in play and popularity in middle childhood. *Sex Roles, 26,* 331–353.

Montare, A., & Boone, S. (1980). Aggression and paternal absence: Racial-ethnic differences among inner-city boys. *Journal of Genetic Psychology, 137,* 223–232.

Montessori, M. (1913). *Pedagogical anthropology*. New York: F.A. Stokes.

Montessori, M. (1917). *The advanced Montessori method: Vol. 1. Spontaneous activity in education*. New York: F. A. Stokes.

Montessori, M. (1964). *The Montessori method*. New York: Schocken Books.

Montessori, M. (1995). *The absorbent mind*. New York: Henry Holt.

Moore, G. T. (1987). The physical environment and cognitive development in child care centers. In C. S. Weinstein & T. G. David (Eds.), *Spaces for children: the built environment and child development* (pp. 117–138). New York: Plenum.

Moore, G. T., & Marans, R. W. (1997). *Advances in environment, behavior, and design*. New York: Plenum.

Moore, M. R. (1992). *An analysis of outdoor play environments and play behaviors*. Unpublished doctoral dissertation, University of Texas, Austin.

Moore, N. V., Evertson, C. D., & Brophy, J. E. (1974). Solitary play: Some functional reconsiderations. *Developmental Psychology, 10,* 830–834.

Moore, R. (1974, October). Anarchy zone: Encounters in a school yard. *Landscape Architecture,* pp. 364–369.

Moore, R. C., Goltsman, S. M., & Iacofano, D. S. (Eds.). (1987). *Play for all guidelines: Planning, design, and management of outdoor play settings for all children*. Berkeley, CA; MIG Communications.

Moore, R. C., & Wong, H. H. (1997). *Natural learning: Creating environments for rediscovering nature's way of teaching*. Berkeley, CA: MIG Communications.

Moore, S. G. (1967). Correlates of peer acceptance in nursery school children. In W. W. Hartrup & N. L. Smothergill (Eds.), *The young child: Reviews of research* (Vol. 1, pp. 229–247). Washington, DC: National Association for the Education of Young Children.

Morgan, J. J. B. (1935). *Child psychology*. New York: Farrar & Rinehart.

Morrow, L. M. (1997). *Literacy development in the early years* (3rd ed.). Boston: Allyn & Bacon.

Morrow, L. M., & Rand, M. K. (1991). Preparing the classroom environment to promote literacy during play. In J. Christie (Ed.), *Play and early literacy development* (pp. 141–165). Albany: State University of New York Press.

Morrow, L. M., & Rand, M. K. (1991). Promoting literacy through play through physical design changes. *Reading Teacher, 44,* 396–402.

Moucha, S., Crawford, S., Drause, J., Stein J. V., et al. (1997). Can students with disabilities be adequately accommodated in today's physical education classes? *Journal of Physical Education, Recreation & Dance, 68,* 7–14.

Moustakas, C. E. (1951). Situational play therapy with normal children. *Journal of Consulting Psychology, 15,* 225–230.

Moustakas, C. E. (1953). *Children in play therapy*. New York: McGraw-Hill.

Moustakas, C. E. (1998). *Reflections on relationship play therapy* [videotape]. Denton: University of North Texas Center for Play Therapy.

Mullen, M. R. (1984). Motor development and child's play. In T. D. Yawkey & A. D. Pellegrini (Eds.), *Child's play and play therapy,* (pp. 7–16). Lancaster, PA: TECHNOMIC.

Muller, A. A., & Perlmutter, M. (1985). Preschool children's problem-solving interactions at computers and jigsaw puzzles. *Journal of Applied Developmental Psychology, 6,* 173–186.

Mullin, C. R., & Linz, D. (1995). Desensitization and resensitization to violence against women: Effects of exposure to sexually violent films on judgements of domestic violent victims. *Journal of Personality and Social Psychology, 69,* 449–459.

Mundy, L. (1957). Therapy with physically and mentally handicapped children in a mental deficiency hospital. *Journal of Clinical Psychology, 13,* 3–9.

Myers, C. L., McBride, S. L., & Peterson, C. A. (1996). Transdisciplinary play-based assessment in early childhood special education: an examination of social validity. *Topics in Early Childhood Special Education, 16,* 102–126.

Myers, G. D. (1985). Motor behavior of kindergartners during physical education and free play. In J. L. Frost & S. Sunderlin, (Eds.), *When children play* (pp. 151–156). Wheaton, MD: Association for Childhood Education International.

Myers, J. B. (1981). *Children's perceived vs. actual choices of playground equipment as viewed by themselves and their teachers*. Unpublished doctoral dissertation, University of Texas, Austin.

Nabhan, G. P., & Trimble, S. (1994). *The geography of childhood: Why children need wild places*. Beacon.

Naisbitt, J. (1994). *Global paradox*. New York: Avon.

Nash, J. M. (1997, February 3). Fertile minds. *Time: Special Report,* pp. 48–56.

National Association for the Education of Young Children. (1988). *Testing of young children: Concerns and cautions*. Washington, DC: Author.

National Association for the Education of Young Children. (1996). Position statement: Technology and young children—ages three through eight. *Young Children, 51*(6), 11–16.

National Association for the Education of Young Children. (1998). *Accreditation criteria and procedures of the National Association for the Education of Young Children.* Washington, DC: NAEYC.

National Association for the Education of Young Children (1998). Early years are learning years: The Internet and young children. Retrieved March 29, 2004, from http://www.naeyc.org/resources/eyly/1998/18.htm

National Center for Injury Prevention and Control. (1999). *Childhood injury fact sheet.* Atlanta, GA: Author. Retrieved March 29, 2004, from http://www.cdc.gov/ncipc/

National Center for Injury Prevention and Control. (2003a). *Playground injuries*. Atlanta, GA: Author. Retrieved March 29, 2004, from http://www.cdc.gov/ncipc/

National Center for Injury Prevention and Control. (2003b). *Water-related injuries*. Atlanta, GA: Author. Retrieved March 29, 2004, from http://www.cdc.gov/ncipc/

National Coalition on Television Violence. (1985, May–June). N.C.T.V. News, 6.

National Program for Playground Safety. (1999). *Playground Safety*. Cedar Rapids, IA: Author.

National Recreation Association. (1931). *Report of Committee on Standards in Playground Apparatus* (Bulletin 2170). New York: Author.

National Recreation and Park Association. (1976) *Proposed safety standard for public playground equipment*. Washington, DC: Consumer Product Safety Commission.

National Safety Council. (1999). *Injury facts*. Itasca, IL: Author.

National Safety Council. (2002). *National Safety Council fireworks advisory*. Itasca, IL: Author. Retrieved May, 2002, from http://www.nsf.org

National Safety Council. (2003). *Amusement ride injury statistics*. News report. Itasca, IL: Author. Retrieved July, 2003, from http://www.nsf.org

National School Boards Foundation (2002). Research and guidelines for children's use of the Internet. Retrieved March 29, 2004, from http://www.nsbf.org/safe-smart/full-report.htm

National Spa and Pool Institute. (1991). *American national standard for public swimming pools*. Alexandria, VA: Author.

National Spa and Pool Institute. (1992). *American national standard for aboveground/onground residential swimming pools*. Alexandria, VA: Author.

Nelson, K. (1989). *Narratives from the crib*. Cambridge, MA: Harvard University Press.

Nelson, K., & Seidman, S. (1984). Playing with scripts. In I. Bretherton (Ed.), *Symbolic play: The development of social understanding* (pp. 45–72). New York: Academic Press.

Neppl, T. K., & Murray, A. D. (1997). Social dominance and play patterns among preschoolers: Gender comparisons. *Sex Roles, 36,* 381–393.

Neuberger, J. J. (1997). Brain development research. *Young Children, 52,* 4–9.

Neuman, S., & Roskos, K. (1991). Peers as literacy informants: A description of young children's literacy conversations in play. *Early Childhood Research Quarterly, 6,* 233–248.

Neuman, S. B., & Roskos, K. (1993). Literacy knowledge in practice: Contexts of participation for young writers and readers. *Reading Research Quarterly, 32,* 10–33.

Nevius, J. (1982). Social participation and culture in play groups of young children. *Journal of Social Psychology, 116,* 291–292.

Nevius, J., Filgo, D., Soldier, L., & Simmons-Rains, B. (1983). Relation of social participation to activity in young children's free choice play. *Educational & Psychological Research, 3,* 95–102.

New, R. (1993). Cultural variations in developmentally appropriate practice. In C. Edwards, L. Gandini, & G. Forman (Eds.), *The hundred languages of children: The Reggio Emilia approach to early childhood education* (pp. 60–69). Norwood, NJ: Ablex.

New, R. S. (1994). Child's play—*una cosanaturale:* An Italian perspective. In J. L. Roopnarine, J. E. Johnson, & F. H. Hooper (Eds.), *Children's play in diverse cultures* (pp. 123–147). Albany: State University of New York Press.

Newman, D., Griffin, P., & Cole, M. (1989). *The construction zone: Working for cognitive change in school*. Cambridge: Cambridge University Press.

Newman, J., Brody, P. J., & Beauchamp, H. M. (1996). Teachers' attitudes and policies regarding play in elementary schools. *Psychology in the Schools, 33,* 61–69.

Newsweek. (1997, Spring–Summer). Special issue on children.

Nicholich, L. M. (1977). Beyond sensorimotor intelligence: Assessment of symbolic maturity through analysis of pretend play. *Merrill-Palmer Quarterly, 23,* 89–99.

Nicholson, M. (1971). *Adventure playgrounds*. London: National Playing Fields Association.

Nicolopoulou, A., Scales, G., & Weintraub, J. (1990). Gender differences in the symbolic imagination in stories of four-year-olds. In A. Dyson & C. Genishi (Eds.), *The need for story: Cultural diversity in classroom and community* (pp. 102–123). Urbana, IL: National Council of Teachers of English.

Nwokah, E. E., & Ikekeonwu, C. (1998). A sociocultural comparison of Nigerian and American children's games. In M. Duncan, G. Chick, & A. Aycock (Eds.), S. Reifel (Series Ed.), *Play and culture studies: Vol. 1. Diversions and divergences in fields of play* (pp. 59–76). Greenwich, CT: Ablex.

O'Brien, J., Boatwright, T., Chaplin, J., Geckler, C., Gosnell, D., Holcombe, J., & Parrish, K. (1998). The impact of positioning equipment on play skills of physically impaired children. In S. Reifel (Ed.), *Play and culture studies: Vol. 1. Diversions and divergences in fields of play* (pp. 149–159). Greenwich, CT: Ablex.

O'Brien, L. M. (2003). The rewards and restrictions of recess: Reflections on being a playground volunteer. *Childhood Education, 79,* 161–168.

O'Connor, K. J. (1991, 2000). *The play therapy primer: An integration of theories and techniques*. New York: Wiley.

Olds, A. (1987). Designing spaces for infants and toddlers. In C. Weinstein & T. David (Eds.), *Spaces for children: The built environment and child development*. New York: Plenum.

Olds, A. R. (1989). Psychological and physiological harmony in child care centers. *Children's Environments Quarterly, 6,* 8–16.

Olds, A. R., & Daniel, P. A. (1987). *Child health care facilities: Design guidelines*. Washington, DC: Association for the Care of Children's Health.

Ollendick, T. H., Weist, M. D., Borden, M. C., & Greene, R. W. (1992). Sociometric status and academic, behavioral, and psychological adjustment: A five-year longitudinal study. *Journal of Consulting and Clinical Psychology, 60,* 80–87.

Olson, M. R. (1981). Enhancing the exploratory behavior of visually impaired preschoolers. *Journal of Visual Impairment & Blindness, 75,* 375–377.

Olson, M. R. (1983). A study of the exploratory behavior of legally blind and sighted preschoolers. *Exceptional Children, 50,* 130–138.

Olweus, D. (1993). Bullies on the playground: The role of victimization. In C. Hart (Ed.), *Children on playgrounds* (pp. 85–128). Albany: State University of New York Press.

Olweus, D. (1993). *Bullying at school: What we know and what we can do*. Oxford: Blackwell.

Olweus, D. (1994). Annotation: Bullying at school: Basic facts and effects of a school-based intervention program. *Journal of Child Psychology and Psychiatry, 35,* 1171–1190.

Olweus, D. (1997). Bully/victim problems in school: Facts and intervention. *European Journal of Psychology of Education, 12,* 495–510.

O'Neill-Wagner, P., Bolig, R., & Price, C. S. (2001). Developmental aspects of play-partner selection in young rhesus monkeys. In J. L. Roopnarine (Ed.), *Play and culture studies: Vol. 4. Conceptual, social-cognitive, and contextual issues in the fields of play* (pp.111-126). Westport, CT: Ablex.

Opie, I. (1993). *The people in the playground*. New York: Oxford University Press.

Opie, I., & Opie, P. (1959). *The lore and language of schoolchildren*. New York: Oxford University Press.

Opie, I., & Opie, P. (1969). *Children's games in street and playground*. New York: Oxford University Press.

Opie, I., & Opie, P. (1997). *Children's games with things*. New York: Oxford University Press.

Oravic, J. A. (Winter 2000/01). Interactive toys and children's education. *Childhood Education, 77,* 81–85.

Ounce of Prevention Fund. (1996). *Starting smart: How early experiences affect brain development*. Chicago: Author.

Owens, K. D., & Sanders, R. L. (1998). Severe weather game. *Science Activities, 35,* 9–12.

Paley, V. (1981). *Wally's stories*. Cambridge, MA: Harvard University Press.

Paley, V. G. (1981). *Boys and girls: Superheros in the doll corner*. Chicago: University of Chicago Press.

Paley, V. G. (1992). *You can't say you can't play*. Cambridge, MA: Harvard University Press.

Palmer, L. A. (1916). *Play life in the first eight years*. Boston: Ginn.

Palmer, P. (1986). *The lively audience*. Sydney: Allen & Unwin.

Pan, H.-L. W. (1994). Children's play in Taiwan. In J. L. Roopnarine, J. E. Johnson, & F. H. Hooper (Eds.), *Children's play in diverse cultures* (pp. 31–50). Albany: State University of New York Press.

Parette, H. P., Jr., & Murdick, N. L. (1998). Assistive technology and IEPs for young children with disabilities. *Early Childhood Education Journal, 25,* 193–196.

Park, Y. S. (1998). *Preschool children's play behaviors and equipment choices on two playgrounds*. Unpublished master's thesis, University of Texas, Austin.

Parke, R. D., & Tinsley, B. R. (1981). The father's role in infancy: Determinants of involvement in caregiving and play. In M. E. Lamb (Ed.), *The role of the father in child development* (2nd ed., pp. 429–458). New York: Wiley.

Parks and Recreation. (1998). [Special issue on aquatic safety.] *33*(2).

Parsons, S. (1986). Function of play in low vision children (Part 2): Emerging patterns of behavior. *Journal of Visual Impairment & Blindness, 80,* 777–784.

Parten, M. B. (1932). Social participation among preschool children. *Journal of Abnormal and Social Psychology, 27,* 243–269.

Patton, M. M., & Mercer, J. (1996). "Hey! Where's the toys?" Play and literacy in first grade. *Childhood Education, 73,* 10–13.

Paul, R. (1993). *Background interpretation with a child placed under government protection by means of play therapy* (Masters Abstracts International 32/01). Unpublished master's thesis, University of Pretoria, South Africa.

Peck, J., & Goldman, R. (1978). *The behaviors of kindergarten children under selected conditions of the physical and social environment*. Paper presented at the meeting of the American Educational Research Association, Toronto, Canada.

Peitgen, H., Jurgens, J., & Saupe, D. (1992). *Chaos and fractals*. New York: Springer.

Pelham, L. E. (1971). *Self-directive play therapy with socially immature kindergarten students*. Unpublished doctoral dissertation, University of Northern Colorado, Greeley.

Pellegrini, A. D. (1984). Children's play and Language: Infancy through early childhood. In T. D. Yawkey & A. D. Pellegrini (Eds.), *Child's play and play therapy* (pp. 45–58). Lancaster, PA: TECHNOMIC.

Pellegrini, A. D. (1988). Elementary school children's rough-and-tumble play and social competence. *Developmental Psychology, 24,* 802–806.

Pellegrini, A. D. (1995). *School recess and playground behavior: Educational and developmental roles*. Albany: State University of New York Press.

Pellegrini, A. D. (1998). Rough-and-tumble play from childhood through adolescence. In D. P. Fromberg & D. Bergen (Eds.), *Play from birth to twelve and beyond: Contexts, perspectives, and meanings* (pp. 401–408). New York: Garland.

Pellegrini, A. D. (2002). Perceptions of playfighting and real fighting: Effects of sex and participant status. In J. L. Roopnarine (Ed.), *Play and culture studies: Vol. 4. Social-cognitive, and contextual issues in the fields of play* (pp. 223–233). Westport, CT: Ablex.

Pellegrini, A. D., & Bjorklund, D. F. (1996, Fall/Winter). The place of recess in school: Issues in the role of recess in children's education and development. *Journal of Research in Childhood Education, 11,* 5–13.

Pellegrini, A. D., & Boyd, B. (1993). The role of play in early childhood development and education: Issues in definition and function. In S. Spodek (Ed.), *Handbook of research on the education of young children* (pp. 105–121). New York: Macmillan.

Pellegrini, A. D., & Galda, L. (1990). Children's play, language, and early literacy. *Topics in Language Disorders, 10,* 76–88.

Pellegrini, A. D., & Galda, L. (1993). Ten years after: A reexamination of symbolic play and literacy research. *Reading Research Quarterly, 28,* 162–177.

Pellegrini, A. D., & Smith, P. K. (1993). School recess: Implications for education and development. *Review of Educational Research, 63,* 51–67.

Pellegrini, A. D., & Smith, P. K. (1998). Physical activity play: The nature and function of a neglected aspect of play. *Child Development, 69,* 577–598.

Peller, L. (1954). Libidinal phases, ego development, and play. *Psychoanalytic Study of the Child, 9,* 178–198.

Pepler, D. (1986). Play and creativity. In G. Fein & M. Rivkin (Eds.), *The young child at play, Reviews of research* (Vol. 4, pp. 143–154). Washington, DC: National Association for the Education of Young Children.

Pepler, D. J. (1979). *Effects of convergent and divergent play experience on preschoolers' problem solving.* Unpublished doctoral dissertation, University of Waterloo, Ontario, Canada.

Pepler, D. J., & Ross, H. S. (1981). The effects of play on convergent and divergent problem-solving. *Child Development, 52,* 1202–1210.

Perkes, K. S. L. (1998, March 22). Amusement ride's owner has troubled past. *Austin American-Statesman*, p. B-l.

Perry, B. D. (1996). Incubated in terror: Neurodevelopmental factors in the "cycle of violence." In J. D. Osofsky (Ed.), *Children, youth and violence: Searching for solutions* (pp. 101–122). New York: Guilford.

Perry, D. G., Williard, J. D., & Perry, L. C. (1990). Peers' perceptions of the consequences that victimized children provide aggressors. *Child Development, 61,* 1310–1325.

Peterson, L., Ewigman, B., & Kivlahan, C. (1993). Judgments regarding appropriate child supervision to prevent injury: The role of environmental risk and child age. *Child Development, 64,* 934–950.

Pettit, G., & Harrist, A. (1993). Children's aggressive and socially unskilled playground behavior with peers: Origins in early family relations. In C. Hart (Ed.), *Children on playgrounds* (pp. 240–270). Albany: State University of New York Press.

Phelps, K. E., & Woolley, J. D. (1994). The form and function of young children's magical beliefs. *Developmental Psychology, 30,* 385–394.

Phillips, R. D. (1985). Whistling in the dark? A review of play therapy research. *Psychotherapy, 22,* 752–760.

Piaget, J. (1951). *Play, dreams and imitation in childhood* (C. Gattegno & F. M. Hodgson, Trans.). New York: International Universities Press. (Originally published 1945.)

Piaget, J. (1952). *The origins of intelligence in children* (M. Cook, Trans.). New York: International Universities Press. (Originally published 1936.)

Piaget, J. (1962). *Play, dreams and imitation in childhood*. New York: Norton.

Piaget, J. (1965). *The moral judgment of the child*. New York: Free Press. (Originally published 1932.)

Piaget, J. (1966). *Psychology of intelligence*. Totowa, NJ: Littlefield, Adams.

Piaget, J. (1970). *Structuralism*. New York: Harper & Row.

Piaget, J. (1976). Mastery play. In J. S. Bruner, A. Jolly, & K. Sylva (Eds.), *Play: Its role in development and evolution* (pp. 12–17). New York: Basic Books.

Piaget, J., & Inhelder, B. (1969). *The psychology of the child*. New York: Basic Books.

Pica, R. (1997). Beyond physical development: Why young children need to move. *Young Children, 52,* 4–11.

Pickett, L. (1998). Literacy learning during block play. *Journal of Research in Childhood Education, 12,* 225–230.

Piers, M. W., & Landau, G. M. (1980). *The gift of play*. New York: Walker.

Plato. (1975). *The laws*. Harmondsworth: Penguin.

Plato. (1993). *The republic*. Oxford, UK: Oxford University Press.

Playground and Recreation Association of America. (1909). *Proceedings of the third annual conference of the Playground Association* (Vol. 3, pp. 2–24). N.p.: Author.

Playground and Recreation Association of America. (1928). *Play areas: Their design and equipment*. New York: Barnes.

Plomin, R., & Daniels, D. (1986). Genetics and shyness. In W. H. Jones, J. M. Cheek, & S. R. Briggs (Eds.), *Shyness: Perspectives on research and treatment* (pp. 63–80). New York: Plenum.

Poest, C. A., Williams, J. R., Witt, D. D., & Atwood, M. E. (1990). Challenge to move: Large muscle development in young children. *Young Children, 45,* 4–10.

Popham, W. J. (2002, February). Today's standardized tests are not the best way to evaluate schools or students: Right task—wrong tool. *American School Board Journal,* p. 21.

Postman, N. (1982) *The disappearance of childhood.* New York: Delacorte.

Poussaint, A. F., & Linn, S. (1997, Spring–Summer). Fragile: Handle with care. *Newsweek Special Issue,* p. 33.

Powell, E. C., Tanz, R. R., & DiScala, C. (1997). Bicycle-related injuries among preschool children. *Annals of Emergency Medicine, 30*(3), 260–265.

Power, T. G. (1985). Mother- and father-infant play: A developmental analysis. *Child Development, 56,* 1514–1524.

Pratt, C. (1948). *I learn from children.* New York: Simon & Schuster.

Preiser, W. F. E. (1972). Work in progress: The behavior of nursery school children under different spatial densities. *Man Environment Systems, 2,* 247–250.

Preisler, G., & Palmer, C. (1989). Thoughts from Sweden: The blind child at nursery school with sighted children. *Child: Care, Health and Development, 15,* 45–52.

Prescott, E. (1987). The environment as organizer of intent in child care. In C. S. Weinstein & T. G. David (Eds.), *Spaces for children: The built environment and child development* (pp. 73–86). New York: Plenum.

Provenzo, E. F. (1991). *Video kids: Making sense of Nintendo.* Cambridge, MA: Harvard University Press.

Pumfrey, P. D., & Elliott, C. D. (1970). Play therapy, social adjustment and reading attainment. *Educational Research, 12,* 183–193.

Quattlebaum, R. F. (1970). *A study of the effectiveness of nondirective counseling and play therapy with maladjusted fifth-grade pupils.* Unpublished doctoral dissertation, University of Alabama.

Quick, R. H. (1896). *Essays on educational reformers.* New York: D. Appleton.

Quinn, J., & Rubin, K. (1984). The play of handicapped children. In T. D. Yawkey & A. Pellegrini (Eds.), *Child's play: Developmental and applied.* Hillsdale, NJ: Erlbaum.

Ramey, C. T., & Ramey, S. L. (1996). *Prevention of intellectual disabilities: Early interventions to improve cognitive development.* Birmingham: University of Alabama Civitan International Research Center.

Ramsey, P. G. (1998). Diversity and play: Influences of race, culture, class, and gender. In D. P. Fromberg & D. Bergen (Eds.), *Play from birth to twelve and beyond: Contexts, perspectives, and meanings* (pp. 23–33). New York: Garland.

Rasmussen, V. (1920). *Child psychology.* London: Gyldendal.

Reams, R., & Friedrich, W. (1994). The efficacy of time-limited play therapy with maltreated preschoolers. *Journal of Clinical Psychology, 50,* 889–899.

Reber, A. S. (1995). *Dictionary of Psychology.* New York: Penguin.

Recchia, S. L. (1987). *Learning to play—Common concerns for the visually impaired preschool child.* Los Angeles: Blind Children's Center (ERIC Document Reproduction Service Number ED 292240).

Recreation Access Advisory Committee. (1994). *Recommendations for accessibility guidelines: Recreational facilities and outdoor developed areas.* Washington, DC: U.S. Architectural and Transportation Barriers Compliance Board.

Reifel, S. (1984). Block construction: Children's developmental landmarks in representation of space. *Young Children, 40*(1), 61–67.

Reifel, S. (1986). Play in the elementary school cafeteria. In B. Mergen (Ed.), *Cultural dimensions of play, games, and sport* (pp. 29–36). West Point, NY: Leisure Press.

Reifel, S. (1995). Preschool play: Some roots for literacy. In B. Immroth & V. Ash-Geisler (Eds.), *Achieving school readiness: Public libraries and national education goal number one* (pp. 10–30). Chicago: American Library Association.

Reifel, S. (Ed.). (1999). *Play and Culture Studies: Vol. 2. Play contexts revisited.* Stamford, CT: Ablex.

Reifel, S. (1999). Play research and the early childhood profession. In S. Reifel (Ed.), *Advances in early education and day care: Vol. 10. Foundations, adult dynamics, teacher education and play* (pp. 201–211). Stamford, CT: JAI.

Reifel, S., Hoke, P., Pape, D., & Wirneski, D. (2004). From context to texts: DAP hermeneutics, and reading classroom play. In S. Reifel & M. Brown

(Eds.), *Advances in early education and day care* (Vol. 13). Oxford, UK: JAI/Elseviev Science.

Reifel, S., & Yeatman, J. (1991). Action, talk, and thought in block play. In B. Scales, M. Almy, A. Nicolopoulou, & S. Ervin-Tripp (Eds.), *Play and the social context of development in early care and education* (pp. 156–172). New York: Teachers College Press.

Reifel, S., & Yeatman, J. (1993). From category to context: Reconsidering classroom play. *Early Childhood Research Quarterly, 8,* 347–367.

Reimer, G. (1985). Effects of a Logo computer programming experience on readiness for first grade, creativity, and self concept. *AEDS Monitor,* 23(7–8), 8–12.

Renken, B., Egeland, B., Marvinney, S., Mangelsdorf, S., & Stroufe, L. A. (1989). Early childhood antecedents of aggression and passive-withdrawal in early elementary school. *Journal of Personality, 57,* 257–281.

Rescorla, L., & Goossens, M. (1992). Symbolic play development in toddlers with expressive specific language impairment. *Journal of Speech and Hearing Research, 35,* 1290–1302.

Rettig, M. (1994). The play of young children with visual impairments: Characteristics and interventions. *Journal of Visual Impairment and Blindness, 88,* 410–420.

Reynolds, G., & Jones, E. (1997). *Master players: Learning from children at play*. New York: Teachers College Press.

Rheingold, H. L. & Cook, K. V. (1975). The content of boys' and girls' rooms as an index of parents' behavior. *Child Development, 46,* 459–463.

Ricco, R. B. (1989). Operational thought and the acquisition of taxonomic relations involving figurative dissimilarity. *Developmental Psychology, 25,* 996–1003.

Riddell, C. J. (1992). *The effects of contrasting playgrounds on the play behaviors of kindergarten children*. Unpublished master's thesis, University of Texas, Austin.

Rivkin, M. (1997). *The great outdoors: Restoring children's right to play outdoors*. Washington, DC: National Association for the Education of Young Children.

Rivkin, M. (1999). Rhetorics redux. In S. Reifel (Ed.), *Advances in early education and day care: Vol. 10. Foundations, adult dynamics, teacher education and play* (pp. 163–168). Stamford, CT: JAI.

Rivkin, M. S. (1998). Children's outdoor play. In D. P. Fromberg & D. Bergen (Eds.), *Play from birth to twelve and beyond: Contexts, perspectives, and meanings* (pp. 225–231). New York: Garland.

Roberts, A. (1980). *Out to play: The middle years of childhood*. Aberdeen: Aberdeen University Press.

Robinson, C. (1978). *The uses of order and disorder in play: An analysis of Vietnamese refugee children's play*. (ERIC Document Reproduction Service No. ED 153 944).

Rogers, C. R. (1942). *Counseling and psychotherapy*. Boston: Houghton Mifflin.

Rogers, C. R. (1951). *Client-centered therapy*. Boston: Houghton Mifflin.

Rogers, C. R. (1962). Toward becoming a fully functioning person. In ASCD Yearbook Committee (Ed.), *Perceiving, behaving, becoming: Yearbook 1962*. Washington, DC: Association for Supervision and Curriculum Development.

Rogers, C. S., Impara, J. C., Frary, R. B., Harris, T., Meeks, A., Semanic-Lauth, S., & Reynolds, M. R. (1998). Measuring playfulness: Development of the Child Behaviors Inventory of playfulness. In M. Duncan, G. Chick, & A. Aycock (Eds.), S. Reifel (Series Ed.), *Play and culture studies: Vol. 1. Diversions and divergences in fields of play* (pp. 151-168). Greenwich, CT: Ablex.

Rogers, C. S., & Sawyers, J. K. (1988). *Play in the lives of children*. Washington, DC: National Association for the Education of Young Children.

Rogoff, B. (1990). *Apprenticeship in thinking: Cognitive development in social context*. New York: Oxford University Press.

Rogoff, B. (1994). Observing sociocultural activity on three planes: Participatory appropriation, guided participation, apprenticeship. In A. Alvarez, P. del Rio, & J. V. Wertsch (Eds.), *Perspectives in sociocultural research*. Cambridge: Cambridge University Press.

Rogoff, B., Mistry, J., & Mosier, C. (1993). Guided participation in cultural activity by toddlers and caregivers. *Monographs of the Society for Research in Child Development, 58,* 8.

Romaine, S. (1984). *The language of children and adolescents: The acquisition of communication competence*. Oxford: Blackwell.

Roopnarine, J. L. (1987). Social interaction in the peer group: Relationship to perceptions of parenting and to children's interpersonal awareness and problem solving ability. *Journal of Applied Developmental Psychology, 8,* 351–362.

Roopnarine, J. L., Johnson, J. E., & Hooper, F. H. (Eds.). (1994). *Children's play in diverse cultures.* Albany: State University of New York Press.

Rosen, C. E. (1974). The effects of sociodramatic play on problem-solving behavior among culturally disadvantaged preschool children. *Child Development, 45,* 920–927.

Rosenberg, D. (2002, June 10). Fighting G-forces. *Newsweek.*

Rosenberg, M. (1979). *Conceiving the self.* New York: Basic Books.

Roskos, K. (1990). A taxonomic view of pretend play among four- and five-year old children. *Early Childhood Research Quarterly, 5,* 495–572.

Roskos, K., Christie, J. F., & Richgels, D. I. (2003). The essentials of early literacy instruction. *Young Children, 58,* 52–60.

Roskos, K., & Neuman, S. B. (1993). Descriptive observations of adults' facilitation of literacy in young children's play. *Early Childhood Research Quarterly, 8,* 77–98.

Roskos, K., & Neuman, S. B. (1998). Play as an opportunity for literacy. In O. N. Saracho & B. Spodek (Eds.), *Multiple perspectives on play in early childhood* (pp. 100–116). Albany: State University of New York Press.

Ross, H. S., & Kay, D. A. (1980). The origins of social games. In K. H. Rubin (Ed.), *Children's play* (pp. 17–31). San Francisco: Jossey-Bass.

Ross, J., & Gilbert, G. (1985). The national children and youth fitness study: A summary of the findings. *Journal of Health, Physical Education, Recreation and Dance, 56,* 45–60.

Ross, S., & Zimiles, H. (1976). The differentiated child behavior observation system. *Instructional Science, 5,* 325–342.

Roth, W. E. (1902). Games, sports, and amusements. *North Queensland Ethnography,* Bulletin No. 4.

Rothschild, J. (1960). Play therapy with blind children. *New Outlook for the Blind, 54,* 329–333.

Rousseau, J.-J. (1972). *Emile* (A. Bloom, trans.). London: Basic Books.

Rubin, K. H. (1982). Nonsocial play in preschoolers: Necessary evil? *Child Development, 53,* 651–657.

Rubin, K. H. (1986). Play, peer interactions, and social development. In A. W. Gottfried & C. C. Brown (Eds.), *Play interactions* (pp. 163–173). Lexington, MA: Lexington.

Rubin, K. H., Bukowski, W., & Parker, J. G. (1998). Peer interactions, relationships, and groups. In N. Eisenberg (Ed.), *Handbook of child psychology: Social, emotional, and personality* (Vol. 3, 5th ed., pp. 619–700). New York: John Wiley & Sons.

Rubin, K. H., Chen, X., McDougall, P., Bowker, A., & McKinnon, J. (1995). The Waterloo Longitudinal Project: Predicting, internalizing and externalizing problems in adolescence. *Development and Psychopathology, 7,* 751–764.

Rubin, K. H., & Coplan, R. J. (1998). Social and nonsocial play in childhood: An individual differences perspective. In O. N. Saracho & B. Spodek (Eds.), *Multiple perspectives on play in early childhood education* (pp. 144–170). Albany: State University of New York Press.

Rubin, K. H., Coplan, R. J., Fox, N. A., & Calkins, S. D. (1995). Emotionality, emotion regulation, and preschoolers' social adaptation. *Development and Psychopathology, 7,* 49–62.

Rubin, K. H., Fein, G. G., & Vandenberg, B. (1983). Play. In E. M. Hetherington (Ed.), *Handbook of child psychology: Vol. 4. Socialization, personality and social development* (pp. 693–774). New York: Wiley.

Rubin, K. H., Fein, G. G., & Vandenberg, B. (1983). In P. H. Mussen (Ed.), *Handbook of child psychology: Vol. 7. Socialization, personality, and social development* (4th ed., pp. 693–774). New York: Wiley.

Rubin, K. H., Maioni, T. L., & Hornung, M. (1976). Free play behaviors in middle and lower class preschoolers: Parten and Piaget revisited. *Child Development, 47,* 414–419.

Rubin, K. H., Watson, K. S., & Jambor, T. W. (1978). Free-play behaviors in preschool and kindergarten children. *Child Development, 49,* 534–536.

Ruble, D. N., & Martin, C. L. (1998). Gender development. In N. Eisenberg (Ed.), *Handbook of child psychology: Social, emotional, and personality development.* (Vol. 3, 5th ed., pp. 933–1016). New York: John Wiley & Sons.

Ruff, H. A., Lawson, K. R., Parniello, R., & Weissberg, R. (1990). Long term stability of individual differences in sustained attention in the early years. *Child Development, 61,* 60–76.

Rutter, M. (1983). Cognitive deficits in the pathogenesis of autism. *Journal of Child Psychology and Psychiatry, 24,* 513–531.

Sale, P., & Carey, D. M. (1995). The sociometric status of students with disabilities in a full-inclusion school. *Exceptional Children, 62,* 6–19.

Saltz, E., Dixon, D., & Johnson, J. (1977). Training disadvantaged preschoolers on various fantasy activities: Effects on cognitive functioning and impulse control. *Child Development, 48,* 367–380.

Saltz, E., & Johnson, J. (1974). Training for thematic fantasy play in culturally disadvantaged children: Preliminary results. *Journal of Educational Psychology, 66,* 623–630.

Saltz, R. (1997). The Reggio Emilia influence at the University of Michigan-Dearborn Child Development Center: Challenges and change. In J. Hendrick (Ed.), *First steps toward teaching the Reggio way* (pp. 167–180). Upper Saddle River, NJ: Merrill/Prentice Hall.

Samaras, A. P. (1999). Implications of the rhetoric of play as progress for preservice and inservice teachers. In S. Reifel (Ed.), *Advances in early education and day care: Vol. 10. Foundations, adult dynamics, teacher education and play* (pp. 177–188). Stamford, CT: JAI.

Sanders, S. W. (2002). *Active for life.* Washington, DC: National Association for the Education of Young Children.

Sandler, A. M. (1963). Aspects of passivity and ego development in the blind infant. *Psychoanalytic Study of the Child, 18,* 343–360.

Sandler, A. M. & Wills, D. M. (1965). Some notes on play and mastery in the blind child. *Journal of Child Psychotherapy, 1,* 7–19.

Santrock, J. W. (2000). *Children*. Dubuque, IA: Wm. C. Brown.

Sapon-Shevin, M., Dobbelaere, A., Corrigan, C., Goodman, K., & Mastin, M. (1998). Everyone here can play. *Educational Leadership, 56,* 42–45.

Sapora, A. V., & Mitchell, E. D. (1948). *The Theory of Play and Recreation*. New York: Ronald.

Sawyer, K. (1997). *Pretend play as improvisation: Conversation in the preschool classroom*. Hillsdale, NJ: Erlbaum.

Sawyer, R.K. (2003). Levels of analysis in pretend play discourse: Metacommunication in conversational routines. In D. Lytle (Ed.), *Play and culture studies: Vol. 5. Play and educational theory and practice* (pp. 137–157). Westport, CT: Praeger.

Sayre, N. E., & Gallagher, J. D. (2001). *The young child and the environment: Issues related to health, nutrition, safety, and physical activity.* Boston: Allyn & Bacon.

Scales, B. (1996). Researching the hidden curriculum. In S. Reifel (Ed.), *Advances in early education and day care: Vol. 8. Theory and practice in early childhood teaching* (pp. 237–259). Greenwich, CT: JAI.

Scales, B., & Cook-Gumperz, J. (1993). Gender in narrative and play: A view from the frontier. In S. Reifel (Ed.), *Advances in early education and day care: Vol 5.* (pp. 167–195). Greenwich, CT: JAI.

Scarr, S. (1968). Environment bias in twin studies. *Eugenics Quarterly, 15,* 34–40.

Schaefer, C. E. (1985). Play therapy. *Early Child Development and Care, 19,* 95–108.

Schaefer, C. E. (Ed.). (1993). *The therapeutic powers of play*. Northvale, NJ: Aronson.

Schaefer, C. E., Johnson, L., & Wherry, J. N. (1982). *Group therapy for children and youth: Principles and practices of group treatment*. San Francisco: Jossey-Bass.

Schafer, M., & Smith, P. K. (1996). Teachers' perceptions of play fighting and real fighting in primary school. *Educational Research, 38,* 173–181.

Schickedanz, J. A., Schickedanz, D. I., Hansen, K., & Forsyth, P. D. (1993). *Understanding children* (2nd ed.). Mountain View, CA: Mayfield.

Schiller, F. (1795). *On the aesthetic education of man*. New York: Ungar.

Schneekloth, L. H. (1989). Play environments for visually impaired children. *Journal of Visual Impairment and Blindness, 83,* 196–201.

Schneider, J. (1997). *Developmental stages of chase play: A proposal*. Unpublished manuscript.

Schnorr, R. F., (1990). "Peter? He comes and goes . . .": First graders' perspectives on a part-time mainstream student. *Journal of the Association for Persons with Severe Handicaps, 15,* 231–240.

Schooley, M. (1995). Students in wonderland. *Teaching PreK–8, 25,* 43.

Schwartzman, H. B. (1978). *Transformations: The anthropology of children's play*. New York: Plenum.

Schwartzman, H. G. (1986). A cross-cultural perspective on child-structured play activities and materials. In A. W. Gottfried & C. C. Brown (Eds.), *Play interactions: The contribution of play materials and parental involvement to children's development* (pp. 13–30). Lexington, MA: Lexington.

Schweinhart, L., & Weikart, D. (1996). Lasting differences: The High/Scope preschool curriculum comparison study through age 23. *Monographs of the High/Scope Educational Research Foundation, No. 12*. Ypsilanti, MI: High/Scope Press.

Schweinhart, L., Weikart, D., & Larner, M. (1986). Consequences of three preschool curriculum models through age 15. *Early Childhood Research Quarterly, 1,* 15–45.

Scully, P., & Roberts, H. (2002). Phonics, expository writing, and reading aloud: Playful literacy in the primary grades. *Early Childhood Education Journal, 30,* 93–99.

Sears, P., & Dowley, E. (1963). Research on teaching in the nursery school: In N. Gage (Ed.), *Handbook of research on teaching* (pp. 814–864). Skokie, IL: Rand McNally.

Seeman, J., & Edwards, B. (1954). A therapeutic approach to reading difficulties, *Journal of Consulting Psychology, 18,* 451–453.

Segal, M., & Webber, N. T. (1996). Nonstructured play observations: Guidelines, benefits, and caveats. In S. J. Meisels & E. Fenichel (Eds.), *New visions for the developmental assessment of infants and young children* (pp. 207–230). Washington, DC: Zero to Three: National Center for Infants, Toddlers, and Families.

Selman, R. L. (1976). Social-cognitive understanding: A guide to educational and clinical practice. In T. Lickona (Ed.), *Moral development and behavior: Theory, research and social issues* (pp. 299–316). New York: Holt, Rinehart, & Winston.

Seo, K. H. (2003). What children's play tells us about teaching mathematics. *Young Children, 58,* 28–35.

Serbin, L. A., & Sprafkin, C. (1986). The salience of gender and the process of sex typing in three- to seven-year-old children. *Child Development, 57,* 1188–1199.

Shantz, D. W. (1986). Conflict, aggression, and peer status: An observational study. *Child Development, 57,* 1322–1332.

Shapiro, L. (1997, May 12). The myth of quality time. *Newsweek*.

Shapiro, M. (1983). *Child's garden*. University Park, PA: Pennsylvania State University Press.

Sharp, D. (1997, July 3). Pools plus toddlers can lead to tragedy. *USA Today*.

Shatz, M., & Gelman, R. (1973). The development of communication skills: Modifications in the speech of young children as a function of listener. *Monographs of a Society for Research in Child Development, 38*(5, Serial No. 152).

Shell, E. R. (1994). Kids don't need equipment, they need opportunity. *Smithsonian, 25*(4), 79–86.

Shin, D. (1994). *Preschool children's symbolic play indoors and outdoors*. Unpublished doctoral dissertation, University of Texas, Austin.

Shin, D., & Frost, J. L. (1995). Preschool children's symbolic play indoors and outdoors. *International Play Journal, 3*(2), 83–96.

Shine, S., & Acosta, T. Y. (1999). The effect of the physical and social environment on parent-child interactions: A qualitative analysis of pretend play in a children's museum. *Play and Culture Studies, 2.*

Shore, R. (1997). *Rethinking the brain: New insights into early development*. New York: Families and Work Institute.

Sigman, M., & Sena, R. (1993). Pretend play in high risk and developmentally delayed children. In M. H. Bornstein & A. W. O'Reilly (Eds.), *The role of play in the development of thought* (pp. 29–42). San Francisco: Jossey-Bass.

Sikes, L., Fise, M. E., & Morrison, M. (1992). *Playing it safe: A nationwide safety survey of public playgrounds*. Washington, DC: U.S. Public Interest Research Group and the Consumer Federation of America.

Silver, M. (1999). Fatal attractions. *U.S. News & World Report, 127,* 56–59.

Silvern, S. B. (1998). Educational implications of play with computers. In D. P. Fromberg & D. Bergen (Eds.), *Play from birth to twelve and beyond: Contexts, perspectives, and meanings* (pp. 530–536). New York: Garland.

Singer, D., & Singer, J. L. (1977). *Partners in play*. New York: Random House.

Singer, D., & Singer, J. L. (1992). *The house of make-believe*. Cambridge, MA: Harvard University Press.

Skellenger, A. C., & Hill, E. W. (1994). Effect of a shared teacher-child play intervention on the play skills of three young children who are blind. *Journal of Visual Impairment and Blindness, 88,* 433–445.

Skellenger, A. C., Rosenblum, L. P., & Jager, B. K. (1997). Behaviors of preschoolers with visual impairments in indoor play settings. *Journal of Visual Impairment and Blindness, 91,* 519–530.

Skinner, B. F. (1957). *Verbal behavior*. New York: Appleton-Century-Crofts.

Skinner, B. F. (1966). What is the experimental analysis of behavior? *Journal of the Experimental Analysis of Behavior, 9,* 1–2.

Slaughter, D. T., & Dombrowski, J. (1989). Cultural continuities and discontinuities: Impact on social and pretend play. In M. N. Bloch & A. D. Pellegrini (Eds.), *The ecological context of children's play* (pp. 282–310). Norwood, NJ: Ablex.

Sluckin, A. (1981). *Growing up in the playground: The social development of children*. London: Routledge & Kegan Paul.

Smilansky, S. (1968). *The effects of sociodramatic play on disadvantaged preschool children*. New York: Wiley.

Smilansky, S. (1990). Sociodramatic play: Its relevance to behavior and achievement in school. In E. Klugman & S. Smilansky (Eds.), *Children's play and learning: Perspectives and policy implications* (pp. 18–42). New York: Teachers College Press.

Smilansky, S., & Shefatya, L. (1990). *Facilitating play: A medium for promoting cognitive, socio-emotional and academic development in young children*. Gaithersburg, MD: Psychosocial & Educational Publications.

Smith, G. A., Dietrich, A. M., Garcia, C. T., & Shields, B. J. (1995). Epidemiology of shopping cart-related injuries to children: An analysis of national data for 1990 to 1992. *Archives of pediatrics & Adolescent Medicine, 149*(11), 1207–1210.

Smith, J. E. (1984). Non-accidental injury to children: I. A review of behavioral interventions. *Behavior Research and Therapy, 22,* 331–347.

Smith, P. K., & Boulton, M. (1990). Rough-and-tumble play, aggression, and dominance: Perceptions and behavior in children's encounters. *Human Development, 33,* 271–282.

Smith, P. K., Dalgleish, & Herzmark, G. (1981). A comparison of the effects of fantasy play tutoring and skills tutoring in nursery classes. *International Journal of Behavioral Development, 4,* 421–444.

Smith, P. K., Smees, R., Pellegrini, A.D., & Menesini, E. (2002). Comparing pupil and teacher perceptions for playful fighting, serious fighting, and positive peer interaction. In J.L. Roopnarine (Ed.), *Play and culture studies: Vol. 4. Social-cognitive, and contextual issues in the fields of play* (pp. 235–245). Westport, CT: Ablex.

Smith, P. K., & Sydall, S. (1978). Play and non-play tutoring in preschool children: Is it play or tutoring which matters? *British Journal of Educational Psychology, 48,* 315–325.

Smith, R. P. (1957). *"Where did you go?" "Out" "What did you do?" "Nothing."* New York: Norton.

Smith, S. J. (1998). *Risk and our pedagogical relation to children: On the playground and beyond*. Albany: State University of New York Press.

Smith, S. T. (1998, July 26). Recess isn't what it used to be. *Boston Globe,* p. F5.

Smolucha, F. (1992). The relevance of Vygotsky's theory of creative imagination for contemporary research in play. *Creativity Research Journal, 5,* 69–76.

Smolucha, L., & Smolucha, F. (1998). The social origins of mind: Post-Piagetian perspectives on pretend play. In O. N. Saracho & B. Spodek (Eds.), *Multiple perspectives on play in early childhood* (pp. 34–58). Albany: State University of New York.

Sobel, D. (1993). *Children's special places: Exploring the role of forts, dens, and bush houses in middle childhood*. Tucson, AZ: Zephyr.

Soefje, A. (1998). Way off Broadway. *Teaching PreK–8, 28,* 44–46.

Software and Information Industry Association (2000). 2000 report on the effectiveness of technology in schools. Retrieved December, 2000, from http://www.siia.net

Sontag, J. C. (1997). Contextual factors influencing the sociability of preschool children with disabilities in integrated and segregated classrooms. *Exceptional Children, 63,* 389–404.

Southern Building Code Congress (1992). *Standard swimming pool code*. Birmingham, AL: Author.

Spariosu, M. (1989). *Dionysus reborn: Play and the aesthetic dimension in modern philosophical and scientific discourse*. Ithaca, NY: Cornell University Press.

Spencer, M. (2003). What do parents need to know about children's television viewing? ERIC Clearinghouse on Elementary and Early Childhood Education. Retrieved July, 2003 from http://interact.uoregon.edu/MediaLit/mlr/home/index.html

Spodek, B., & Saracho, O. (1988). The challenge of educational play. In D. Bergen (Ed.), *Play as a medium for learning and development* (pp. 9–22). Portsmouth, NH: Heinemann.

Stahmer, A. C., & Schreibman, L. (1992). Teaching children with autism appropriate play in unsupervised environments using a self-management treatment package. *Journal of Applied Behavior Analysis, 25,* 447–459.

Stevenson, M. B. (1989). The influences on the play of infants and toddlers. In M. N. Bloch & A. D. Pellegrini (Eds.), *The ecological content of children's play* (pp. 84–103). Norwood, NJ: Ablex.

Stiber, J. A. (1991). *The effect of play therapy on the temper tantrums of a seven-year-old-boy* (Masters Abstracts International 30/01). Unpublished master's thesis, Southern Connecticut State University, New Haven.

Stipek, D. J., & Sanborn, M. E. (1985). Teachers' task-related interactions with handicapped and non-handicapped preschool children. *Merrill-Palmer Quarterly, 31,* 285–300.

Stone, M., & Sagstetter, M. (1998). Simple technology. . . : It's never too early to start. *The Exceptional Parent, 28,* 50–51.

Stone, S. J., & Christie, J. F. (1996). Collaborative literacy learning during sociodramatic play in a multi-age (K–2) primary classroom. *Journal of Research in Childhood Education, 10,* 123–133.

Strasburger, V. C., & Wilson, B. J. (2002). *Children, Adolescents, and the Media*. Thousand Oaks, CA: Sage.

Stremmel, A., Fu, V., Patet, P., & Shah, H. (1995). Images of teaching: Prospective early childhood teachers' constructions of the teacher-learning process of young children. In S. Reifel (Ed.), *Advances in early education and day care: Vol. 7* (pp. 253–270). Greenwich, CT: JAI.

Stringer, L. (1971). *The sense of self: A guide to how we mature*. Philadelphia: Temple University.

Stroufe, L. A. (In press). Psychotherapy as development. *Psychopathology.*

Subbotsky, E. V. (1994). Early rationality and magical thinking in preschoolers: Space and time. *British Journal of Developmental Psychology, 12,* 97–108.

Subrahmanyan, K., & Greenfield, P. M. (1994). Effects of video game practice on spatial skills in girls and boys. *Journal of Applied Developmental Psychology, 15*(1), 13–32.

Suddendorf, T. (2000). A developmental link between the production of gestural representation and understanding of mental states. In S. Reifel (Ed.), *Play and culture studies: Vol. 3. Play in and out of context*. Stamford, CT: Ablex.

Suito, N., & Reifel, S. (1993). Aspects of gender role in American and Japanese play. *Journal of Play Theory & Research, 1,* 26–54.

Super, C. M. (1981). Cross-cultural research on infancy. In H. Trianis & A. Heron (Eds.), *Handbook of cross-cultural psychology* (Vol. 4, pp. 11–53). Boston: Allyn & Bacon.

Supple, C. (1997, July). Robot revolution. *National Geographic, 192*(1), 76–95.

Sutterby, J. A. (2001). Todos somos amigas: Cross-cultural and cross-linguistic play interactions in a two-way immersion prekindergarten classroom. Unpublished doctoral dissertation. Austin, TX: University of Texas.

Sutterby, J. A., & Frost, J. L. (2002). Making playgrounds fit for children and children fit on playgrounds. *Young Children, 57*(3), 36–42.

Sutton-Smith, B. (1972). *The folkgames of children*. Austin: University of Texas Press.

Sutton-Smith, B. (1976). Current research and theory on play, games, and sports. In T. Craig (Ed.), *The humanistic and mental health aspects of sports, exercise and recreation*. Chicago: American Medical Association.

Sutton-Smith, B. (Ed.). (1979). *Play and learning*. New York: Gardner.

Sutton-Smith, B. (1981). *A history of children's play: The New Zealand playground 1840–1950*. Philadelphia: University of Pennsylvania Press.

Sutton-Smith, B. (1983). Commentary on social class differences in socio-dramatic play in historical context: A reply to McLoyd. *Developmental Review, 3,* 1–5.

Sutton-Smith, B. (1984). In B. Sutton-Smith & D. Kelly-Byrne (Eds.), *The masks of play*. New York: Leisure Press.

Sutton-Smith, B. (1985). Play research: State of the art. In J. Frost & S. Sunderlin (Eds.), *When children play*. Washington, DC: Association for Childhood Education International.

Sutton-Smith, B. (1988). War toys and childhood aggression. *Play and Culture, 1,* 57–69.

Sutton-Smith, B. (1990). Playfully yours. *TASP Newsletter, 16,* 2–5.

Sutton-Smith, B. (1990). The school playground as festival. *Children's Environments Quarterly, 7,* 3–7.

Sutton-Smith, B. (1992). Foreword. In J. Frost (Ed.), *Play and playscapes* (pp. vii–viii). Albany, NY: Delmar.

Sutton-Smith, B. (1993). Dilemmas in adult play with children. In K. MacDonald (Ed.), *Parent-child play: Descriptions and implications* (pp. 15–40). Albany: State University of New York Press.

Sutton-Smith, B. (1993). Play rhetorics and toy rhetorics. *Journal of Play Theory & Research, 1*(4), 239–250.

Sutton-Smith, B. (1995). Conclusion: The persuasive rhetorics of play. In A. D. Pellegrini (Ed.), *The future of play theory* (pp. 275–295). Albany: State University of New York Press.

Sutton-Smith, B. (1997). *The ambiguity of play*. Cambridge, MA: Harvard University Press.

Sutton-Smith, B. (1999). The rhetorics of adult and child play theories. In S. Reifel (Ed.), *Advances in early education and day care: Vol. 10. Foundations, adult dynamics, teacher education and play* (pp. 149–162). Stamford, CT: JAI.

Sutton-Smith, B. (Undated). *The rhetorics of adult and child play theories*. Unpublished manuscript.

Sutton-Smith, B., Gerstmyer, J., & Meckley, A. (1988). Playfighting as folkplay amongst preschool children. *Western Folklore, 47,* 161–176.

Swaminathan, S., & Yeiland, N. (2003, annual theme issue). Global perspectives on educational technology. *Childhood Education*. Olney, MD: Association for Childhood Education International. 79(5). 258–260.

Sweeney, D. S., & Rocha, S. L. (2000). Using play therapy to assess family values. In R. E. Watts (Ed.), *Techniques in marriage and family counseling* (Vol. 1, pp. 33–47). Family Psychology and Counseling Series. Alexandria, VA: American Counseling Association.

Sweeney, T. (1974). *Petition to develop safety standards for playground equipment*. Washington, DC: Consumer Product Safety Commission.

Switzky, H. N., Ludwig, L., & Haywood, H. C. (1979). Exploration and play in retarded and nonretarded preschool children: Effects of object complexity and age. *American Journal of Mental Deficiency, 83,* 637–644.

Sylva, K., Roy, C., & Painter, M. (1980). *Childwatching at playgroup & nursery school*. Ypsilanti, MI: High/Scope Press.

Sylwester, R. (1995). *A Celebration of neurons: An educator's guide to the human brain*. Alexandria, VA: Association for Supervision and Curriculum Development.

Szala-Meneok, K. (1994). Christmas janneying and Easter drinking: Symbolic inversion, contingency, and ritual time in coastal Labrador. *Arctic Anthropology, 31*(1), 103–116.

Taft, J. (1933). *The dynamics of therapy in a controlled relationship*. New York: Macmillan.

Tait, P. E. (1972a). Behavior of young blind children in a controlled play situation. *Perceptual and Motor Skills, 34,* 963–969.

Tait, P. E. (1972b). A descriptive analysis of the play of young blind children. *Education of the Visually Handicapped, 4,* 12–15.

Tait, P. E. (1972c). The implications of play as it relates to the emotional development of the blind child. *Education of the Visually Handicapped, 4,* 52–54.

Takeuchi, M. (1994). Children's play in Japan. In J. L. Roopnarine, J. E. Johnson, & F. H. Hooper (Eds.), *Children's play in diverse cultures* (pp. 51–72). Albany: State University of New York Press.

Takhvar, M., & Smith, P. K. (1990). A review and critique of Smilansky's classification scheme and the "nested hierarchy" of play categories. *Journal of Research in Childhood Education, 4,* 112–122.

Talbot, J., & Frost, J. L. (1989). Magical playscapes. *Childhood Education, 66*(1), 11–19.

Tamis-LeMonda, C. S., & Bornstein, M. H. (1991). Individual variation, correspondence, stability, and change in mother and toddler play. *Infant Behavior and Development, 14,* 143–162.

Tanner, J. M. (1990). *Foetus into man* (2nd ed.). Cambridge, MA: Harvard University Press.

Tanner, L. N. (1997). *Dewey's laboratory school: Lessons for today*. New York: Teachers College Press.

Tarini, E. (1997). Reflections on a year in Reggio Emilia: Key concepts in rethinking and learning the Reggio way. In J. Hendrick (Ed.), *First steps toward teaching the Reggio way* (pp. 56–69). Upper Saddle River, NJ: Merrill/Prentice Hall.

Taylor, J. (1998). A garden where plants, children, and imaginations grow. In J. C. Kimmel & M. R. Moore (Eds.), *The world of play: Proceedings of the International World of Play Conference*. San Antonio: University of the Incarnate Word.

Taylor, M., Carlson, S. M., & Gerow, L. (2000). Imaginary companions: Characteristics and correlates. In S. Reifel (Ed.), *Play and culture studies: Vol. 3. Play in and out of context*. Stamford, CT: Ablex.

Taylor, S. I., Rogers, C. S., & Kaiser, J. (1999). A comparison of playfulness among American and Japanese preschoolers. In S. Reifel (Ed.), *Play and Culture Studies: Vol. 2. Play contexts revisited* (pp. 143–150). Stamford, CT: Ablex.

Tegano, D. W., & Burdette, M. P. (1991). Length of activity periods and play behaviors of preschool children. *Journal of Research in Childhood Education, 5,* 93–99.

Terrell, B., & Schwartz, R. (1988). Object transformations in the play of language-impaired children. *Journal of Speech and Hearing Disorders, 53,* 459–466.

Tharp, R. G., & Gallimore, R. (1988). *Rousing minds to life: Teaching, learning, and schooling in social contexts*. New York: Cambridge University Press.

Thatcher, R. W., Lyon, G. R., Rumsey, J., & Krasnegor, N. (Eds.). (1996). *Developmental neuroimaging: Mapping the development of brain and behavior*. New York: Academic Press.

Therrell, J. A., Brown, P., Sutterby, J. A., & Thornton, C. D. (2002). *Age determination guidelines: Relating children's ages to toy characteristics and play behavior.* Washington, DC: U. S. Consumer Product Safety Commission.

Thomas, A., & Chess, S. (1977). *Temperament and development*. New York: Brunner/Mazel.

Thomas, D. (1954). Waiting for cats. *A child's Christmas in Wales*. Norfolk, CT: New Directions.

Thomas, J. R. (1984). Children's motor skill development. In J. R. Thomas (Ed.), *Motor development during childhood and adolescence* (pp. 91–104). Minneapolis: Burgess.

Thomas, R. M. (1996). *Comparing theories of child development* (4th ed.). Pacific Grove, CA: Brooks/Cole.

Thompson, D., & Bowers, L. (Eds.). (1989). *Where our children play: Community park playground equipment*. Reston, VA: American Alliance for Health, Physical Education, Recreation and Dance.

Thompson, G. (1998, December 14). More diabetes cases found in obese children. *Austin American-Statesman,* pp. A-1, A-3.

Thompson, L., & Walker, A. J. (1989). Gender in families: Women and men in marriage, work, and parenthood. *Journal of Marriage and the Family, 5,* 845–871.

Thompson, R. A. (1997). *Early brain development and early intervention*. Lincoln: University of Nebraska.

Thompson, R. J. (1990). From the president. *Child Life Council Bulletin, 7,* 2.

Thompson, R. J., & Stanford, G. (1981). *Child life in hospitals*. Springfield, IL: Thomas.

Thompson, W. R., & Heron, W. (1954). The effects of restricting early experience on the problem-solving capacity of dogs. *Canadian Journal of Psychology, 8,* 17–31.

Thorndike, R. L., Hagen, E. P., & Sattler, J. P. (1986). *Stanford-Binet Intelligence Scale* (4th ed.). Chicago: Riverside.

Thorne, B. (1995). *Gender play: Girls and boys*. New Brunswick, NJ: Rutgers University Press.

Tietz, J., & Shine, S. (2000). The interaction of gender and play style in the development of gender segregation. In S. Reifel (Ed.), *Play and culture studies: Vol. 3. Play in and out of context* (pp. 131–146). Stamford, CT: Ablex.

Tilton, J. R., & Ottinger, D. R. (1964). Comparisons of the toy play of and behavior of autistic, retarded, and normal children. *Psychological Reports, 15,* 967–975.

Tizard, B., Philps, J., & Plewis, I. (1976). Play in preschool centers: II. Effects on play of the child's social class and of the educational orientation of the center. *Journal of School Psychology and Psychiatry, 17,* 265–274.

Tjossem, T. D. (Ed.) (1976). *Intervention strategies for high risk infants and young children*. Baltimore: University Park Press.

Tobin, J., Wu, D., & Davidson, D. (1989). *Preschool in three cultures: Japan, China, and the United States*. New Haven, CT: Yale University Press.

Tompkins, G. E., & Hoskisson, K. (1995). *Language arts: Content and teaching strategies*. Upper Saddle River, NJ: Merrill/Prentice Hall.

Tracy, D. M. (1987). Toys, spatial ability, and science and mathematics achievement: Are they related? *Sex Roles, 17,* 115–138.

Trawick-Smith, J. (1992). The physical classroom environment: How it affects learning and development. *Dimensions of Early Childhood, 20,* 34–42.

Trawick-Smith, J. (1993, April). *Effects of realistic, nonrealistic, and mixed-realism play environments on young children symbolization, social interaction, and language.* Paper presented at the annual meeting of the American Educational Research Association, Atlanta.

Trawick-Smith, J. (1994a). *Interactions in the classroom: Facilitating play in the early years.* Upper Saddle River, NJ: Prentice Hall.

Trawick-Smith, J. (1994b, April). *A qualitative study of young children's metaplay.* Paper presented at the annual meeting of the American Educational Research Association, New Orleans.

Trawick-Smith, J. (1997). *Early childhood development: A multicultural perspective*. Upper Saddle River, NJ: Merrill/Prentice Hall.

Trawick-Smith, J. (1998a, April). *A socio-cultural perspective on children's play: Lessons from an ethnographic study in Puerto Rico.* Paper presented at the annual meeting of the American Educational Research Association, San Francisco.

Trawick-Smith, J. (1998b). Why play training works: An integrated model for play intervention. *Journal of Research in Childhood Education, 12,* 117–129.

Trawick-Smith, J. (2000). *Early childhood development: A multicultural perspective.* Upper Saddle River, NJ: Merrill/Prentice Hall.

Trawick-Smith, J. (2001). The play frame and the "Fictional Dream": The bidirectional relationship between metaplay and story writing. In S. Reifel & M. Brown (Eds.), *Advances in early education and day care, Vol. 11. Early Education and care, and reconceptualizing play.* New York: JAI.

Trawick-Smith, J., & Landry-Fitzsimmons, K. (1992). A descriptive study of spatial arrangement in a family child care home. *Child and Youth Care Quarterly, 21,* 97–114.

Trawick-Smith, J., & Picard, T. (2003). Literacy play: Is it really play anymore? *Childhood Education, 79, (4),* 229–231.

Tronick, E. Z. (1989). Emotions and emotional communication in infants. *American Psychologist, 44,* 112–119.

Troster, H., & Bambring, M. (1992a). Early social-emotional development in blind infants. *Child: Care, Health and Development, 18,* 207–227.

Troster, H., & Bambring, M. (1993). Early motor development in blind infants. *Journal of Applied Developmental Psychology, 14,* 83–106.

Troster, H., & Bambring, M. (1994). The play behavior and play materials of blind and sighted infants and preschoolers. *Journal of Visual Impairment and Blindness, 88,* 421–432.

Trostle, S. L. (1984). *An investigation of the effects of child-centered group play therapy upon sociometric, self-control, and play behavior ratings of three- to six-year-old bilingual Puerto Rican children* (Dissertation Abstracts International 46/05A). Unpublished doctoral dissertation, Pennsylvania State University, University Park.

Tuan, Y. (1998) *Escapism*. Baltimore: Johns Hopkins University Press.

Tudge, J., Lee, S., & Putnam, S. (1998). Young children's play in socio-cultural context: South Korea and the United States. In M. C. Duncan, G. Chick, & A. Aycock (Eds.), S. Reifel (Series Ed.), *Play and culture studies: Vol. 1. Diversions and divergences in fields of play* (pp. 77–90). Greenwich, CT: Ablex.

Tyler, E. B. (1871). *Primitive culture: Researches into the development of mythology, philosophy, language, art and custom*. London: Murray.

Tyler, E. B. (1971). The history of games. In E. M. Avedon & B. Sutton-Smith (Eds.), *The study of games* (pp. 63–76). New York: Wiley. (Originally published in 1879.)

Ude-Pestel, A. (1977). *Betty: History and art of a child in therapy*. Palo Alto, CA: Science and Behavior Books.

Udwin, O. (1983). Imaginative play training as an intervention method with institutionalized preschool children. *British Journal of Educational Psychology, 53,* 32–39.

Udwin, O., & Shmukler, D. (1981). The influence of sociocultural, economic and home background factors on children's ability to engage in imaginative play. *Developmental Psychology, 17,* 66–72.

Underwood, A., & Plagens, P. (1997, Spring–Summer). Little artists and athletes. *Newsweek Special Issue,* pp. 14–15.

Unger, R., Kruger, L., & Christoffel, K. K. (1990). Childhood obesity: Medical and family correlates and age of onset. *Clinical Pediatrics, 29,* 368–372.

U.S. Consumer Product Safety Commission. (1981). *Handbook for public playground safety: Volumes I and II*. Washington, DC: Author.

U.S. Department of Health and Human Services. (2002). *Path to positive child outcomes.* Washington, DC: Author.

USA Today. (2003, February 10) Head Start resists efforts to give pupils a real boost. *USA Today,* p. 14A.

Uzgiris, I., & Hunt, J. M. (1975). *Assessment in infancy*. Urbana: University of Illinois Press.

Van Alstyne, D. (1932). Play behavior and choice of play materials of preschool children. Chicago: University of Chicago Press.

Van Fleet, R., Lilly, J. P., & Kaduson, H. (1999). Play therapy for children exposed to violence. *International Journal of Play Therapy, 8,* 27–42.

Van Hoorn, J., Scales, B., Nourot, P. M., & Alward, K. R. (1999). *Play at the center of the curriculum* (2nd ed.). Upper Saddle River, NJ: Merrill/Prentice Hall.

Van Rheenan, D. (2000). Boys who play hopscotch: The historical divide of a gendered space. In S. Reifel (Ed.), *Play and culture studies: Vol. 3. Play in and out of context* (pp. 111–130). Stamford, CT: Ablex.

Vandenberg, B. (1985). Beyond the ethology of play. In C. C. Brown & A. W. Gottfried (Eds.), *Play interactions* (pp. 3–10). Lexington, MA: Heath.

VanderVen, K. (1998). Play, Proteus, and paradox: Education for a chaotic and supersymmetric world. In D. Fromberg & D. Bergen (Eds.), *Play from birth to twelve and beyond: Contexts, perspectives, and meanings* (pp. 119–132). New York: Garland.

VanderVen, K. (in press). Beyond fun and games towards a meaningful theory of play: Can a hermeneutic perspective contribute? In S. Reifel & M. Brown (Eds.), *Advances in early education and day care* (Vol. 13). Oxford, UK: JAI/Elsevier Science.

Vaughter, R. M., Sadh, D., & Vozzola, E. (1994). Sex similarities and differences in types of play in games and sports. *Psychology of Women Quarterly, 18,* 86–103.

Vobejda, B. (1998, November 9). Study: Children watch less TV, spend more time on homework. *Austin American-Statesman,* p. A-4.

Von Marenholz-Bulow, Baroness. (1897). *Reminiscences of Friedrich Froebel*. Boston: Lee & Shepard.

Vukelich, C. (1989, December). *A description of young children's writing in two play settings with and without adult support*. Paper presented at the 39th National Reading Conference, Austin, TX.

Vukelich, C. (1991, December). *Learning about the functions of writing: The effects of three play interventions on children's development and knowledge about writing.* Paper presented at the annual meeting of the National Reading Conference, Palm Springs.

Vygotsky, L. (1977). Play and its role in the mental development of the child. In M. Cole (Ed.), *Soviet developmental psychology* (pp. 76–99). White Plains, NY: Sharpe.

Vygotsky, L. S. (1962). *Thought and language*. Cambridge, MA: MIT Press.

Vygotsky, L. S. (1966). Play and its role in the mental development of the child. *Soviet Psychology, 12*(6), 62–76.

Vygotsky, L. S. (1976). Play and its role in the mental development of the child. In J. S. Bruner, A. Jolly, & K. Sylva (Eds.), *Play: Its role in development and evolution* (pp. 536–552). New York: Basic Books.

Vygotsky, L. S. (1978). *Mind in society: The development of higher psychological processes*. Cambridge, MA: Harvard University Press.

Vygotsky, L. S. (1984). *Thought and language*. Cambridge, MA: MIT Press.

Wachs, T. D. (1979). Proximal experience and early cognitive-intellectual development: They physical environment. *Merrill-Palmer Quarterly, 25,* 3–41.

Waggoner, J. E., & Palermo, D. S. (1989). Betty is a bouncing bubble: Children's comprehension of emotion-descriptive metaphors. *Developmental Psychology, 25,* 152–163.

Waldrop, M. M. (1992). *Complexity: The emerging science at the edge of order and chaos*. New York: Simon & Schuster.

Walker C., Kragler, S., Martin, L., & Arnett, A. (2002). Facilitating the use of informational texts in a 1st-grade classroom. *Childhood Education, 79,* 152–159.

Wallach, F. (1992, April). What did we do wrong? *Parks and Recreation, 26,* 53–57, 83.

Walsh, D. (2001). Too much television alters a young child's brain. For Kid's Sake Feature. Retrieved October, 2001, from http://thekidsshow.org/

Walsh, D., Gentile, D., VanOverbeke, M., & Chasco, E. (2002). *Video game report card*. National Institute on Media and the Family. Retrieved March 29, 2004, from http://www.mediafamily.org/research/report_vgrc_2002-2.shtml

Warren, D. (1984). *Blindness and early childhood development*. New York: American Foundation for the Blind.

Waters, E., Wippman, J., & Sroufe, L. (1979). Attachment, positive affect, and competence in the peer group: Two studies in construct validation. *Child Development, 50,* 821–829.

Watson, J. (1976). Smiling, cooing, and "The Game." In J. S. Bruner, A. Jolly, and K. Sylva (Eds.), *Play: Its role in development and evolution* (pp. 268–276). New York: Basic Books.

Watson, M. W., & Fischer, K. W. (1977). A developmental sequence of agent use in late infancy. *Child Development, 48,* 828–836.

Watson, M. W., & Jackowitz, E. R. (1984). Agents and recipient objects in the development of early symbolic play. *Child Development, 55,* 1091–1097.

Wear, B. (1998, March 21). Fatal accidents rare on amusement rides. *Austin American-Statesman,* p. A-7.

Webb, N. B. (1991). *Play therapy with children in crisis*. New York: Guilford.

Webb, N. B. (Ed.). (1999). *Play therapy with children in crisis: Individual, group, and family treatment* (2nd ed.). New York: Guilford.

Wegener-Spohring, G. (1989). War toys and aggressive games. *Play and Culture, 2,* 35–47.

Weinberg, S. (1992). *Dreams of a final theory*. New York: Pantheon.

Weiner, B. J., Tilton, J. F., & Ottinger, D. R. (1969). Comparison of the play behavior of autistic, retarded, and normal children: A re-analysis. *Psychological Reports, 25,* 223–227.

Weiner, E. A., & Weiner, B. J. (1974). Differentiation of retarded and normal children through toy-play analysis. *Multivariate Behavioral Research, 8,* 245–252.

Weir, R. (1976). Playing with language. In J. S. Bruner, A. Jolly, & K. Sylva (Eds.), *Play: Its role in development and evolution* (pp. 609–618). New York: Basic Books.

Weisler, A., & McCall, R. B. (1976). Exploration and play: Resume and redirection. *American Psychologist, 31,* 492–508.

Wertsch, J. V., & Hickmann, M. (1987). *Problem solving in social interaction: A microgenetic analysis*. In M. C. Hickmann (Ed.), *Social and functional approaches to language and thought* (pp. 251–266). San Diego: Academic Press.

West, W. B. (1969). *An investigation of the significance of client-centered play therapy as a counseling technique*. Unpublished doctoral dissertation, University of North Texas, Denton.

Wheatley, M. (1992). *Leadership and the new science*. San Francisco: Berrett-Koehler.

Whitebrook, M., Howes, C., & Phillips, D. (1990). *Who cares? Child care teachers and the quality of care in America*. Oakland, CA: Child Care Employee Project.

Whiting, B., & Whiting, J. (1975). *Children of six cultures*. Cambridge, MA: Harvard University Press.

Whiting, B. B. (1980). Culture and social behavior. *Ethos, 2,* 95–116.

Whiting, B. B., & Edwards, C. P. (1988). *Children of different worlds: The formation of social behavior*. Cambridge, MA: Harvard University Press.

Whitton, S. (1998). The playful ways of mathematicians' work. In D. P. Fromberg & D. Bergen (Eds.), *Play from birth to twelve and beyond: Contexts, perspectives, and meanings*. New York: Garland.

Wick, D. T., Wick, J. K., & Peterson, N. (1997). Improving self-esteem with Adlerian Adventure Therapy. *Professional School Counseling, 1,* 53–56.

Wilcox-Herzog, A., & Kontos, S. (1998). The nature of teacher talk in early childhood classrooms and its relationship to children's play with objects and peers. *Journal of Genetic Psychology, 159,* 30–39.

Williams, L. (1996). Does practice lead theory? Teachers' constructs about teaching: Bottom-up perspectives. In S. Reifel (Ed.), *Advances in early education and day care: Vol. 8. Theory and practice in early childhood teaching* (pp. 153–184). Greenwich, CT: JAI.

Willner, A. H. (1991). Behavioral deficiencies of aggressive 8–9 year old boys: An observational study. *Aggressive Behavior, 17,* 135–154.

Willock, B. (1983). Play therapy with the aggressive, acting-out child. In C. E. Schaefer & K. L. O'Connor (Eds.), *Handbook of play therapy* (pp. 387–411). New York: Wiley.

Wills, D. M. (1965). Some observations on blind nursery school children's understanding of their world. *Psychoanalytic Study of the Child, 20,* 344–364.

Wills, D. M. (1968). Problems of play and mastery in the blind child. *British Journal of Medical Psychology, 41,* 213–222.

Wills, D. M. (1970). Vulnerable periods in the early development of blind children. *Psychoanalytic Study of the Child, 25,* 461–480.

Wills, D. M. (1972). Problems of play and mastery in the blind child. In E. P. Trapp & P. Himmelstein (Eds.), *Readings on the exceptional child* (pp. 335–349). New York: Meredith.

Wills, D. M. (1979). The ordinary devoted mother and her blind baby. *Psychoanalytic Study of the Child, 34,* 31–49.

Wills, D. M. (1981). Some notes on the application of the diagnostic profile to young blind children. *Psychoanalytic Study of the Child, 36,* 217–237.

Wilson, L. C. (1990). *Infants and toddlers: Curriculum and teaching*. Albany, NY: Delmar.

Wilson, M. H., Baker, S. P., Teret, S. P., Shock, S., & Garbarino, J. (1991). *Saving children: A guide to injury prevention*. New York: Oxford University Press.

Winegar, L. T. (1989). *Organization and process in the development of children's understanding of social events*. In L. T. Winegar (Ed.), *Social interaction and the development of children's understanding* (pp. 45–65). Norwood, NJ: Ablex.

Wing, L., Gould, J., Yeates, S. R., & Brierly, L. M. (1977). Symbolic play in severely mentally retarded and autistic children. *Journal of Child Psychology and Psychiatry, 18,* 167–178.

Winn, E. V. (1959). *The influence of play therapy on personality change and the consequent effect on reading performance*. Unpublished doctoral dissertation, Michigan State University, Lansing.

Winnecott, D. (1971). *Playing and reality.* New York: Basic Books.

Winston, P. (1984, October 31). Despite fitness boom the young remain unfit. *Education Week*, p. 9.

Winter, S. M. (1983). *Toddler play behaviors and equipment choices in an outdoor playground*. Unpublished doctoral dissertation, University of Texas, Austin.

Wohlwill, J. F. (1984). Relationships between exploration and play. In T. D. Yawkey & A. D. Pellegrini (Eds.), *Child's play: Developmental and applied* (pp. 143–170). Hillsdale, NJ: Erlbaum.

Wolery, M., Werts, M. G., Caldwell, N. K., Snyder, E. D., & Lisowski, L. (1995). Experienced teachers' perceptions of resources and supports for inclusion. *Education and Training in Mental Retardation and Developmental Disabilities, 30,* 15–26.

Wolfberg, P. J., & Schuler, A. L. (1993). Integrated play groups: A model for promoting the social and cognitive dimensions of play in children with autism. *Journal of Autism and Developmental Disorders, 23,* 467–489.

Wolfe, J. (2002). *Learning from the past: Historical voices in early childhood education*. Mayerthorpe, Alberta: Piney Branch Press.

Wolfe, P., & Brandt, R. (2000). What do we know from brain research? In E. N. Nunn & C. J. Boyatzis (Eds.), *Child growth and development* (7th ed., pp. 25–28). Guilford, CT: Dushkin/McGraw-Hill.)

Wolfenstein, M. (1954). *Children's humor: A psychological analysis*. Glencoe, IL: Free Press.

Wood, B., Fise, M. E., & Morrison, M. (1994). *Playing it safe: A second nationwide safety survey of public playgrounds*. Washington, DC: U.S. Public Interest Research Group and the Consumer Federation of America.

Wood, D., McMahon, L., & Cranstoun, Y. (1980). *Working with under fives*. Ypsilanti, MI: High/Scope Foundation.

Woods, I. C. (1995). *Rethinking Froebel's kindergarten metaphor: Culture and development in multiple settings*. Unpublished doctoral dissertation, University of Texas at Austin.

Woolley, J. D. (1995). The fictional mind: Young children's understanding of imagination, pretense, and dreams. *Developmental Review, 15,* 172–211.

Woolley, J. D., & Wellman, H. M. (1990). Young children's understanding of realities, nonrealities, and appearances. *Child Development, 61,* 946–961.

Wortham, S. C. (1996). *The integrated classroom. The assessment-curriculum link in early childhood education*. Upper Saddle River, NJ: Merrill/Prentice Hall.

Wortham, S. C., & Frost, J. L. (Eds.). *Playgrounds for young children: American survey and perspectives*. Reston, VA: American Alliance for Health, Physical Education, Recreation, and Dance.

Wright, L. (1990). The social and nonsocial behavior of precocious preschoolers during free play. *Roeper Review, 12,* 268–273.

Yawkey, T., & Alverez-Dominques, J. (1984). *Comparisons of free play behaviors of Hispanic and Anglo middle-class SES five-year-olds*. Paper presented at the annual meeting of the American Educational Research Association, New Orleans.

Yawkey, T. D., & Diantoniis, J. M. (1984). Relationship between child's play and cognitive development and learning in infancy birth through age eight. In T. D. Yawkey & A. D. Pellegrini (Eds.), *Child's play and play therapy* (pp. 31–43). Lancaster, PA: TECHNOMIC.

Yeatman, J., & Reifel, S. (1997). Conflict and power in classroom play. In *International Journal of Early Childhood Education, 2,* 77–93.

Yelland, H. (1999). Technology as play. *Early Childhood Education Journal, 26,* 217–220.

Yerkes, R. (1982). *Caring spaces, learning places: Children's environments that work.* Redmond, WA: Exchange.

Young, J. (1985). The cultural significance of (male) children's playground activities. *Alberta Journal of Educational Research, 31,* 125–138.

Youngblade, L. M., & Dunn, J. (1995). Individual differences in young children's pretend play with mother and sibling: Links to relationships and understanding of other people's feelings and beliefs. *Child Development, 66,* 1472–1492.

Youngerman, S. (1998). The power of cross-level partnerships. *Educational Leadership, 56,* 58–60.

Zaun, C. G. (1952). It's not what you fall on: It's how you land. *Safety Education, 32*(1), 3–4.

Zaun, C. G. (1955). Four conclusions. *Safety Education, 34*(5), 8.

Zeisel, S. H. (1986). Dietary influences on neurotransmission. *Advances in Pediatrics, 33,* 23–48.

Zigler, E., & Lang, M. E. (1990). *Child care choices.* New York: Free Press.

Zimiles, H. (1986). The Bank Street approach. In J. L. Roopnarine & J. Johnson (Eds.), *Approaches to early childhood education* (pp. 163–178). Upper Saddle River, NJ: Merrill/Prentice Hall.

Zippiroli, S., Bayer, D., & Mistrett, S. (1988). *Use of the microcomputer as a social facilitator between physically handicapped and non-handicapped preschoolers.* N.p.: Handicapped Children's Early Education Program.

Name Index

Subject Index